THE PRONUNCIATION OF ENGLISH IN

The Pronunciation of English

in the

Atlantic States

BASED UPON THE COLLECTIONS OF THE
LINGUISTIC ATLAS OF THE EASTERN UNITED STATES

by

HANS KURATH

RAVEN I. McDAVID, JR.

ANN ARBOR
THE UNIVERSITY OF MICHIGAN PRESS

PREFACE

THE organization of this book on the pronunciation of the English spoken on the Atlantic seaboard of the United States of America was planned by the senior author. He is also responsible for the scheme of phonemicizing the syllabic sounds (the vowels), which is consistently adhered to in presenting the phonemic (structural), the phonic (subphonemic), and the incidental (largely distributional) differences between the regional and the social dialects current on the Atlantic seaboard. Whatever the merits of this scheme may be from a theoretical point of view, it is eminently serviceable in dealing with the regional and the social dissemination of features of pronunciation, whether phonemic, phonic, or incidental, and in comparing the dialects in an orderly manner, the two sets of problems with which this investigation is primarily concerned.

The first four chapters are chiefly the work of Hans Kurath, the very full fifth chapter chiefly that of Raven I. McDavid, Jr. As stated below, McDavid has also gathered much of the source material in South Carolina, Georgia, and New York State.

Brief comments on the organization of this volume should be helpful to the reader.

In Chapter 1 some important preliminary matters are considered, such as the character of the source material, the problem of interpreting the phonic record in phonemic terms, the approach to the analysis of the vowel system, and an outline of the vowel system set up from this point of view. It has also seemed advisable to comment briefly on the extent to which features of pronunciation are systematized and to what extent dialects and idiolects exhibit and tolerate oddities that cannot be regarded as normal features of the system.

The chief regional types of cultivated speech, based upon the usage of 157 speakers, are discussed in Chapter 2. Here the configurations of phonemic and phonic features (to some extent also of incidental features) that characterize the dialects are briefly outlined for the following areas: Eastern New England, the Lower Connecti-

cut Valley, Metropolitan New York, Upstate New York and Western New England, Pennsylvania, the South Midland, the Upper South, and the Lower South. It is a highly significant fact that in the various areas the speech of the middle class and of the folk rarely deviates from cultivated usage in phonemic structure, though differences in the phonic character of some of the phonemes and in their incidence may be very marked.

Regional and social differences in the pronunciation of the vowel phonemes—the *diaphones* of these phonemes—are presented in Chapter 3. If a vowel has positional allophones in one area or another, that too is pointed out. The term *diaphone* as used here comprises all regional and social variants of a phoneme or its allophones. Needless to say, whether a regional difference in pronunciation is regarded as diaphonic, as involving different phonemes, or as exhibiting a divergence in the incidence of the phonemes depends upon one's conception of the phonemic system.

The complicated problem of the incidence of the vowel phonemes before /r/ and the regionally corresponding unsyllabic /ə/ is treated in Chapter 4. Since the differences between the dialects are very great in this respect and the identification of the phonemes in this position offers considerable difficulty, a rather full treatment is given. The vowels before tautosyllabic /r ~ ə/, as in *ear*, *care*, *four*, *poor*, are taken up first, then those before intersyllabic /r/, as in *syrup*, *merry*, *Mary*, *tomorrow*.

Chapter 5 deals with the regionally and socially varying incidence of vowel and consonant phonemes in the vocabulary. Though rarely of structural significance, such variations as /æ ~ ɑ ~ a/ in *aunt*, *glass*, *pasture*, /æ ~ ɛ/ in *radish*, /ɑ ~ ɒ ~ æ/ in *calm*, *palm*, /ʌ ~ ʊ/ in *bulge*, /e ~ æ ~ ɑ/ in *tomato*, /u ~ ʊ/ in *broom*, *hoof*, *soot*, /s ~ z/ in *greasy*, /f ~ v/ in *nephew*, /š ~ s/ in *sumac*, and /ð ~ θ/ in *without* are nevertheless characteristic features of the regional and the social dialects, and relatively of considerable importance because structural differences in American English are so few in number.

For most of the illustrative examples used in Chapters 3, 4, and 5, full-page maps showing the regional dissemination of the variants are provided, to which the reader will want to turn when he reads the text. Whenever cultivated usage differs more or less strikingly from that of the middle class and/or the folk, it is exhibited on an insert. On some of the maps, English folk usage is shown on a small-scale map of the southern counties of England to point out connections of American variants with English folk speech—whether certain, probable, or merely possible.

The area under consideration is somewhat larger than the one treated in Hans Kurath's *A Word Geography of the Eastern United States*. It includes the northern and the western parts of New York State, the section of Georgia settled by 1810, four communities on the coast of Florida, and three in Ontario, Canada, all of which were investigated by Raven I. McDavid, Jr. after the *Word Geography* had been written. Moreover, McDavid brought the survey of South Carolina, for which Lowman had done the exploratory sampling, up to scale.

All of the data from the Middle and the South Atlantic States used in this study were gathered in the field by the late Dr. Guy S. Lowman (1934–41) and by Raven I. McDavid, Jr. (1941–48), two highly trained investigators. Lowman also had a large share in the survey of New England (1931–33), in which others participated (see Hans Kurath, Miles L. Hanley, Bernard Bloch, and others, *Linguistic Atlas of New England*, Vol. 1 [1939], map facing the Preface).

The design of the Atlas survey, the work sheets, and the finely graded phonetic alphabet are described in Hans Kurath, Bernard Bloch, and others, *Handbook of the Linguistic Geography of New England* (1939, reprinted 1954 by the American Council of Learned Societies). A salient feature of the sampling plan is the systematic inclusion of speakers from all social levels: the highly cultured, the middle group, and the folk. As a result, our collections provide the data for *cultivated* speech, *common* speech, and *folk* speech, and point up the existence or absence of social differences in usage. Social dissemination, taken to-

gether with the regional dissemination of variants, often leads to fairly safe inferences concerning trends in usage.

The regional dissemination of variant pronunciations is described in terms of the major speech areas and their subdivisions as established on the basis of vocabulary in Hans Kurath, *A Word Geography of the Eastern United States* (1949). For the convenience of the reader this scheme of speech areas is here reproduced on Map 2. Features of pronunciation clearly exhibit the same types of regional dissemination as features of the vocabulary, the same expansive and recessive subareas, and the same transition belts. However, the relative importance of the phonetic boundaries between subareas often differs noticeably from that of the lexical boundaries. The most striking instance is the boundary between the North Midland (Pennsylvania) and the South Midland (West Virginia), which is relatively unimportant in matters of vocabulary but very prominent in features of pronunciation. The construction of a refined scheme of dialect areas based upon lexical, phonetic, and morphological isoglosses is reserved for later publication. It involves the evaluation of the various types of isoglosses from the structural point of view, a count of the isoglosses of each type established in the survey, and an evaluation of the isoglosses thus established with reference to their frequency in the dialects as a whole.

Though fully aware of the hazards involved, an attempt is made to point out the probable British sources of American usage when it differs from Standard British English of today. Unsettled usage in Standard English during our Colonial period, both within the London area (the Home Counties) and in other sections of England (about which very little is known), stands back of some of these divergencies; others have their sources in English folk speech. Most American practices can with some probability be related to specific features once current in Standard British English or still in use in one or another of the regional folk dialects of England. It is also fairly clear that most, if not all, regional variants in American cultivated speech of today can be traced to British cultivated usage of the seventeenth and the eighteenth centuries, and that features of pronunciation confined to certain subareas of the Atlantic seaboard, notably the loss of postvocalic /r/ as such and the /ɑ ~ a/ vowel in *half*, *glass*, etc., were not fashionable in the London area until shortly before the American Revolution.

Much help in mastering the data contained in the records of the pronunciation of nearly 1500 speakers and in developing techniques for handling a great variety of problems has been received from doctoral candidates working under my direction. Herbert Penzl has dealt with the /æ ~ a/ in *half*, *glass*, *aunt*, etc.; Walter S. Avis with the /o ~ ə/ in *road*, *stone*, *know*, etc.; Thomas Wetmore with /ɑ ~ ɒ ~ ɔ/ in *lot*, *law*, *loss*, *log*, *wash*, etc.; Helen W. Kao with the /u ~ ʊ ~ ʌ/ in *room*, *roof*, *soot*, etc.; Bernard Bloch and William R. Van Riper with postvocalic /r ~ ə/ in *ear*, *care*, *four*, *poor* and the /ɜ/ vowel in *thirty*, *sermon*. Yakira H. Frank has described the pronunciation of Metropolitan New York, James W. Downer the dialect of J. R. Lowell's *Biglow Papers* in its relation to the present rustic speech of northeastern New England. I am grateful to them for their painstaking work in assembling the data, determining the regional and social dissemination of the variants, disentangling phonemic entities from the mass of phonic data, describing the phonic range of the phonemes area by area, establishing present and recent trends in usage, and reconstructing the probable history of these features on the Atlantic seaboard. Their work has lightened our labor immeasurably.

Since the description and the interpretation presented here rest solely upon the first systematic survey of usage in the Atlantic States, no reference to the work of others, as of Leonard Bloomfield, Charles H. Grandgent, John S. Kenyon, George P. Krapp, and Charles K. Thomas, has been thought necessary. Needless to say, a good many hints have been received from these sources and are gratefully acknowledged.

It is a pleasure to acknowledge with thanks substantial grants from the Faculty Research Fund of the Horace H. Rackham School of Graduate Studies of the University of Michigan and from the Linguistic Atlas Fund of the American Council of Learned Societies for mapping and tabulating the Atlas data on which this treatment of the pronunciation of English on the Atlantic seaboard rests. This preliminary task was carried out with accuracy and dispatch by Helen W. Kao and Raven I. McDavid, Jr. The American Council of Learned Societies has also granted a subsidy to the University of Michigan Press for publishing this volume, the third of the *Studies in American English* issued by the Press. Part of the funds for publication were derived from a grant from the Horace H. Rackham School of Graduate Studies, the University of Michigan.

For the careful drafting of the maps we are greatly indebted to Professor Charles M. Davis and to Mr. D. Peruzzi of the Geography Department of the University of Michigan. The lettering of the synopses in Chapter 2 was done by Professor Leonard W. Zamiska of the College of Architecture.

May 1, 1959   HANS KURATH

It is a pleasure to join in the acknowledgment of the assistance to the project rendered by the American Council of Learned Societies and the Horace H. Rackham School of Graduate Studies. In addition to this assistance, I wish to acknowledge the assistance of the Research Fund of the Modern Language Association of America toward the charting of items and the preparation of the manuscript, and of my wife, Dr. Virginia McDavid, in every stage of the project from preliminary charting to the reading of proofs.

November 10, 1960   RAVEN I. McDAVID, JR.

CONTENTS

CHAPTER 1

INTRODUCTION

1.1 THE CHARACTER OF THE SOURCE MATERIAL

All field recordings of the Linguistic Atlas are *phonic* in intention. Particular utterances of the informants are recorded as heard by trained observers without reference to a general scheme of phonemicization or to the phonemic structure of the separate idiolects. When several variant utterances of the same expression by one and the same speaker are taken down, the observer may classify them as "fast" or "slow," "natural" or "guarded," "old" or "modern," etc., but he does not change the phonic record or attempt to establish the full phonic range of the variant sound. The observer may also comment on the phonemic status of any given phone in a particular idiolect, as often happens, but he does not obliterate the phonic entity. Thus all records of pronunciation are deliberately phonic.

The instrument for phonic recording is a finely graded phonetic alphabet, which is described in full detail in Hans Kurath, Bernard Bloch, and others, *Handbook of the Linguistic Geography of New England* (1939; second printing 1954, by the American Council of Learned Societies, 345 East 46th Street, New York 17, N. Y.), pp. 122–46. Here only the scheme of vowel symbols is reproduced from the *Handbook*, p. 123. Rounded vowels are enclosed in parentheses.

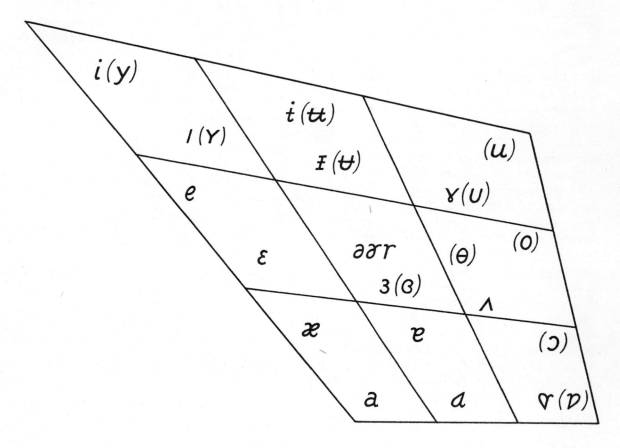

A phonic record of pronunciation is needed for all attempts at establishing the system of phonemes and describing the phonic range of the several phonemes (i.e., their positional and prosodic allophones or their free variations). The preservation of the phonic record is all the more important since all schemes of phonemicization are to some extent arbitrary in view of the present state of our knowledge of the segmentation of utterances. On the other hand, all features of pronunciation must of course be presented from a phonemic point of view. If the basis of the adopted scheme of phonemicization is explicitly stated and each phoneme in that system is described in phonic terms, the phonic data thus preserved can be interpreted in terms of different systems of phonemicization.

For comparative dialectology and historical linguistics in general a phonic record is of the utmost importance. The splitting of phonemes, the merging of one phoneme with another—whether partial or total— are readily comprehensible when the allophones of the phonemes in question are known.

For the study of American English, whose dialects differ rather little in phonemic structure but exhibit rather marked differences in the phonic character of many of the vowel phonemes, a phonic record is of peculiar importance, as shown in Chapter 3. This observation holds whether one accepts the unitary interpretation of phonically complex syllabics or not.

To emphasize the importance of the phonic data is not to detract from the overriding importance of the system of phonemes, however conceived. Phonic differences between idiolects or between regional and social dialects must be kept strictly apart from differences in the system of phonemes, and these in turn from differences in the incidence of the phonemes in the vocabulary. *Phonemic*, *phonic*, and *incidental* heteroglosses are of unequal value in determining the degree of difference between dialects and in evaluating the relative importance of the boundaries between speech areas. Of the three types, phonemic heteroglosses obviously outrank the others.

1.2 THE DESIGN OF THE QUESTIONNAIRE

The work sheets of the Linguistic Atlas of the Eastern States are sufficiently inclusive to provide the phonic data for describing the pronunciation of each of the 1500 speakers interviewed in phonemic and in phonic terms. This expectation was expressed in the *New England Handbook* (1939), p. 148, in these words:

> Care was taken to provide sufficient material for a rather full description, both phonemic and phonic, of the pronunciation of each informant, and hence for determining the regional and social distribution of the phonic variations of all the phonemes of American English, and for establishing differences in phonemic structure.

The work sheets used in New England are printed in the *Handbook*, pp. 150–58. They contain 814 words and phrases. The work sheets for the Middle and the South Atlantic States are somewhat fuller and include all of the key words of the New England set selected for matters of pronunciation.

Extensive experience with the Atlas records over two decades, both in connection with the preparation of the present volume and the direction of doctoral dissertations devoted to particular problems in the pronunciation of English in the Eastern States, leaves no doubt of the essential soundness of the expectation expressed in 1939. There are, however, some minor reservations.

(1) Although examples are available for all vowel phonemes in their major positions (e.g., before stops, fricatives, and tautosyllabic /r/ as well as finally), there are some minor omissions, notably the type of *story, glory*.

(2) Although the sampling is adequate for describing the pronunciation of speakers living in areas of relatively uniform usage (such as Maine, Metropolitan New York, Philadelphia and vicinity, the Virginia piedmont, the Low Country of South Carolina, and western North Carolina), the speech of informants living in transition belts, and especially in rapidly growing cities located on or near major dialect boundaries (such as Newark, N. J., Baltimore, Md., Roanoke, Va., and Atlanta, Ga.), is at times so mixed and unsettled that some questions have to be left open for lack of sufficient evidence.

1.3 HOW SYSTEMATIC IS SPEECH?

The task of presenting a complicated and fluid linguistic situation in readily intelligible simplified form exposes one to the risk of making the dialects look more regular and systematized than the observed facts warrant. One should, of course, uncover all the regularities; but one should not overlook recalcitrant data or play them down. We have tried to avoid oversystematization and oversimplification in our statements and have taken pains to present the data on which our generalizations rest as fully as we could within our means. Much corroborative material, and some that may require modifications of some of our statements, is available in the collections of the Linguistic Atlas of the Eastern States awaiting publication.

As a means of communication between the members of a community, whether small or large, language is essentially systematic in its sounds and forms. This is as true of the speech ways of the folk as of the dialects of the cultured. It is the first task of the linguist to discover the system and to describe it. Operating on the theory that language is essentially systematic and using a technique for identifying the systematic features, he analyzes the structure of the language or dialect and formulates descriptive statements. Sooner or later he finds features that don't follow the rule, that do not conform to the system; these too he must recognize for what they are. For, though language is essentially systematic, it is never wholly without irregularities and oddities, whatever their origin. This is a simple matter of observation and should surprise no one who is unwilling to forget that all natural languages are historical products developed in the give–and–take between individuals and social groups of a speech community and between speech communities. In this complicated historical process, so different from the creation, once and for all, of an artificial code, features taken from other social and regional dialects are not always adapted to the native system, and innovations in the native system may as yet not be established with consistency, so that elements of an older system survive as relics. To treat such tangible irregularities, current in all natural languages and dialects, as if they were built into the system is to misjudge linguistic realities for the sake of a working theory. The more ingenious the formulations of certain structuralists who are bent upon making oddities look systematic, the more suspect they become.

In our handling of the data we single out the inconsistencies and the vacillations in usage after the regularities have been established. Such deviations from the system are indicative of change in progress, of trends in usage. In fact, changes in systematization, which all living dialects undergo from time to time, are inconceivable without temporary disorganization.

1.4 FROM PHONE TO PHONEME

The analysis, on a purely phonic basis, shows (1) that the preconsonantal segments in such pairs as *grease:crib*, *eight:ten*, *tooth:wood*, *bag:fog*, *nine:down*, etc., are contrastive; (2) that the segments contained in *grease*, *eight*, *tooth*, *fog* occur also at the end of words, as in *three*, *day*, *two*, *law*, *nine*, *down*, whereas those contained in *crib*, *ten*, *wood*, *bag* do not occur in this position; (3) that the "free" segments—those that occur both before consonants and word-finally—are predominantly upgliding, while the "checked" segments—those restricted to preconsonantal position—are usually monophthongal or ingliding.

At this point in the analysis of the phonic data the question must be raised whether the contrastive diphthongal segments should be treated as unit phonemes or broken down into a syllabic and a following unsyllabic element. No clear-cut answer can be given to this question in the present state of phonemic theory. Some scholars advocate a "unitary" interpretation of such segments, others favor a "binary" analysis, and some hold that the choice is a matter of convenience—not a matter of definitive cognition of a linguistic reality.*

Although admitting that a binary interpretation of diphthongal phones of American English more satisfactory than any advanced so far may in time be devised, a unitary interpretation seems more realistic, and certainly more convenient for comparing the dialects of English spoken in the Atlantic States and establishing degrees of diversity or kinship between them on a stated basis. It has been adopted here and is consistently applied to all features of pronunciation dealt with.

From this point of view the stressed vowels of English fall into two classes: (1) FREE VOWELS, as

---

* This problem has recently been discussed by Hans Kurath and James H. Sledd in *Language* 33.111–33.122 (1957) and 34.252–34.260 (1958).

in *three, two, day, know, law, bur, high, boy, now,* which are usually upgliding diphthongs but have monophthongal allophones and diaphones; they occur also in checked position, as in *grease, tooth, eight, road, frost, worm, five, boil, down.* (2) CHECKED VOWELS, as in *crib, wood, ten, sun, bag, crop,* which are often monophthongal but have ingliding allophones and diaphones.

The phonic characteristics of vowels, upglides *vs.* inglides, are most clearly perceptible under heavy stress, especially at the end of a phrase or utterance, where they are apt to be prolonged. They are less noticeable before voiceless stops, somewhat more prominent before voiced stops, fricatives, and sonorants (in ascending order). The upglide of free vowels is most striking in word-final position.

In rapid speech, and especially under half-stress, the "drift" in quality resulting from upglides or inglides may not be observable at all. Hence free and checked vowels of similar quality that are clearly differentiated under heavy stress are less distinct under weaker stress, or even merged in one phonic entity (neutralization).

The unitary interpretation of diphthongal vowels adopted here recommends itself for several reasons.

(1) In most dialects diphthongal and monophthongal variants occur side by side under observable (hence statable) conditions, i.e., in certain positions or under certain prosodic conditions. For instance, a speaker may have [ɪ] in *bit*, [ʊ] in *put*, [æ] in *bat*, and [ɑ] in *lot* but [ɪ⁹] in *crib*, [ʊ⁹] in *good*, [æ·] in *half*, and [ɑ·] in *rod*. From a unitary point of view, [ɪ ∼ ɪ⁹] and [æ ∼ æ·], etc. are positional and/or prosodic allophones of the checked phonemes /ɪ/ and /æ/. Again, some speakers have [e¹] in *day*, [oᵁ] in *know*, and [a·ᵋ] in *nine*, but [e] in *make*, [o] in *coat*, and [ɐɪ] in *twice*; here [e¹ ∼ e, oᵁ ∼ o, a·ᵋ ∼ ɐɪ] are best treated as allophones of the free vowels /e, o, ai/.

The binary interpretation of diphthongal segments as vowel plus "semivowel," if applied consistently, would have to separate [e¹, oᵁ] from [e, o], [a·ᵋ] from [ɐɪ], and certainly also [ɪ⁹, ʊ⁹] from [ɪ, ʊ], and [æ·, ɑ·] from [æ, ɑ] in such cases. For, if [e¹, oᵁ] are taken as /ey, ow/, the segments [ɪ⁹, ʊ⁹] cannot be taken as unit phonemes; nor can the segments [æ·, ɑ·] be taken as units, if length is treated as phonemic in other "syllabic nuclei."

(2) The vowels in *eight* and *road* vary regionally as [ɛɪ ∼ eɪ ∼ e¹ ∼ e· ∼ e⁹] and [ɐʊ ∼ o‹ʊ ∼ oʊ ∼ o·ᵁ ∼ o· ∼ o⁹] but occupy the same position in the system of vowels of the several dialects. All these variants are here taken as regional diaphones of the unit phonemes /e/ and /o/.

In current binary phonemicizations, the variants showing an upglide to [ɪ] and [ʊ] are taken as the sequences /ey/ and /ow/, [e·] and [o·] as /eh/ and /oh/ or /e·/ and /o·/, and the variants [e⁹] and [o⁹] are presumably thrown in with [e·] and [o·] but could be interpreted as /eǝ/ and /oǝ/. In other words, some dialects are said to have an /h/ or /·/, a phoneme of length, in *eight* and *road*, others a /y/ in *eight* and a /w/ in *road*. Since all speakers of American English distinguish /h/ from /y/ and /w/ before vowels, as in *hell : yell : well*, it is rather incredible that speakers who are said to have /y/ and /w/ in *eight* and *road* should not detect the posited postvocalic /h/ in speakers of another dialect. If the untenable /h/ is replaced by another "semivowel," say /ǝ/ or /x/, this difficulty is not resolved. Moreover, there are dialects in which the vowels exemplified in *eight* and *road* vary positionally as [e¹ ∼ e, oᵁ ∼ o] or as [e⁹ ∼ e, o⁹ ∼ o] and must, it seems to us, be taken as the unit phonemes /e/ and /o/.

(3) The vowels before an /r/ of the same syllable, or before the derivative unsyllabic /ǝ/ in certain coastal dialects, present a challenge to any plan of phonemicization. They differ phonically from vowels in other positions in most, if not all, of the dialects, vary strikingly from dialect to dialect, and frequently exhibit a wide range of phonic variation not only within the regional dialects but also in the speech of one and the same person. Clearly, the vowels occurring in this position must be treated with reference to a scheme of vowel phonemes based upon the phonic characteristics of the syllabics in other positions.

The unitary interpretation of syllabics adopted here provides an approach for dealing effectively with vowels before tautosyllabic /r ∼ ǝ/, although some of the decisions may be somewhat arbitrary because of the instability of certain phones or their peculiar character.

The procedure is as follows. After the phonic

character and range of all the phonemes in the major dialects have been determined for other positions, the phones appearing before /r ∼ ə̣/ are compared with the allophones of the several phonemes and assigned to phonemes they most closely resemble. One soon discovers that the phonemic contrasts shown in *beat: bit, tooth: put, eight: set: hat* do not occur before tautosyllabic /r ∼ ə̣/ and that in this position some dialects also lack the contrast exhibited in *coat: caught*. Since there is only one high-front, one high-back, and one mid-to-low front vowel before /r ∼ ə̣/, one is faced with the problem of assigning the phones occurring in *ear, poor* and *care* to /i/ or /ɪ/, to /u/ or /ʊ/, and to /e/ or /ɛ/ or /æ/, respectively. Similarly, in dialects that have one and the same mid-back vowel in *four* and in *forty*, the question arises whether the vowel is that of *coat* or of *caught*. In view of the well-known historical fact that /r/ favors a lowered tongue position of the preceding high and mid vowels, the phones occurring in *ear, poor* and *care* are assigned to the /i, u, e/ of *beat, tooth, eight*, if the tongue position is higher than in the vowels of *bit, put, set*, otherwise to /ɪ, ʊ, ɛ/; and so forth. Decisions must of course be made independently for each dialect, if not for each idiolect.

The practice adopted in some binary interpretations of positing vowel plus /h/ when the vowel before /r ∼ ə̣/ is said to be long is not admissible, if only for the fact that /h/, or whatever other "semivowel" is posited in its place, does not account for the peculiar allophonic deviations of the vowels in this position.

(4) A plausible account of the allophones of phonemes in terms of the articulatory features of adjoining sounds and of prosodic factors is an important matter that no scheme of phonemicization can set aside. Satisfactory handling of this aspect of the phonemes is demanded by sound method in structural linguistics itself and is absolutely required for the understanding of phonemic splits and mergers with which the historian of language is intimately concerned. We believe that the unitary interpretation used in this book does in a large measure account for allophonic variations in realistic terms, whereas the binary approach has signally failed to do so. This failure has repeatedly been pointed out.

1.5 THE STRESSED VOWELS

A systematic comparison of the major dialects of English spoken in the Eastern States shows that they have largely the same system of vowel phonemes, though they differ rather markedly in the phonic character of some of the vowels and in their incidence in the vocabulary. Briefly stated, this is the situation.

(1) All dialects have the five checked vowels /ɪ, ʊ, ɛ, ʌ, æ/, as in *six, wood, ten, sun, bag*. In addition, all dialects except that of Eastern New England and that of Western Pennsylvania have the checked vowel /ɑ/, as in *crop*.

(2) All dialects have the nine free vowels /i, u, e, o, ɜ, ɔ, ai, au, ɔi/, as in *three, two, April, know, sermon, law, five, boil, down*. In addition, those dialects in which postvocalic /r/ is not preserved as such have a free low vowel /a/ or /ɑ/, as in *car, garden*.

(3) The following vowel phonemes are regionally restricted:

(a) The free low vowel /a ∼ ɑ/ occurs only in areas in which postvocalic /r/ is not preserved as such, that is, in Eastern New England, Metropolitan New York, the Upper South, and the Lower South. It appears in such words as *car, garden* and *calm, palm, father*, in Eastern New England also in *half, glass*, etc., though without any consistency. In New England this vowel ranges from low-front [aˑ] to mid-central [ɑˑ] and will be symbolized by /a/; elsewhere it is low-back or low-central-retracted and will be represented by the symbol /ɑ/. Free /a ∼ ɑ/ contrasts with checked /ɑ/, as in *hard* /had ∼ hɑd/ vs. *hod* /hɑd/, except in Eastern New England, which lacks checked /ɑ/.

(b) A checked mid-back vowel /ɵ/, as in *coat, stone*, occurs in New England, chiefly along the Atlantic coast. In this area checked /ɵ/ is in contrast with free /o/, as in *road: rode*; but many New Englanders avoid /ɵ/ entirely or use it rarely. Relics of /ɵ/ survive sporadically in Western New England and in Upstate New York.

(c) A back-gliding free vowel /iu/, as in *music, new* /miuzɪk, niu/, is current in parts of the North alongside the sequence /ju/ or the vowel /u/. It is sharply recessive. As a decrescendo diphthong it must be treated as a unit phoneme, if the [eɪ, oʊ, aɪ, aʊ] of *eight, know, five, down* are so interpreted.

(4) As pointed out above, Eastern New England and Western Pennsylvania lack the checked low vowel /ɑ/ which occurs in all other dialect areas. Here the free low-back phoneme /ɒ/ corresponds to two phonemes, the checked /ɑ/ of *crop, lot* and the free /ɔ/ of *law, frost,* of the other dialects.

These relatively minor differences in the vowel system of the dialects of American English produce four somewhat divergent types of organization, none of which is exactly the same as that of Standard British English. In listing the vowels, checked and free vowels of similar quality are placed side by side, sometimes perhaps rather arbitrarily. The brief comments following the lists point out the existence of such "paired" vowels. The cognitive value of these groupings is by no means clear, but they have a practical bearing on the presentation of differences in the incidence of the vowels in the several dialects, e.g., the incidence of /ɪ ∼ i, ʊ ∼ u, ε ∼ e/ before /r ∼ ɚ/, of /ʊ ∼ u/ in *room, root,* etc.

Type I: *Upstate New York, Eastern Pennsylvania, and the South Midland*

crib:three	ɪ	i			ʊ	u	*wood:tooth*
ten:eight	ε	e		ɜ	ʌ	o	*sun:road*
bag	æ			ɑ		ɔ	*law*
five		ai		au		ɔi	*boil*
			thirty				
			crop				
			down				

The checked high-front, high-back, mid-front, and mid-back vowels are paired with phonically similar free vowels. The other vowels are not so paired. See 2.5, 2.6, and 2.7.

Type II: *Metropolitan New York, the Upper South, and the Lower South*

crib:three	ɪ	i			ʊ	u	*wood:tooth*
ten:eight	ε	e		ɜ	ʌ	o	*sun:road*
bag	æ					ɔ	*law*
					ɑ	ɝ	*crop:car*
five		ai		au		ɔi	*boil*
			thirty				
			down				

The checked high-front, high-back, mid-front, and mid-back vowels are paired with phonically similar free vowels, and the checked low-central vowel with the free low-back vowel. The other vowels are not so paired. See 2.4, 2.8, and 2.9.

Type III: *Eastern New England*

crib:three	ɪ	i			ʊ	u	*wood:tooth*
ten:eight	ε	e		ɜ	θ	o	*road:rode*
bag:car	æ	a			ʌ	ɒ	*sun:law, crop*
five		ai		au		ɒi	*boil*
			thirty				
			down				

The six checked vowels /ɪ, ε, æ, ʌ, θ, ʊ/ are paired with phonically more or less similar free vowels. The free vowels /ɜ, ai, au, ɒi/ are not so paired; in the speech of those who no longer use /θ/, the free vowel /o/ is also unpaired. See 2.2.

Type IV: *Western Pennsylvania*

crib:three	ɪ	i				ʊ	u		*wood:tooth*
ton:oight	ɤ	ɵ		ɞ		ʌ	ꞏ		*sun:road*
bag	æ							ɒ	*law, crop*
five		ai		au		ɒi			*boil*

thirty
down

The high-front, high-back, mid-front, and mid-back checked vowels are paired with phonically similar free vowels. The other vowels are not so paired. See 2.6.

Type V: *Standard British English*

crib:three	ɪ	i				ʊ	u		*wood:tooth*
ten:eight	ɛ	e		ɜ			o		*road*
bag	æ		ʌ	ɤ		ɒ	ɔ		*crop:law*
five		ai		au		ɔi			*boil*

thirty
sun:car
down

The checked vowels /ɪ, ɛ, ʌ, ɒ, ʊ/ are paired with phonically similar free vowels. Checked /æ/ and free /ɜ, o, ai, au, ɔi/ are not so paired.

Inspection of these dialectal vowel systems shows that the differences are largely confined to the low and the raised low vowels. Hence a brief consideration of the origin of these differences may prove helpful. A further reason for outlining the sources of the low vowels at this point is the great diversity in the incidence of the low vowels, as shown in the table given below.

The low vowels of American English are derived from three vowel phonemes of Early Modern English (EMnE): (1) the short checked vowel /æ/ of *bag, glass, car*, etc.; (2) the short checked vowel /o/ of *lot, fog, frost*, etc.; (3) the free diphthongal vowel /au/ of *law, daughter, salt*, etc. The short checked vowels /æ/ and /o/ had positional allophones in some regional varieties of EMnE (as we must infer from their later history), which are phonemicized in various ways in the several dialects of American English. Thus, short /æ/ splits into /æ/ and /ɤ ~ a/ in some dialects, but not in others; short /o/ splits into /ɑ/ and /ɔ/ in certain dialects (the latter joining the /ɔ/ derived from EMnE /au/), but not in others; the EMnE sequence /ær/, passing through [ɑr > ɑ̯ə], develops

The Low Vowel Phonemes and Their Incidence in the Vocabulary

Examples of the Several Historical Types	Standard British English	Eastern New England	Metropolitan New York	Upper South	Lower South	Upstate New York	Eastern Pennsylvania	South Midland	Western Pennsylvania
hat, bag, ashes	æ	æ	æ	æ	æ	æ	æ	æ	æ
glass, calves, can't	ɤ	a	æ	æ	æ	æ	æ	æ	æ
car, father, calm	ɤ	a	ɤ	ɤ	ɤ	ɑ	ɑ	ɑ	ɒ
crop, lot, rod	ɒ	ɒ	ɑ	ɑ	ɑ	ɑ	ɑ	ɑ	ɒ
frost, long, fog	ɒ	ɒ	ɔ	ɔ	ɔ	ɔ	ɔ	ɔ	ɒ
law, daughter, salt	ɔ	ɒ	ɔ	ɔ	ɔ	ɔ	ɔ	ɔ	ɒ
Number of Contrasts	4	3	4	4	4	3	3	3	2

into a new free vowel phoneme /ɑ ~ a/ in several dialects spoken on the Atlantic seaboard, as in Standard British English, but appears as the sequence /ɑr/, containing the checked vowel /ɑ/, in other dialects of American English.

The highly complicated divergent developments and their results in Standard British English (SBE) and in the chief dialects of the Eastern States can be briefly summarized as follows.

In SBE, (1) the EMnE checked vowel /æ/ remains before stops and nasals, as in *bag, man*, etc., and in some other positions. (2) The EMnE sequence /ær/ develops into a free vowel /ɑ/, as in *car, garden*, whereupon the allophone of /æ/ before certain fricatives, as in *laugh, bath, glass, calves*, and before /n/ plus front consonants, as in *can't, dance, branch*, is phonemicized as /ɑ/, though not consistently. (3) Checked EMnE short /o/ remains /ɒ/ before all consonants, as in *lot, fog, frost*, etc. (4) EMnE /au/ becomes the free vowel /ɔ/, as in *law, daughter, salt*. Hence, SBE has two checked low vowels, /æ/ and /ɒ/, and two free low vowels, /ɑ/ and /ɔ/.

In the dialect of Eastern New England, (1) EMnE short /æ/ survives as /æ/ in the same positions as in SBE, but to a considerable extent also before fricatives and especially before /n/ plus front consonants. (2) EMnE /ær/ appears as the free vowel /a/, articulated low-front or low-central (whereas the corresponding SBE /ɑ/ is low-central to low-back); and this /a/ occurs also to some extent in *laugh, bath, glass, can't, aunt*, and occasionally in *dance, France*. (3) EMnE short /o/ and /au/ are completely merged in a free vowel /ɒ/. Thus Eastern New England has only three low vowels, checked /æ/ and free /a/ and /ɒ/.

Metropolitan New York, the Upper South, and the Lower South have the same system of low vowels, although the phonic characteristics of these vowels vary regionally. In these three major dialects, (1) EMnE short /æ/ remains /æ/ in all positions, except before historical /r/, after /w/, and sporadically elsewhere. (2) EMnE /ær/ becomes a free low-back vowel /ɑ/, as in SBE. This vowel occurs also in *father, calm* in all three areas, in *pasture, master* in parts of the South, in *can't, aunt, glass, after*, etc. only occasionally in Virginia and in Metropolitan New York. (3) EMnE short /o/ splits into /ɑ/ and /ɔ/. Unrounded low-central /ɑ/ appears regularly in *lot, crop, cob*, etc., rounded /ɔ/ regularly before voiceless fricatives, as in *cough, frost*, and before /ŋ/, as in *long*, and usually before /g/, as in *dog, fog*. (4) EMnE /au/ appears as /ɔ/, with which the /ɔ/ from earlier short /o/ is merged. These three dialects, therefore, have two checked low vowels, /æ/ and /ɑ/, and two free low vowels, /ɑ/ and /ɔ/.

In three areas—Upstate New York with Western New England, Eastern Pennsylvania, and the South Midland (West Virginia to northernmost Georgia)—three low vowels are current: checked /æ/ and /ɑ/, and free /ɔ/. Here the development is as follows: (1) EMnE /æ/ remains unchanged, except before /r/ and after /w/. (2) /au/ becomes /ɔ/. (3) /o/ splits into /ɑ/ and /ɔ/, and this /ɔ/, as in *cough, frost, dog, long*, is merged with the /ɔ/ derived from EMnE /au/. (4) Earlier /ær/ becomes /ɑr/, the vowel being subsumed under the /ɑ/ from earlier /o/.

In the dialect of Western Pennsylvania, (1) EMnE short /æ/ remains unchanged, except before /r/ and after /w/. (2) EMnE short /o/ and /au/ are completely merged in /ɒ/. (3) The sequence /ær/, as in *car, garden*, becomes phonically [ɑr], which in the absence of an /ɑ/ phoneme must be taken as the phoneme sequence /ɒr/; earlier /wæ/, as in *wash, water*, appears as /wɒ/. Owing to the merging of EMnE short /o/ and /au/ and the preservation of /r/ after vowels, this dialect has only two low vowels, checked /æ/ and free /ɒ/.

In the brief sketches presented above the terms "develop" and "become" are used quite broadly to refer to changes arising either from the rephonemicization of allophones or from dialect mixture. When either one or the other factor is hinted at, the statement must be accepted with proper caution, since we are as yet not in a position to identify the complicated historical changes with finality. Dialect mixture doubtless had a considerable share in these "developments" both in SBE and in AE, as one may safely infer from the many inconsistencies and from unsettled usage in all varieties of English.

1.6 Vowels in Unstressed and Weakly Stressed Syllables

(1) All dialects of American English have a free vowel /ə/ that occurs only in unstressed

syllables. It appears in *sofa* /sofə/, *again* /əgɛn/, etc., in all dialects; in *father* /faðə ∼ fʊðə/, *afternoon* /æftənun/, etc., in dialects that lack postvocalic /r/; in *bucket, houses* /bʌkət, hauzəz/, etc., only in certain dialects. In *borrow, value,* etc., /ə/ alternates with /o, u/, etc., dialectally or prosodically.

(2) Checked /ɪ/, as in *laughing* /læfɪŋ/, occurs frequently in *sausage* /sɔsɪǰ/, etc., in certain dialects also in *bucket, houses* /bʌkɪt, hauzɪz/, etc.

(3) Free /i, u, e, o/, as in *foggy, value, Tuesday, borrow* /fɔgi, vælju, tjuzde, baro/, occur in all dialects. Although /i, u/ often resemble checked /ɪ, ʊ/ under weak stress, these phones must be regarded as prosodic allophones of free vowels because they occur in free position and are often articulated as upgliding diphthongs. The /u, o/ of *value, borrow* alternate dialectally and prosodically with /ə/, the /e/ of *Tuesday* with /i/.

Free /ɜ/ is restricted to dialects that preserve postvocalic /r/. It occurs in *father, further, afternoon* /faðɜ, fɜðɜ, æftənun/, etc.

1.7 The Consonants

All dialects of English spoken in the Eastern States have the same system of consonants, except that the dialects lacking postvocalic /r/ have an additional consonant, /ə̣/, as in *here, care, four, poor* /hiə̣, keə̣, foə̣, puə̣/.

The consonants are:

stops	p	t		č	k	
	b	d		ǰ	g	
fricatives	f	θ	s	š		h
	v	ð	z	ž		
sonorants	m	n	l r		ŋ	
semivowels	w			j	(ʔ)	

The segments preceding the vowel in such words as *chin* /čɪn/ and *gin* /ǰɪn/ are here treated as units, although they exhibit peculiarities in clustering. They enter into clusters with sonorants after syllabics, as do other stops; compare, for instance, *branch, mulch* /brænč, mʌlč/ with *bank, milk* /bæŋk, mɪlk/, and *singe, bulge* /sɪnǰ, bʌlǰ/ with *bend, build* /bend, bɪld/. On the other hand, they do not enter into clusters with sonorants and semivowels before vowels, as other stops actually do, as, for instance, in *clean, crib, cube, quit* and *glass, green, argue, guano*. To regard the initial segments of *chin* and *gin* as phonemically complex, i.e., as consisting of a stop plus a fricative, is to recognize a type of cluster unparalleled in English, one that, in addition, exhibits after vowels the sequence stop-fricative, as in *peach* /pitš/ and *edge* /ɛdž/, whereas in other clusters containing a stop and a fricative the sequence is fricative-stop, as in *loft, lost*. Neither treatment can do away with a patently peculiar feature of the English consonant system.

CHAPTER 2

REGIONAL DIALECTS OF CULTIVATED SPEECH

2.1 INTRODUCTORY REMARKS

THE DESCRIPTION of the chief regional types of cultivated speech in the Eastern States is based upon field records of 157 speakers in 136 different communities. All of these records were made in the homes of the informants by trained observers. Synopses of relevant features of pronunciation are presented for only about one half of the speakers, though the data for all of them were taken into consideration in framing the statements concerning regional usage. Hence it seems desirable to give in an appendix to this chapter a brief account of all the speakers interviewed for this purpose. Their location is shown on Map 1 by numbers.

The notes on the lives of the speakers contain, as far as available, the following information: (1) the name of the community, with the population figure for 1930 (unless under 2,000); (2) occupation and sex, age at the time of the interview, religious denomination, membership in clubs and societies; (3) extent and character of formal education, reading habits; (4) family background; (5) the fieldworker's comments on social class, attitude, etc., of the informant (enclosed in single quotation marks); (6) comments on tempo and articulation; (7) the initial of the fieldworker, the year of the interview.

Unless otherwise indicated, all of the speakers whose lives appear in the appendix were born, grew up, and lived continuously in the communities they represent, are descendants of local families, and were educated locally or within the region. Most of them have attended finishing school or college, and many of them play—or have played—leading roles in their communities.

The speakers classified here as "cultured" are representatives of a group comprising the social and cultural elite and the upper middle class. They differ considerably among themselves with regard to social position and the kinds of social contacts they enjoy in their communities; they come from many walks of life (physicians, lawyers, bankers, merchants, farmers, writers, scholars, men of leisure, housewives, etc.); some are well to do, others not; many are college graduates, others largely self-taught; some have wide intellectual and esthetic interests, others are largely absorbed in their professional activities; some read widely, others not. Though most of them were between 45 and 65 at the time of the interview, others were considerably older and a few younger. Despite all the diversity among these speakers, they all belong to a social class distinct from the lower middle class and the folk.

A rather marked social cleavage exists in the Eastern States only in the old plantation country (linguistically, the South) and in the old cities on the Atlantic seaboard, notably Boston, New York, Philadelphia, Baltimore, Richmond, and Charleston. Elsewhere there is rather a gradation from the cultured to the folk, especially in rural areas, both the cultured and the folk merging into the dominant middle class.

This well-known fact was taken into account in selecting cultured speakers in the several areas and communities. It is, of course, not to be expected that the 157 cultured speakers chosen from a total population of about 50 million can tell the whole story of cultivated usage in the Eastern States. The sampling is too limited to reflect differences and trends in usage within the group, and it gives no indication of the relative size of the cultured class in the several regions and communities. However, it has sufficient validity to establish the existence of regional types of cultivated speech; it furnishes sufficient data for delineating the characteristic phonemic and phonic features of these regional types (even for showing some of the more common incidental features); and it permits at least a tentative delimitation of the areas occupied by the several regional types of cultivated speech. The very fact that in such focal areas as Eastern New England, Metropolitan New York, and the Upper and Lower South the cultured speakers—selected from various walks of life, with rather different backgrounds, and from several age groups—are in substantial agreement would seem to guarantee the validity of the sample. This claim is further substantiated by the fact that in areas that exhibit diversity in word usage, and in the margins of the focal areas, cultured speakers often are shown to differ among themselves in matters of pronunciation.

The brief outlines presented below of the major regional types of cultivated English spoken in the Eastern States would therefore seem to be trustworthy. In any event, they are based upon data collected systematically and vastly more extensive than any that have been available hitherto. It is a highly significant fact that in the major focal areas cultivated speech rarely diverges from the speech of the middle class, or even from that of the folk, in the system of phonemes or the phonic character of the phonemes, whereas in the margins of these areas cultured speakers often differ from other speakers, since they are the first to adopt features of the culturally dominant focal areas.

Conservative as the outlines of regional usage are, they nevertheless involve generalizations. For this reason a rather large number of "synopses" of the practices of individual speakers is appended to each section of this chapter. The symbols representing the vowel phones occurring in key words are entered in columns headed by phonemic symbols. If a phone is not clearly assignable to a particular phoneme, the entry is followed by an arrow pointing away from the column to suggest that its phonemic status is in doubt. Some entries have been slightly simplified, but otherwise they merely reproduce the field worker's notation. It should be noted that for words with a historical /r/ after the vowel the /r/ or its reflex (if any) has been included in the tabulation.

Features in which the usage of the middle class and the folk differs from that of the cultured are referred to only in passing. Deviations from the phonemic system of the cultured are rare, purely phonic differences rather uncommon. On the other hand, the folk and the middle group often use vowel phonemes in certain words that the cultured avoid. Such instances are rather fully treated in the chapter on the incidence of vowels.

2.2 EASTERN NEW ENGLAND

Synopses 3–21

Although considerable variation occurs in the cultivated speech of Eastern New England in the pronunciation of some of the vowel phonemes and their incidence, the entire area has the same configuration of distinctive phonemic features.

As in other areas where postvocalic /r/ is lost as such, (1) an unsyllabic /ə/ is current after the high and mid vowels of *ear, poor, care, four,* and (2) *car, garden* /ka, gadɪn/ have a free low-front or low-central vowel /a/ contrasting with the free low-back vowel /ɒ/ of *law, crop, John,* etc.

A regional feature not found elsewhere in the Eastern States (except as a relic in Western New England and in parts of Upstate New York) is a checked vowel /ɵ/ in such words as *coat, road, home,* contrasting with the free vowel /o/ of *know, rode,* etc. This phonemic feature, traditionally known as the "New England short *o*," is much more common in the speech of the folk and the middle class than in cultivated speech, and its incidence in the vocabulary varies greatly from section to section and from person to person. However, all cultured speakers have it, if only as a relic in a few "homely" words.

Another regional phonemic feature, a back-gliding free vowel /iu/ instead of /u/ or the sequence /ju/, as in *new, tube, music,* is much less common in Eastern New England than to the west of it; one hears it from Narragansett Bay to Cape Cod and in New Hampshire and Maine, rarely in eastern Massachusetts.

The phonic characteristics of the vowel phonemes of this regional dialect are as follows.

The checked high and mid vowels /ɪ, ʊ, ɛ, ʌ/, as in *six, wood, head, sun,* are usually short monophthongs, but have ingliding positional and/or prosodic allophones. The raised low-front vowel /æ/, as in *ashes, bag, glass,* is often long and has ingliding allophones. The checked /ɵ/, as in *coat, road, home*, is a fronted mid-back vowel, more or less rounded, usually very short, and often ingliding; it is never confused with the /ʌ/ of *sun*, which is unrounded and has a lower tongue position.

The free high and mid vowels /i, u, e, o/, as in *three, two, eight, know*, usually have a rather close beginning and a brief upglide (often so brief that several of the fieldworkers wrote them down as monophthongs). /ai, au/, as in *five, down*, usually have a swift upglide from a low-front or low-central position; in folk speech they appear also as [ɐɪ, ɐʊ], with a centralized beginning. /au/ as [æʊ, ɛʊ] occurs only in rural folk speech. The /ɒi/ of *boil, joint* varies from [oˇɪ] to [ɔɪ].

The free low vowels /a/ and /ɒ/, as in *car* and *law*, and the free mid-central vowel /ɜ/ of *thirty, sermon*, are monophthongal and usually prolonged at the end of a word or syllable; in other positions their length varies considerably.

The free vowel /a/ ranges phonically from low-front [aˑ, a] to low-central [ɑˑ, ɑ], the latter variant being apparently preferred by some cultured persons in urban areas. This phoneme (from earlier /ɑ̹ < ɑr/) appears regularly in *car, barn, garden* /ka, ban, gadɪn/, and in *father, palm, calm*; in *half, glass, aunt, dance*, etc., the incidence of /a/ varies greatly both regionally and individually.

The free vowel /ɒ/ is most commonly a low-back-raised [ɒˇˑ, ɒˇ] sound, more or less rounded; however, it varies all the way from low-back-unrounded [ɑ] to well-rounded [ɔ], partly by position or prosody, partly in regional and social dissemination. This phoneme occurs regularly in *law, water, dog, frost*, etc., in *forty, morning, corn*, /fɒti, mɒnɪŋ, kɒn/, etc. (from earlier /ɒ̹ < ɒr/), and in *crop, rod, John, college, borrow*. It should be noted that in this regional dialect, as in that of Western Pennsylvania, *crop, rod, John*, etc., have the same vowel phoneme as *law, dog, frost*, etc.; on the other hand, *car, barn, garden*, etc., and *father, palm*, which have /ɒ/ in Western Pennsylvania, have contrastive /a/ in this area.

The free vowel /ɜ/ of *thirty, Thursday, sermon, girl*, etc., is usually an unrounded mid-central vowel [ɝ, ɜ], but in the Boston area it is often raised and rounded to [ɞˇˑ, ɞˇ], in New Hampshire and Maine backed to [ɝ>, ʌ̹]. Moreover, a slightly constricted variant [ɝ] is not uncommon along the western margin of this area (central New England) and from Narragansett Bay to Cape Cod in the speech of those who do not have postvocalic /r/ in *ear, care, four*, etc. (It should be noted that Martha's Vineyard and Marblehead preserve a fully constricted /ɜ/ along with postvocalic /r/.)

Five vowel phonemes occur before unsyllabic /ɘ/ (derived from postvocalic /r/): /i ~ ɪ/ as in *ear, beard*, /æ ~ ɛ ~ e/ as in *chair, care*, /ɒ/ as in *war, forty, horse*, /o/ as in *four, hoarse*, and /u ~ ʊ/ as in *poor*; after /ɒ/ the unsyllabic /ɘ/ is sometimes lost, so that *war* rimes with *law*. *Wire, flower* /waiɘ, flauɘ/ are disyllabic, ending in the vowel /ɘ/. Occasionally such words as *chair* and *four*, which normally are pronounced in one syllable as /čæɘ/ and /foɘ/, become disyllabic /čæɘ ~ čæjɘ, foɘ ~ fowɘ/ under heavy stress, ending in syllabic /ɘ/.

Before intersyllabic /r/, free /e/ and checked /ɛ/ remain distinct, as in *Mary* and *merry*, respectively.

The unstressed syllables of *houses, haunted, bucket* have checked /ɪ/, pronounced as a lowered high-central [ɪˇ].

In summary, the characteristic features of the cultivated speech of Eastern New England are:

(1) The presence in the phonemic system of a free vowel /a/, as in *car, garden*; a checked vowel /ɵ/, as in *coat, home*; an unsyllabic /ɘ/, as in *ear, care, war, four, poor*.

(2) The pronunciation of the free vowel of *car, garden* as a predominantly low-front [aˑ]; of the vowel of *law* as a weakly rounded [ɒˇˑ]; of the /ɜ/ of *thirty, sermon* as unconstricted; of the vowels in *five, down* as fast diphthongs starting low-front or low-central; and of the vowels of *three, April, know, two* as fast upgliding diphthongs with close beginning.

(3) The occurrence of the /a/ of *car* in *half, glass, aunt*, though without consistency, and of the /ɒ/ of *law* in *lot, John*, etc.; the restriction of /r/ to prevocalic position and the resulting positional allomorphs in such words as *ear* /iɘ ~ iɘr/, *four* /foɘ ~ foɘr/, *war* /wɒɘ ~ wɒɘr/, etc. (analogically also in *law* /lɒ ~ lɒɘr/), the forms

with /r/ occurring prevocalically in such phrases as *ear and eye, four apples, war and peace, law and order*.

Of these features, the unique checked vowel /ɵ/ of *road, home* is clearly recessive; the incidence of /a/ in *half, glass, aunt*, etc., is quite variable and subject to conflicting trends; and in some urban communities the vowel in such words as *lot, John* /lɒt, ǰɒn/ tends to merge with that of *car, garden* /ka, gadɪn/ in an [ɑ·]-like sound.

2.3 THE LOWER CONNECTICUT VALLEY
Synopses 25–32

In the Lower Connecticut Valley and the New Haven area usage varies considerably, both socially and regionally. Cultured speakers in urban areas usually have two unrounded low vowels, a free low-front to low-central vowel /a/, as in *car, barn, father, palm, half, aunt*, and a checked low-central to low-back vowel /ɑ/, as in *crop, rod, John, college*; but the two are not always kept apart. Another feature of cultivated city speech in this area is the loss of postvocalic /r/ as such, which however is not universal, and the consequent emergence of unsyllabic /ə̯/ after high and mid vowels. Speakers who retain post-vocalic /r/ tend to merge /a/ and /ɑ/ in a low-central vowel.

The checked high and mid vowels /ɪ, ʊ, ɛ, ʌ/, as in *six, wood, head, sun*, are short monophthongs, but may be positionally or prosodically ingliding; the checked low vowels /æ, ɑ/, as in *bag, John*, are monophthongal and not infrequently prolonged.

The free vowels /i, u, a, ɔ, ɜ/, as in *three, two, car, law, sermon*, tend to be long, but may be positionally or prosodically short. /ɜ/ is usually unconstricted, but may have slight constriction; upgliding [ɜ�^ɪ] occurs sporadically. /a/ ranges from low-front [a] to low-central [ɑ]; some speakers have [a] rather consistently, some fluctuate between [a] and [ɑ], others have predominantly [ɑ] (by preference, it seems). This phoneme occurs in *car, garden* /ka, gadən/, etc., in *father, palm*, and —though rather erratically—in *half, glass, aunt*, etc. /ɔ/ is usually well-rounded and long, but has less rounded short [ɒ]-like variants.

The free vowels /e, o, ai, au/, as in *eight, coat,*

five, down, have a swift upglide, which is rather brief in /e, o/; /ɔi/, on the other hand, is often a "slow" diphthong. /ai, au/ have a low-front to low-central beginning; the variants [ɐɪ] and [æʊ] occur only in folk speech.

Postvocalic /r/ is often lost after the low vowels of *car, garden* /ka, gadən/ and *corn, horse* /kɔn, hɔs/ and appears as unsyllabic /ə̯/ after the high and mid vowels of *ear, poor, care, four*. *Care, chair, stairs* have /ɛ ~ e/, rarely /æ/; *Mary* and *merry* usually have contrastive vowels.

The speech of the Lower Connecticut Valley and the New Haven area has some structural features in common with that of Eastern New England, though these features do not occur with the same regularity: (1) the loss of postvocalic /r/ as such; and (2) the consequent emergence of a free vowel /a/ in *car, garden* and of unsyllabic /ə̯/ after the high and mid vowels in *ear, poor, care, four*. It differs from it: (1) in having the contrasting vowels /ɑ/ and /ɔ/ in *crop, John* and *law, frost, dog*, respectively, which are merged in /ɒ/ in Eastern New England; (2) in having a rather unstable low-front /a/ in *car, father, calm* contrasting, at times, with low-central /ɑ/ in *lot, John*; and (3) in the rather uncommon use of /a ~ ɑ/ in *calf, glass, aunt*, etc.

2.4 METROPOLITAN NEW YORK
Synopses 41–43 and 60–65

The speech of Metropolitan New York (comprising Manhattan, the Bronx, Brooklyn, and Staten Island) possesses a rather distinctive configuration of phonemic, phonic, and incidental features, most of which are shared by all social groups in this densely populated urban area.

The most important characteristics of the speech of Metropolitan New York are the loss of postvocalic /r/ as such and the consequent structural innovations: (1) the emergence of an unsyllabic phoneme /ə̯/ after high and mid vowels, as in *ear, poor, care, four* /iə̯, puə̯, kɛə̯, fɔə̯/, and (2) the rise of a free low-back vowel /ɒ/, as in *car, garden* /kɒ, gɒdən/, contrasting with the checked low-central vowel /ɑ/ of *lot, John*. These changes in phonemic structure, it should be noted, occur in all other areas on the Atlantic seaboard where postvocalic /r/ is not preserved as such—

Eastern New England, the Upper South, and the Lower South—although there are many differences in detail.

The phonic characteristics of the vowel phonemes in the cultivated speech of this area are as follows.

The checked high and mid vowels /ɪ, ʊ, ɛ, ʌ/, as in *six, wood, head, sun,* are short monophthongs, with occasional inglides. The low vowels /æ, ɑ/ are positionally and/or prosodically long or short, and occasionally ingliding. Long [æ·, æ·ᵊ] is especially common in *bag, half, glass, aunt.* Long [ɑ·] is usual in *John,* regular in *glass, bath, aunt, can't,* in the speech of those cultured New Yorkers who do not have /æ/ in these words; it occurs sometimes in *car, barn, garden* in place of the free vowel /ɑ/.

The free vowels /i, u, ɜ, ɔ, ɑ/, as in *three, two, thirty, law, car,* are long monophthongs. /i, u/ sometimes have a slight upglide, /ɔ, ɑ/ a brief inglide; /ɔ/ is well-rounded. The /ɑ/ of *car, garden* and *father, palm* is low-back-fronted [ɑ‹·] or low-central-backed [a›·] and not always differentiated from the long allophone [ɑ·] of the checked vowel /ɑ/ in *John, log* (so that *barn* may rime with *John*). The free vowel /ɜ/, as in *thirty, sermon,* is a long mid-central monophthong [ɜ˄·, ɵ˄·] in the speech of most cultured informants (especially in Manhattan), but others use an upgliding diphthong [ɜɪ, ɵɪ], which is regular among middle-class speakers.

The free vowels /e, o, ai, ɔi, au/, as in *eight, know, five, boil, down,* are upgliding diphthongs. /e, o/ have a rather close beginning, /o/ appearing as fronted or centralized [oʂʊ, ɵʊ]. /ai, au/, as in *five, down,* have a low-front beginning and usually a rather quick upglide. The /ɔi/ of *join, boil,* pronounced as [ɔɪ, oˇɪ], is clearly distinguished from the /ɜ/ of *learn, curl* in cultivated speech. Only some of the less educated speakers merge /ɔi/ and /ɜ/, so that *join, boil* rime with *learn, curl* either on /ɔi/ or on /ɜ/.

The incidence of checked /ɑ/ and free /ɑ/ in the vocabulary varies considerably and the usage of some speakers is obviously unsettled. Checked /ɑ/ occurs regularly in *crop, John, college,* pronounced as low-central [a, a˄], often prolonged, as in *John, log.* Free /ɑ/, pronounced as a long backish [ɑ‹·, a›·], is fairly regular in *car, barn,*

garden, and in *father, palm.* On the other hand, in *half, glass, aunt,* etc., cultured speakers who avoid /æ/ in some of these words have a longish [a›·, a·], which does not clearly fall in with either /ɑ/ or /ɑ/, since checked /ɑ/ is often long in *John, log,* etc.

Before unsyllabic /ə/ (derived from postvocalic /r/) only two high and two mid vowels actually occur: /i/ in *ear, beard* [ɪ˄·ə, bɪ˄·əd]; /u/ in *poor* [pʊ˄·ə]; /ɛ/ in *care, stairs* [kɛ·ə, stɛ·əz]; /ɔ/ in *four, door* [fɔ·ə, dɔ·ə]. All four vowels are long monophthongs in this position and are articulated with lowered tongue position (as indicated in brackets above), the original /o/ of *four, door* being merged with the /ɔ/ of *law, loss,* etc., and of *forty, horse,* etc.

As pointed out above, earlier /ɑr/ yields the free vowel /ɑ/ in this dialect, presumably by way of /ɑə/; in similar fashion, earlier /ɔr/, passing through a stage /ɔə/, yields /ɔ/ in *forty, horse* /fɔti, hɔs/, the vowel being articulated as [ɔ· ~ ɔ·ᵊ], exactly as in *water, frost.* In *hoarse, mourning,* which had earlier /or/ before a consonant, some speakers seem to retain the sequence /ɔə/ in the same way as in *four, door,* but most of them reduce it to /ɔ/ in this position, so that *hoarse, mourning* rime with *horse, morning.*

Before intersyllabic /r/, *Mary, dairy* have the sequence /ɛə/, pronounced [ɛ·ə], as in *care,* whereas *merry, cherry* have simply the /ɛ/ of *head, egg.*

Several of the most striking features of the speech of Metropolitan New York (notably /ə/ for postvocalic /r/ in *ear, care, poor, four;* the free vowel /ɑ/ of *car, garden;* to a lesser extent the pronunciation of /ɜ/ as [ɜɪ] in such words as *thirty, sermon*) are now also current across the Hudson River in Jersey City and Newark and vicinity, and have been adopted by some cultured speakers in the Hudson Valley as far north as Albany, though rarely with any consistency. See the synopses for Jersey City, Poughkeepsie, Kingston, and Albany.

2.5 UPSTATE NEW YORK AND WESTERN NEW ENGLAND

Synopses 35–39 and 44–56

The cultivated speech of Upstate New York and adjoining parts of Western New England is remarkably uniform in phonemic structure, in the phonic characteristics of the vowel phonemes, and even in the incidence of the phonemes.

The checked high and mid vowels /ɪ, ʊ, ɛ, ʌ/, as in *six, wood, ten, sun,* are short monophthongs with occasional prolonged or ingliding allophones. The checked low vowels /æ, ɑ/ are positionally and/or prosodically short or long. /æ/ occurs regularly not only in *bag, ashes, married,* etc., but also in *half, glass, aunt,* etc., although some cultured speakers may deliberately use /ɑ/ in some words of the latter group. Checked /ɑ/, pronounced as low-central [ɑ], sometimes fronted toward [a], is normal in *drop, John, college,* etc., in *car, garden,* etc., and in *father, palm;* it occurs also beside the more common /ɔ/ in *log, foggy,* etc., and sporadically in *half, glass, aunt* in place of the usual /æ/.

The free high and mid vowels /i, u, e, o/, as in *three, two, April, know,* have a rather close beginning and a brief upglide; however, the high vowels /i, u/ may be monophthongal, occasionally also the mid vowels /e, o/. The back vowels /u, o/, though usually fully back, are sometimes somewhat fronted.

The free vowels /ai, au, ɔi/, as in *five, down, boil,* are upgliding diphthongs. /ai/ and /au/ usually start in a somewhat fronted and raised low-central position and glide swiftly upward; although a higher initial position is common in the speech of other social groups in this area, pronunciations such as [ɐɪ ~ əɪ, ɐu ~ əu] are now rare in cultivated speech.

The free vowels /ɔ/ and /ɜ/, as in *law* and *sermon,* are monophthongal and positionally long. /ɔ/ has a rather low tongue position and is but slightly rounded; it occurs in *law, daughter, water,* in *frost, off,* in *dog, fog,* and in *corn, forty* /kɔrn, fɔrti/, etc. The mid-central vowel /ɜ/ of *sermon, thirty,* etc., is usually fully constricted, but some cultured speakers (as in Rochester, N. Y., and Burlington, Vt.) waver between weak and full constriction.

The back-gliding diphthong /iu/ in place of /ju/ or /u/, as in *music, Tuesday,* is quite rare in the cultivated speech of this area, but not uncommon in the speech of the other social groups.

Postvocalic /r/ is pronounced as a more or less constricted [ɚ ~ ə]. Before it, the following vowels occur: /i ~ ɪ/, as in *ear, beard;* /u ~ ʊ/, as in *poor;* /ɛ ~ e ~ æ/, as in *stairs, care;* /o/, as in *four, hoarse;* /ɔ/ as in *forty, horse;* and /ɑ/, as in *barn, garden.* All the vowels are monophthongal or ingliding in this position, and usually short. It should be noted that /o/ and /ɔ/ are not merged before /r/ in this dialectal type, as they are in Metropolitan New York and in Pennsylvania, but they differ less in quality than in Eastern New England.

Although in this area /e, ɛ, æ/ do not occur in contrast before an /r/ of the same syllable, these three phonemes are distinguished before intersyllabic /r/, as in *Mary* [ɛˑ, ɛə] vs. *merry* [ɛ] vs. *married* [æ], but *Mary,* though usually /meri/, sometimes rimes with *merry* /mɛri/.

In the Genesee Valley area of western New York State (Rochester, Bath) some speakers vacillate between a more or less constricted postvocalic /r/ and unsyllabic /ə/ in such words as *ear, care, garden, four,* etc. This is a relic of usage brought into this area from Eastern New England, whereas in the Hudson Valley the same phenomenon is more probably due to a rather recent influence of Metropolitan New York. In the lower Hudson Valley some cultured speakers have also adopted the unconstricted diphthongal [ɜɪ ~ ɞɪ] of Metropolitan New York in such words as *thirty, sermon* /θɜti, sɜmən/, etc.

2.6 PENNSYLVANIA

Synopses 72–88

The distinctive features of all varieties of cultivated speech current in Pennsylvania (exclusive of the New England settlements in the northern counties) are: (1) the preservation of /r/ after vowels, as in *ear, care, barn, four, poor,* articulated as a fully constricted [ɚ] or, as in parts of the western section, as a retroflex apical [r]; (2) short vowels both before tautosyllabic and intersyllabic /r/, as in *ear, care* and *Mary, merry;* (3) the pronunciation of the mid-central vowel /ɜ/, as in *thirty, sermon,* with full constriction; and (4) the merging of /o/ and /ɔ/ before tautosyllabic /r/, as in *four, forty,* and of /e/ and /ɛ/ before intersyllabic /r/, as in *Mary, merry.*

The articulation of some of the vowel phonemes varies regionally: the Delaware Valley (Philadelphia), the lower Susquehanna Valley (York, Harrisburg), the Great Valley with its German centers (Reading), and the valley of the upper Ohio and its tributaries (Pittsburgh, Wheeling) all have certain distinctive phonic features, which are pointed out below.

The most important isogloss within Pennsylvania follows roughly the crest of the Allegheny Mountains. To the east of this divide, the /ɔ/ of *law, salt, dog*, etc., is in contrast with the /ɑ/ of *lot, crop, father*; to the west /ɔ/ and /ɑ/ are merged in /ɒ/.

Eastern Pennsylvania

The four cultured speakers interviewed in Philadelphia are remarkably uniform in their practice. They all exhibit the general Pennsylvania (North Midland) features listed above, distinguish between the /ɔ/ of *law* and the /ɑ/ of *lot*, and pronounce the various vowels in very similar ways.

The phonic characteristics of the vowels are as follows.

The checked high and mid vowels /ɪ, ʊ, ɛ, ʌ/, as in *six, wood, ten, sun*, are short monophthongs but have ingliding positional allophones. The checked low vowels /æ/ and /ɑ/, as in *bag, half* and *crop, father, palm*, have long and short positional allophones and are often ingliding. /ɑ/ is low-central, occasionally slightly backed; before /r/, as in *barn, garden*, it is a back [ɑ] and sometimes slightly rounded.

The free vowels /ɔ/ and /u/, as in *law*, and *two*, are longish monophthongs, /u/ being slightly fronted; /i/, as in *three, grease*, is slightly upgliding or monophthongal. The free mid vowels /e/ and /o/, as in *April* and *know*, are pronounced as [ɛɪ] and [ɤʊ]; both have an open beginning and a marked upglide, and /o/ starts in or near mid-central position. The upgliding free vowels /ai, au, ɔi/, as in *five, down, boil*, vary from slow to fast (as in the Delaware Valley generally); /ai, au/ start low-front rather than low-central.

As to the vowels occurring before /r/, *care, Mary, merry* clearly have the checked /ɛ/ of *egg*, and *barn, garden* a backed allophone of the /ɑ/ of *lot*. The vowels occurring in *ear, poor, four* usually have a somewhat higher tongue position than the

vowels in *crib, wood, law*, respectively, and are to be regarded as lowered allophones of the free vowels in *three, two, know* rather than as raised variants of the corresponding checked vowels.

Three cultured speakers interviewed within 25 miles of Philadelphia (Burlington, N. J., Chester, Pa., Wilmington, Del.) differ only slightly from the Philadelphians, if at all. The Burlington informant uses [æ·ʊ, æʊ] in *down, out*, which is common enough in West Jersey; the Wilmington speaker has contrasting vowels in *four : forty*, which is usual on Delmarva.

Divergences from Philadelphia usage increase markedly with distance. Thus, Easton, Pa., has a close beginning in upgliding /e, o/; Reading, with its German background, has close monophthongal [i·, u·, e·, o·] in *three, two, eight, know* and fast diphthongs [aɪ, aʊ] in *five, down*; the cities on the lower Susquehanna (Lancaster, York, Harrisburg) have the slow diphthongs [a·ɪ, æ·ʊ] in *five* and *down*, while /e/ and /o/ vary as [ɛɪ ∼ eɪ ∼ e·] and [ɤʊ ∼ oʊ ∼ o·]; Wilkes-Barre on the West Branch of the Susquehanna conforms rather to the New York State type of cultivated speech with its fast diphthongs /ai, au/, close upgliding /e, o/, and contrasting vowels in *four : forty*. Thus, Philadelphia influence upon the cultivated speech of eastern Pennsylvania, while undeniable, appears to be limited to a radius of from fifty to seventy-five miles; even here the sharp regional differences of earlier days, created by the settlement of three national stocks (English, Ulster Scots, and Germans), have persisted rather extensively.

Western Pennsylvania

In addition to the features common to cultivated Pennsylvania speech, the western part of the state has a number of regional characteristics shared by the cultured with the middle class and the folk.

First of all, the checked vowel /ɑ/ of *lot, John, palm, barn* is merged with the free vowel /ɔ/ of *law, frost, dog* in a free vowel /ɒ/. This /ɒ/ has a considerable range of allophones; it is usually a raised low-back vowel [ɒˑ], more or less rounded and prolonged, but may be positionally short and even unrounded, as before the voiceless stops in *lot, daughter,* and especially before /r/, as in *barn, garden.*

The phonic characteristics of the other vowels in this area agree in part with those of the Philadelphia area, but differ in other respects.

The checked high and mid vowels /ɪ, ʊ, ɛ, ʌ/, as in *six, wood, ten, sun,* are short monophthongs with positionally ingliding allophones (as in *crib, brush*). The checked low vowel /æ/ has long and short positional allophones and ingliding variants. As pointed out above, this dialect has no checked low phoneme /ɑ/.

Of the free high vowels, the /i/ of *three, grease* is a slightly upgliding [iˇi] or a long monophthong [i·], the /u/ of *two, shoes* a high-central monophthong [ʉ· ~ ʉ·]. The free mid vowels /e/ and /o/, as in *eight, April* and *road, know,* are upgliding diphthongs [ɛɪ ~ eˇɪ] and [ɵʊ ~ o‹ʊ] with a more or less open beginning, the latter being centralized or fronted. The upgliding free vowels of *five, down, boil* are usually "fast" diphthongs, /ai/ and /au/ beginning low-front.

The free mid-central vowel /ɜ/ of *thirty, sermon* is pronounced as an apical [ᵊr], less commonly as a constricted [ɚ]. The consonant /r/ after vowels, as in *ear, care, barn, four, poor,* exhibits a corresponding diversity in articulation.

As in Eastern Pennsylvania, the number of vowels occurring before tautosyllabic and intersyllabic /r/ is severely limited. *Care, Mary, merry* have the checked /ɛ/ of *egg; ear* and *poor* have free /i/ and /u/ rather than checked /ɪ/ and /ʊ/; *four, forty* have a lowered allophone [ɔ] of the free /o/ of *know, road;* the vowel in *barn, garden,* though usually unrounded, must be assigned to the free /ɒ/ of *lot, law,* etc. All vowels before /r/ are short.

The cultivated speech of Western Pennsylvania is even less uniform than that of the eastern section. The type described above is best exemplified in the immediate vicinity of Pittsburgh and the valleys of the Allegheny and the Beaver to the north. The cultivated speech of Wheeling, W. Va., though agreeing substantially with that of the Pittsburgh area, distinguishes the /ɑ/ and /ɔ/ of *lot* and *law;* in the valley of the Monongahela in West Virginia *four* and *forty* have contrastive phonemes; and so forth.

It is a significant fact that two rather striking phonic features shared by southeastern and western Pennsylvania, the [ɛɪ, ɵʊ] of *eight, road* are uncommon or absent in the central part of the state, and that, on the other hand, they are current in areas adjoining the Philadelphia and the Pittsburgh areas. Southeastern Pennsylvania shares these features with West Jersey and Delaware, Western Pennsylvania with the West Virginia side of the Ohio Valley. It is very likely that these features were brought to the Pittsburgh area by the many settlers who came from eastern Pennsylvania and from New Jersey.

2.7 THE SOUTH MIDLAND

Synopses 89, 91, 117, 129

The South Midland area, comprising the far-flung Appalachians and the Blue Ridge from the Pennsylvania line to northern Georgia (a stretch of some 500 miles), is a linguistically graded area without any one dominant population center. Nevertheless, it has a unique configuration of dialect features that sets it off from the North Midland (Pennsylvania) and from the South. None of the features in this complex are unique in themselves; all of them occur either in the North Midland or the South. But the configuration of features is peculiar to the South Midland.

In this area the checked high and mid vowels /ɪ, ʊ, ɛ, ʌ/, as in *crib, wood, ten, sun,* are predominantly ingliding and not infrequently prolonged, especially south of the Kanawha River. The /ʌ/ of *sun, brush, judge* is decidedly raised and sometimes slightly rounded, the /ʊ/ of *wood, pull* fronted and sometimes centered to [ʉ]. The checked low vowel /æ/ of *bag, glass, aunt,* etc., is often prolonged; it is ingliding north of the Kanawha, upgliding to the south of it. The checked low vowel /ɑ/, as in *lot, John,* in *car, garden,* and in *father, palm,* is a low-central [ɑ, ɑ·], positionally prolonged, as in *John, father.*

The free high vowels /i, u/, as in *three, two,* are long monophthongs, but occasionally slightly upgliding; /u/ is fronted or fully centered to [ʉ·]. The free mid vowels /e, o/ of *April, road,* etc., are upgliding and have a close beginning. /ɔ/, as in *law, frost, dog* and in *forty, corn,* is well-rounded and prolonged, less commonly an upgliding [ɒə]. The mid-central vowel /ɜ/ of *thirty, sermon* is fully constricted; it occurs rather frequently also in *ear, beard* /jɜ, bjɜd/.

The free vowels /ai/ and /au/, as in *five, twice* and *down, out*, vary regionally. North of the Kanawha they are slow diphthongs in all positions, /ai/ being pronounced as [a·ɪ], /au/ as [æ·ɵ]; in the valley of the Kanawha (as in Charleston) and farther south, the fast variants [aɪ ∼ ɐɪ] and [au ∼ ɐu] occur not infrequently before voiceless consonants, as in *twice* and *out*.

Postvocalic /r/ is preserved as a fully constricted [ɚ] sound. Before it, the following vowels occur: /i ∼ ɪ/ in *ear, beard*; /ɛ ∼ æ/ in *care, stairs* (/æ/ only south of the Kanawha); /ɑ/ in *car, garden* and occasionally also in *wire, tired*; /o/ in *four, door* and in *poor*; /ɔ/ in *forty, corn*. In this position all vowels are short. The /o/ of *four, door* is sharply differentiated from the /ɔ/ of *forty, corn. Wire, flower*, etc. are often disyllabic /waiɜ, flauɜ/. Before /r/, the /ai/ commonly merges with /ɑ/ in folk speech, occasionally also in the speech of the better educated, so that *wire* rimes with *car*.

North of the Kanawha, *Mary, dairy* have the vowel /ɛ/ of *merry, cherry*, south of it the /e/ of *April*.

All of the South Midland shares with the North Midland (Pennsylvania) the fully constricted vowel /ɜ/ of *thirty, sermon* and the postvocalic /r/ in *car, care, ear*, etc., and hence lacks the free low vowel /ɑ/ and the unsyllabic /ə/ of the South. Moreover, the lack of marked positional variants in /ai, au/ and the occurrence of checked /ɛ/ in *care, stairs* links the northern part of the South Midland with Pennsylvania.

On the other hand, all of the South Midland has some phonic and incidental features in common with the Upper South (Virginia) and the Upcountry of the Lower South: the high-central [ʉ·] in *two, shoes*; the slow diphthongs [a·ɪ ∼ a·ɛ] and [æ·ɵ] in *good-bye, five* and *cow, down*; and contrasting /o/ : /ɔ/ in *four, hoarse* vs. *forty, horse*. Furthermore, the section south of the Kanawha often has upgliding variants of the /æ/ and the /ɔ/ in *glass, dance* and *law, dog*, and the phoneme /æ/ in *care, stairs*, which are of Southern origin.

Although the dialect of the South Midland has hardly a single feature that does not occur either in the North Midland or the South, we must recognize it as a distinct regional type because of its unique configuration of phonemic, phonic, and incidental features. Historically, to be sure, it is a blend of Pennsylvanian and Southern features, graded from north to south.

2.8 THE UPPER SOUTH

Synopses 98–128

The dialect of the Upper South, of which the Virginia Piedmont is the geographic and historic center, has a rather distinctive configuration of phonemic and phonic features. The most important and pervasive of these are:

(1) The loss of postvocalic /r/ as such. It is replaced by unsyllabic /ə̬/ after /i ∼ ɪ/, as in *ear, beard* (/iə̬/ not infrequently changing to /jɜ/ in *beard*); after /æ/, as in *stairs, care*; and after /o/, as in *four, door*. It appears as syllabic /ə/ after /ai, au/, as in *wire, flower* (which are thus disyllabic), occasionally also in *stairs, care* [stæˈəz, kæˈə]. It is lost after /ɔ/, so that *corn* rimes with *lawn*; in folk speech /ə̬/ is lost also after /o/, so that *four* rimes with *know*.

(2) The earlier sequence /ɑə̬/, as in *car, garden*, has developed into a free vowel /ɑ/, phonemically distinct from the checked vowel /ɑ/ in *crop, college*.

(3) /ai/ and /au/ have striking positional allophones before voiceless consonants, as in *twice, right* and *house, out*, the former appearing here as [ɐɪ], the latter as [ɐu ∼ əu]. In other positions /ai/ is a slow diphthong [a·ɛ ∼ a·ᵉ ∼ a·ə], as in *five, good-bye*, /au/ a slow diphthong [æ·u ∼ æ·ɵ], as in *down, cow*.

(4) The low free vowels /ɔ/ and /ɑ/, as in *law, frost, dog, corn* and in *car, garden, father, palm*, respectively, are usually diphthongal, but appear also as long monophthongs.

(5) The free mid-central vowel /ɜ/ of *thirty, sermon*, etc., is usually a slightly constricted and rounded [ɵ· ∼ ɵ·ᵊ], but unconstricted and unrounded varieties also occur.

(6) The /u/ of *two, music*, etc., is a high-central [ʉ· ∼ ɵu].

(7) /æ/ appears regularly before unsyllabic /ə̬/ in *care, stairs*.

(8) /o/ contrasts with /ɔ/ in *four, poor* vs. *forty, corn.*

(9) *Mary* and *merry* have /e/ and /ɛ/, respectively.

On the periphery of this speech area, which extends from Baltimore, Md., to north-central North Carolina and westward to the Blue Ridge, various deviations from this configuration of features occur, especially in folk speech, and there are also rather marked variations within this large area. It is, therefore, desirable to present synopses of a rather large number of idiolects.

The cultivated speech of the Upper South has the following phonic and incidental features.

The checked high and mid vowels /ɪ, ʊ, ɛ, ʌ/, as in *crib, wood, head, sun*, are predominantly ingliding, but monophthongal variants are not uncommon before voiceless stops in monosyllables, in words of two or more syllables also in other positions. /ɛ/ is often raised, /ʌ/ raised, fronted, and occasionally slightly rounded. Along the western margin of this area /ʊ/ is apt to be fronted. Prolongation is not infrequent, especially of the mid vowels /ɛ/ and /ʌ/. Upgliding positional allophones of /ʊ, ɛ, ʌ/ occur in *bush, egg, brush*, etc.

The checked low vowel /ɑ/, as in *crop, John*, is predominantly an ingliding low-central [ɑ°] sound, but monophthongal [ɑ ~ ɑ·] also occurs. A backish [ɑ› ~ ɑ›·] occurs rather frequently in southern Maryland and in the District of Columbia, occasionally also elsewhere. The checked low vowel /æ/ is long in most positions and frequently ingliding; however, parts of Virginia and North Carolina have upgliding [æ¹] in *bag, half, can't*, etc., and even in *stairs, care.*

The free high vowels /i/ and /u/, as in *three* and *two*, are long monophthongs or slightly upgliding diphthongs; /u/ is nearly always high-central [ʉ· ~ ʉ·ʌ·ʉ].

The free mid vowels /e/ and /o/, as in *April* and *know*, have a rather close beginning and a brief upglide. A more open beginning and a longer glide is current in Maryland and, at the other extreme, in northeastern North Carolina; /o/ is more or less fronted in these two subareas, in northeastern North Carolina even centralized to [ɵʊ]. Monophthongal or ingliding variants of /e/ and /o/ are rare in cultivated speech, but

survive rather extensively in folk speech, especially along Chesapeake Bay.

The free mid-central vowel /ɜ/, as in *thirty, sermon*, is usually rounded and slightly constricted, or ends in slight constriction, but unconstricted diaphones also occur.

The rounded and raised free back vowel /ɔ/ of *law, dog* is usually an upgliding diphthong with progressive rounding; but long monophthongs are not uncommon, either as positional allophones or as regional and social diaphones. This phoneme occurs in such words as *law, salt, daughter; moth, frost, dog; corn, horse* /kɔn, hɔs/, in tidewater Virginia and on Delmarva also in *barn, garden, calm, father, aunt*, etc.

The free vowel /ɑ˞/ of *car, father* /kɑ˞, fɑ˞ðə/ has a wide phonic range within this area and its incidence in the vocabulary varies considerably. It is most commonly a back-gliding diphthong [ɑɑ˞ ~ ɑɒ] or a long low-back monophthong [ɑ˞·], contrasting with the short low-central [ɑ˄ ~ ɑ˄°] of *crop, college*. On the periphery of this area the phonic difference between the free /ɑ˞/ of *father* and the checked /ɑ/ of *college* is rather slight and there seems to be some overlapping or fluctuation between the two.

The free vowel /ɑ˞/ occurs in *car, barn, garden*, in *father, calm*, in *pasture*, frequently in *aunt* (but not in *can't*), occasionally in *John*. The two speakers who do not use /æ/ in *half, glass*, etc., waver uneasily between free /ɑ˞/ and checked /ɑ/.

As pointed out above, the free /ɑ˞/ of *car, barn, father, calm*, etc., is merged in the /ɔ/ of *corn, law, frost*, pronounced as [ɒɒ˄], in the tidewater of Virginia. One cultured speaker within this area has this phoneme also in *half, glass, master, aunt*. On Delmarva, where postvocalic /r/ survives, *car, barn, garden* also have /ɔ/.

/ai/ and /au/ are slow diphthongs in all positions except before voiceless consonants, pronounced [a·ɛ ~ a·ᵋ ~ a·°] and [æ·ʊ ~ æ·ʉ], as in *good-bye, five* and *cow, down, houses*. The /ai/ of *five, nine* is sometimes nearly monophthongal [a·], but nevertheless distinct from the /ɑ˞/ of *barn* and the /ɑ/ of *John*; thus *nine* /nain/ never rimes with *barn* /bɑn/ or *John* /ǰɑn/. Before voiceless consonants, /ai/ and /au/ have the swiftly upgliding allophones [ɐɪ] and [ɐʊ ~ əu], as in *twice, right* and *house, out*; the extreme variant [əu], with full centralization of the initial tongue position, is largely confined to the James River Valley (the core of the Virginia Piedmont area). Contrary to the general rule of the distribution of the slow and the fast allophones of /au/, the fast variants [ɐu ~ əu] appear also in word-final position in parts of tidewater Virginia, as in *cow, plow*; furthermore, they are extended to the plural forms of these nouns, so that the positional distribution of the slow and the fast allophones is no longer strictly complementary.

Postvocalic /r/ is lost after the low vowels /ɑ/ and /ɔ/, as in *barn* /bɑn/ and *corn* /kɔn/. It survives as unsyllabic /ə̦/ after the front vowels /i ~ ɪ/ and /æ/, as in *ear, beard* and *stairs, care*, usually also after the mid-back vowel /o/ of *four, hoarse*, etc., and of *poor*. These three vowels are monophthongal before unsyllabic /ə̦/; however, *care, four*, etc. often are pronounced as [kæˈə, foᵛə], with syllabic /ə/. In folk speech, *four, poor* /fo, po/ often rime with *know* /no/; *ear, here* /jɜ, hjɜ/ with *fur* /fɜ/; and *care, chair* with *ear* /iə̦ ~ jɜ/. After /ai, au/, as in *wire, flower*, the original postvocalic /r/ appears as syllabic /ə/.

The unstressed syllables of *houses, haunted, bucket* have checked /ɪ/, pronounced as a lowered high-central [ɨ].

The description of the dialect of the Upper South presented above is based upon the usage of cultured speakers and applies most fully to the focal area centering on Richmond, Va. The folk speech of this area, though varying regionally, exhibits the same general pattern, but often differs from cultivated speech phonically, and especially in the incidence of the phonemes. These differences are most marked on the periphery of this large area, where cultured speakers have adopted, in part, the usage of the Virginia Piedmont, while the middle group and the folk have retained the features of the local dialects.

2.9 THE LOWER SOUTH

Synopses 131–57

The Lower South (chiefly South Carolina and Georgia) has the same phonemic system as the Upper South, but differs from it rather strikingly in many phonic and incidental features. As in the Upper South, (1) postvocalic /r/ is lost as such, which leads to the emergence of a free low vowel /ɑ/ in *car, barn*, etc., and to the rise of unsyllabic /ə̦/ after the high and mid vowels, as in *ear, care, four*; (2) the /ɜ/ of *thirty, sermon*, etc., is unconstricted (in Virginia more often slightly constricted than wholly unconstricted); (3) the /ai/ and the /au/ have striking positional allophones before voiceless consonants, as in *twice* and *out*; (4) *four* and *forty* have /o/ and /ɔ/, respectively, *Mary* and *merry* contrastive /e/ and /ɛ/. Of these features, the marked allophones of /au/ occur only in the coastal plain from the Pee Dee southward.

Within the Lower South, the Low Country of South Carolina and the adjoining coast of Georgia and Florida form a rather distinctive subarea. Here the free mid vowels /e/ and /o/, as in *day, eight* and *know, road*, are very close monophthongs, with ingliding allophones in checked position; and, as pointed out above, /ai/ and /au/ have centralized allophones before voiceless consonants. The Upcountry, on the other hand, has upgliding /e, o/ and lacks marked allophones of /au/. Other differences in the cultivated speech of these two major subareas of the Lower South are pointed out below. It is fairly clear that the speech of the cultured in the Upcountry (above the fall line) has been more extensively influenced by the usage of the Charleston area, once politically and culturally dominant, than that of the other social groups.

In the Lower South, the checked high and mid vowels /ɪ, ʊ, ɛ, ʌ/, as in *crib, wood, ten, sun*, are normally ingliding and often positionally and/or prosodically prolonged, except for a narrow coastal belt extending from the Santee to the Savannah (including the cities of Charleston, Beaufort, and Savannah), where they are monophthongal and short. /ʊ/ is often fronted and sometimes centralized to [ʉ̈ə]. In the Upcountry, the /ʌ/ of *sun, brush* is decidedly raised and sometimes slightly rounded, but not in the coastal section. The checked low-front vowel /æ/, as in *bag, half, aunt*, is usually longish and ingliding in the Low Country, but upgliding above the fall line. The checked vowel /ɑ/ of *crop, college*, etc. is a low-back [ɑ], sometimes even a slightly rounded [ɒ], and rather short, whereas the free vowel /ɑ/ of *car, barn* is always prolonged and articulated farther forward.

The high free vowels /i/ and /u/, as in *three, grease* and *two, tooth*, are monophthongal in the Low Country and often ingliding in checked position, but monophthongal or upgliding in the Upcountry. /u/ is a high-central [ʉ· ∼ ʊˆʉ] throughout the Lower South. The free mid vowels /e/ and /o/, as in *day, eight* and *know, road*, have a decidedly close beginning; in the Low Country they are monophthongal and positionally ingliding, in the Upcountry usually upgliding. The mid-central vowel /ɝ/ of *thirty, sermon*, etc., is unconstricted and often more or less rounded; in the Charleston area it is usually monophthongal, in the Upcountry (especially in Georgia) predominantly an upgliding [ɝɪ]. The free low vowel /ɔ/, as in *law, dog, frost* and in *forty, corn*, rather well-rounded, is monophthongal or ingliding below the fall line, but appears almost invariably as an upgliding [ɒɔ ∼ ɔo] in the Upcountry. To summarize: the free vowels /i, u, e, o, ɔ/ of *three, two, day, know, law* have marked regional diaphones in the Lower South, being monophthongal or ingliding in the Low Country, but upgliding in the Upcountry.

On the other hand, the free low vowel of *car, barn, garden* /kɑ, bɑn, gɑdən/ and of *father, palm* /fɑðə, pɑm/ is a long ingliding [ɑ·ᵊ ∼ ɑˀ·ᵊ] throughout the Lower South, contrasting with the checked /ɑ/ of *crop, college*, etc., articulated as [ɑ] or [ɒ], primarily in length. Since checked /ɑ/ has longish positional variants, these two phonemes sometimes overlap phonically, so that *John* rimes with *barn* in some idiolects. When free /ɑ/ and checked /ɑ/ differ in quality, the latter is more backish and sometimes weakly rounded, whereas in the Upper South free /ɑ/ is low-back, checked /ɑ/ low-central.

The free vowels /ai/ and /au/ are upgliding diphthongs throughout the area, but exhibit very marked regional diaphones. In the Low Country /ai/ and /au/ consistently have striking positional allophones (as in the Upper South), being articulated as slow [ɑ·ɪ] and [ɑ·o] finally and before voiced consonants, as in *good-bye, five* and *cow, down*, but as fast [ɐɪ ∼ əɪ] and [ʌu], with centralized starting position, before voiceless consonants, as in *twice, right* and *house, out*. The Upcountry has marked allophones in /ai/ but not in /au/. Here the slow variant of /ai/ occurring in *good-bye, five* is pronounced as [a·ᵊ], gliding from low-front to mid-central position, the fast variants in *twice, right* as [ɐɪ ∼ aɪ]. The vowel /au/ of *cow, down, out*, etc., is articulated as [au] or [æu] in all positions, but the upglide is usually faster before voiceless consonants.

In the treatment of vowels before historical /r/ the two subareas of the Lower South are in substantial agreement. /r/ is lost after the low vowels /ɑ/ and /ɔ/, as in *car, barn* /kɑ, bɑn/ and *corn, forty* /kɔn, fɔti/. It survives as unsyllabic /ə̣/ after /i, e ∼ æ, o/, as in *ear, care, four* /iə̣, keə̣ ∼ kæə̣, foə̣/. The incidence of /i/ in *ear, here, beard* is restricted and rather erratic; some speakers have /i/ fairly regularly in such words, others /e/, still others vary or vacillate. In *care, stairs*, etc., the Low Country has /e/, articulated as [e· ∼ ɛˆ], the Upcountry /e/ or /æ/. Since *ear, beard* often have /e/ in this subarea, *ear* sometimes rimes with *care*; but most speakers who have /e/ in *ear* have /æ/ in *care*. No other dialect of the Atlantic States has this vowel contrast before tautosyllabic /r/ or its derivative /ə̣/.

Though /ə̣/ is usually preserved after the /o/ of *four, door, poor* in cultivated speech, it is often lost in the speech of the other social groups, especially in the Upcountry, so that *four, door*, pronounced with final [o· ∼ ou], rime with *know*.

It is of interest to note that in the Lower South some speakers seem to lack the high vowels /i, u/ before unsyllabic /ə̣/, that others rarely have /i/ in *ear, beard*, etc., and that /u/ is decidedly rare in *poor* throughout the area. Nevertheless, there is a fairly clear trend toward introducing the high vowels in this position.

2.10 Appendix

Notes on the Lives of the Cultured Speakers

The investigators are identified by the following initials: B = Bernard Bloch; C = Marguerite Chapallaz; H = Miles L. Hanley; Hs = Rachel S. Harris; J = Martin Joos; K = Hans Kurath; L = Guy S. Lowman, Jr.; M = Raven I. McDavid, Jr.; R = Cassil Reynard. Outside of New England all records are either by Lowman (10 years of field work) or by McDavid (5 years).

1. Brewer, Me., pop. 6,000. Folklorist (woman), aged 68 in 1932. College graduate (Smith). Has observed folk speech. "Natural speech of a cultured person." Moderate tempo; rather precise articulation.—L.

2. Machias, Me., pop. 2,000. Lumber dealer, aged 66 in 1932. Mason. Interested in state politics; well-to-do. Attended college preparatory school in Providence, R. I. Deliberate tempo.—L.

3. Nobleboro, Me. (Lincoln Co.). Woman, aged 50 in 1932. Roman Catholic; D.A.R. Attended private school in Portland. Has spent winters in Cambridge, Mass. Rapid tempo.—L.

4. Farmington, Me., pop. 3,500. College student (Colby), aged 22 in 1932. Lawyer's son.—L.

5. Portland, Me., pop. 71,000. Music teacher, aged 67 in 1932. Swedenborgian. Studied music in Boston, New York, and Berlin. Interested in dramatics; adept at conversation. Unguarded cultivated speech. Rapid tempo; precise articulation.—L.

6. Concord, N. H., pop. 25,000. Woman, aged 70 in 1932. Congregationalist. Attended private school in Haverhill, Mass. Member of D.A.R., Woman's Club, etc. Well read; dignified. Deliberate tempo.—C.

7. Keene, N. H., pop. 14,000. Woman, aged 77 in 1932; taught school in her youth. Congregationalist; active in church work. Reads a great deal; good conversationalist. "Short staccato vowels."—C.

8. Billerica, Mass. (Middlesex Co.). Psychiatrist, aged 48 in 1931. Graduate of Tufts Medical School. Brilliant mind. Can report the speech of the older generation. Rapid tempo.—L.

9. Beverly, Mass., pop. 25,000. Woman, aged 74 in 1931. Episcopalian. Officer of historical society. Attended Abbot Academy in Andover. "Natural, unaffected speech; precise articulation."—H.

10. Boston, Mass., pop. 781,000. Woman, aged 74 in 1932. "Accustomed to wealth and social position." Her father was a man of strict literary taste. "Careful pronunciation, entirely natural to her."—H.

11. Boston, Mass. Woman (lawyer's wife), aged 46 in 1932. Had German governess; attended private school until 18. Wide reading. Extensive contacts in Boston and vicinity. Medium tempo.—H.

12. Bridgewater, Mass., pop. 9,000. Teacher (woman), aged 45 in 1931. Attended normal school. Active in church affairs.—R.

13. Plymouth, Mass., pop. 13,000. Engineer, aged 42 in 1931. Graduate of Massachusetts Institute of Technology. Wide social contacts.—R.

14. Rochester, Mass. (Plymouth Co.). Farmer, aged 73 in 1931. Has taught school. Graduate of normal school. Reads widely.—R.

15. Barnstable, Mass. (Cape Cod). Town officer and farmer, aged 73 in 1931. Former lecturer for the Grange. Well read; highly regarded.—R.

16. Newport, R. I., pop. 28,000. Woman, aged 63 in 1931. Attended private school in Newport and Boston. Officer of historical society. Aristocratic manner. "Speech typical of the older generation."—Hs.

17. Newport, R. I. Woman, aged 51 in 1931. Attended normal school, but never taught school. Writes articles and composes music. Club member; many contacts.—Hs.

18. Wakefield, R. I. (Washington Co.). Woman, aged 56 in 1931. Attended high school; children in college. Fairly active socially. Somewhat self-conscious.—Hs.

19. New London, Conn., pop. 30,000. Director of local museum, aged 73 in 1932. Attended high school. Extensive reading and travel; many contacts.—Hs.

20. Willimantic, Conn., pop. 12,000. Teacher (woman), aged 58 in 1932. Attended normal school. Considerable reading. "Conscious of grammatical proprieties, but natural."—Hs.

21. Providence, R. I., pop. 253,000. Woman, aged 63 in 1931. Congregationalist. College graduate (Smith). Member of clubs. "Sure of her own speech."—Hs.

22. Providence, R. I. Librarian and scholar, aged 46 in 1931. Episcopalian. College graduate (Pembroke in Brown U.). Member of learned societies.—Hs.

23. Worcester, Mass., pop. 195,000. Manufacturer, aged 83 in 1931. Graduate of Harvard U. Officer of American Antiquarian Society. "A leading citizen; fine example of New England aristocracy." Deliberate tempo. —B.

24. Springfield, Mass., pop. 150,000. Woman, aged 73 in 1931. Attended private schools. Member of several clubs. "An aristocrat, keenly intelligent; ridicules improper pronunciations." Slow tempo; clear articulation.—B.

25. Springfield, Mass. Woman, aged 55 in 1931. Wife of local historian. Attended private school in Springfield and finishing school in Boston. Remembers the rural speech of her childhood. Rather slow tempo; careful articulation.—B.

26. Granby, Mass. (Hampshire Co.). Farmer, aged 77

in 1931. College graduate (Amherst), as also his wife (Holyoke). Active in church and Grange. "Guarded and consciously correct speech."—B.

27. Northampton, Mass., pop. 25,000. Secretary of college administrator, aged 51 in 1931. Graduate of Smith College. "Distinguishes native from acquired usage." Medium tempo; clear articulation.—B.

28. Deerfield, Mass. (Franklin Co.). Insurance agent and newspaper correspondent, aged 66 in 1931. Attended high school. Reads considerably. Many social contacts. "Example of local cultivated speech."—J.

29. Farmington, Conn., pop. 4,500. Civil engineer and farmer, aged 77 in 1931. Graduate of Sheffield Scientific School, Yale U. Member of state legislature for many years. "Excellent representative of the older generation."—H.

30. Middletown, Conn., pop. 25,000. Manufacturer, aged 60 in 1931. Attended boarding school in Worcester Co., Mass. Of prominent cultured family. Extensive reading and travel. "Speaks with ease and assurance; can quote popular speech."—K.

31. Guilford, Conn. (New Haven Co.). Woman, aged 30 in 1931. College graduate (Connecticut College for Women). Speaks much like her father, who is prominent in town affairs. Slow tempo.—K.

32. New Haven, Conn., pop. 163,000. Librarian of historical society, aged 45 in 1931. Attended normal school. —K.

33. Milford, Conn. (New Haven Co.). Fruit farmer, aged 57 in 1931. Congregationalist. Attended Hopkins Grammar School (New Haven) and Yale U. Many social and business contacts. Officer of historical society. "Consciously cultivated speech, but not affected." Fast tempo; precise articulation.—H.

34. Danbury, Conn., pop. 22,000. Farmer, aged 47 in 1931. College graduate (Harvard). Well read and well informed. "Cultivated urban speech." Moderate tempo. —H.

35. Litchfield, Conn., pop. 3,500. Lawyer, aged 75 in 1931. Episcopalian. Graduate of Yale Law School. "Old-fashioned cultivated speech."—H.

36. Cornwall, Conn. (Litchfield Co.). Farmer, aged 69 in 1931. Congregationalist. Attended Hopkins Grammar School (New Haven); college graduate (Yale). Influential in town affairs.—H.

37. Pittsfield, Mass., pop. 50,000. Businessman, aged 85 in 1932. Congregationalist. Has held municipal offices. Attended high school. Reads a good deal. "Old-fashioned cultivated speech." Slow tempo.—B.

38. Pawlet, Vt., pop. 1,500. Woman, aged 55 in 1932. Attended high school. Associates with prosperous farmers' wives. "Proud of her social standing; local speech overlaid with self-conscious gentility." Slow tempo; rather careful articulation.—B.

39. Burlington, Vt., pop. 25,000. University professor (classics), aged 40 in 1932. Attended U. of Vermont and Harvard. "Feeling for his native idiom is very keen." Slow tempo; clear articulation.—B.

40. Goshen, N. Y. (Orange Co.). Woman, aged 63 in

1940. Episcopalian. Attended high school. Reads widely. Clear articulation.—L.

41. Poughkeepsie, N. Y., pop. 40,000. Librarian and historian (woman), aged 65 in 1940. Episcopalian. Rapid tempo.—L.

42. Hurley, N. Y. (near Kingston, pop. 28,000). Woman, aged 68 in 1940. Dutch Reformed church. Attended high school.—L.

43. Albany, N. Y., pop. 127,000. Manufacturer and banker, aged 84 in 1940. Attended high school.—L.

44. Fort Edward, N. Y., pop. 4,000. Woman, aged 61 in 1940. Episcopalian. Attended college.—L.

45. Utica, N. Y., pop. 102,000. Woman, aged 52 in 1941. Episcopalian. Attended private school and college (in Garden City, L. I.).—L.

46. Oswego, N. Y., pop. 23,000. Merchant, aged 81 in 1949.—M.

47. Ontario, Can., Kingston, pop. 22,000. Secretary (woman), aged 59 in 1949. Attended college (Queens U.). Club member. "Some British influence."—M.

48. Binghamton, N. Y., pop. 77,000. Woman, aged 47 in 1941. Episcopalian. Attended high school. Moderate tempo.—L.

49. Elmira, N. Y., pop. 47,000. Teacher and newspaper writer (woman), aged 72 in 1949. Congregationalist; club member. Attended Elmira College. Rather fast tempo. —M.

50. Bath, N. Y., pop. 4,000. Teacher and historian (woman), aged 80 in 1949. Christian Scientist. Attended private school and summer sessions at Cornell U.—M.

51. Geneva, N. Y., pop. 16,000. Prominent businessman, college trustee, aged 89 in 1949. Christian Scientist. Attended high school; well read.—M.

52. Rochester, N. Y., pop. 328,000. Woman, aged 60 in 1949. Presbyterian; member of historical society. Attended private school; college graduate (Columbia U.). Rather fast tempo.—M.

53. Rochester, N. Y., pop. 328,000. Woman, aged 65 in 1949. Episcopalian; member of clubs. College graduate (Smith College in Mass.). Rather fast tempo.—M.

54. Albion, N. Y., pop. 5,000. Businessman, aged 74 in 1949. Attended military school at Niagara Falls. Rapid tempo; clear articulation.—M.

55. Lima, N. Y. (Livingston Co.). Woman, aged 83 in 1949. Presbyterian; W. C. T. U. College graduate (Syracuse U.). Well read. Rather fast tempo.—M.

56. Orchard Park, N. Y. (near Buffalo, pop. 573,000). Justice of the Peace (woman), aged 73 in 1949. Quaker. Graduate of normal school (in Buffalo). Fast tempo; clear articulation.—M.

57. Salamanca, N. Y., pop. 10,000. Lawyer and bank director, aged 72 in 1949. Congregationalist; member of several societies. College graduate (Hamilton College); well read. Slow tempo.—M.

58. Westfield, N. Y., pop. 4,000. Teacher and librarian, aged 65 in 1949. College graduate (Michigan and Columbia). Member of D.A.R., A.A.U.W. Slow tempo. —M.

59. Manhattan, N. Y., pop. 1,867,000. Woman, aged

59 in 1940. Episcopalian. Attended private schools. "Vigorous speech."—L.

60. Manhattan, N. Y. Lawyer, aged 60 in 1940. Attended private schools and Columbia U.—L.

61. Manhattan, N. Y. Writer (woman), aged 76 in 1940. Episcopalian. Had French governess and attended private schools.—L.

62. Manhattan, N. Y. Woman, aged 62 in 1940. Episcopalian. Had governess and attended private schools. —L.

63. Brooklyn, N. Y., pop. 2,670,000. Businessman (executive), aged 68 in 1940. Episcopalian. Attended private school and college (Columbia U.).—L.

64. Flushing, N. Y. (Queens Co.). Manufacturer and banker, aged 54 in 1940. Congregationalist. College graduate (Yale U.).—L.

65. Jersey City, N. J., pop. 317,000. Teacher (woman), aged 65 in 1941. Dutch Reformed church. Attended Bergen School for Girls.—L.

66. Newark, N. J., pop. 442,000. Social service director, aged 57 in 1941. Presbyterian. Attended private schools.—L.

67. Orange, N. J., pop. 35,000. Music teacher (woman), aged 54 in 1941. Presbyterian. College graduate (Vassar).—L.

68. New Brunswick, N. J., pop. 35,000. Engineer and executive, aged 59 in 1941. Dutch Reformed church. College graduate (Rutgers).—L.

69. Burlington, N. J., pop. 11,000. Woman, aged 49 in 1941. Quaker. Attended college in Philadelphia.—L.

70. Philadelphia (Germantown), Pa., pop. 1,950,000. Businessman (executive), aged 62 in 1939. Quaker. Attended college (Haverford).—L.

71. Philadelphia, Pa. Merchant, aged 70 in 1939. Episcopalian. Attended college (Haverford).—L.

72. Philadelphia (Germantown), Pa. Woman, aged 59 in 1939. Quaker. Attended Friends School. Well-to-do; gracious. Moderate tempo; precise articulation.—L.

73. Lancaster, Pa., pop. 60,000. Merchant, aged 39 in 1939. Lutheran. Attended college (Marshall and Franklin).—L.

74. York, Pa., pop. 55,000. Woman, aged 62 in 1939. Episcopalian. Attended private school in York and Philadelphia. "A charming cultivated person."—L.

75. Harrisburg, Pa., pop. 80,000. Secretary (woman), aged 68 in 1939. Presbyterian. Attended private school. Quick tempo; precise articulation.—L.

76. Reading, Pa., pop. 111,000. Architect, aged 69 in 1939. Lutheran. Attended college in Boston, Mass. "Cultivated person of the old school."—L.

77. Easton, Pa., pop. 34,000. Architect, aged 60 in 1939. Presbyterian. Attended college (Lafayette). Quick tempo.—L.

78. Kingston, Pa., pop. 22,000 (near Wilkes-Barre, pop. 87,000). Druggist, aged 62 in 1939. Presbyterian. Attended college (Lafayette). Prominent family.—L.

79. Williamsport, Pa., pop. 46,000. Woman, aged 50 in 1939. Presbyterian. Attended college. Well-to-do family. —L.

80. Cassville, Pa. (Huntington Co.). Farmer, aged 37 in 1940. Methodist. Attended high school. "Intelligent middle-class informant."—L.

81. Boon, Pa. (Somerset Co.). Farmer, aged 43 in 1940. Lutheran. Attended high school. "Middle-class speaker with distinct traces of Pennsylvania German."—L.

82. Summerville, Pa. (Jefferson Co.). Woman, aged 41 in 1940. Lutheran. Attended high school. "Highly intelligent and quick of response."—L.

83. Jefferson, Ohio, pop. 2,000 (near Ashtabula, pop. 23,000). Woman, aged 53 in 1940. Congregationalist. Attended college (Lake Erie). "Very modern." Clear articulation.—L.

84. Beaver, Pa., pop. 6,000. Farmer, aged 48 in 1940. Presbyterian. Attended normal school. "Somewhat self-conscious."—L.

85. Elizabeth, Pa. (near Pittsburgh, pop. 670,000). Farmer, aged 47 in 1940. Presbyterian. Attended high school. "Intelligent middle-class speaker."—L.

86. Sugar Run, Pa. (Washington Co.). Farmer, aged 44 in 1940. Presbyterian. Attended high school and business college. Upper-middle class.—L.

87. Coliers, W. Va. (near Steubenville, O., pop. 35,000). Farmer and postmaster, aged 43 in 1940. Presbyterian. Attended high school. "A local cultivated type." Good articulation.—L.

88. Wheeling, W. Va., pop. 62,000. Manufacturer, aged 70 in 1940. Episcopalian. Attended college preparatory school in Providence, R. I.—L.

89. Farmington, W. Va. (near Fairmont, pop. 23,000). Farmer, aged 59 in 1940. Official of agricultural association; member of school board. Methodist. Attended teachers college. Deliberate tempo.—L.

90. Parsons, W. Va., pop. 2,000. Farmer, aged 58 in 1940. Presbyterian. Attended high school.—L.

91. Charleston, W. Va., pop. 60,000. Teacher, aged 45 in 1940. Episcopalian. Attended high school and college (one year).—L.

92. Point Pleasant, W. Va., pop. 3,000. Woman, aged 69 in 1940. Methodist. "Local cultivated type, somewhat self-conscious."—L.

93. Marietta, Ohio, pop. 14,000. Woman, aged 70 in 1940. Episcopalian. Of New England stock. Attended college (Goucher and U. of Chicago). Very precise articulation.—L.

94. Wilmington, Del., pop. 107,000. Woman, aged 62 in 1937. Episcopalian. Attended private school. Very rapid tempo.—L.

95. Dover, Del., pop. 5,000. Farmer and lobbyist, aged 66 in 1937. Episcopalian. Attended college (Swarthmore) and medical school (in Philadelphia). "His mother insisted on proper speech."—L.

96. Salisbury, Md. (Eastern Shore), pop. 11,000. Interior decorator (man), aged 55 in 1937. Episcopalian. Attended Philadelphia School of Design. "Local cultivated type; rather precise and opinionated."—L.

97. Baltimore, Md., pop. 805,000. Woman, aged 70 in 1937. Episcopalian. Had French governess. Husband an engineer.—L.

98. Baltimore, Md. Woman, aged 76 in 1937. Episcopalian. Had governess; extensive travel. Prominent family. Organizer of social work. "Many Southern features."—L.

99. Baltimore, Md. Woman, aged 45 in 1937. Episcopalian. Had governess and attended private school. Of good family. "Poised and sure of her usage."—L.

100. Annapolis, Md., pop. 13,000. Secretary (man), aged 33 in 1937. Episcopalian. Attended college (St. John's). Cultured background. "Distinctly Southern intonation; moderate tempo."—L.

101. Leonardtown, Md. (St. Marys Co.). Woman, aged 65 in 1937. Roman Catholic. Had governess and attended private school. "Delightful cultivated speech; rapid tempo; precise articulation."—L.

102. Washington (Georgetown), D. C., pop. 487,000. Woman, aged 50 in 1936. Presbyterian. Attended Friends School. Drawling tempo.—L.

103. Alexandria, Va., pop. 24,000. Woman, aged 45 in 1935. Episcopalian. Attended Arlington Institute. Club member. "Has cultivated the art of being charming." —L.

104. Shepherdstown, W. Va. (near Martinsburg, pop. 15,000). Woman, aged 71 in 1940. Episcopalian. Attended private school and college.—L.

105. Winchester, Va., pop. 11,000. Woman, aged 55 in 1935. Episcopalian. Attended Fairfax Hall. Spends winters in Richmond or Norfolk. "An aristocrat."—L.

106. Stafford, Va. (on Northern Neck). Woman, aged 71 in 1935. Episcopalian. Had private tutor. "An old-fashioned provincial cultivated type."—L.

107. Fredericksburg, Va., pop. 7,000. Woman, aged 62 in 1935. Presbyterian. Attended high school. Active in historical and literary societies. "A provincial cultivated type."—L.

108. Wiconico Church, Va. (Northern Neck). Woman, aged 46 in 1936. Episcopalian. Private schooling. Good family background. "A local cultivated type."—L.

109. Gloucester, Va. (Middle Neck). Woman, aged 55 in 1936. Episcopalian. Private schooling. Aristocratic family. Club member. "Distinctly cultivated type."—L.

110. Richmond, Va., pop. 183,000. Woman, aged 85 in 1934. Baptist. Attended private school and college (Farmville). Well-to-do family; highly respected. "Cultivated speech of the older generation."—L.

111. Richmond, Va. Woman, aged 83 in 1936. Presbyterian. Attended private school (Southern Female Institute). Well-to-do family; father a banker. Member of Colonial Dames, Woman's Club. "Somewhat concerned with correctness."—L.

112. Richmond, Va. Woman, aged 49 in 1936. Episcopalian. Attended private school (Miss Ellett's). Member of Colonial Dames, Woman's Club. "Distinctly modern type." Tends to prolong vowels.—L.

113. Petersburg, Va., pop. 29,000. Woman, aged 70 in 1936. Episcopalian. Attended St. Paul's School. Member of Colonial Dames, D.A.R., etc. "Charmingly cultured person, modern in spirit and yet delightfully old-fashioned."—L.

114. Norfolk, Va., pop. 130,000. Artist (woman), aged 47 in 1935. Episcopalian. Attended college. Club member. "A trustworthy, cultured informant."—L.

115. Lynchburg, Va., pop. 41,000. Singer (woman), aged 55 in 1935. Methodist. Attended college (Randolph Macon). Club member. Deliberate tempo; clear articulation.—L.

116. Charlottesville, Va., pop. 15,000. Woman, aged 54 in 1935. Episcopalian. Attended college and art school. Aristocratic background. Club member. "Somewhat affected."—L.

117. Lexington, Va., pop. 4,000. Merchant, aged 54 in 1935. Presbyterian. Attended high school. "Refined local type." Rapid tempo.—L.

118. Roanoke, Va., pop. 69,000. Woman, aged 35 in 1935. Episcopalian. Attended college (Bryn Mawr and Barnard). Family well-to-do.—L.

119. Edenton, N. C., pop. 4,000. Woman, aged 57 in 1936. Episcopalian. Attended Salem Academy (Winston-Salem). Good family; father a lawyer. "Speech somewhat guarded."—L.

120. New Bern, N. C., pop. 12,000. Woman, aged 67 in 1936. Episcopalian. Attended New Bern Academy. Old local family; secluded life.—L.

121. Wilmington, N. C., pop. 32,000. Nurse, aged 48 in 1935. Attended high school. Good local family. Rapid tempo.—L.

122. Wilmington, N. C. Woman, aged 55 in 1935. Episcopalian. Cultured background. Moderate tempo. —L.

123. Fayetteville, N. C., pop. 13,000. Woman, aged 37 in 1935. Episcopalian. Attended high school. Distinguished ancestry. Tends to lengthen vowels.—L.

124. Tarboro, N. C., pop. 6,000. Woman, aged 59 in 1936. Baptist. Attended college in Tarboro and in Greensboro. "Poised and natural."—L.

125. Stoval, N. C. (near Oxford, pop. 4,000). Woman, aged 45 in 1937. Presbyterian. Had governess (from Richmond, Va.); attended college (Statesville Female College, western N. C.). "Charming cultured person." —L.

126. Raleigh, N. C., pop. 37,000. Woman, aged 54 in 1937. Episcopalian. Attended college. Club member (Colonial Dames). Good family; father an M.D. Slow tempo.—L.

127. Greensboro, N. C., pop. 54,000. Secretary of Girl Scouts, aged 48 in 1937. Presbyterian turned Methodist. College graduate. "Perhaps somewhat affected."—L.

128. Charlotte, N. C., pop. 83,000. Wife of a physician, aged 45 in 1935. Baptist turned Episcopalian. Attended college. "Of the best old Charlotte stock." Rapid tempo; vowels often prolonged.—L.

129. Asheville, N. C., pop. 50,000. Lawyer's wife, aged 49 in 1936. Methodist. College graduate (Converse College, Spartanburg, S. C.). "Thoroughly natural."—L.

130. Pawleys Island, S. C. (near Georgetown, pop. 5,000). Teacher (woman), aged 68 in 1948. Episcopalian. Had governess and attended private school. Club mem-

ber (U.D.C., etc.). "Typical plantation speech." Very fast tempo.—M.

131. Georgetown, S. C., pop. 5,000. Woman, aged 50 in 1946. Episcopalian. College graduate (Winthrop). "Good example of cultivated speech." Fast tempo.—M.

132. Florence, S. C., pop. 15,000. Plantation owner's wife, aged 67 in 1946. Presbyterian. College graduate (Winthrop). Member of U.D.C. "Enthusiastic informant; can quote folk forms." Fast tempo.—M.

133. Mt. Pleasant, S. C. (near Charleston). Woman, aged 64 in 1946. Presbyterian. Attended normal school and taught for four years. Member of many clubs, including D.A.R. Moderate tempo; clear articulation.—M.

134. Charleston, S. C., pop. 62,000. Physician, aged 24 in 1946. Roman Catholic. Attended College of Charleston and Medical College of S. C. "Normal colloquial speech, though aware of correctness."—M.

135. Charleston, S. C. Administrator, aged 52 in 1946. Episcopalian. Graduate of the U. of South Carolina. Member of many societies. "Has the natural assurance of an aristocrat." Rapid tempo.—M.

136. Charleston, S. C. Woman, aged 51 in 1935. Episcopalian. Attended private school. "Of the best Charleston families; highly intelligent." Extremely fast tempo. —L.

137. Charleston, S. C. Artist and writer (woman), aged 69 in 1946. Attended private schools. Member of many societies. Honorary Lit. D. from Mt. Holyoke College, Mass. "Charleston aristocracy at its best."—M.

138. Beaufort, S. C., pop. 3,000. Woman, aged 61 in 1946. Episcopalian. College graduate (Winthrop); well read. Of good family. "Completely natural." Fast tempo. —M.

139. Bluffton, S. C. (near Savannah, Ga.). Rice planter, aged 67 in 1946. Episcopalian. College graduate (Sewanee). Club member. "Good example of locally rooted cultivated speech." Fast tempo.—M.

140. Moncks Corner, S. C. (Berkeley Co.). Lawyer. Incomplete record.—M.

141. Barnwell, S. C., pop. 2,000. Secretary (of a state senator), aged 19 in 1946. Attended high school. "Unaffected speech; can report older usage." Fast tempo. —M.

142. Columbia, S. C., pop. 52,000. Commercial artist (woman), aged 30 in 1946. Episcopalian. Graduate of the U. of South Carolina (where her father is dean of the college). Rapid tempo; clear utterance.—M.

143. Camden, S. C., pop. 5,000. Cotton planter, aged 74 in 1946. Episcopalian. College graduate (Citadel, in Charleston); taught school for 12 years. Well informed and widely known.—M.

144. Newberry, S. C., pop. 7,000. Librarian (woman), aged 59 in 1946. Lutheran. Attended Newberry College and the Peabody Conservatory in Baltimore, Md. Father born in Newberry, mother in Charleston. Fast tempo. —M.

145. Greenville, S. C., pop. 29,000. Woman, aged 67 in 1946. Episcopalian. Attended finishing school in New York City and Greenville Women's College. Of prominent family. Club member.—M.

146. Greenville, S. C. Businessman (banking and real estate), aged 58 in 1941. Episcopalian. College graduate (Davidson). Member of city council and state legislature; many contacts. Rather slow tempo.—M.

147. Savannah, Ga., pop. 85,000. Woman, aged 78 in 1945. Episcopalian. Had governess. Prominent family; cultured background. "Horrified by folk speech." Precise utterance.—L.

148. Egypt, Ga. (near Savannah). Dentist (practiced in Savannah for 50 years), aged 83 in 1946. Graduate of Baltimore Dental College. Member of clubs (Mason). —M.

149. Valona, Ga. (McIntosh Co.). Woman, aged 58 in 1946. Episcopalian. Had governess and attended boarding school. Wide interests; well read. "Fine example of regional cultivated speech."—M.

150. St. Marys, Ga. (near Florida line). Merchant and postmaster, aged 78 in 1946. Has been city and county treasurers; writes on local history. Not much formal education, but reads widely. "A self-possessed middle-class speaker." Fast tempo; vowels short.—M.

151. Jacksonville, Fla., pop. 130,000. Merchant and manufacturer, aged 85 in 1946. Methodist. College graduate (Vanderbilt U.). Club member; highly respected. "A fine example of coastal cultivated speech." Moderate tempo.—M.

152. St. Augustine, Fla., pop. 12,000. Surveyor, farmer, and local historian; aged 76 in 1946. Roman Catholic. Attended college in Macon and in Baltimore. Widely read and highly respected. Fast tempo; somewhat on guard.—M.

153. Augusta, Ga., pop. 60,000. Woman, aged 54 in 1946. Presbyterian. Attended Mary Baldwin College (Staunton, Va.). Club member; wide acquaintance among old families. Reads widely. "Excellent informant; keen observer of folk speech." Fast tempo; clear articulation.—M.

154. Macon, Ga., pop. 54,000. Woman, aged 62 in 1946. Baptist. College graduate. Member of Colonial Dames. Parents born near Augusta. Slow tempo.—M.

155. Atlanta, Ga., pop. 270,000. Woman, aged 84 in 1946. Wife of one of the "empire builders" of Atlanta. Presbyterian. Attended private school in Abingdon, Va.; college graduate (Agnes Scott). Moderate tempo.—M.

156. Atlanta, Ga. College professor (Emory U.), aged 50 in 1946. Methodist. Attended Emory U. and U. of Chicago. Rural background; born north of Atlanta. Slow tempo.—M.

157. Atlanta, Ga. Writer and journalist (son of Joel Chandler Harris), aged 73 in 1946. Pulitzer Prize winner. Roman Catholic. Privately educated. Has lived briefly in New York and Chattanooga. "Excellent example of cultivated speech." Fast tempo.—M.

2.11 SYNOPSES

	i	ɪ	e	ə	ɛ	ɜ	æ	ɒ	ɑ	ɑ	ai	ɔi	au	ɑ	ɔ	ʌ	ɵ	o	ʊ	u	
three	iˇj																				two
grease	iˇj																			ʊˆw	tooth
six		ɪ																	ʊ		wood
crib		ɪᵊ																	ʊ		pull
ear	iˇˑ																			ʊˆˑ	poor
beard	ɪˆˑ																	oˇʊ			ago
eight			ɛˆj															oˇʊ			coat
April			ɛɟˆ															oˇʊ			road
ten				ɛᵊ													oˑʏˑ				home
egg				ɛ														oˇʊ			know
head				ɛ														oˇʊˑ			four
Mary			ɛɟ															oˇʊˑ			door
stairs							æˑᵊ											oˇʊˑ			hoarse
care							æᵊ											oᵊ			mourn
merry				ɛ																	
thirty						3,3ˑ										ʌˇ					sun
sermon						3ˇ										ʌˇ					brush
furrow						3ˆ															
ashes							æˑ						ɒᵊ								frost
bag							æˑᵊ						ɒ								log
married							æ						ɔˇ								dog
half								ɑˑɑˑ						ɒˆ							water
glass								ɑˑ						ɒˇˑ							daughter
aunt								ɑˑˑ						ɒˇˑ							law
father								ɑˑˑ													
palm								ɑˑˑ													
barn								æˑɑˑ						ɒᵊ							forty
garden								æˑᵊ						ɒˆ							morning
crop														ɒˑᵊ							corn
John														ɒˆᵊ							horse
college														ɒ							
borrow														ɒ							
five										ɑɟ			au								down
twice										ɒɟ			ɑˑʊ								out
wire										ɒjᵊ			æwᵊ								flower
												ɟɔ									joint
												ɟɔ									boil
	i	ɪ	e	ə	ɛ	3	æ	ɒ	ɑ	ɑ	ai	ɔi	au	ɑ	ɔ	ʌ	ɵ	o	ʊ	u	

31

	i	ɪ	e	ɜ	ɛ	æ	ɑ	ɒ	ai	ɔi	au	ɵ	a	ɔ	ʌ	θ	o	ʊ	u	
three	—																		ʊ˞ᵘ	two
grease	i j																		ʊ˞ᵘ	tooth
six		ɪ																ʊ˞ᵊ		wood
crib		ɪ																ʊ		pull
ear	—																o˙ᵊ			poor
beard	—																ou			ago
eight			eᶤ														ou			coat
April			eᶤ														ou			road
ten					ɛ												o˖			home
egg					ɛᶤ												—			know
head					ɛ,ɛ˞ᵊ												o˙ᵊ			four
Mary			eᶤ														o˙ᵊ			door
stairs						æ˞ᵊ											o˞˙ᵊ			hoarse
care						æ˞ᵊ											o˞˙ᵊ			mourn
merry					ɛ˞															
thirty				ɜ˞											ʌ					sun
sermon				ɝ˞											ʌ					brush
furrow				ɝ																
ashes						æ˙							ʋ˞ᵊ							frost
bag						æ˞ᶤ							ɔᵛ˙							log
married						æ˯ᵛ							ɔ˙							dog
half							a˙							ɔᵊ						water
glass							a˙							ɔᵛ						daughter
aunt						æ˞ᵊ								ɔᵛ˙						law
father							a˙													
palm							a˙													
barn							a˞ᵊ						ʋˮ˙							forty
garden							a˙						ʋˮ							morning
crop														ɔ˞ᵊ						corn
John													ʋ˞ᵊ							horse
college													ʋˮ							
borrow														ɔᵛ						
five									aˀᶤ		aᵛʊ									down
twice									—		aᵛʊ									out
wire									ɐˮᵊ		—									flower
										ɪˮᶜ										joint
										ɔˮᶜ										boil
	i	ɪ	e	ɜ	ɛ	æ	ɑ	ɒ	ai	ɔi	au	ɵ	a	ɔ	ʌ	θ	o	ʊ	u	

	i	i	ɪ	e	ə	ɛ	ɜ	æ	ɑ	ɒ	ai	ɔi	au	ɑ	ɔ	ʌ	θ	o	ʊ	u	
three	ij																				two
grease	ij																			ʊᴧ·ʷ	tooth
six		ɪ																		ʊ	wood
crib		ɪᵛ																		ʊ	pull
ear	i·ᵛə																			ʊᵛə	poor
beard	i·ᵛə																	oːᵛʊ			ago
eight			eɨ												c						coat
April			eɨ															ɔːʊ			road
ten					ɛᵛə											ŏᵛ					home
egg			eᵛɨ															—			know
head				ɛ														oːᵛə			four
Mary			eɨ															ɔᵛə			door
stairs					æᵛə													oːᵛə			hoarse
care					æᵛə													oᵛə			mourn
merry				ɛ																	
thirty					ʒˑʏ̈											ʌ					sun
sermon					ʒᵛ											ʌɨ					brush
furrow																ʌᵛ					
ashes					—					ʋᵛə											frost
bag					æɨ					ʋᵛə											log
married					æᵛ					ʋᵛə											dog
half						a·				ɔᵛ											water
glass						a·				ʋᵛ											daughter
aunt						a··				ʋᵛˑ											law
father						a··															
palm						a··															
barn						a··				ʋᵛ											forty
garden						a··				ʋᵛə											morning
crop										ʋᵛə											corn
John										ʋᵛə											horse
college										ʋᵛ											
borrow										ʋᵛ											
five								æɨ	ɑᵛʊ												down
twice								æɨ	ʌ·ɑ												out
wire								æɨə	—												flower
joint										ɔɨ											joint
boil										ɨɔ											boil

| | i | i | ɪ | e | ə | ɛ | ɜ | æ | ɑ | ɒ | ai | ɔi | au | ɑ | ɔ | ʌ | θ | o | ʊ | u | |

33

	i	ɪ	e	ɛ	ɜ	æ	ɒ	ɑ	aɪ	ɔɪ	au	ɒ	ɔ	ʌ	ɵ	o	ʊ	u	
three	iᵛj																	ᵁW	two
grease	ij																	ᵁW	tooth
six		ɪ															ʊ		wood
crib		ɪ															ʊ		pull
ear	iᵛɘ																ʊə		poor
beard	iᵛɘ															ou			ago
eight			eɪ												oᵛɘ				coat
April			eɪ												oᵛɘ				road
ten				ɛɘ											oᵛ				home
egg				ɛ̄											oᵛu				know
head				ɛ											o ɘ				four
Mary			eɪ												o ɘ				door
stairs						æᵛɘ									oᵛɘ				hoarse
care						æᵛɘ									o ɘ				mourn
merry			ɛ																
thirty					ɜ									ʌᵛ					sun
sermon					ɜˈ									ʌ					brush
furrow					ɜ														
ashes						æ						ɒᵛɘ							frost
bag						æˈ						ɒᵛ							log
married						æ						ɒᵛ							dog
half								aˈ				ɒᵛɘ							water
glass								aˈˈ				ɒᵛ							daughter
aunt								aˈˈ				ɒ							law
father								aˈ											
palm								aˈˈ											
barn								aˈɘ				ɒᵛ							forty
garden								aˈ				ɒᵛɘ							morning
crop												ɒᵛ							corn
John												ɒᵛɘ							horse
college												ɒ							
borrow												ɒ							
five									aɪ		au								down
twice									aɪ		au								out
wire									aɪɘ		auɘ								flower
joint										ɔɪ									joint
boil										ɔɪ									boil
	i	ɪ	e	ɛ	ɜ	æ	ɒ	ɑ	aɪ	ɔɪ	au	ɒ	ɔ	ʌ	ɵ	o	ʊ	u	

34

	i	ɪ	e	ɛ	ɜ	æ	ɒ	ɑ	aɪ	ɔɪ	au	ʊ	o	ɔ	ʌ	ɵ	o	ʊ	u	
three	iˑi																			two
grease	ɪ i																	ʊ ɯ		tooth
six		ɪˑɪᵊ																ʊˀᵊ		wood
crib		ɪ																ʊ		pull
ear	iˑᵊ																		ʊˀᵊ	poor
beard	iˑᵊ												ɔˑʊ							ago
eight			eˑɪ										ʙˀʊ							coat
April			eˑɪ										ɔˑʊ							road
ten				ɛ									ʙˀʊ							home
egg				ɛ									oˑʊ							know
head				ɛˑɜᵊ									ɔˀwᵊ							four
Mary			ɛˑɜᵊ										ɔˑᵊ							door
stairs			ɛˑᵊ										ɔˀ							hoarse
care			ɛˑᵊ										ɔˀᵊ							mourn
merry				ɛᵊ																
thirty					ɜˀ										ʌˑ					sun
sermon					ɜˀˑ										ʌˑ					brush
furrow															ʌˀ					
ashes						æˑɪ								ɔˀˑ						frost
bag						æˀˑɛ		ɑˑᵛ												log
married						æˑᵊ								ɔˑᵌ						dog
half							ɑˀˑ							ɔˀˀ						water
glass							ɑˀˑ							ɔˀ						daughter
aunt							ɑˀˑᵊ							ɔˀˑ						law
father							ɑˀˑ													
palm							ɑˀˑ													
barn							ɑˑᵊ							ɔˑ						forty
garden							ɑˑ							ɔˀˑᵊ						morning
crop								ɒ						ɔˀˑ						corn
John								ɒ						ɔˀˑᵊ						horse
college								ɒ												
borrow								ɒ												
five									ɑˑɛ	ɑˑo										down
twice									ɑˀɪ	ɑˑo										out
wire									ɑˀɪᵊ	auᵊ										flower
										ɔˀɪ										joint
										ɪˀɔ										boil
	i	ɪ	e	ɛ	ɜ	æ	ɒ	ɑ	aɪ	ɔɪ	au	ʊ	o	ɔ	ʌ	ɵ	o	ʊ	u	

	i	ɪ	e	ɛ	ɜ	æ	a	ɑ	aɪ	ɔɪ	au	ɒ	ɔ	ʌ	ɵ	o	ʊ	u	
three	i																	ʮʮ	two
grease	i																	u	tooth
six		ɪ															ʊ		wood
crib		ɪ															ʊ		pull
ear	iˤə																	uˤə	poor
beard	iˤə															oᵁ			ago
eight			e												oˑ				coat
April			e													oᵁ			road
ten				ɛ												oᵁʊ			home
egg				ɛ												oᵁ			know
head				ɛ												oˤə			four
Mary			e													oˤə			door
stairs				ɛə												oˤə			hoarse
care						æˤə										oˤə			mourn
merry				ɛ															
thirty					ɜ									ʌ					sun
sermon					ɜˑ									ʌᵛ					brush
furrow					ɞ														
ashes						æ						ɒ							frost
bag						æ						ɒ							log
married						æ							ɔˤ						dog
half							aˑ						ɔᵛ						water
glass							aˑˑ						ɔᵛ						daughter
aunt							aˑ						ɔ						law
father							aˤˑ												
palm							aˑ												
barn							aˑˑ						ɔ						forty
garden							aˑ						ɔ						morning
crop													ɒɔ						corn
John													ɒˣ						horse
college												ɒ							
borrow												ɒ							
five									aɨ		ao								down
twice									aɨ		ɑʊ								out
wire									—		—								flower
										oɨ									joint
										ɨɔ									boil

| | i | ɪ | e | ɛ | ɜ | æ | a | ɑ | aɪ | ɔɪ | au | ɒ | ɔ | ʌ | ɵ | o | ʊ | u | |

	i	ɪ	e	e	ɛ	ɜ	æ	ɑ	ɑ	ai	ɔi	au	ɒ	ɔ	ʌ	ɵ	o	ʊ	u	ʊ	
three	i																			ʊ	two
grease	i																			ʊ	tooth
six		ı																ʊə			wood
crib		ı																ʊ			pull
ear	iɘ																			—	poor
beard	iɘ																oʊ				ago
eight			eɪ														o:o				coat
April			e														oʊ				road
ten					ɛ												oʊ				home
egg					ɛ												oʊ				know
head					ɛ,ɛɘ												oɘ				four
Mary			e														oɘ				door
stairs					ɛʌɘ									ɔʌ·							hoarse
care					ɛʌɘ												oɘ				mourn
merry					ɛ																
thirty						ɜ									ʌ						sun
sermon						ɜ									ʌ						brush
furrow						ɜʌ															
ashes							æ							ɔɘ							frost
bag							æɘ						ɒ								log
married							æ							ɔɘ							dog
half								a					ɒ								water
glass							æ						ɒʌ								daughter
aunt								a,a·					ɒ·								law
father								a													
palm								a													
barn								a,a·						ɔ							forty
garden								a·						ɔ							morning
crop													ɒ,ɒ·								corn
John													ɒ,ɔ								horse
college													ɒ·								
borrow													ɒ·								
five										aɪ		au									down
twice										ʌɪ		au									out
wire										aɪɘ		auɘ									flower
joint											ɔɪ										
boil											ɔɪ										
	i	ɪ	e	e	ɛ	ɜ	æ	ɑ	ɑ	ai	ɔi	au	ɒ	ɔ	ʌ	ɵ	o	ʊ	u	ʊ	

	i	ɪ	e	ɛ	ɜ	æ	a	ɑ	ɒ	ai	ɔi	au	a	ɒ	ɔ	ʌ	ɵ	o	ʊ	u	
three	iᵛ																			ʊ	two
grease	i																			ʊ	tooth
six		ɪ																	ʊ		wood
crib		ɪ																	ʊ		pull
ear	iᵛɘ																			uɘ	poor
beard	ɪᵛɘ																	oʊ			ago
eight			eɨ														oᵊ				coat
April			e														oᵊ				road
ten				ɛ														oʊ			home
egg				ɛ														oʊ			know
head				ɛᶺ														oɘ			four
Mary			e															oᵛɘ			door
stairs				ɛᵛɘ														oᵛɘ			hoarse
care				ɛᵛɘ														oᵛɘ			mourn
merry				ɛ																	
thirty					ɜᵛ,ɜɨ											ʌ					sun
sermon					ɜᵛ,ɜɨ											ʌ					brush
furrow					ɜ'																
ashes						æ									ɔᵊ						frost
bag						æᵊ									ɔᵊ						log
married						æ									ɔᵛᵊ						dog
half							a							ɒᶺ							water
glass						æ									ɔᵛ						daughter
aunt							a								ɔ						law
father							a														
palm							aᵛ														
barn							ɑɘ								ɔᶺ						forty
garden							a								ɔ						morning
crop															ɔ						corn
John														ɒᶜ,ɔᵛᵊ							horse
college														ɒᶜ							
borrow															ɔᵛ						
five								aɨ		au											down
twice								aɨ		au											out
wire								aɨɘ		auɘ											flower
									oᶥɨ												joint
									oɟo												boil

	i	ɪ	e	ɛ	ɜ	æ	ɒ	ɑ	aɪ	ɔɪ	aʊ	ɒ	ɔ	ʌ	ɵ	o	ʊ	u	
three	i																	ʊ	two
grease	i																	ʊʻ	tooth
six		ɪ															ʊ		wood
crib		ɪ															ʊˑ		pull
ear	iə																ʊˠə		poor
beard	iˠə															o			ago
eight			eᵻ													o			coat
April			e													oˑ			road
ten				ɛ												oˑ			home
egg				ɛᵻ												oʊ			know
head				ɛ												oə			four
Mary			e													oˠə			door
stairs				ɛˠə												oə			hoarse
care				ɛˠə												—			mourn
merry				ɛʼ															
thirty					ɜ									ʌ					sun
sermon					ɜ									ʌə					brush
furrow					ɜʼ														
ashes						æ							ɒˠ,ɔˠə						frost
bag						æ							ɒˑˤ						log
married						æ							ɔə						dog
half								ɑ					ɔˠ						water
glass						æ							ɒ						daughter
aunt								ɑ					ɔ						law
father								ɑ											
palm								ɑˑˑ											
barn								ɑ;ɑ					ɔ						forty
garden								ɑ					ɒ						morning
crop													ɔ,ɒˠə						corn
John													ɔ;,ɔ						horse
college													ɒ;						
borrow													ɒˤ						
five									aᵻ		aʊ								down
twice									aᵻ		aʊ								out
wire									aᵻə		aʊə								flower
joint										oᵻ									joint
boil										oᵻ									boil
	i	ɪ	e	ɛ	ɜ	æ	ɒ	ɑ	aɪ	ɔɪ	aʊ	ɒ	ɔ	ʌ	ɵ	o	ʊ	u	

	i	ɪ	e	ɛ	ʒ	æ	ɒ	ɑ	aɪ	ɔɪ	aʊ	ɑ	ɔ	ʌ	ɵ	o	ʊ	u	
three	ii																	u·	two
grease	i·																	ʊu	tooth
six		ɪ															ʊ		wood
crib		ɪ															ʊ		pull
ear	i·ə																	ʊə	poor
beard	i ə															oʊ			ago
eight			eɪ													o·ʊ			coat
April			eɪ													oʊ			road
ten				ɛ												oʊ			home
egg				ɛ												oʊ			know
head				ɛ												ɔ·ə			four
Mary				ɛ ə												ɔ·ə			door
stairs				ɛ ə												o·ə			hoarse
care				ɛ ə												ɔ·ə			mourn
merry				ɛ															
thirty					ʒ·ʒɪ									ʌ					sun
sermon					ʒ·ʒʼ									ʌ					brush
furrow														ʌ					
ashes						æ							ɔ						frost
bag						æ							ɒ						log
married						æ							ɔ·						dog
half							ɑ						ɔ						water
glass						æ							ɔ						daughter
aunt							ɑ·ʼ						ɔ·						law
father							ɑ·												
palm							ɑ·												
barn							ɑ·						ɔ·						forty
garden							ɑ·						ɔ·						morning
crop							ɑ						ɔ·						corn
John							ɑ·						ɔ·						horse
college								ɑ											
borrow								ɑ											
five									aɛ	ao									down
twice									ɑ·ɛ	ɑ·o									out
wire									ɛɹə	ɑoə									flower
									ɔ·ɪ										joint
									ɔɪ										boil
	i	ɪ	e	ɛ	ʒ	æ	ɒ	ɑ	aɪ	ɔɪ	aʊ	ɑ	ɔ	ʌ	ɵ	o	ʊ	u	

	i	ɪ	e	ɛ	ɜ	æ	ɑ	ɒ	a	ai	ɔi	au	ɒ	ɔ	ʌ	ɵ	o	ʊ	u	
three	i˙																			two
grease	i˙																		ᵾ˙	tooth
six		ɪ																	ᵾ˙	wood
crib		ɪ																ʊ		pull
ear	iˇᵊ																	ʊ		poor
beard	iˇᵊ															oᵁ		—		ago
eight			eᵛɪ														oᵁ			coat
April			eᵛɪ														oᵁ			road
ten				ɛ													oᵁ			home
egg				ɛ													oᵁ			know
head				ɛ													ɔˇᵊ			four
Mary			eⱻ														ɔˇᵊ			door
stairs				ɛᵊ													ɔᵊ			hoarse
care				ɛᵊ													oᵊ			mourn
merry				ɛ																
thirty					3˙										ʌ					sun
sermon					3˙										ʌ					brush
furrow					3															
ashes						æ								ɔˇ˙						frost
bag						æ		ɑ						ɔ						log
married						æ								ɔ						dog
half							aˑ							ɔᵛ						water
glass						æᵛ								ɔˑ						daughter
aunt							aˑˇ							ɔˑ						law
father							aˑˇ													
palm							aˑˇ													
barn							aˑˇ							ɔˑ						forty
garden							aˑˇ							ɔˑ						morning
crop								ɑ						ɔˑ						corn
John								ɑˑ						ɔˑ						horse
college		ɪ						ɒ												
borrow								ɒ												
five									aˑɪ		au									down
twice									ɑˑɪ		au									out
wire									aˑɪᵊ		aˑʊᵊ									flower
joint										ɔɪ										joint
boil										ɔˑɪ										boil
	i	ɪ	e	ɛ	3	æ	ɑ	ɒ	a	ai	ɔi	au	ɒ	ɔ	ʌ	ɵ	o	ʊ	u	

	i	ɪ	e	ɛ	ɜ	æ	ɑ	ɑ	ai	ɔi	au	ɒ	ɔ	ʌ	θ	o	ʊ	u	
three	iˑ																	uˑ	two
grease	iˑ																	uˑ	tooth
six		ɪ˄															ʊ		wood
crib		ɪ															ʊ		pull
ear	ɪ˄ə																ʊ˅ə		poor
beard	ɪ˄ə															oˑ			ago
eight			e˅ɪ													oᵘ			coat
April			e˅ɪ													oᵘ			road
ten				ɛ												o˅ʊ			home
egg				ɛ												o˅ᵘ			know
head				ɛ												ɔ˄ə			four
Mary			e˅ɪ̶													ɔ˄ə			door
stairs			ɛ˄ə													o˅ə			hoarse
care			ɛ˄ə													—			mourn
merry				ɛ															
thirty					ɜ									ʌ					sun
sermon					ɜˑ									ʌ˅					brush
furrow														ʌ˅					
ashes						æ						ɔ˅							frost
bag						æ						ɔ˅ˑ							log
married						æ						ɔ˅ˑ							dog
half							ɑ˂					ɔ							water
glass							a					ɔˑ							daughter
aunt							aˑ					ɔˑ							law
father							aˑ												
palm							a˃ˑ												
barn							a˃ˑ					ɔ˅ˑ							forty
garden							aˑ					ɔˑ							morning
crop												ɒ,ɔˑ							corn
John												ɒˑ,ɔˑ							horse
college												ɒ							
borrow												ɒ							
five									ɑe		a˃ʊ								down
twice									ɐɪ		ɑ˂ʊ								out
wire									ɑɪə		ɑʊə								flower
										ɔ˅e									joint
										ɔ˅ɪ									boil
	i	ɪ	e	ɛ	ɜ	æ	ɑ	ɑ	ai	ɔi	au	ɒ	ɔ	ʌ	θ	o	ʊ	u	

	i	ı	e	ɛ	ɜ	æ	a	ɑ	ai	ɔi	au	ɒ	ɔ	ʌ	θ	o	ʊ	u	
three	i																		two · u
grease	i																		tooth · u
six		ı																ʊ	wood
crib		ı																ʊ	pull
ear	ıˑə																	ʊə	poor
beard	ıə															oʊ			ago
eight			e													oʊ			coat
April			e													oʊ			road
ten				ɛˀ												oʊ			home
egg				ɛ												o			know
head				ɛ												ɔˀə			four
Mary			ɛˑɜ													oə			door
stairs				ɛˑɜ												oˀʲə			hoarse
care				ɛˑɜ												—			mourn
merry				ɛ															
thirty					ɜ									ʌ					sun
sermon					ɜˑ									ʌ					brush
furrow					ɜ̬														
ashes						æ							ɔ						frost
bag						æ						ɒ							log
married						æ							ɔˑ						dog
half							aˀ						ɔ						water
glass							aˑ						ɔ						daughter
aunt							a						ɔˑ						law
father								ɑˑ											
palm								ɑˑˑ											
barn								ɑˑ					ɔˀə						forty
garden							aˑ						ɔˀə						morning
crop							a						oʲə						corn
John							—						ɒˀ						horse
college							ɑ												
borrow												ɒ							
five									aɨ		au								down
twice									aı		au								out
wire									aˀıˑə		auə								flower
										ɔɨ									joint
										ɔˀ									boil

| | i | ı | e | ɛ | ɜ | æ | a | ɑ | ai | ɔi | au | ɒ | ɔ | ʌ | θ | o | ʊ | u | |

	i	ɪ	e	ə	ɛ	ɜ	æ	ɒ	ɑ	aɪ	ɔɪ	au	ɒ	ɔ	ʌ	ɵ	o	ʊ	u	
three	i´																			ú̇	two
grease	i´																			u̇	tooth
six		ɪ																	ʊ		wood
crib		ɪ																	ʊ		pull
ear	i̯ə																		—		poor
beard	i̯ə																oʊ				ago
eight			e´														oᵛ				coat
April			e´														oᵛ				road
ten					ɛ												oʊ				home
egg					ɛ												oᵘ				know
head					ɛ												o̯ə				four
Mary			eᵊ		ɛ												o̯ə				door
stairs			ɛ̯ɜ														o̯ᵊ				hoarse
care			ɛ̯ɜ														o̯ᵊ				mourn
merry			ɛ˒																		
thirty						ɝ									ʌ						sun
sermon						ɜ									ʌ						brush
furrow						ɜ															
ashes							æ							ɔᵊ							frost
bag							æ·		ɑᵊ												log
married							æ							ɔ´							dog
half							æᵛ							ɔ							water
glass							æ							ɔ´							daughter
aunt							æ·							ɔ´							law
father									ɑ·												
palm									ɑ·												
barn									ɑɝ					ɔᵊ							forty
garden									ɑɝ					ɔᵊ							morning
crop									ɑ					ɔ̯ə							corn
John									ɑ					ɔɝ							horse
college									ɑ												
borrow														ɔᵛ							
five										ɜɛ		au									down
twice										ɜɛ		au									out
wire										—		auə									flower
joint											ɜɔ										joint
boil											ɔɜ										boil
	i	ɪ	e	ə	ɛ	ɜ	æ	ɒ	ɑ	aɪ	ɔɪ	au	ɒ	ɔ	ʌ	ɵ	o	ʊ	u	

	i	ɪ	e	ǝ	ɛ	ɜ	æ	a	ɑ	ai	ɔi	au	ɒ	ɔ	ʌ	ɵ	o	ʊ	u	
three	i																			two
grease	i																			tooth
six		ɪ																		wood
crib		ɪˀ																ʊ		pull
ear	iˑɚ																		ʊᵊɚ	poor
beard	iˑɚ																oᵁ			ago
eight			eˆ														ɵ			coat
April			eˑ														o			road
ten					ɛˇ												o			home
egg					ɛˆ												o			know
head					ɛ									ɔᵊɚ						four
Mary					ɛ												oᵊɚ			door
stairs			ɛˑɚ														oᵊɚ			hoarse
care					ɛɚ												oˑɚ			mourn
merry					ɛ															
thirty						ɚ									ʌ					sun
sermon						ɚ									ʌ					brush
furrow						ɚ														
ashes							æɨ						ʋˆ							frost
bag							æɨ							ɔˑ						log
married							æˆ							ɔˑ						dog
half							æ,æ						ʋ							water
glass							æ							ɔˑ						daughter
aunt							æ							ɔ						law
father									ɑˑˑ											
palm									ɑˑɑˑ											
barn									ɑɚ								oɚ			forty
garden									ɑɚ								oˑɚ			morning
crop									ɑˑ					ɔɚ						corn
John									ɑˑ					ɔɚ						horse
college									ɑ											
borrow													ʋ							
five										ɑɨ		ɑo								down
twice										ɑɨ		au								out
wire										ɑɨɚ		auᵊɚ								flower
											ɔɨ									joint
											ɔɨ									boil

	i	ɪ	e	ɪ	ɛ	ɜ	æ	ɒ	ɑ	ai	ɔi	au	ɒ	ɔ	ʌ	ɵ	o	ʊ	u	
three	ļi																		ʋɯ	two
grease	ļi																		—	tooth
six		ɪ																—		wood
crib		ɪˑ																ʊ		pull
ear	iˑə̗																	—		poor
beard		ɪə̗														oʊ				ago
eight			eɪ													ð				coat
April			eɪ														oʊ			road
ten					ɛ												oʊ			home
egg					ɛ,ɛˑ												oˑʊ			know
head					—												oˑə̗			four
Mary			eɪ														oˑə̗			door
stairs							æˑə̗										o ə̗			hoarse
care																	oˑə̗			mourn
merry					ɛ̗															
thirty						ɜˀ										ʌˑ̗				sun
sermon						ɜˑˀ										ʌ				brush
furrow						ɜ̗														
ashes							æ							ɔ						frost
bag							æ							ɔ						log
married							æˑ							ɔˀ						dog
half								ɑ						ɔ						water
glass							æ							ɔ						daughter
aunt								ɑˑ						ɔˑ						law
father								ɑˑˀ												
palm								ɑˑˀ												
barn								ɑˑ						ɔˀ						forty
garden								ɑˑ						ɔˑ						morning
crop									ɑ					ɔˀ						corn
John									ɑ					ɔˀ						horse
college									ɑˀ											
borrow									ɒˀ											
five										ɑɛ	ɑo									down
twice										ɑɛ	ɑo									out
wire										ɑɛə̗	ɑoə̗									flower
											ɔɛ̗ˀ									joint
											ˑɛ̗c									boil

| | i | ɪ | e | ɪ | ɛ | ɜ | æ | ɒ | ɑ | ai | ɔi | au | ɒ | ɔ | ʌ | ɵ | o | ʊ | u | |

	i ɪ e ɪ ɛ ɜ æ ɒ ɑ ɑ ai ɔi au ɒ ɔ ʌ θ o ʊ u	
three	ʃi	two · ʊu
grease	ʃi	tooth · ʊu
six	ɪ	wood · ʊ
crib	ɪ	pull · ʊ̠
ear	iˇə̰	poor · ʊˆɚ
beard	ɪˆə̰	ago · ou
eight	eɪ	coat · oˇʊ
April	eɪ	road · ou
ten	ɛˇ	home · oːʊ
egg	ɛ	know · ou
head	ɛ,ɛə	four · oˇɚ
Mary	ɛ	door · oˇə̰
stairs	ɛə	hoarse · oˇɚ
care	ɛə	mourn · oə̰
merry	ɛ	
thirty	ɝ · ʌ	sun
sermon	ɜ,ɝ̣ · ʌ	brush
furrow	ʌ	furrow
ashes	æ · ɒ,ɒˇ	frost
bag	æ · ɔˇ	log
married	æ · ɔˇɔ	dog
half	æ · ɔˇ	water
glass	æ · ɔ	daughter
aunt	æə · ɒˇʷ	law
father	ɑˑ	
palm	ɑˑ	
barn	ɑˑɚ · ɔˇ	forty
garden	ɑˑ,ɑ · ɒˇʌˇ	morning
crop	ɑ · ɔˇ	corn ·
John	ɑ · ɔ̣ɔ	horse
college	ɑ	
borrow	ɑˀ	
five	ɑɛ · ɑo	down
twice	ɑɛ · æo	out
wire	ɑeə · ɑoə̰	flower
	ɔɪˇ	joint
	ɔɪ	boil
	i ɪ e ɪ ɛ ɜ æ ɒ ɑ ɑ ai ɔi au ɒ ɔ ʌ θ o ʊ u	

	i	ɪ	e	ə	ɛ	æ	ɒ	ɑ	ai	au	ɒ	ɔ	ʌ	θ	o	ʊ	u	
three	i˙																	ᴜˇ˙	two
grease	i˙																	ᴜ˙	tooth
six		ɪ															ʊ		wood
crib		ɪˀ															ʊ		pull
ear	ɪˀə																	ᴜˇᵛə	poor
beard	ɪˀə														o˙ʊ			ago
eight			eɪ̵												oʊ			coat
April			eˀɪ̵												o˙ʊ			road
ten				ɛˀ											o˙ʊ			home
egg				ɛ											oʊ			know
head				ɛ											ɔˀə			four
Mary			ɛˀˀə												o˙ˀə			door
stairs			ɛˀˀə̣												ɔˀə̣			hoarse
care			ɛˀˀə												ɔˀə̣			mourn
merry				ɛˀ														
thirty					ɓʌˀə								ʌ					sun
sermon					ɓʌˀə̣								ʌˋ					brush
furrow													ʌ					
ashes						æ					ɔˀ˙ə							frost
bag						æˀ˙					ɔ˙							log
married						æ					ɔ˙							dog
half						æˀ˙					ɔ˙							water
glass						æ					ɔ˙							daughter
aunt						æˀˀ,æˀə					ɔˀ˙							law
father							ɑˀ˙˙											
palm							ɑ˙											
barn							ɑˀ˙˙					ɔˀ˙ə							forty
garden							ɑˀ˙ə̣					ɔˀ˙ə							morning
. crop								ɑˀ˙				ɔˀ˙ə							corn
John								ɑ˙				ɔˀ˙ə̣							horse
college								ɑˀ										
borrow								ɑˀ										
five									əɪ̵	au								down
twice									əɪ̵	aˀ˙u								out
wire									əˀɪ̵ə	auə								flower
joint											ɪ̵ɔ							joint
boil											ɪ̵ɔ							boil

| | i | ɪ | e | ə | ɛ | æ | ɒ | ɑ | ai | au | ɒ | ɔ | ʌ | θ | o | ʊ | u | |

	i	ɪ	e	ɜ	ɛ	æ	a	ɑ	ɒ	ai	ɔi	au	ʊ	ɔ	ʌ	θ	o	ʊ	u	
three	i˙																			u̇ː	two
grease	i˂˙																			u̇˙	tooth
six		ɪ																ʊ			wood
crib		ɪˑ																ʊ			pull
ear	ɪˑɚ																		ʊˑɚ		poor
beard	ɪˑɚ																oʊ				ago
eight			eɪ														oʊ				coat
April			eˑɪ														oʊ				road
ten					ɛɚ												oʊ				home
egg					ɛ												oᵁ				know
head					ɛˀ									ɔˑɚ							four
Mary				ɛˑɚ										ɔɚ							door
stairs				ɛˑɚ										ɔɚ							hoarse
care				ɛˑɚ										ɔɚ							mourn
merry				ɛ																	
thirty					ɜᵉ										ʌˑ						sun
sermon					ɜɪᵛ										ʌ̤						brush
furrow															ʌ̤						
ashes						æ								ɔˑɚ							frost
bag						æˀ		ɑ						ɔˑ							log
married						æᵛ								ɔˑ							dog
half						æɚ								ɔˑ							water
glass						æɚ								ɔˑ							daughter
aunt						æɚ								ɔˑ							law
father							aː														
palm							aˑ														
barn							aː							ɔˑɚ							forty
garden							aˑɚ							ɔɚ							morning
crop								ɑˀ						ɔˑɚ							corn
John								ɑˑ						ɔˑɚ							horse
college								ɑ													
borrow								ɑ													
five										ɑɪ		aᵁ									down
twice										ɒɪ		ɑ̈ᵁ									out
wire										ɑɪɚ		—									flower
joint											ɪˑɔ										joint
boil											ɪˑɔ										boil
	i	ɪ	e	ɜ	ɛ	æ	a	ɑ	ɒ	ai	ɔi	au	ʊ	ɔ	ʌ	θ	o	ʊ	u	

	i	ɪ	e	ɛ	ɜ	æ	a	ɑ	ai	ɔi	au	a	ɒ	ɔ	ʌ	θ	o	ʊ	u	
three	i˅i																			two
grease	i˙																		u˙	tooth
six		ɪ																ʊ		wood
crib		ɪ																ʊ		pull
ear		ɪɚ																ʊɚ		poor
beard		ɪɚ														oˇʊ				ago
eight			eɪ													oˇʊ				coat
April			eɪ													oˇʊ				road
ten				ɛᵊ												oˇʊ				home
egg				ɛ												oˑʊ				know
head				ɛ												oˇɚ				four
Mary				ɛ												oˇɚ				door
stairs						æˑɚ										oˇɚ				hoarse
care				ɛɚ												oˇɚ				mourn
merry				ɛ																
thirty					ɚ										ʌ					sun
sermon					ɚˑ										ʌˇ					brush
furrow				ɛ																
ashes						æ						ɒˇᵊ								frost
bag						æˑ						ɒˑ								log
married						æᵊ						ɒˑ								dog
half						æᵊ						ɒˑ								water
glass						æˑᵊ						ɒˑ								daughter
aunt						æˑᵊ						ɒˑ								law
father							aˑˑ													
palm							aˑˑ													
barn							aˑɚ					ɒˑɚ								forty
garden							aˑɚ					ɒˑɚ								morning
crop							aˑˑ					ɒˑɚ								corn
John							aˑˑ					ɒˑɚ								horse
college							aˑˑ													
borrow							a													
five									aˑɪ		aˑʊ									down
twice									aˑɪ		aʊ									out
wire									aˑɪɚ		aʊɚ									flower
										ɔɪ										joint
										ɔɪ										boil
	i	ɪ	e	ɛ	ɜ	æ	a	ɑ	ai	ɔi	au	a	ɒ	ɔ	ʌ	θ	o	ʊ	u	

	i	ɪ	e	ɛ	ɜ	æ	ɑ	ɑ	ɒ	ai	ɔi	au	ɒ	ɔ	ʌ	ɵ	o	ʊ	u	
three	i´																		ṵ̆	two
grease	i´																		ṵ´	tooth
six		ɪ																ʊ		wood
crib		ɪ																ʊ		pull
ear	ɪɚ																		ṵɚ	poor
beard	ɪɚ																oʊ			ago
eight			eɪ														oʊ			coat
April			eɪ														oʊ			road
ten				ɛə													oʊ			home
egg				ɛ													oʊ			know
head				ɛə													oɚ			four
Mary				ɛə													oɚ			door
stairs				ɛɚ													oɚ			hoarse
care				ɛɚ													oɚ			mourn
merry				ɛ																
thirty					ɚ										ʌ					sun
sermon					ɚ										ʌ					brush
furrow					ɚ															
ashes						æ							ɒɚ							frost
bag						æ							ɒ							log
married						æ							ɒ							dog
half						æ							ɒ							water
glass						æɚ							ɒ							daughter
aunt						æ							ɒ							law
father							ɑ´													
palm							ɑ													
barn							ɑɚ						ɔɚ							forty
garden							ɑɚ						ɔɚ							morning
crop							ɑ´						ɔɚ							corn
John							ɑ						ɔɚ							horse
college							ɑ													
borrow							ɑ													
five										aɪ		aʊ								down
twice										aɪ		aʊ								out
wire										aɪɚ		aʊɚ								flower
joint											ɔi									joint
boil											ɔi									boil
	i	ɪ	e	ɛ	ɜ	æ	ɑ	ɑ	ɒ	ai	ɔi	au	ɒ	ɔ	ʌ	ɵ	o	ʊ	u	

	i	ɪ	e	ɜ	ɛ	æ	ɑ	ɒ	aɪ	ɔɪ	aʊ	ɒ	ɔ	ʌ	θ	o	ʊ	u	
three	i																	ʊ˝	two
grease	i																	ʊ˙	tooth
six		ɪ															ʊ		wood
crib		ɪ															ʊ		pull
ear		ɪɚ																ʊɚ	poor
beard	iˑɚ															oːʊ			ago
eight			eɪ̯													oːʊ			coat
April			eɪ̯													oːʊ			road
ten					ɛ											oːʊ			home
egg					ɛ											o ʊ			know
head					ɛ											oˑɚ			four
Mary						æ˝										oˑɚ			door
stairs			ɛˑɚ													oˑɚ			hoarse
care				ɛɚ												oˑɚ			mourn
merry					ɛ														
thirty				ɝ										ʌ					sun
sermon				ɝ										ʌ					brush
furrow				ɝ															
ashes						æ						ɒ˞							frost
bag						æ	ɑ												log
married						æ						ɒˑ							dog
half						æˑ						ɒ							water
glass						æˑ						ɒˑ							daughter
aunt						æˑ						ɒˑ							law
father							ɑ												
palm							ɑˑ												
barn							ɑɚ						ɔɚ						forty
garden							ɑɚ						ɔɚ						morning
crop							ɑ						ɔɚ						corn
John							ɑˑ						ɔɚ						horse
college							ɑ˝												
borrow												ɒˑ							
five									aɪ̯		aʊ								down
twice									aɪ̯		aʊ								out
wire									aɪ̯ɚ		aʊɚ								flower
										ɔɪ									joint
										ɔɪ									boil
	i	ɪ	e	ɜ	ɛ	æ	ɑ	ɒ	aɪ	ɔɪ	aʊ	ɒ	ɔ	ʌ	θ	o	ʊ	u	

	i	ɪ	e	ɛ	ɜ	æ	a	ɑ	ɒ	ai	ɔi	au	ʊ	ɑ	ɔ	ʌ	ɵ	o	ʊ	u	
three	iˣi																			ʊˣʊ	two
grease	iˣi																			ʊ˙˙	tooth
six		ɪ																	ʊ		wood
crib		ɪ																	ʊ		pull
ear	ɪˣɚ																		—		poor
beard		ɪ ɚ																oˣʊ			ago
eight			eˣɨ															oˑʊ			coat
April			eˣɨ															oˑʊ			road
ten				ɛˆ														ɐˑʊ			home
egg				ɛˆɨ														oˑʊ			know
head				ɛˆ														ǫˑɚ			four
Mary			eˣɨ															oˑɚ			door
stairs				ɛɚ														ǫˣɚ			hoarse
care				ɛɚ														ɔˣɚ			mourn
merry				ɛ																	
thirty					ɝˣɚ											ʌˆ					sun
sermon					ɝˣɚ											ʌˆ					brush
furrow					ɝˑ																
ashes						æ									ɔˣˑ						frost
bag						æˣᵊ		ɑ													log
married						æ									ɔˣᵊ						dog
half						æᵊ									ɔˣ						water
glass						æ									ɔˣ						daughter
aunt							ɑˣᵊ								ɔˣ						law
father							ɑ														
palm							ɑ														
barn							ɑˑɚ								ɔˣɚ						forty
garden							ɑˑɚ								ɔˣɚ						morning
crop							ɑˑᵊ								ɔˣɚ						corn
John							ɑˑᵊ								ɔˣɚ						horse
college							ɑˑ														
borrow							ɑ˙														
five										ɑˣɨ		ɑˣʊ									down
twice										ɑˣɨ		ɑˣʊ									out
wire										ɑˣɨɚ		ɑˣʊɚ									flower
											ɔˣɨ										joint
											ɔˣɨ										boil
	i	ɪ	e	ɛ	ɜ	æ	a	ɑ	ɒ	ai	ɔi	au	ʊ	ɑ	ɔ	ʌ	ɵ	o	ʊ	u	

	i	ɪ	e	ɛ	ɜ	æ	a	ɑ	ai	ɔi	au	u	ɒ	ɔ	ʌ	ɵ	o	ʊ	u	
three	i																		ʊˑˮ	two
grease	iˑ																		ʊˑ	tooth
six		ɪ																ʊ̆		wood
crib		ɪ̡ˑ																ʊ		pull
ear	ɪˑɚ																		ʊɚ	poor
beard		ɪ̡ˑɚ															oˑˮʊ			ago
eight			eɟ														oˑʊ			coat
April			eɟ														oˑˮɚ			road
ten				ɛˆ													oˮʊ			home
egg				ɛˆ													—			know
head				ɛ													o̡ɚ			four
Mary				ɛˑ													o o̡			door
stairs				ɛɚ													o̡ɚ			hoarse
care				ɛ̡ˮɚ													o̡̡ɚ			mourn
merry				ɛˑ																
thirty					ɝˑɚ										ʌᵋ					sun
sermon					ɝˑɚ										ʌᵋ					brush
furrow					ɝˮˑ															
ashes						æˮˑ								ɔˮˑ						frost
bag						æˮᵋ								ɔˮˑ						log
married				ɛ̣ˮ										ɔ̇ᴧᵟ						dog
half						æˮˑ								ɔᵋ						water
glass						æ								ɔˮ						daughter
aunt						æˑ								ɔˑ						law
father							ɑˑ													
palm							ɑˑ													
barn							ɑ̣ᵋɚ							ɔ̣ᵋɚ						forty
garden							ɑ̣ɚ							ɔ̣ᵋɚ						morning
crop							ɑ							ɔ̣ɚ						corn
John							ɑˑ							ɔ̣ɚ						horse
college							ɑˀ													
borrow							ɑˀ													
five									ɜ̣ɟ		ɑˑᴧ̣ʊ									down
twice									ɪɟ		ɑ̣ɟʊ									out
wire									eɟˑɚ		ɑ̣ʊɚ									flower
										ɔɟ										joint
										ɟɔ										boil
	i	ɪ	e	ɛ	ɜ	æ	a	ɑ	ai	ɔi	au	u	ɒ	ɔ	ʌ	ɵ	o	ʊ	u	

	i	ɪ	e	ɪ	ɛ	ɜ	æ	ɒ	ɑ	ai	ɔi	au	ɒ	ɔ	ʌ	ɵ	o	ʊ	u	
three	iᵛ·																			two
grease	i·																		u̓	tooth
six		ɪ																		wood
crib		ɪ																ʊ		pull
ear	ɪᵊ																	ʊə		poor
beard	ɪᵊ																o̤ʊ			ago
eight			eɪ														o̤ʊ			coat
April			eɪ														oᵛʊ			road
ten					ɛᵊ												oᵛʊ			home
egg					ɛ												o̤ʊ			know
head					ɛᵊ									ɔᵊc						four
Mary			ɛ·ᵊ											ɔᵊc						door
stairs			ɛ·ᵊ											ɔᵊc						hoarse
care			ɛᵊ											ɔᵊc						mourn
merry					ɛᵊ															
thirty						ɜ·ᵊ									ʌ					sun
sermon						ɜ·ᵊ									ʌᶜ					brush
furrow															ʌᶜ					
ashes							æ							ɔᵛ						frost
bag							æ·	a						ɔ						log
married							æ							ɔᵊc						dog
half							æᵊ							ɔ·						water
glass							æᵊ							ɔ·						daughter
aunt							æ·							ɔ·						law
father							ɑᵛ·													
palm							ɑᵛ··													
barn							ɒᵛ·ᵊ							ɔᵊc						forty
garden							ɑᵛ··							ɔᵊc						morning
crop									ɑ					ɔᵊc						corn
John									ɑ·					ɔᵊc						horse
college									ɑᵛ											
borrow									ɑ											
five										a·ɪ		a·ʊ								down
twice										aɪ		aʊ								out
wire										æᵛɪᵊ		ɛᵛᵊʊə								flower
											ɔɪ									joint
											ɔɪ									boil
	i	ɪ	e	ɪ	ɛ	ɜ	æ	ɒ	ɑ	ai	ɔi	au	ɒ	ɔ	ʌ	ɵ	o	ʊ	u	

	i	ɪ	e	ɛ	ɜ	æ	ɑ	ɑ	aɪ	ɔɪ	au	ɒ	ɔ	ʌ	θ	o	ʊ	u	
three	jᵛ																	uˑ	two
grease	jˑ																	uˑᶜ	tooth
six		ɪ															ʊ		wood
crib		ɪᵊ															ʊ		pull
ear	ɪᶦᵊ																	ʊᶦᵊ	poor
beard	ɪᶦᵊ															oᵛʊ			ago
eight			eᵛɪ													ʙᵊʊ			coat
April			eᵛɪ													ʙᵊʊ			road
ten				ɛ												ʙʊᶺ			home
egg				ɛ												ʙᵊʊᶺ			know
head				ɛᵊ						ɔːᵊ									four
Mary			ɛᶦᵊ							ᵊɔ									door
stairs			ɛˑᵊ							ɔˑ									hoarse
care			ɛˑᵊ							ɔˑ									mourn
merry				ɛ															
thirty					ɜᶺˑ									ᴧᶜ					sun
sermon					ɜᵎˑ									ᴧᶜ					brush
furrow														ᴧᶜ					
ashes						æˑ				ɔᶜᵊ									frost
bag						æˑ		ɑᶺˑ											log
married						æ				ɔː									dog
half						æᵛᵊ				ɔˑ									water
glass								ɑᶺˑ		ɔˑ									daughter
aunt						æᵎ				ɔː									law
father							ɑᶜˑː												
palm							ɑᵎˑː												
barn							ɑᵎˑː						ɔˑ						forty
garden							ɑᶜˑː						ɔˑː						morning
crop								ɑᵎ					ɔˑ						corn
John								ɑᶺˑ					ɔᶜᵊ						horse
college								ɑᶺᵊ											
borrow								ɑᶺ											
five									aᵎɜ		aʊ								down
twice									aᵎɪ		aʊ								out
wire									aᵎɪɐ		æᵛʊɐ								flower
joint										ɔᵎɪ									
boil										ɪ									
	i	ɪ	e	ɛ	ɜ	æ	ɑ	ɑ	aɪ	ɔɪ	au	ɒ	ɔ	ʌ	θ	o	ʊ	u	

	i	ɪ	e	ǝ	ɪ	ɛ	æ	a	ɑ	ai	ɔi	au	ɒ	ɔ	ʌ	θ	o	ʊ	u	
three	i¨																		u̶¨	two
grease	i¨																		u̶˙	tooth
six		ɪ																ʊ		wood
crib		ɪᵊ																ʊ		pull
ear	ɪ˄ᵊ																	ʊ˄ᵊ		poor
beard	ɪ˄ᵊ														ɞ̗ᵕ					ago
eight			ℓɟ												o̗ᵕ					coat
April			ℓɟ												o̗ᵕ					road
ten				ɛ											o˄ᵕ					home
egg				ɛ˄											ɞ˄ᵕ					know
head				ɛ										ɔ̇ᵊ						four
Mary			ɛ˄ᵊ											ɔ̇ᵊ						door
stairs			ɛ˄ᵊ											ɔᵊ						hoarse
care			ɛ˄ᵊ											ɔᵊ						mourn
merry				ɛ																
thirty					ɞɟ										ʌ					sun
sermon					ɞɟ										ʌᵊ					brush
furrow					ɜ															
ashes						æ								ɔᵛᵊ						frost
bag						æ˄¨		ɑ˄												log
married						æ								ɔᵛ						dog
half						æᵊ								ɔᵊ						water
glass						æᵛᵊ								ɔ˙						daughter
aunt						æᵊ								ɔ˙						law
father							ɑ̈˙													
palm							ɑ̈˙													
barn							ɑ̈˙							ɔᵊ						forty
garden							ɑ̈˙							ɔᵊ						morning
crop								ɑ̇ɑ						ɔᵊ						corn
John								ɑ̇						ɔᵊ						horse
college								ɑ												
borrow								ɑ												
five									ɑɟ		au									down
twice									ɑɟ		æᵕ									out
wire									ɑ˄ᵊ		ɞᵕᵊ									flower
										ɔɟ										joint
										ɔɟ										boil
	i	ɪ	e	ǝ	ɪ	ɛ	æ	a	ɑ	ai	ɔi	au	ɒ	ɔ	ʌ	θ	o	ʊ	u	

57

	i	ɪ	e	ɛ	ɜ	æ	ɒ	ɑ	aɪ	ɔɪ	aʊ	ɒ	ɔ	ʌ	ɵ	o	ʊ	u	
three	i·																	u·	two
grease	i·																	u·	tooth
six		ɨ															ʊ		wood
crib		ɪ															ʊ		pull
ear	ɪ·ɚ																	ʊ·ɚ	poor
beard	ɪ·ɚ															o·ʊ			ago
eight			eɨ													o·ʊ			coat
April			eɨ													o·ʊ			road
ten				ɛ·												o·ʊ			home
egg				ɛ												oʊ			know
head				ɛ·									ɔ·ɚ						four
Mary				ɛ·ɚ									ɔ·ɚ						door
stairs				ɛ·ɚ									ɔ·ɚ						hoarse
care				ɛ·ɚ									ɔ·ɚ						mourn
merry				ɛ															
thirty					ɜɨ									ʌ·					sun
sermon					ɜ·ɚ									ʌ					brush
furrow														ʌ					
ashes						æ·							ɔ·						frost
bag						æ·	ɑ·												log
married						æ							ɔ·						dog
half						æ·							ɔ·						water
glass						æ·ɚ							ɔ·						daughter
aunt						æ·							ɔ·ɚ						law
father							ɑ·:												
palm							ɑ·												
barn							ɑ·ɚ						ɔ·ɚ						forty
garden							ɑ·						ɔ·ɚ						morning
crop								ɑ					ɔ·ɚ						corn
John								ɑ·					ɔ·ɚ						horse
college								ɑ											
borrow								ɑ											
five									aɨ		aʊ								down
twice									aɨ		aʊ								out
wire									aɨɚ		aʊɚ								flower
joint										ɔɨ									joint
boil										ɔɨ									boil
	i	ɪ	e	ɛ	ɜ	æ	ɒ	ɑ	aɪ	ɔɪ	aʊ	ɒ	ɔ	ʌ	ɵ	o	ʊ	u	

	i	ɪ	e	ɛ	ɜ	æ	a	ɑ	ɒ	ai	ɔi	au	ɒ	ɔ	ʌ	θ	o	ʊ	u	
three	iˑi																		uˑ	two
grease	iˑi																		uˑ	tooth
six		ɪ																ʊ		wood
crib		ɪᵊ																ʊ		pull
ear	ɪʳɚ																		uɚ	poor
beard	ɪʳɚ																oˑʊ			ago
eight			ɛɪ														θʊ			coat
April			ɛɪ														θʊ			road
ten				ɛ													θʊ			home
egg				ɛ													oˑʊ			know
head				ɛ													ɔˑɚ			four
Mary				ɛɚ													ɔɚ			door
stairs				ɛɚ													oˑɚ			hoarse
care				ɛɚ													ɔɚ			mourn
merry				ɛɚ																
thirty					ɚ										ʌ					sun
sermon					ɚ										ʌᵊ					brush
furrow					ɚ															
ashes						æˑ								ɔˑᵊ						frost
bag						æˑ								ɔʌᵊ						log
married						æᵊ								ɔˑᵊ						dog
half						æᵊ								ɔˑ						water
glass						æᵊ								ɔˑᵊ						daughter
aunt						æˑ								ɔˑ						law
father							ɑˑ													
palm							ɑˑ													
barn							ɑɚ							ɔˑɚ						forty
garden							ɑɚ							ɔˑɚ						morning
crop							ɑ							ɔɚ						corn
John							ɑᵊ							ɔɚ						horse
college							ɑᵊ													
borrow							ɑ													
five										ɑɛ		aʊ								down
twice										ɑɪ		aʊ								out
wire										aɛɚ		aʊɚ								flower
											oˑɪ									joint
											oɪ									boil
	i	ɪ	e	ɛ	ɜ	æ	a	ɑ	ɒ	ai	ɔi	au	ɒ	ɔ	ʌ	θ	o	ʊ	u	

	i	ɪ	e	ɛ	ɜ	æ	ɑ	ɒ	ɑ	ai	ɔi	au	ɔ	ʌ	θ	o	ʊ	u	
three	ɪˑi																	ʊˑˑ	two
grease	iˑi																	ʊˑ	tooth
six		ɪ															ʊ		wood
crib		ɪ															ʊ		pull
ear	ɪˑɚ																	uˑɚ	poor
beard	ɪˑɚ															ɔˑʊ			ago
eight			ɛɪ													ɐˑʊ			coat
April			ɛɪ													ɔˑʊ			road
ten				ɛ												ɔˑʊ			home
egg				ɛ												—			know
head				ɛ									ɔˑɚ						four
Mary				ɛˑ									ɔ ɚ						door
stairs				ɛɚ									ɔ ɚ						hoarse
care				ɛɚ									ɔ ɚ						mourn
merry				ɛ															
thirty					ɚ									ʌˑ					sun
sermon					ɚ									ʌ,ʌˑ					brush
furrow					ɚ														
ashes						æ							ɔˑˑ						frost
bag						æˑ	ɑ												log
married						æ							ɔˑ						dog
half						æˑ							ɔˑ						water
glass						æˑ							ɔˑ						daughter
aunt						æˑ							ɔˑ						law
father									ɑˑ										
palm									ɑˑ										
barn									ɑɚ				ɔɚ						forty
garden									ɑɚ				ɔɚ						morning
crop									ɑˑ				ɔɚ						corn
John									ɑˑ				ɔɚ						horse
college									ɑ										
borrow									ɑ										
five										aɪ		æˑʊ							down
twice										aɪ		æˑʊ							out
wire										aɪɚ		ɑˑʊɚ							flower
											ɪɔ								joint
											ɔɪ								boil
	i	ɪ	e	ɛ	ɜ	æ	ɑ	ɒ	ɑ	ai	ɔi	au	ɔ	ʌ	θ	o	ʊ	u	

	i	ɪ	e	e	ɛ	ɜ	æ	a	ɑ	ɑ	ai	ɔi	au	ɒ	ɔ	ʌ	ɵ	o	ʊ	u	
three	iᵛˑ																				two (uˑ)
grease	iˑ																				tooth (uˑˑ)
six		ɪ																	ʊ		wood
crib		ɪᵊ																	ʊ		pull
ear		ɪɚ																		uˑɚ	poor
beard		ɪɚ																oˑ			ago
eight			eˑ															oˑ			coat
April			eˑ															oˑ			road
ten					ɛ													oˑ			home
egg					ɛ													o			know
head					ɛ									ɔɚ							four
Mary					ɛᵊ									ɔɚ							door
stairs					ɛɚ												ɚɚ				hoarse
care					ɛɚ									ɔɚ							mourn
merry					ɛ																
thirty						ɚ										ʌ					sun
sermon						ɚ										ʌᵊ					brush
furrow						ɚˑ															
ashes							æ							ɒᵛ							frost
bag							æᵛˑ							ɒᵛ							log
married							æ							ɔᵛˑ							dog
half							æᵛᵊ							ɔ							water
glass							æˑᵊ							ɔᵛˑ							daughter
aunt							æˑᵊ							ɔᵛˑ							law
father								ɑᵛˑ													
palm								ɑˑ													
barn								ɑᵛˑɚ						ɔɚ							forty
garden								ɑᵛˑɚ										ɔɚ			morning
crop								ɑˑ										ɔɚ			corn
John								ɑ						ɔɚ							horse
college								ɑˑ													
borrow								ɑ													
five											aɪ		au								down
twice											aɪ	—	—								out
wire											aɪɚ		auɚ								flower
												ɔɪ									joint
												ɔɪ									boil
	i	ɪ	e	e	ɛ	ɜ	æ	a	ɑ	ɑ	ai	ɔi	au	ɒ	ɔ	ʌ	ɵ	o	ʊ	u	

	i	ɪ	e	ɪ	ɛ	æ	ɑ	ɒ	ai	ɔi	au	ɑ	ɔ	ʌ	θ	o	ʊ	u	
three	iˇi																		two
grease	iˊ																	uˊˊ	tooth
six		ɪ															ʊ		wood
crib		ɪᵊ															ʊ		pull
ear	ɪɚ																	uɚ	poor
beard	ɪˊɚ															oˑʊ			ago
eight			eˇɪ													oᵛ			coat
April			eˇɪ													o ʊ			road
ten					ɛ											oˑʊ			home
egg					ɛ											oˑʊ			know
head					ɛ							ɔɚ							four
Mary					ɛ							ɔɚ							door
stairs					ɛɚ							ɔɚ							hoarse
care					ɛɚ							ɔɚ							mourn
merry					ɛ														
thirty						ɝ								ʌ					sun
sermon						ɝ								ʌᵛ					brush
furrow						ɝ													
ashes						æˑ						ɒᵛᵊ							frost
bag						æ						ɒᵛ							log
married						æ						ɒˑ							dog
half						æ						ɔᵊ							water
glass						æˑᵊ						ɒˑ							daughter
aunt						æᵊ						ɒᵛ							law
father							ɑˑ												
palm							ɑˑ												
barn							ɒˑɚ					ɔɚ							forty
garden							ɑˑɚ					ɔɚ							morning
crop							ɑˑ					ɔɚ							corn
John							ɑˑ					ɔɚ							horse
college							ɑˑ												
borrow							ɑ												
five									aɪ		au								down
twice									aɪ		au								out
wire									aɪɚ		auɚ								flower
										ɔɪ									joint
										ɔɪ									boil
	i	ɪ	e	ɪ	ɛ	æ	ɑ	ɒ	ai	ɔi	au	ɑ	ɔ	ʌ	θ	o	ʊ	u	

	i	ɪ	e	ə	ɛ	ɜ	æ	ɑ	ɑ	ai	ɔi	au	ɒ	ɔ	ʌ	ɵ	o	ʊ	u	
three	iˑi																			ʊˑʊ	two
grease	iˑi																			ʊˑ	tooth
six		ɪ																ʊ			wood
crib		ɪᵊ																ʊ			pull
ear	ɪɚ																			ʊˑɚ	poor
beard	ɪˑɚ																oˑʊ				ago
eight			eˑɪ														ʙˑʊ				coat
April			eˑɪ														ʙˑʊ				road
ten					ɛᵊ												oˑʊ				home
egg					ɛ												oˑʊ				know
head					ɛ												ɔˑɚ				four
Mary					ɛ												ɔˑɚ				door
stairs					ɛɚ												ɔˑɚ				hoarse
care					ɛɚ												ɔɚ				mourn
merry					ɛ																
thirty						ɚ									ʌ						sun
sermon						ɚ									ʌ						brush
furrow						ɚˑ															
ashes							æ						ɒˑᵊ								frost
bag							æ						ɒˑ								log
married							æ						ɒˑ								dog
half							æ						ɒˑ								water
glass							æˑᵊ						ɒ								daughter
aunt							æˑᵊ						ɒˑ								law
father													ɒˑ								
palm													ɒˑ								
barn								ɑɚ									ɔˑɚ				forty
garden								ɑˑɚ									ɔˑɚ				morning
crop													ɒˑ				ɔˑɚ				corn
John													ɒˑᵊ				ɔˑɚ				horse
college													ɒ								
borrow													ɒˑ								
five								ɑˑɪ		aʊ											down
twice								ɑˑɪ		ɑˑʊ											out
wire								ɑɚ		aʊɚ											flower
										ɔˑɪ										joint
										oˑɪ										boil
	i	ɪ	e	ə	ɛ	ɜ	æ	ɑ	ɑ	ai	ɔi	au	ɒ	ɔ	ʌ	ɵ	o	ʊ	u	

	i	ɪ	e	ə	ɛ	ɜ	æ	ɒ	ɑ	ai	ɔi	au	ɒ	ɔ	ʌ	ɵ	o	ʊ	u	
three	iˇi																		uˇˑ	two
grease	iˑ																		uˑ	tooth
six		ɪ																ʊ		wood
crib		ɪə																ʊ,ʊə		pull
ear		ɪʏ																	uˑʏ	poor
beard	iˑʏ																oˈʊ			ago
eight			eɪ														oˈʊ			coat
April			eɪ														oˑʊ			road
ten					ɛə												oˑʊ			home
egg					ɛ												ɐˑʊ			know
head					ɛə												ɔʏ			four
Mary					ɛ												ɔʏ			door
stairs					ɛʏ												ɔʏ			hoarse
care					ɛʏ												ɔʏ			mourn
merry					ɛ															
thirty						əʏ									ʌˇ					sun
sermon						əʏ									ʌˇ					brush
furrow						əʏ														
ashes							æ		ʋˈə											frost
bag							æ·		ʋˈ											log
married							æ		ʋə											dog
half							æˆ								ʌˈ					water
glass							æ·		ʋˈ											daughter
aunt							æˑə		ʋˈˑ											law
father									ʋˑ											
palm									ʋə											
barn									ɑr								ɔʏ			forty
garden									ɑr								ɔʏ			morning
crop									ʋə								ɔʏ			corn
John									ʋˈə								ɔʏ			horse
college									ʋˈ											
borrow														ɔˆ						
five										aɪ		aˈʊ								down
twice										aɪ		aˈʊ								out
wire										aɪʏ		aˈʊʏ								flower
											ɔɪ									joint
											ɔɪ									boil
	i	ɪ	e	ə	ɛ	ɜ	æ	ɒ	ɑ	ai	ɔi	au	ɒ	ɔ	ʌ	ɵ	o	ʊ	u	

	i	ı	e	ɛ	ɜ	æ	ɑ	ɑ	ai	ɔi	au	ɒ	ɔ	ʌ	θ	o	ʊ	u	
three	ˡˆi																		two	ʉˀ
grease	ˡi																		tooth	ʉˀ
six		ɪ															ʊ		wood
crib		ɪˀ															ʊ		pull
ear		ˡˀɹ																ʉˀɹ	poor
beard		ˡˀɹ													ɘˀʊ				ago
eight			ɛɨ												ɘʊ				coat
April			ɛɨ												ɘʊ				road
ten				ɛˀ											ɘˀʊ				home
egg				ɛ											ɘʊ				know
head				ɛ											ɔɹ				four
Mary				ɛˀ											ɔɹ				door
stairs				ɛɹ											ɔɹ				hoarse
care				ɛˀɹ											ɔɹ				mourn
merry				ɛˀ															
thirty					ˀɹ									ʌ					sun
sermon					ˀɹ									ʌˀˀ					brush
furrow					ˀɹ														
ashes						æ						ɒˀ							frost
bag						æˀ						ɒ							log
married						æ						ɒˀˀ							dog
half						æˀ						ɒˀ							water
glass						æˀ						ɒˀ							daughter
aunt						æˀ						ɒˀ							law
father												ɒ							
palm						æˀ													
barn							ɑɹ						ɔɹ						forty
garden							ɑɹ						ɔɹ						morning
crop							ɒ						ɔɹ						corn
John							ɒˀ						ɔɹ						horse
college							ɒˀ												
borrow													ɔ						
five									aɨ		aˀʊ								down
twice									aɨ		æˀʊ								out
wire						æˀɹ					aʊɹ								flower
joint										ɔɨ									joint
boil										ɔˀɨ									boil
	i	ı	e	ɛ	ɜ	æ	ɑ	ɑ	ai	ɔi	au	ɒ	ɔ	ʌ	θ	o	ʊ	u	

	i	ɪ	e	ɛ	ɜ	æ	ɒ	ɑ	ai	ɔi	au	ʊ	ɒ	ɔ	ʌ	θ	o	ʊ	u	
three	iˇi																			two
grease	iˊ																		ʉˇˑ	tooth
six		ɪ																ʊˊ		wood
crib		ɪᵊ																ʊ,ʊᵊ		pull
ear		ɪɚ																ʉˑɚ		poor
beard		ɪɚ														ɔˊʊ				ago
eight			ɛˊɸ													ɞˀʊ				coat
April			ɛˊɸ													ɞˀʊ				road
ten				ɛᵊ												ɞˀʊ				home
egg				ɛ												ɔˑʊ				know
head				ɛᵊ												ɔɚ				four
Mary				ɛˊ												ɔˊɚ				door
stairs				ɛɚ												ɔɚ				hoarse
care				ɛɚ												ɔɚ				mourn
merry				ɛᵊ																
thirty					ɚ										ʌ					sun
sermon					ɚ										ʌᵊ					brush
furrow					ɚˑ															
ashes						æˑ							ʋˑᵊ							frost
bag						æˑ							ʋˑ							log
married						æᵊ							ɔˑ							dog
half						æᵊ	ɐ													water
glass						æᵊ							ʋ							daughter
aunt						æᵊ							ʋˑ							law
father							ɑˑˑ													
palm							ɑˑ													
barn							ɑɚ							ɔɚ						forty
garden							ɑɚ							ɔɚ						morning
crop							ɐ							ɔɚ						corn
John							ɑˑ							ɔɚ						horse
college							ɑ													
borrow							ɑ													
five								ɑɸ	aʉ											down
twice								aɸ	aʉ											out
wire								ɑɸɚ	æʋɚ											flower
										ɸɔ										joint
										ɸɔ										boil
	i	ɪ	e	ɛ	ɜ	æ	ɒ	ɑ	ai	ɔi	au	ʊ	ɒ	ɔ	ʌ	θ	o	ʊ	u	

	i	ɪ	e	ɪ	ə	ɛ	ɜ	æ	ɒ	ɑ	ɒ	ai	ɔi	au	ɑ	ɔ	ʌ	θ	o	ʊ	u	u	
three	i˙																					ʉ˙	two
grease	i˙																					u˱	tooth
six		ɪ																		ʊ˱			wood
crib		ɪ˒																		ʊ			pull
ear		ɪɚ																	oɚ				poor
beard	i˞ɚ																		o˙ʊ				ago
eight			eɪ																o˙ʊ				coat
April			eɪ																o˙ʊ				road
ten						ɛ˙ə													o˙ʊ				home
egg						ɛ													o˙ʊ				know
head						ɛ													oɚ				four
Mary						ɛ˒													oɚ				door
stairs								æ˞ɚ											oɚ				hoarse
care						ɛɚ													oɚ				mourn
merry						ɛ																	
thirty							ɚ									ʌ˱							sun
sermon							ɚ									ʌ˙ə							brush
furrow							ɚ˙																
ashes								æɪ								ɔ˙ə							frost
bag								æɪ								ɔ˙ə							log
married								æ								ɔɔ							dog
half								æə	ɒ˙														water
glass								æ˙								ɔ˙							daughter
aunt								æ˙								ɔ˙							law
father									ɑ˙														
palm								æə															
barn									ɒ˞ɚ							ɔɚ							forty
garden									ɑ˒ɚ							ɔɚ							morning
crop									ɒ˒ɑ							ɔɚ							corn
John									ɑ							ɔɚ							horse
college									ɒ˱														
borrow									ɑ														
five												aɪ		æ˞ʉ									down
twice												aɪ		æ˞ʉ									out
wire									ɑ˞ɚ					aʊɚ									flower
													ɔɪ										joint
													ɔɪ										boil
	i	ɪ	e	ɪ	ə	ɛ	ɜ	æ	ɒ	ɑ	ɒ	ai	ɔi	au	ɑ	ɔ	ʌ	θ	o	ʊ	u	u	

	i	ɪ	e	ɛ	ʒ	æ	ɒ	ɑ	ai	ɔi	au	ɐ	ɔ	ʌ	θ	o	ʊ	u	
three	i˅i																		two
grease	i˅i																	uˑ	tooth
six		ɪ																	wood
crib		ɪˀ																ʊˑ	pull
ear	ɪˀɚ														oɚ		ʊˑ		poor
beard				ˀɚ												oʊ			ago
eight			ɛˀɪ													oʊ			coat
April			eˀɪ													oʊ			road
ten				ɛˀˀ												oʊ			home
egg				ɛ												oʊ			know
head				ɛˀ												oˀɚ			four
Mary				ɛˀ												oˑɚ			door
stairs				ɛɚ												oˀɚ			hoarse
care				ɛɚ												oˀɚ			mourn
merry				ɛ															
thirty					ˀɚ									ʌˀ					sun
sermon					ˀɚ									ʌˀˀ					brush
furrow					ˀɚ														
ashes						æ̱							ɔ˅ˀ						frost
bag						æ̱							ɔ˅						log
married						æ							ɔ˅						dog
half						æ							ɔˑ						water
glass						æˀ							ɔ˅						daughter
aunt						æˀ							ɔ˅						law
father							ɑˑ												
palm							ɑˑ												
barn							ɑɚ						ɔɚ						forty
garden							ɑɚ						ɔɚ						morning
crop							ɑ						ɔɚ						corn
John							ɑˑ						ɔɚ						horse
college							ɑˑ												
borrow							ɑ												
five								æˑɛ	ɐˑæ										down
twice								aˀɪ	æ˅ɐ										out
wire								æɛɚ	ɐˀɐ										flower
										ɔɪ									joint
										ɔɪ									boil
	i	ɪ	e	ɛ	ʒ	æ	ɒ	ɑ	ai	ɔi	au	ɐ	ɔ	ʌ	θ	o	ʊ	u	

	i	ɪ	e	ɜ	ɛ	ɜ	æ	ɒ	ɑ	ai	ɔi	au	ɒ	ɔ	ʌ	ɵ	o	ʊ	u	
three	i˞ˇᵛ																		ʧ˞ˇᵛ	two
grease	iˆiˇᵛ																		u˞ˇ	tooth
six		ɪ																ʊ		wood
crib		ɪᵊ																ʊ		pull
ear	ɪ˞ᵊ											ɔ˞ᵊ								poor
beard	ɪ˞ᵊ˙															oᵛᵁ				ago
eight			e˙													o˙				coat
April			eᵛᵊ													oˇᵛ				road
ten				ɛᵊ												oˉ				home
egg				ɛ												oᵛ				know
head				ɛᵊ								ɔ˞ᵊ								four
Mary					æˆᵊ							ɔˉᵊ								door
stairs					æˆᵊ							ɔ˞ᵊ								hoarse
care					ɛˆᵊ							ɔ˞								mourn
merry				ɛ																
thirty					ɜˆᵊ									ʌˉ						sun
sermon					ɜˉˉ									ʌˉ						brush
furrow					ɜᵊ															
ashes					æ˙							ɔᵛᵊ								frost
bag					æ˙		ɑˆᵊ													log
married					æᵊ							ɔˉ								dog
half					æ							ɔˉ								water
glass					æˉᵊ							ɔˉ								daughter
aunt					æ˙							ɔˉ								law
father						ɑˉᵊ														
palm						ɑˉ														
barn						ɑˉˉ						ɔˉᵊ								forty
garden						ɑˉ						ɔˉ								morning
crop							ɑˉ					ɔˉ								corn
John							ɑᵊ					ɔˉ								horse
college							ɑˉ													
borrow							ɑˉᵊ													
five								aɛ	æˆᵁ											down
twice								aˆɪ	aˉᵁ											out
wire								a˙ɛ	a˙ᵊ											flower
joint									ɪɔ											joint
boil									ɪɔ											boil
	i	ɪ	e	ɜ	ɛ	ɜ	æ	ɒ	ɑ	ai	ɔi	au	ɒ	ɔ	ʌ	ɵ	o	ʊ	u	

	i	ɪ	e	ə	ɜ	ɛ	æ	a	ɑ	ɑ	aɪ	ɔɪ	aʊ	u	ɑ	ɔ	ʌ	θ	o	ʊ	u	
three	ɪˆi																				ʉˆʉ	two
grease	ɪˆi																				ʉˈʉˁ	tooth
six		ɪˇ,ɪˀ																		ʊˇˑˀ		wood
crib		ɪˇˑˀ																		ʊˑˀ		pull
ear		ɪˇˀ	ɛˇˀ																ʊˇˑˀ			poor
beard		ɪˇˀ	ɛˇˀ																oˈʊˑ			ago
eight			ɛˆj																oˈʊˑ			coat
April			ɛˆɫˆ																oˈʊˑ			road
ten				ɛˀ															θʊˀ			home
egg			ɛˇˀ																oˈʊˑ			know
head			ɛˀ,ɛˀ																ɔˀˀ			four
Mary			ɛˇˀ			æˑˀ													ɔˀˀ			door
stairs						æˇˀ													ɔˀˑ			hoarse
care						æˑˀ													ɔˀˑ			mourn
merry				ɛ																		
thirty					ɜə												ʌˀ					sun
sermon					ɜə												ʌˇˀ					brush
furrow																	ʌˑ					
ashes						æˀ									ɔˑ							frost
bag						æˀ		ɒˀ														log
married						æˀ										ɔˑ						dog
half						æˀ										ɔˀ						water
glass						æˑ										ɔˀˀ						daughter
aunt						æˀ										ɔˀˑ						law
father							ɑˑɐ															
palm							ɑˑɐ															
barn							ɐˑɐ												ɔˀˀ			forty
garden							ɑˑɐ												ɔˀˀ			morning
crop								ɑˀ											ɔˑˀ			corn
John								ɑˇˀ											ɔˑˀ			horse
college								ɑˇˀ														
borrow								ɑ														
five										ɑˑɛ	ɑˀʊ											down
twice										ɑˀɫ	ɔˑʊˀ											out
wire										ɑˀɛə	æˀʊɐ											flower
joint											oˀɫ											joint
boil											ɔˀɫ											boil
	i	ɪ	e	ə	ɜ	ɛ	æ	a	ɑ	ɑ	aɪ	ɔɪ	aʊ	u	ɑ	ɔ	ʌ	θ	o	ʊ	u	

	i	ɪ	e	ɛ	ɜ	æ	ɒ	ɑ	ai	ɔi	au	ɒ	ɔ	ə	ʌ	ɵ	o	ʊ	u	
three	iᶦˇ																			ɫ'ɫ	two
grease	i'																			ɫ'ᵗᵗˏ	tooth
six		ɪ																	ʊ		wood
crib		ɪᵊ																	ʊ		pull
ear		ɪˑᵊ										ɔˑᵊ									poor
beard		ɪˑᵊ															oᵘʊ				ago
eight			eɫ														oˑʊ				coat
April			eɫ														oˑʊ				road
ten				ɛᴧᵊ													oˑʊ				home
egg				ɛᴧ													oᵘʊ				know
head				ɛ									ɔˑ								four
Mary				ɛᵊᵊ								ɔˑᵊ									door
stairs						æᵘᵊ						ɔˑᵊ									hoarse
care						æᵘᵊ						ɔˑᵊ									mourn
merry				ɛ																	
thirty					ɜᵊ										ʌ						sun
sermon					ɜᵊ										ʌˏ						brush
furrow				ɛˏ																	
ashes						æˑ						ɔˑᵊ									frost
bag						æˑ		ɒᵊ													log
married						æ							ɔˑ								dog
half						æˑ						ɔᵊᵊ									water
glass						æˑᵊ							ɔˑ								daughter
aunt						æ							ɔˑ								law
father							ɒˑ														
palm							ɒˑ														
barn							ɒˑᵊ						ɔˑᵊ								forty
garden							ɒˑ						ɔˑ								morning
crop								ɑˏ					ɔˑᵊ								corn
John								ɑˏ					ɔˑᵊ								horse
college								ɑ													
borrow								ɑ													
five									ɑˏɛ	ɑˏʊ											down
twice									ʊɫ	ʌᵘʊ											out
wire									aɛᵊ	ɛᵘᵊ											flower
joint										ɔˏɫ											
boil										ɔˏɫ											
	i	ɪ	e	ɛ	ɜ	æ	ɒ	ɑ	ai	ɔi	au	ɒ	ɔ	ə	ʌ	ɵ	o	ʊ	u	

71

	i	ɪ	e	ɛ	ɜ	æ	a	ɑ	ɑi	au	ɔi	au	ɒ	ɔ	ʌ	ɵ	o	ʊ	u	
three	iˑ																		ʊˑʉ	two
grease	iˑ																		ʉˑˑ	tooth
six		ɪ																ʊ		wood
crib		ɪˑᵊ																ʊˑᵊ		pull
ear	iˑᵊ													ɔˑᵊ						poor
beard	iˑᵊ													oˑʊ						ago
eight			eˑɨ											oˑʊ						coat
April			eˑɨ											oˑʊ						road
ten				ɛˑᵊ										oˑʊ						home
egg				ɛ										oˑʊ						know
head				ɛˑᵊ										ɔˑᵊ						four
Mary				ɛᵊ										ɔˑᵊ						door
stairs						æˑᵊ								ɔˑᵊ						hoarse
care						æˑᵊ								ɔˑᵊ						mourn
merry				ɛ																
thirty					ɜˑˑ										ʌˑ					sun
sermon					ɜˑˑ										ʌ, ʌᵊ					brush
furrow															ʌˑ					
ashes						æˑ								ɔˑˑ						frost
bag						æˑ								ɔˑ						log
married						æ								ɔˑ						dog
half						æˑ								ɔˑ						water
glass						æˑᵊ								ɔˑ						daughter
aunt						æˑᵊ								ɔˑᵊ						law
father								ɑˑ												
palm								ɑˑ												
barn								ɑˑᵊ						ɔˑ						forty
garden								ɑˑ						ɔˑ						morning
crop							aˑ							ɔˑᵊ						corn
John							aˑᵊ							ɔˑ						horse
college								ɑˑ												
borrow							aˑᵊ													
five									aˑɛ	æˑʊ										down
twice									aˑɨ	aˑʊ										out
wire									aˑɨᵊ	aˑʊ										flower
										ɔɨ										joint
										ɔɵ										boil
	i	ɪ	e	ɛ	ɜ	æ	a	ɑ	ɑi	au	ɔi	au	ɒ	ɔ	ʌ	ɵ	o	ʊ	u	

	i	ɪ	e	ɜ	ɛ	æ	a	ɑ	ɒ	aɪ	ɔɪ	au	ɒ	ɔ	ʌ	ɵ	o	ʊ	u	
three	i˅i																		ʉˀ˅	two
grease	i˅i																		ʉˀ	tooth
six		ɪ																ʊˆ		wood
crib		ɪᵊ																ʊˆ		pull
ear	iˀᵊ																oᵊ			poor
beard	iˀᵊ																oᵁ			ago
eight			eᴵ														oᵁ			coat
April			eᵻ														oᵁ			road
ten				ɛᵊ													oᵁ			home
egg				ɛˆ													oᵁ			know
head				ɛᵊ													oᵊ			four
Mary			eˀᵊ														oˀᵊ			door
stairs					æˀᵋ												oᵊ			hoarse
care					æᵻᵊ												oˀˀᵊ			mourn
merry				ɛˆ																
thirty						ɞˀ̈									ʌ					sun
sermon						ɞˀ̈									ʌˆ					brush
furrow															ʌ̈					
ashes						æᵻ							ɒˀ̈							frost
bag						æᵻ							ɒˀ̈							log
married						æˀᵊ							ɒˀᵋ							dog
half							ɒɒˀ →						ɔˀᵊ							water
glass							ɒɒˀ →						ɒɒˀ							daughter
aunt							ɒɒˀ →						ɒɒˀ							law
father							ɒɒˀ →													
palm							ɒɒˀ →													
barn							ɒɒˀ →						ɒɒˀ							forty
garden							ɑɒˀ →						ɒɒˀ							morning
crop								aˆ̈					ɒɒˀ							corn
John							ɒɒˀ →						ɒɒˀ							horse
college								aˆ̈												
borrow								aˀᵊ												
five									aˀᵊ	ᴂʉ										down
twice									ɒᵻ	ɒᵘˆ										out
wire									aˀᵋ	ᴂᵁᵊ										flower
joint											ɔᵻ									
boil											ɔᵻ									
	i	ɪ	e	ɜ	ɛ	æ	a	ɑ	ɒ	aɪ	ɔɪ	au	ɒ	ɔ	ʌ	ɵ	o	ʊ	u	

73

	i	ɪ	e	ɛ	ɜ	æ	ɒ	ɑ	ai	ui	ɔi	au	ɒ	ɔ	ʌ	θ	o	ʊ	u	
three	iˇi																			two	ʉˈ
grease	iˇˈ																			tooth	ʊˇˈ
six		ɪ																ʊᵛᵊ		wood
crib		ɪˑᵊ																ʊᵛᵊ		pull
ear	ɪˆᵊ																		ʊⁱᵊ	poor
beard				ɪᵊˑ													oˇʊ			ago
eight			eˑɨ														oˈʊ			coat
April			eˑɨ														oˑʊ			road
ten				ɛˑᵊ													oˈʊ			home
egg				ɛˈɨ													oˇʊ			know
head				ɛᵊ													oˑᵊ			four
Mary			eᵊ	ɛˑ													ɔˆᵊ			door
stairs						æˑᵊ											oˑᵊ			hoarse
care						æˑᵋᵊ											oˇᵊ			mourn
merry				ɛ																
thirty					ɝ										ʌˑᵊ					sun
sermon					ɝˑ										ʌᵊ					brush
furrow															Δˆ					
ashes						æɨ							yˑᵊ							frost
bag						æˆᵊ	ɑˆᵊ													log
married						æ							ɔˑ							dog
half							ɑˑᵊ						ɔᵊ							water
glass							ɑˑ						ɔˆˑ							daughter
aunt							ɒˆˑ						yˆ							law
father							ɑˑˑ													
palm							ɑˆˑ													
barn							ɒˆɒˆ						ɔᵊ							forty
garden							ɒˑˑ						ɔᵊ							morning
crop								ɑˆ					ɔˆ							corn
John								ɑˆᵊ					ɔˑ							horse
college								ɑˆᵊ												
borrow								ɑˆᵊ												
five								ɑˑɛ		æᵛʊ										down
twice								ʌˆɨ		ʋˆɑʊ										out
wire								ɑᵋᵊ		ɐɑᵛᵊ										flower
joint									ɨɨ											joint
boil									ɨɨ											boil
	i	ɪ	e	ɛ	ɜ	æ	ɒ	ɑ	ai	ui	ɔi	au	ɒ	ɔ	ʌ	θ	o	ʊ	u	

	i	ɪ	e	e	ɪ	ɜ	æ	ɑ	a	aɪ	ɔɪ	aʊ	ɑ	ɔ	ʌ	ɵ	o	ʊ	u	
three	iˠi																		ʉˑ˙ʉ	two
grease	iˠj																		ʉˑ˙	tooth
six		ɪ																ʊˑᵊ		wood
crib		ɪ																ʊ		pull
ear	ɪˆᵊ																oˑ			poor
beard					ɪᵊː												oˑˑ			ago
eight			eˑꞮᵊ														oˑ:			coat
April			eˑꞮ														oˑᵘ			road
ten					ɛᵊ												oˑ			home
egg					ɛꞮ												—			know
head					ɛᵊ												oˑ			four
Mary			eꞮˑˠ														oˑᵒ			door
stairs					æˠᵊ												oᵛᵘ			hoarse
care					ɪᵊː												oᵛᵘ			mourn
merry					ɛˠ															
thirty					зᵊ										ʌ					sun
sermon					зᵊ,зˆᵊ										ʌˠˆᵊ					brush
furrow					ᶚ															
ashes							æꞮ							ɔˆᵊ						frost
bag							æ							ɔᵛˑ						log
married							æˠ							ɔˑˠˠ						dog
half							æᵊ							ɔᵊ						water
glass							æᵊ							ɔː						daughter
aunt							æˠᵊ							ɔᵛˑ						law
father								ɑˠˑ												
palm							æˠᵊ													
barn								ɑˠˑ						ɔˠˠ						forty
garden								ɑˠˑ						ɔː						morning
crop									ɑˠ					ɔˠᵊ						corn
John									ɑˠᵊ					ɔˠˠ						horse
college									ɑˠ											
borrow									ɑˠ											
five										ɑˑˠ		æˠʉ								down
twice										Ɪɑ		ɑʊ								out
wire										ɑˠꞮᵊ		ɑᵛˠᵊ								flower
joint										ɑꞮ										joint
boil										ɑꞮ	ɔꞮ									boil
	i	ɪ	e	e	ɪ	ɜ	æ	ɑ	a	aɪ	ɔɪ	aʊ	ɑ	ɔ	ʌ	ɵ	o	ʊ	u	

	i	ɪ	e	ɛ	ɜ	æ	ɒ	ɑ	ai	ɔi	au	ɒ	ɔ	ʌ	θ	o	ʊ	u	
three	li˅																	ʉᵗᵗ	two
grease	i˽˙																	ʦ˙	tooth
six		ɪ															ʊᵊ		wood
crib		ɪᵊ															ʊ		pull
ear		ɪᵊ														o˙			poor
beard		ɪᵊ														ou			ago
eight			eɫ													ou			coat
April			eɫ˅													ou			road
ten				ɛᵊ												o˙u			home
egg				—												ou			know
head				ɛᵊ												oə,o˙			four
Mary			e													o˙ᵊ			door
stairs						æᵊ										o˙ᵊ			hoarse
care						æᵊ										—			mourn
merry				ɛ															
thirty					ɞˆᵊ									ʌ					sun
sermon					ɞ˙									ʌ˂ɫ					brush
furrow					ɜ														
ashes						æɫ						ɒ˖ᵓ							frost
bag						æ˙ɫ	ɑ˂ᵊ												log
married						æᵊ	ɑˆᵊ												dog
half						æᵊ						ɒɒ							water
glass						æ˙						ɒɒ							daughter
aunt						ɑ˙ɒ˖ →						ɒ˙ɒ							law
father						ɒɒ˖ →													
palm						ɒ˙ɒ →													
barn						ɒ˙ɒˆ →						ɒ˙ɒ˖							forty
garden						ɒɒˆ →						ɒ˙ɒˆ							morning
crop							ɑˆ					ɒ˙ɒˆ							corn
John												ɒɒˆ							horse
college							ɑˆ												
borrow							ɑ˖ᵊ												
five								ɑɛ	æʊ										down
twice								ɫɑ	ᵊɯ̈										out
wire								ɑˆᵊ	—										flower
joint										—									joint
boil										ɫɫ									boil
	i	ɪ	e	ɛ	ɜ	æ	ɒ	ɑ	ai	ɔi	au	ɒ	ɔ	ʌ	θ	o	ʊ	u	

	i	ɪ	e	ɛ	ɜ	æ	ɑ	ɑ	aɪ	ɔɪ	aʊ	ɒ	ɔ	ʌ	θ	o	ʊ	u	
three	iᵛⁱ																	ᵗᵗᵛᵗᵗ	two
grease	jⁱᴧ																	ᵗᵗᵛᵗᵗ	tooth
six		ɪ															ʊᵊ		wood
crib		ɪᵊ															ʊˑᵊ		pull
ear	iᵛᵊ˞															oᵊ			poor
beard	iᵊ˞															oʊ			ago
eight			eⱻᵊ													oʊ			coat
April			eⱻ													oʊ			road
ten				ɛᵊ												oˈ			home
egg				ɛᴧ												oʊ			know
head				ɛᵊ												oᵊ			four
Mary			eⱻ													oᵊ			door
stairs						æᵊ										oᵊ			hoarse
care						æˑᵊ										oᵊ			mourn
merry				ɛˀ															
thirty					ɞˑᵊ									ʌᴧᵊ					sun
sermon					ɞˑᵊ									ʌᵊ					brush
furrow														ʌᵊ					
ashes						æᵊ˞							ɔᵛᵊ						frost
bag						æˑᵊ		ɑᵊ											log
married						æˀ							ɔᵛᵊ						dog
half						æˑᵊ						ɒᴧᵊ							water
glass						æˀᵊ						ɒᴧᵊ							daughter
aunt							ɑˑʊ					ɒᴧᵊ							law
father							ɑʊ												
palm							ɑˑʊ												
barn							ɑˑʊ					ɒᴧᵊ							forty
garden							ɑˑʊ					ɒᴧᵊ							morning
crop								ɑᴧᵊ					ɔᵛ						corn
John												ɒᴧᵊ							horse
college								ɑˀᵊ											
borrow								ɑᴧᵊ											
five									ɑˑᵛᵋ		æʊ								down
twice									ɐˈɪ		ɔˈʊˈ								out
wire									ɑˀᵋᵊ		æˀʊᵊ								flower
										ɪɔ									joint
										ɔˈɪ									boil
	i	ɪ	e	ɛ	ɜ	æ	ɑ	ɑ	aɪ	ɔɪ	aʊ	ɒ	ɔ	ʌ	θ	o	ʊ	u	

	i	ɪ	e	ɪ	e	ɛ	ɜ	æ	ɑ	ɒ	ai	ɔi	au	ɒ	ɔ	ʌ	θ	o	ʊ	u	
three	ɪ⁀i																			u̜⁀ᵘ	two
grease	i⁀i																			u⁀ᵗ	tooth
six		ɪ																	ʊ·ᵊ		wood
crib		ɪᵊ																	ʊ·ᵊ		pull
ear	i̯ᵊ																	oᵊ			poor
beard	i̯ᵊ																	oᵛʊ			ago
eight			eᵛɪ															oᵛ			coat
April			eᵛɪ															oᵛʊ			road
ten						ɛᵛᵊ												oᵛ			home
egg						ɛᵻ												oᵛ			know
head						ɛᵛᵊ												oᵊ			four
Mary			eᵛɪ															oᵊ			door
stairs								æ·ᵊ										oᵊ			hoarse
care								æᵛᵊ										oᵊ			mourn
merry						ɛ															
thirty							ɜ··									ʌᵊ					sun
sermon							ɜ··ᵊ									ʌᵊ					brush
furrow																ʌᵊ					
ashes								æᵃᵛ							ɒᵛ						frost
bag								æᵻ	aᵛᵊ												log
married								æᵊ							ɔᵛ						dog
half								æᵻ							ɔ·ᵊ						water
glass								æ·ᵊ							ɒᵛᵛ						daughter
aunt									ɑ·ᵛ						ɔᵛ·ᵊ						law
father									ɑ·ᵛ												
palm									ɑ·ᵛ												
barn									ɑ·ᵛ						ɔᵛ·						forty
garden									ɑ·ᵛ						ɒᵛᵊ						morning
crop										aᵛᵊ					ɒᵛᵊ						corn
John									ɑ·ᵛ						ɔᵛᵊ						horse
college										aᵛᵊ											
borrow										aᵛᵊ											
five											a·ᵊ		æᵛʊ								down
twice											ɒɪ		ᵊʊᵛ								out
wire											aᵋᵊ		æʊᵊ								flower
												ɔɪ									joint
												ɔɪ									boil
	i	ɪ	e	ɪ	e	ɛ	ɜ	æ	ɑ	ɒ	ai	ɔi	au	ɒ	ɔ	ʌ	θ	o	ʊ	u	

	i	ɪ	e	ɪ	ɛ	ɜ	æ	ɑ	ɒ	ai	ɔi	au	ɒ	ɔ	ʌ	ɵ	o	ʊ	u	
three	ɪˆɪᵛ																		ʉ˕ʉ	two
grease	iᵛi																		ʉᵛ	tooth
six		ɪ																ʊᵊʊ		wood
crib		ɪˑᵊ																ʊᵊ		pull
ear	ɪˆᵊ															oᵊ				poor
beard	ɪˆᵊ															oˁᵘ				ago
eight			eᵛɪ̵													oˁᵘ				coat
April			eᵛɪ̵													oˁᵛᵘ				road
ten					ɛˆᵊ											oˁᵛᵘ				home
egg					ɛˑ											oˁᵘ				know
head					ɛˆᵊ											oᵊ				four
Mary			eᵛɪ̵													oᵊ				door
stairs							æˣᵊ									oˑᵊ				hoarse
care							æˣᵊ									oᵊ				mourn
merry					ɛᵛ															
thirty						ʚˑᵊ									ʌᵊ					sun
sermon						ʚˆˑ									ʌˆɪ̵					brush
furrow															ʌᵊ					
ashes							æɪ̵						Cᵛᵊ							frost
bag							æˑɪ̵	aˆᵊ					ɒᵛᵊ							log
married							æᵊ						ɒˆᵊ							dog
half							æˑᵊ						ɒˆᵊ							water
glass							æˑᵊ						ɒˑɒᵛ							daughter
aunt							æˑᵊᵛ						ɒᵛɒᵛ							law
father													ɒˑɒᵛ							
palm													ɒˑɒᵛ							
barn							ɒˑɒᵛ →						ɒˑɒᵛ							forty
garden							ɒˑɒᵛ →						ɒˑɒᵛ							morning
crop								aˆ					ɒˑɒᵛ							corn
John								aˆˑᵊ					ɒˑɒᵛ							horse
college								aˆˑᵊ												
borrow								aˆᵊ												
five										aˑᵋ	æˑʊ									down
twice										ɒɪ̵	ɒʊˆ									out
wire										ɒᵛᵊ	ɒˑwᵊ									flower
											ɔɪ̵									joint
											ɔɪ̵									boil
	i	ɪ	e	ɪ	ɛ	ɜ	æ	ɑ	ɒ	ai	ɔi	au	ɒ	ɔ	ʌ	ɵ	o	ʊ	u	

79

Column headers: i ɪ e ɜ ə æ ɑ ɒ ɑ ai ɔi au ɒ ɔ ʌ θ o ʊ u u

word	left transcription	right transcription	word
three	iᵛj	ʉᵛᵗᵗ	two
grease	iᵛj	ʉᵗᵗ	tooth
six	ɪ	ʊᵊ	wood
crib	ɪᵊ	ʊᵛᵊ	pull
ear	iᵛᵊ	oᵛᵊ	poor
beard	ɪᵛᵊ	oᵛʋ	ago
eight	ɛɪ	oᵛʋ	coat
April	ɛɪ	oᵛʋ	road
ten	ɛˑ	oʋ	home
egg	ɛˑ	oᵛʋ	know
head	ɛˑᵊ	ɔᵛᵊ	four
Mary	eˑɪ	ɔᵛᵊ	door
stairs	æᵊ	ɔᵛᵊ	hoarse
care	ɛˑᵊ	ɔᵛᵊ	mourn
merry	ɛᵊ		
thirty	ɞᵛˑᵊ	ʌᵊ	sun
sermon	ɞᵛˑᵊ	ʌᵊ	brush
furrow		ʌᵛᵊ	
ashes	æᵊ	ʋᵛʋ	frost
bag	æˑɪ aᵛᵊ		log
married	æᵊ	ʋᵛʋᵛ	dog
half	æᵥᵛɪ	ʋʋᵛ	water
glass	æɪ	ʋᵛʋ	daughter
aunt	ʋᵛʋᵛ →	ʋᵛʋᵛ	law
father	ʋᵛʋᵛ →		
palm	ʋᵛʋᵛ →		
barn	ʋᵛʋᵛ →	ʋᵛʋᵛ	forty
garden	ʋᵛʋᵛ →	ʋᵛʋᵛ	morning
crop	ɑᵛᵊ	ʋᵛʋᵛ	corn
John	ɑᵛᵊ	ʋᵛʋᵛ	horse
college	ɑᵛᵊ		
borrow	ɑᵛᵊ		
five	æˑɛ / æu		down
twice	ɪɪ / ɔᵛʋᵛ		out
wire	ɑˑᵛɛ / ɛɑᵊ		flower
	ɛɪ		joint
	ɪɛ		boil

Column footers: i ɪ e ɜ ə æ ɑ ɒ ɑ ai ɔi au ɒ ɔ ʌ θ o ʊ u u

word	i	ɪ	e	ɛ	ʒ	æ	a	ɑ	ai	ɔi	au	ɒ	ɔ	ʌ	ɵ	o	ʊ	u	word
three	iⱽi																ʊ˙		two
grease	iⱽˑ																	ʉⱽᵗ	tooth
six		ɪ															ʊ˄ᵊ		wood
crib		ɪˑᵊ															ʊᵊ		pull
ear	ɪ˄ᵊ																	ʊᵊ	poor
beard	ɪ˄ᵊ															oᵛʊ			ago
eight			eⱽɪ													oᵛʊ			coat
April			eⱽɪ													oʊ			road
ten				ɛ˄ᵊ												oʊ			home
egg				ɛˑ												oᵛʊ			know
head				ɛˑᵊ												oᵊ			four
Mary			ɛɪ													oˑᵊ			door
stairs						æᵊ										oᵊ			hoarse
care						æᵊ										oᵊ			mourn
merry				ɛ															
thirty					ʒ˙									ʌᵊ					sun
sermon					ʒ˙									ʌᵊˑ					brush
furrow														ʌᵊ					
ashes						æˑ							ɔᵛᵊ						frost
bag						æː	aᵛᵊ												log
married						æᵊ							ɔᵛᵊ						dog
half						æɨ							ɔˑ						water
glass							aˑ						ɔᵛ						daughter
aunt							aˑ						ɔᵛˑ						law
father							aː												
palm							aː												
barn							aˑː						ɔᵛ						forty
garden							aˑː						ɔᵛᵊ						morning
crop								ɑ					ɔᵛᵊ						corn
John								ɑᵊ					ɔᵛᵊ						horse
college								ɑᵛᵊ											
borrow								ɑᵛᵊ											
five									aᵛˑᵊ		æʊ								down
twice									aɨ		ɑʊ								out
wire									aᵛᵊ		æwᵊ								flower
										ɔɨ									joint
										ɔɨ									boil
	i	ɪ	e	ɛ	ʒ	æ	a	ɑ	ai	ɔi	au	ɒ	ɔ	ʌ	ɵ	o	ʊ	u	

	i	ɪ	e	ɛ	з	æ	ɑ	ɒ	ai	ɔi	au	ɒ	ɔ	ʌ	ɵ	o	ʊ	u	
three	iᵛj																	ʉ·̈	two
grease	iᵛ·																	ʉᵛ	tooth
six		ɪ															ʊᵊ		wood
crib		ɪᵊ															ʊᵊ		pull
ear	iɚ															oɚ			poor
beard	iᵛɚ															ou			ago
eight			eɪ													ou			coat
April			eɪ													oᵛu			road
ten				ɛᵛᵊ												oᵛu			home
egg			eɪ													ou			know
head				ɛᵛ												oᵊ			four
Mary			eɪ													oᵊɚ			door
stairs				ɛɚ												oᵊɚ			hoarse
care						æᵛɚ										oɚ			mourn
merry				ɛᵛ															
thirty					ɚ·									ʌ					sun
sermon					ɚ·									ʌᵢᵊ					brush
furrow					ɚ·														
ashes						æɨ							ɔᵛᵊ						frost
bag						æɨ							ɒᵛᵊ						log
married						æᵛ							ɔ·						dog
half						æᵛ·							ɒᵢᵊ						water
glass						æᵋ							ɒᵢᵊ						daughter
aunt						æɨ							ɒᵢ··						law
father								ɑᵢ·											
palm						æ·ᵋ													
barn								ɑᵢɚ					ɔᵢᵛ						forty
garden								ɑᵢɚ					ɔᵛ·						morning
crop								ɑᵢᵊ					ɔɚ						corn
John								ɑᵛᵊ					ɔɚ						horse
college								ɑᵢᵊ											
borrow								ɑᵢᵊ											
five									æ·ᵋ		æʊ								down
twice									ɒɨ		ʊᴧw								out
wire									æᵋɚ		æʊɚ								flower
										ɪɨ									joint
										ɪɨ									boil
	i	ɪ	e	ɛ	з	æ	ɑ	ɒ	ai	ɔi	au	ɒ	ɔ	ʌ	ɵ	o	ʊ	u	

	i	ɪ	e	ɜ	ɛ	ʒ	æ	ɑ	ɒ	aɪ	ɔɪ	au	ɒ	ɔ	ʌ	ɵ	o	ʊ	u	
three	iˇj																			ʉʸʷ	two
grease	ɪˆj																			ʉˇʷ	tooth
six		ɪ																Uᵊ		wood
crib		ɪ																Uˑᵊ		pull
ear	ɪˑᵊ																Oᵛˑᵊ			poor
beard	ɪˆᵊ																Oᵘ			ago
eight			eˇɪ														Oᵛᵘ			coat
April			eᵛɪ														Oᵛᵘ			road
ten					ɛˑᵊ												O ᵘ			home
egg			eᵛɪ														O ᵘ			know
head					ɛˑᵊ												O ᵗ			four
Mary			eɪ		ɛˑᵊ												Oᵛᵊ			door
stairs							æᵋᵊ										Oᵛˑᵊ			hoarse
care							æˑᵊ										O ᵘ			mourn
merry					ɛᵊ															
thirty				ɞˆˑᵊ											ʌˑ					sun
sermon				ɞˑˑ											ʌˆᵊ					brush
furrow															ʌˑᵊ					
ashes							æɪ						ʋᵛˑᵊ							frost
bag							æˑᵊ	aᵊ												log
married							æᵊ						ɔᵛˑᵊ							dog
half							æɪ						ɔˑᵊ							water
glass							æˑᵊ						ɔᵛˑ							daughter
aunt							æɪ						ɔᵛˑ							law
father								aˑᵊ												
palm								aˑᵛ												
barn								aˑːᵊ						ɔᵛᵊ						forty
garden								aˑːᵊ						ɔᵛˑ						morning
crop									aˑ					ɔᵛˑᵊ						corn
John									aˑᵊ					ɔᵛˑᵊ						horse
college									aˑ											
borrow									aˑᵊ											
five										aˑᵋ	æˑʉ									down
twice										ʋɪ	ʋʊ									out
wire										æˑᵋ	æˑʋᵊ									flower
joint											ɪˇɪ									
boil											ɔᵛɪ									

| | i | ɪ | e | ɜ | ɛ | ʒ | æ | ɑ | ɒ | aɪ | ɔɪ | au | ɒ | ɔ | ʌ | ɵ | o | ʊ | u | |

	i	ɪ	e	ɛ	ɜ	æ	ɑ	ɒ	ai	ɔi	au	ə	ɔ	ʌ	ɵ	o	ʊ	u	
three	iˬʲi																	ʊᵗᵗ	two
grease	iˬʲi																	ʊᵗᵗ	tooth
six		ɪ															ʊᵊ		wood
crib		ɪᵊ															ʊˬᵊ		pull
ear		ɪᵛˑᵊ											oˑᵊ						poor
beard		ɪᵊ											oˑʊ						ago
eight			eˤɪˆ										oˑʊˆ						coat
April			ɛˤɪˆ										oˑʊˆ						road
ten				ɛˑᵊ									oˑʊ						home
egg				ɛᵊ									oˑʊ						know
head				ɛˑᵊ									oˑᵊ						four
Mary			eˤɪ										oˑᵊ						door
stairs						æˑᵊ							oˑᵊ						hoarse
care						æɪᵊ							oˑᵊ						mourn
merry				ɛᵊ															
thirty					ʚɪ									ʌˑᵊ					sun
sermon					ʚˑᵊˆ									ʌˑᵊ					brush
furrow														ʌˑᵊ					
ashes						æɪ							ɔˑɔ						frost
bag						æˑᵊ		aˑᵊ											log
married						æᵊ							ɔˑɔ						dog
half						æɪ							ɔˑ						water
glass						æˑɪ							ɔɔ						daughter
aunt						æɪ							ɔˑˑ						law
father						ɑˤˑᵊ													
palm						ɑˤˑᵊ													
barn						ɑˤˑᵊ							ɔˑᵊ						forty
garden						ɑˤˑᵊ							ɔˑɔ						morning
crop							ɑˑᵊ						ɔˑᵊ						corn
John							ɑˑᵊ						ɔˑɔ						horse
college							ɑˑᵊ												
borrow							ɑˑᵊ												
five									aˑᵊˬ		æˑʊ								down
twice									aˑɪ		æʊˆ								out
wire									aˤᵊ		ɛᵛʊᵊ								flower
										ɔɪ									joint
										ɔɪ									boil
	i	ɪ	e	ɛ	ɜ	æ	ɑ	ɒ	ai	ɔi	au	ə	ɔ	ʌ	ɵ	o	ʊ	u	

	i	ɪ	e	ɪ	ᴈ	ɛ	ɜ	æ	ɒ	ɑ	aɪ	ɔɪ	au	ɒ	ɔ	ʌ	ɵ	o	ʊ	u	
three	iˇi																			ʊˊᵘ	two
grease	iˑ																			ʊˊᵘ	tooth
six		ɪ																	ʊᵊ		wood
crib		ɪᵊ																	ʊᵊ		pull
ear		ɪˑᵊ																	ʊᵊ		poor
beard				ɪᵊˑ													ɵˑʊˊ				ago
eight			eˊɪ														ɵˑʊˊ				coat
April			ɛˊɪ														ɵˑʊˊ				road
ten						ɛᵊ											ɞʊ				home
egg						ɛᵊ											oˊʊ				know
head						ɛᵊ											oˑᵘᵊ				four
Mary			eˊɪ														oˑᵊ				door
stairs								æˑᵊ									oˑᵊ				hoarse
care								æˊᵊ									oˑᵊ				mourn
merry						ɛᵊ															
thirty							ɞɪ									ʌᵊ					sun
sermon							ɞɪ									ʌˑᵊ					brush
furrow																ʌᵊ					
ashes								æ						ɒˊʌ						frost
bag								æˑ	ɒˊˑᵊ												log
married								æᵊ							ɔˊɔ						dog
half								æᵊˑ							ɔˊɔ						water
glass								æᴵᵊ						ɔˊʌ							daughter
aunt								æᴵᵛ						ɒˊɒˊ							law
father									ɑˑᵊ												
palm								æˑᵊ													
barn									ɒˊˑᵊ						ɒˊɒˊ						forty
garden									ɒˑᵊ						ɔˊᵊ						morning
crop										ɑˊ					ɔˊᵊ						corn
John										ɑˑᵊ					ɔˊɔ						horse
college									ɒˊˑ												
borrow										ɑˑᵊ											
five											aˑɛˑ		æˊʊ								down
twice											aˑˑɛˑ		æˊʊˊ								out
wire											aᴵᵊ		æˊʊᵊ								flower
joint												ɔˊɪ									joint
boil												ɔˊɪ									boil
	i	ɪ	e	ɪ	ᴈ	ɛ	ɜ	æ	ɒ	ɑ	aɪ	ɔɪ	au	ɒ	ɔ	ʌ	ɵ	o	ʊ	u	

	i	ɪ	e	ɜ	ɛ	ɝ	æ	ɑ	ɑ	ai	ɔi	au	ɒ	ɔ	ʌ	θ	o	ʊ	u	
three	iˇi																		tʰˈᵗᵗ	two
grease	iˑ																		tʰˈᵗᵗ	tooth
six		ɪ																ʊᵊ		wood
crib		ɪᵊ																ʊ		pull
ear			ɛˇᵊ														o̜ᵊo̜ᵘ			poor
beard			ɛˑᵊ														oᵘ			ago
eight			eɪ														oʊ			coat
April			eˑɪ														oˇᵘ			road
ten				ɛᵊ													oˑʊ			home
egg				ɛᵊ													oˑʊ			know
head				ɛᵊ													o̜ᵊo̜ᵘ			four
Mary				ɛᵊ													oᵘo̜ᵊ			door
stairs				ɛᵊ													oʊᵊ			hoarse
care				ɛᵊ													oʊᵊ			mourn
merry				ɛ																
thirty					ɞˑ										ʌᵊ					sun
sermon					ɞˑˈ										ʌˈᵊ					brush
furrow															ʌ					
ashes							æᵊ							ɔˈˈᵊ						frost
bag							æˈᵊ	ɑ̰ᵊ												log
married							æ							ɔɔ						dog
half							æᵊ							ɔᵊ						water
glass							æᵊ							ɔˑ						daughter
aunt							æˈᵊ							ɔɔ						law
father								ɑ̰ˑᵊ												
palm								ɑ̰ˑ												
barn								ɑˈɒˈ						ɔˈᵊ						forty
garden								ɑˈɒˈ						ɔɔ						morning
crop									ɑᵊ					ɔˈᵊ						corn
John									ɑᵊ					ɔˈɔ						horse
college									ɑ											
borrow									ɑ̰											
five										æˑɛ	æˈʊ									down
twice										ɨɑ	ʌɑˈ									out
wire										ɑɛᵊ	æˈʊᵊ									flower
											ɔɨ									joint
											ɔɨ									boil
	i	ɪ	e	ɜ	ɛ	ɝ	æ	ɑ	ɑ	ai	ɔi	au	ɒ	ɔ	ʌ	θ	o	ʊ	u	

	i	ɪ	e	ə	ɛ	ɜ	æ	ɑ	ɑ	ai	ɔi	au	ɒ	ɔ	ʌ	ɵ	o	ʊ	u	
three	i˒ˑi																			two
grease	i˒ˑi																			tooth
six		ɪ																ʊᵊ		wood
crib		ɪˑᵊ																ʊᵊ		pull
ear	iˇᵊ																oᵊ			poor
beard	iˇᵊ																oʊ			ago
eight			eˇɪ														oˑʊ			coat
April			eˇɪ														oᵘ			road
ten					ɛˇᵊ												oˑʊ			home
egg					ɛɪ												oʊ			know
head					ɛᵊ												oᵊ			four
Mary			eˇɪ														oᵊ			door
stairs							æᵋᵊ										oᵘᵊ			hoarse
care							æˇᵋᵊ										oᵊ			mourn
merry					ɛˇ															
thirty						ɞˑˑᵊ										ʌˇᵊ				sun
sermon						ɞˑˑ										ʌ				brush
furrow																ʌ				
ashes							æɪ							ɔˇᵊ						frost
bag							æᵊ							ʋˇʏ						log
married							æᵊ							ɔˇɔ						dog
half							æᵊ							ɔˇɔ						water
glass							æɪ							ɔɔˇ						daughter
aunt							æᵊ							ɔɔ						law
father								ɑˑᵊ												
palm								ɑˇʋ												
barn								ɑˇʋ						ɔˇɔ						forty
garden								ɑˇʋ						ɔˇɔ						morning
crop								ɑˑ						ɔˇɔ						corn
John								ɑˑᵊ						ɔˇᵊ						horse
college								ɑˑᵊ												
borrow								ɑˑᵊ												
five										æˑɛ	æˇʋ									down
twice										ʋˇɪ	ʋˇʋ									out
wire										æˇɛᵊ	æˇʋᵊ									flower
											ɔɪ									joint
											ɔɪ									boil
	i	ɪ	e	ə	ɛ	ɜ	æ	ɑ	ɑ	ai	ɔi	au	ɒ	ɔ	ʌ	ɵ	o	ʊ	u	

	i	ɪ	e	ɪ	ɛ	ɜ	æ	ɑ	ɒ	ai	ɔi	au	ɑ	ɔ	ʌ	ɵ	o	ʊ	u	
three	i˰j																		ʊu˞	two
grease	i˞i																		ʉ˞ᵘ	tooth
six		ɪ																ʊᵊ		wood
crib		ɪᵊ																ʊᵋᵊ		pull
ear		ɪᵊ˞															oˑᵊ			poor
beard				ɪᵊˑˑ													oˑ			ago
eight			eɬ														oˑ			coat
April			eˑ														oʊ			road
ten					ɛᵌᵊ												oʊ			home
egg					ɛᵊ												oᵁ			know
head					ɛᵊ												oᵁᵊ			four
Mary			eˑɬ														oᵊ			door
stairs							æˑᵊ										oᵁᵊ			hoarse
care							æˑᵊ										oᵁᵊ			mourn
merry					ɛᵌ															
thirty					ʚᵌ										ʌ˞					sun
sermon					ʚᵌ										ʌᵊ					brush
furrow															ʌ˞					
ashes							æˑᵊ							ɒ˞ᵊ						frost
bag							æᵊ		ɑ˞ᵊ											log
married							æᵊ							ɒᵛ˞						dog
half							æˑᵊ							ɒᵛᵊ						water
glass							æˑᵊ							ɔ˞ˑ						daughter
aunt							æˑᵊ							ɒᵛ˞						law
father								ɑ˞ᵊ												
palm								ɑᵛˑ												
barn								ɑᵛˑᵊ		ɑˑʊ				ɔ˞ˑ						forty
garden								ɑᵛˑ						ɒɑ˞						morning
crop									ɑ˞					ɒɑ˞						corn
John									—					ɔ˞ᵊ						horse
college									ɑ˞ᵊ											
borrow									ɑ˞ᵊ											
five									ɑˑᵋ	æˑʊ										down
twice									ɐɬ	æᵛʊᵛ										out
wire									æˑᵋɐ	æᵛᵛᵊ										flower
											ɔɬ									joint
											ɔɬ									boil
	i	ɪ	e	ɪ	ɛ	ɜ	æ	ɑ	ɒ	ai	ɔi	au	ɑ	ɔ	ʌ	ɵ	o	ʊ	u	

88

	i	ɪ	e	ɛ	ɜ	æ	ɑ	a	ai	ɔi	au	ɒ	ɔ	ʌ	ɵ	o	ʊ	u	
three	i·																	ʉ˄ʉ	two
grease	iᵛ·																	ʉ˅ʉ˃	tooth
six		ɪ															ʊə		wood
crib		ɪə															ʊ˂ə		pull
ear	ɪ˄·ə															oə			poor
beard	ɪ˄·ə															o˂˅ʊ			ago
eight			ɛ˄·˃ᵻ													o˂˅ʊ			coat
April			e˅·˃ᵻ													o˂˅ʊ			road
ten				ɛ˄·ə												o˅ʊ			home
egg				ɛə												o˂˄ʊ			know
head				ɛə												oʊə			four
Mary			e˅ᵻ													oʊ			door
stairs						æ˄ɛə										oʊə			hoarse
care						æᵻ˄ə										o·ə			mourn
merry				ɛ															
thirty					ɜ̣ə									ʌ˄					sun
sermon					ɜ̣·ə									ʌ˂·ə˄					brush
furrow														ʌ˄ə					
ashes						æ							ɒ˄ɔ						frost
bag						æ	ɒ˂·ə˄												log
married						æə							ɒ˄ɔ						dog
half						æə							ɒ˄ɔ̰						water
glass						æ·ə˂˄							ɒ˄ɔ						daughter
aunt						æ·ə							ɒ ɔ						law
father							ɑ˄·ə												
palm							ɑ˃·												
barn							ɒɒ̰ə						ɒ˄ɔ						forty
garden							ɒ˂·						ɒ˄ɔ						morning
crop								ɒ˂ə˄					ɒ˄ɔ						corn
John								ɑ˄ə					ɒ˄ɔə						horse
college								ɑ˃˄ə											
borrow								ɑ˃˄ə											
five									a·ɛ˃		æ˅ʉ								down
twice									a·ᵻ˅		æʊ								out
wire									a·ɛə										flower
										ɔ·ᵻ									joint
										ɔ·ᵻ˄									boil
	i	ɪ	e	ɛ	ɜ	æ	ɑ	a	ai	ɔi	au	ɒ	ɔ	ʌ	ɵ	o	ʊ	u	

	i	ɪ	e	ɪ	ə	ɛ	ɜ	æ	a	ɑ	ɒ	ai	ɔi	au	ɒ	ɔ	ʌ	ɵ	o	ʊ	u	
three	i˙ⁱi																				ʊˑʊ	two
grease	iᵛ˙																				ᵗʊᵘ	tooth
six		ɪ																		ʊᵊ		wood
crib		ɪˑᵊ																		ʊˑᵊ		pull
ear	ɪᵊ																		oˑᵊ			poor
beard				ɪˑᵊ															o ʊ			ago
eight			eˑɪ																oˑʊ			coat
April			ɛˑɪ																oˑʊ			road
ten						ɛᵊ													oˑʊ			home
egg						ɛᵊ													oˑʊ			know
head						ɛᵊ													oˑᵊ			four
Mary			eᵛɪ																oˑᵛᵊ			door
stairs								æᵊ											o ᵊ			hoarse
care								æⁿᵊ											oˑᵊ			mourn
merry						ɛᵊ																
thirty							ᵊˑ										ʌˑᵊ					sun
sermon							ᵊˑ										ʌˑᵊ					brush
furrow						ɛ																
ashes								æˑ								ɒˑᵛ						frost
bag								æˑᵊ								ɒˑᵛ						log
married								æᵊ								ɔˑɒ						dog
half								æˑ		ɒˑᵊ												water
glass								æᵊ								ɔˑᵛ						daughter
aunt								æᵊ								ɔɒ						law
father										ɒˑ												
palm										ɒˑ												
barn										ɑˑᵊ						ɔᵊ						forty
garden										ɑˑᵊ						ɔˑᵊ						morning
crop										ɑˑ						ɔᵊ						corn
John										ɒˑᵊ						ɔᵊ						horse
college										ɒˑ												
borrow										ɒˑ												
five											aˑɛˑ	æˑʊ										down
twice											aˑɛˑ	æˑʊ										out
wire										aⁿᵊ	—											flower
												ɔɪ										joint
												ɔɪ										boil
	i	ɪ	e	ɪ	ə	ɛ	ɜ	æ	a	ɑ	ɒ	ai	ɔi	au	ɒ	ɔ	ʌ	ɵ	o	ʊ	u	

	i	ɪ	e	ɪ	ɛ	ɜ	æ	ɑ	ɑ	ai	ɔi	au	ɒ	ɔ	ʌ	θ	o	ʊ	u	
three	iˑ																			two
grease	i·;iˑ																		ʉ	tooth
six		ɪˆ·ᵊ																ʊˆ·ᵊ		wood
crib		ɪˆ·ᵊ																ʊˣ·ᵊ		pull
ear	iˑᵊ																			poor
beard			ɛˆ·ᵊ														oˆˑᵊ			ago
eight			eˆ·ᵊ														ʊˆˑ·ᵊ			coat
April			eˆˑ														oˆˑ·ᵊ			road
ten					ɛˆ·ᵊ												oˣ·ᵊ			home
egg					ɛˆ·ᵊ												—			know
head					ɛˆ·ɫ												oˆ·			four
Mary			eˑ														oˆ·ᵊ			door
stairs			eˆ·ᵊ														oˆˑ·ᵊ			hoarse
care			ɛˆ·ᵊ														oˆˑ·ᵊ			mourn
merry					ɛˑ															
thirty						ɜˆ·ɫ									ʌˆ·ᵊ					sun
sermon						ɜˆˑ·ᵊ									ʌˣ·ᵊ					brush
furrow						ɜˑ									ɜˣ·ᵊ					
ashes							æˆ·ᵊ							ɔˆ·ᵊ						frost
bag							æˆ·ᵊ							ɔˆ·ᵊ						log
married							æˑ							ɔˆ·ᵊ						dog
half							æˆ·ᵊ							ɔˆ·ᵊ						water
glass							æˑᵊ							ɔˣ·ᵊ						daughter
aunt							æˑᵊ							ɔˆˑ						law
father								ɑˣ·ᵊ												
palm								ɑˣ·ᵊ												
barn								ɑˣ·ᵊ						ɔˆ·ᵊ						forty
garden								ɑˣ·ᵊ						ɔɔᵊ						morning
crop								ɒ;ɒᵊ						ɔˆ·ᵊ						corn
John								ɑˣ·ᵊ						ɔˣ·ᵊ						horse
college								ɒᵊ												
borrow								ɒˣˑ												
five									ɑˑɫ	ɑˑo										down
twice									ɒˆɑ	ʌˣʊ										out
wire								ɑˑᵊᵊ			ɑˑʊwᵊ										flower
joint										ɔˆɫ											joint
boil										oɔˑɫ											boil
	i	ɪ	e	ɪ	ɛ	ɜ	æ	ɑ	ɑ	ai	ɔi	au	ɒ	ɔ	ʌ	θ	o	ʊ	u	

	i	ɪ	e	ɪ	ɛ	з	æ	a	ɑ	ai	ɔi	au	ɒ	ɔ	ʌ	ɵ	o	ʊ	u	
three	jˑ																			two (ʦˑ)
grease	jˑᵻ																			tooth (ʦˑ·ᵊ)
six		ɪˆ																ʊˁ		wood
crib		¯																		pull
ear		ɪˑᵊ												ɔˁˑᵊ						poor
beard		¯												ɔˁˑ						ago
eight			eˑᵊ											ɔˁˑᵊ						coat
April			eˑ											ɔˁˑᵊ						road
ten					ɛˆ									ɔˁˑᵊ						home
egg					ɛˆᵻ									ɔˁˑ						know
head					ɛˆᵻ									ɔˁˑ						four
Mary			eˑ											ɔˁˑᵊ						door
stairs					ɛˑᵊ									ɔˁˑᵊ						hoarse
care			eˑᵊ											ɔˁˑᵊ						mourn
merry					ɛˑ															
thirty						зˆᵻ									ʌˆ					sun
sermon						ɞˆᵻ									ʌˁ					brush
furrow						зˆ														
ashes							¯							ɔˑᵊ						frost
bag							æˑ							ɔˑᵊ						log
married							æˑ							ɔˑᵊ						dog
half							æˑᵊ							ɔˑᵊ						water
glass							æˑᵊ							ɔˑᵊ						daughter
aunt							æˑᵊ							ɔˑ						law
father								ɑˑᵊ												
palm							æˑᵊ													
barn								ɑˑᵊ						ɔˑᵊ						forty
garden								ɑˑᵊ						ɔˑᵊ						morning
crop									ɒ					ɔˑᵊ						corn
John														ɔˑᵊ						horse
college									ɒ											
borrow									ɒˑˑ											
five										ɑˑᵻ		ɑˑʊ								down
twice										ɑˑᵻ		ʌˑʊ								out
wire										ɑˑjᵊ										flower
											ɔˑᵻ									joint
											ɔˑᵻ									boil
	i	ɪ	e	ɪ	ɛ	з	æ	a	ɑ	ai	ɔi	au	ɒ	ɔ	ʌ	ɵ	o	ʊ	u	

92

	i	ɪ	e	ɛ	ɜ	æ	ɑ	ɑ	ai	ɔi	au	ɒ	ɔ	ʌ	θ	o	ʊ	u	u	
three	iˇ																		uˑ	two
grease	iˇ																		uˑ	tooth
six		ɪˇ															ʊ			wood
crib		ɪ															ʊˇ			pull
ear	iˇə																ʊə			poor
beard	iˇə															oˑˇ				ago
eight			eˇə													oˑ;oˑə				coat
April			eə													oˑ				road
ten				ɛ												o				home
egg				ɛ												o				know
head				ɛ												oə				four
Mary			eə													oˑə				door
stairs			eˑə													oəˇ				hoarse
care			eə														uˇə			mourn
merry				ɛ																
thirty					ɞˇ									ʌˇ						sun
sermon					ɞˇˑ									ʌˇ						brush
furrow														ʌˇ						
ashes						æˇ							ɔˑə							frost
bag						æˇə		ɑ̆												log
married						æˇə							ɔˑ							dog
half						æˇ							ɔˑ							water
glass						æˇˑ							ɔˑ							daughter
aunt						æˑ							ɔˇˑ							law
father							ɑˑə													
palm							ɑˑə													
barn							ɑɑˇ						ɔˑ							forty
garden							ɑə						ɔˑ							morning
crop								ɒ̆ə					ɔ							corn
John								ɒ̆ə					ɔˇˑ							horse
college								ʋ̆												
borrow								ɒ̆												
five									ɑɪ		au									down
twice									ɑɪ		ʋa									out
wire									eɪə		awə									flower
joint										ɔɪ										joint
boil										ɔɪ										boil
	i	ɪ	e	ɛ	ɜ	æ	ɑ	ɑ	ai	ɔi	au	ɒ	ɔ	ʌ	θ	o	ʊ	u	u	

	i	ɪ	e	ɛ	ɜ	æ	ɑ	a	ai	ɔi	au	ɒ	ɔ	ʌ	θ	o	ʊ	u	
three	i˃																	ʉ	two
grease	i·˃																	ʉ˂·	tooth
six		ɪ˄															ʊ˂		wood
crib		ɪ˃															ᵿ˃		pull
ear			ɛ·ə													—			poor
beard			ɛ˄·ə													o̝˂·ə			ago
eight			e˄·ə													o̝˂·ə			coat
April			e˄·													o̝˂·ə			road
ten				ɛ˄												o̝˂·ə			home
egg				ɛ·ɨ												o̝˂			know
head				ɛ·ɨ												o̝˂·ə			four
Mary			e·													o˄·ə			door
stairs			e˅·ə													o̝˂·ə			hoarse
care			ɛ˄·ə													o̞˂·			mourn
merry				ɛ˃·															
thirty					ɜ̰ɨ									ʌ˄					sun
sermon					ɜ˅ɨ									ʌ̝˂					brush
furrow														ʌ·					
ashes						æ							ɔ̞˂·ə						frost
bag						æ·ɛ							ɔ˂·ə						log
married						æ˅							ɔ˂·ə						dog
half						—							ɔ˂·ə						water
glass						æ˅							ɔ˂·						daughter
aunt						æ·ɛ							ɔ˂						law
father							ɑ·ə												
palm							ɑ·												
barn							ɑ·ə						ɔ̞˂						forty
garden							ɑ·ə						ɔ˂·ə						morning
crop								ɑ					ɔ˂·						corn
John								ɑ					ɔ˂·ə						horse
college								ɑ											
borrow								ɑ·											
five									ɑ·ɨ		ɑ·ʊ								down
twice									ə˅ɪ		ʌ˅ʊ								out
wire							ɑ̝˂·ə				ɑʊʷə								flower
										ɒ˅ɨ									joint
										ɔ̝˂ɨ									boil
	i	ɪ	e	ɛ	ɜ	æ	ɑ	a	ai	ɔi	au	ɒ	ɔ	ʌ	θ	o	ʊ	u	

	i	ɪ	e	e	ɪ	ɛ	ɜ	æ	a	ɑ	ɒ	ai	ɔi	au	ʊ	ʌ	θ	o	ʊ	u	u	
three	i˙																				ᵗt˙	two
grease	i˒																				ᵗt˙	tooth
six		ɪ˄																	ʊᶜ			wood
crib		ɫ																	ʊᶜ			pull
ear	i˙ɔ																	—				poor
beard			ɛ˙ɔ															o˂˙				ago
eight			e˄˙															oˑ˄				coat
April			e˄˙															oˑ˙				road
ten						ɛ˄ɔ												oˑ˄				home
egg						ɛᵻ												—				know
head						ɛᵻ												o˄ɔ				four
Mary			e˄˙															o˄ɔ				door
stairs			e˙ɔ															o˙ɔ				hoarse
care			e˙ɔ															o˄ɔ				mourn
merry					ɛ˄																	
thirty						ɜ˄ᵻ										ɣ˄ɔ						sun
sermon						ɜ˄									ɜ˄ɔ							brush
furrow						ɜ˒˄																
ashes								æɔ								ɔ˙ɔ						frost
bag								æ˄ɛ								ɔ˄ɔ						log
married								æ˙								ɔ˄ɔ						dog
half									a˄							ɔ						water
glass								æɛ								ɔ˙ɔ						daughter
aunt								æɛ								ɔ						law
father									ɑ˒˙ɔ													
palm									ɒ˙ɔ													
barn									ɑ˒˙ɔ							ɔ˙ɔ						forty
garden									ɒ˙ɔ							ɔ˄ɔ						morning
crop										ɒ˙ɔ						ɔ˄˙						corn
John									ɑ˒˙ɔ							ɔ˙ɔ						horse
college										a˂												
borrow									ɑ˒˙													
five											a˒˙ɔ		aᵻo									down
twice											ɒᵻ		ʌᵻʊ									out
wire											aᵻ˙ɔ		ɑ˙wɔ									flower
joint													ɔ˄ᵻ									joint
boil													ɔ˄ᵻ									boil
	i	ɪ	e	e	ɪ	ɛ	ɜ	æ	a	ɑ	ɒ	ai	ɔi	au	ʊ	ʌ	θ	o	ʊ	u	u	

	i	ɪ	e	ə	ɛ	ɜ	æ	a	ɑ	ɒ	aɪ	ɔɪ	aʊ	ɒ	ɔ	ʌ	θ	o	ʊ	u	
three	i·j																			ʉ·ʷ	two
grease	i·j																			ʉ·ʷ	tooth
six		ɪ^																	ʊ˕		wood
crib		ɪ^																	ʊ		pull
ear	ɪ·ə															o˓·ə			ʉ·ə		poor
beard	ɪ^·ə															o˕·ʊ					ago
eight			e^·ɪ													o˓·ʊ					coat
April			e·ɪ													o˓·ʊ					road
ten		ɪ^			ɛ^											o˓·ʊ					home
egg					ɛ·ɪ											o˓·ʊ					know
head					ɛ·											o·ʊ					four
Mary			e·ɪ													o˓·ə					door
stairs			ɛ^·ə				æ^·ə									o˓·ə					hoarse
care							æ·ə									o˓·ə					mourn
merry				ɛ·																	
thirty					ɜ·ɪ										ʌ˅						sun
sermon					ɞ·										ʌ˕						brush
furrow					ɜ^																
ashes							æ·ɛ							ʋ·ɔ							frost
bag							æ·ɛ							ɔc							log
married							æ·							ɔ·o							dog
half							æ·ɛ							ʋa							water
glass							æ·ɛ							ʋɑ							daughter
aunt							æ^·ə							ʋ·ɔ							law
father								ɑ·ə													
palm								ɑ·ə													
barn								ɑ·ə						ʋ·a							forty
garden								ɑ·ə						ɔ·c							morning
crop									ɑ					ʋ·ɔ ɔ·ə							corn
John								ɑ·ə						ʋɑ							horse
college									ɑ												
borrow									ʋ^												
five										æ·ə	aɪ·ʊ										down
twice										aɪ	æ·ʊ										out
wire										æ·ə	aɪ·wə										flower
											ɔɪ										joint
											ɔc										boil
	i	ɪ	e	ə	ɛ	ɜ	æ	a	ɑ	ɒ	aɪ	ɔɪ	aʊ	ɒ	ɔ	ʌ	θ	o	ʊ	u	

	i	i	e	e	ɛ	ɜ	æ	a	ɑ	ɑ	ai	ɔi	au	ɒ	ɔ	ʌ	ɵ	o	ʊ	u	
three	iiˆ																				two
grease	iiˆ																			ʉˑuˑ	tooth
six		ɪˑ																	ʊˑ		wood
crib		ɪˆ																	ʉˑ		pull
ear	ɪˑˑɘ																—				poor
beard	ɪˑˑɘ															oˑʊˑ					ago
eight			eˆɪ													oˑʊˆ					coat
April			eˑɪ													ʌˑʊ					road
ten					ɛˑ											oˑʊ					home
egg					ɛˑɪ											oˑʊ					know
head					ɛˆ											oˑˑɘ					four
Mary			eˆɪ,ɪeˆ													oˑʊɘ					door
stairs							æˑˑɘ									oʊɘ					hoarse
care				ɛˑɘ												ọˑʊˑ					mourn
merry					ɛˑˑ																
thirty						ɜˆˑɘ										ʌˆ					sun
sermon						ɜˑɪ										ɤˑ					brush
furrow						ɜˑˑ															
ashes							æˑˑɛ								ɔˑoˑ						frost
bag							æˑˑ		ɒˑˑ												log
married							æˑˑ								ʋˑˑo						dog
half							æˑɛ								ʋˑˑɘ						water
glass							æˑɛ								ʋˑoˑ						daughter
aunt							æˑɛ								ʋˑoˑ						law
father								ɒˑˑ													
palm								ɒˑˑɘ													
barn								ɒˑˑ							ʋoˑ						forty
garden								ɒˑˑɘ							ɔˑoˑ						morning
crop									ɒˑ						ɔˑʌ						corn
John									—						ɔˑʌ						horse
college									ɒ												
borrow									ɒˑ												
five										ɐˑɪ,ɑˑɘ	aˑʊˑ										down
twice										ɐˑɪ	aoˑ										out
wire										ɑˑˑɘ	æˑoˑ										flower
joint												ɔoˑɪ									
boil									ɔˑɪ												
	i	i	e	e	ɛ	ɜ	æ	a	ɑ	ɑ	ai	ɔi	au	ɒ	ɔ	ʌ	ɵ	o	ʊ	u	

97

	i	ɪ	e	ɛ	ɜ	æ	ɒ	ɑ	ai	ɔi	au	u	ɒ	ɔ	ʌ	ɵ	o	ʊ	u	
three	i˞i																		ɨ˞tt	two
grease	i˞i'																		ʊ˞tt	tooth
six		ɪ˞																ʊ˞		wood
crib		ɪ˞ᵊ																ʊ˞ᵊ		pull
ear		ɪ˞ᵊ															o˞ᵊ			poor
beard			e˞ᵊ														o˞ᵘ			ago
eight			e˞ɨ														o˞			coat
April			e˞ɨ														o˞ᵘ			road
ten				ɛ˞													o˞ᵊ			home
egg				ɛ˞ɨ													o˞ᵘ			know
head				ɛ˞													o˞			four
Mary			e˞														o˞ᵊ			door
stairs			ɛ˞ᵊ														o˞ᵊ			hoarse
care			e˞ᵊ														o˞ᵊ			mourn
merry				ɛ˞																
thirty					ɜ˞ɨ										ʌ˞					sun
sermon					ɜ˞ɨ										ʌ˞					brush
furrow															ʌ˞					
ashes						æ˞								ɔ˞ᵊ						frost
bag						æ˞ᵊ								ɔ˞ᵊ						log
married						æ˞								ɔ˞ᵊ						dog
half						æ˞								ɔ˞						water
glass						æ˞ɛ								ɔ˞						daughter
aunt						æ˞ᵊ								ɔ˞ᵊ						law
father							ɑ˞													
palm							ɑ˞ᵊ													
barn							ɑ˞ᵊ							ɔ˞ᵊ						forty
garden							ɑ˞ᵊ							ɔ˞ᵊ						morning
crop								ɑ						ɔ˞ᵊ						corn
John								ɑ˞						ɔ˞ᵊ						horse
college							ɑ˞ᵊ	ɑ˞												
borrow								ɑ												
five									a˞ᵊ		a˞o									down
twice									ɨ˞a		ʌ˞u									out
wire									ɑ˞ᵊ		ao˞ᵊ									flower
										ɔɨ										joint
										ɔɨ										boil
	i	ɪ	e	ɛ	ɜ	æ	ɒ	ɑ	ai	ɔi	au	u	ɒ	ɔ	ʌ	ɵ	o	ʊ	u	

	i	ɪ	e	ə	ɪ	ɜ	ɛ	æ	ɒ	ɑ	ai	ɔi	au	ɒ	ɔ	ʌ	ɵ	o	ʊ	u	
three	i·																			ʉˑʉ	two
grease	i·ɪ																			ʉˑʉ	tooth
six		ɪ̌																	ʊˤ		wood
crib		ɪˤ																	ʊˤə		pull
ear			eˑə															—			poor
beard			eˤə															oˤʊ			ago
eight			eˤɪ															oˑ			coat
April			eˑ															oˑ			road
ten				ɛˑə														oˤʊ			home
egg				ɛˤə														oˤ			know
head				ɛˤɪ														oˑə			four
Mary			eˤ															oˑə			door
stairs								æˤə										oˑə			hoarse
care			eˑə															oˑə			mourn
merry				ɛˤ																	
thirty						ɜˑɪ									ɤˤ						sun
sermon						ɜˑə									ɤˤə						brush
furrow															ʌˑ						
ashes								æˤə						ɔˑ							frost
bag								æə	ɑˑə					ɔˑə							log
married								æˤ						ɔˑə							dog
half								æɛ						ɔˑə							water
glass								æə						ɔˑə							daughter
aunt								æɛ						ɔˑ							law
father									ɑˑə												
palm									ɑˑə												
barn									ɑˑə					ɔˤə							forty
garden									ɑˤə					ɔˤə							morning
crop										ɑˤ				ɔˑə							corn
John									ɑˑə					ɔˑ							horse
college									ɑ												
borrow									ɑˤ												
five											ɑˑɪ	ɑˑo									down
twice											ɐˤɑ	ɑˑo									out
wire											ɑˤjə	æˤ ə									flower
												ɔɪ									joint
												ɔˑɪ									boil
	i	ɪ	e	ə	ɪ	ɜ	ɛ	æ	ɒ	ɑ	ai	ɔi	au	ɒ	ɔ	ʌ	ɵ	o	ʊ	u	

	i	ɪ	e	ɛ	æ	a	ɑ	ɒ	ai	ɔi	au	ɒ	ɔ	ʌ	ɵ	o	ʊ	u	
three	iʲ																	tɬʼ	two
grease	iʲ																	tɬʷ	tooth
six		ɪˆ															ʊˢ		wood
crib		ɪˆᵊ															ʊˢ		pull
ear			eˆᵊ																poor
beard	ɪˆᵊ														oˑʊˢ				ago
eight			eˑɪ												oˑʊˢ				coat
April			eˑɪ												oˆʊˢ				road
ten				ɛˆᵊ											oˆʊˢ				home
egg				ɛˆᵊ											oˆʊˢ				know
head				ɛˆᵊ											oˆᵊ				four
Mary			eˑɪ												oˑᵊ				door
stairs					æˆᵊ										oˑᵊ				hoarse
care				ɛˑᵊ											oˆᵊ				mourn
merry				ɛˑᵊ															
thirty				ɜˑɪ									ɣˢ						sun
sermon				ɜˑɪ									ɣˆᵊ						brush
furrow				ɜˑ															
ashes					æˆᵋ							ɔˆᵊ							frost
bag					æˑᵋ	aˀᵊ													log
married					æˑ							ɔɣˢ							dog
half					æᵋ							ɔˆᵊ							water
glass					æᵋ							ʋˆɔ							daughter
aunt					æᵋ							ɔɣˢ							law
father						ɑˆᵊ													
palm						ɑˑᵊ													
barn						ɑˑᵊ							ɔɔ						forty
garden						ɑˑᵊ							ɔˆᵊ						morning
crop						ɑ						ɔˑᵊ							corn
John						ɑˀ						ɔˆᵊ							horse
college						ɑˀ													
borrow						ɑˑ													
five							aˑˆᵊ		æˆo									down
twice							aˑɪ		æˑo									out
wire							aˑˆᵊ		ɛˆoᵊ									flower
joint								ɔɪ										joint
boil								ɔɪ										boil
	i	ɪ	e	ɛ	æ	a	ɑ	ɒ	ai	ɔi	au	ɒ	ɔ	ʌ	ɵ	o	ʊ	u	

CHAPTER 3

THE REGIONAL AND SOCIAL DISSEMINATION OF THE DIAPHONES OF STRESSED VOWELS

3.1 INTRODUCTORY REMARKS

THE VOWELS are dealt with in this order: the checked vowels (3.2–3.8) and the free vowels (3.9–3.18) current in all of the dialects; the vowels restricted to certain dialects (3.19–3.21). The treatment of vowels before /r ∼ ə̣/ has been reserved for a separate chapter because of the complicated interrelations between phonemic, phonic, and incidental aspects of the vowels in this position.

For each of the vowel phonemes the regional variants or diaphones are pointed out, traced in their dissemination, and presented on Maps 4–33. Whenever more or less marked positional allophones are current in one area or another, that fact is pointed out and sometimes shown on separate maps. Articulatory or prosodic factors determining the character of the allophones can usually be pointed out. In addition to the regional diaphones, socially restricted phones are noted; occasionally a regional trend in the phonic characteristics of a vowel phoneme can be shown to be in process.

The description of the diaphones and allophones of the phonemes rests upon the behavior of the several vowels in three or more words selected from a larger number of instances. The words are chosen to display the vowels in different contexts in order that the more striking allophones may be exhibited. Hence, although the descriptions refer to particular examples, they can be safely taken as being generally applicable, unless a statement to the contrary is made.

The mapping of the phonic types of a vowel in representative words and the assignment of the phonic types to phonemes provide the basis for dealing with the incidence of different phonemes in one and the same word, as in *creek, room, road, fog, stairs, Mary*. If the regional and social dissemination of the diaphones of the several phonemes is known, their incidence in the vocabulary can usually be safely determined; without such information a decision is often impossible and always hazardous. For instance, when the diaphones of /u/ as in *two* and of /ʊ/ as in *wood* have been determined, it is nearly always possible to decide whether a given speaker in any of the communities investigated has /u/ or /ʊ/ in such words as *room, roof, root*; or again, if the diaphones of the /e/ of *paper*, the /ɛ/ of *head*, and the /æ/ of *ashes* are known, one can determine fairly safely which of the three phonemes a speaker has in *stairs* or *Mary*.

3.2 THE CHECKED VOWELS

(Map 4)

The checked high and mid vowels, as in *crib, wool, bed, judge*, have rather marked regional diaphones. Monophthongal phones characterize the Northern area, ingliding diphthongs the South and the South Midland. The North Midland varies. Within the North ingliding phones are common in northeastern New England; in the South the coastal cities of South Carolina and the westernmost part of the state have monophthongs; the urban areas of Pennsylvania incline toward monophthongal pronunciation of these checked vowels.

Before voiceless stops, inglides are less common and briefer, and in words of more than one syllable they are infrequent.

The manifold regional and positional variants of the checked low vowels /æ/ and /ɑ/ are discussed separately.

3.3 THE VOWEL IN *whip, crib, chimney*

(Map 5)

/hwɪp, krɪb, čɪmni/

Both monophthongal [ɪ ∼ ɨ] and ingliding [ɪᵊ ∼ ɨᵊ] are current, largely in regional dissemination.

In the North and in the Hudson Valley monophthongal [ɪ] is in general use; centralized [ɨ] occurs in scattered fashion in New England and in Upstate New York. Ingliding [ɪ̯ə] is rare throughout this area.

In the South and the South Midland ingliding [ɪ̯ə] predominates and is well-nigh universal in the greater part of Virginia and West Virginia, in all of North Carolina, and in parts of South Carolina and Georgia. Centralized [ɪ̯ə] occurs along with [ɪ̯ə] in parts of South Carolina, less commonly in Eastern Virginia, especially after /w/ in *whip*.

Monophthongal /ɪ/ is rather frequent on Chesapeake Bay, including Baltimore (in *chimney* also along the Potomac); it predominates in the coastal communities of South Carolina (Charleston has only the monophthong), Georgia (Savannah), and Florida (Jacksonville), and in Western South Carolina.

In the North Midland usage varies regionally. The Hudson Valley, Metropolitan New York, and East Jersey generally have monophthongal [ɪ], which also predominates in Southeastern Pennsylvania (Philadelphia and the German area). The greater part of Pennsylvania has the ingliding diphthong [ɪ̯ə] in the monosyllables *whip*, *crib*, but not in the disyllabic *chimney*, as do the adjoining parts of Maryland and West Virginia.

In English folk speech ingliding [ɪ̯ə] is fairly common in *whip*, *chimney*, etc.

3.4 THE VOWEL IN *wood, wool, push*

(Maps 6–7)

/wud, wul, puš/

Monophthongal [ʊ] prevails in the North, diphthongal [ʊ̯ə ~ ʉ̯ə] in the South and the Southern Appalachians. However, the ingliding diphthong is common in northeastern New England, especially in Maine, and occurs sporadically in other parts of New England and in New York State. On the other hand, monophthongal [ʊ] is a characteristic feature of the coastal counties of South Carolina, Georgia, and Florida (Charleston, Savannah, Jacksonville), and of the westernmost counties of South Carolina.

Pennsylvania has both [ʊ] and [ʊ̯ə], partly in regional distribution, partly as positional or prosodic allophones. Ingliding [ʊ̯ə] is more common before the /š/ of *push* than before the /l/ of *wool*, *pull* and does not occur in the trisyllabic *woodpecker*.

Delaware, Maryland, and West Virginia are a transition belt in which the diphthongal variant increases in frequency as one goes southward.

High-central variants [ʉ ~ ʉ̯ə] occur beside fronted [ʊ ~ ʊ̯ə] in West Virginia and in parts of South Carolina. Fronted [ʊ ~ ʊ̯ə] are widespread.

Before the /š/ of *push* an upgliding allophone [ʊ̯ᵻ ~ ʉ̯ᵻ] is not uncommon in Eastern New England and in Virginia, West Virginia, and South Carolina. Moreover, such variants as [ʊ ~ ʉ ~ ʉ̯ᵻ] occur not infrequently in West Virginia and occasionally in South Carolina, which must be taken as the phoneme /u/ of *two*.

English folk speech has [ʊ̯ə] beside [ʊ] in *wool*, *push*, etc. Central [ʉ ~ ʉ̯ə] do not occur in the Midland and the South, but Devonshire has a long high-front [y·] in these words.

3.5 THE VOWEL IN *bed, egg, fence*

(Maps 8–9)

/bɛd, ɛg, fɛnts/

Monophthongal [ɛ] has general currency in the North and in the Hudson Valley, including Metropolitan New York and Long Island. However, the ingliding diphthong [ɛ̯ə] predominates in northeastern New England in words of one syllable, as in *bed*, *fence*, and occurs more or less sporadically in all parts of the North.

Diphthongal [ɛ̯ə] is almost universal in the South, except for the upper reaches of Chesapeake Bay (including Baltimore and Annapolis), the immediate vicinity of Charleston, S. C., and the westernmost part of South Carolina.

Within the North Midland, monophthongal [ɛ] predominates in Eastern Pennsylvania, but [ɛ̯ə] is not uncommon in Philadelphia and vicinity. In the remainder of Pennsylvania the ingliding diphthong [ɛ̯ə] becomes more and more common in fully stressed monosyllables the farther west one goes, and predominates decidedly in the western part of the state and the adjoining parts of Ohio and West Virginia. However, under half-stress, as in *heads* in the phrase *heads of lettuce*, the inglide is uncommon even in western Pennsylvania and the northernmost parts of West Virginia. Pennsylvania and Maryland thus constitute a transition area between the North with its monophthongal [ɛ] and the South Midland and the South with its diphthongal [ɛə].

Positional allophones of /ɛ/ and phonemic shifts occur before certain consonants.

Before the voiced velar /g/ in *egg*, monophthongal [ɛ], often raised, predominates in western New England and New York State, is almost universal in the North Midland (New Jersey, Pennsylvania, and all but the southernmost part of West Virginia), and of common occurrence in Maryland and Delaware. Ingliding [ɛə] occurs in an area extending from Chesapeake Bay, through eastern North Carolina, to the Low Country of South Carolina and adjoining parts of Georgia. A third type, upgliding [ɛ ͥ ~ ɛɪ ~ eͥ ~ eɪ], is widely used in most of the South and the South Midland. It is also common in Eastern New England and occurs to some extent in the greater part of the New England settlements of Upstate New York and Pennsylvania. Such pronunciations of the vowel in *egg* are most frequent in folk speech and almost entirely avoided by cultured speakers. The phonemic status of these upgliding phones is not always clear: with some speakers they are positional allophones of checked /ɛ/ (phonically parallel to upgliding [æͥ] in *bag* and [ʊͥ] in *push*); but in Eastern New England, in the South, and in the South Midland the checked /ɛ/ has actually been replaced by the free vowel /e/ of *eight*.

Before /n/, as in *fence, ten*, the /ɛ/ is often raised in the South, and some speakers in Georgia, South Carolina, and eastern North Carolina have the high vowel /ɪ/ of *six* instead of /ɛ/. Elsewhere /ɪ/ is rare (see Map 9).

3.6 THE VOWEL IN *sun, judge, brush*

(Maps 10–11)

/sʌn, ǰʌǰ, brʌš/

In *sun*, monophthongal [ʌ] prevails in the North, diphthongal [ʌə ~ ɤə] in the South and the South Midland. Diphthongal variants are rare in the North. On the other hand, monophthongal [ʌ ~ ɤ] is fairly common in parts of the South: south-central Virginia; all of North Carolina

except Albemarle Sound and the Blue Ridge; the coastal cities of South Carolina, Georgia, and Florida; and the western third of South Carolina with the adjoining parts of Georgia. The ingliding diphthong is most common in Virginia north of the James River, on Albemarle Sound, and in South Carolina.

There are marked regional differences in tongue position: [ʌ] is general in the North and the North Midland, and in all of West Virginia; raised and frequently somewhat rounded [ʌ ~ ʌə] and [ɤ ~ ɤə] prevail in the South, in Maryland west of Chesapeake Bay, and on the lower Susquehanna in Pennsylvania. Centralized [ɜ ~ ɜə] occurs sporadically in northeastern North Carolina and in the western tip of Virginia.

Mid-central [ɜ˞ ~ ɜ] phones are much more common in *judge*, where the vowel is flanked by palatal affricates. They occur with varying frequency in the folk speech of the South. In dialects with constricted /ɝ/, these phones are positional variants of the /ʌ/ of *sun*; in dialects with unconstricted /ɝ/, as that of the Low Country of South Carolina, they are either members of the /ɝ/ phoneme of *thirty* or hover uneasily between /ʌ/ and /ɝ/.

Upgliding allophones [ʌͥ ~ ɤͥ ~ ɜͥ] of /ʌ/ (or /ɝ/) appear before the /ǰ/ of *judge* and before the /š/ of *brush* in Southern folk speech (see Map 11).

3.7 THE VOWEL IN *sack, ashes, half, dance, glass*

(Maps 12–14)

/sæk, æšəz, hæf, dæns, glæs/

The raised low-front vowel /æ/ varies markedly by position in the word and regionally. Like the checked low-central vowel /ɑ/ of *rod* it is often quite long in monosyllables.

Before the voiceless velar stop in *sack*, monophthongal [æ] prevails in the North and the Midland and the greater part of the South. Ingliding [æə] predominates in the Low Country of South Carolina and adjoining parts of Georgia, and is not uncommon along Albemarle Sound in North Carolina. Upgliding [æͥ, æᵉ], often followed by fronted or palatalized /k/, is common in the Upcountry of South Carolina, the greater part of Georgia, and on the Florida coast; it occurs rather frequently in northeastern North Carolina, rarely in western Virginia. Upgliding diphthongs predominate also in southern New Hampshire and adjoining parts of Maine, but are exceedingly rare in other parts of the North and entirely lacking in the Midland.

Before the voiced velar stop in *bag*, both upgliding [æ¹] and ingliding [æə] are much more widespread. Upgliding [æ¹], often followed by fronted or palatalized /g/, and ingliding [æə] are common on all social levels in most of the South. The variant [æə] predominates in the Richmond area, in all of North Carolina except the northeastern part, and in the Low Country of South Carolina, [æ¹] elsewhere. In *bag* upgliding [æ¹, æᵉ] is of frequent occurrence also in parts of the North: from Boston to Portland and northwestward to the Green Mountains in Vermont, in the Adirondacks and the St. Lawrence Valley, and in the Genesee Valley (Rochester) in New York State. It does not occur in the Midland.

Before the voiceless fricatives of *ash(es)*, *glass*, *half*, upgliding [æ¹] is widespread in the South, except in the Low Country of South Carolina and on the coast of Georgia and Florida. It is most common in North Carolina but occurs also fairly frequently in Tidewater Virginia. In *ash(es)*, [æ¹] is found as far north as the Potomac and prevails in the Upcountry of South Carolina and the greater part of Georgia, which rarely have [æ¹] in *glass* and *half*.

In New England [æ¹] occurs only in *ash(es)* (New Hampshire and adjoining parts of Maine); here *glass*, *half* have the vowel of *car*.

3.8 THE VOWEL IN *crop, oxen, college*

(Map 15)

/krɑp, ɑksən, kɑləǰ/

The checked low vowel /ɑ/ occurs in all parts of the Eastern States, except Eastern New England and Western Pennsylvania where it is merged with the free vowel /ɒ/ of *law, salt, loss* (see 2.2 and 2.6). Its incidence varies regionally. It appears regularly before the stops /p, b, t, d, k/, as in *crop, cob, lot, rod, oxen*, before intersyllabic /l/, as in *college*, and before /r/, as in *car, barn*, in those dialects that preserve /r/ in this position. In other positions the incidence of /ɑ/ varies regionally, as before /g/ in *log, fog*, after /w/ in *wash, water, swallow*, and before intersyllabic /r/ in *tomorrow, orange*.

The checked low vowel /ɑ/ contrasts with the free low vowel /ɑ ~ a/ of *car, barn, father, calm* in Eastern New England, in Metropolitan New York, and in the Upper and the Lower South, where earlier /ɑr/, passing through /ɑə/, has yielded the free vowel /ɑ ~ a/. Checked /ɑ/ differs in these areas from free /ɑ ~ a/ in quality and length, or only in being shorter than the free vowel.

The phonic character of checked /ɑ/, as in *crop, oxen, college*, ranges from a backed low-front [a‹] through low-central [ɑ] to low-back unrounded or slightly rounded [ɑ ~ ɒ]. The most widely used phone is low-central [ɑ], not infrequently fronted in the North and backed in the Upper South and the South Midland. Unrounded low-back [ɑ], sometimes fronted, is common in the Carolinas and in Georgia, not uncommon in West Virginia, and has some currency along the western shore of Chesapeake Bay and in Eastern Pennsylvania. In the Low Country of South Carolina and along the Georgia and Florida coast rounded low-back [ɒ] stands beside unrounded [ɑ]; here checked /ɑ/ differs from the free vowel of *car, barn* in being articulated farther back, whereas in the Upper South (Virginia) the reverse is true.

The checked /ɑ/ of *rod, crop, college* is often prolonged in the North and the Midland and noticeably ingliding in the South Midland and parts of the South.

Crop, oxen, college, etc., have a more or less rounded low-back [ɒ] in Western Pennsylvania and in Eastern New England; however, in these two areas this [ɒ] is not the checked vowel /ɑ/ but the free vowel /ɒ/ occurring in *law, seesaw*, etc.

The complicated interrelations of checked /ɑ/ with the free /ɔ ~ ɒ/ of *law, loss*, and the incidence of these vowels in the various dialect areas on the Atlantic seaboard, are discussed in great detail in Thomas Wetmore's monograph.

English folk speech exhibits the same wide phonic range of the vowel, as in *crop*.

3.9 THE FREE VOWELS

Free vowels tend to be upgliding diphthongs, except in certain subareas.

The mid vowels /e/ and /o/, as in *day* and *ago*, exhibit parallel treatment. For instance, the diaphones [ɛɪ] and [ɔu ∼ ɤu] appear (1) along the New England coast, (2) in an area including most of New Jersey, Southeastern Pennsylvania (Philadelphia), and Delaware, (3) the Ohio Valley (Pittsburgh), and (4) northeastern North Carolina; monophthongal [e· ∼ e] and [o· ∼ o] (1) in the Low Country of South Carolina, (2) in the German settlements of eastern Pennsylvania, and (3) as relics along Chesapeake Bay.

The diphthongal vowels /ai/ and /au/, as in *nine*, *twice*, and *mountain*, *out*, also show parallel regional diaphones. Thus "slow" [a·ɪ ∼ a·ᵋ ∼ a·ᵊ] and [a·ʊ ∼ æ·ʊ] prevail finally and before voiced consonants (1) in all of the South and the South Midland, except the Low Country of South Carolina, and (2) in an area extending from the Metropolitan New York area to Philadelphia and vicinity. Before voiceless consonants, on the other hand, two subareas of the South, (1) eastern Virginia with adjoining sections of Maryland and North Carolina and (2) the Low Country of South Carolina and coastal Georgia and Florida, have the "fast" allophones [əɪ ∼ ʊɪ] and [əʊ ∼ ʊʊ], as in *twice* and *out*.

3.10 THE VOWEL IN *three, grease, bean*

(Map 16)

/θri, gris, bin/

Three phonic types are current: an upgliding diphthong [ɪi, ij], a monophthong [i·, i], and an ingliding diphthong [iᵊ].

Upgliding diphthongs, ranging from [ɪi], with a lowered beginning, to [ij], with a close beginning, predominate (1) in northern New England; (2) in an area including New Jersey, the southeastern corner of Pennsylvania (Philadelphia), and Delmarva (roughly from the Raritan in New Jersey to Chesapeake Bay); and (3) in all of the South except the Low Country of South Carolina and coastal Georgia and Florida. They are also fairly common along Lake Ontario in New York State, and in western Pennsylvania and parts of

West Virginia (the valleys of the Allegheny and the Ohio). The diphthongal glide is more marked in final position, as in *three*, especially under heavy stress, than in checked position, as in *grease, bean*. A relatively open beginning is common in parts of New Jersey, in Philadelphia, in western Pennsylvania (Pittsburgh), on lower Chesapeake Bay, and in northeastern North Carolina.

Monophthongal [i·, i] predominate (1) in southern New England and New York State, including Metropolitan New York; (2) in the Pennsylvania German area of eastern Pennsylvania; (3) in Maryland west of the Bay (Baltimore); and (4) especially in the Low Country of South Carolina (to Columbia and Augusta, Ga.) and along the Georgia and Florida coast.

Ingliding [iᵋ, iᵊ] is confined to the Low Country of South Carolina and coastal Georgia and Florida, where it occurs fairly regularly in checked position, as in *grease, bean*, rarely in free position, as in *three*.

All of these phonic types occur in English folk speech.

3.11 THE VOWEL IN *two, shoes, tooth, school*

(Map 17)

/tu, šuz, tuθ, skul/

Like the high-front vowel /i/, this vowel is either an upgliding diphthong, a monophthong, or an ingliding diphthong. The regional dissemination of these phonic types of /u/ corresponds very closely to that of the diaphones of /i/. In all of these types the tongue may be high-back, high-central, or in an intermediate position.

Fully high-back [u· ∼ ʊu] predominates only in the North. It occurs, along with fronted [u· ∼ ʊu], in Metropolitan New York and Philadelphia and, beside central [ʉ· ∼ ʊʉ], in parts of North Carolina, sporadically also in other parts of Pennsylvania and the South.

High-central [ʉ· ∼ ʊʉ] predominates in all of the South except parts of North Carolina and the Eastern Shore of Maryland. It is common in the South Midland, in the Pittsburgh area, around Baltimore, and on Delaware Bay, and not infrequent in parts of New Jersey. Central [ʉ· ∼ ʊʉ]

is especially widespread after the blade consonant /š/ in *shoes* and after /j/, as in *music, dues,* and decidedly less frequent before the velarized /l/ in *school*.

Fronted high-back [u· ∼ ʊu] is current in an irregular belt along the northern margin of the [ʉ· ∼ ᵿu] area: in large parts of Pennsylvania, in New Jersey, and on the lower Hudson with Metropolitan New York. It has also considerable currency in parts of Eastern New England (especially Maine, New Hampshire, and Cape Cod) and along Lake Ontario and the St. Lawrence River in Upstate New York.

All of these phonic types are current in English folk speech.

3.12 THE VOWEL IN *day, April, eight, bracelet*

(Maps 18–19)

/de, eprəl, et, breslət/

Three types of pronunciation are current, largely in regional dissemination: upgliding [eɪ, ɛɪ], monophthongal [e·, e], and ingliding [eə].

Upgliding [eɪ, ɛɪ] predominate in the greater part of the Eastern States. The variants [eɪ, eˢ], with relatively close beginning, are most widespread.

The variant [ɛɪ], with a more open beginning, is concentrated in four geographically separate subareas: (1) the New England coast from Boston northeastward (especially the valleys of the Androscoggin and the Kennebec in Maine); (2) an area including New Jersey (but excluding Newark and vicinity), Philadelphia and the lower Susquehanna Valley in Pennsylvania, and Delmarva; (3) western Pennsylvania (Pittsburgh) and the upper Ohio Valley to the mouth of the Kanawha in West Virginia; and (4) northeastern North Carolina, from Albemarle Sound to the valley of the Neuse.

Monophthongal [e·, e] and ingliding [eə] are a distinctive feature of the speech of the Low Country of South Carolina and the coast of Georgia and Florida. Monophthongal [e·, e] predominates here in word-final and syllable-final position, as in *day, April*, ingliding [eə] in checked position, as in *afraid, bracelet*. Relics of this usage survive in eastern Virginia and the southern tip of Maryland.

Monophthongal [e·] is common in the Pennsylvania German area, reflecting German usage, and stands out sharply from the [ɛɪ] of Philadelphia and vicinity. Elsewhere the monophthong is rare and appears to be a prosodic variant of the slightly diphthongal [eˢ].

All American variants have their counterparts in English folk speech.

3.13 THE VOWEL IN *ago, coat, road*

(Maps 20–21)

/əgo, kot, rod/

Four types of pronunciation occur: an upgliding diphthong [ou ∼ oᵛ] with a rather close mid-back beginning, an upgliding diphthong [ɤu] with a more or less open mid-central beginning, monophthongal close [o· ∼ o], and ingliding [oə].

[ou ∼ oᵛ] are current in the greater part of the Eastern States.

[ɤu] occurs in three separate areas: (1) the Delaware Valley (including Philadelphia), (2) western Pennsylvania (including Pittsburgh) and the upper Ohio Valley, and (3) northeastern North Carolina.

Monophthongal [o· ∼ o] predominates along with ingliding [oə] in the Low Country of South Carolina and coastal Georgia and Florida, the former in free position (as in *ago*), the latter in checked position (as in *coat, road*). Pronunciations of this type occur also in eastern Virginia and the southern tip of Maryland, but are here largely confined to folk speech.

As a Germanism, [o·] occurs also in Eastern Pennsylvania.

New England has upgliding [ou ∼ oᵛ], occasionally also [ɔu], both in free and in checked position. In addition, Eastern New England has a variety of ingliding vowels in checked position, as in *road, coat*, which constitute a phoneme distinct from that in *ago, know*. See 3.19.

3.14 THE VOWEL IN *law, salt, dog*

(Maps 22–24)

/lɔ ∼ lɒ, sɔlt ∼ sɒlt, dɔg ∼ dɒg/

Three major phonic types are widely current in the Eastern States: a well-rounded monophthongal raised low-back [ɔ], usually prolonged; a slightly rounded low-back [ɒ]; and an upgliding diphthong [ɒə], with progressive lip rounding.

Well-rounded [ɔ·] predominates (1) in Western New England, the lower Hudson Valley, Metropolitan New York, and Long Island; (2) along Lake Ontario and the St. Lawrence River in Upstate New York; (3) in southeastern Pennsylvania (Philadelphia) and Maryland west of Chesapeake Bay; and (4) in the Low Country of South Carolina and along the coast of Georgia and Florida.

In tidewater Virginia and on the coast of North Carolina monophthongal [ɔ·] competes with diphthongal [ɒə]. The greater part of West Virginia has [ɔ·] along with [ɒə] and [ɒ].

Diphthongal [ɒə] is common in the South from the Potomac to the Pee Dee in South Carolina, in the southern Appalachians, the Upcountry of South Carolina, and the greater part of Georgia. [ɒə] is not current in the Low Country of South Carolina, the lower Savannah Valley, and coastal Georgia and Florida. On the coast of North Carolina and Virginia monophthongal [ɔ·] is not uncommon, but seems to be yielding ground to [ɒə]. Upgliding [ɒə] is more common before the velar stop /g/ of *dog* and the velarized /l/ of *salt* than in other positions, appearing not only in the South, in West Virginia, and in Maryland, but also in New England.

Slightly rounded [ɒ· ~ ɒ] predominates (1) in Eastern New England, (2) in parts of Upstate New York, (3) in the greater part of Pennsylvania and adjoining parts of Ohio and West Virginia, and (4) in an extensive coastal area comprising West Jersey and Delmarva (from the Raritan to Chesapeake Bay).

It should be noted that Eastern New England and Western Pennsylvania have [ɒ] phones not only in *law, salt, dog*, etc., but also in *rod, crop, college*, etc., whereas other areas have a different phoneme, checked /ɑ/, in the latter set. Because of this striking difference in incidence, the vowel phoneme occurring in words of these historical types is represented by the symbol /ɒ/ in the description of these two dialects.

3.15 THE VOWEL IN *thirty, Thursday, sermon, girl*

(Map 25)

/θɜti, θɜzdi, sɜmən, gɜl/

This mid-central vowel has striking regional variants. (1) It may be fully constricted, i.e.,

articulated with the sides of the tongue drawn away from the gums and the body of the tongue bulging upward, or it may be only slightly constricted or entirely unconstricted. (2) Both constricted and unconstricted /ɜ/ may be monophthongal or diphthongal. (3) Both types may be pronounced without or with rounding of the lips.

The constricted variety occurs as monophthongal [ɝ] or [ɝ] (the former fully constricted, the latter slightly), or as an upgliding diphthong [ɜɝ] with progressive constriction. The unconstricted variety appears as monophthongal [ɜ ~ ɵ], with or without lip rounding, as ingliding [ɜə ~ ɵə], or as upgliding [ɜ¹ ~ ɵ¹]. All varieties may be prolonged.

Constricted [ɝ ~ ɜɝ] prevail in all of the North except Eastern New England, in all of the North Midland except Metropolitan New York and Western Pennsylvania, in all of the South Midland and the Valley of Virginia, and in the greater part of North Carolina.

Unconstricted [ɜ ~ ɵ ~ ɜ¹ ~ ɵ¹] are confined to four geographically separated coastal areas: Eastern New England, Metropolitan New York, Eastern Virginia, and South Carolina–Georgia.

In New England unconstricted mid-central [ɜ, ɵ] are in general use along the Atlantic seaboard from the Boston area northeastward to the eastern boundary of Maine, and westward to the Green Mountains in Vermont and the Berkshires in Massachusetts. They predominate also in southeastern Massachusetts (Plymouth to Cape Cod, Nantucket), Rhode Island, and eastern Connecticut, but a slightly constricted [ɝ] still survives in these sections. Unconstricted and slightly constricted varieties occur here and there on the lower Connecticut (Hartford, Middletown) and on Long Island Sound (Saybrook, New Haven, Milford), apparently in the speech of the old stock and the better educated.

Within the area in which the unconstricted phonic types predominate, more or less constricted varieties survive in some rural or secluded spots: on Martha's Vineyard, on lower Cape Cod, in Marblehead, on Cape Ann, in the Scotch-Irish settlements of south-central New Hampshire, and in the upper Connecticut Valley.

The St. John Valley in New Brunswick, settled in large part by loyalists from western Connecticut, New York, and New Jersey, has the constricted [ɚ], and this type prevails also in northeastern Maine (Fort Kent, Fort Fairfield, Houlton).

Metropolitan New York has unconstricted diphthongal [ɜɪ], in cultivated speech also monophthongal or ingliding [ɜ, ɜ°]; but slight constriction also occurs. Diphthongal [ɜɪ] and slightly constricted [ɜ] appear sporadically in the Hudson Valley as far north as Albany, in the Newark area in New Jersey, and along Long Island Sound in Connecticut. The diphthongal [ɜɪ] of *girl* is kept apart from the [ɔɪ] of *boil*, except by some less educated speakers in Metropolitan New York (especially Brooklyn).

In Virginia east of the Blue Ridge and adjoining parts of Maryland and North Carolina usage varies considerably. Slightly constricted [ɜ] predominates. The unconstricted variants [ɜ, ɜ°, ɜᴵ] are not uncommon north of the James River (Richmond, Charlottesville, Fredericksburg), but elsewhere they are rather rare. South of the lower James fully constricted [ɚ] still occurs along with slightly constricted [ɜ]; full constriction survives also in scattered points in the tidewater area to the north of the James. Throughout eastern Virginia the trend appears to be toward weaker constriction or its elimination.

Nearly all of South Carolina, the greater part of Georgia, and the Florida coast have unconstricted [ɜ ~ ɜ°] or [ɜɪ], the former predominating before labials and /l/, as in *purpose*, *sermon*, *girl*, the latter before alveolar stops, as in *thirty*, *heard*.

Constriction, often quite marked, occurs in South Carolina along the northern and western margin, rarely elsewhere; in Georgia, full constriction prevails in the mountains north of Atlanta and in the pine barrens along the coast.

The eastern half of North Carolina, lying between Virginia and South Carolina where constriction is weak or lacking, is highly diversified. Fully constricted [ɚ], which prevails in western North Carolina, predominates south of the Neuse River (especially along the Cape Fear), less constricted [ɜ] to the north of it (especially along the Virginia border). In these areas, younger and better educated speakers tend to reduce constriction (Wilmington), and some cultured speakers north of the Neuse (New Bern, Edenton) use the unconstricted type.

The phonemic interpretation of the syllabic in *Thursday*, *sermon*, *girl*, etc., as the unit phoneme /ɜ/, whatever its articulation, is consistent with our treatment of the free vowels /i, u, e, o/ of *three*, *two*, *eight*, *know*, all of which exhibit diphthongal and monophthongal regional diaphones and considerable variation in tongue height.

It will be observed that unconstricted /ɜ/ is confined to areas in which postvocalic /r/ is not preserved (see Maps 156 and 157). Here /ɜ/ derives from an earlier sequence /ər > əə̯/—ultimately from earlier /ɪr, ʊr, ɛr/, as in *girl*, *Thursday*, *sermon*, respectively—in the same manner as the free vowel /ɑ ~ a/ of *car*, *garden* arises from earlier /ɑr > ɑə̯/ and the /ɔ ~ ɒ/ of *corn*, *forty* from /ɔr > ɔə̯/.

Areas that keep postvocalic /r/ consistently have constricted /ɜ/, a phonically unique type of vowel, which occurs also to some extent in areas where postvocalic /r/ does not survive as such (notably in the Upper South). No phonemic formulation can do away with the unique character of syllabic [ɚ ~ ɜ]. If one takes it as /ə/ plus /r/ articulated simultaneously, as some do, its phonic uniqueness is not removed.

English folk speech of today exhibits all the major phonic types occurring as diaphones of American /ɜ/, except upgliding [ɜɪ]. The southern, the central, and the western counties have a fully constricted [ɚ ~ ɚ] vowel. Unconstricted [ɜ ~ ʌ ~ ɐ] is used in Middlesex, Hertford, Essex, Suffolk, Norfolk, and in southern Lincoln and Leister (probably also farther north), and of course in Standard British English, which has its roots in Middlesex-Essex. See the inserts on Maps 25 and 156. The constricted [ɚ] of American English, it is clear, came to this country from England with the first settlers and throughout the Colonial period, the unconstricted type probably not until the eighteenth century. At any rate, the confinement of the diaphones [ɜ, ɞ, ɜɪ], pronounced without constriction, to four coastal areas, each with one or several seaports through which close commercial and social relations were maintained with London and those who spoke Standard British English, points to a later adoption and dissemination of this manner of pronouncing the syllabic of *thirty*, *Thursday*, *sermon*, *girl*, etc.

Western Pennsylvania lacks the /ɜ/ phoneme.

It has instead the sequence /ʌr/, articulated as [ər ~ ɜr], the /r/ being an alveolar tongue tip consonant as after other vowels in this area. Similar pronunciations occur sporadically in northern West Virginia.

3.16 THE VOWEL IN *nine, twice, wire*

(Maps 26–27)

/nain, twais, waiɜ ~ waiə/

This diphthongal vowel varies regionally and positionally in four respects: (1) in initial quality, which may be low-front [a], low-central [ɑ], low-back [ɒ], or centralized [ɐ, ə, ʌ]; (2) in the relative length of the initial element, which results in "slow" and "fast" diphthongs; (3) in the distance, and hence the relative prominence, of the upglide (or inglide); and (4) in the presence or absence of marked positional variants.

A low-front beginning is widespread in all of the Eastern States. The North and the North Midland have [aɪ], less commonly [a·ɪ] (as in Metropolitan New York and Philadelphia); the South Midland and the South, except for the coastal area, have [a·ᵉ, a·ᵊ].

A low central beginning is common along the Atlantic coast from New Jersey to Florida. New Jersey and northern Delaware Bay have [ɑ·ɪ, ɑɪ], the Virginia tidewater and coastal North Carolina [ɑ·ᵉ] beside [a·ᵉ], and the Low Country of South Carolina and coastal Georgia and Florida predominantly [ɑ·ɪ]. A low-back beginning occurs sporadically on the South Atlantic coast.

Variants with a centralized beginning, [əɪ, ʌɪ, ɐɪ], occur in three geographically separated areas.

In northeastern New England and in parts of Upstate New York this type of "fast" diphthong occurs in all positions, chiefly in rustic and in old-fashioned speech; scattered instances have also been observed in southern New England.

In two rather sharply delimited areas of the South, (1) Virginia and adjoining parts of Maryland and North Carolina, and (2) the coastal belt of South Carolina, Georgia, and Florida, these "fast" diphthongs with centralized beginning occur only before voiceless consonants, as in *twice, night*, and differ sharply from the "slow" diphthongs [a·ᵉ, a·ᵊ, ɑ·ɪ] current in these areas

before voiced consonants and finally, as in *five, nine, good-bye*. In Virginia the difference between these positional variants is especially great, as in *twice* [əɪ] vs. *nine* [ɑ·ᵉ, ɑ·ᵊ]. In South Carolina less so, usually [ɐɪ] vs. [ɑ·ɪ].

All variants beginning in mid-central or in raised low-central position are "fast" diphthongs, that is, the first element is relatively short and the upglide swift and prominent. Northern [ʌɪ, ɐɪ] occurs in all positions; it is yielding ground to [aɪ] and has been largely replaced by it in southern New England and in the Hudson Valley. In Virginia and in coastal South Carolina, Georgia, and Florida these "fast" diphthongs, [əɪ] in Virginia and [ɐɪ] in South Carolina, are firmly entrenched before voiceless consonants and appear to be spreading.

Variants beginning in low position are either "fast" or "slow" diphthongs. "Fast" [aɪ] predominates in large parts of the North and in Pennsylvania and is not uncommon in Metropolitan New York, in the Hudson Valley, and on Long Island. "Slow" [a·ɪ] occurs along with "slow" [ɑ·ɪ] in Metropolitan New York, in New Jersey, and in the Philadelphia area.

"Slow" diphthongs with a short upglide or an inglide predominate before voiced consonants and finally in all of the South and the South Midland except the Low Country of South Carolina and coastal Georgia and Florida, which have [ɑ·ɪ]. The most widespread variants are [a·ᵉ] and [ɑ·ᵉ], the latter chiefly along the coast (sporadically also [ɒ·ᵉ]). Within this area, ingliding [a·ᵊ, ɑ·ᵊ] is of common occurrence in parts of Virginia and North Carolina and predominates in the Up-country of South Carolina and in Georgia.

As has been pointed out above, these "slow" diphthongs with a vanishing glide occur before voiced consonants and finally throughout the South and the South Midland, except along the coast of South Carolina, Georgia, and Florida. Before voiceless consonants they are current only in the Southern Appalachians and the Blue Ridge, and in parts of eastern North Carolina (the valley of the Neuse and the area between the Cape Fear River and the Pee Dee). Elsewhere in the South and the South Midland we find more or less marked positional allophones before voiceless and voiced consonants, as in *twice* vs. *five*: [aɪ] ~

[a·ᵉ] in West Virginia, [əɪ] ~ [a·ᵉ] in Virginia, [aɪ] ~ [a·ᵊ, a·ᵉ] in most of South Carolina and Georgia, and [ɐɪ ~ ɑ·ɪ] in coastal South Carolina and along the coast of Georgia and Florida.

For the vowel in *tired, wire* see 4.10.

In the folk speech of England slow and fast diphthongs occur in regional dissemination, without any marked positional variation. Slow [ɑ·ɪ ~ ɑ·ɨ], as in *nine* and *twice*, appear in a widening corridor extending from Middlesex-Essex northward to Leicester-Lincoln, fast [ɐɪ] (rarely [ʌɪ ~ əɪ]) everywhere else. The latter type is the obvious source of the recessive [ɐɪ ~ ʌɪ] of the New England settlement area. The northern and North Midland [aɪ ~ ɑɪ ~ ɑ·ɪ] resemble Standard British usage, which is in agreement with the folk speech of the corridor described above. Southern [a·ᵉ ~ a·ᵊ] is presumably derived from this type. The striking positional variants [a·ᵉ ~ əɪ] of Virginia are probably an American innovation, since this feature is not found in Standard British English or the folk speech of the Midland and the south of England, though northern England and Scotland have it to some extent.

3.17 The Vowel in *down, mountain, house, out*

(Maps 28–29)

/daun, mauntən, haus, aut/

This diphthongal vowel varies regionally, socially, and positionally in three respects: (1) in initial quality, which may be low-front [a], low-central [ɑ], raised low-front [æ], mid-front [ɛ], or centralized [ɐ, ə, ʌ]; (2) in the relative length of the initial element, which results in "slow" and "fast" diphthongs; and (3) in the presence or absence of marked positional variants.

The type of [aʊ], with low-front beginning, is in general used in the North Midland, from the Hudson Valley and Metropolitan New York to Ohio. In New England and Upstate New York it is the predominant pronunciation, but the types [æʊ, ɛʊ] and [ɐʊ, əʊ] still have considerable currency in northern New England and in Upstate New York, especially in folk speech.

A "slow" diphthong [ɑ·ʊ, a·ʊ] has general currency in nearly all of South Carolina and in coastal Georgia and Florida. It is not uncommon in the Cape Fear Valley of North Carolina and occurs sporadically in other parts of the South, especially in folk speech. Outside of South Carolina [a·ʊ] is here clearly yielding ground to [æ·ʊ].

The type of [æ·ʊ, æʊ] predominates, when followed by a voiced consonant or ending a word, in all of the South Midland and the South, except in the greater part of South Carolina and the adjoining coastal sections of North Carolina and Georgia. Throughout Virginia and the Appalachians this type is used in these positions by all social classes, in the cities (Baltimore, Richmond, Norfolk, Charlottesville, Roanoke, Atlanta, etc.) as well as in the countryside. In large parts of North Carolina [æ·ʊ] competes with [a·ʊ]; it seems to be especially common in the cities (Raleigh, Wilmington, Charlotte, Asheville) and among the better educated.

[æ·ʊ, æʊ] is not uncommon in West Jersey, on the Delaware and the lower Susquehanna in Pennsylvania, and in all of Delmarva; Philadelphians tend to avoid it, but in Lancaster and York well-educated older speakers still use it.

In New England [æʊ, ɛʊ] are rare except in some rural northern areas; in parts of New York State and the northern counties of Pennsylvania they are somewhat more common. There, as in New England, this type of pronunciation is regarded as rustic and old-fashioned and is being replaced by [aʊ].

Relics of [ɐʊ, ʌʊ], with centralized beginning, are found both before voiceless and voiced consonants on the coast of Maine, in southern New Hampshire, in Upstate New York, and on Chesapeake Bay.

In two sections of the South, (1) Virginia and adjoining parts of Maryland and North Carolina, and (2) coastal South Carolina, Georgia, and Florida, the "fast" diphthongs [əʊ, ɐʊ], with centralized beginning, occur regularly before voiceless consonants, as in *out, house*. The extreme variant [əʊ] is characteristic of the Virginia Piedmont, [ɐʊ] of its periphery and of the South Carolina coast. In a much more restricted area of eastern Virginia, in a belt extending from the lower Rappahannock southwestward to the Roanoke, these variants occur also at the end of a word, as in *cow, plow*; on the South Carolina coast this usage is rare.

These two subareas of the South have thus very striking allophones before voiced and voiceless consonants, as in *down* and *out*, respectively: Virginia [æ·ʊ] ~ [əu, ɐʊ], South Carolina [ɑ·ʊ] ~ [ɐʊ]. Elsewhere in the South, and in all of the Midland and the North, the phoneme /au/, whatever its regional pronunciation, has no marked positional allophones.

Except before voiceless consonants in the two areas just discussed, all of the South and the South Midland have the "slow" diphthongs [æ·ʊ] and [a·ʊ, ɑ·ʊ], the latter predominating in South Carolina, the former everywhere else. The "slow" diphthongs [a·ʊ] and [æ·ʊ] also occur commonly in New Jersey (except for the Newark area), in southeastern Pennsylvania (Philadelphia), and on the upper Ohio (Pittsburgh, Wheeling), but not elsewhere in the Midland. The North has only "fast" diphthongs, although at the end of a phrase prolongation may occur under heavy stress.

The [aʊ ~ ɑʊ] type of the American North and North Midland agrees with Standard British usage. American [æʊ ~ ɛʊ] and [ɐʊ ~ əu] have their counterparts in English folk speech, the former type prevailing in the eastern counties (with the exception of Norfolk and eastern Suffolk and Essex), the latter in the west and in parts of East Anglia. Marked positional variants are not current in English folk speech, except perhaps in the northern counties and in Scotland; hence Virginian usage is presumably an innovation, as in the case of /ai/.

3.18 The Vowel in *oil, boiled, poison, joint*

/ɔil, bɔild, pɔizən, ǰɔint/

The vowel /ɔi/ varies regionally in the quality and the length of the initial element and the relative prominence of the upglide. In folk speech the phoneme /ai/ is widely current in place of /ɔi/, especially in the South and the South Midland and in northeastern New England (see 5.15). In Metropolitan New York some less educated speakers merge the vowels of *oil* and *girl*.

Diphthongs beginning with rounded and raised low-back [ɔ ~ ɔ·] predominate in most of the Eastern States. A higher and fully rounded beginning, mid-back [o ~ o·], predominates in the Low Country of South Carolina; it occurs rather commonly on Delaware Bay, on upper Chesapeake Bay (Maryland), and in parts of eastern New England.

"Fast" diphthongs, [ɔɪ ~ oɪ], prevail in the North and the North Midland, "slow" diphthongs in the South and the South Midland. The greater part of the South has the type of [ɔ·ᵉ], lower South Carolina [o·ɪ]; ingliding [ɔ·ᵊ] occurs along with [ɔ·ᵉ] in western South Carolina.

3.19 The Vowel in *coat, stonewall, whole*

(Map 30)

/kөt, stөnwɒl, hөl/

The dialect of New England possesses a checked mid-back vowel /ө/, traditionally called "the New England short *o*," in such words as *coat, road, smoke, stone, home, whole*, which does not occur outside the New England settlement area, i.e., the Northern dialect area. Checked /ө/ contrasts with the checked high-back vowel /ʊ/ of *put, pull* and the checked raised low-back vowel /ʌ/ of *cut, stun, hull*. It differs markedly from the normally upgliding free mid-back vowel /o/ of *know, ago* and appears in contrast with it in such pairs as *road* vs. *rode* /rөd:rod/, *coat* vs. *shoat* /kөt:šot/, *stone* vs. *own* /stөn:on/, and *whole* vs. *knoll* /hөl:nol/.

The checked vowel /ө/ is normally a fronted and lowered mid-back [o̞ ~ ɔ̈] sound, clearly ingliding before alveolar stops, as in *coat, road*, and before /n/, as in *stone, bone*, less commonly before other consonants, as in *folks, whole, home, most*. It is usually short, especially in words of more than one syllable, as in *toadstool, stonewall, smokestack*, and under half-stress, as in *whetstone, railroad*, but may be prosodically prolonged, as in *I'll take you home*.

This vowel phoneme, a hallmark of the New England dialect, is sharply recessive at the present time and has obviously been receding for several generations. It is preserved most extensively in northeastern New England (from the Green Mountains in Vermont eastward), less so in the southeast. In the lower Connecticut Valley and westward it is now rather uncommon, except among the older generation, and in the New England settlements of Upstate New York, northern Pennsylvania, and east-central New Jersey it survives only as a rare relic.

Checked mid-back /ɵ/ is being replaced by the free mid-back vowel /o/ of *know*, presumably under the influence of American national usage. Many speakers waver between /ɵ/ and /o/ in certain words, using the latter when they are on guard. Occasionally the /ɵ/ is replaced by /ʌ/, especially in the word *whole* /hʌl/, which survives in this pronunciation in the New England settlements of Upstate New York, northern Pennsylvania, and the Western Reserve of Ohio, often as a lone reminder of a New England pronunciation.

The incidence of /ɵ/ within New England varies not only regionally, socially, by age groups, and from person to person, but also from word to word. In general, words that are frequently used in the home or on the farm, and therefore less subject to school influence, retain /ɵ/ more extensively. But there is little apparent consistency in the replacement of checked /ɵ/ by free /o/.

The ingliding checked /ɵ/ of New England is not an American innovation. Ingliding [oᵊ, uᵊ] and [ʊ, ʌ, ə] are the normal derivatives of Middle English open /ǭ/, as in *stone, road, coat*, in the folk speech of England south of Yorkshire, except for London-Middlesex and the adjoining counties of Surrey, Hertford, Bedford, and western Essex and Kent. Only in these counties has ME /ǭ/ been merged with ME /ou/, as in *know, grow, own*, into an upgliding [oʊ ~ ɔʊ ~ ʌʊ] sound, from which the usually upgliding free /o/ of American English is derived. Though New England preserves ME /ǭ/ and /ou/ as ingliding checked /ɵ/ and upgliding free /o/, respectively, the incidence of these two phonemes no longer corresponds strictly to the two sources. To be sure, ME /ou/, as in *know, grow, own*, is always represented by free /o/, and checked /ɵ/ occurs only in words that had /ǭ/ in Middle English. However, the upgliding free /o/ has become established regularly in word-final position even where ME had the monophthong /ǭ/, as in *no, ago, so*, and is gradually replacing /ɵ/ in checked position, as described above.

3.20 THE VOWEL IN *car, barn, father, calm*

(Maps 31–32)

/kɑ˞ ~ ka, bɑ˞n ~ ban, fɑ˞ðə ~ faðə, kɑ˞m ~ kam/

The free low vowel /ɑ˞ ~ a/, as in *car, barn, father, calm*, is confined to the four areas on the Atlantic seaboard in which postvocalic /r/ is not preserved in such words as *ear, poor, care, four, corn, car*, namely Eastern New England, Metropolitan New York, Virginia east of the Blue Ridge with adjoining parts of Maryland and North Carolina, and South Carolina–Georgia. Dialects in which postvocalic /r/ is in use have checked /a/ not only in *lot, rod, ox, college*, etc., but also in *car, barn, father, calm*, etc. Western Pennsylvania and Delmarva form exceptions to this rule. In Western Pennsylvania *lot, rod*, etc., and *car, father*, etc. have the phoneme /ɒ/ of *law, loss*, etc. On Delmarva *car, garden, barn*, etc., have the /ɔ/ phoneme of *corn, morning*, etc.

The free low vowel differs rather markedly from area to area. In Eastern New England it ranges in quality from low-front [a] to low-central [ɑ] (hence symbolized by /a/), and contrasts sharply with the more or less rounded low-back /ɒ/ phoneme of *law, loss, rod, crop*, etc.

In Metropolitan New York the free low vowel is always a prolonged [ɑ˞· ~ ɑ·], the checked low vowel nearly always a short [ɑ ~ ɑ˄]. For approximately half of our informants in this area the contrast between the free and the checked vowel is purely one of quantity; the other half has a backish long [ɑ˞˂·] in *car, garden, father* /kɑ˞, gɑ˞dən, fɑ˞ðə/ over against a short low-central [ɑ ~ ɑ˄] in *crop, rod, bother* /krɑp, rɑd, bɑðə/.

In Virginia and adjoining parts of Maryland and North Carolina, the free low vowel /ɑ˞/ of *car, barn, garden, father* is always long, the checked low vowel of *crop, oxen*, etc., short. On the periphery of this area the contrast is primarily one of length, both vowels being low-central. Along the fall line (including Richmond) and in the tidewater area, the free /ɑ˞/ is a low-back [ɑ˞· ~ ɑ˞ɒ ~ ɒ·] sound, unrounded or rounded, and contrasts sharply with the checked low-central /a/ both in quality and in quantity. Free low-back [ɑ˞· ~ ɒ·] is also current in Annapolis and Baltimore, Md.

In South Carolina and Georgia, the free vowel /ɑ/ is consistently long, the checked vowel /ɑ/ short. For many speakers in this area the two vowels differ only in length, predominantly so in Charleston, Savannah, and Atlanta, both articulated as unrounded low-back [ɑ] sounds. When the two phonemes differ in quality, the free vowel of *car, garden, father, calm*, etc., tends to be a low-central [ɑ· ∼ ɑ›·], the checked vowel of *crop, oxen*, etc., a low-back [ɑ ∼ ɒ], often more or less rounded. It should be noted that in Virginia the articulation of these two vowels is precisely the reverse, the free vowel being low-back and often rounded, the checked vowel low-central and unrounded.

In all four areas that have the free /ɑ ∼ a/ it occurs regularly in *car, barn, garden*, etc., and in *father*. In Eastern New England it appears also in *half, laugh, bath, rather, glass, past*, though not consistently (see 5.3), and occasionally also in Metropolitan New York and in Virginia. For the incidence of /ɑ ∼ a/ in *calm, palm, ma, pa*, see 5.4 and 5.12.

The dialects that preserve postvocalic /r/ lack the free /ɑ ∼ a/ as a feature of their vowel system. A word-final low vowel occurs in these dialects only in a number of peculiar words, the exclamations *bah, hurrah*, the affectionate *ma, pa*, and several loan words such as *shah, pasha*, and should therefore be regarded as an exceptional use of the checked vowel /ɑ/ of *rod*, with which it agrees both in quality and in length.

3.21 THE VOWEL IN *music, dues, Tuesday, new*

(Map 33)

/miuzɪk, diuz, tiuzde, niu/

The diphthongal vowel /iu/, gliding from high-front-unround to high-back-round with decreasing stress, is confined to the New England settlement area. After labials and velars, as in *music, beautiful, cube*, this phoneme stands beside the sequence /ju/; after alveolars, as in *dues, Tuesday, new*, beside the vowel /u/ or the sequence /ju/.

/iu/ is clearly recessive. It is most common in rural Northern New England and in Upstate New York with the adjoining counties of Pennsylvania, and has considerable currency in western Massachusetts and Connecticut. It is uncommon to rare in southeastern New England, and urbanites and better educated speakers largely avoid it throughout the area. Thus the pronunciation /miuzɪk/ is being replaced by /mjuzɪk/, and /diuz, tiuzde, niu/ are giving way to /duz, tuzde, nu/ or, less commonly, to /djuz, tjuzde, nju/. The pace of the replacement varies from word to word.

In English folk speech of the present day the phoneme /iu/ is still widely used in the eastern counties.

CHAPTER 4

THE CONSONANT /r/ AND THE VOWELS BEFORE /r∼ɚ/

4.1 THE CONSONANTS /r/ and /ɚ/

ALL DIALECTS on the Atlantic seaboard have an alveolar /r/ before vowels in which the tip of the tongue approaches, but does not touch, the upper gums or the prepalatal region of the roof of the mouth. After the dental fricative /θ/, as in *three*, the tip may approach the base of the teeth. The middle or the back of the tongue is usually more or less arched toward the roof of the mouth and laterally constricted.

After vowels, as in *ear, poor, care, door, corn, car*, the incidence of the /r/ phoneme is regionally restricted, as described below. In dialects that have /r/ after vowels, it is articulated in this position without tongue-tip action. In forming this positional allophone of /r/, the body of the tongue is arched toward the roof of the mouth and the sides of the tongue are drawn away from the gums. This lateral constriction of the tongue creates a very complicated resonance chamber, the vibrating breath passing both over the tongue and along its sides. The degree of constriction and elevation of the tongue varies regionally, but the essential features of the articulation remain the same. There is one notable exception to this rule: in western Pennsylvania the postvocalic /r/ is articulated like the prevocalic /r/.

The articulation of the intervocalic /r/, as in *merry, Mary, harrow, tomorrow*, in *clearing, pouring*, and in *far out, your aunt*, varies regionally. In general, dialects that retain postvocalic /r/ have the *constricted* allophone [ɚ] in this position, and dialects that lack postvocalic /r/ have the alveolar tongue-tip [r]. Western Pennsylvania forms an exception in that both postvocalic and intervocalic /r/ are articulated with the tip of the tongue against the gums. Southerners usually lack [r] in such phrases as *far out, your aunt* (see 5.20).

Postvocalic /r/, as in *ear, poor, care, door, corn, car*, is in regular use in all of the Midland and the North, except for Eastern New England and Metropolitan New York. It survives to some extent on the South Atlantic coast, notably on the Eastern Shore of Chesapeake Bay (Delmarva) and in Eastern North Carolina with adjoining parts of South Carolina; in Eastern New England it is rare and, except on the island of Martha's Vineyard, sharply recessive.

In the greater part of the South, in Metropolitan New York, and in Eastern New England tautosyllabic postvocalic /r/ does not survive as such. After the high and the mid vowels it appears normally as unsyllabic /ɚ/, as in *ear, poor, care, door* (see 5.20); after /ɔ ∼ ɒ/, as in *corn, horse*, it is usually lost, so that these words rime with *lawn, loss*; after the checked low vowel of *car, barn* it merges with the vowel to create a new free vowel /ɑ ∼ a/, presumably passing through a stage /ɑɚ/ (see 3.20). Thus in these dialects *hard* contrasts with *hod* as /hɑrd : hɑd/ or as /had : hɒd/ (the latter in Eastern New England), whereas in dialects that retain postvocalic /r/ *hard* vs. *hod* are phonemically /hɑrd : hɑd/ or /hɒrd : hɒd/ (the latter in Western Pennsylvania).

For the positionally developed intrusive /r/, as in *wash*, and the analogically created /r/, as in *law-r and order*, see 5.20.

The stressed vowel in *thirty, sermon* /θɝti, sɝmən/, etc., will be treated as a unit phoneme, whether it is constricted, as in areas that have postvocalic /r/ in *ear, care, car, corn*, etc., or unconstricted, as usually within the areas that lack postvocalic /r/. See 3.15.

4.2 VOWELS BEFORE /r ∼ ɚ/

The incidence of vowels before an /r/ of the same syllable, or before the derivative unsyllabic /ɚ/, is severely restricted in all dialects: (1) None have more than one high-front and one high-back vowel, that is, the contrasts exhibited in *beat* : *bit* /i : ɪ/ and *boot* : *foot* /u:ʊ/ is lacking. Some dialects seem to lack high vowels altogether. (2) Except for parts of the Lower South, none has more than one front vowel between high and low, that is, the contrast shown in *eight* : *head* : *bag* /e:ɛ:æ/ does not occur. (3) Some dialects that preserve postvocalic /r/ have two mid-back vowels in this position, as in *hoarse* vs. *horse* /o:ɔ ∼ ɒ/, others only one (i.e., *hoarse* and *horse* are homophonous). Most dialects that lack post-vocalic /r/ have one mid-back vowel before the derivative /ə̣/, as in *four, hoarse* /foə̣, hoə̣s/ or /fɔə̣, hɔə̣s/; but in Metropolitan New York /ɔə̣/ is often reduced to /ɔ/, as commonly in Standard British English. (4) Dialects that pre-serve postvocalic /r/ have the checked low vowel /ɑ/ of *lot* before it, as in *barn, garden*, except that Western Pennsylvania has /ɒ/ both in *lot* and in *barn*. Dialects that have lost postvocalic /r/ have the free vowel /a ∼ ɑ̈/ in *car, barn*, corre-sponding historically to the sequence /ɑr/ of the other dialects.

Since the vowel contrasts occurring in *beat* vs. *bit*, *boot* vs. *foot*, *bait* vs. *bet* vs. *bat* either do not exist before an /r ∼ ə̣/ of the same syllable, or are exceptional, and some dialects lack the contrast exhibited in *boat* vs. *bought* before /r/, the identification of the vowel phonemes offers certain difficulties, especially in view of the fact that all vowels have rather marked allophones in this position and a wide range of prosodic variation. They are often lowered and/or cen-tralized; they are short in some dialects but prolonged in others; unless monophthongal, they are ingliding (though upgliding variants occur in some dialects under certain prosodic con-ditions). Moreover, in dialects that have post-vocalic /r/ as a constricted [ɚ], the preceding vowels are sometimes partially constricted. However, there are certain clues that usually lead to a fairly plausible decision, except in some transition areas, in cities located on or near major dialect boundaries (such as Baltimore and Atlanta), and in areas where the social dialects diverge from each other.

Three factors have been taken into considera-tion in the attempt to phonemicize vowels before

tautosyllabic /r/ and /ə̣/: (1) the height of the tongue as inferred from the timbre of the vowel; (2) the presence of upgliding prosodic allophones; and (3) the incidence of vowels before inter-syllabic /r/, as in such pairs as *experience* and *spirit, Mary* and *merry, glory* and *orange*.

The procedure adopted here can be briefly described as follows:

(1) If the vowels in *ear, poor, care, four* have a higher initial tongue position than in *fit, foot, bet, bought*, they are taken as the vowels /i, u, e, o/ of *feet, boot, bait, boat*, respectively, otherwise as the vowels /ɪ, ʊ, ɛ, ɔ/ of *fit, foot, bet, bought*. If the vowel in *care* is more like the vowel of *bat* than that of *bet*, it is taken as /æ/.

(2) If *ear, poor, care, four*, which normally have monophthongal vowels before tautosyllabic /ə̣/, have prosodic disyllabic allomorphs with upgliding vowels, i.e., are pronounced as [ijə, puwə, kejə, fowə], that fact is taken to mean that they are normally monosyllabic /iə̣, puə̣, keə̣, foə̣/, but disyllabic /iə, puə, keə, foə/ ending in syllabic /ə/ when heavily stressed and prolonged. This feature, occurring only in dialects in which postvocalic /r/ has become /ə̣/, corroborates the inference made from tongue height.

(3) If *Mary* and *merry* have different vowels before the intersyllabic /r/ and the latter clearly has the /ɛ/ of *met*, *Mary* is taken to have the vowel /e/ of *mate*, if the vowel is pronounced as [eɪ ∼ e], as in Eastern New England and the South. However, if the segment preceding the /r/ in *Mary* is identical with the segment at the end of *care* /keə̣/, as in Metropolitan New York, *Mary* is taken as /meə̣ri/.

Although the decisions made in accordance with this procedure may not be conclusive, they seem to be preferable to solutions offered from other points of view.

4.3 THE INCIDENCE OF VOWELS BEFORE /r ∼ ə̣/

The incidence of vowels before /r ∼ ə̣/ in the speech of eight cultured informants repre-senting the major dialect areas is shown in the tables on page 117, the first presenting the phonic data, the second the phonemic interpretation of these data.

Table I: *Phonic Data*

	ear	care	barn	corn	door	poor
1. Elmira, N. Y.	ɪˆɚ	ɛɚ	ɑˆɚ	ɔɚ	oɚ	ʊɚ
2. Philadelphia, Pa.	ɪˆɚ	ɛɚ	ɒˁɚ	ɔˆɚ	ɔˆɚ	uˇɚ
3. Pittsburgh, Pa.	ɪˆᵊr	ɛˆɚ	ɑr	ɔr	ɔr	ʉˇˑr
4. Asheville, N. C.	ɪˆɚ	æᵉɚ	ɑɚ	ɔɚ	oᵁɚ	oˑɚ
5. Billerica, Mass.	iˇə̰	æˆˑə̰	aˀˑᵊ	ɒˆˑᵊ	oˇə̰	ʊˆə̰
6. Manhattan, N. Y.	ɪˆə̰	ɛˀˑə̰	ɑˀː	ɔː	ɔːə̰	ʊˆˑə̰
7. Richmond, Va.	iˇə̰	æᵉə̰	ɑˀɒˆ	ɒɔˇ	oə̰	oə̰
8. Charleston, S. C.	iˑə̰	ɛˑə̰	ɑˀˑᵊ	ɔˑᵊ	oˑə̰	oˑə̰
9. Atlanta, Ga.	eˇˑə̰	æˆˑə̰	ɑˀˑᵊ	ɔˑᵊ	oˑə̰	oˑə̰

Table II: *Phonemic Interpretation*

	ear	care	barn	corn	door	poor
1. Elmira, N. Y.	ir	ɛr	ɑr	ɔr	or	ʊr
2. Philadelphia, Pa.	ir	ɛr	ɑr	or	or	ur
3. Pittsburgh, Pa.	ir	er	ɒr	or	or	ur
4. Asheville, N. C.	ir	ær	ɑr	ɔr	or	or
5. Billerica, Mass.	iə̰	æɛ̰	a	ɒ	oə̰	uə̰
6. Manhattan, N. Y.	iə̰	ɛɛ̰	ɑ̰	ɔ	ɔə̰	uə̰
7. Richmond, Va.	iə̰	æə̰	ɑ̰	ɔ	oə̰	oə̰
8. Charleston, S. C.	iə̰	ɛə̰	ɑ̰	ɔ	oə̰	oə̰
9. Atlanta, Ga.	eə̰	æə̰	ɑ̰	ɔ	oə̰	oə̰

4.4 THE VOWELS IN *ear, here, beard, queer*

(Maps 34–37)

/ɪr ~ iə̰ ~ eə̰ ~ jɜ/

Three (or four) different vowel phonemes occur in *ear, beard,* etc.: high-front /i ~ ɪ/, mid-front /e/, and mid-central /ɜ/.

High-front /i ~ ɪ/ has general currency in the North and the North Midland. It is used by a majority in the South Midland and the Upper South, especially among better educated speakers, but here its incidence varies considerably from word to word. In the Lower South, especially in South Carolina, the high-front vowel is decidedly uncommon and appears mostly in the speech of the cultured.

In dialects that preserve postvocalic /r/, the vowel is apt to be pronounced as a short [ɪ], as in Upstate New York and Pennsylvania; dialects that have /ɜ/ instead of /r/ usually have a prolonged [iˇˑ] or [ɪˆˑ]. But the elevation of the tongue and the length vary greatly, since checked /ɪ/ and free /i/ do not contrast in this position. Disyllabic *ear, beard* [ijə, bijəd], phonemically /iə, biəd/ as distinct from /iə̰, biə̰d/, appear occasionally under heavy stress in Eastern New England and in other areas that lack postvocalic /r/.

Mid-front /e/ is the usual vowel in *ear, beard,* etc., in South Carolina and Georgia. It is usually articulated as a longish [eˇˑ ~ ɛˆˑ] sound and contrasts sharply with the /æ/ phoneme of *care, stairs,* etc., except in the tidewater area of South Carolina, where *care* /keə̰/ rimes with *ear* /eə̰/.

Outside the Lower South, mid-front /e/ is uncommon or rare and its incidence in *ear, here, beard,* etc., varies greatly. It appears with some frequency in parts of North Carolina and on the western shore of Chesapeake Bay, in *beard* also in the folk speech of western Pennsylvania, Upstate New York, and northeastern New England. The word *queer* is exceptional in that /e/ is rather widely used in the Upper South and the South Midland.

The phoneme /ɜ/, constricted or unconstricted, is of common occurrence in *beard, here, ear* /bjɜd, hjɜ, jɜ/ in North Carolina, Virginia, and southern West Virginia, and appears with some frequency also in Maryland, especially on the Eastern Shore. It is rare in South Carolina and Georgia, which have /e/, and unknown in the North Midland and the North, where /ɪ ~ i/ prevail. The segment /jɜ/, it should be noted, is derived from /ir ~ iə/ by a shift of the syllabic peak.

In areas where /ɜ/ predominates, it occurs on all social levels but tends to be replaced by the high vowel /ɪ ~ i/, especially among the cultured. Its incidence varies markedly from word to word, being most widely used in *beard*, less so in *here* (recorded in the phrase *look here!*), and least in *ear*.

All three pronunciations are current at present in English folk speech: /e/ chiefly in East Anglia, constricted /ɜ/ in the western counties, and /i/ in the central counties, but also elsewhere. As in the Eastern United States, the incidence of /e/ and /ɜ/ varies greatly from word to word, an indication that they are being replaced by /i ~ ɪ/. Standard British English has *ear, here, beard* /iə, hiə, biəd/, but according to Daniel Jones, *English Pronouncing Dictionary* (1956), also /jɜ, hjɜ, djɜ, njɜ/, presumably as a recent development. There can be little doubt but that all three types of pronouncing *ear, here, beard* were brought to America from England during the Colonial period and that /i ~ ɪ/ has been spreading, partly under the influence of Standard British English.

4.5 THE VOWELS IN *stairs, theirs, care, chair*

(Maps 38–41)

/keə ~ kɛr ~ kɛə ~ kær ~ kæə ~
kɪr ~ kiə ~ kjɜ/

Stairs, care, etc., have one of three vowels, the /e/ of *eight*, the /ɛ/ of *head*, or the /æ/ of *bag*, in rather clearly defined regional dissemination. In addition, high-front /i ~ ɪ/ and mid-central /ɜ/ occur after the /k, č/ of *care, chair* in the folk speech of certain areas. All vowels tend to be short if the /r/ is preserved, longish or long if they are followed by /ə/, especially in Metropolitan New York.

In some areas usage is rather uniform, particularly in cultivated speech (see the insert on Map 38). Thus the phoneme /ɛ/ of *head* prevails in *stairs, care,* etc., throughout New York State, New Jersey, and Pennsylvania, the /æ/ of *bag* in the Upper South. Other areas, notably New England and the Lower South, are remarkably diversified and unsettled; here even cultured speakers differ from each other and fluctuate in their practice from word to word.

Setting aside for the moment the incidence of /i ~ ɪ/ and /ɜ/ in *care, chair*, the dissemination of the front vowels in *stairs, care,* etc., is as follows.

The vowel /ɛ/ of *head* (1) occurs regularly in the North Midland: in Pennsylvania with adjoining parts of Ohio, West Virginia, and Maryland; in New Jersey; and in Metropolitan New York. In Metropolitan New York *stairs, care* [stɛ˄·ə̯z, kɛ˄·ə̯] have a raised long [ɛ˄·] which could be taken as an allophone of the /e/ of *eight* rather than as /ɛ/. However, since *Mary* contrasts with *merry* as /mɛə̯ri : mɛri/ the latter interpretation is preferable.

/ɛ/ is (2) common in Upstate New York, western Vermont, and large parts of southern New England, competing with and apparently gaining ground from /æ/.

A third area in which /ɛ/ has extensive currency is the Lower South, especially the Low Country of South Carolina. Here it has the /e/ of *eight* or the /æ/ of *bag* as a competitor, the former in the Low Country, the latter in the Upcountry.

The raised low-front vowel /æ/ of *bag* occurs in *stairs, care,* etc. in three major speech areas: (1) the Upper South, including Virginia with adjoining parts of Maryland, southern West Virginia, and most of North Carolina; (2) the Upcountry of the Lower South; and (3) New England and the New England settlements to Lake Erie.

In the Upper South /æ/ is in rather general use on all social levels, in the Upcountry of the Lower South less so. The vowel is often prolonged in the Virginia piedmont, *stairs, care* being pronounced as [stæ·ə̯z, kæ·ə̯].

In New England /æ/ is common in the northeastern section (as far south as northeastern Massachusetts) and not uncommon on Cape Cod and in western Connecticut. Scatterings occur elsewhere in New England and in the New England settlements to the west beside the predominant /ε/. In Eastern New England disyllabic *care, theirs* [kæjə, ðæjəz] appear occasionally beside monosyllabic [kæə̯, ðæə̯z] under heavy stress, as in *I don't care, it's theirs*, which look like a blend of /kæə̯, ðæə̯z/ with the disyllabic prosodic variants [kejə, ðejə] of the type of /keə̯, ðeə̯z/ current in the same area.

The vowel /e/ of *eight* is much less widely used in *stairs, care, theirs*, etc., than either /ε/ or /æ/. It is characteristic of the Low Country of South Carolina and occurs more or less sporadically in New England. As pointed out above, the raised [ε^·] of Metropolitan New York could be taken as /e/ rather than as /ε/.

Besides the three vowels discussed above, three other pronunciations occur in folk speech in certain words: a high-front vowel /i ~ ɪ/, the mid-central vowel /ɜ/, and a low vowel [a ~ ɑ].

High-front /i ~ ɪ/ is widely used in *care, chair* throughout the South and the South Midland, and more or less scattered instances survive in parts of Pennsylvania and New England. The type of /kjɜ, ǰɜ/, derived from /kɪr ~ kiə̯, čɪr ~ čiə̯/, though occurring in the same general area, is regionally more restricted and less common. Virginia seems to lack it altogether. On the other hand, the folk speech of the piedmont of Virginia and adjoining parts of North Carolina have a low vowel [a ~ ɑ] in *stairs, theirs* (rarely in *chair*), which is partly merged with the /ɑr/ of *barn*, partly in contrast with it. All three folk pronunciations are clearly losing ground.

With the exception of the Virginian [a ~ ɑ], the American variants have their counterparts in the folk speech of England, though /æ/ and /ε/ are rare. /e/, pronounced as [e· ~ ε^·], is current chiefly in the eastern counties, /i ~ ɪ/ in the central and the western counties, while *care* as

/kjɜ/ occurs in the west. See the inserts on Maps 39 and 40. Standard British English has /stεə̯z, kεə̯/. The precise historical connections of the American variants with English variants is a problem for future investigation. However, one thing is clear: the extensive use of /æ/ in the South and the [a ~ ɑ] of Virginia are American developments.

4.6 THE VOWELS IN *poor, sure*

(Map 42)

/pur ~ puə̯ ~ pʊr ~ pʊə̯ ~ por ~ poə̯/

In *poor, sure* the high vowels /u ~ ʊ/ are in almost exclusive use in the North Midland and the North, except for northeastern New England. All of the South and the South Midland, on the other hand, have predominantly the mid vowel /o/, so that *poor, sure* rime with *four, shore*. Maryland west of Chesapeake Bay agrees with the South.

The high-back vowel current in the North and the North Midland ranges from a lowered [uˇ ~ uˇ·] to [ʊ ~ ʊ·], and its length varies. In Metropolitan New York the usual pronunciation of *poor* is [pʊ·ə̯], in Eastern New England [pʊə̯ ~ puˇə̯], in Upstate New York and Pennsylvania [puˇɚ ~ pʊɚ]. The variants [uˇ ~ ʊ^] are phonemically /u/; but since free /u/ does not contrast with checked /ʊ/ in this position, the phonemic status of the vowel is not always clear.

South of Pennsylvania the high vowels /u ~ ʊ/ are rare. In the South Midland they occur both in folk speech and in the speech of the better educated, in the South mostly in the speech of the cultured (presumably as an innovation). It is worthy of note that in Virginia all the cultured informants interviewed in the survey use the mid vowel /o/ in *poor* and *sure*.

In the South and the South Midland the /o/ of *poor, sure* /poə̯ ~ po ~ por, šoə̯ ~ šo ~ šor/ exhibits the same diaphones as in *four, door*.

As indicated above, the mid vowel /o/ occurs in *poor, sure* with some frequency in northeastern New England, notably in coastal Maine and New Hampshire. Only relics are found in eastern Massachusetts and in Upstate New York.

According to D. Jones (1956), Standard British

English usage is unsettled; though *poor, sure,* etc., are usually /puə, šuə/, such pronunciations as /poə ~ pɔə ~ pɔ/ also occur. The latter phonic types have widespread currency in the folk speech of the eastern counties lying north of the Thames, the former in the central and the southern counties. It is important to note that the dialects of the American North and North Midland agree with Standard British English in having contrasting vowels in *poor, sure* vs. *four, boar,* and that, on the other hand, the dialects of the American South and South Midland agree with the majority of the folk dialects of England in merging the vowels of these two sets.

4.7 THE VOWELS IN *four, boar, door, hoarse*

(Maps 43–44)

/for ~ foə ~ fo ~ fɔr ~ fɔə ~ fɔ/

Four, door, hoarse, etc., have either the phoneme /o/ of *road, know* or the /ɔ/ of *dog, law,* in rather clear-cut regional dissemination.

Dialects in which the vowel is articulated as [oˇ ~ o ~ o· ~ ou] clearly have the phoneme /o/ in this position, contrasting with the /ɔ ~ ɒ/ of *forty, horse, corn,* etc. On the other hand, dialects in which the vowel in *four, hoarse, torn,* etc., is pronounced as [ɔ ~ ɔˆ ~ ɔˆ·] have the same vowel in *forty, horse, corn,* etc., which may be a positional allophone either of the /o/ of *know, road* or of the /ɔ/ of *law, dog.*

The /o/ vowel is universal in the South and the South Midland, and nearly so in the New England settlements of the North.

In the South—from the Potomac to Georgia—*four, door,* etc., are usually pronounced as [fo·ə, do·ə], phonemically /foə, doə/, especially by cultured speakers. However, in the speech of the folk [fou] is common in the Virginia piedmont, [fo·] in South Carolina. The loss of /ə/ occurs here also to some extent in the speech of the middle group, but rarely among the cultured who occasionally use disyllabic [fouə, douə], phonemically /foə, doə/. In eastern North Carolina, where postvocalic /r/ is often retained, such pronunciations as [fouɚ ~ fouə, douɚ ~ douə], phonemically /for ~ foə, dor ~ doə/, are not uncommon.

The South Midland regularly has /for, dor/,

pronounced as [foˑɚ ~ foɚ], etc., the [o] being close and usually long. This pronunciation occurs as far north as the southwestern corner of Pennsylvania.

In New England and Upstate New York the vowel in *four, door,* etc. is usually rather short and not infrequently lowered. In Eastern New England, *four, hoarse* /foə, hoəs/ and *forty, horse* /foti, hɒs/ have strikingly different vowels. In Western New England and Upstate New York, such pairs as /for/ and /fɔrti/ have rather similar vowels, [oˇ ~ ɔˆ] and [ɔ ~ ɔˇ] respectively, and some speakers seem to merge them.

As pointed out above, the South, the South Midland, and the greater part of the North have contrasting /o/:/ɔ ~ ɒ/ in *four, hoarse* vs. *forty, horse,* etc. This contrast is lacking in a large area extending from Metropolitan New York and the lower Hudson Valley westward through New Jersey and Pennsylvania into Ohio, and from Pennsylvania southward to the Potomac River. The northern and the southern boundaries of this area are remarkably sharp, the former coinciding with a settlement boundary, the latter not; in the East, New York usage seems to be expanding into New England. Throughout this area the vowel in both sets of words is pronounced [ɔ ~ ɔˆ], long or short, but its phonemic status varies regionally.

In Metropolitan New York *four, hoarse* and *forty, horse* have exactly the same vowel phones as *law, loss, all,* long [ɔ· ~ ɔ·ə], which can only be taken as the phoneme /ɔ/. In word-final position, as in *four, door,* the vowel is usually followed by unsyllabic /ə/, so that *four* /foə/ often does not rime with *law* /lɔ/; but *hoarse, corn* /hɔs, kɔn/ regularly rime with *loss, lawn* /lɔs, lɔn/. It should also be pointed out that *law, seesaw* /lɔ, sisɔ/, etc., are sometimes pronounced with final ingliding [ɔ·ə], whose phonemic status is ambiguous. Shall we say that both *four, door* and *law, seesaw* have free variation /ɔə ~ ɔ/, or is the variation prosodic?

In Pennsylvania and in Maryland west of Chesapeake Bay, *four, hoarse,* etc. have the same vowel phoneme as *forty, horse,* etc., which is usually articulated as a raised [ɔˆ· ~ ɔˆ], but at times phonically identical with the [ɔ· ~ ɔ] of *law, loss,* etc.

In Western Pennsylvania, where *law*, *loss* have the same weakly rounded /ɒ/ phoneme as *lot*, *rock*, etc., *four*, *hoarse* and *forty*, *horse* clearly have the /o/ phoneme, articulated as a well-rounded [ɔ^ ~ ɔ], contrasting with the /ɒ/ of *car*, *garden*, etc.

In Eastern Pennsylvania and in Maryland the phonemic status of [ɔ^ ~ ɔ] before tautosyllabic /r/ is not so clear. However, since in these dialects the constricted /r/ tends to lower, or has lowered, the other high and mid vowels, as in *ear*, *poor*, *care*, the phones [ɔ^· ~ ɔ^] must be taken as lowered positional allophones of the /o/ of *know* rather than as raised allophones of the /ɔ/ of *law*. On the other hand, when the vowel in *four*, *forty*, etc. is phonically identical with that in *law*, *loss*, etc., we must recognize it as a member of the /ɔ/ phoneme. Such diversity of usage in dialects that lack contrastive /o : ɔ/ before /r/ is after all not too surprising.

The extensive preservation of contrasting vowels in *four*, *hoarse* vs. *forty*, *horse* in the Eastern States reflects the situation in the folk dialects of England. Coalescence occurs only in some of the eastern counties, and even here rather sporadically. According to Daniel Jones the merging is now complete in the cultivated speech of the London area; but this may well be of rather recent date. Though the usage of Metropolitan New York is practically identical with that of London at the present time, it may well have developed independently, as that of Pennsylvania surely has. The preservation of the contrast both in Eastern New England and in the South points to a late coalescence in Standard British English.

4.8 THE VOWELS IN *forty*, *morning*, *horse*

(Map 45)

/fɔrti ~ forti ~ fɔti ~ fɒti/

Except for Pennsylvania and adjoining parts of New Jersey and Maryland, all areas have the /ɔ ~ ɒ/ phoneme of *law*, *loss* in *forty*, *morning*, *horse*, which exhibits the usual regional diaphones in dialects that lack postvocalic /r/, but has more or less marked positional allophones in some dialects that retain it.

In areas that lack /r/ after vowels, *horse* /hɔs ~ hɒs/ rimes with *loss*, and *corn* /kɔn ~ kɒn/ with *lawn*. In Eastern New England the vowel

ranges from weakly rounded [ɒ· ~ ɒ] through raised [ɒ^·] to lowered [ɔ^·]; in Metropolitan New York it appears as [ɔ· ~ ɔ·ə], in Virginia as [ʊ· ~ ɔ·ə] or diphthongal [ɒɔ ~ ɔʌɔ], in the Low Country of South Carolina as [ɔ·ə ~ ɔ·], in the Upcountry as [ɒɔ] or [ɔ· ~ ɔ·ə]. With the exception of Metropolitan New York, these areas have the /o/ of *know* in *four*, *hoarse*, etc.

In areas that preserve postvocalic /r/, the /ɔ/ vowel in *forty*, *horse* /fɔrti, hɔrs/, etc., is usually shorter than in other positions, e.g., than in *loss*, *lawn*; it may be articulated as in other positions, or somewhat raised or constricted.

In Upstate New York and Western New England the /ɔ/ of *forty*, *horse* is extremely variable, ranging from [ɒ^ ~ ɔ] to [ɔ^ ~ oʌ]; the latter variants are nearly always raised positional allophones of /ɔ/, but some speakers seem to merge the vowel of *forty*, *horse* with the /o/ of *four*, *hoarse*.

In Pennsylvania, Maryland, and New Jersey the /ɔ/ of *forty*, *horse*, etc. usually has a somewhat higher tongue position than that of *law*, *loss*, etc., and must therefore be regarded as an allophone of /o/. Here the same vowel occurs also in *four*, *hoarse*, etc., so that *horse*, *morning* and *hoarse*, *mourning* are homophonous. The South Midland, however, has contrastive /ɔ : o/ in these pairs.

Western Pennsylvania has the phoneme /o/ in *forty*, *morning*, *horse* as well as in *four*, *mourning*, *hoarse*, as pointed out above.

On Delmarva the /ɔ/ in *forty*, *horse* /fɔrti, hɔrs/ is a weakly rounded [ɒ^] sound, as also in *law*, *loss*, etc. It is a unique feature of this dialect that this phoneme occurs also in *barn*, *garden* /bɔrn, gɔrdən/, so that *barn* rimes with *corn*.

Standard British English and the folk dialects of eastern England have /ɔ/. The unrounded [ɑ ~ ɑ] of the western counties of England is not reflected in American English.

4.9 THE VOWELS IN *barn*, *car*, *garden*

(Map 46)

/bɑrn ~ bɒrn ~ bɔrn ~ bɝn ~ ban/

With the exception of Western Pennsylvania and Delmarva, areas that preserve postvocalic /r/ as such have the checked vowel /ɑ/ of *crop*, *pot*, *rod*, etc. in *barn*, *car*, *garden*, etc. In Upstate New York and adjoining parts of New

England and Pennsylvania, the /ɑ/ is usually a low-central [ɑ], occasionally a low-front [a]; elsewhere it ranges from a low-back [ɒ] to a low-central [ɑ]. The low-back variant is especially common in the Philadelphia area, where it may even have slight rounding.

Western Pennsylvania has [ɑ ∼ ɒ] phones in *barn, garden*, etc., which must be taken as allophones of the /ɒ/ phoneme occurring both in *law, loss*, etc. and in *crop, lot*, etc. in this area.

Delmarva has a rounded low-back [ɒˆ] in *car, garden, barn*, so that *barn* /bɔrn/ rimes with *corn* /kɔrn/.

As pointed out in 3.20, the areas which do not retain word-final and preconsonantal /r/ as such, have the free vowel /ɒ ∼ a/ in *car, barn* /kɒ ∼ ka, bɒn ∼ ban/. In these dialects, /ɒ ∼ a/ occurs before intersyllabic /r/, as in *barring*, in Eastern New England and Metropolitan New York also in phrase sandhi, as in *far out*, occasionally even intrusively, as in *Ma and I* /mar ənd ai/. In the South this "linking" /r/ is uncommon.

4.10 The Vowels in *wire, tired*

(Map 47)

Three different vowel phonemes are current in *wire, tired, fire*: the /ai/ of *nine*, the /ɑ/ of *crop*, and the /ɔ/ of *corn*. Their dissemination is regional.

The phoneme /ai/, exhibiting largely its normal regional diaphones, (1) has general currency in the North, in the Hudson Valley with Metropolitan New York, and in East Jersey, (2) is nearly universal in the South, except for Delmarva, and well established in the Valley of Virginia, (3) predominates decidedly in Pennsylvania east of the Susquehanna, but is much less common to the west of it, and (4) is rare in the South Midland, from West Virginia to the South Carolina line, though apparently preferred by cultured speakers.

In Eastern New England, Metropolitan New York, and the Upper South—areas in which postvocalic /r/ does not occur—*wire, tired* are disyllabic /waiə, taiəd/; wherever the /r/ is preserved, these words are predominantly monosyllabic /wair, taird/, as in Western New England, Upstate New York, and Pennsylvania.

In the piedmont of South Carolina and adjoining parts of Georgia, where the /ai/ in *nine, five*, etc., is usually pronounced as an ingliding [a·ə] and postvocalic /r/ is largely lost as such, *wire, tired* are often pronounced as monosyllabic [wa·ə, ta·əd], phonemically /wai, taid/; but disyllabic [wa·ə ∼ wa·ˈə, ta·əd ∼ ta·ˈəd], phonemically /waiə, taiəd/, are also current. It is important to note that in this area *wire, tired* do not rime with *car, tarred* /kɒ, tɒd/, pronounced as [kɒ·, tɒ·d].

The phoneme /ɑ/ (Western Pennsylvania /ɒ/) occurs in *wire, tired* /wɑr, tɑrd/ throughout the Midland, except the Hudson Valley with Metropolitan New York. In the South Midland (West Virginia to North Carolina, but not the Valley of Virginia) it is nearly universal. In the North Midland, where it is clearly recessive, its frequency varies, being rather high in south-central Pennsylvania and adjoining parts of Maryland, low in eastern Pennsylvania. The merging of /ai/ with /ɑ/ before tautosyllabic /r/, which makes *fire, tired* homophonous with *far, tarred*, is a characteristic feature of Midland speech.

The merging of the sequence /air/ with /ɑr/ occurs also to some extent in eastern North Carolina.

The dialect of the Delmarva Peninsula and southern New Jersey is unique in that the three earlier sequences /air, ɑr, ɔr/, as in *wire, barn, corn*, coalesce in /ɔr/. Here *wire* rimes with *far* and *war, iron* with *barn* and *corn*.

Standard British English and the folk dialects of England seem to have only /ai/ in *fire, tired*, etc.

4.11 The Vowels in *flower*

In *flower*, the phoneme /au/ exhibits the usual regional and social diaphones. Disyllabic /flauə/, pronounced as [flaʊə ∼ flawə ∼ flæʊə ∼ flæwə], is regular in areas where postvocalic /r/ is lost as such. Elsewhere disyllabic /flauə/ occurs beside the usual monosyllabic /flaur/, especially under heavy stress and in phrase-final position.

A few speakers in eastern and western Pennsylvania have the /ɑ ~ ɒ/ phoneme in *flower*, pronouncing the word as [flɑɚ ~ flɒɚ], so that it rimes with *car* /kɑr ~ kɒr/.

4.12 THE VOWELS BEFORE INTERSYLLABIC /r/

Derivatives of monosyllabic words like *clearing, caring, barring, warring, boring, poorer* have, in the several dialects, the same vowel phonemes as the base forms. For this reason they do not require extensive treatment here. In a dialect, say that of Upstate New York, where *clear, care, bar, war, bore, poor* are /klɪr, kɛr, bɑr, wɔr, bor, pur/, the derivatives will appear as /klɪrɪŋ, kɛrɪŋ, bɑrɪŋ, wɔrɪŋ, borɪŋ, purər/. On the other hand, a dialect that has /klɪə̯, kæə̯, ba, wɒ, boə̯, puə̯/, as that of Eastern New England, will have /klɪə̯rɪŋ, kæə̯rɪŋ, barɪŋ, wɒrɪŋ, boə̯rɪŋ, puə̯rə/.

In plurisyllables not derived from monosyllables ending in historical /r/, such as *Mary, merry, marry*, etc., the incidence of vowels before the intersyllabic /r/ varies greatly from dialect to dialect, and there is considerable inconsistency and instability.

Some dialects have the vowel of *ear* /ɪr/ both in *diphtheria* /dɪfθɪrɪə/ and *syrup* /sɪrəp/, and that of *care* /kɛr/ both in *Mary* /mɛri/ and *merry* /mɛri/. Others have contrastive vowels in /dɪfθiə̯rɪə/ vs. /sɪrəp/ and in /meri ~ meə̯ri/ vs. /mɛri/, or the two sets differ in that *diphtheria* and *Mary* have an unsyllabic /ə̯/ between the vowel and /r/. Free /i, e/ contrasting with checked /ɪ, ɛ/ are largely restricted to dialects that lack postvocalic /r/, dialects in which the intersyllabic /r/ of *syrup, merry, Mary, glory*, etc., is articulated like a prevocalic /r/, i.e., as an apical alveolar consonant. Dialects that preserve the postvocalic /r/ usually lack these vowel contrasts and have a constricted /r/ in this position.

Only a few of the pertinent examples available in the collections of the Linguistic Atlas can be presented here. Tables in 4.3 exhibit the incidence of vowels before intersyllabic /r/ in a number of dialects. To convey their relation to vowels occurring before tautosyllabic /r/, examples for the latter have been included. It is only fair to warn the reader that the diversity in usage is greater than the simplified table indicates, and that some of the phonemic interpretations are not clearly established.

4.13 THE VOWELS IN *diphtheria*

(Map 48)

In large parts of the North and the Midland, *diphtheria* has the same vowel before the intersyllabic /r/ as *spirit, syrup*, namely the checked high-front vowel /ɪ/ of *six*, frequently lowered and/or centralized to [ɪˇ ~ ɨ]. In Eastern New England and in the South, on the other hand, *diphtheria* usually has the free high-front vowel /i/ of *three* before the /r/, and in Metropolitan New York and vicinity the sequence /iə̯ ~ ɪə̯/. Other vowels occur sporadically, as noted below.

In Eastern New England the stressed free vowel /i/ of *diphtheria* ranges from an upgliding [ij] to monophthongal [i ~ iˇ ~ ɪˆ], varying in length. Since high and mid vowels are usually lowered before /r/, the raised [ɪˆ] can safely be taken as a positional variant of free /i/. In Connecticut, western Vermont, and Upstate New York free /i/ is rare in this position.

The South, from the Potomac to Georgia, also has the free vowel /i/ in *diphtheria*, pronounced as a long [i· ~ iˇ· ~ ɪˆ·] or as a short [i ~ iˇ ~ ɪˆ], the long variants predominating in the Lower South, the short in the Upper South. This usage has spread into the eastern margin of the South Midland and has some currency north of the Potomac (Washington, Baltimore). On the other hand, the checked /ɪ/ of *syrup, spirit* is fairly common in *diphtheria* in parts of North Carolina, survives to some extent in Tidewater Virginia, and predominates decidedly north of the Potomac and on Delmarva.

A third area in which *diphtheria* has free /i/ contrasting with the checked /ɪ/ of *syrup* centers on the German settlements of eastern Pennsylvania (including Allentown, Reading, Lancaster, York). Since Pennsylvania German has long /i·/ before /r/ (as in /di·r/ "door") but lacks short /i/ in this position (German *wirt* "innkeeper" is /vɑrt/ in this dialect), this usage clearly reflects German speech habits. The fact that neither the vicinity of Philadelphia nor central Pennsylvania exhibit this usage confirms this interpretation.

Metropolitan New York and the lower Hudson Valley are unique in having the sequence /iə̯ ~ ɪə/ in *diphtheria* /dɪfθiə̯rɪə/, which in this dialect occurs also in *ear*, *here*, etc. This pronunciation is decidedly more common in Manhattan than in Brooklyn; it has been adopted by some speakers on the New Jersey shore and by many in the lower Hudson Valley east of the river.

Metropolitan New York shares this feature with Standard British English, but it would be rash to assume that the latter is its immediate or only source.

Two other pronunciations of the stressed vowel of *diphtheria* occur sporadically: the /ɛ/ of *merry* in Eastern New England, along the South Atlantic coast, in western North Carolina, and in West Virginia; the /ɜ/ of *furrow* in West Virginia, and in scattered instances from Chesapeake Bay to Albemarle Sound in North Carolina.

As pointed out above, the checked /ɪ/ of *syrup*, *spirit* predominates in *diphtheria* in the North, except for Eastern New England and Metropolitan New York, and in the North Midland, excepting only the Pennsylvania German area, and as far south as the Potomac. In the South Midland, /ɪ/ is common enough, but has several competitors, old and new.

4.14 THE VOWELS IN *cherry*, *merry*

(Map 49)

The word *cherry*, recorded in the compound *cherry tree*, predominantly has the checked vowel /ɛ/ of *ten* in all parts of the Eastern States, regularly so in cultivated speech.

In folk speech, and to some extent in the speech of the middle group, four other vowels occur besides /ɛ/: the checked /ɪ/ of *crib* in parts of New England and Upstate New York, the /ɜ/ of *first* chiefly in parts of Pennsylvania and West Virginia, the /ʌ/ of *sun* in parts of the Lower South, and the free /e/ of *eight* in parts of South Carolina and Georgia. Thus *cherry* sometimes has the same vowel as *spirit* in the Northern area; it rimes occasionally with *hurry* /hɜi ~ hʌri/ in parts of the Midland and the Lower South, and

with *Mary* /meri/ in South Carolina and Georgia. However, because of the great variability of the vowels in this position the phonemic interpretation of the phones often remains in doubt for lack of sufficient evidence.

In *merry*, recorded in the salutation *merry Christmas!*, the variants /ɪ/ and /ɜ/ are much less common than in *cherry*, where they are favored by the initial /č/. Since this salutation is little used south of Pennsylvania, the Atlas collections provide only fragmentary evidence for the South and the South Midland.

American is almost regularly pronounced /əmɛrɪkən ~ əmɛrəkən/. In folk speech, /əmɜəkən ~ əmɜrɪkən/ and /əmærɪkən/ occur sporadically, the former in New England, western New York State, western Pennsylvania, West Virginia, and the Eastern Shore of Maryland, the latter in northeastern New England and northeastern North Carolina.

4.15 THE VOWELS IN *Mary*, *dairy*

(Map 50)

Broadly speaking, *Mary* rimes with *merry* /mɛri/ in the Midland, but not in the South, while the North exhibits a rather complicated situation. In general, areas that lack postvocalic /r/ and have an apical /r/ between syllabics distinguish *Mary* from *merry*.

The area in which *Mary* is regularly homophonous with *merry* includes all of Pennsylvania, nearly all of New Jersey, Delaware, and Maryland, and all of West Virginia. This type predominates in the Valley of Virginia and in western North Carolina, is not uncommon in northeastern North Carolina and parts of Upstate New York, and occurs as a minority pronunciation in parts of New England.

Mary has the vowel /e/ of *eight* in two major areas: the South and New England.

From the Potomac southward /e/ has rather general currency, pronounced as an upgliding diphthong [eɪ] or, as in the Low Country of South Carolina, as monophthongal [e·] or ingliding [e·ə ~ eə]. This type appears to be spreading into western Virginia and North Carolina, replacing there the Midland /ɛ/, and is now fully established in the Upcountry of South Carolina and Georgia.

It has only a tenuous foothold north of the Potomac, is not current on the Eastern Shore of Maryland, and is still in competition with /ɛ/ on Albemarle Sound in North Carolina.

Mary /meri/ with the /e/ of *eight* predominates over other pronunciations in all of New England except southwestern Connecticut. In this position the /e/ is pronounced either as [eɪ] or as [e· ~ eᵊ ~ e], and thus clearly different from the /ɛ/ of *merry*. Relics of this /e/ survive in the New England settlements of Upstate New York, the northern counties of Pennsylvania, and even in Marietta, Ohio.

A third type of pronunciation is in regular use in Metropolitan New York and vicinity, and occurs with varying frequency in Upstate New York, in New England, on upper Chesapeake Bay (Maryland), and in Wilmington, N. C. Here *Mary* contrasts with *merry* as /mɛəri/ vs. /meri/, much as in Standard British English.

4.16 THE VOWELS IN *married, wheelbarrow, harrow, barrel*

(Maps 51–52)

Married has the /æ/ phoneme in all parts of the Eastern States, but /ɛ/ competes with it in several areas, and /ɑ ~ ɒ/ is rather common in the folk speech of Western Pennsylvania.

The vowel /ɛ/ predominates in northern West Virginia (where *marry* is often homophonous with *merry* and *Mary*); it is rather common in southwestern New England and in western New York State (Buffalo, Rochester and vicinity), and has some currency also in coastal New Hampshire, on Martha's Vineyard and Nantucket, in northeastern Pennsylvania, and on the lower Cape Fear River in North Carolina.

The vowel /ɒ/ is a characteristic feature of the folk speech of Western Pennsylvania. Elsewhere only scattered instances of /ɑ/ survive in *married*.

In *wheelbarrow*, a farm word, the vowel /ɑ/, varying regionally from [a ~ ɑ] to [ɒ], is much more common than in *married*. In folk speech it is rather generally used in all parts of the Eastern States, except southeastern New England, the rather densely populated area extending from the lower Hudson Valley to the lower Potomac (including New York City, Philadelphia, Balti-more, and Washington), parts of the Virginia Piedmont (Richmond and vicinity), and the Low Country of South Carolina with the lower Savannah Valley (Charleston, Savannah, Augusta). In an area extending from western Pennsylvania southward to western North Carolina, even middle-class speakers predominantly use /ɑ/ in this word, and not all cultured speakers avoid it.

In *harrow*, another farm term, the incidence of /ɑ/ and /ɛ/ is nearly the same as in *wheelbarrow*, but /ɑ/ is somewhat less common. On the other hand, the dissemination of these two vowels in *barrel* resembles that in *married*, though /ɑ ~ ɒ/ is more widely used in western Pennsylvania and occurs with some frequency in the Low Country of South Carolina.

In English folk speech the /æ/ phoneme in *married*, *harrow*, and *wheelbarrow* is confined to the eastern counties lying between the Thames and the Wash. Elsewhere [a ~ ɑ] sounds are in general use, which clearly stand back of the widespread occurrence of /ɑ/ in American farm words. American cultivated usage agrees with Standard British English in having /æ/ in these words, a fact that accounts for the extensive elimination of /ɑ/ in words that are not largely rustic.

The phoneme /ɛ/ occurring in these words in certain parts of the Eastern States seems to have no parallel in British English and may therefore be an American innovation.

4.17 THE VOWELS IN *tomorrow, borrow, orange*

(Maps 53–54)

Tomorrow has either the stressed vowel of *forty*, that is /ɔ ~ ɒ/, or that of *barn*, namely /ɑ ~ a ~ ɒ/; in some areas it is not clear whether *tomorrow* has an allophone of the vowel of *forty* or of *barn*.

An unrounded low vowel /ɑ ~ a ~ ɒ/ occurs in nearly all parts of the Eastern States, though with varying frequency, a rounded low-back vowel /ɔ ~ ɒ/ only in certain areas.

The South and the South Midland have /ɑ ~ ɒ/ regularly, with the possible exception of the Low Country of South Carolina. This type of pronunciation is also current almost universally in a large area extending from Maryland through eastern Pennsylvania to the Hudson Valley, including Metropolitan New York; less generally, though still predominantly, in Upstate New York and adjoining parts of Pennsylvania. It is relatively uncommon in Western New England.

More or less rounded low-back vowels occur in several separate areas.

New England predominantly has a more or less rounded [ɒ] sound in *tomorrow*, less commonly a well-rounded [ɔ]. In Eastern New England, where *forty*, *fog*, *frost* as well as *John*, *rod* have the phoneme /ɒ/, *tomorrow* clearly has /ɒ/. In Western New England, where *forty*, *fog*, *frost* have the phoneme /ɔ/ contrasting with the /ɑ/ of *John*, *rod*, the variants [ɔ] and [ɑ] are phonemically unambiguous; but the phonically intermediate variant [ɒ] can be as readily assigned to /ɔ/ as to /ɑ/, since these vowels do not appear in contrast before intersyllabic /r/ (*harrow*, *barrel* regularly have /æ/ here).

Western and central Pennsylvania usually have sounds ranging from [ɒ] to [ɔ˄]. In this area *law*, *lot*, *barn* generally have the phoneme /ɒ/; *four*, *forty* the phoneme /o/ of *road*, pronounced [ɔ˄ ~ ɔ]. Read against this background, the [ɒ ~ ɑ] phones in *tomorrow* belong to the /ɒ/ phoneme of *law*, *lot*, *barn*, the [ɔ ~ ɔ˄] phones to the /o/ of *forty*, *four*, *road*.

The [ɒ]-like phones occurring in *tomorrow* along with [ɑ ~ ɑ]-like phones in the Low Country of South Carolina and along the coast of Georgia and Florida belong to the /ɑ/ phoneme of *lot* (see 3.8 and Map 15).

Borrow exhibits the same pattern in the dissemination of the variants as *tomorrow*. *Orange*, on the other hand, though it follows the same pattern in the South and the South Midland and to some extent also in New England, exhibits a decided predominance of rounded [ɒ ~ ɔ], members of the /ɔ/ phoneme, in Upstate New York and the adjoining counties of Pennsylvania (in some parts to the exclusion of [ɑ ~ ɑ]), and is widely current in the Ohio Valley, including the greater part of West Virginia, where *tomorrow* and *borrow* have the unrounded vowel /ɑ/ almost universally.

In English folk speech, *tomorrow* and *borrow* have a rounded vowel in most of the eastern counties, hence also in Standard British English. All of the western and the central counties have unrounded varieties ranging from [ɑ] to [ɑ]. The diversity in American English and the predominance of the unrounded vowel before intersyllabic /r/ are, therefore, not surprising, especially since such words as *John*, *rod*, etc. have rounded vowels only in relatively small sections of the Eastern States.

4.18 THE VOWELS IN *furrow*, *worry*

(Map 55)

The pronunciation of these words varies regionally on all social levels. The chief types of variants are these:

(1) Disyllabic [fɚ·ə ~ fɝɚ] with constricted syllabic /ɜ/ and [fr·ə] with apical syllabic /ɜ/, the latter chiefly in western Pennsylvania, West Virginia, and adjoining parts of Ohio. Since the stressed syllabic exhibits the same regional diaphones as in *sermon*, *thirty*, etc., these variants of *furrow*, *worry* are to be taken phonemically as /fɜə, wɜi/. This type is current throughout the Midland except Metropolitan New York and vicinity, in Upstate New York and western New England, on the Delmarva Peninsula, and along the coast of North Carolina. In all of these areas *worry* rimes with *furry*.

(2) Disyllabic [fərə ~ fɵrə ~ fɝrə ~ fərə] with apical unsyllabic /r/, phonemically *furrow* /fərə/. These variants predominate in eastern New England and in the South (except for Delmarva and the coast of North Carolina), and have some currency in the German settlements of eastern Pennsylvania and in the southern part of the South Midland. Here, too, *worry* /wɜri/ rimes with *furry* /fəri/.

(3) Disyllabic [fʌrə ~ fɤrə] with apical /r/, phonemically /fʌrə/. This type is in regular use in Metropolitan New York and vicinity and occurs by the side of /fərə/ in eastern New England and the South. Speakers who use this type have contrasting vowels in *worry* /wʌri/ vs. *furry* /fəri/.

Types (2) and (3), which are current side by side in eastern New England and the South, are not always clearly differentiated in these two areas. Only further investigation will permit a definitive phonemic interpretation of phones ranging between [ɜ] and [ʌ].

Disyllabic [fɚ·ə] and [fɜrə] are occasionally reduced to monosyllabic [fɚ·] and [fɜ·], respectively, both of which are phonemically /fɜ/, homophonous with *fur* /fɜ/.

In cultivated speech *furrow* usually ends in /o/ rather than /ə/.

Standard British English has the type of /fʌro/, which, as we have seen, is now fully established in Metropolitan New York and occurs to some extent in other parts of the Atlantic seaboard. In English folk speech this type occurs only in the eastern counties north of the Thames, alongside of the more common /fɜrə/, which is the obvious source of the pronunciation that predominates in eastern New England and the South Atlantic States. The American Midland type of /fɜə ~ fɜo/, with constricted syllabic [ɚ], has its counterpart in the folk speech of the south of England and of the south-central counties of the Midland; it may well have been current in London English during our Colonial period.

4.19 THE VOWELS IN *squirrel, stirrup, syrup*

(Maps 56–58)

These three words exhibit the same regional types of pronunciation as *furrow, worry*, earlier /ɪ/ merging with earlier /ʊ/ before intersyllabic /r/. However, though earlier /ɪ/ and /ʊ/ regularly coalesce before tautosyllabic /r/, as in *fir* and *fur*, /ɪ/ sometimes remains distinct from /ʊ/ before intersyllabic /r/. The incidence of /ɪ/, or its derivative /ɛ/, varies greatly from word to word in American English.

Squirrel rather generally appears as disyllabic /skwɜəl ~ skwɜrəl ~ skwʌrəl/, exhibiting the same three regional types as *furrow*; but monosyllabic /skwɜl/, riming with the regional variants of *girl* /gɜl/, is not uncommon. Only scattered instances of /skwɛrəl ~ skwɛrɪl/ and /skwɪrəl ~ skwɪrɪl/ survive, notably in Eastern New England, on the Middle Neck of Virginia, and in the Low Country of South Carolina.

All American variants of *squirrel* have their counterparts in the folk speech of England: /skwɜəl ~ skwɜl/, with constricted syllabic [ɚ], in the southern counties (Kent to Devon and Gloucester); /skwɜrəl ~ skwʌrəl/ in East Anglia and parts of the Midland; /skwɪrəl ~ skwɛrəl/ in Essex, Middlesex, and parts of the Midland. Standard British /skwɪrəl/, rooted in the folk speech of Middlesex and Essex, has had no apparent effect on American usage, except perhaps in Boston, Mass., and Charleston, S. C.

In *stirrup* the variants /stɪrəp/ and /stɛrəp/ are much more widespread, though the variants /stɜəp ~ stɜrəp ~ stʌrəp/ occur everywhere and predominate decisively in the greater part of the Eastern States. /stɪrəp ~ stɛrəp/ are common in New England (but not in the usually conservative "Down East") and occur with some frequency in parts of Upstate New York, in Metropolitan New York, and in South Carolina. Elsewhere, as in southeastern Pennsylvania, eastern Virginia, and the Ohio Valley, they are rare. Outside New England, /stɪrəp/ seems to have prestige, as in the cities of Manhattan, Albany, Rochester, Buffalo, Newark, Philadelphia, Baltimore, Charleston, Savannah, Augusta, and Atlanta.

All American variants have their parallels in English folk speech; but the type of /stɪrəp/, fairly common in parts of the Eastern United States and accepted as Standard in England, is exceedingly rare in folk speech.

In *syrup* the vowel /ɪ/ occurs in the same areas as in *stirrup*, but is considerably more frequent, especially in Metropolitan New York and vicinity and in southeastern Pennsylvania. In all areas that have /sɪrəp/ at all, it is clearly preferred by many of the better educated speakers.

The Atlas collections do not contain the evidence for *spirit, mirror*, etc., but it may be safely assumed that /ɪ/ is much more common in these words than in *syrup, stirrup*, and *squirrel*, which were included in the survey because their pronunciation was known to vary regionally and socially.

CHAPTER 5

REGIONAL AND SOCIAL DIFFERENCES IN THE INCIDENCE OF VOWELS AND CONSONANTS

INTRODUCTORY REMARKS

FROM THE wealth of materials available in the collection of the Linguistic Atlas words are selected in which different phonemes occur in more or less clearly marked regional and/or social dissemination. Some of the words chosen are representative of a group of words that had the same vowel in earlier English; others illustrate divergent dissemination of the variants derived from one and the same source; yet others are isolated instances.

For each word included here the regional and the social dissemination of the several phonemic variants is briefly described. Prestige forms and relics are identified; trends in usage are pointed out whenever the record warrants such an inference from the distribution by social groups or age groups, or from comments of the informants and the field workers.

Most items are accompanied by one or more maps on which *selected* variants—usually the less common ones—are shown in full detail. If cultivated speech varies regionally, a small-scale insert exhibiting the usage of the cultured informants is included. Since the brief summaries of the dissemination of regional and social variants do not provide a complete picture, the reader will do well to consult these maps.

Although it would obviously be rash to relate American variants in precise terms to attested variants in Standard British English of the seventeenth and the eighteenth centuries or of the present, and to variants in the folk speech of present-day England, it has nevertheless seemed desirable to point out probable and possible connections. It is clear that many of the widely disseminated variants in American English stem from unsettled usage in cultivated British English of earlier days, and that other variants are derived from regional English folk speech or from regional adaptations of the Standard pronunciation about which so little is known. Statements made with respect to probable or possible connections should be regarded as suggestive rather than as definitive.

No attempt has been made to document Standard British English pronunciation in any detail or to report scholarly opinion regarding American usage exhaustively or consistently. Citations are made from the following works as the occasion arises:

Century = *The Century Dictionary:* An encyclopedic lexicon of the English language. Prepared under the superintendence of William Dwight Whitney. New York: The Century Company, 1889–95.

Jones = Jones, Daniel. *Everyman's English Pronouncing Dictionary.* Eleventh edition. New York: E. P. Dutton and Co., Inc., 1956.

Kenyon-Knott = Kenyon, John Samuel, and Knott, Thomas Alva. *A Pronouncing Dictionary of American English.* Revised edition. Springfield, Mass.: G. and C. Merriam Co., 1953.

OD = Oxford English Dictionary. Oxford: Oxford University Press, 1884–1933.

Walker = Walker, John. *A Critical Pronouncing Dictionary and Expositor of the English Language.* The second edition, with considerable improvements and large additions. London, 1797.

Webster = Webster, Noah. *An American Dictionary of the English Language.* Revised and enlarged by Chauncey A. Goodrich. Springfield, Mass.: G. and C. Merriam Co., 1847.

Webster 1934 = Webster, Noah. *Webster's New International Dictionary of the English Language.* Second edition. Springfield, Mass.: G. and C. Merriam Co., 1934.

Worcester 1860 = Worcester, Joseph E. *A Dictionary of the English Language.* Boston: Hickling, Swan, and Brewer, 1860.

Wright *EDD* = Wright, Joseph. *The English Dialect Dictionary.* London: Henry Frowde, 1898–1905.

Wright *EDG* = Wright, Joseph. *The English Dialect Grammar.* London: Henry Frowde, 1905.

Statements concerning pronunciations occurring in the English dialects are based almost entirely upon the wide-meshed field survey of the southern and the South Midland counties made by the late Dr. Guy S. Lowman, Jr. in 1937–38. Since Lowman used the same system of notation in England and in America, phonic types common to America and to the part of England investigated by him can be pointed out with assurance; but the phonemic status of these phonic types in the several dialects of the mother country cannot be determined with finality until the vowel structure of these dialects has been systematically analyzed. Hence, the comparison of American with English pronunciations is usually kept on a phonic basis.

Occasionally Lowman's data are supplemented from Joseph Wright's *English Dialect Dictionary* (1898–1905) and his *Dialect Grammar* (1905). Though Wright's notation differs markedly from Lowman's, rough correspondences between the two systems can be set up on the basis of their record for the southern and the South Midland counties, which furnish a key to Wright's notation of the dialects current farther north.

Needless to say, all statements concerning the regional dissemination of phonic types in England, in Scotland, and in Ireland are subject to revision. For England the survey now in progress under the direction of Harold Orton will furnish the data, for Scotland and Northern Ireland that of Angus McIntosh; for a survey of the English of Eire we may have to wait longer.

STRESSED VOWELS

5.1 /ɪ/ AND VARIANTS

bristle (Map 59)

The vowel /ɪ/ of *six* is current in *bristles* in all sections of the Eastern States. In the Midland and the South, this pronunciation is in universal use among all social classes. Under the influence of the preceding /r/, the vowel is frequently backed (sometimes to high-central [ɨ]) and occasionally slightly rounded.

In the North, usage is divided. Cultured speakers use only /ɪ/, as do most of the middle group and many old-fashioned speakers in urbanized

areas, such as Boston and vicinity, the cities of the Connecticut Valley, and especially Metropolitan New York and surroundings. On the other hand, *bristle* usually has the vowel /ʌ/ of *sun* in the rural folk speech of New England and Upstate New York, and in northern New England this pronunciation has considerable currency among middle-class speakers. This usage occurs also along the Atlantic coast in southern New Jersey. In general, /ʌ/ decreases in frequency as one goes west; it has been nearly eliminated in the vicinity of New York City.

This New Englandism has its counterpart in the folk speech of East Anglia and Essex. (Lincolnshire has the historically corresponding /ʊ/ in this word.) Moreover, /ʌ/ is current in the folk speech of the southern counties of England (Sussex, Dorset, Somerset). Under these circumstances it is a surprising fact that only two instances of /ʌ/ and one of /ʊ/ have been observed outside the New England settlement area.

rinse

In *rinse* the vowels /ɪ/ and /ɛ/ are current nearly everywhere, more or less in social dissemination.

Cultivated speech has predominantly /ɪ/, but instances of /ɛ/ occur, for instance, in Hartford, Conn., Brooklyn and Rochester, N.Y., York and Pittsburgh, Pa., and Richmond, Va. In such cities as Portland, Boston, New Haven, Philadelphia, Baltimore, Richmond, and Charleston, usage is divided, the cultured and some of the middle class using /ɪ/, the others /ɛ/; in other cities, as in Providence, Springfield, and Buffalo, /ɛ/ seems to have been eliminated.

In folk speech, *rinse* has predominantly the vowel /ɛ/ of *ten*, except in parts of southern New England, in western New York State, and perhaps in the Low Country of South Carolina. This pronunciation is also commonly used by middle-class speakers in northeastern New England, the rural parts of Pennsylvania, throughout the South Midland, and in the Upper South. All in all, there are social gradations in the use of /ɪ/ and /ɛ/ rather than sharp social boundaries, the drift being away from /ɛ/.

Other vowels are rare in *rinse*. In the southern Appalachians, the /æ/ of *pan* occurs beside /ɛ/ in folk speech, in eastern North Carolina, the /e/ of *pain*.

Both /ɪ/ and /ɛ/ were brought to this country from England. The variants existed in Middle English, survive in English folk speech of today, and had a social rating in London English of the eighteenth century not unlike that in present-day American English. Says John Walker (1797): "This word is often corruptly pronounced as if written *rense* . . . but this impropriety is daily losing ground."

5.2 /ɛ/ AND VARIANTS

again (Maps 60–61)

Again rimes either with *pen*, *pin*, or *pain*. The dissemination of the variants is largely social, but the frequency of their incidence varies markedly from section to section.

The /ɛ/ of *pen* is in fairly general use in cultivated speech throughout the Eastern States. Among the middle group of speakers, this vowel predominates in the North and the North Midland (except northeastern New England and Western Pennsylvania) and in the Low Country of South Carolina and Georgia; it is not uncommon in other parts of the South, but not between the James River and the Pee Dee. In folk speech, /əgɛn/ is in rather general use in most of southern New England, the Hudson Valley with Metropolitan New York and vicinity, Eastern Pennsylvania, and again in coastal South Carolina–Georgia; elsewhere it is much less common or not used at all.

Again with the vowel /ɪ/ of *pin* is widely used in folk speech in nearly all parts of the Eastern States. It is almost universal in northeastern New England, Upstate New York, Northern and Western Pennsylvania, West Virginia, and all of the South except coastal South Carolina–Georgia; it is fairly common elsewhere, except in Southern New England, the Hudson Valley with Metropolitan New York, and Eastern Pennsylvania. In middle-class speech, /əgɪn/ is much more restricted; it predominates over /əgɛn/ in large parts of the South, in West Virginia, and in Western Pennsylvania, but is uncommon to

rare elsewhere and lacking in metropolitan areas. Scattered relics of /əgɪn/ survive in old-fashioned cultivated speech.

The vowel /e/ of *pain* is decidedly uncommon in *again* and exhibits no marked social dissemination. It occurs especially in parts of New England, on Delaware Bay, in Tidewater Virginia and northeastern North Carolina (highly conservative areas), and again in the Savannah Valley; only scattered instances are found elsewhere.

Rare cases of /əgæn/, with the vowel of *pan*, occur in the North and the North Midland.

In English folk speech, *again* has the /ɛ/ of *pen* in the central counties (from Hampshire northward to Leistershire), the /ɪ/ of *pin* in the eastern counties (from Sussex to the Wash, including Middlesex), and various other vowels in the western counties. The vowel of *pain* is exceedingly rare in this word and shows no regional concentration. According to the *Oxford Dictionary* and Daniel Jones, Standard British English now varies between the /ɛ/ of *pen* and the /e/ of *pain*; John Walker (1797), Webster (1847), and Worcester (1860) record only /əgɛn/. The present diversity of usage in the Eastern States thus reflects the situation in the mother country at the time of settlement: the American prestige form /əgɛn/ is derived from its counterpart in Standard British English and the folk usage of the central counties, the folk variant /əgɪn/ from a regional English folk form, while the variant /əgen/ (from ME *again*) has a peculiar status both in England and in America.

deaf (Map 62)

Three different vowel phonemes occur in this word: the /ɛ/ of *left*, the /i/ of *leaf*, and the /ɪ/ of *stiff*.

/ɛ/ is current throughout the Eastern States. All cultured speakers have it (but six aged informants in New England, interviewed in 1931–32, still used /i/); it is the predominant and preferred pronunciation of the middle group everywhere except in parts of the South Midland (West Virginia and western North Carolina); it is regularly used on all social levels in some urbanized areas, notably in a belt extending from Metropolitan New York to Philadelphia, in the Buffalo-Rochester-Binghamton area in western New York State, and in the lower Hudson Valley.

In folk speech, partly also in common speech, *deaf* often rimes either with *leaf* or with *stiff* in the greater part of the Eastern States.

The vowel /ɪ/ of *stiff* is widely current in folk speech, and to some extent in the speech of the middle class, in a well-defined area extending from the lower Potomac southward to the valley of the Neuse in North Carolina, that is, in Tidewater Virginia (but not in Richmond) and in northeastern North Carolina (the Albemarle Sound settlement area). A fair number of relics of /ɪ/ survive also on Delmarva and in South Carolina; scattered instances are found in western Pennsylvania and the South Midland, and even in New Jersey.

Outside the /ɪ/ area described above, *deaf* has predominantly the vowel /i/ of *leaf* in the folk speech of the Eastern States, except for the urbanized areas mentioned above, in which /ε/ is universal or nearly so. In common speech its currency is more or less restricted to New England, central Pennsylvania, and the South Midland; even here it is yielding ground to /ε/, as the wavering usage of the middle group shows.

Rare instances of /e/, as in *safe*, have been observed in northwestern New England.

In Standard British English, *deaf* has the vowel /ε/ of *left*, and this pronunciation now predominates in the folk speech of the southern and the Southeast Midland counties. However, the /ɪ/ of *stiff* is regular in the southwest (Dorset, Somerset, Devon) and survives to some extent on the Wash, in East Anglia, and in coastal Sussex. The /i/ of *leaf* (the normal derivative of older /ē/) is not attested south of the Wash-Severn line, but is current in northern Lincolnshire, and (according to Joseph Wright, *EDD*) from northern Yorkshire northward, probably also in Lancashire and Shropshire.

English usage thus accounts for the use of /ε/ as the preferred pronunciation in America and the occurrence of /ɪ/ in the folk speech of the South Atlantic coast. On the other hand, the use of /i/ as the predominant folk pronunciation in the Eastern States is puzzling. Can it be that /i/ has sharply receded in the folk speech of England since the eighteenth century under the influence of Standard English?

egg (Map 63)

Egg has either the vowel /ε/ of *bet* or the /e/ of *eight*.

The checked vowel /ε/ is (1) universal in the North Midland, in all of New Jersey, the lower Hudson Valley (including Metropolitan New York), and on Long Island (except the southeastern prong). It is (2) in general use among cultured and middle-class speakers, though not among the folk, in the areas adjoining Pennsylvania to the south (Delaware, northern Maryland, West Virginia) and to the north (Upstate New York), as well as in large parts of western and southern New England. (3) Except for a few relics in folk speech, /ε/ also has general currency in the Low Country of South Carolina and in nearly all of Georgia. (4) Elsewhere in the Eastern States, checked /ε/ competes with the free vowel /e/ of *eight*, predominating two to one in the cultivated speech of New England and Virginia, and gaining ground among the middle class.

In two areas on the Atlantic seaboard, (1) parts of New England, and (2) the Upper South and parts of the South Midland (including all of North Carolina and the Upcountry of South Carolina), *egg* commonly has the vowel /e/ of *eight*, fairly regularly in folk speech, less so among middle-class speakers, least among the cultured (who prefer /ε/ two or three to one).

In New England, /e/ is most common in the northeast (New Hampshire and Maine), fairly common from Rhode Island to Cape Cod, and again in the rural parts of western Connecticut; elsewhere in New England it is rare even in folk speech, as also in the New England settlements to the west.

In the Upper South, /e/ is the predominant vowel in *egg*, except in cultivated speech, especially in Virginia and adjoining parts of North Carolina. However, the checked /ε/ of *bet* is clearly spreading. As pointed out above, relics of /e/ are found in folk speech to the north of this area (Delaware, Maryland, West Virginia), and rare instances survive in South Carolina and Georgia.

Since the checked front vowels /ɪ, ɛ, æ/ frequently have upgliding allophones before the fronted /g/ of *big, egg, bag* in the two areas in which *egg* has the vowel /e/ of *eight*, the replacement of /ɛ/, pronounced as [ɛ¹], by /e/, pronounced as /eɪ, e¹/, is easily understood. On the other hand, one is sometimes in doubt whether a particular pronunciation is to be taken as /ɛ/ or as /e/, especially when a speaker's articulation varies, as it often does. A comparison with the phones occurring in *ague*, which the Linguistic Atlas also records, usually leads to a decision.

In England, *egg* is pronounced as [ɛ¹g] by some folk speakers in the eastern counties (from Norfolk to Kent and Sussex), rarely elsewhere. Without deciding whether this pronunciation is to be taken as /e/ or as /ɛ/, one can safely say that it stands back of American /e/.

keg (Map 64)

Keg rimes either with *bag, beg,* or *plague.*

The /æ/ of *bag* occurs nearly everywhere in the Eastern States, but varies greatly in frequency, both regionally and by social groups. In the South Midland (all of West Virginia and the Southern Mountains), in Delmarva and Southern New Jersey, and in North Carolina it is in rather general use, except among cultured speakers. It is somewhat less common in Virginia, South Carolina (especially in Charleston and vicinity), and Georgia, where it competes both with /keg/ and /kɛg/. In the North, /kæg/ is the predominant variant in folk speech, but is uncommon among the middle group, except in Maine; even some cultured speakers still use it in New England. It is rare in the vicinity of Metropolitan New York and in large parts of Pennsylvania, and no longer current in New York City, Philadelphia, and other cities in this section.

Keg riming with *beg* is used by the great majority of cultured speakers in all parts of the Eastern States, has rather general currency on all social levels in the cities of the North and the North Midland, and is extensively used by middle-class speakers in the greater part of these areas. South of Pennsylvania, /kɛg/ is distinctly a cultured and middle-class pronunciation (except in Charleston, S. C. and vicinity). Among the middle group it is fairly common in South Carolina and Tidewater Virginia, rare in the rest of Virginia, in North Carolina, and in Georgia.

Beside the widely used /kæg/ and /kɛg/, a variant riming with *plague* (historically derived from /kɛg/) occurs not infrequently in three separate areas: New England, Virginia, and South Carolina. As in *egg*, which has /e/ much more extensively, it is sometimes hard to decide whether the upgliding phones [ɛ¹ ~ ɛɪ] before fronted /g/ are to be assigned to the checked vowel /ɛ/ or to the free vowel /e/.

Along the South Carolina–Georgia coast (Charleston to Brunswick), three elderly Negroes and one uneducated white offered /kag/, the Gullah variant corresponding to /kæg/.

The extensive use of /kæg/ in the Eastern States is not surprising. According to the *Oxford Dictionary*, the spelling *cag* is attested from 1452 to 1797, *keg* only from 1617 onward. Webster's *American Dictionary*, revised by C. A. Goodrich in 1847, recommends the spelling *cag*, and J. E. Worcester enters both *cag* and *keg* without comment in 1860. The recession of the pronunciation /kæg/ in cultivated and in middle-class speech is thus clearly a development of rather recent times. The survival of /æ/ in the speech of some elderly cultured informants in all parts of the Eastern States supports this interpretation.

kettle

With few exceptions, cultured speakers have the vowel /ɛ/ of *bet* in kettle. On the other hand, the /ɪ/ of *bit* is rather regular in folk speech, except for highly urbanized areas. The usage of the middle group varies, /ɪ/ being common in rural areas, as in northern New England, central Pennsylvania, the Appalachians, and the greater part of North Carolina, /ɛ/ elsewhere. In the more densely populated areas, especially in the cities, the middle group has largely abandoned the older /ɪ/.

Both pronunciations were brought to America from England. According to Joseph Wright's *EDG*, /ɪ/ is now current in the folk speech of all the southern and South Midland counties, /ɛ/ in the North Midland and the northern counties. American cultivated usage agrees with SBE.

muskmelon (Map 65)

This word is popularly pronounced *mushmillon* in the greater part of the South and the South Midland, much less commonly among the middle group than among the folk. This pronunciation is especially frequent along the Atlantic coast, from Chesapeake Bay to the Neuse in North Carolina, and again in western North Carolina; here a fair number of better educated speakers use it along with the folk. Elsewhere /mʌšmɪlən/ is not widely used by the middle group, and in Georgia, the Upcountry of South Carolina, and West Virginia even many of the folk have /ɛ/ in the second syllable.

In Pennsylvania, *-millon* is a fairly common pronunciation east of the crest of the Alleghenies, but not in the vicinity of Philadelphia; in New Jersey it still flourishes along Delaware Bay, but is rare in other parts of the state. In New York State and in northeastern New England only a few relics of *mushmillon* survive.

Scattered instances of the variant *-million* are found in sections where *-millon* is common.

yellow

The color name yellow regularly has the vowel /ɛ/ of *sell* in cultivated speech, although the vowel may be more or less backed before velarized intersyllabic /l/. This pronunciation is also generally used by middle-class speakers in the Eastern States, except for some sections of the South and the South Midland. It is, moreover, the predominant variant in the folk speech of New York State, New Jersey, and Pennsylvania with adjoining parts of Maryland.

In the folk speech of the South an almost bewildering variety of other pronunciations are current; some of them are also used in common speech, but largely avoided by the better educated.

The most common folk form of *yellow* is /jælə/, with the vowel of *Sally*. It is widespread in the South Midland and the South (except Georgia) and extends northward into Pennsylvania, though it is much less common there and does not occur in urbanized areas (Philadelphia, Pittsburgh, etc.). Relics are found even in New York State (and presumably in New England, where this word was not investigated). In parts of North Carolina

(the Blue Ridge and the Cape Fear Valley) this pronunciation reaches up into the middle class, rarely elsewhere.

The type of /jɑlə/, with the vowel of *hollow*, which is historically derived from /jælə/, occurs chiefly in Tidewater Virginia folk speech.

Yellow with the vowel of *silly* has a wider dissemination. It occurs in rather scattered fashion along the Southern coast from Delmarva to Florida, with some concentration in the Low Country of South Carolina and the Savannah Valley. A few instances have also been observed in the Blue Ridge. /jɪlə/, not infrequently pronounced with high-central [ɨ], is derived from /jɛlə/, probably before "clear" intersyllabic /l/.

The variant /jʌlə/, with the vowel of *color*, is also current in the South Atlantic States, especially in South Carolina and Georgia, where even middle-class speakers use it to some extent. [ə]-like phones are not uncommon in South Carolina and Georgia, which cannot safely be assigned to either /ʌ/ or /ɛ/. Similar phones observed in *yellow* by McDavid, a South Carolinian, in Upstate New York are most probably backed allophones of /ɛ/ before velarized /l/.

Confused as usage is in the South Atlantic States, there is nevertheless a rather well-defined trend toward /ɛ/.

All the variant pronunciations of *yellow* occurring in the Eastern States are found also in the folk speech of England, and in more or less the same proportion: /ɛ/ predominates in the eastern counties; /ɑ/ (corresponding historically to /æ/) in the west; /ʌ/ is attested in the counties of Norfolk and Hertford; /ɪ/ in Lincoln, Cambridge, and Devon, though sparingly.

yesterday (Map 66)

In folk speech, the first syllable of *yesterday* predominantly has the vowel /ɪ/ of *six* (1) in the South and the South Midland and (2) in large parts of New England. This pronunciation is less common in Upstate New York, rather infrequent anywhere in Pennsylvania, and decidedly rare in the heavily populated belt extending from eastern Pennsylvania (the Susquehanna Valley) to the lower Hudson Valley. In such cities as New York, Newark, Philadelphia, and Baltimore it is no longer heard even from the folk.

Among middle-class speakers, /ɪ/ is not uncommon in parts of the South (eastern North Carolina and the Blue Ridge province of the Carolinas) and in northern New England; elsewhere it is rather rare or not used at all. Cultured speakers use /ɛ/ almost without exception.

The centralized [ɪ]-like sound observed in the speech of some informants may be taken either as an allophone of /ɛ/ or of /ɪ/. Several speakers in South Carolina and Georgia have the vowel /ʌ/ of *just* in *yesterday*.

In English folk speech, the /ɪ/ of *six* is used in *yesterday* all the way from East Anglia to Gloucester and Somerset. Although rejected by John Walker (1797), it was widely current in Standard British English during the latter part of the eighteenth century, as also in *yes* (see Walker's comments).

5.3 /æ/ AND VARIANTS

aunt (Map 67)

Three different vowel phonemes are current in *aunt*: the /æ/ of *pant*, the /a ~ ɑ/ of *car*, and the /e/ of *paint*.

Outside of New England, /æ/ is nearly universal on all social levels in the North and the North Midland; only some cultured speakers in Metropolitan New York and Philadelphia use the /ɑ/ of *car* or the /ɑ/ of *lot* in this word, one of three cultured informants in Rochester, N.Y., and one highly educated speaker in the New England town of Marietta in Ohio. In the South Midland and the South, /æ/ is also the usual vowel on all social levels, except for a part of Tidewater Virginia.

In two areas, Eastern New England and Tidewater Virginia, *aunt* has predominantly the vowel occurring in *car*, *garden*, etc.: that is, low-front /a/ in New England, low-back to low-central /ɑ/ in Virginia.

In New England, the /a/ area extends from the Atlantic coast westward to the Green Mountains in Vermont, to the New York State line in Massachusetts, farther south only to the western boundary of Rhode Island. Within this area, /a/ is not universal; nearly everywhere some speakers

use /æ/, and in some localities—Nantucket, Marblehead, and the southern tip of Maine—/æ/ is in general use. No social prestige seems to attach to /a/ in this area; in fact, some speakers regard /a/ as old-fashioned.

Outside this area, /a ~ ɑ/ is partly a prestige pronunciation in Connecticut, and definitely so in New York City and Philadelphia, where it occurs only in cultivated speech. Whether Standard British usage has influenced the speech of some cultured New Yorkers and Philadelphians in recent times is an open question.

In Virginia, the /ɑ/ area is very restricted: it extends in the Tidewater area from the Rappahannock to the lower James Valley, an area dominated by Richmond. Outside this area, /ɑ/ occurs almost exclusively in cultivated city speech—as in Alexandria, Winchester, Charlottesville, Roanoke. As a prestige pronunciation it has also been adopted by better educated speakers on Albemarle Sound, N. C.

The few instances of /a/ recorded in *aunt* from Charleston, S. C. southward occur in folk speech (four of the six in the speech of Negroes). Here cultured speakers avoid /a/.

Aunt with the vowel /e/ of *paint* occurs in the folk speech of parts of the South and the South Midland. It is not very common, except in eastern North Carolina and southern West Virginia. Only a fraction of those who have /e/ in *can't* use it also in *aunt*.

Standard British English has the vowel /ɑ/ of *car* in *aunt*. This vowel, or /a/, is widely current in the folk speech of England south of the Wash-Severn line. The /æ/ of *pant*, on the other hand, is now confined to the eastern margin of East Anglia and to the southern counties (Sussex to Dorset and Somerset).

At first blush, the predominance of /æ/ in America is therefore rather surprising; but on second thought the mystery disappears. (1) Except for some relics of /ɑ/ in folk speech, as in *hammer*, *Saturday*, American English has /æ/ in such words as *apple*, *man*, etc., in agreement with East Anglia, Essex, Middlesex, Surrey, and Kent (all of the central, western, and northern counties still have an [a] sound). (2) Such words as *aunt*, *dance*, etc. had /æ/ in Standard British English until the latter part of the eighteenth century, and this pronunciation must have been current until the eighteenth century in the area that has retained /æ/ in *apple, man*, etc. Hence /æ/ was brought to America in *aunt, dance*, etc., along with the /æ/ in *apple, man*, etc., from the eastern counties of England.

The establishment of /a ~ ɑ/ in Eastern New England and in the Virginia Tidewater in such words as *aunt* is a more vexing problem. Was it imported from Standard British English during the latter part of the Colonial period and after, or had the split of /æ/ into /æ/, as in *man, apple*, and /a ~ ɑ/, as in *aunt, half, glass,* respectively, taken place, say in Middlesex-Essex, early enough to be introduced in America in the course of the settlement of Eastern New England and coastal Virginia? The striking fact is that this split is reflected only in two areas of early settlement which continued to have intimate commercial and cultural relations with London and with cultured Englishmen throughout the Colonial period and after. It is also significant that Eastern New England, which demonstrably derives other dialect features from East Anglia and the London area, is the area in which this split into /æ/ and /a/ has become most fully established.

calf, glass, dance (Map 68)

Words of the type of *calf, glass, dance*, in which the vowel is followed by a voiceless fricative or by /n/ plus a dental, have the vowel /æ/ of *bag* in all sections of the Eastern States, except that (1) in Eastern New England many speakers of all social levels use the /a/ of *car*, (2) some cultured urban speakers in other areas strive to adopt the /ɑ/ of *car*, and (3) some of the common folk (not the cultured) have a low-front [a] in such words along the coast of South Carolina and Georgia (from Charleston southward).

In New England, the type of /kaf, glas, dans/ is most common along the Atlantic coast, from Rhode Island to Maine, rather common in the upper Connecticut Valley, relatively infrequent in eastern Connecticut, rare in the western fringe of New England. Even in Eastern New England the incidence of /a/ in such words varies greatly. Many speakers freely shift from /a/ to /æ/ and back again in one and the same word. Some regard /a/ as refined, others as rustic.

Outside New England and the coastal belt in South Carolina, this type appears only as an occasional prestige pronunciation, as in Manhattan and Philadelphia, and along the Rappahannock in northern Virginia.

can't (Map 69)

In this word three different vowel phonemes occur in the Eastern States, largely in regional dissemination: the /æ/ of *pant*, the /e/ of *paint*, and the /a ~ ɑ/ of *car*.

/æ/, pronounced variously as [æ ~ æ· ~ æᵊ ~ æ¹], is nearly universal in the North and the North Midland, except for Eastern New England, and predominates decisively on all social levels in Virginia-Maryland (except for the Eastern Shore), and in the greater part of South Carolina–Georgia.

Low-front /a/, as in *car*, predominates in large parts of Eastern New England from Rhode Island to Maine. But there are two sizable pockets—southeastern New England (the Plymouth Colony) with the offshore islands and a coastal area extending from Marblehead, Mass., through New Hampshire into southern Maine (York County)—where it is rare. There is no marked social dissemination of /a/ and /æ/ in Eastern New England, but /a/ seems to be well established in such important cities as Boston, Providence, and Newport. In the lower Connecticut Valley, where /a/ is not common, it is apparently in part a prestige pronunciation (as in Hartford and Northampton), and clearly so in Manhattan, Rochester, and Philadelphia, where only some cultured informants use it.

In Virginia only four cultured speakers in widely scattered cities (Winchester, Fredericksburg, Gloucester, Roanoke—not Richmond) use the /ɑ/ of *car* in *can't*. In coastal South Carolina and Georgia, on the other hand, the occasional /a/ occurs only in folk and common speech.

In large parts of the South and the South Midland, *can't* has the vowel /e/ of *paint* in folk speech and in some sections also in common speech. This pronunciation predominates in folk speech, partly also in common speech, in the greater part of North Carolina and in adjoining parts of western South Carolina and Virginia, as well as in the southernmost counties of West

Virginia and in northern Georgia. It is rare, even in folk speech, in the greater part of Virginia, South Carolina, and Georgia, but has considerable currency on Delmarva. The location of the communities in Virginia and on the Eastern Shore of Chesapeake Bay in which *can't* is now pronounced as /kent/ by the folk suggests that this pronunciation has rather recently been eliminated in eastern Virginia, the major focal area of the Upper South. On the other hand, there is no evidence that it was ever current in the Low Country of South Carolina.

All three pronunciations of *can't* are current in English folk speech of today. The /æ/ of *pant*, the most widely used pronunciation in the Eastern United States, occurs only in scattered instances in eastern Norfolk, in Kent and Sussex, and again in Somerset and Gloucester. The /e/ of *paint*, pronounced as [e·ə], rarely as [e·ɪ], appears fairly regularly in the southern counties of Hampshire, Wiltshire, and Dorset and occasionally in the Midland counties of Cambridgeshire, Bedford, Northampton, and Warwick. The /a ~ ɑ/ of *car* is current everywhere else as well as in Standard British English. It appears to be clear that all three variants were brought to this country from England, and that /æ/ was much more widely current in England when the colonies were founded and during the Colonial period.

pasture (Map 70)

If the /a ~ ɑ/ area for *aunt* is extensive in New England and severely restricted in Virginia, the situation is reversed in *pasture*.

In this word /a/ is common only (1) in the Massachusetts Bay area and (2) in Maine from Casco Bay (Portland) eastward. Southeastern Massachusetts (Plymouth Colony) and Rhode Island lack it almost entirely, as do New Hampshire and adjoining parts of Maine. There is only a scattering of /a/ in the Connecticut Valley.

In Virginia, on the other hand, *pasture* is pronounced as /pɑstə/ from Chesapeake Bay to the Blue Ridge and southward into the north-

ern counties of North Carolina; it predominates, moreover, in highly conservative northeastern North Carolina from Albemarle Sound to the lower Neuse Valley.

In English folk speech this word is now rare in this sense; the few instances noted in the eastern counties have /a/, except for one /æ/ in eastern Kent. The common occurrence of /a ~ ɑ/ in Virginia, and especially in conservative eastern North Carolina and eastern Maine, can hardly be attributed to the influence of Standard British English after the settlement of these areas. It must have been brought to this country by the early settlers. It is presumably derived from the /a/ that prevails in English folk speech over large areas not only in *glass*, *bath*, etc., but also in *man*, *hammer*, etc.

raspberry (Map 71)

Raspberry has the vowel /æ/ of *bat* in all of the Eastern States. But in New England and the New England settlements to the west, rarely elsewhere, several other pronunciations are also current, although /æ/ predominates decidedly in cultivated speech (as in Boston, Providence, New Haven, Springfield) and has extensive currency among the middle group.

In northeastern New England the /ɒ/ of *law*, *loss* is rather common in *raspberry*, in Upstate New York the corresponding /ɔ/, which is also still heard to some extent in the folk speech of Western New England. /ɔ/ also has some currency along the Ohio River in West Virginia. It is largely a folk pronunciation.

A third vowel, the /a ~ ɑ/ of *car*, occurs with some frequency in southern New England and northwestern Vermont, and in scattered instances along the Great Lakes. In Eastern New England this vowel is associated with the free vowel /a/ of *car*, *glass*, *half*, elsewhere with the checked vowel /ɑ/ of *lot*. Outside the New England settlements only a few instances of an unrounded low vowel, either /ɑ/ or /ɑ/, have been observed (see the map).

Standard British English has /ɑ/; no information on folk usage in England is now available. American /ɒ ~ ɔ/ point to an early variant *rosp*-by the side of *rasp*-.

rather (Maps 72–73)

Rather was usually recorded in the phrase *I'd rather not*. It rimes with *gather*, *father*, *feather*, or *brother*. All four types can be heard in any major area of the Eastern States, but their regional incidence and their social dissemination vary markedly.

Rather with the vowel /æ/ of *gather* is the usual pronunciation among the middle class in the North and the North Midland. In southern New England, in Metropolitan New York, and in parts of Pennsylvania it is also fairly frequent in folk speech. The usage of cultured speakers varies within these areas: /æ/ is widely used by this group in Pennsylvania, except for Philadelphia and vicinity, in New York State, except for Metropolitan New York and vicinity, and in Connecticut; others have the /ɑ ∼ a ∼ ɒ/ of *father*.

South of Pennsylvania, /æ/ is the usual pronunciation of the vowel among the cultured, except in coastal South Carolina, Georgia, and Florida. Among the middle group, /æ/ is not as common here as farther north, and in folk speech it is decidedly rare.

Rather riming with *father* is strictly a cultivated pronunciation. It is fairly common in Massachusetts and Rhode Island, in Metropolitan New York and vicinity, in Philadelphia and surroundings, in Baltimore and Annapolis, in the Virginia piedmont (not in Richmond, Petersburg, or Norfolk), and in the Low Country of South Carolina. Elsewhere only scattered instances have been observed, as in Rochester, N. Y., Marietta, O., Greenville, S. C., and Atlanta, Ga.

In folk speech, *rather* has the vowel /ʌ/ of *brother* fairly generally throughout the South and the South Midland, in Delmarva, in New Jersey, and in northeastern New England, less commonly in western and northern Pennsylvania, rather infrequently in Upstate New York and southern New England, and rarely in or near the cities of the North and the North Midland. Among middle-class speakers this pronunciation is fairly common in parts of the South and the South Midland (but not in Virginia), in Delmarva and New Jersey, and in northeastern New England, rather rare elsewhere. In cultivated speech, /ʌ/ is rare, except along the coast of South Carolina, Georgia, and Florida.

Rather with the /ɛ/ of *feather* occurs to some extent in all of the major speech areas. It is not uncommon in New England, in Upstate New York, in parts of the North Midland, and in the Lower South. Though largely restricted to the speech of the folk and the middle group, it is used by some cultured speakers in the New England settlement area and in the Lower South.

As observed above, cultivated usage in the pronunciation of *rather* varies considerably within the Eastern States. The vowels /ɑ ∼ a ∼ ɒ/ of *father*, strictly an urban phenomenon, and the /æ/ of *gather*, exhibiting a much wider dissemination, have prestige; on the other hand, the /ɛ/ of *feather* and the /ʌ/ of *brother* are sharply recessive among cultured speakers, except along the coast of the Lower South.

All four types of pronouncing *rather* are derived from British English. Long low vowels [ɒ· ∼ ɑ· ∼ a·] occur in the folk speech of the eastern counties of England on which Standard British usage is based, [æ ∼ æ·] and the historically corresponding short [a] in the southwestern counties, [ʌ] chiefly in East Anglia, and [ɛ] in the central counties of the Midland. The extensive use of /ɛ/ and /ʌ/ in American folk and common speech is thus not surprising. American /æ/ as a prestige pronunciation derives from Standard British usage of the eighteenth century; the cultivated urban /ɒ ∼ a ∼ ɑ/ of the Atlantic seaboard must almost certainly be attributed to later importation from Standard British English.

It is of some interest to observe that *rather* with the vowel of *bathe*, current in Lincolnshire and, according to Joseph Wright, *EDG*, throughout the northern counties, has no counterpart in American English. This confirms the general impression that distinctive features of the dialects of the northern counties of England, of Scotland, and of Northern Ireland rarely survive in American English.

stamp (one's foot)

In this expression the verb *stamp* has a great variety of vowels in the Eastern States: the /æ/ of *lamp*, the /ɔ ∼ ɒ/ of *lawn*, the /ɑ ∼ ɒ/ of *calm*, and the /ʌ/ of *stump*. All of these pronunciations, except /ʌ/, are widely used and occur to some extent in all major areas and on all social levels.

The /æ/ of *lamp* predominates in most of New England, in Metropolitan New York and vicinity, and in southeastern Pennsylvania (also in Baltimore, Md.), notably in urban centers. In these areas most cultured speakers use this pronunciation, though some have /ɑ ∼ ɑ̈ ∼ ɒ ∼ ɔ/. Elsewhere in the Eastern States, /æ/ is largely a cultivated pronunciation.

The /ɔ ∼ ɒ/ of *lawn* is current in this expression in all dialect areas, excepting only the subareas where /æ/ is heavily predominant. South of Pennsylvania, /ɔ/ occurs on all social levels. It is here the usual pronunciation in folk speech, fairly evenly matched with /ɑ ∼ ɑ̈/ in common speech, and not infrequent in cultivated usage, especially in the Carolinas and in Georgia (but Charleston and Savannah have /æ/). /ɔ/ is also fairly common in central Pennsylvania, parts of Upstate New York, and western New England, but not in cultivated speech. The historically corresponding /ɒ/ prevails in western Pennsylvania and survives to some extent in Eastern New England.

The type of /stɑmp ∼ stɑ̈mp/ is extensively used in all areas with the exception of Eastern New England, Metropolitan New York, western Pennsylvania, and parts of the South Midland. It exhibits no marked social dissemination, occurring alongside of /æ/ in cultivated speech and of /ɔ/ in folk and common speech.

It should be pointed out that in the expression *stamp one's foot* the verb exhibits the same diversity of vowels as *launch* in the phrase *launch the boat*. In addition, *stamp* is occasionally homophonous with *stump* in areas where Pennsylvania Germans have settled in larger numbers.

In English folk speech of today, /stæmp/ is confined to the eastern counties (Kent to Norfolk) and the southwest (Somerset, Dorset, Devon). /stɒmp/ occurs in Middlesex and along the estuary of the Thames in Kent and Essex. [a ∼ ɑ ∼ ɑ̈] sounds, corresponding historically either to /æ/ or to /ɒ/, prevail everywhere else. In agreement with the eastern counties (but not Middlesex!) Standard British English has /æ/. Clearly, all American types of pronouncing *stamp* in this context, except /stʌmp/, have a British

background, and Standard British usage has lent prestige to /stæmp/ over the years.

catch (Map 74)

Catch rimes either with *match*, with *fetch*, or with *pitch*.

Of these three variants the /ɛ/ of *fetch* is by far the most common in the Eastern States. It is nearly universal in folk speech, except for parts of Pennsylvania and the vicinity of Metropolitan New York; it predominates decisively among middle-class speakers throughout the South and the South Midland (except Baltimore), and only less so in Upstate New York and Northeastern New England; moreover, it still has considerable currency in cultivated speech, especially in New England, western New York State, and the Low Country of South Carolina (where /æ/ is rare, except in Charleston).

Catch with the vowel /ɪ/ of *pitch* occurs with some frequency in the folk speech of New Hampshire and adjoining parts of Maine, and again on Cape Cod in Massachusetts; elsewhere only rare instances of /kɪč/ appear beside /kɛč/.

The incidence of the vowel /æ/ of *match* is decidedly restricted in *catch*, both socially and regionally. It occurs most frequently in cultivated speech; but /ɛ/ still predominates in South Carolina and western New York State, is fairly common in New England, and occurs sporadically elsewhere. In middle-class speech, /æ/ is fairly common in Pennsylvania, New Jersey, Metropolitan New York and vicinity, and southern New England; elsewhere it is unusual or rare, except in such cities as Baltimore and Charleston, S. C. Folk speakers have adopted /æ/ in fairly large numbers in Pennsylvania, Metropolitan New York and vicinity, and parts of southern New England (excluding eastern Massachusetts); but in other sections of the Eastern States /kæč/ is rare in folk speech or not used at all (except in the cities of Baltimore, Charleston, W. Va., and Charleston, S. C.).

All three variants of *catch* occur in the folk speech of England: /kɛč/ in all the eastern counties from the Wash to the Thames (including Middlesex), in all the southern counties from Kent to Devon, and northward to southern Warwick and Worcester; /kač/, corresponding historically to Standard British English and American /kæč/, in the central counties (west of the Ouse); /kɪč/ in scattered fashion within the /kɛč/ area. In Standard British English the pronunciation /kɛč/ was still common by the end of the eighteenth century, if John Walker (1797) can be trusted. He says: "This word is almost universally pronounced in the capital like the noun *ketch*; but this deviation from the true sound of *a* is only tolerable in colloquial pronunciation, and ought, by correct speakers, to be avoided even in that."

In view of the fact that /kɛč/ is current among the folk in such large sections of England to this day and was rather widely used by cultured Englishmen until after the American Revolution, its widespread currency in America and partial survival in cultivated usage is not surprising.

hammer, Saturday (Map 75)

These words regularly have the /æ/ of *bag*, except in three coastal areas, where relics of [a ∼ ɑ ∼ ɒ] sounds survive in folk speech: Eastern New England, the Virginia tidewater and piedmont, and the coast of South Carolina and Georgia. In New England and in Virginia, this type of pronouncing the stressed vowel in *hammer, Saturday* is almost entirely confined to the areas in which *pasture* usually has the free vowel /a ∼ ɒ/ of *father* on all social levels; in South Carolina, it is restricted to the coastal belt, where raised low-front [a^] is a social diaphone of the vowel /æ/ of *bag* (regularly so in Gullah, not infrequently in the speech of uneducated whites).

In New England and in Virginia these relics survive, or have been adapted, from English folk speech; in South Carolina their history is probably more complicated, because of the possible influence of Gullah upon the speech of the poor white. See the insert on the *hammer* map.

The extensive survival of /a/ in *hammer, Saturday* in northeastern New England supports the view that the /a/ in *half, glass, bath,* etc., more strongly entrenched in conservative Maine and New Hampshire than in Massachusetts, derives from English folk speech, but was later supported by Standard British English, which did not admit /ɒ/ in such words until the latter part of the eighteenth century.

radish (Map 76)

In cultivated speech *radish* has the vowel /æ/ of *bad*, except for a few scattered instances. This pronunciation also has rather general currency among the middle group, except in West Virginia, Maryland, Virginia north of the James River, and in parts of the Carolinas.

The vowel /ɛ/ of *bed* predominates decisively in the folk speech of the Eastern States, except in parts of New England, being in nearly universal use in the South and the South Midland. In middle-class speech it is rather uncommon in the North and the North Midland, but is widely used in West Virginia, Maryland, Virginia north of the James, and some parts of the Carolinas. Only a few elderly cultured speakers have retained it.

Several informants along the South Carolina coast say [radɪš].

The social dissemination of the variants clearly shows a trend toward /æ/ in common speech, except perhaps in some rural sections.

Standard British English has /æ/, as does cultivated American English; but as late as 1797 John Walker says in his *Pronouncing Dictionary* that *radish* is "commonly, but corruptly, pronounced as if written *Reddish*." In English folk speech of the present day /rɛdɪš/ is in rather general use north of the Thames, including Middlesex and Essex, /rædɪš/ and its western counterpart /radɪš/ to the south of it. The two American variants were obviously brought over from England.

sumac

The second syllable of *sumac* has either the vowel /æ/ of *back* or the /e/ of *take*, occasionally also the vowel /ɛ/ of *deck* or the /ɑ/ of *dock*.

/æ/ is almost universal in cultivated speech, except in parts of the Lower South (especially the piedmont of South Carolina and Atlanta, Ga.) and of West Virginia. Among the middle group, on the other hand, it is largely confined to the North and the North Midland, predominating decidedly over the /e/ of *take* in urbanized areas and only less so in the countryside. It is not common in folk speech, except in parts of New England and New York State.

Sumac with the vowel /e/ of *take* occurs everywhere, except in urban areas of the North and the North Midland (including Baltimore, Md.). In the South and the South Midland it is regular in common and in folk speech, and appears even in cultivated speech in parts of the Lower South and West Virginia. In the North Midland and the North, /e/ is rather frequent in rural folk speech but uncommon among middle-class speakers; only a few elderly cultured informants offered it in these areas.

The vowel /ɛ/ of *deck* occurs with some frequency on both sides of lower Chesapeake Bay and in west-central North Carolina (Raleigh to Charlotte), rarely elsewhere. It is a folk pronunciation, probably derived from half-stressed or ingliding /e/.

Scattered instances of the /ɑ/ of *dock* occur in *sumac* in the Hudson Valley and in Philadelphia, mostly in the speech of the better educated and the cultured (so in Albany, Manhattan, Newark, and Philadelphia), presumably as an overrefinement.

The seventeenth-century spellings *shoemake*, *shoomake* illustrated in the *OD* are good evidence for the currency of /e/ beside /æ/ in England at the time the American colonies were founded. Indeed, the widespread use of /e/ in the Atlantic States points to its extensive occurrence in England at that time, if only in folk speech.

tassel

Various vowels occur in this word: the /æ/ of *sack*, the /ɔ ∼ ɒ/ of *loss*, the /ɑ/ of *lot*, and the /a ∼ ɑ/ of *father*.

/æ/ is the usual vowel in cultivated speech throughout the Eastern States, though /ɔ ∼ ɒ/ are occasionally heard from cultured speakers in New England and South Carolina, and /ɑ ∼ a ∼ ɑ/ are attested in Providence, Manhattan, and Philadelphia. Among the other social groups usage varies regionally.

The /æ/ of *sack* predominates decidedly in the Upper South, in eastern Pennsylvania, in Metropolitan New York, and in southern New England; it is also common in the Lower South. Elsewhere this pronunciation is less frequent in common and in folk speech, and relatively unusual in parts of Upstate New York and the South Midland.

Tassel with the vowels /ɔ ∼ ɒ/ predominates in western Pennsylvania and the South Midland and is rather common in the Lower South, in Eastern New England, and in parts of New York State (especially the Mohawk Valley). It is not unknown in other sections of the Eastern States, but definitely uncommon in the Upper South. Only a few cultured speakers use it.

The vowels /ɑ/ of *lot* and /ɑ ∼ a/ of *father* are not very common in *tassel* but occur to some extent in most parts of the Eastern States, apparently without social implications.

5.4 /ɑ/ AND VARIANTS

calm (Map 77)

Calm was recorded in three different contexts: *the sea is calm*, in New England; *calm down!* (addressed to an excited person) and *the wind is calming down*, in the Middle and the South Atlantic States. Since the dissemination of the variants appears to be nearly the same in all three contexts, all instances of the word will be treated together.

With few exceptions (chiefly along the Southern coast), cultured speakers have the vowel of *barn* (i.e., either checked /ɑ/ or free /a ∼ ɑ/) in *calm*, with the usual regional variants ranging from front [a] through [ɑ] to back [ɑ] and [ɒ]. Throughout the North, including East Jersey and the northern counties of Pennsylvania, this pronunciation is also used almost without exception by the middle group and by the great majority of the simple folk. Elsewhere this vowel is much less frequent in common speech and rare in folk speech. Among middle-class speakers it is usual in Pennsylvania east of the Susquehanna (Philadelphia and the German settlements) and in South Carolina–Georgia, not uncommon in Western Pennsylvania, Virginia, and parts of North Carolina, rare in Maryland, Delmarva, and throughout the Blue Ridge and the Appalachians. In folk speech, *calm* with the vowel of *barn* is rather rare outside the North and eastern Pennsylvania, except for parts of South Carolina.

Calm with the vowel /æ/ of *bag* has extensive currency in the Midland and the South, except in cultivated speech. It is the predominant folk pronunciation throughout this far-flung area, being nearly universal outside of eastern Pennsylvania and parts of South Carolina. Though less common among the middle class, /kæm/ nevertheless predominates decisively in large parts of the Midland and the South, especially on Chesapeake Bay and in the mountains. On the other hand, in the New England settlement area this pronunciation survives only in the speech of a minority of the folk and has been completely eliminated in Metropolitan New York and its extensive hinterland (Long Island, the lower Hudson Valley, and East Jersey).

Several other phonemes occur sporadically in *calm*: the /ɔ/ of *law* in eastern Pennsylvania, the /ɒ/ of *John* in central and western Pennsylvania, and the /e/ of *eight* in eastern North Carolina.

In English folk speech of today, /æ/ (or a derivative [ɛ]) is current from Kent to Dorset (sporadically elsewhere), a low-front [a] sound in East Anglia and the Midland (here also in *man*, *bag*), a low-central or low-back [ɑ ~ ɑ̈] in the London area (as in Standard British English) and in the southwestern counties, and a low-back-round [ɒ ~ ɔ] apparently from northern Lincolnshire to Scotland. Though the precise relation of the variants occurring in the Eastern States is a matter for future investigation, it seems safe to say that all variants, except perhaps /e/, were brought to America from England and Scotland-Ulster. The /ɔ/ and the /ɒ/ survive in Pennsylvania from the speech of the Scotch-Irish, who settled there in large numbers; /a ~ ɑ ~ ɑ̈/ have their English counterparts in folk speech and the Received Standard; /æ/ must come partly from the /æ/ of the southern counties of England, but perhaps largely from Midland /a/, by replacement, as in *man*, *bag*, etc.

palm

Palm (of the hand) exhibits a regional and social dissemination of variants similar to that observed in *calm*, but in the Midland and the South the vowel of *barn* is decidedly more common in *palm* than in *calm*. In Pennsylvania, /ɔ ~ ɒ/ occurs as in *calm*, but rather more frequently; /e/, however, does not appear in North Carolina, since in the folk speech of the South and the South Midland *palm* has been largely replaced by *pan*.

cartridge (Map 78)

Beside the usual /ɑ ~ ɑ̈ ~ a/ of *car*, *garden*, etc., the stressed syllable of *cartridge* often has the /æ/ of *bag* in folk speech, in certain areas also in common speech. This pronunciation, resulting from the early loss of /r/ by dissimilation, is very common in northern New England and the greater part of West Virginia, less so in southern New England, Upstate New York, New Jersey, Pennsylvania, the Virginia Piedmont, and on Delmarva. It rarely survives in the Carolinas, and has been eliminated in Metropolitan New York and adjoining parts of New Jersey, the lower Hudson Valley, and western Connecticut. Cultured speakers avoid it altogether.

marsh (Map 79)

/ɑ ~ ɑ̈ ~ a/, as in *car*, are the usual vowels in *marsh*, but along the coast the /æ/ of *ashes*, pronounced as [æ· ~ æ] or [æɪ], survives to some extent in folk speech (owing to early loss of /r/ before /š/). The word nearly always refers to a salt marsh, and therefore has only limited currency in the upland.

hearth (Map 80)

Hearth, denoting either the floor of a fireplace or the firebox of a cast-iron stove, has several different vowel phonemes: the /ɑ ~ a ~ ɑ̈/ of *barn*; the /ɜ/ of *earth*, *thirty*; or the /æ/ of *care*.

The vowel of *barn* is regularly used in this word by all cultured speakers, except for a few in western Pennsylvania and along the coast of South Carolina who use also the /ɜ/ of *thirty*.

Among the middle group usage varies regionally: in the Upper South and the South Midland, the vowel of *barn* is nearly universal; in the Lower South and in urbanized parts of the North Midland and the North (especially in a broad belt extending from Washington-Baltimore to Metropolitan New York and vicinity) this pronunciation predominates; but in large parts of the North Midland and the North as well as the coastal plane of South Carolina–Georgia the vowel of *barn* is rather uncommon in *hearth* among this class of speakers.

In folk speech, /hɑrθ ~ hɑ̈θ/ is very common in the Appalachians and the Blue Ridge, in Maryland, in the densely populated area extending from Baltimore to the lower Hudson Valley, and in other urbanized sections from New England to Georgia; it is rather infrequent in rural parts of the North and the North Midland, and again along the coast of South Carolina and Georgia.

Of the two variants /hɜθ/ and /hæθ/, the latter is largely confined to the folk speech of the South, although a few instances occur in southern New Jersey and in the New England settlement area. Historically derived from earlier /hērθ/, with lengthening of the vowel before /rθ/, or from /hærθ/, with early loss of /r/ before a dental consonant, the pronunciation of *hearth* as /hæθ/ occurs only in areas that have /æ/ in *care, stairs*, etc.

Hearth with the vowel /ɜ/ of *thirty, sermon* is characteristic (1) of the North and the North Midland, and (2) of the Lower South, areas where it predominates decisively in folk speech and is rather common among the middle group, except in urbanized areas. In the Upper South it occurs only in coastal communities. Relics of /hɜθ/ survive in cultivated speech along the coast of South Carolina and in western Pennsylvania.

In the folk speech of England, *hearth* has the vowel of *barn*, except in the southwestern counties (Hampshire, Wiltshire, Dorset, Somerset, Gloucester), where the vowel of *earth* is current. Relics of /æ/ survive in the counties of Cambridge, Essex, and Oxford. All three American types have therefore an English background.

In Standard British English /hɑᵊθ/ was not fully established until the latter part of the eighteenth century. John Walker's comment (1797) makes this clear: "Till I had inspected the Dictionaries, I could not conceive there were two pronunciations of this word; but now I find that Mr. Elphinston, W. Johnston, and Buchanan, sound the diphthong as in *earth* and *dearth*." In cultivated American usage, /hɜθ/ survived regionally until recent times, though Webster (1847) and Worcester (1860) do not mention it.

crop (Map 81)

The usual vowel in *crop* is the checked /ɑ/ of *lot* with its normal regional diaphones; Eastern

New England and Western Pennsylvania have the /ɒ/ of *law, lot*.

The /æ/ of *cat* appears in *crop* in the folk speech of two areas: (1) the Atlantic coast from Chesapeake Bay to the Neuse River in North Carolina, and (2) the Appalachians south of the Kanawha River. It is rather more common along the Atlantic coast than in the Appalachians. Scattered instances survive in Pennsylvania and elsewhere.

yonder (Map 82)

This word was usually recorded in the phrase *over yonder*, an expression that has rather limited currency in the North and in urbanized areas of the Midland and the South.

The /ɑ ∼ ɒ/ of *lot* is the usual vowel in *yonder*, but a variety of other vowels have some currency, mostly in folk speech: in the North and the North Midland, the /ʌ/ of *sun* and the /ɛ/ of *ten*; in parts of the South and the South Midland, the /æ/ of *man*. See Map 82. It is not clear without further investigation whether South Carolina and Georgia have /ɔ/ beside /ɑ/ in *yonder*.

5.5 /ʌ/ AND VARIANTS

brush (Map 83)

Except for some relics of /ɛ/ in folk speech, *brush* regularly has the vowel /ʌ/ of *sun* in the North and the North Midland. In the South and the South Midland, even in the southern counties of Pennsylvania, this pronunciation is socially restricted. It is here used by all cultured speakers and by the great majority of the middle group, while the vowel /ɛ/ of *ten* predominates decisively in folk speech, except for the Low Country of South Carolina and most of Georgia. In the speech of the middle group, /ɛ/ is largely confined to the southern Appalachians and to the points of land along Chesapeake Bay.

A small number of informants in North Carolina, Virginia, and West Virginia have the vowel /ɜ/ of *thirty* in this word, pronounced as constricted [ɝ] or as [ɜr, ᵊr] in West Virginia, as unconstricted mid-central [ɜ, ɜ¹] elsewhere. This variant derives from /ʌ/ through the influence of the adjoining consonants and occurs more commonly among the middle group than among the folk.

bulge, bulk (Map 84)

Bulge has either the vowel of *hull* /ʌ/ or that of *bull* /ʊ/.

/ʌ/ is (1) nearly universal in the North and the North Midland, an area extending southward to the middle of Delmarva and the northern watershed of the Kanawha River in West Virginia. Baltimore has /ʌ/ on all social levels, but in Annapolis and Washington only the cultured speakers use it. Within this /ʌ/ area, a few informants still use /ʊ/ in New England, Upstate New York, Ontario, on the lower Susquehanna, and in northern West Virginia; in Ohio west of the Scioto River and in Ontario /ʊ/ seems to be more common. All in all, the line between /ʌ/ and /ʊ/ is clearly defined and coincides in its eastern sector with the well-known boundary between the Midland and the South, and in its western sector with that between the North Midland and the South Midland.

/ʌ/ is (2) also in general use on the South Atlantic coast from the mouth of Chesapeake Bay (Norfolk, Va.) to Florida. In the Carolinas this belt is about 100 miles in width and includes part of the lower piedmont (Raleigh, N. C. and Augusta, Ga. lie just beyond it, but Columbia, S. C. is in it). Some instances of /ʊ/ survive along the western edge of this belt and in the Savannah Valley; on the other hand, /ʌ/ has been adopted by some cultured informants in the cities of the upper piedmont as far west as Asheville, N. C., Greenville, S. C., and Atlanta, Ga.

Aside from the coastal area mentioned above, the South and the South Midland have the vowel of *bull* in *bulge*. This /ʊ/ area extends westward and southwestward from Chesapeake Bay in a broad sweep. Within this area, /ʊ/ is common to all social levels. The few instances of /ʌ/ in southern Maryland, in West Virginia, and in the Upcountry of the Carolinas occur almost exclusively in cultivated speech and may therefore be recent innovations.

In the word *bulk*, /ʌ/ and /ʊ/ exhibit the same patterns of regional dissemination.

In the folk speech of England, /ʌ/ is current in *bulge* throughout the South and East Anglia,

/ʊ/ from Northampton (the valley of the Nene) northward (as also in *thunder, sun*, etc.). Both pronunciations were obviously brought from England to all the colonies, whereupon either /ʌ/ or /ʊ/ became established in the several areas, so that *bulge* now has either the unrounded vowel /ʌ/ of *hull, gull* (as in Standard British English) or the rounded /ʊ/ of *bull, pull*, in regional dissemination.

gums (Map 85)

In the South and the Midland, *gums* regularly has the vowel /ʌ/ of *sun*.

Throughout the New England settlements of the Northern area usage varies. Cultured speakers use /ʌ/ almost without exception, but among the middle group and the folk the /u/ of *two* is as common as /ʌ/, and the /ʊ/ of *book* not infrequent. In northeastern New England and in the northern counties of Pennsylvania, /u ～ ʊ/ are especially common and firmly established; in southern New England and in New York State, there is a clear trend toward /ʌ/ among the middle group.

In English folk speech, /ʊ/ prevails in areas where *sun* also has /ʊ/, /ʌ/ elsewhere, except that the /u/ of *two* appears in some of the central counties beside /ʊ/. New England's /u ～ ʊ/ in *gum* is a normal descendant of the OE ō of *gōma*, but its immediate British background is far from clear.

judge (Map 86)

The vowel /ʌ/ of *sun* has universal currency in *judge* among all social groups in the North (except northeastern New England) and in the Midland; also in Delaware, Maryland, and the Valley of Virginia. South of the Potomac cultured speakers use it almost without exception, but not the folk or the middle group. Here the vowel /ɝ/ of *thirty*, with or without constriction, is fairly common in folk speech and not unknown in the speech of the middle class, but avoided in such cities as Richmond, Norfolk, Charleston, Savannah, Augusta, and Atlanta.

When the vowel in *judge* is more or less constricted, as often in Virginia and North Carolina, or an upgliding diphthong [ɝɪ], as occasionally in

South Carolina and Georgia, we clearly have the vowel /ɜ/ of *thirty*. When it is an unconstricted mid-central [ɜ ~ ɵ] sound, a decision can usually be made, but not always with certainty. In South Carolina, where *thirty* has an unconstricted [ɜ] sound that is markedly different from the [ʌ] of *hut, sun*, the phone [ɜ] in *judge* must obviously be taken as the phoneme /ɜ/ of *thirty*; the same is true of the unconstricted [ɜ ~ ɵ] of eastern Virginia. On the other hand, the [ɜ] phone in northeastern North Carolina and in the western tip of Virginia—areas in which *thirty, sermon* have both constricted and unconstricted /ɜ/ (varying from speaker to speaker or even in the speech of one and the same person)—it is not always easy to decide whether [ɜ] is to be taken as the phoneme /ɜ/ or as an allophone of /ʌ/, fronted to [ɜ] between the two palatal stops. In fact, one may have to admit that with some speakers the phonemic status of the phone [ɜ] is ambiguous in this word.

The transition from older [ʌ] to unconstricted [ɜ] between the two palatals is a simple case of assimilation; its replacement by constricted [ɝ] must have occurred in areas that had both the unconstricted and the constricted articulation of /ɜ/ in *thirty, sermon*, etc.

Other folk pronunciations of the vowel in *judge* occur sporadically in the North (especially northeastern New England) and in the Carolinas: the /ɛ/ of *egg* and (very rarely) the /ɪ/ of *big*, both obviously derived from /ʌ/ between the two palatal consonants.

mush, mushmelon (Map 87)

The checked vowel /ʌ/, which is current in *mush* in all parts of the Eastern States, commonly has an upgliding allophone [ʌᶦ ~ ʌɪ] before the /š/ sound on Delaware Bay in New Jersey, in Maryland, Virginia, and North Carolina, less commonly in West Virginia and adjoining parts of Ohio, and rather infrequently in South Carolina and Georgia. Scattered instances of this articulation of /ʌ/ occur also in Pennsylvania and in New England. It is less common in cultivated speech than in the speech of other social groups.

In Western Pennsylvania and in West Virginia, *mush* frequently has the constricted vowel /ɝ/ of *first*, especially in folk speech, a pronunciation

that occurs sporadically also in the Valley of Virginia and—with or without constriction—in the westernmost parts of Virginia and North Carolina. This /ɝ/ is derived from an earlier /ʌr/, with intrusive /r/ before /š/ (which also appears in *wash, Washington* within the same general area).

Several uneducated speakers in Manhattan and on Long Island say /muš/, riming the word with *bush*.

In *mushmelon*, a popular variant of *muskmelon*, the pronunciation of /ʌ/ as [ʌᶦ ~ ʌɪ] occurs in the same areas as in *mush*, but constricted /ɝ/ is confined to a rather small area in northwestern West Virginia (the valleys of the Monongahela and the Ohio), though scattered instances appear elsewhere in the Midland.

nothing (Map 88)

Throughout the South and the South Midland, *nothing* has only the vowel /ʌ/ of *nut*. This vowel is also regularly used by speakers of all social groups in the Philadelphia-Baltimore area, in Metropolitan New York, and in the valley of the Ohio and its tributaries in Pennsylvania, West Virginia, and Ohio. Moreover, /ʌ/ is used by all cultured speakers in the North Midland and the North and by a majority of the middle group, except in the rural northeastern section of New England.

In the North, the vowel of *lot, rod* competes in this word with the vowel /ʌ/ of *nut*. In folk speech, /ɑ ~ ɒ/ predominate decidedly over /ʌ/ in most of New England and Upstate New York and the greater part of New Jersey and Pennsylvania, as well as in the Yankee settlements of Northern Ohio. In middle-class speech they are largely confined to northeastern New England and some rural sections of the New England settlement area; in cultivated speech they have been abandoned. As in *lot, rod*, etc., the vowel in *nothing* is a more or less rounded low-back vowel /ɒ/ in Eastern New England and parts of Western Pennsylvania, an unrounded low-central or low-back /ɑ/ everywhere else.

Both /ʌ/ and /ɑ ~ ɒ/ came to this country from England. In present-day English folk speech, *nothing* has /ʌ/ in the central and the western counties, and /ɑ ~ ɒ/ in East Anglia and Lincolnshire, as well as in eastern Essex and in Kent and Sussex. The New England and Pennsylvania /ɒ ~ ɑ/ obviously derives from the usage of the eastern counties of England, which represents the normal phonemic development of a shortened ME /ọ/, whereas the /ʌ/ of Standard British and American English is aberrant.

Russia (Map 89)

The vowel /ʌ/ of *rush* is regularly used in *Russia* by cultured speakers, and with few exceptions also by members of the middle group. In folk speech, the /u/ of *two* and the /ʊ/ of *bush* occur beside /ʌ/, fairly commonly in northeastern New England and parts of West Virginia, less so in other parts of the North and the Midland, rarely in the South.

shut (Map 90)

The verb in the phrase *shut the door!* usually rimes with *bet* in the folk speech (1) of the South and the South Midland and (2) of northeastern New England, rarely elsewhere. In large parts of the South, this pronunciation is used also by some middle-class speakers, but not by the better educated. It is almost entirely avoided in cultivated speech.

In the Low Country of South Carolina and in Georgia, rarely elsewhere, the vowel in *shut* is rather frequently pronounced as a mid-central [ɜ] by speakers who pronounce the vowel in *worm* /wɜm/ without constriction, so that *shut* would seem to rime with *shirt* /šɜt/. Whether the speakers who use this pronunciation actually have the phoneme /ɜ/ of *shirt* in *shut*, or whether their [ɜ] is a fronted allophone of the vowel /ʌ/ of *hut*, induced by the preceding /š/, calls for a closer analysis than can be undertaken here.

The verb in the Southern expression *get shet (shed) of*, "get rid of (somebody)," current among the folk and in informal common speech, regularly rimes with *bet*. It contains a variant of *shed*, but some speakers "improve" upon folk speech by saying *shut* /šʌt/.

touch (Map 91)

This word, recorded in the sentence *Don't touch it!*, commonly has the vowel /ɛ/ of *fetch* in the folk speech of the South and the South Midland and not infrequently in that of northeastern New England (Maine). Elsewhere it is of rare occurrence, though some instances have been noted in all major dialect areas.

Touch as /tɛč/ is less common in Maryland, West Virginia, and Georgia than in most parts of Virginia and the Carolinas, where even some speakers of the middle group use it. It is rare in the cities of the South and is not used by any cultured speakers.

Two other pronunciations occur sporadically: (1) an [ɜ]-like sound in western New York State (here clearly a fronted allophone of the vowel /ʌ/ of *hut*) and in the Carolinas and Georgia (here either an allophone of /ʌ/ or of the /ɜ/ of *hurt*); (2) an [ɪ] or [ɨ]-like sound (only two instances in New Hampshire and one in South Carolina), which can be assigned to the /ɪ/ of *hit*.

Cultured speakers use only the /ʌ/ of *hut* in this word, and, except for parts of the South, also the middle group.

tushes (Map 92)

In the Eastern States *tushes* is the usual variant for *tusks* (of a boar), except in cultivated speech. It has the vowel /ʌ/ of *sun* regularly (1) in the North and the North Midland (except for rare instances in southern New Jersey and the southwestern corner of Pennsylvania) and (2) in South Carolina and Georgia, and overwhelmingly elsewhere, except in parts of West Virginia.

In northwestern West Virginia *tushes* is commonly pronounced with the constricted vowel /ɜ/ of *first*, both in folk speech and in common speech; this variant occurs also in the southern part of the state and, though less frequently, in parts of Virginia and North Carolina, rarely elsewhere.

Intrusion of constricted [ɚ] before /š/ occurs here also after the vowel in *wash*; in *tushes* the resulting [ʌɚ] was phonemicized as /ɜ/, whereas in *wash* /wɔrš ~ wɑrš/ the /r/ survives as a separate phoneme. It is worth noting that throughout the area in which *tushes* occurs as /tɜšəz/ many other speakers have an upgliding allophone [ʌᴵ] in this word as well as in *brush*.

5.6 /ʊ/ AND VARIANTS

butcher (Map 93)

In all of the Midland and the South, *butcher* has the vowel /ʊ/ of *foot*, except for a few relics of /u/ in the South, chiefly along the coast (Delmarva, Albemarle Sound, the estuary of the Neuse). /ʊ/ is also the predominant and favored vowel in the greater part of the North (the New England settlement area). It is used by most cultured speakers and, except for northeastern and southeastern New England, by the great majority of the middle group; urban areas (Metropolitan New York, Boston) have only /ʊ/.

Within the New England settlement area (the North without Metropolitan New York), *butcher* has /u/, the vowel of *boot*, with varying frequency. In northeastern New England (Maine and eastern New Hampshire), /u/ predominates decidedly on all social levels. In southeastern New England (from New London, Conn. to Cape Cod) this pronunciation is still very common, especially on the islands of Nantucket and Martha's Vineyard, west of Narragansett Bay in Rhode Island, and around New London; here even some cultured speakers use it, as in Providence and New London (but not in Newport). Elsewhere in New England, and in the New England settlements in New York State, northern Pennsylvania, and New Jersey, /u/ is now largely a folk pronunciation; it is rare in the greater part of Massachusetts, in all of Western New England, in the valleys of the Hudson and the Mohawk, and in New Jersey. Only a few relics have been observed along Lake Erie.

The pronunciation of *butcher* with the vowel of *boot* was brought to New England (and to other parts of the Atlantic coast) from the mother country, where it survives as a relic in the folk speech of eastern Essex County and still has extensive currency in Devonshire (which frequently reflects east country usage), pronounced as high-front [y·]. It is worth noting that /ʌ/, current in the folk speech of the southernmost counties of England (Kent to Dorset) as well as in Norfolk, has not survived in the Eastern States.

bushel, push (Map 94)

Three vowels are current in *push, bushel*: the /ʊ/ of *pull*, the /u/ of *pool*, and the /ɜ/ of *girl*.

Excepting West Virginia, *push* and *bushel* quite generally have the vowel /ʊ/ of *pull*. In large areas of the South and the South Midland, to some extent also in the North Midland and in New England, /ʊ/ occurs as an upgliding allophone [ʊ¹ ~ ɞ¹] before the /š/ of *push* and *bushel*. Retention of the rounding during the upglide has often changed the checked vowel /ʊ/ into the free upgliding vowel /u/ in West Virginia north of the Kanawha, less frequently elsewhere within the [ʊ¹]-pronouncing area. On the other hand, an intrusive constricted [ɚ] before the /š/ sound has led to the substitution of constricted /ɜ/ for /ʊ/ in the speech of several informants in northern West Virginia and adjoining parts of Pennsylvania. Both /u/ and /ɜ/ occur in the speech of the folk as well as in the speech of the better educated, but not in cultivated use.

In England only the [y·] of Devonshire appears to correspond to the /u/ of *bushel* current in West Virginia.

put (Map 95)

In the North and the North Midland, *put* has the vowel /ʊ/ of *book* on all social levels. From the Potomac southward and on the Delmarva Peninsula, only cultured speakers use this pronunciation consistently. In these areas *put* has the vowel /ʌ/ of *cut* rather generally in folk speech and not infrequently in the speech of the middle group. This usage prevails also in the upcountry of the Carolinas and to some extent in the valley of the Kanawha in West Virginia. Relics of /ʌ/ survive in the southern counties of Pennsylvania, in northern West Virginia, and in northeastern New England.

took (Map 96)

Besides the usual /ʊ/ of *book*, the vowel /ʌ/ of *luck* occurs in *took* rather frequently in the folk speech of the Carolinas, and of Georgia, West Virginia, Delmarva, and New Hampshire. Elsewhere only scattered relics have been recorded.

It is of some interest to observe that /tʌk/ is restricted to areas that have /ʌ/ in *hoof* or in *roof*.

5.7 /i/ AND VARIANTS

bleat

This word for the crying of a calf (or sheep) is used only in the North and the South; in the entire Midland calves are said to *bawl* (see Figure 16 in Hans Kurath, *Word Geography*), and city dwellers are apt to use *cry*.

In the North the word rimes with *bat* /bæt/, in the South with *bait* /bet/, with remarkable regularity. The variant *blat* occurs also in southern New Jersey and is known to one cultured informant in Philadelphia.

Within the /æ/ area of Eastern New England, two subareas — northeastern Massachusetts (Middlesex and parts of Essex County) and coastal Maine (from Casco Bay eastward)—commonly have the vowel /a/ of *car* in *blat*, and scattered instances of /a/ survive from Cape Cod to Narragansett Bay and elsewhere in New England.

Bleat with the vowel of *beat* is exceedingly rare.

In Standard British English (as in literary American English) *bleat* has the vowel /i/ of *beat*. In English folk speech, however, the /e/ of *bait* is widely used in this word, except perhaps in the central counties (see Wright, *EDG*, §§131, 132), and the /a/ of *car* is attested in the counties of Cheshire, Oxford, Buckingham, and Bedford. No evidence is available at present for the /æ/ of *mat*, which corresponds historically to the /a/ current in the counties mentioned above.

It is thus clear that Southern /e/, New England /a/, and almost certainly also Northern /æ/ were brought to America by the early settlers. In this rural expression, /e/ (from OE æ) has escaped the raising of /e/ to /i/ in our South. The history of /æ ~ a/ in this word is not clear; it could be of imitative origin or be influenced by *bah* /bæ, ba/, a synonym of *bleat*.

creek (Map 97)

Creek has either the vowel /i/ of *peak* or the /ɪ/ of *pick*. The dissemination of the variants is largely regional.

/i/ is in general use in the South, except for the South Carolina coast, and in the South Midland from the Kanawha River southward. Within this extensive area, the /ɪ/ of *pick* has some currency along the lower Potomac and in a pocket in western North Carolina (here clearly a survival of Pennsylvania usage). On the other hand, /i/ is used to some extent on upper Chesapeake Bay: by older persons on the Eastern Shore of Maryland; by younger and by cultured speakers—clearly as a prestige pronunciation—on the Western Shore, especially in Annapolis and Baltimore. /i/ has also been adopted by some younger and better educated speakers in the Valley of Virginia and in West Virginia north of the Kanawha (Charleston to Wheeling).

In coastal South Carolina, from the Pee Dee to the Savannah, /i/ and /ɪ/ are equally common. There is no marked social cleavage in usage, and in Charleston and elsewhere many speakers waver. Here the /ɪ/ of *pick* is clearly old in *creek*; it is noteworthy that it has not been accepted in the piedmont, as so many Low Country features have been adopted there.

The vowel /ɪ/ of *pick* predominates throughout the North Midland and the North, except for southern New England and, perhaps, Metropolitan New York. It has nearly universal currency in New Jersey, Delaware, Pennsylvania, and northern West Virginia, as well as in the valleys of the Hudson and the Mohawk in New York State and in northeastern New England and New Brunswick.

In southern New England, from Plymouth to the Housatonic in western Connecticut, /ɪ/ and /i/ are equally common, and the usage of some speakers fluctuates. The dissemination of the variants is local rather than social (e.g., Martha's Vineyard and the communities on the lower Connecticut have only /ɪ/, Rhode Island more commonly /i/).

Long Island has /ɪ/, which also predominates in Brooklyn. In Manhattan usage seems to be equally divided, but cultured speakers use the /i/ of *peak*.

In western Vermont (where *creek* means a fresh-water stream, as farther west), and in the northern and western parts of New York State, /i/ runs a close second to /ɪ/, especially in the speech of the better educated. Here /i/ is presumably derived in part from coastal New England (where *creek* means a tidal inlet of the sea; see Kurath, *Word Geography*, Figure 92); but the spelling of the word has doubtless been a contributing factor in favor of /i/. The rather frequent use of /i/ in Ontario and in northern Ohio has a similar background. In southern Ohio, however, /i/ is a contribution of the South Midland.

either, neither (Map 98)

These words were recorded in the phrases *nor I either* (*neither*), *me neither*, usually in emphatic utterance.

The vowel /i/ of *three* predominates decidedly on all social levels in all sections of the Eastern States (except parts of Pennsylvania, New Jersey, and Delmarva), and is almost the only pronunciation current in the North and the Lower South.

The most frequent variant has the vowel /ɪ/ of *pith*, which is rather common in parts of the North Midland (Delmarva, New Jersey, central Pennsylvania, and the section of West Virginia adjoining the Ohio River); it occurs also in parts of western Pennsylvania and is scattered through the Blue Ridge to western Virginia. Though most frequent in folk speech, it is also used to some extent by the middle group.

The second most common variant of the vowel in *neither* is /ʌ/, as in *mother*, which is fairly common in the folk speech of North Carolina and occurs in scattered instances elsewhere in the South as well as in northeastern New England.

The vowel /ɛ/ of *ten* is rare in this word; only a few instances have been observed in the Alleghenies and the Blue Ridge alongside the rather common /ɪ/.

Either with the vowel /ai/ of *five* is distinctly a sporadic feature of the cultivated speech of Metropolitan New York and Philadelphia, although scattered instances occur elsewhere in the North Midland and the North, even among the less educated.

In English folk speech (according to Wright, *EDG*) the types corresponding to American /i/ and /ai/ are widespread. Both have been current in Standard British English for centuries (see the note in the *Oxford Dictionary*), /aiðə/ apparently coming into favor during the nineteenth century. It is exceedingly unlikely that /ai/ has survived in America from Colonial times; it is in all probability a recent adoption from British English.

The English background of American /i/ and /ʌ/ in *either, neither* is not clear; they are presumably related somehow to the short [e] sounds current in large parts of England and Scotland.

Negro (Maps 99–100)

The pronunciation of this word varies greatly regionally and socially. In addition, many informants have both neutral (polite) and derogatory variants of this word; others avoid the word and use only the neutral or polite expressions *colored man, colored woman*, etc.

The most common pronunciations are /nɪgrə, nigro, nigro/ and /nɪgə, nigə/.

In the old plantation country of the South the usual neutral pronunciation of *Negro* is /nɪgrə/, with the vowel of *big*. In Maryland and in the South Midland (West Virginia to northern Georgia) this type is uncommon, elsewhere exceedingly rare.

/nɪgro/, with the vowel /ɪ/ of *big*, predominates in West Virginia, Maryland, Delaware, and New Jersey, and is rather evenly matched with /nigro/ in Pennsylvania and parts of northern New England. /nɪgro/ occurs also, along with other more common pronunciations, in parts of New England and New York State (including Long Island with Brooklyn), the Southern coast (including Charleston, S. C.), and in the Blue Ridge.

The type of /nigro/, with the vowel of *three*, is characteristic of most of New England and New York State (including Manhattan, but not Long Island with Brooklyn), and of Newark, N. J., and vicinity. In Pennsylvania, /nigro/ is as common as /nɪgro/, and is clearly preferred by cultured speakers in Philadelphia (and even in Baltimore); in the Ohio Valley it is used by a minority. Scattered instances of /nigro/ occur in parts of the South beside the usual /nɪgrə/, notably along the coast of South Carolina from Georgetown to Savannah. (In Charleston, five informants offered /nɪgrə/, five /nigro/, three /nɪgro/, and two /nigrə/ as neutral variants, and nine use /nɪgə/ contemptuously.)

The usage of cultured speakers exhibits the same regional diversity as that of the less educated. Northerners and Pennsylvanians say

/nigro/, less commonly /nɪgro/, Southerners predominantly /nɪgrə/.

The variant *nigger* /nɪgə ∼ nɪgɜ/ occurs fairly regularly in all parts of the Eastern States. Although it is the only variant of *Negro* that is used with disrespect or insultingly, it is nevertheless a neutral (even affectionate) expression in the speech of many. This is especially true of folk speech. It is significant that ten of the twenty-two Negroes interviewed in the South regard *nigger* as a normal neutral expression and only twelve (seven out of eight in South Carolina) avoid it as objectionable. A detailed analysis of usage as reflected in the 1450 informants interviewed for the Linguistic Atlas would give us a picture of the intricacies of relations and attitudes between black and white in the major speech and culture areas of the Eastern States.

5.8 /e/ and Variants

afraid

The vowel /e/ of *eight* is regularly used in this word, except in Virginia east of the Blue Ridge. Here *afraid* predominantly rimes with *bed* among all social groups; only three out of ten cultured informants interviewed in this area have the /e/ of *eight* in this word.

Scattered instances of the /ɛ/ of *bed* occur in the southern peninsula of Maryland, in the northern counties of North Carolina, and apparently in the Upcountry of South Carolina and Georgia.

There seems to be no evidence for /ɛ/ in English folk speech. The Virginian pronunciation of *afraid* may be due to shortening of earlier long *ē*, as in *bread*, or to an adaptation of the ingliding diaphone of the /e/ of *eight*, for which there is some evidence in tidewater Virginia.

drain (Map 101)

Drain rimes either with *rain* or with *bean*. The vowel /e/ of *rain* is used by all cultured speakers throughout the Eastern States. Among the middle group its frequency varies regionally, being fairly regular in the North and in Pennsylvania, but considerably less so in large parts of the South Midland and the South. In folk speech, /dren/ predominates only in Pennsylvania, the lower

Hudson Valley with Metropolitan New York, and parts of southern New England.

Drain with the vowel /i/ of *bean* is nearly universal in the folk speech of the South and the South Midland, rather common in the New England settlement area (except for Massachusetts and parts of New York State), but decidedly infrequent in Pennsylvania (except for the northern counties) and no longer current in the cities of the North and the North Midland. Among the middle group, /drin/ predominates in West Virginia and is not uncommon along Chesapeake Bay and on Albemarle Sound; it has some currency in other parts of the South and the South Midland, but is rare elsewhere (except for parts of northern New England).

Both types of pronunciation are still current in the folk speech of England, /drin/ especially in the eastern counties (from Kent and Sussex to Yorkshire; see Joseph Wright, *EDG*). According to the *OD*, the spelling *drean* occurs as late as 1615, which indicates that /drin/ was in cultivated use beside /dren/ when the colonies were founded along the Atlantic coast.

parents (Maps 102–4)

The vowel in this word exhibits all the variants occurring before the intersyllabic /r/ in *Mary*, *dairy* (see Map 50), and in addition the /æ/ current before the tautosyllabic /r ∼ ɜ/ in *chair*, *care* in certain areas (see Maps 38 and 39). The regional dissemination of the variants is analogous to that in *Mary* and in *stairs*.

English folk speech has all of these variants except /æ/, which appears to be an American innovation. /æ/ was presumably introduced in the monosyllabic pronunciation of *parents*, which has tautosyllabic /r ∼ ɜ/.

scarce (Map 105)

In addition to the great variety of vowels current in *care*, *chair* (see 4.5), *scarce* has the vowel phoneme /e/ of *eight* in the South and the southern sector of the South Midland. This pronunciation, resulting from the early loss of /r/ before /s/, is especially common in the Carolinas and in Georgia, and only less so along Chesapeake Bay. /skes/ is rarely used by cultured speakers and is not as frequent in the speech of the middle group as among the folk.

This expression was not investigated in New England.

tomato (Map 106)

Three different vowels occur in the stressed syllable of *tomato*: the /e/ of *eight*, the /æ/ of *mat*, and the /a ∼ ɑ/ of *car*.

/e/ is by far the most common pronunciation. It is universal, or nearly so, (1) in all of the Midland, from New Jersey and Pennsylvania to northern Georgia, (2) in the Carolinas and in Georgia, (3) in Maryland and Delaware, and (4) in an area including the Hudson Valley, southwestern Connecticut, Long Island, Metropolitan New York, and East Jersey. However, in areas (3) and (4) some cultured urbanites, and a few others, use the /ɑ ∼ a/ of *car*. In other parts of the North, even in some sections of Eastern New England, /e/ is at least as common as other pronunciations. In Virginia, /e/ predominates decidedly south of the James River, but has a serious competitor in the /ɑ/ of *car* to the north of it.

Tomato with the vowel /æ/ of *mat* is predominantly a folk pronunciation of the Northern area, but scattered instances of it occur on lower Chesapeake Bay and along the coast of the Carolinas. /æ/ is rather common in western New England and only less so in northern and western New York State; in rural areas even middle-class speakers use it, especially in western Vermont. In Eastern New England /æ/ turns up in scattered fashion from Cape Cod to eastern Connecticut (but not in Rhode Island), and again in New Hampshire and Maine. It is doubtless an old folk pronunciation in all of New England.

The /a ∼ ɑ/ of *car* has widespread currency only in two subareas of the Atlantic coast, Eastern New England and Eastern Virginia north of the James River. Within these two areas, its social dissemination is highly complicated.

In New England, /a/ is definitely preferred by cultured urbanites (as in Boston, Worcester, Providence, Newport, New London, Middletown, Springfield). On the other hand, it is rare in folk speech, except in parts of Maine, and not very common among the middle group.

In Upstate New York, /a ∼ ɑ/ occurs only in cultivated urban speech, perhaps in imitation of New England usage. Whether the preference for /ɑ ∼ ɑ/ among cultured speakers in Metropolitan New York, Newark, and Philadelphia is to be attributed to British or to New England influence, or to both, is an open question. Such supraregional cultural spreading of prestige pronunciations actually does occur in the Eastern States, but is rather unusual.

In Virginia north of the James the social status of /ɑ/ in *tomato* is not unlike that of /a/ in New England. It is widely used by cultured speakers in the cities (Richmond, Fredericksburg, Charlottesville, Alexandria, Winchester) and has been adopted as a prestige pronunciation in cities outside this area (Norfolk, Petersburg, Raleigh, Roanoke to the south, and Annapolis, Baltimore to the north). In the speech of the folk and the middle group it is decidedly less common than /e/.

On the coast of South Carolina only a scattering of /ɑ/ occurs. Charlestonians use /e/ predominantly, but /ɑ/ and /æ/ are also used here, seemingly without favoring one or the other.

In England, the /e/ of *eight* does not seem to occur at all in *tomato*, the /æ/ of *mat* only in the folk speech of some of the western counties (Devon, Dorset, Somerset) and in scattered instances elsewhere. The /a ∼ ɑ/ of *car* is in regular use elsewhere (even in the eastern counties that have /æ/ in *apple*), and of course in Standard British English.

The word *tomato* (earlier *tomate*) is an adaptation of Spanish *tomate* (from Nahuatl *tomatl*), which gradually replaced *love-apple* after 1775 both in England and in America. The foreign pronunciation with /a ∼ ɑ/ survives in British English and in eastern New England and Virginia—here largely in cultivated speech. Elsewhere in America, *tomato* was Anglicized either on the model of *potato* (current in English since c. 1550) or of such words as *matter*. The American adaptation is thus largely independent of British usage.

5.9 /u/ AND VARIANTS

broom (Map 107)

Broom has either the vowel /u/ of *two* or the /ʊ/ of *pull* in rather striking regional dissemination.

/u/ is decidedly the most widespread pronunciation, occurring with varying frequency in all parts of the Eastern States except northeastern New England and eastern Virginia. It is nearly universal in all of the Midland, from New Jersey to Ohio and southward through the Appalachians to Georgia; it predominates decidedly in New York State (including Metropolitan New York), in North Carolina, and in the greater part of the Lower South; moreover, /brum/ is nearly as common as /brʊm/ in large sections of southern New England.

Broom with the vowel /ʊ/ of *pull*, on the other hand, is largely restricted to three subareas of the Atlantic seaboard: New England, Eastern Virginia, and the Lower South.

In New England, /brʊm/ is nearly universal from the Green Mountains eastward as far as New Brunswick, predominates decidedly in Boston and vicinity, and is fairly evenly matched with /brum/ in the greater part of southern New England. It is of interest to note that Cape Cod, usually conservative, has predominantly /u/, while the equally conservative islands of Nantucket, Martha's Vineyard, and Aquidneck (with Newport) have only /ʊ/. There is no clear evidence that either of the two pronunciations has more prestige, except perhaps locally.

In the New England settlement area to the west and in Metropolitan New York, /brʊm/ is uncommon; it occurs sporadically on all social levels, but is perhaps somewhat more frequent in cultivated speech (as in Manhattan). In southeastern Pennsylvania, /brʊm/ is equally unusual, though four out of eight informants in Philadelphia offered it; here it is probably a prestige form, conceivably a Southernism.

Eastern Virginia and southern Maryland have the /ʊ/ of *pull* in *broom* almost without exception, and this pronunciation now has extensive currency northward to the head of Chesapeake Bay; but the less educated Baltimore informants and the majority of the older country people on the Eastern Shore of Maryland still say /brum/. In North Carolina /brʊm/ is uncommon, even along the Virginia line; it is clearly a prestige pronunciation in Edenton, Raleigh, Wilmington, Fayetteville, and Charlotte, adopted from Virginia and South Carolina.

In the Low Country of South Carolina and parts of the piedmont, /brum/ occurs as a minority pronunciation by the side of /brum/. Charleston and its hinterland between the Edisto and the Santee have almost exclusively the /u/ of *two*; the adjoining areas, both north and south, have the /ʊ/ of *pull* rather frequently, especially the coastal cities of Georgia and Florida (Savannah to St. Augustine). Scattered instances of /ʊ/ occur in the Upcountry of South Carolina and Georgia, largely in the speech of better educated urbanites (as in Greenville, Augusta, Atlanta).

A rather large number of speakers in nearly all sections of the Eastern States use a lowered monophthongal [uˇ] or a raised and ingliding [ʊ^·ᵊ, ʊ^ᵊ] in *broom* instead of the normal regional diaphones of /u/ or /ʊ/. These intermediate phones, shown on the map, are clearly positional allophones of /u/ in the Lower South, but are more probably unsystematized "compromise" pronunciations in other areas.

The word *room* exhibits a very similar pattern in the dissemination of /u/ and /ʊ/. On the other hand, before the /f/ of *hoof* and *roof* the regional dissemination of these two phonemes is radically different, and a third phoneme, the /ʌ/ of *cuff*, makes its appearance.

In English folk speech of the present day both types of pronunciation are current: /rʊm/ with the vowel of *pull*, *book* in the eastern counties (from Norfolk to Sussex, including Middlesex), /rum/ with the vowel of *two*, *tooth* everywhere else. American usage is therefore clearly derived from the mother country.

Standard British English must have had both pronunciations all along, although Daniel Jones is the first to report /rʊm/ as current in cultivated London speech besides /rum/. The location of London on the /u ~ ʊ/ isogloss and the prevalence of /rʊm/ in the three areas on the Atlantic seaboard that had the most intimate contact with the London area during the Colonial period and after permit this inference despite the silence of the dictionaries. It is even more surprising that the two Yankee lexicographers, Webster and Worcester, who must have heard /rʊm/ every day from the best of speakers, should have failed to book it in the middle of the 19th century. Following this tradition, *Webster's New International*

Dictionary (1934), though stating on p. xlix that "cultivated usage is divided" in *broom, room,* does not record /rʊm, brʊm/ in the body of the dictionary.

coop (Map 108)

The two different vowels occurring in *coop* (and its variant *coob*) exhibit a rather clear-cut regional dissemination: the North and the North Midland have predominantly, if not exclusively, the vowel /u/ of *two,* the South and the South Midland the /ʊ/ of *pull.*

The isogloss follows the state line between Pennsylvania and Maryland almost exactly, continuing eastward through New Jersey and westward through the panhandle of West Virginia into Ohio. To the north of this line, /kʊp/ is current to some extent along the Ohio River and again in the vicinity of Philadelphia. In the city itself /kʊp/ is rare now, although Philadelphia is unquestionably the old center of the /kʊp ∼ kʊb/ area on Delaware Bay and the Delaware Valley. In the Northern speech area, /kʊp/ occurs with some frequency only in western Connecticut, on Long Island, and in Metropolitan New York, but there are sporadic instances also in other parts of southern New England; here this pronunciation is chiefly found in the folk speech of rural districts and must therefore be old.

South of the isogloss described above, more or less scattered instances of /kup/ occur within this extensive /kʊp ∼ kʊb/ area: (1) in the Appalachians and the Blue Ridge, here doubtless of Pennsylvanian descent; and (2) in the Low Country of South Carolina, a long established pronunciation now largely confined to folk speech, but fairly common in Charleston.

On Delaware Bay and in the coastal plane of the Carolinas /kʊb/ predominates over /kʊp/, except in cultivated speech. Within this area the vowel is often pronounced as [ʊ·ə], and this prolongation occurs also in the Appalachians and the Blue Ridge (see the map) where the word ends in /p/. This phone has here been interpreted as a diaphone of the checked vowel /ʊ/ of *pull,* since the prolongation of checked vowels, especially before voiced consonants, is quite common in these areas; it may, however, be an unsystematized variant that cannot be unambiguously assigned either to /ʊ/ or to /u/.

Both /kup/ and /kʊp/ are now current in English folk speech, the latter much more widely than the former. Standard English has /kup/, which in folk speech is current in the eastern counties, though not in Suffolk and parts of Essex, Hertford, and Cambridge. The dictionaries, both English and American, deal with *coop* as they do with *broom.*

Cooper (Map 109)

In the family name *Cooper* the /u/ of *two* and the /ʊ/ of *book* occur in rather clear-cut regional distribution, /u/ prevailing in the North and in Pennsylvania (except Philadelphia and vicinity), /ʊ/ everywhere south of Pennsylvania. In the South and the South Midland, the clusters of /ʊ/ in West Virginia, the Valley of Virginia, and western North Carolina reflect Pennsylvania settlements. The only area in which usage is fairly evenly divided between /u/ and /ʊ/ is the thickly populated belt extending from western Connecticut through Metropolitan New York to Philadelphia and vicinity. No clear trend in usage is apparent, though cultured Manhattanites and Philadelphians use the /ʊ/ of *book* in this word.

Both /u/ and /ʊ/ are current in English folk speech, the former in the Home Counties and in a corridor leading northward, the latter in the southwestern counties and in parts of East Anglia and Essex. New England and Metropolitan New York usage seems to reflect the divided usage of the eastern counties of England; Southern /ʊ/ may be derived primarily from the western counties.

hoop (Map 110)

In *hoop,* the incidence of the /u/ of *two* is much more restricted than in *coop* or *Cooper.* It predominates over the /ʊ/ of *book* only in central and western Pennsylvania and in central and western Massachusetts. In other parts of southern New England and in parts of New York State it is used by a minority. Some instances of /u/ occur in the Pennsylvania settlements of the southern upland, and a few in the Low Country of South Carolina.

English folk speech has both /u/ and /ʊ/, disseminated much as in *Cooper*.

roof (Map 111)

Roof has either the vowel /u/ of *tooth* or the /ʊ/ of *wood*, chiefly in regional dissemination, in folk speech also relics of the /ʌ/ of *brush*.

/u/ is current to some extent in nearly all sections of the Eastern States, but with greatly varying frequency. It is universal in the Lower South and, except for some points of land along the coast, in the Upper South, as far north as Baltimore. It predominates decisively in Pennsylvania and in Metropolitan New York and vicinity, and is rather common in large parts of New England. In Upstate New York and the adjoining counties of Pennsylvania, /ruf/ is in the minority, as also in Connecticut and parts of eastern Massachusetts. It is rare on Delaware Bay, though regular in Philadelphia, and in West Virginia north of the Kanawha Valley together with the adjoining counties of Ohio.

Roof with the vowel /ʊ/ of *wood* is largely confined to three areas: (1) New England and its settlements to the west, (2) Delaware Bay, and (3) West Virginia north of the Kanawha. In West Virginia and the adjoining counties of Ohio it is nearly universal; on Delaware Bay (including all of southern New Jersey) it predominates decisively (but Philadelphia has /u/); in New England and its settlements it varies greatly in frequency, predominating decisively in Connecticut, Upstate New York, and parts of eastern Massachusetts, evenly matched with /u/ in northern New England, less common to rare from Narragansett Bay to Cape Cod and the islands. Scatterings of /ʊ/ survive along the Southern coast from Chesapeake Bay to the Neuse in North Carolina, and in the Valley of Virginia and the Pennsylvania settlements in the upper piedmont of North Carolina.

In areas where both /ruf/ and /rʊf/ are common, the former is apt to be used by the better educated speakers, especially in the cities; but there is no clear-cut class cleavage. In areas where one or the other pronunciation predominates, cultivated usage reflects the regional majority usage described above, with the possible exception of Boston and Philadelphia, which

have /u/ on the periphery of areas where /ʊ/ predominates.

Relics of /rʊf/ in the folk speech of the Southern coast permit the inference that the predominance of /ruf/ is of rather recent date in the Upper South; relics of /ʊ/ in Pennsylvania and the Pennsylvania settlements of the Valley of Virginia and western North Carolina, and especially the almost universal use of /ʊ/ in West Virginia (which cannot be of Southern origin), make it perfectly clear that /rʊf/ has given way to /ruf/ fairly recently in Pennsylvania.

The pronunciation of *roof* as /rʌf/ occurs only in folk speech; as such it is not too uncommon in northern New England, on Delmarva and Albemarle Sound, and in the Southern Appalachians, but rare elsewhere.

All three pronunciations were brought over from England, where they are still current in folk speech. Standard British English has /u/, the only pronunciation recorded in English and American dictionaries, except for Kenyon-Knott and Kenyon's note, §200, in Webster 1934.

hoofs (Map 112)

Hoofs, hooves have the same diversity in the vowel as *roof*, but the regional dissemination of the variants and their relative frequency is strikingly different.

The /u/ of *tooth*, which is almost universal in *roof* throughout the South and the South Midland, predominates in *hoofs* only in the Virginia piedmont and the southern upland; in North Carolina it is barely as common as /ʊ/ and /ʌ/, in most of South Carolina decidedly rare. Pennsylvania has /u/ in both words, but less extensively in *hoofs, hooves* than in *roof* (e.g., Philadelphians say /ruf/ but /hʊfs/). Elsewhere in the Eastern States /u/ is rare or not used at all. (Though this word was not investigated in New England, this assertion can be safely made by inference from usage in Upstate New York.)

All the areas that have the /ʊ/ of *wood* in *roof* have it also in *hoofs*, and with greater frequency. Moreover, /hʊfs/ has wide currency in parts of the South (as pointed out above) and is almost universal in Metropolitan New York and vicinity. Thus New Yorkers say /ruf/ but /hʊfs/.

The vowel /ʌ/ of *brush*, rare in *roof*, has rather extensive currency in *hoofs* in the folk speech of the Carolinas, parts of West Virginia, and Delmarva.

All three vowels are current in this word in English folk speech, nearly with the same regional dissemination as in *roof*. Standard British English has /u/. Except for Kenyon-Knott, American dictionaries record only /huf/, although /hʊf/ with the vowel of *wood* predominates in cultivated speech in all parts of the Eastern States, except perhaps Pennsylvania.

root (Map 113)

In *root* the vowel /u/ of *two, tooth* is universal in the South and the South Midland, and nearly so in the North Midland, the lower Hudson Valley with Metropolitan New York, and southeastern New England (Rhode Island, Cape Cod with the offshore islands, and the immediate vicinity of Boston). In the remainder of New England and in the New England settlements to the west, /rʊt/ is either in the minority or of rare occurrence.

Root with the vowel /ʊ/ of *pull, book* is largely confined to the New England settlement area. It predominates decisively in Connecticut, central and western Massachusetts, New Hampshire, Vermont, and Upstate New York, less so in Maine. There seems to be no marked social cleavage in usage, although /u/ is rather frequent in cultivated speech. Scattered instances of /rʊt/ occur in Metropolitan New York, New Jersey, parts of Pennsylvania, and the Ohio Valley (Marietta).

The type of /rʊt/ with the vowel /u/ of *two, tooth* predominates in English folk speech, but /rʊt/ is current in Suffolk, Sussex, and Hampshire, and not unknown elsewhere. American usage reflects this situation.

Standard British English has /u/, and, except for the *Century Dictionary* (1889), this pronunciation is the only one recorded in American dictionaries until recently.

soot (Maps 114–15)

Three different vowel phonemes occur in *soot*: the /ʊ/ of *foot*, the /ʌ/ of *flood*, and the /u/ of *food*. Their dissemination is partly regional and partly social.

/sʊt/ is the predominant pronunciation in the North and in large parts of Pennsylvania, but /sʌt/ and/or /sut/ are used by a considerable minority, the former especially in folk speech. This diversity is found even in the cities, although /sʊt/ predominates decidedly in Boston, Metropolitan New York, and Philadelphia, as well as in Baltimore. South of Pennsylvania this variant is uncommon and clearly a prestige pronunciation.

In the South and the South Midland *soot* has the vowel /ʌ/ of *flood* quite regularly in the speech of the folk and, with some exceptions, in that of the middle class; even cultured speakers use it, especially in South Carolina. /sʌt/ also predominates in some of the southern counties of Pennsylvania and adjoining parts of West Virginia and Maryland, in southern New Jersey, and again in northeastern Pennsylvania, but does not occur in cultivated speech. In the remainder of the North Midland and in the North it is rather strictly a folk pronunciation.

Soot with the vowel /u/ of *food* is much less widespread than /sʊt/ and /sʌt/ and has the earmarks of a prestige pronunciation. It occurs most frequently in the New England settlement area, but scattered instances make their appearance in all parts of the Eastern States, especially in cultivated speech.

The dissemination of the variants is far too complicated to be presented here in detail.

English folk usage appears to be equally confused, /ʊ/ being widely used, /ʌ/ chiefly in the central counties, /u/ only in scattered instances, except for Devonshire.

Some dictionaries give only /ʊ/, others /ʊ/ and /u/; none, except Kenyon-Knott, admit /ʌ/ as a pronunciation in good standing, although it is used unblushingly by cultured speakers in the Lower South and to some extent also in Virginia.

food (Map 116)

The vowel /u/ of *two* is in general use in *food*, except for Pennsylvania and some adjoining districts. In Pennsylvania the /ʊ/ of *good* predominates west of the Susquehanna, where it is used even by some cultured speakers. In Eastern

Pennsylvania, /ʊ/ is less common and sharply recessive. This pronunciation occurs also in the folk speech of northern New Jersey and the Catskills in New York State, and relics of /ʊ/ survive on Delaware Bay and in the Blue Ridge.

The word was not investigated in New England. From scattered relics of /ʊ/ along Lake Erie and in northern New Jersey, which cannot be of Pennsylvania origin, one may infer that this pronunciation has (or had) some currency in New England.

It is probable that Pennsylvanian *food* with the /ʊ/ of *good* is of Ulster Scots origin, since Joseph Wright, *EDG*, reports /ʊ/ from Cumberland, Westmoreland, and the Isle of Man.

wound, wounded (Map 117)

Except for New England, *wound* has the vowel /u/ of *two* among all social groups, either exclusively or predominantly. The vowel /au/ of *down* is common only in parts of New England. Here it predominates decisively in the folk speech of Vermont, New Hampshire, Maine, and rural sections of western Connecticut; in New Hampshire and Maine it is common enough in the speech of the middle group (though usually by the side of /u/), but rare elsewhere in New England; in cultivated speech it persists only in New Hampshire and Maine.

Outside of New England, *wound* with the vowel of *down* occurs only in folk speech; it is rather rare even on this social level, and large parts of the Midland and the South don't have it at all.

Rare instances of *wound* with the vowel /ʊ/ of *wood* have been observed in Upstate New York, and the vowel /o/ of *home* has some currency in folk speech along the coast of the Carolinas and Georgia.

According to Wright's *EDG*, English folk speech has the /u/ type in the northern counties and in Scotland (but not exclusively); /ʊ/ is current south of the Thames from Sussex to Wiltshire; /au/ in East Anglia, the southwestern counties of Dorset, Somerset, and Devon, and throughout a large area extending from Northampton-Gloucester into Yorkshire and Lancashire.

Standard British English had both /au/ and /u/ in the latter part of the eighteenth century.

John Walker (1797) puts /u/ ahead of /au/, but says: "The first pronunciation of this word, though generally received among the polite world, is certainly a capricious novelty . . . that the other pronunciation was the established sound of this word, appears from the poets, who rhyme it with *bound*. . . . This pronunciation [i.e., /u/] ought to be entirely banished. But where is the man bold enough to risk the imputation of vulgarity by such an expulsion?" This is a clear enough exposition of cultivated London usage at the turn of the eighteenth century; needless to say, the *Oxford Dictionary* (1928) recognizes only /wund/.

The New England lexicographers Webster (1847) and Worcester (1860) give both pronunciations, the former putting /au/ first, the latter /u/; *Webster's New International Dictionary* (1934) and Kenyon-Knott still recognize /au/ along with /u/, presumably as cultivated usage.

As far as the Eastern States are concerned, it is obvious that *wound* with the vowel /u/ of *two* has had predominant currency on all social levels in the South and the Midland. In New England alone has *wound* with the vowel of *down* been in cultivated use to any extent.

goober, cooter (Map 118)

Goober 'peanut' and *cooter* 'turtle,' taken from African languages spoken by the slaves in the South, have either the /ʊ/ of *book* or the /u/ of *two*. *Goober* is more widely current in Virginia than in the Carolinas and in Georgia; *cooter*, on the other hand, is confined to South Carolina and adjoining parts of North Carolina and Georgia. In *goober*, checked /ʊ/ prevails in the Virginia piedmont and stands beside free /u/ in the upcountry of the Carolinas and Georgia; in *cooter* /ʊ/ is restricted to the coastal plain of South Carolina and Georgia.

spook (Map 119)

This word came into American English from two sources: from the Dutch of the Hudson Valley with the /u/ of *two*, and from Pennsylvania German with the /ʊ/ of *book*. The word is unfamiliar to many Southerners and not generally current in New England, western Pennsylvania, and the Appalachians.

/u/ is the usual pronunciation in the North, /ʊ/ in areas where Pennsylvania Germans settled in large numbers. It is possible, but not very likely, that Pennsylvania German *spuck* is itself an adaptation of the Hudson Valley Dutch *spoek*, since this Dutch and Low German word appears in High German in the seventeenth century.

ewe (Maps 120-21)

Four types of pronouncing *ewe* are current in the Eastern States: /ju/, /jiu/, /iu/, and /jo/.

/ju/ is common in the North and in parts of the North Midland, especially in urbanized areas where the word is normally acquired in school or through reading. It is generally current among cultured speakers throughout the Eastern States, although many of them are familiar with the pronunciation /jo/ and some Southerners and South Midlanders do not hesitate to use it. Among the middle group, /ju/ is uncommon to rare south of Pennsylvania.

/iu/ and /jiu/ are confined to the New England settlement area, an area in which *beautiful, music,* etc., often have the decrescendo diphthong /iu/ instead of the sequence /ju/.

The type of /jo/ is heard in all parts of the Eastern States. In the South and the South Midland it has rather general currency, except among the cultured; in the North Midland it is common in rural areas but not in and around the large population centers; in the North it has been largely abandoned, except in the Catskills, in northeastern New England, and on the offshore islands of Nantucket, Martha's Vineyard, and Block Island.

In English folk speech, the type of *ewe* /jo/ has by far the widest dissemination. It is used quite generally in all of the southern and the southwestern counties and (according to Joseph Wright, *EDG*) from Lincoln and Yorkshire northward into Scotland, less commonly in the central counties. This obviously accounts for its widespread use in the Atlantic States.

The type of /iu/ is current in the eastern counties, from Kent and eastern Sussex northward to the Wash, whence it was brought to

New England along with /jiu/. According to Wright, /iu/ occurs, besides other pronunciations, also in some of the West Midland counties (southern Lancashire to Stafford, Derby, and Leicester), and Dr. Lowman recorded it in Warwick and Worcester.

Ewe as /ju/ has very limited currency in English folk speech, unless the variants [jʌu, jɑu, jɛu] historically belong to this type. It is common in Middlesex and Surrey and occurs in addition to other pronunciations in the valleys of the Severn and its tributaries, and besides /iu/ in Stafford, Derby, and southern Lancashire. This type, whatever its origin in precise terms, has been adopted from Standard British English into American cultivated speech and has acquired rather general currency in urbanized areas of the North and the North Midland, supported by the spelling.

5.10 /o/ AND VARIANTS

goal (Map 122)

The word *goal*, as used in children's games, regularly rimes with *pole* in all of the South and the Midland as well as in Northern cultivated speech.

In the North, from New England to the Great Lakes, usage varies socially and regionally. *Goal* with the vowel /u/ of *pool* is fairly general in the folk speech of this area (except in the cities), especially in New England. In northern New England, from Maine to Vermont, and in rural eastern Connecticut, this pronunciation predominates also in middle-class usage, a practice not unknown in Upstate New York and adjoining parts of Pennsylvania, though decidedly less common here.

Outside the New England settlement area, /u/ is rare in *goal*, except in the highly conservative southern section of Delmarva.

Is it possible that in this children's word /u/ is derived from those English dialects in which such words as *road, stone* now have the vowel phones [uə, ʊə]?

home (Map 123)

Besides the usual free vowel /o/ of *know*, two other vowels occur with some frequency in *home* as recorded in the expression *not at home*: checked /ə/ in New England, and checked /ʊ/ in Virginia.

Checked /ə/ occurs in *home* with about the same frequency as in *stone, road, coat* (cp. 3.19). It is common in northeastern New England and not infrequent in eastern Massachusetts, Rhode Island, and Connecticut. Though recessive, it is still used by some cultured speakers. In the New England settlements of Upstate New York, checked /ə/ has been nearly eliminated, except in the St. Lawrence Valley and along the shore of Lake Ontario.

Home with the vowel /ʊ/ of *book* has rather wide currency in large parts of eastern Virginia (not north of the upper Rappahannock or in the Norfolk area). It is common among the folk, less so among the middle class, rare among the cultured. Scattered instances occur in Delaware and in the Carolinas. The /ʊ/ in *home* is an isolated relic in Virginia speech; *stone, road,* etc., which had the same vowel as *home* in earlier English, regularly have the /o/ of *know* in this area.

In addition to the two regional variants discussed above, scattered instances of the /ʌ/ of *sun* and the /u/ of *two* occur in *at home*. The phonemic status of the short [o] sounds recorded sporadically in the Southern area is not clear; they may be prosodic variants of the /o/ of *know*, or blends of checked /ʊ/ with free /o/ as yet unsystematized.

Standard British English has the upgliding free /o/ in *home*. In English folk speech this type is rather narrowly restricted to the counties adjoining London—the so-called Home Counties. Elsewhere short ingliding [ʊᵊ ∼ oᵊ ∼ ɔᵊ] and short monophthongal [ʊ ∼ o ∼ ɔ˄ ∼ ʌ] prevail, which are reflected in the New England /ə/ and the Virginian /ʊ/, or else long ingliding [o·ᵊ ∼ u·ᵊ], with which the South Carolinian ingliding articulation of free /o/, as in *home, road, no*, etc., is doubtless connected. The prevalence of upgliding /o/ in America is a measure of the dominant influence of Standard British English.

loam (Map 124)

Loam has either the vowel of *home* or that of *room*.

The vowel /o/ of *home* prevails everywhere in cultivated speech and is very common in the speech of the middle group, except in some rural areas of the North and the North Midland.

Although this word was not systematically investigated in the South and the South Midland (since the wide-meshed preliminary survey showed that /o/ was in rather general use on all social levels), it is safe to say that *loam* riming with *room*, either with the free /u/ of *two* or the checked /ʊ/ of *book*, is confined to the North and the North Midland.

Checked /ʊ/ predominates decidedly in northeastern New England and New Brunswick, both in folk speech and in common speech, and is even used by some cultured speakers. It is also regular on the islands of Martha's Vineyard and Nantucket. Scattered instances survive in southern Vermont and on Long Island. (Cp. the incidence of /ʊ/ in *room, broom*.)

The free vowel /u/ of *two* is common in this word elsewhere in New England, and only less so in New York State, East Jersey, Pennsylvania (except the southeastern and south-central counties, including the Pennsylvania German settlements), and the Ohio Valley from Pittsburgh to Huntington, W. Va. As pointed out above, this pronunciation is characteristic of folk speech, but is also more or less widely used by the middle group in rural sections. It is rare in urbanized areas and not current in cultivated speech.

In the folk speech of England, checked /ʊ/ is largely confined to Suffolk, though not unknown in eastern Essex and in Hertfordshire; this is the obvious source of the New England /ʊ/ in *loam*. Free /u/, on the other hand, is widely used in the Midland and the south-central counties as far west as Hampshire and Oxfordshire, whence it was brought to New England and to Pennsylvania. Standard British /o/, which appears to be rare in English folk speech, is clearly the source of that pronunciation in America.

won't (Map 125)

Five different vowels are current in *won't*, that of *stone*, of *sun*, of *moon*, of *bull*, and of *lawn*. The /o/ of *stone* occurs in all parts of the

Eastern States, but with great variation in frequency. It is nearly universal (1) in the Midland, from Pennsylvania to northern Georgia; (2) in the Upper South, including the northern counties of North Carolina; and (3) in Georgia and adjoining parts of South Carolina. In the North, /o/ is rather uncommon, except in southern New England; in Metropolitan New York and vicinity it is rare. In the Low Country of South Carolina, coastal Georgia and Florida, and southeastern North Carolina usage is rather evenly divided between /o/ and /u ∼ ʊ/.

Won't with the vowel /ʌ/ of *sun* predominates in New England and in the New England settlements along the Great Lakes and in the northern counties of Pennsylvania. It is nearly universal on all social levels in northern New England and large parts of Upstate New York. In southern New England, /o/ is replacing, or has replaced, /ʌ/ in cultivated urban speech, as in Boston, Worcester, Providence, Newport, New London, New Haven, Hartford, and Springfield; a similar trend is noticeable in Upstate New York. Whether some New Englanders substitute the checked /ɵ/ of *home* rather than the free /o/ of *know* for /ʌ/ is an open question.

Outside the New England settlement area, the /ʌ/ of *sun* is exceedingly rare in *won't*.

Won't with the vowel /u/ of *moon* is a striking feature of the speech (1) of Metropolitan New York and vicinity and (2) the Carolina coast, and is not unknown (3) on the Eastern Shore of Maryland.

In New York City, on Long Island, in the lower Hudson Valley, and on the Jersey shore, /u/ is used rather generally by all social groups, but cultured Manhattanites seem to avoid it in favor of /o/. On the periphery of this densely populated area, some speakers have checked /ʊ/ rather than free /u/.

On the Southern coast, the /u/ of *moon* occurs in *won't* from Albemarle Sound southward to Florida. In South Carolina, free /u/ competes with the checked /ʊ/ of *bull*, which is nearly as frequent here, and with the /o/ of *stone* (in Charleston, as in Savannah, /u/ is preferred by cultured speakers); in coastal North Carolina and Georgia it is overshadowed by /o/.

Relics of /u/ and /ʊ/ occur on Chesapeake Bay (especially on the Eastern Shore), in central Pennsylvania, in New York State, and in southeastern New England (on Martha's Vineyard and Nantucket the seven informants interviewed use the /ʊ/ of *bull* without exception).

In parts of North Carolina, chiefly in the valleys of the Neuse and the Yadkin, *won't* often rimes with *want*, the /ɔ/ being pronounced as an upgliding diphthong [ɒə]. Scattered instances of /ɔ/ have also been noted in the North and the North Midland.

Of the variant pronunciations of *won't* current in the Eastern States, /wunt, wʊnt, wɔnt/ have remained pretty well confined to the coastal plain. The type of /wont/, with the vowel of *stone*, is firmly established everywhere west of the Alleghenies and the Appalachians; but along the Great Lakes the type of /wʌnt/ is still fairly common, and /wʊnt, wunt/ hang on (especially in Ontario).

The two most common pronunciations of *won't* in the Eastern States, /wont/ and /wʌnt/, have their counterparts in English folk speech of today: the former is current in the eastern counties from Norfolk to Kent and Sussex (hence also in Standard British English, which has doubtless supported the use of /o/ in America); the latter in the central and western counties.

The types of /wʊnt/ and /wunt/ now appear to be rare in England, but scattered relics on the Wash, in Herts, eastern Essex, Sussex, and Hampshire point to a wider currency of these types at the time when the American colonies were peopled.

yolk (Maps 126–28)

The most common pronunciations of *yolk* are: /jok/, riming with *folk*; /jɛlk/, riming with *elk*; and /jolk ∼ jɵlk/, riming with the first syllable of *polka*. Other pronunciations are: /jʌlk/, riming with *bulk* (75 instances, chiefly in New England and New York State); /jɒlk ∼ jalk/, riming with the first syllable of *falcon* (60 instances, mostly in Maine and New Hampshire); and /jælk/, riming with the first syllable of *balcony* (6 instances in Maine and New Hampshire).

The type of /jok/ is current in all major areas, but with greatly varying frequency. It is very common in Metropolitan New York and the greater part of Pennsylvania, where nearly all cultured speakers use it. In Eastern New England and in the coastal plain of the South it is decidedly infrequent and hardly ever occurs in folk speech; even among the cultured it is here outnumbered by other pronunciations.

/jɛlk/, riming with *elk*, is the most common folk pronunciation of *yolk* in the greater part of the Eastern States. It is also widely used by middle-class speakers in parts of New England, New Jersey, and West Virginia, and throughout the tidewater area of the South (assuming that South Carolinian [jɔlk] is phonemically /jɛlk/ rather than /jʌlk/). This pronunciation is even current in the cultivated speech of the South, occasionally also elsewhere. On the other hand, /jɛlk/ is of rare occurrence in Pennsylvania (except for the northern counties settled from New England) and the greater part of the southern upland, where /jok/ prevails or, as in the Appalachians, the synonym *yellow*.

The type of /jolk ~ jəlk/, riming with the first syllable of *polka*, is regionally more restricted than /jok/ and /jɛlk/.

It is especially common in New England, and only less so in the New England settlements to the west. In this entire area the checked /ɵ/ of *stone*, *coat* occurs besides the free /o/ of *no*, and predominates decidedly in Eastern New England. Cultured speakers use /jolk ~ jəlk/ as freely as /jok/.

Outside the New England settlement area, /jolk/ occurs fairly frequently in the Lower South, rarely elsewhere, apparently as a prestige pronunciation.

Cultivated usage in the Eastern States presents a rather bewildering diversity. /jok/ is fairly well established in the Midland, in Metropolitan New York, in Maryland, and in North Carolina. Elsewhere it is matched or outranked by /jolk ~ jəlk/ and/or /jɛlk/. Even /jʌlk/ and /jɒlk/ still survive among the better educated, notably in New England.

Standard British English now has /jok/. But as late as 1797 John Walker championed *yelk* in his *Pronouncing Dictionary*, and the *Oxford Dictionary* records the spelling *yelk* up to 1884. Noah Webster (1847), though making *yolk* his main entry, defines it as "the yelk of an egg," regarding *yelk* as "the proper word."

In English folk speech, the type of /jɛlk/ is largely confined to the eastern counties between the Thames and the Welland. All other sections of England, as well as Scotland, have the type of /jok/ or derivatives of it, except that /jolk/ occurs along the western margin of the /jɛlk/ area (Oxfordshire), clearly as a blend of the two types. Both /jok/ and /jɛlk/ are normal regional derivatives of OE *geolca*.

American /jok/ and /jɛlk/, current on all social levels, though with varying frequency in the several dialect areas, are obviously derived in part from English folk speech and in part from Standard British English, which tolerated both types well beyond the American Revolution. The predominance of /jok/ in Pennsylvania and the South Midland can safely be attributed to the Ulster Scots, since (according to Joseph Wright) this type is regular in Scotland and northern England. The frequency of /jɛlk/ in New England is at least partly due to the numerous settlers from the eastern counties of England, but was strongly supported by Standard British usage of the seventeenth and eighteenth centuries. As far as the extensive use of /jɛlk/ along the South Atlantic coast is concerned, the background is not as clear; however, one can hardly doubt that Standard British usage is its primary source.

The type of /jolk ~ jəlk/, though attested in English folk speech, is largely an American innovation. Occurring mostly alongside of /jɛlk/, it is a blend of /jok/ and /jɛlk/. /jʌlk/ may come from /jɛlk/ through backing of /ɛ/ before velarized /l/. Other variants cannot be accounted for without further evidence.

5.11 /ɔ/ AND VARIANTS

daughter (Map 129)

In the greater part of the Eastern States, *daughter* has the vowel /ɔ/ of *law*, in Eastern New England and Western Pennsylvania usually the corresponding /ɒ/ of *law*, *lot*.

Three other phonemes occur in limited areas.

The checked vowel /ɑ/ of *lot* is common in the Ohio Valley (both in Ohio and in West Virginia), in central West Virginia, and in the Alleghenies of central Pennsylvania. Scattered instances of /ɑ/ survive in the Valley of Virginia as relics of Pennsylvania speech. Elsewhere /ɑ/ is rare.

The folk speech of northeastern New England preserves to some extent an [a ~ ɑ] sound in *daughter*, which is clearly the free /a/ phoneme of *car, calm, half*, contrasting with the free /ɒ/ of *law, lot*. There are in this area (and on Martha's Vineyard) a few relics of the historically related /æ/, of which a few scattered instances survive also in eastern North Carolina and elsewhere in the South.

All of these variants came to this country from England. Standard British /ɔ/ agrees with folk usage of the eastern counties from the Thames northward; unrounded [ɑ· ~ ɑ·] is current in the dialects of the southern and the southwestern counties; [ɑ· ~ a·] survives in East Anglia and Essex, and [æ] in coastal Sussex and Hampshire. Usage of the eastern counties, with the London area, stands back of American /ɔ/ in *daughter*; New England /a/ reflects East Anglian [ɑ· ~ a·]; the /ɑ/ of Pennsylvania and West Virginia may derive in part from Ulster (see Wright, *EDG*, p. 398).

faucet (Map 130)

This term is largely confined to the North, including Metropolitan New York. The Midland and the South have the synonym *spicket, spigot* (see Hans Kurath, *Word Geography*, Figure 69); when *faucet* is used in these areas, it has the vowel /ɔ ~ ɒ/ of *law* or the /ɑ/ of *lot*.

A variety of vowels are used in *faucet* in the Northern area, where the term has general currency: the /ɔ ~ ɒ/ of *law*; the /ɑ/ of *lot*; the /a/ of *car, half*; and the /æ/ of *bag*. /ɔ ~ ɒ/ predominates in cultivated speech and is rather common in the speech of the middle group. /æ/ is chiefly a folk pronunciation, but is still used by some elderly cultured speakers (as in Boston, Newport, Hartford, Albany, Manhattan, and Newark). [ɑ ~ a] sounds are less common; in Eastern New England they belong to the /a/ phoneme of *car, half*, elsewhere to the checked /ɑ/ of *lot*.

In the Midland and the South cultured speakers

who use *faucet* at all have /ɔ/, presumably as a spelling pronunciation.

haunted (Map 131)

This word was recorded in the contexts *a haunted house, the house is haunted*. It has four different vowel phonemes in the Eastern States: the /ɔ ~ ɒ/ of *law*, the /a ~ ɑ/ of *car*, the /æ/ of *bag*, or the /e/ of *eight*. Many speakers use two pronunciations interchangeably, usually with social implications, since the folk variants are traditionally associated with a well-known folk belief.

The /ɔ/ of *law* predominates on all social levels from the Connecticut Valley westward to the Great Lakes, in Metropolitan New York and vicinity, and in all of Pennsylvania except the south-central and southwestern sections. In Eastern New England, /ɒ/ is much less widely used: it competes here with the /a/ of *car* among all social groups, in folk speech also with the /æ/ of *bag*. In the southern counties of Pennsylvania west of the Susquehanna and adjoining parts of Maryland and West Virginia, /ɔ/ is fairly definitely restricted to cultivated and middle-class speech, south of the Potomac more or less to the speech of the cultured.

In Eastern New England *haunted* has the vowel /a/ of *car* approximately to the same extent as in *aunt*; in Massachusetts this usage is current as far west as the Berkshires, in Vermont to the crest of the Green Mountains, but in Connecticut /ɔ/ has largely taken over. In Massachusetts and on Narragansett Bay, /a/ is now all but universal, but the older /æ/ of *bag* survives extensively in New Hampshire-Maine and on the islands of Martha's Vineyard and Nantucket. Outside of New England, /a ~ ɑ/ survives in scattered instances in parts of the New England settlement area, in the North Midland, along Chesapeake Bay, and in parts of the South Carolina–Georgia coast, without any marked social dissemination.

In the South and the South Midland *haunted* regularly has the /æ/ of *bag* in folk speech and predominantly so in the speech of the middle group, except in some of the cities (Richmond, Va., Charleston, W. Va., Wilmington, N. C., Savannah, Ga., and some others). In South

Carolina and Georgia even cultured speakers often say /hæntɪd/. Elsewhere this variant is confined to folk speech (as in parts of Pennsylvania, Delmarva, southern New Jersey, and New England) or entirely avoided; only in northeastern New England does it have wider currency.

A fourth variant of *haunted*, with the vowel /e/ of *eight*, occurs in parts of the Carolinas, in Georgia, and in West Virginia, well within the areas in which *can't*, *aunt* have this vowel.

English folk speech exhibits similar diversity: /ɔ/ is current in the eastern counties north of the Thames, /a ~ ɒ/ everywhere else, except for the southwestern counties (Hampshire to Devonshire), which have /æ/. John Walker (1797) recommends /ɒ/ for cultivated speech and deliberately rejects /ɔ/ as a recent intruder; the two New Englanders, Webster (1847) and Worcester (1860), list only /a/; the *Oxford Dictionary* (1901) puts /ɔ/ ahead of /ɒ/; and Daniel Jones gives only /ɔ/. Clearly, /ɔ/ is a relative newcomer in Standard British English, as it is in large parts of the Eastern States, where it is fully established only in the North Midland and in New York State with adjoining parts of New England, but is clearly spreading in other areas. In Eastern New England, to be sure, /hantɪd/ will not as readily be replaced by /hɒntɪd/ as /hæntɪd/ has been replaced, or is being replaced, in the cultivated use of other areas.

sausage (Map 132)

In *sausage* the rounded vowels /ɔ ~ ɒ/ predominate everywhere except in tidewater Virginia and in Maryland, being nearly universal in New York State, most of Pennsylvania, and the South Midland. Outside the Southern area nearly all cultured speakers use them.

Unrounded [ɑ ~ ɒ ~ a], which belong to the checked /ɑ/ of *lot*, except in Eastern New England where they fall in with the free /a/ of *car*, *half*, appear with greatly varying frequency in most parts of the Eastern States. On both sides of Chesapeake Bay, /ɑ/ is in rather general use on all social levels, as for instance in Richmond and Baltimore. In the Carolinas this pronunciation is much less frequent but exhibits no marked class cleavage. In the Midland and in New England,

/ɑ/ is rather infrequent and cultured speakers avoid it; in New York State only a few relics of it survive.

Yet another phoneme, the /æ/ of *bag*, occurs with some frequency in the folk speech of northeastern New England; only scattered relics remain elsewhere.

Standard British English has /ɔ/ in agreement with folk usage in the eastern counties to the north of the Thames. Unrounded [ɒ ~ ɑ] prevails in the south and the west of England and is not uncommon in some of the eastern counties (Northampton, Norfolk, Essex). Of all American variants only /æ/ seems to be unknown in English folk speech.

because (Map 133)

The vowels /ɔ ~ ɒ/ are fairly generally used in *because* throughout the Eastern States. However, one other pronunciation, the /ʌ/ of *sun*, is rather widely current and several others appear regionally or prosodically.

/ʌ/ is especially common in the New England settlement area and in South Carolina, but occurs also elsewhere. With some speakers, /ʌ/ and the related [ə ~ ɪ] are confined to unstressed position in the sentence, but others use these variants also under half-stress and full stress. Though more frequent in the speech of the folk and the middle group, not all cultured speakers avoid /ʌ/.

Because with the vowel /e/ of *eight* occurs in the folk speech of the South and the South Midland; it is sharply recessive. Scattered instances of the /ɑ/ of *lot* appear in various places, but especially in the New England settlements.

Standard British English has /ɔ/, a type confined in folk speech to a corridor leading from Middlesex northward to Lincolnshire. American /ɔ/ thus stems largely from Standard British English. The other East Midland counties have /ʌ/ or /ʊ/, with which the New England /ʌ/ is historically connected. The type of /ɑ/, uncommon in America, is widely used in the west of England. There is at present no evidence in English dialects for the /e/ of our Southern folk speech.

water (Map 134)

A rounded back vowel, ranging regionally from [ɒˆ ~ ɔ] to [ɔˆ·] and [ɒɔ], is current in all areas, except the greater part of the South Midland. It is nearly universal in the South and in Metropolitan New York, and predominates decidedly in the North, in parts of New Jersey, in Eastern Pennsylvania (Philadelphia), and in all of Maryland and Delaware. Except for Eastern New England and Western Pennsylvania, which lack the /ɔ:ɑ/ contrast, these phones clearly belong to the /ɔ/ phoneme of *law*.

An unrounded low-back vowel [ɑ] (occasionally even low-central [ɑ]), clearly the /ɑ/ phoneme of *lot*, is nearly universal in West Virginia, in eastern Ohio (but Marietta has /ɔ/), and in the westernmost section of North Carolina. In adjoining parts of the South Midland, /ɑ/ stands beside /ɔ/. The unrounded vowel occurs as a minority pronunciation in parts of the North and in Eastern Pennsylvania.

A slightly rounded [ɒ] sound—not shown on the map—has some currency in Western New England and Upstate New York, which can safely be taken as a positional allophone of /ɑ/ following the /w/. [ɒ] phones occur also in Eastern New England and in Western Pennsylvania, where /ɑ/ and /ɔ/ have been merged in the phoneme /ɒ/.

In large parts of New Jersey, a subarea of Western Pennsylvania, and on the Eastern Shore of Maryland, *water* often has the /ʌ/ phoneme of *sun*. In these areas, /ʌ/ occurs also in *want* and *watch*.

Standard British English and the folk speech of the eastern counties of England have /ɔ/ in *water*, the southwestern counties /ɑ/. Both pronunciations thus came to America from England.

wash (Map 135)

In *wash*, the regional dissemination of the /ɔ/ and the /ɑ/ phonemes is almost the reverse of that in *water*. In this word, the /ɔ/ of *law* is characteristic of the South Midland, the /ɑ/ of *lot* of the South, the Philadelphia area, New Jersey, Metropolitan New York, and all but the western end of Upstate New York. Eastern New England and Western Pennsylvania have /ɒ/, of course. Only a few subareas having the /ɔ:ɑ/ contrast have achieved relative uniformity in usage: Metropolitan New York and the Hudson Valley, Philadelphia and vicinity, and the Upper South, which have /ɔ/; and West Virginia north of the Kanawha, which has /ɑ/.

Both pronunciations are current in English folk speech. Standard British English /wɔš/ has had no influence upon usage in the old urban centers on the Atlantic seaboard, with the possible exception of Boston.

The regional incidence of /ɔ/ and /ɑ/ after /w/ varies from word to word. The following table exhibits the predominant usage in selected subareas of the Eastern States along with the usage of substantial minorities. There seems to be no marked social cleavage anywhere.

	wash	watch	water	wasp	want	swamp
Upstate N. Y.	ɑ ~ ɔ	ɑ	ɔ ~ ɑ	ɑ	ɔ ~ ɑ	ɔ ~ ɑ
Metrop. N. Y.	ɑ	ɑ	ɔ	ɔ ~ ɑ	ɑ	ɑ
Phila. area	ɑ	ɑ	ɔ	ɔ ~ ɑ	ɔ ~ ɑ	ɑ
W. Va.	ɔ	ɑ	ɑ	ɔ	ɔ ~ ɑ	ɔ ~ ɑ
Eastern Va.	ɑ	ɑ	ɔ	ɔ	ɔ	ɔ
Eastern S. C.	ɑ ~ ɔ	ɔ ~ ɑ	ɔ	ɔ	ɔ	ɔ

fog (Map 136)

Fog has either the phoneme /ɔ ~ ɒ/ of *law* or the /ɑ/ of *lot*. The dissemination of these variants is largely regional.

/ɒ/ is regular in Eastern New England and in Western Pennsylvania, areas that lack the contrast /ɔ:ɑ/ of *law* vs. *lot*.

/ɔ/ is nearly universal in the Midland, except for Western Pennsylvania and the vicinity of Philadelphia, and rather common in Maryland, Virginia, and South Carolina. It is infrequent to rare in Eastern North Carolina, New York State, and Western New England.

Fog with the vowel /ɑ/ of *lot* is regularly used in Western New England, in New York State with the adjoining counties of Pennsylvania, in Metropolitan New York and vicinity, in the Philadelphia area, and in Eastern North Carolina. In Virginia east of the Blue Ridge, in South Carolina, and in Georgia, /ɑ/ is not infrequent, but definitely less common than /ɔ/. However, in Virginia and adjoining parts of Maryland all cultured speakers say /fɑg/, which obviously has prestige.

The /ɒ/-like phones occurring in South Carolina are slightly rounded allophones of /ɑ/ before the velar stop /g/. Similar phones current in Western New England may be allophones of /ɑ/ or they may be survivals of the /ɒ/ phoneme of Eastern New England.

The incidence of the phonemes /ɔ ∼ ɒ/ and /ɑ/ in *log* and *frog* is much the same as in *fog*, but *dog* nearly always has /ɔ ∼ ɒ/ in all areas.

long, strong (Map 137)

The North, the North Midland, large sections of the South Midland, and the Lower South have the /ɔ ∼ ɒ/ of *law* in *long*, *strong* almost universally. On the other hand, Virginia east of the Blue Ridge and all of North Carolina have in these words the /ɑ/ of *lot* with similar regularity. Outside this large section of the South, more or less scattered instances of /ɑ/ appear in southern West Virginia, eastern Pennsylvania, northeastern New Jersey, Brooklyn, and western New England.

It should be noted that before the velar stop, as in *fog*, *log*, /ɑ/ has a much wider dissemination than before the velar nasal /ŋ/ of *long*, *strong*.

on (Map 138)

The adverb *on*, as in *put it on!*, has either the vowel /ɔ ∼ ɒ/ of *law*, *frost* or the vowel /ɑ/ of *lot* in rather well-defined regional dissemination.

The phoneme /ɑ/ is confined to a single area extending from Western New England to the New England settlements on the Great Lakes. It includes Metropolitan New York and the Hudson Valley. In this area the vowel in *on* contrasts sharply with the vowel in *law*, *lawn*. Along the eastern and southern boundaries of this area, and especially along the Great Lakes, /ɔ ∼ ɒ/ occurs as a minority usage, apparently in individual rather than social dissemination, although two cultured speakers in Brooklyn, N. Y. use it. Outside of this area, /ɑ/ occurs only sporadically; only in Philadelphia, which is well

within the /ɔ/ area, do cultured speakers exhibit a preference for it.

In the South and the South Midland the phoneme /ɔ/, always well rounded and often an upgliding diphthong, is nearly universal in the adverb *on*. Here upgliding /ɔ/ occasionally merges with /o/. With few exceptions /ɔ/ has general currency also in Eastern Pennsylvania and adjoining sections of New Jersey and Maryland; it is universal in northern West Virginia and in all of Ohio, except for a narrow belt along Lake Erie.

In Western Pennsylvania, the phoneme /ɒ/, usually only slightly rounded (if at all), occurs both in *law*, *lawn*, *frost* and in *lot*, *rot*, *John*, *car*, and, of course, also in *on*, which here rimes both with *lawn* and *John*.

In Eastern New England, *on* also rimes both with *lawn* and with *John*, the vowel being a more or less rounded [ɒ] sound, which we take to be the phoneme /ɒ/. This phoneme is sharply differentiated from the unrounded low-front vowel /a/ occurring in *car*, *half*, *glass*, etc., which here never is used in *on*.

No reliable information is as yet available on English folk usage. Standard British /ɒn/ (written /ɔn/ by Daniel Jones) corresponds historically to the American English variants /ɑn/ and /ɒn/, not to /ɔn/.

5.12 /ɚ/ AND VARIANTS

grandma, grandpa, ma, pa

The final syllable in *grandma* has a great variety of vowels, in marked regional dissemination: the /ɑ ∼ ɚ ∼ a/ of *father*, the /ɔ ∼ ɒ/ of *law*, the /æ/ of *bad*, the /ə/ of *sofa*, and the /i/ of *happy*.

The /ɑ ∼ ɚ ∼ a/ of *father* is used (1) throughout the North, including Metropolitan New York, and (2) in large parts of the South.

The /ɔ ∼ ɒ/ of *law* (1) predominates in the Midland from the Susquehanna Valley westward to Ohio and from there southward to the Carolinas and northern Georgia. It is universal in West Virginia; in western Pennsylvania, /æ/ occurs alongside of it, in the Carolinas and Georgia /ɑ ∼ ɚ/. (2) /ɔ/ occurs also, besides /ɚ/, from Albemarle Sound northward to lower Chesapeake Bay.

The /æ/ of *bad* predominates (1) in the Low Country of South Carolina, (2) on the Eastern Shore of Maryland and in southern New Jersey, and occurs (3) as a minority variant in western Pennsylvania (probably introduced from the Delaware Valley).

The /ə/ of *sofa* is current, along with /a ∼ ɑ/, in nearly all of the North (rarely in Metropolitan New York), the /i/ of *happy* in New Hampshire and Maine.

There is no marked social dissemination of any of these variants. It would seem that family tradition has been decisive in preserving regional pronunciations and a certain degree of diversity within nearly all the areas, irrespective of social class.

In *grandpa*, *pa*, and *ma*, the regional dissemination of the variants is nearly the same as in *grandma* (except that *pa* and *ma*, being stressed, lack /ə/ and /i/). However, *ma* (not *pa*) often has the /ʌ/ of *hut* or the /ɜ/ of *her* in the folk speech of the Neuse Valley in North Carolina (Raleigh to the sea), and scattered instances have been noted elsewhere in the Carolinas and in Virginia. In *grandma* a few relics of /ʌ ∼ ɜ/ occur on the lower Neuse.

5.13 /ai/ AND VARIANTS

appendicitis (Map 139)

This learned word was coined on the model of *neuritis* in the last decades of the nineteenth century. As in Standard British English, the /ai/ of *sight* is in general use in the Eastern States. However, the /i/ of *seat* occurs in addition to it as a minority usage in New England, Eastern Virginia, and South Carolina (areas in which /i/ is current also in the last syllable of *iodine*), rarely elsewhere. The incidence of /i/ does not follow social lines, except in Philadelphia, and perhaps in Richmond, Va., and Charleston, S. C.

iodine (Map 140)

This word, coined in 1814 on the model of *chlorine*, *fluorine* (see the *Oxford Dictionary*), has either the vowel /ai/ of *dine* or the /i/ of

dean (as in Standard British English), occasionally also the /ɪ/ of *din*.

/ai/ predominates in the North and the North Midland, including all of West Virginia, on Delmarva, in North Carolina, and in Georgia; it is nearly universal in Eastern New England, in Pennsylvania (except for Philadelphia and vicinity), and in West Virginia. In Virginia /ai/ is not uncommon, except in cultivated speech; in South Carolina it is rare, but definitely preferred by educated speakers in the coastal cities (Charleston, Beaufort, as well as Savannah, Ga.).

The /i/ of *dean* is nearly universal in South Carolina, except for the cities on the coast, and predominates decisively in Virginia. In North Carolina, lying between these two distinctive subareas of the South, /i/ occurs as a minority pronunciation with varying frequency (rarely between Albemarle Sound and the Neuse).

In the North, /i/ is uncommon, occurring most frequently in the Connecticut Valley and in western Vermont, less often in Upstate New York. In the lower Hudson Valley, Metropolitan New York, New Jersey, Delmarva, Pennsylvania, and West Virginia, the /i/ of *dean* is rare in *iodine*, but cultured speakers in Manhattan, Philadelphia, and Baltimore have a strong preference for it.

Iodine riming with *din* occurs in scattered instances in New England (especially Rhode Island) and the New England settlement area, rarely elsewhere. It is usually a prestige pronunciation (as in Boston, Newport, New Haven, Albany, Rochester, Richmond, Va., Columbia, S. C.).

The pronunciation of this learned word, which came into popular use along with this antiseptic in rather recent times, epitomizes rather neatly the persistence of the dialectal structure of the Eastern States. Created by the settlement and preserved by economic and cultural cohesion, such subareas as Eastern New England, the Connecticut Valley, the Hudson Valley with New York City, the Virginia Piedmont, and South Carolina continue to control the dissemination of dialectal features. On the other hand, the preference for /i/ on the part of cultured speakers in the cities of the /ai/ area—Manhattan, Philadelphia, Baltimore—is presumably connected with the learned origin of *iodine*, which was coined on the model of *chlorine, fluorine*, etc.

quinine (Map 141)

Three types of pronunciation are fairly widely current in the Eastern States: /'kwainain/, with main stress on the first syllable and half-stress on the second; /'kwɪnain ~ kwɪ'nain/, with the main stress predominantly on the first syllable; and /kwɪ'nin/, riming with *bean*, stressed on the final syllable.

/'kwainain/ has by far the widest dissemination. It is in nearly universal use in the Midland (from New Jersey and Pennsylvania to western North Carolina) as well as in Maryland and in Upstate New York; it predominates decisively in the Hudson Valley and in southwestern New England. In the South it is fairly evenly matched with other pronunciations, except for the Low Country of South Carolina and Georgia and parts of eastern Virginia. /'kwainain/ is uncommon to rare only in parts of the Lower South and of Eastern New England.

The type of /'kwɪnain ~ kwɪ'nain/ is largely confined to two areas on the Atlantic coast: New England and the South. In New England it predominates decisively in Maine, New Hampshire, and most of Vermont, and only less so in eastern Massachusetts and adjoining parts of Rhode Island. In western New England and New York State it is of rare occurrence, except for the St. Lawrence Valley.

In the South this type is fully established in the Low Country of South Carolina and adjoining parts of Georgia. It is only less common in eastern North Carolina and in the Upcountry of South Carolina, but apparently little used in Atlanta, Ga., and vicinity. Eastern Virginia presents a complicated situation. Here /'kwɪnain ~ kwɪ'nain/ predominate between the lower James River and the Rappahannock, especially in Richmond and vicinity, but not elsewhere. As a prestige pronunciation, usually with end stress, this type has been adopted by cultured speakers as far north as Annapolis and Baltimore, Md. Some cultured Philadelphians also use this pronunciation of *quinine*.

An occasional /'kwinain/, with the /i/ of *three* in the first syllable, occurs along the coast of the Carolinas.

The type of /kwɪ'nin ~ kɪn'in/, riming with *canteen*, is used by a minority in southwestern New England and the Hudson Valley, including Metropolitan New York. Its social standing varies: clearly preferred by cultured speakers in Manhattan and Newark, it occurs also in the speech of elderly rustics. Elsewhere in the Eastern States this pronunciation is exceedingly rare. On the other hand, it seems to be common in Canada, predominating in the valley of the St. John in New Brunswick and, judging by the three border communities investigated, also in Ontario.

The medicinal drug known as quinine, obtained from the bark of a South American tree, came into use early in the nineteenth century. Spanish *quinina* /ki'nina/, derived from Quechuan, entering American and British English independently (probably in part by way of French *quinine* or Latinized *chininum*), was Anglicized in various ways, to a large extent on the basis of the spelling. SBE /kwɪ'nin ~ 'kwɪnin/, a pronunciation current to some extent in the Hudson Valley and in southwestern New England, and as a Briticism in Canada, retains the vowels and the stress pattern, but has /kw/ for /k/. The most widespread American type, /'kwainain/, with shifted stress, is an out-and-out spelling pronunciation. The American regional type /'kwɪnain ~ kwɪ'nain/ is yet another adaptation.

A full account of the present dissemination of the several American variants cannot be attempted here. The medical schools, physicians and pharmacists, and the organization of the drug trade have doubtlessly had a major share in establishing regional usage. Nevertheless, it is a striking phenomenon that the less widely used variants, /'kwɪnain/ and /kwɪ'nin/, have their centers in areas that stand out as highly distinctive dialect areas in other respects. As far as Southern usage is concerned, it is perhaps not idle to point out that *quinine* came into use about a generation before the Civil War. One feels tempted to suggest that the out-and-out spelling pronunciation /'kwainain/ was disseminated largely by that unique institution, the American drugstore.

5.14 /au/ AND VARIANT

drought (Map 142)

Drought rimes either with *out*, with *mouth*, with *tooth*, with *bought*, or with *moth*. Many, who normally use *dry spell*, know this expression only from print.

The vowel /au/ of *out* has nearly universal currency everywhere, except in western Pennsylvania, where the word is rather generally pronounced /druθ/, riming with *tooth*. This is one of the very few Scotticisms that have survived in any area in which the Ulster Scots were numerous among the early settlers (cp. *hap* for *quilt* in Hans Kurath, *Word Geography*, Figure 89).

The vowel /ɔ/ of *bought* (presumably a spelling pronunciation of an unfamiliar word) occurs in scattered instances in New England, New York State, and the German section of eastern Pennsylvania, rarely elsewhere.

The final consonant is either /t/ or /θ/. /draut/, riming with *out*, is common only in cultivated speech, but has some currency among the middle class, especially in urbanized areas (Boston with its hinterland, Metropolitan New York, Philadelphia and vicinity, and Charleston-Beaufort-Savannah). Except for western Pennsylvania, /drauθ/, riming with *mouth*, is nearly universal in folk speech and predominates decidedly in the speech of the middle group; in cultivated speech it occurs not infrequently by the side of /draut/ in the New England settlement area, but is rather rare elsewhere.

English folk speech south of Yorkshire has /draut/, as does Standard British English of today; however, some instances of /drauθ/ are reported in Joseph Wright's *EDG* (p. 414) from the western counties of England. The vowels /u, ʊ/ are current in this word from Yorkshire-Lancashire northward and in Northern Ireland, but the type of /druθ/ is confined to Scotland and Northern Ireland, whence it was brought to Pennsylvania.

Both *drought* and *drouth* were current in written English until the middle of the nineteenth century (Tennyson rimes it with *south*; see the *OD*). Most dictionaries from John Walker to *Webster's International Dictionary* (1934) recognize the existence of both pronunciations, giving *drought* first; but Daniel Jones lists only /draut/. As pointed out above, this pronunciation is now clearly expansive in the Eastern States, but not yet in general use among the cultured.

5.15 /ɔi/ AND VARIANTS

joint (Maps 143–46)

The word *joint* (used with reference to the knee or the elbow) has the vowel /ɔi/ of *boy* in cultivated and in common speech. Except for parts of New Hampshire and Maine, this pronunciation predominates in the North and the North Midland also in folk speech.

In the South and the South Midland, on the other hand, the currency of /ɔi/ is regionally restricted on the folk level. It is nearly universal in Georgia and large parts of South Carolina, quite frequent in parts of North Carolina and Virginia, but rather uncommon elsewhere.

Joint with the vowel /ai/ of *five* predominates in folk speech (1) in the coastal plane from Chesapeake Bay to the Pee Dee in South Carolina and (2) in the Appalachians and the Blue Ridge; it is much less frequent in the intervening area, the piedmont of Virginia and North Carolina, and rather rare in the Lower South.

In the North Midland and the North, the /ai/ of *five* is rather rare in *joint*, except for parts of New Hampshire and Maine. Scattered instances of this pronunciation survive in the Hudson Valley and in the New England settlements of northeastern Pennsylvania; elsewhere it has been eliminated.

In the folk speech of Metropolitan New York the earlier /ɔi/ is often merged with the /ɜ/ of *learn*, pronounced as diphthongal [ɜɪ]; hence it occurs rather frequently in *joint*.

A similar pattern in the incidence of the phonemes /ɔi, ai, ɜ/ appears in *joined, boiled, spoiled,* and *boil* (furuncle), although their frequency varies and many speakers vacillate or are inconsistent in their practice. On the other hand, *hoist, oyster,* and *oil* behave very differently.

As far as *boiled, spoiled, oil,* and *boil* are concerned, a rather important deviation occurs. Before the velarized /l/ in these words, the earlier /ɔi/ has either been merged with the /ɔ/ of *dog* (pronounced as an upgliding [ɒɔ ~ ɔo]), as in the western part of the Carolinas (where *oil* rimes with *all*), or developed into the sequence /ɔr/ (with constricted [ɚ] arising through the anticipation of the lateral constriction of the tongue for /l/), as in scattered instances in the Midland. This feature occurs both in folk speech and in common speech.

Oil predominantly has the vowel /ɔi/ of *boy* on all social levels in the Eastern States, the /ai/ of *five* being exceedingly rare, except in parts of New Hampshire and Maine; scattered instances of it occur chiefly in coastal communities from Chesapeake Bay to Georgia. As pointed out above, /ɔ/ and /ɔr/ are current in *oil* where *boiled* and *spoiled* also have them. In Metropolitan New York /ɜ/ appears as in *joint*.

Oyster (not investigated in New England) normally has the /ɔi/ of *boy·* only a few instances of /ai/ occur. Metropolitan New York has /ɜ/ rather more frequently in *oyster* than in *joint, boiled*, etc. and /ɔ ~ ɔr/ are much more widely disseminated than in *boiled*, being especially common in folk speech along the South Atlantic coast, where *boiled, spoiled, oil* do not exhibit this variant.

Although *boil* (furuncle), which had /ī/ in Old and Middle English, shows the same dissemination of /ɔi/ and /ai/ as *joint* in the Eastern States, *hoist*!, which came into English (c. 1500) from Dutch with /ī/ (in the expression *hoist sail*!), regularly retains /ai/ when it is used as a command (addressed to sailors, or at milking time to a cow).

In the folk speech of England the /ai/ type (pronounced regionally as [ɐɪ ~ əɪ ~ ɑɪ ~ ɒɪ]) is most common in East Anglia and the central counties from Hampshire northward. The /ɔi/ type (appearing regionally as [oɪ ~ ɔɪ ~ ʊɪ ~ we]) is concentrated (1) in the vicinity of London (especially Middlesex, Surrey, Kent), (2) in Northampton-Lincolnshire, and (3) in the southwestern counties. The /ai/ type is most widely disseminated in *joint, oil* and appears with decreasing frequency in *boil, boiled, spoiled*. In England there seems to be no trace of the phoneme /ɔ/ or the sequence /ɔr/ in *oil, boil, boiled, spoiled*; hence these variants must have arisen

in this country, as the /ɜ/ of Metropolitan New York most certainly did.

5.16 /iu/ AND VARIANTS

blew, chew, suit (Map 147)

After /l, č, s/, as in *blew, chew, suit* (of clothes), all dialects on the Atlantic seaboard have /u/, without a preceding /j/. However, in the New England settlement area a fair number of the less educated speakers say /bliu, čiu, siut/, using the decrescendo vowel /iu/ which they also have in *music, new, due*, etc.

This pronunciation is widely current in the folk speech of eastern England. The type of Standard British *suit* /sjut/ does not occur in the Eastern United States.

UNSTRESSED VOWELS

5.17 /ə ~ ɪ/

bucket, skillet, careless, houses, towel, funnel, mountain (Map 148)

A clear regional pattern appears in the dissemination of the phonemes /ə/ and /ɪ/ in the unstressed syllable of *bucket, careless, towel, mountain*, etc.

The entire Midland as well as Metropolitan New York and the lower Hudson Valley have /ə/ before the stops and fricatives of *bucket, careless*, etc., the New England settlement area and the entire South checked /ɪ/, usually articulated as a high-central [ɨ].

Before the sonorants /n/ and /l/, as in *mountain* and *towel*, the incidence of /ɪ/ is largely confined to coastal subareas of the North and the South and appears to be more common among older speakers, especially in western and central New England. When *mountain, towel*, etc., do not have /ɪ/, they end in /-ən, -əl/, articulated as [-ən, -əl] or as syllabic [n̩, l̩].

5.18 /ə ~ ɜ ~ i/

sofa, china (Map 149)

These words usually end in /ə/. But in folk speech [ɨ ~ ɪ] occur with some frequency in northern New England, in West Virginia, and in the

Upper South, and relics of it appear elsewhere. Moreover, in areas that have constricted /ɜ/ in *father* this phoneme appears occasionally also in *sofa*.

All three pronunciations are current in English folk speech: [ɪ] from Lincolnshire to Suffolk, [ɚ] chiefly in the southern counties from Kent to Dorset, and [ə] everywhere else.

Missouri, Cincinnati (Map 150)

These place names end in [ə] or in [ɪ ~ ɪ], the former predominating in Western New England, New Jersey, Pennsylvania, Virginia, and parts of North Carolina, the latter in Eastern New England, Metropolitan New York, Philadelphia, and the Lower South. Elsewhere the two pronunciations are rather evenly matched. There is no marked class cleavage in usage, but urbanites have a preference for [ɪ ~ ɪ], a prosodic allophone of the free /i/ of *three*. All in all, /ə/ is somewhat more frequent in *Cincinnati* than in *Missouri*.

father, mother (Map 151)

In phrase-final position and before words beginning with a consonant, *father, mother*, etc., end in the phoneme /ə/ in those areas in which /r/ is not preserved after stressed vowels: Eastern New England, Metropolitan New York and vicinity, Eastern Virginia with adjoining parts of Maryland and North Carolina, and the greater part of South Carolina and Georgia.

In the South this pronunciation is clearly spreading, as evidenced by the fact that in sections or communities in which usage is divided it is the better educated and the younger speakers who use /ə/. The trend is especially marked in North Carolina and in the cities located on the periphery of the /ə/ areas. Metropolitan New York influence is reflected in the cities on the Jersey shore and in the Hudson Valley as far north as Albany. In the lower Connecticut Valley and the New Haven area usage is divided without any noticeable drift. The scattered instances of /ə/ in the St. Lawrence Valley and along Lake Ontario (Rochester) are at least in part relics of the usage of Eastern New England.

Outside of the four subareas along the Atlantic coast discussed above, *father, mother*, etc., end in [ɚ], a prosodic allophone of the constricted /ɜ/ of *thirty*. In the Midland and in Upstate New York with western New England, this unstressed /ɜ/ is fully constricted. On the periphery of the /ə/ areas and in the large transition area of North Carolina, the constriction is often rather slight and many speakers waver between weakly constricted [ɚ] and unconstricted [ə].

It is of historical interest to note that pockets of /ɜ/ survive within some of the /ə/ areas, as Martha's Vineyard, Marblehead and Cape Ann on the Massachusetts coast, Cape Henry at the mouth of Chesapeake Bay, and the sand hills of coastal Georgia. The relative uniformity of the /ə/ areas is obviously of rather recent date.

5.19 /o ~ ə ~ ɜ/

borrow (Maps 152–53)

The final syllable of *borrow* ends either in /o/, in /ə/, or in /i/ (pronounced as [ɪ] or [ɪ']). All three variants are widely used, partly in regional and partly in social dissemination.

The variant ending in /o/ is common in most sections of New England and in Metropolitan New York, with adjoining parts of the Hudson Valley and East Jersey. In these areas most cultured speakers use it and also a majority of the middle group. It is much less common than /ə/ in the remainder of New York State and in Eastern Pennsylvania, but clearly preferred in cultivated speech. In the greater part of Pennsylvania and throughout the South Midland and the South /o/ is rare (or not used at all) even among the cultured.

The variant /ə/ is current in all parts of the Eastern States, but with greatly varying frequency. It is most common in Pennsylvania and in a wide belt extending from Vermont westward to Lake Erie, where it is used by all social groups. In New England it is a more or less common folk pronunciation, whereas in the South and the South Midland it is most widely used by the cultured, less so by the middle group, and rather infrequently, or not at all, by the folk.

The variant ending in /i/ is characteristic of

Southern and South Midland folk speech; it occurs here also, with varying frequency, in the speech of the middle class, but is rare in cultivated speech. Outside the South and the South Midland only scattered instances of /i/ have been observed, except in southeastern Maine and adjoining parts of New Hampshire.

All three variants were brought to this country from England: /o/ derives from Standard British English, /ə/ and /i/ from English folk speech. The variant ending in /i/ is now current chiefly in the southern counties from Sussex to Devonshire, but relics of it are scattered through the /ə/ area as far north as Lincolnshire. Hence the widespread use of /i/ south of Pennsylvania is not too surprising.

tomato (Map 154)

Tomato ends in /o/, /ə/, or /ɜ/ = [ɚ]. The variant in /o/ predominates on all social levels in New England (except western Vermont) and in Metropolitan New York, and is nearly universal among cultured speakers. In Upstate New York it is much less common, but is the usual pronunciation in cultivated speech, except for the western part of the state. In Pennsylvania final /o/ is rare, but is clearly preferred by cultured speakers in Philadelphia. Throughout the South and the South Midland final /o/ occurs only sporadically, even in cultivated urban speech.

The variant ending in /ə/ predominates decisively among all social classes in the South and the Midland, except for parts of North Carolina, where constricted /ɜ/ is common in folk speech, and Philadelphia, where the cultured use /o/. In Upstate New York final /ə/ and /o/ are fairly evenly matched in some parts, but /ə/ predominates in others, as also in western Vermont. Connecticut has it as a minority form. In all of Eastern New England /ə/ is rare (except on Martha's Vineyard and Nantucket), and cultured speakers avoid it.

Tomato ending in constricted [ɚ] predominates in the folk speech of eastern and western North Carolina, but is infrequent in the central section of the state. This pronunciation is also current in the northern and western margins of South Carolina and in the hill country of northern Georgia. Sporadic instances occur in the Valley of Virginia, in West Virginia, on Delmarva, and in western New York State.

All three pronunciations are now current in England: final /o/ in Standard British English, and occasionally in folk speech; /ɜ/, pronounced as constricted [ɚ], in the folk speech of the counties south of the Thames (Kent to Dorset) and of Buckingham with adjoining sections of the surrounding counties; /ə/ everywhere else. The American variant ending in /ə/, by far the most widely used, is thus deeply rooted in English folk speech, the variant in /o/ in cultivated British usage, and the /ɜ/ of North Carolina (which survives in relics elsewhere) apparently in the folk speech of the southern counties of England. We are here not concerned with the troublesome problem of the origin of /ɜ/ in southern England.

widow, meadow, yellow (Map 155)

These words end in /o/, /ə/, or /ɜ/. In cultivated speech, the /o/ of *ago* predominates in the North and the North Midland, the final /ə/ of *Martha* in the South Midland and the Lower South; in Virginia the two vowels are rather evenly matched. Among the folk and the middle class, /o/ is common in the North and in Eastern Pennsylvania, but infrequent to rare throughout the South, the South Midland, and Pennsylvania west of the Susquehanna, where /ə/ prevails.

In some areas where *father* ends in constricted /ɜ/, *widow, meadow, yellow* also end in /ɜ/. This pronunciation is common in the mountains of the South (from the Kanawha southward), in eastern North Carolina, and on the Delmarva Peninsula, being most frequent among the folk. Relics of /ɜ/ survive in the folk speech of the North. Cultured speakers avoid it altogether.

CONSONANTS

5.20 /r/ AND VARIANTS

door (Map 156)

Postvocalic /r/, as in *door, care, poor, ear*, is preserved in all of the Midland (from New Jersey and Pennsylvania to northernmost Georgia), in the North from western New England to the Great Lakes, on Delmarva, and to a considerable extent in coastal North Carolina. Pockets of post-vocalic /r/ survive along the coast of New England (Cape Ann, Marblehead, Martha's Vineyard) and in the sand hills of coastal Georgia. This postvocalic /r/ is generally a velarized constricted [ɚ], but is often articulated as an apical [r] in Western Pennsylvania and as a weak velar fricative in the German settlements of Eastern Pennsylvania.

Instead of postvocalic /r/, four geographically separated subareas have a mid-central semivowel /ə̯/: Eastern New England as far west as the Connecticut Valley (to the crest of the Green Mountains in Vermont), Metropolitan New York, the Upper South (the southern peninsula of Maryland, Virginia to the Blue Ridge, and north-central North Carolina), and the Lower South (South Carolina and Georgia).

On the margin of the Southern subareas cultured and younger speakers frequently have /ə̯/, others /r/ (as in Baltimore, Roanoke, Va., and Spartanburg, S. C.), a clear indication that this type is spreading in the South. In eastern North Carolina, where usage varies greatly, this trend is quite clear. The /ə̯/ of Metropolitan New York is a prestige pronunciation in the lower Hudson Valley. In the lower Connecticut Valley usage is divided, as in Springfield, Hartford, and New Haven, without any clear trend. The /ə̯/ of Eastern New England survives to some extent in the Genesee Valley of Upstate New York, as in Rochester.

In Southern folk speech, /ə̯/ is often lost, door, four, poor /doə̯, foə̯, poə̯/ thus becoming /do, fo, po/. This pronunciation has also some currency among the middle class, but is avoided by cultured speakers.

In English folk speech of today, door, care, ear end in unsyllabic /ə̯/ in the eastern counties north of the Thames, in /r/, articulated as a constricted [ɚ], in the south and the west. In all probability both types came to this country with the first colonists and could be heard in all of the colonies. With the acceptance of /doə̯, keə, iə̯/ in Standard British English during the eighteenth century, it would seem that this type acquired prestige in the chief American seaports on the Atlantic coast—Boston, New York, Richmond, Charleston—and spread from there to the hinter-land. In the inland, on the other hand, the post-vocalic /r/, common from the beginning, came to be generally established, as also in the Quaker-dominated port of Philadelphia and vicinity.

your aunt (Map 157)

In all the areas where historical postvocalic /r/ is lost before consonants, as in garden, corn, bastard, or has become unsyllabic /ə̯/, as in beard, board, etc., these developments also occur in word-final position, as in car, for, father and in ear, care, for, four, poor, if these words end a phrase or are followed within a phrase by a word beginning with a consonant. On the other hand, if such a word is followed without a pause by a word beginning with a vowel, the treatment varies regionally.

In Eastern New England and Metropolitan New York, /r/ is regularly preserved in this position, that is, it is treated like the intersyllabic /r/ in such words as merry, borrow, or arrange, derive. Consequently, such words as car, for, father have the contextual allomorphs (sandhi doublets) /ka(r, fɒ(r, faðə(r/ in New England, /kɑ(r, fɔ(r, fɑðə(r/ in New York City, and ear, care, four, poor appear as /iə̯(r, kæə̯(r ~ keə̯(ˌr foə̯(r ~ fɔə̯(r, puə̯(r/.

In the Upper South (Virginia and the adjoining counties of Maryland and North Carolina) such doublets are uncommon, the /r/-less forms being used predominantly in all contexts. In the Lower South (South Carolina and Georgia) sandhi forms with /r/ are more common than in the Upper South, but are nevertheless only half as frequent as the variants without /r/. In the greater part of eastern North Carolina, and the sand hills of South Carolina and Georgia, where /ə̯/ and /r/ occur side by side in barn, corn, etc., historical final /r/, as in car, four, exhibits the same variability and instability, irrespective of context.

The regional treatment of historical word-final /r/ before the initial vowel of a word following it within the phrase without pause is illustrated by the phrase your aunt.

The folk speech of England has "linking" /r/ fairly regularly in the phrase your aunt within the area that has lost phrase-final /r/ or has changed it to /ə̯ ~ ə/, and Standard British usage conforms to this rule. In America only

Eastern New England and Metropolitan New York follow this practice. Of the other two areas on the Atlantic seaboard where phrase-final /r/ is lost, the Upper South has nearly eliminated the "linking" /r/ and the Lower South wavers in usage, as pointed out above. Southern usage is clearly an American innovation, although the loss of /r/ in *your aunt* is sporadically attested in the English counties of Northampton, Suffolk, and Essex.

law and order (Map 158)

It has been pointed out above that in the phrase *your aunt* word-final /r/ is treated as intersyllabic /r/ before the initial vowel of the following word in Eastern New England and in Metropolitan New York. The same treatment of historical word-final /r/ occurs in these two areas whatever the preceding vowel may be, so that *ear, poor, care four* have in these two dialects the positional allomorphs /iə ∼ iər, puə̯ ∼ puə̯r, kæə̯ (keə̯) ∼ kæə̯r (keə̯r), foə̯ (fɔə̯) ∼ foə̯r (fɔə̯r)/, and *car, for* (stressed), *father* the allomorphs /ka (kɑ) ∼ kar (kɑr), fɒ (fɔ) ∼ fɒr (fɔr), faðə ∼ faðər/.

On the analogy of such doublets as *for* /fɒ (fɔ) ∼ fɒr (fɔr)/, *car* /ka (kɑ) ∼ kar (kɑr)/, and *father* /faðə ∼ faðər/, positional allomorphs ending in /r/ are often created in Eastern New England and Metropolitan New York for words that historically end in the vowels /ɒ ∼ ɔ, a ∼ ɑ, ə/, as *law, ma, Martha*. Thus one hears *law and order* /lɒr ənd ɒdə, lɔr ənd ɔdə/, *ma and pa* /mar ən(d) pa, mɑr ən(d) pɑ/, *Martha and I* /maθər (mɑθər) ənd ai/.

The incidence of this "intrusive" linking /r/ is illustrated on the map for the phrase *law and order*. In Eastern New England it occurs in about one third of the responses, most commonly on Narragansett Bay (Rhode Island), in the back country of Boston, and in New Hampshire and Maine (especially along the coast). Cultured speakers use it as freely as the other social groups (e.g., in Providence, Newport, Plymouth, Boston, Portland). In Metropolitan New York it occurs with slightly greater frequency, but seems to be avoided by cultured informants (only two in nine offered it). It is still rare on the Jersey shore and in the lower Hudson Valley.

This analogical linking /r/ appears also within words in morpheme-final position, as in *sawing wood, seesawing*, but no systematic investigation of this feature has been undertaken.

Intrusive linking /r/ is rather common in *law and order, the law of the land* in the eastern counties of England (from Middlesex-Essex to Northampton-Norfolk), an area in which phrase-final /r/ is lost as such. The precise historical connection between English folk usage and that of New England and Metropolitan New York is not clear, since even in Standard British English the chronology of the loss of postvocalic /r/ is still in doubt.

In the American South intrusive linking /r/ does not occur in *law and order*. This is not surprising, since even the historical /r/, as in *your aunt, far out*, etc., has been largely eliminated in the Upper South and is not securely established in the Lower South.

It is worth noting that after the normally up-gliding free vowels /i, u, e, o/, as in *three, two, day, know*, an analogical "intrusive" /r/ never occurs. The reason for this is clear: since /θri, tu, de, no/ do not end like the phrase-final /r/-less allomorphs of *ear, poor, care, four* /iə, puə̯, keə̯, foə̯/, the basis for creating allomorphs ending in /r/ is lacking.

swallow it (Map 159)

In the phrase *swallow it*, a "linking" /r/ occurs chiefly in the South and the South Midland, and again in eastern New England. It is articulated as a constricted [ɚ] in areas that regularly preserve postvocalic /r/, and as a tongue tip /r/ elsewhere.

In the South and the South Midland, the linking /r/ is exceedingly common in this phrase; only urban speakers, especially the cultured, tend to avoid it (as in Baltimore, Charleston, and Atlanta). In eastern New England, on the other hand, the /r/ is rather clearly confined to folk speech, except for New Hampshire and Maine, where it is common enough among the middle group. It has been largely eliminated in urbanized southern New England and is avoided in cultivated speech.

In Western New England and the New England settlements to the west, /r/ is uncommon even in folk speech, and in Metropolitan New York and

Pennsylvania only scattered relics of it have been observed.

In Eastern New England the occurrence of /r/ in the phrase *swallow it* follows the pattern of *father is (away)* /faðər ɪz/: that is, *swallow* like *father* has positional allomorphs with and without /r/. In the South and the South Midland, the historical background of this /r/ is rather different. A glance at present-day usage in English folk speech leads the way to a satisfactory explanation.

In England /r/ appears in *swallow it* not only in the East Midland counties (from Essex to southern Lincoln), where *swallow* has allomorphs modeled on *father*, but also in the southern counties (from Kent to Devonshire) and in Buckingham and adjoining parts of Middlesex, Hertford, Northampton, and Oxford, where *father, order* end in constricted /r/ in all positions. The origin of /r/ in *swallow, sofa, yellow, widow* in these English dialects does not concern us here. For our purposes it is sufficient to point out that usage in the American South and South Midland clearly derives from British folk speech, both in areas that lack postvocalic /r/ (as Virginia and South Carolina) and in areas that have it (as the South Midland).

wash, ought to (Map 160)

In Pennsylvania west of the Susquehanna River and in West Virginia, an /r/ rather generally makes its appearance between the /ɔ ∼ ɒ/ and the /š/ of *wash* and *Washington*. This usage survives also in the Valley of Virginia and the Pennsylvania settlements farther south. In other areas that preserve postvocalic /r/, this intrusive /r/ is rare.

Between /ɔ ∼ ɒ/ and /t/, as in *daughter, water*, intrusive /r/ is rare, except in the expression *ought to*, where it occurs with some frequency in the South Midland and in eastern North Carolina, occasionally also in Pennsylvania, New Jersey, and on the Delmarva peninsula.

library (Maps 161–62)

Two major types of pronunciation are current in the Eastern States: (1) trisyllabic /'laɪˌbrɛri ∼ 'laiˌbɛri/, with half-stress on the second syllable; and (2) /'laibrəri ∼ 'laibəri ∼ 'laibri/. Type (1) occurs everywhere, but with greatly varying frequency; type (2) is largely confined to several subareas on the Atlantic seaboard.

The disyllabic variant /'laibri/ predominates in Eastern New England, in Maryland (along with Philadelphia and vicinity), in northeastern North Carolina, and in the Low Country of South Carolina and Georgia. In New England, trisyllabic /'laibrəri ∼ 'laibəri/ stand beside the disyllabic variant, occasionally also in the other subareas mentioned above. Scatterings of /laibri/ and its variants are found in Upstate New York (from New England), in Manhattan, in Tidewater Virginia (as relics), and in the Upcountry of the Carolinas (presumably introduced from the Low Country).

Trisyllabic /'laiˌbrɛri ∼ 'laiˌbɛri/, with half-stressed second syllable, predominates in all of the Eastern States except for the subareas along the coast mentioned above, being almost universal in some sections, especially toward the west. There is fairly clear evidence that these types are spreading into New England, where many cultured speakers now say /'laiˌbrɛri/ (as in Boston, Providence, Springfield, Hartford, New Haven). On the other hand, in northeastern New England, Maryland, Philadelphia, northeastern North Carolina, and the Low Country of South Carolina, disyllabic /laibri/ is firmly established on all social levels.

Trisyllabic /'laiˌbɛri/, with loss of /r/ in the second syllable, is of frequent occurrence in folk speech and not uncommon among the middle group in West Jersey, the Virginias, and North Carolina. It is rare in cultivated speech.

Besides disyllabic /laibri/, trisyllabic /laibəri/ is current in New England, and this pronunciation survives among less educated speakers in Manhattan along with /'laiˌbɛri/.

Cultivated usage in the Eastern States varies regionally; it is remarkably unsettled, but appears to be drifting toward trisyllabic /'laiˌbrɛri/.

According to the *Oxford Dictionary* and Daniel Jones (1956), Standard British English has only trisyllabic /laibrəri/. English folk speech of the Midland and the South has this type, but also disyllabic /laibri/, as in East Anglia-Essex and in the southwestern counties. These are the variants that became established along the Atlantic coast.

The predominant American types /ˈlaɪˌbreri/ and /ˈlaɪˌbɛri/ presumably represent earlier English usage. Among others, John Walker (1797) assigns the vowel of *fat* to the second syllable (which he also records in *February, secretary, literary*, etc.).

5.21 /j/ AND VARIANTS

new, due, Tuesday (Maps 163–65)

The alveolar consonants in *new, due, Tuesday,* etc., are followed either by the vowel /u/ of *two*, the sequence /ju/, or the back-gliding vowel /iu/ (for which see 3.21). The dissemination of the variants is largely regional.

The type of /nu, du, tuzde/ is current throughout the North and the North Midland. In Pennsylvania, northeastern West Virginia, New Jersey, and Metropolitan New York, /u/ is universal; in the New England settlement area it is the predominant pronunciation, but not the only one.

The type of /nju, dju, tjuzde/ has general currency in the South and the South Midland (south of the Potomac and the Kanawha). Here the sporadic [iu] phone may be a prosodic variant of the /ju/ sequence. In the North /ju/ is infrequent, though preferred by some cultured speakers, as in Metropolitan New York.

The type of /niu, diu, tiuzde/, with back-gliding decrescendo vowel, is largely confined to New England and the Yankee settlements to the west. It is especially common in folk speech, but is also used by some cultured speakers in New England (not in Upstate New York, it seems).

[iu] phones occur not infrequently in Maryland, rarely farther south; whether these are to be taken as prosodic allophones of the sequence /ju/ or as the vowel /iu/ is not clear.

Within the /ju/ area of the South and the South Midland, the sequences /dju, tju-/ are partly replaced by assibilated [džu, tšu-], phonemically /ǰu/ as in *June* and /ču-/ as in *chew*. This pronunciation is fairly common in folk speech, but is avoided by cultured speakers.

Standard British English has /nju, dju, tju-/,

historically derived from /niu, diu, tiu-/ of East Midland folk speech. New England /iu/ obviously reflects a folk usage of eastern England. Our southern /dju ∼ ǰu/ and /tju- ∼ ču-/, on the other hand, clearly derive from English folk speech of the western counties, supported by Standard British usage. American /nu, du, tu-/ of the North and the Midland was also introduced from England, where it is still rather common in the folk speech of some of the Home Counties and of East Anglia.

yeast (Map 166)

Two pronunciations are widely current in the Eastern States: /jist/, beginning like *yield*; and /ist/, homophonous with *east*.

Except for relics of /ist/ (chiefly in the folk speech of Eastern New England), /jist/ prevails on all social levels throughout the Northern area, including Metropolitan New York and the northern counties of Pennsylvania.

In the Midland and the South, on the other hand, /ist/ is the most common pronunciation of *yeast*. It is in almost exclusive use in Virginia and adjoining parts of Maryland, West Virginia, and North Carolina, and predominates decisively in most of Pennsylvania (including the cities of Philadelphia and Pittsburgh) and in South Carolina–Georgia (except for some of the cities, as Charleston, Columbia, Savannah, Augusta, and Atlanta). Cultured speakers use /ist/ unhesitatingly in Philadelphia, Baltimore, Richmond, Raleigh, Wilmington, Greenville; but in the cities of the Lower South, as in Charleston and Atlanta, they have shifted to the spelling pronunciation /jist/.

Standard British English now appears to have only /jist/, but the type of /ist/ is still widespread in English folk speech. It is current in the southern counties from Sussex to Devon and northward to western Essex, Middlesex, Oxford, Gloucester, and Worcester; it is used also in Lincolnshire and (according to Wright) in Yorkshire. It must have been used by well-educated Englishmen as late as 1800, since John Walker (who regards the pronunciation /jɛst/ as preferable to /jist/ and spells the word *yest*) goes out of his way to comment as follows: "The vulgar do not only pronounce the diphthong long, but sink the *y*, and reduce the word to *east*." The usage of the American Midland and South thus has a broad basis in British pronunciation. The silence of all the large American dictionaries with regard to /ist/ reflects the New England bias in American lexicography. Even the well-informed G. P. Krapp calls the pronunciation /ist/ "dialectal" in his *Comprehensive Guide to Good English* (1927).

It is worth noting that only two instances of the pronunciation /jɛst/, riming with *guest*, have been recorded in the New England settlement area (one near Boston, the other near Buffalo), a pronunciation widely used in the English Midland along with /jɪst/, riming with *fist*. These are the normal derivatives of OE *gist*, *gest*, whereas both *yeast* /jist/ and *east* /ist/ show deviant phonemic changes.

garden (Map 167)

From the Potomac to the Savannah, the initial consonant of *garden* is frequently a palatal stop [ɟ] followed by a [j]-like glide, whether the vowel following it is a low-front [a·], a low-back [ɑ· ~ ɑɒ], or a low-central [ɑ· ~ ɑ]. This palatal [ɟ] with its [j] glide must be taken as a cluster /gj/, unless one is willing to posit a palatal stop /ɟ/ that occurs only before a low vowel (that is, before the free vowel /ɑ/ or the checked vowel /ɑ/, depending upon the absence or presence of postvocalic /r/). Southerners who have the cluster /gj/ in *garden* /gjɑdɪn/ have a corresponding cluster /kj/ in *car* /kjɑ/.

The pronunciation of *garden* as /gjɑdɪn/ is especially common (1) between the Potomac and the James in Virginia and (2) in the Low Country of South Carolina, where it occurs on all social levels, although it is clearly recessive. Some cultured informants, indeed, use this regional pronunciation with some pride.

In eastern North Carolina and in the Upcountry of both of the Carolinas, /gjɑdɪn ~ gjɑrdən/ is largely restricted to folk speech. Only rare instances occur between the lower James and Albemarle Sound, in central North Carolina, and in southeastern West Virginia.

It is of interest to observe that this way of pronouncing *garden* does not survive north of the Potomac and but rarely south of the Savannah, although Maryland and Georgia usually share Virginian and South Carolinian features to some extent, and that, on the other hand, /gj/ was carried westward from the plantation country into the Upcountry of the Carolinas.

Before the vowel /ɜ/ of *girl*, the cluster /gj/ is much less frequent. It occurs chiefly along the coast of South Carolina (Georgetown, Charleston, Beaufort) and on the points of land in tidewater Virginia.

In English folk speech a palatalized velar stop is common in *garden* north of the Thames (East Anglia to Gloucester), and a palatal stop occurs in Leicester, Warwick, and Worcester (according to Joseph Wright also in Derby). Whatever the phonemic interpretation of these phones in the several English dialects may be, they are the immediate source of the /gj/ in Southern American English.

Massachusetts (Map 168)

The syllable next to the last, which bears the main stress, is pronounced as /ču/, /ǰu/, /tju/, or /tu/.

The variant /ču/, homophonous with *chew*, is in regular use in the North Midland, and with few exceptions also in the North outside of New England. In the South this pronunciation is uncommon, except in cultivated speech.

/ǰu/, identical with *Jew*, is fairly common in the folk speech of New England, less so in the speech of the middle group, rare in cultivated speech. Relics of this variant survive in the central part of Upstate New York.

In the South, /tju/ as in *tube* is the usual pronunciation of this syllable of *Massachusetts*, although some cultured informants say /ču/.

In the transition belt between North Midland /ču/ and Southern /tju/, especially in Delmarva and West Virginia, some speakers say /tu/ as in *two*, and scattered instances of this variant occur also in the coastal plain of the Carolinas. Here this syllable of *Massachusetts* exhibits the same three variants as *tube*.

No dictionary mentions the usual Southern pronunciation of *Massachusetts*.

5.22 FRICATIVES

nephew (Map 169)

/nɛfju/ is the usual pronunciation of this word throughout the Eastern States. Relics of /nɛvju/ survive, both in folk speech and in cultivated speech, in Eastern New England, on Chesapeake Bay, and especially in South Carolina, rarely elsewhere. Several instances of /nɛvi/ have been observed in the folk speech of New Hampshire.

In English folk speech the type of /nɛvju/ is in general use in the southern counties (except Somerset and Devonshire) and from Essex to Oxfordshire and Gloucestershire. In the Midland counties to the north of this area the type of /nɛfju/ predominates. (For Yorkshire and Scotland Joseph Wright reports both types.) Standard British English has /nɛvju/, but /nɛfju/ is recognized by the OD and by Daniel Jones as an alternate pronunciation.

Both /nɛvju/ and /nɛfju/ thus came to America from England. The former, representing the spoken tradition of Old French neveu (taken into English shortly before 1300), now predominates in England; the latter, conforming to the spelling nephew (introduced shortly before 1600 as a pseudolearned spelling), has all but ousted the older pronunciation /nɛvju/ in America.

hoofs

The plural form of hoof, whether pronounced with the /ʊ/ of wood or the /u/ of tooth, has the voiceless fricative /f/ nearly everywhere in the Eastern States. /huvz/ is common only in central Pennsylvania (from the Susquehanna to the Allegheny River, where it may well derive from the dialect of the Ulster Scots) and in the westernmost part of South Carolina; elsewhere only scattered instances have been observed. /hʊvz/, with the vowel of wood, is exceedingly rare. See Map 112.

without (Map 170)

Without has the voiced fricative /ð/ in all parts of the Eastern States, but with greatly varying frequency. It is nearly universal in all of the North, from New England to the Great Lakes; it predominates decisively in a wide belt extending from Metropolitan New York to Delaware Bay and the lower Susquehanna Valley, and again in most of the Upper South, including all of North Carolina. Elsewhere voiceless /θ/ is as frequent as voiced /ð/.

The voiceless fricative is common in without in two extensive areas: (1) Pennsylvania with West Virginia and the Valley of Virginia, but excluding Philadelphia and its hinterland to the Susquehanna and the Blue Mountains; (2) the Lower South. /θ/ also occurs with some frequency in parts of the Virginia Tidewater; it is not unknown in Richmond, but rare everywhere else.

Within the two large areas where /θ/ and /ð/ are nearly equally common, there is no marked social distribution of the variants, although the voiceless fricative appears to be more common in the cultivated speech of the Lower South.

Standard British English has /ð/, and, with a few exceptions noted in Middlesex, Berkshire, and Somerset, this variant is current in English folk speech. Joseph Wright gives no information on without, but reports /wɪθ/ from southern Scotland, Northumberland, Cumberland, and Ulster. It is highly probable that the /θ/ of Pennsylvania and West Virginia in without is of Ulster Scot derivation, but the sources of this variant in the Lower South and in Tidewater Virginia are probably more complex.

greasy (Map 171)

Voiceless /s/ and voiced /z/ are current in this word in remarkably clear-cut regional dissemination.

Voiceless /s/ is nearly universal (1) in New England and throughout the New England settlement area along the Great Lakes and in northern Pennsylvania, as also in the Hudson Valley north of Metropolitan New York. As a New Englandism it survives in a compact enclave around Marietta on the Ohio River and in scattered instances in the southern two-thirds of Ohio, especially also in Cincinnati. It predominates decisively (2) in Eastern Pennsylvania as far west as the valleys of the Susquehanna and the Juniata, but not in Philadelphia.

Voiced /z/ (1) is in universal use throughout

the South and the South Midland, except for a few instances along the coast of the Carolinas, on the Potomac, and in Baltimore; (2) predominates decisively in Metropolitan New York (seventeen out of thirty instances) and in New Jersey (except for the Newark area), and is used by five of the eight informants in Philadelphia; and (3) is in exclusive use in southwestern and south-central Pennsylvania and predominates in the southern two-thirds of Ohio.

In areas of divided usage—Metropolitan New York, the Newark area in New Jersey, Philadelphia and vicinity, and Ohio—the social and age distribution is erratic and does not permit of any inference as to present trends in usage. The isolated instances of /z/ in the North and of /s/ in the South occur both in folk speech and in cultivated speech and may well survive for some time to come.

In English folk speech of the present day /z/ and /s/ occur in clear-cut dissemination: the eastern counties (Kent and Essex to Lincolnshire) have /z/, the central and western counties /s/. According to Daniel Jones and the *Oxford Dictionary* (H. Bradley), Standard British English wavers between /z/ and /s/, which is not surprising, since London straddles the isogloss. In America, usage must have been unsettled in all sections of the Atlantic seaboard before uniformity was achieved in the North and the South. It is rather peculiar that New England, which often shows agreement with the eastern counties of England, should have discarded /z/ in this word.

vase

The usual pronunciation of this word is /ves/. However, a variant ending in /z/ occurs by the side of /ves/ in most of the cities on the Atlantic seaboard from Maine to Georgia, especially in cultivated speech. It is especially common in Metropolitan New York and in Philadelphia and vicinity, where one may even hear British /vɑz ∼ vɑz/.

/vɑz/ and /vɔz/ of Standard British English and of English folk speech represent the oral tradition in the pronunciation of this word (taken from French in this sense early in the seventeenth century), whereas American English /ves/ and /vez/ are spelling pronunciations (which formerly were also current in England; see the *Oxford Dictionary*).

Mrs. (Map 172)

The manifold regional, social, positional, and prosodic variants of *Mrs.*, the title of a married woman, have been discussed by E. Bagby Atwood in *American Speech* 25.10 (1950). Here only some of the more common variants will be considered.

The type of /mɪsɪz/ prevails throughout the North and the North Midland, but /mɪsɪs/ is rather common in New England and occurs with some frequency in the northern and the eastern counties of Pennsylvania. In these areas, /mɪsɪz/ and /mɪsɪs/ are reduced to monosyllabic /mɪz/ and /mɪs/, respectively, in rapid speech.

In the South, with the exception of parts of North Carolina, the prevalent types are /mɪzɪz/ and its reduced form /mɪz/. Even in North Carolina /mɪsɪs/ is rare, but its reduced variant /mɪs/—inconveniently homophonous with the title *Miss*—is rather widely used and not unknown in South Carolina and Georgia. The South Midland presents the same confused situation as North Carolina.

sumac (Map 173)

This word is generally pronounced with initial /š/, as in *shoe*. However, many cultured urbanites along the Atlantic seaboard from Maine (Portland) to Georgia (Savannah), and some living farther inland, say /sumæk/. Among less educated speakers this type is rare outside of New England.

Both /sjumæk/ and /šumæk/—with assimilation of /sj/ to /š/, as in *sugar*, *sure*—are current in England. The spelling with *sh* is attested in the *OD* from 1580 to 1860 for the popular name of the sumac preparations used in tanning and dyeing. American English has rather generally retained this folk pronunciation of the word; whether /sumæk/ is merely a school-taught spelling pronunciation or in part a recent importation of the preferred British pronunciation is an open question.

wheelbarrow, whinny, wharf

(Maps 174–75)

In the greater part of the Eastern States, initial /h/ is preserved before /w/ in stressed syllables, as in *wheelbarrow, whip, whinny, whicker*. However, it is lost, either wholly or in part: (1) in an extensive coastal section of the Middle Atlantic States, (2) in a narrow coastal strip of New England extending from Boston to the Kennebec in Maine, and (3) in a narrow belt along the coast of South Carolina and Georgia.

The /h/-less area of the Middle Atlantic States extends from the Hudson Valley southward to Chesapeake Bay, including the metropolitan areas of Greater New York and Philadelphia where the loss of /h/ is nearly universal. In the Hudson Valley and on Long Island usage is still divided; New Jersey, Delaware, and Eastern Pennsylvania to the Susquehanna Valley (including the Pennsylvania German area) lack the /h/ almost entirely (as do the Loyalist settlements of New Brunswick and their derivative settlements in northern Maine); from the Susquehanna to the crest of the Alleghenies usage is still divided, as also in adjoining parts of Maryland (in Baltimore the cleavage is clearly social, the cultured informants using the Southern /hw/).

In the coastal belts of New England and South Carolina the /h/ is being restored in *wheelbarrow, whip, whinny, whicker*, etc.; here the cultured speakers clearly have a preference for initial /hw-/ in such words.

In the British Isles, initial /hw/ has been reduced to /w/ in all except the northernmost counties of England. It survives in Northumberland, Westmoreland, Cumberland, and in Scotland and Northern Ireland (see Joseph Wright, *EDG*, pp. 673–79). The widespread use of /hw/ in the Eastern States points to a rather extensive preservation of this initial cluster in parts of England at the time the American colonies were established, since the widespread use of /hw/, especially in the South, cannot be attributed to the influence of this spelling. Moreover, the geographic restriction of initial /w/ in such words to several coastal areas centering on prominent seaports definitely points to post-settlement influence of Standard British English. That the coastal section of the Middle Atlantic States lacked /h/ in *whip, wheelbarrow, whinny*, etc., to a considerable extent at the time of the War for Independence is strikingly shown by present-day usage in the Loyalist settlements of New Brunswick, Canada, where initial /hw/ is rare.

It is of considerable interest to observe that *wharf*, a seaside term, appears to be the only word in which initial /w/ is widely used outside the area in which *wheelbarrow*, etc., have this feature. It is now current (1) throughout the coastal plain of the Southern States, and (2) in Western Pennsylvania and the Ohio Valley as far downstream as the mouth of the Scioto in Ohio (here obviously brought in from the Middle Atlantic coast). In New York State and in the southern upland most speakers use *dock* instead of *wharf*.

humor (Map 176)

The prevalent pronunciation of *humor* is /jumɜ ~ jumə/. With few exceptions, initial /h/ occurs only in New England and Upstate New York. It is most common in the Connecticut Valley. Within the areas that have the /ʊ/ of *book* in *broom, room* (see Map 107), /ʊ/ appears also in *humor*, but to a very limited extent.

5.23 MISCELLANEOUS CONSONANTS

(Maps 177–80)

coop

Commonly pronounced as /kup/ or /kʊp/, this word has a variant /kʊb/ in two well-defined areas: (1) on Delaware Bay and the lower Susquehanna (but not in Philadelphia, its original center of dissemination); and (2) in the coastal plain of Georgia and the Carolinas (but not in the immediate vicinity of Albemarle and Pamlico Sound), and in scattered fashion northward on Chesapeake Bay to the Potomac. Except for South Carolina, /kʊb/ is confined to folk speech and to common speech; in South Carolina it is frequent enough in cultivated speech, but no longer so in Charleston. See Map 108.

The variant /kʊb/ is not an American innovation; it comes from the western counties of England, where it is still widely current in folk speech.

mushroom (Map 177)

A pronunciation of *mushroom* in three syllables is current in nearly all sections of the Eastern States, though with greatly varying frequency.

The trisyllabic type, ending in /n/ or /m/, predominates in the folk speech of most of the South and the Midland, in West Virginia and in western Pennsylvania also in common speech. It does not occur in cultivated speech, is almost completely absent in the larger cities (e.g., Philadelphia, Baltimore, Richmond, Charleston, Atlanta), relatively infrequent in the Upcountry of South Carolina and the greater part of Georgia, and lacking in the bilingual German section of Eastern Pennsylvania (where the word is learned in school).

Trisyllabic variants are much less common in the North, surprisingly so in normally conservative New Hampshire and Maine. Rhode Island stands out as favoring /mʌšərun/, as do some sections of Upstate New York and the northern counties of Pennsylvania; on the other hand, this type has been eliminated in Metropolitan New York, the lower Hudson Valley, and on Long Island.

Disyllabic *mushroom* ending in /n/ is very common in New England, Upstate New York, New Jersey, Pennsylvania, West Virginia, Delmarva, and Tidewater Virginia, but rather infrequent in the rest of Virginia, the Carolinas, and Georgia. In the North and the Midland one hears /mʌšrun/ even from older cultured speakers (though not in Boston, Metropolitan New York, or Philadelphia), occasionally also in the South.

In summary, one can say that disyllabic variants ending in /n/ are characteristic of the North, trisyllabic variants ending in /m/ or /n/ of the South and the Midland, though both types occur in all major areas.

Both trisyllabic variants of *mushroom* and variants ending in /n/ are still widely current in the folk speech of the southern counties of England (Kent to Somerset). Trisyllabic variants ending in /m/ occur also north of the Thames (Middlesex-Essex to eastern Norfolk, with a scattering in Bucks, Oxford, and Warwick). Though Standard British English has had final /m/ since 1550 (along with final /mp/ until c. 1675), forms ending in /n/ appear in written English as late as c. 1650 (see the *OD*). Hence this type (the direct descendant of OF *mousseron*) must have been current on all social levels in England when the American colonies were founded, which accounts for its extensive dissemination in the Eastern States at the present time and its survival in the cultivated speech of the older generation. American dictionaries are silent on this point, with the honorable exception of Kenyon-Knott.

walnut (Map 178)

In two subareas of the Atlantic coast—Southern New England with Long Island, and Eastern Virginia with adjoining parts of Maryland and North Carolina—/l/ is often lost in *walnut*. Elsewhere this loss is rare, except perhaps in the Low Country of South Carolina.

In two other areas—the Carolinas and Delmarva—the velarized /l/ is frequently replaced by /r ∼ ə̯/.

Both pronunciations are widely current in English folk speech of today, the former in the east, the latter in the west.

once, twice (Map 179)

An added /t/ occurs in *once* and *twice* throughout the Midland and the South, excepting only the piedmont of Virginia. It is more frequent in *once* than in *twice*. Though most common in folk speech, it is widely used by middle-class speakers, especially in the South Midland.

turtle (Map 180)

The /t/ in *turtle* is largely replaced by /k/ in the folk speech of the South and the South Midland. This substitution occurs occasionally also in New Jersey and New York State. The term was not investigated in New England. The Lower South has the synonym *cooter* for the turtle.

INDEX

MAPS 1–180

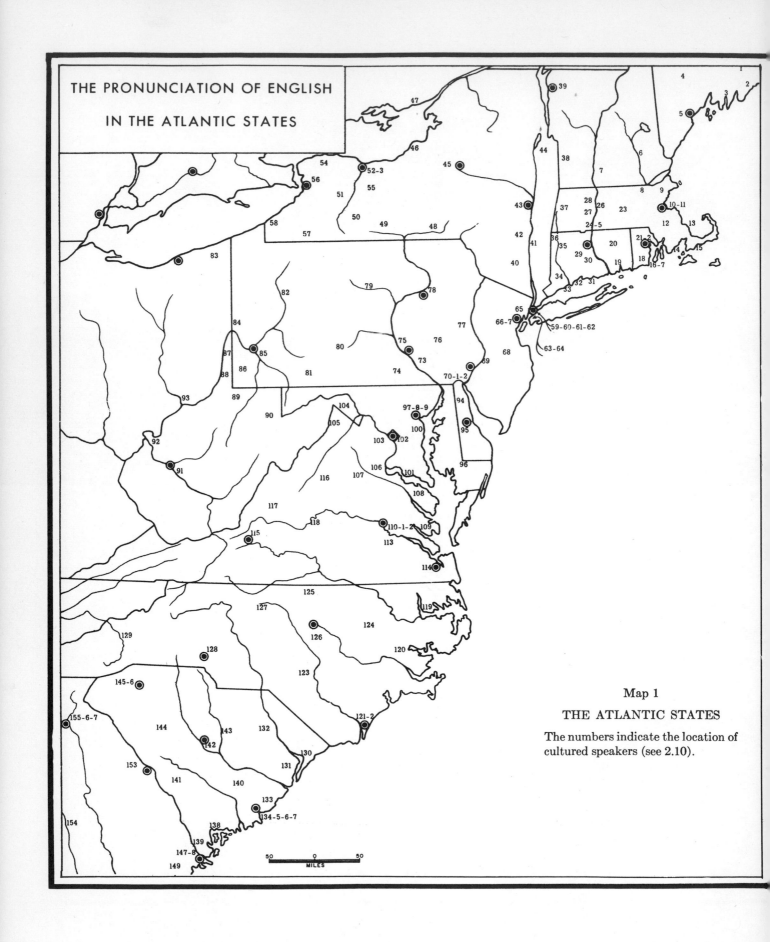

THE PRONUNCIATION OF ENGLISH

IN THE ATLANTIC STATES

Map 1

THE ATLANTIC STATES

The numbers indicate the location of
cultured speakers (see 2.10).

MILES

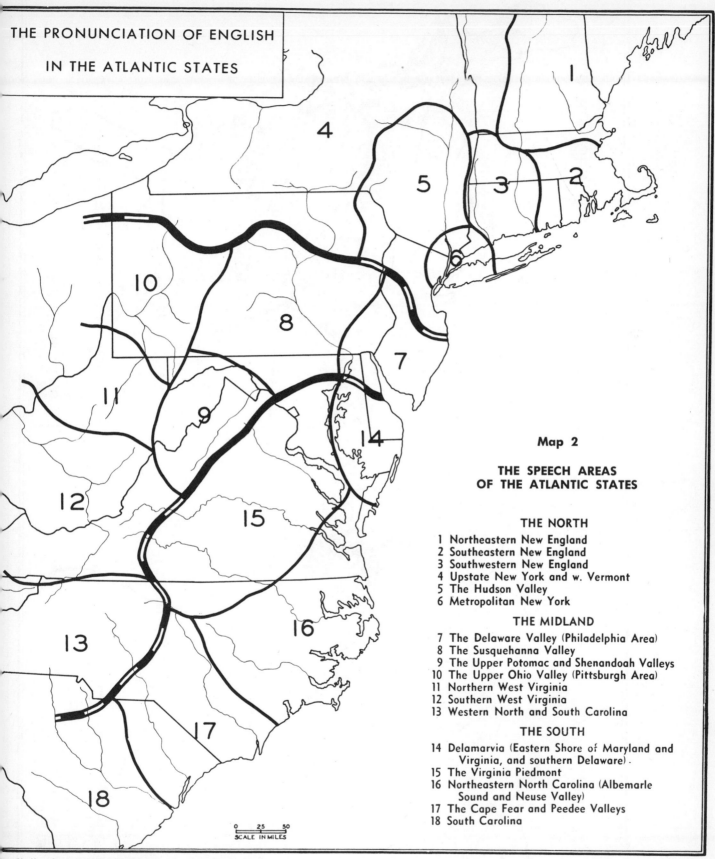

THE PRONUNCIATION OF ENGLISH

IN THE ATLANTIC STATES

Map 2

THE SPEECH AREAS
OF THE ATLANTIC STATES

THE NORTH

1 Northeastern New England
2 Southeastern New England
3 Southwestern New England
4 Upstate New York and w. Vermont
5 The Hudson Valley
6 Metropolitan New York

THE MIDLAND

7 The Delaware Valley (Philadelphia Area)
8 The Susquehanna Valley
9 The Upper Potomac and Shenandoah Valleys
10 The Upper Ohio Valley (Pittsburgh Area)
11 Northern West Virginia
12 Southern West Virginia
13 Western North and South Carolina

THE SOUTH

14 Delamarvia (Eastern Shore of Maryland and
      Virginia, and southern Delaware)
15 The Virginia Piedmont
16 Northeastern North Carolina (Albemarle
      Sound and Neuse Valley)
17 The Cape Fear and Peedee Valleys
18 South Carolina

0   25   50
SCALE IN MILES

om H. Kurath, A WORD GEOGRAPHY OF THE EASTERN STATES.

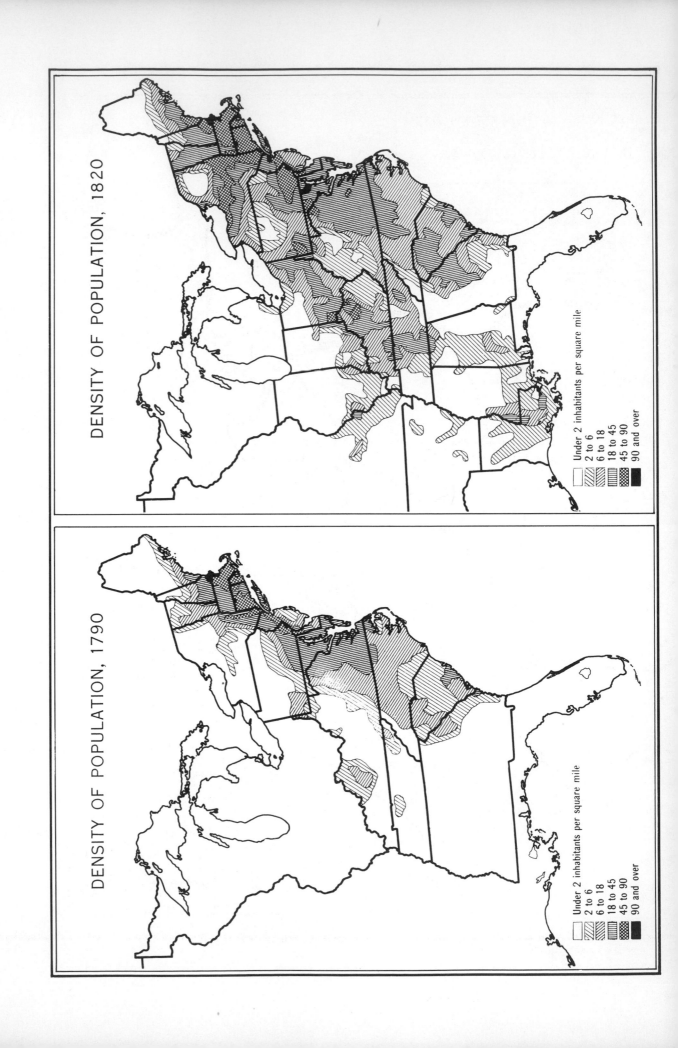

DENSITY OF POPULATION, 1820

Under 2 inhabitants per square mile
2 to 6
6 to 18
18 to 45
45 to 90
90 and over

DENSITY OF POPULATION, 1790

Under 2 inhabitants per square mile
2 to 6
6 to 18
18 to 45
45 to 90
90 and over

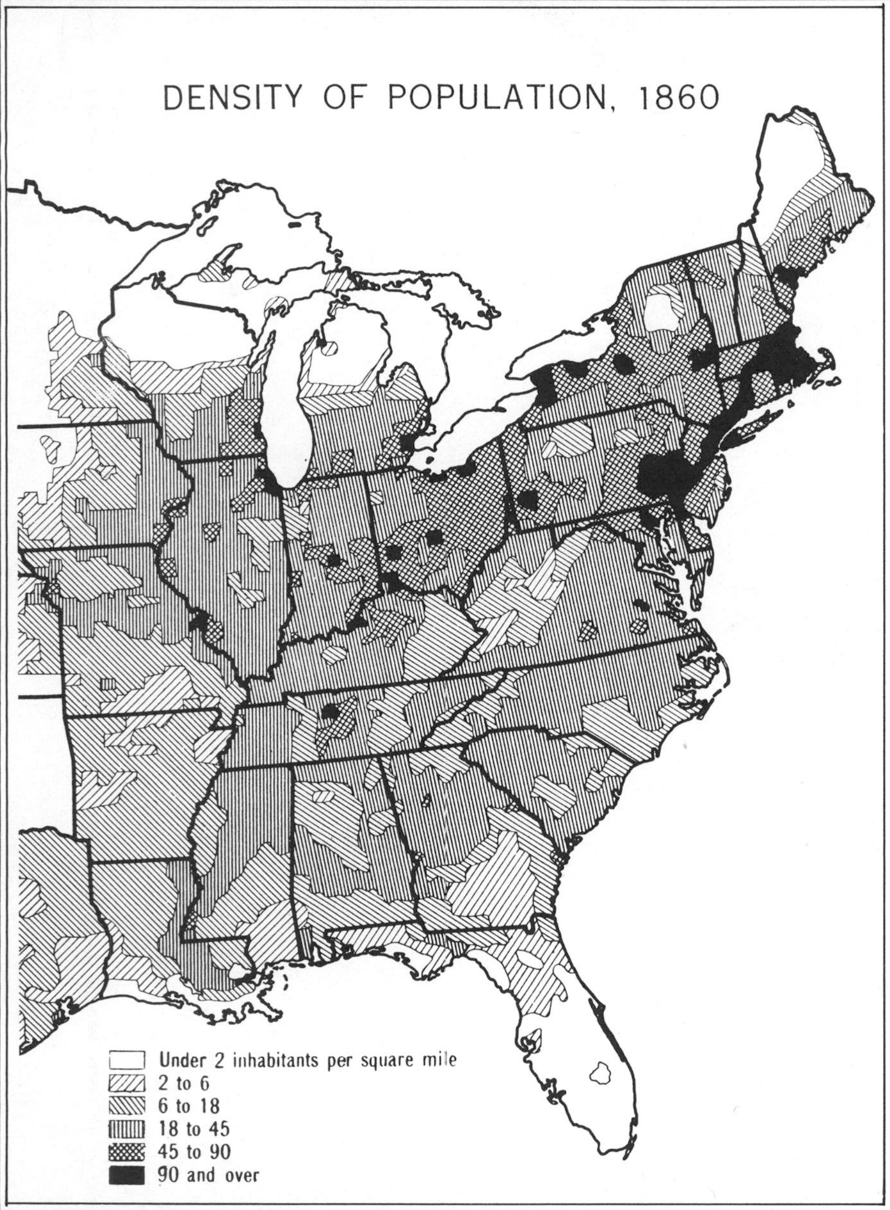

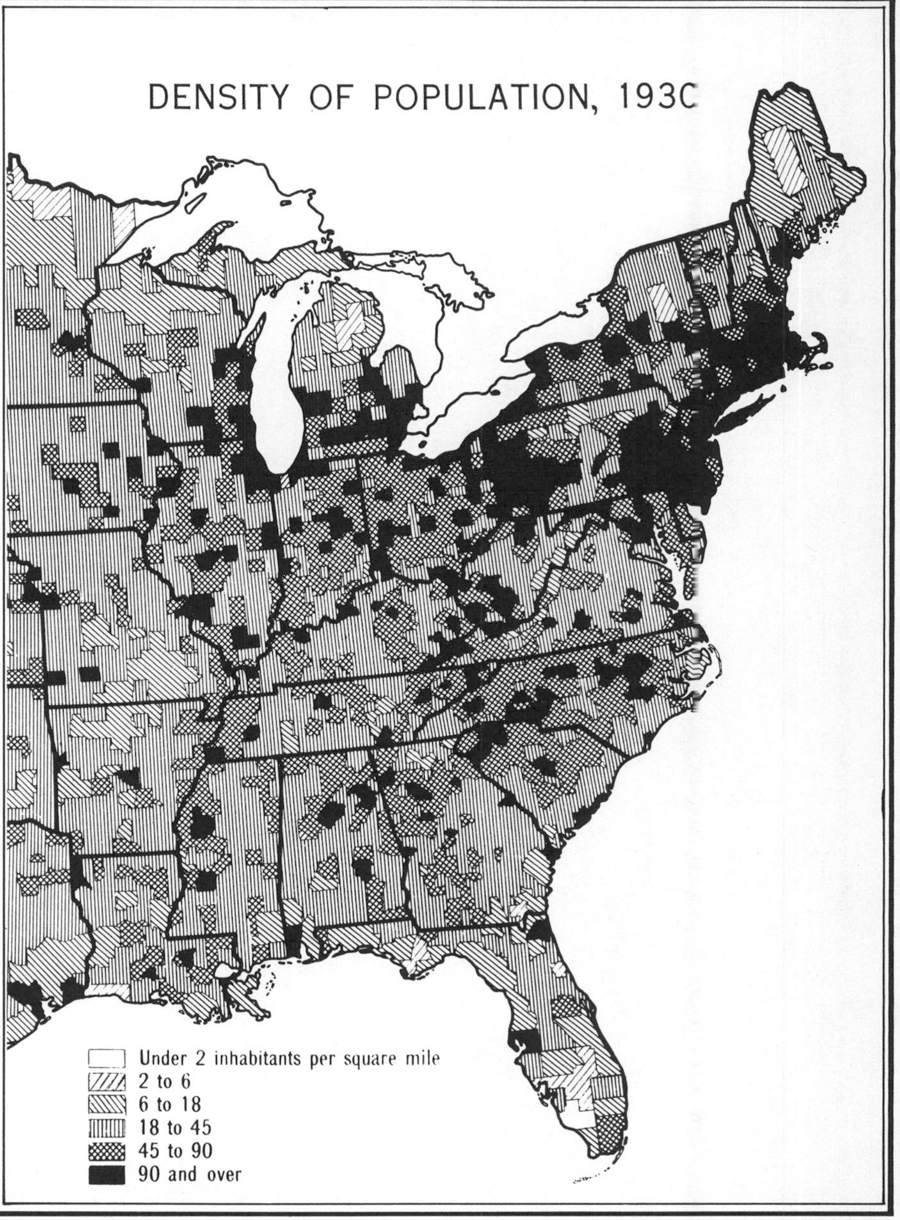

DENSITY OF POPULATION, 1930

DENSITY OF POPULATION, 1860

Under 2 inhabitants per square mile
2 to 6
6 to 18
18 to 45
45 to 90
90 and over

Under 2 inhabitants per square mile
2 to 6
6 to 18
18 to 45
45 to 90
90 and over

From C. Paullin and J. Wright, ATLAS OF THE HISTORICAL
GEOGRAPHY OF THE UNITED STATES.

Map 3

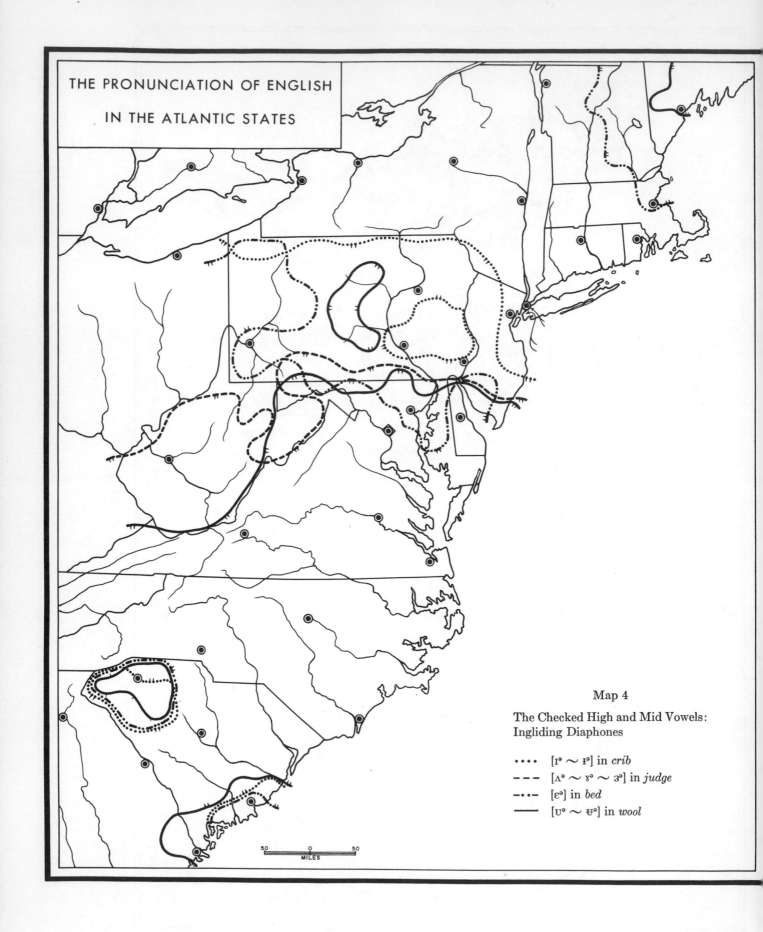

THE PRONUNCIATION OF ENGLISH

IN THE ATLANTIC STATES

Map 4

The Checked High and Mid Vowels:
Ingliding Diaphones

•••• [ɪ˒ ∼ ɪ̵˒] in *crib*

‐ ‐ ‐ [ʌ˒ ∼ ɤ˒ ∼ ɝ˒] in *judge*

‐·‐·‐ [ɛ˒] in *bed*

──── [ʊ˒ ∼ ʊ̵˒] in *wool*

50 0 50
MILES

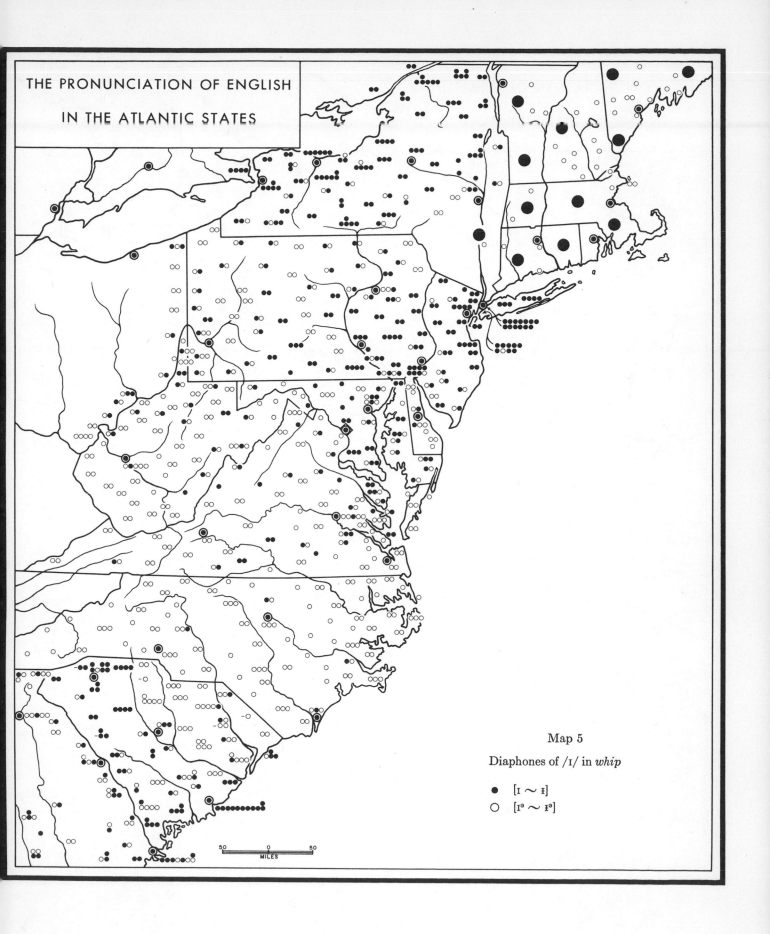

THE PRONUNCIATION OF ENGLISH
IN THE ATLANTIC STATES

Map 5

Diaphones of /ɪ/ in *whip*

● [ɪ ∼ ɨ]

○ [ɪᵊ ∼ ɨᵊ]

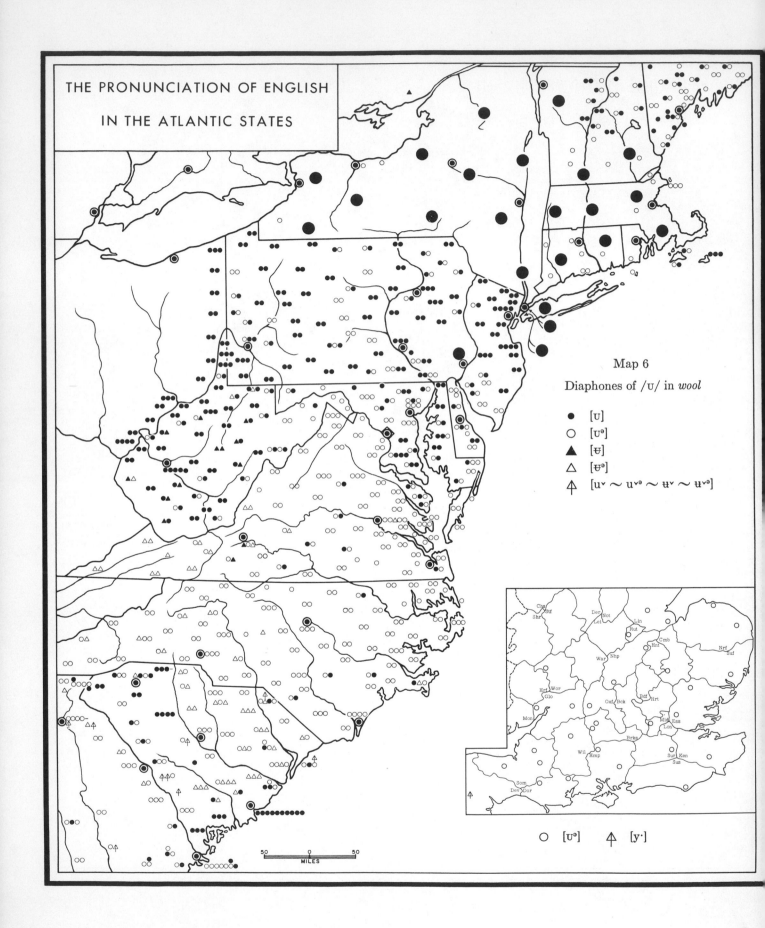

THE PRONUNCIATION OF ENGLISH

IN THE ATLANTIC STATES

Map 6

Diaphones of /ʊ/ in *wool*

- ● [ʊ]
- ○ [ʊᵊ]
- ▲ [ʉ]
- △ [ʉᵊ]
- ⚡ [uˇ ~ uˇᵊ ~ ʉˇ ~ ʉˇᵊ]

50   0   50
MILES

○ [ʊᵊ]   ⚡ [yˑ]

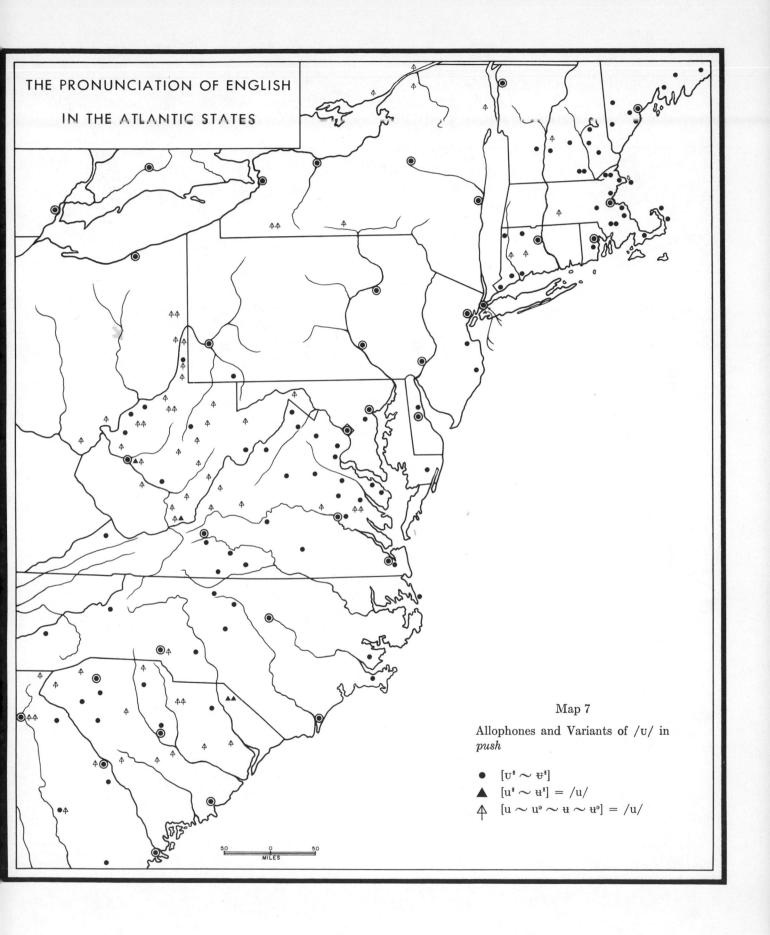

THE PRONUNCIATION OF ENGLISH
IN THE ATLANTIC STATES

Map 7

Allophones and Variants of /ʊ/ in
push

●   [ʊˣ ~ ᵾˣ]

▲   [uˣ ~ ᵾˣ] = /u/

⚶   [u ~ uᵊ ~ ᵾ ~ ᵾᵊ] = /u/

50   0   50
MILES

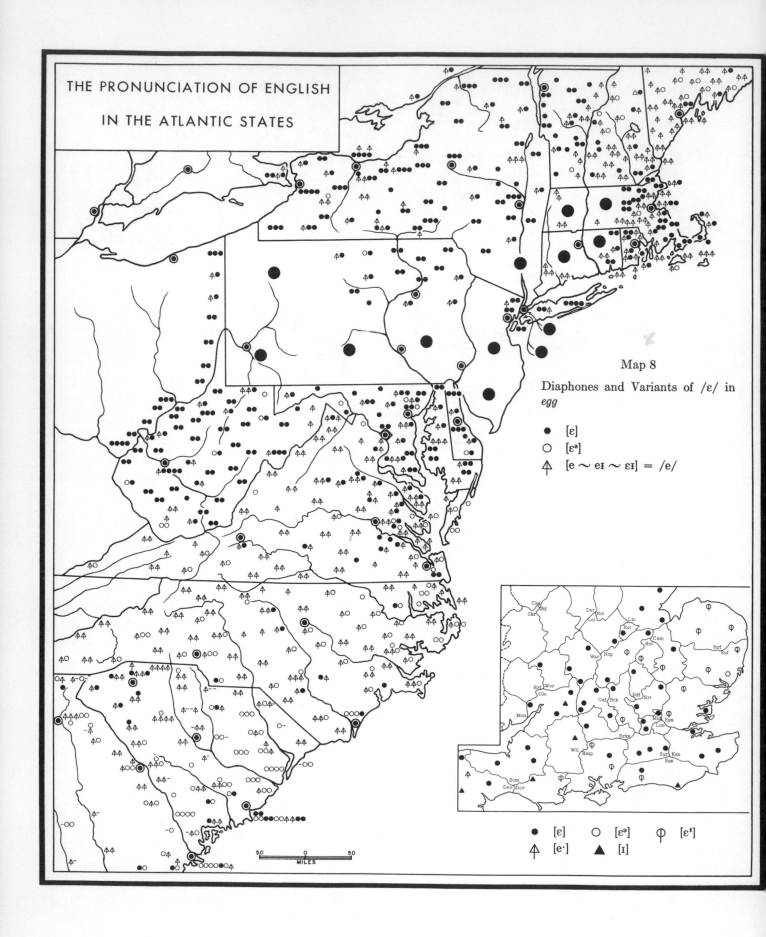

THE PRONUNCIATION OF ENGLISH

IN THE ATLANTIC STATES

Map 8

Diaphones and Variants of /ɛ/ in
egg

● [ɛ]

○ [ɛə]

⚹ [e ~ eɪ ~ ɛɪ] = /e/

MILES

● [ɛ]   ○ [ɛə]   φ [ɛ²]

⚹ [e·]   ▲ [ɪ]

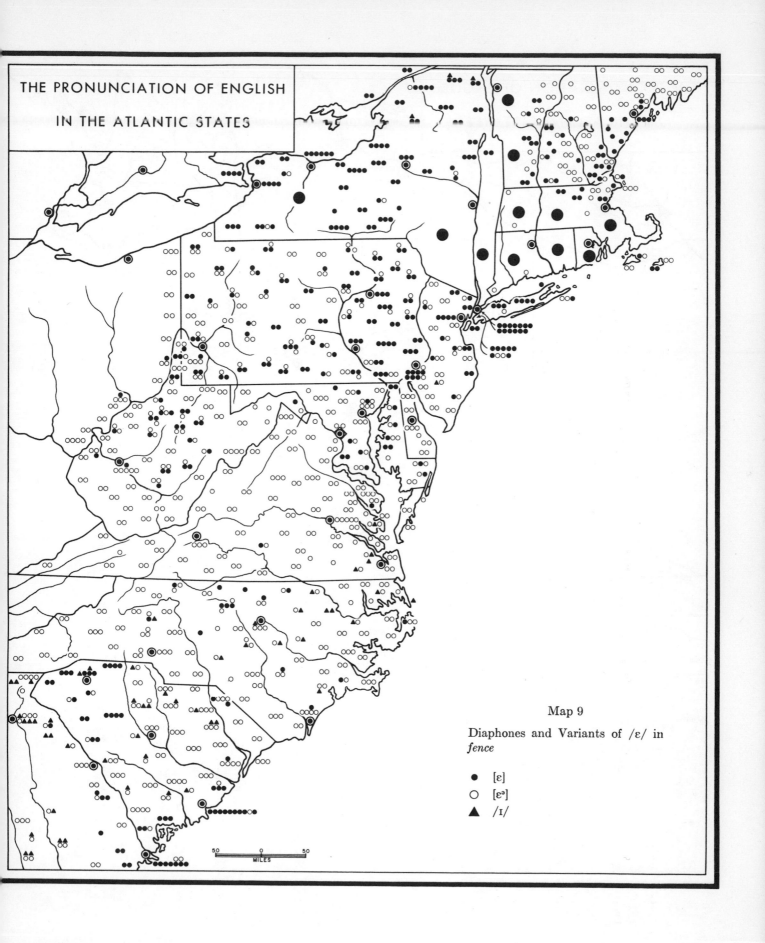

THE PRONUNCIATION OF ENGLISH

IN THE ATLANTIC STATES

Map 9

Diaphones and Variants of /ɛ/ in
fence

● [ɛ]

○ [ɛᵊ]

▲ /ɪ/

50   0   50
MILES

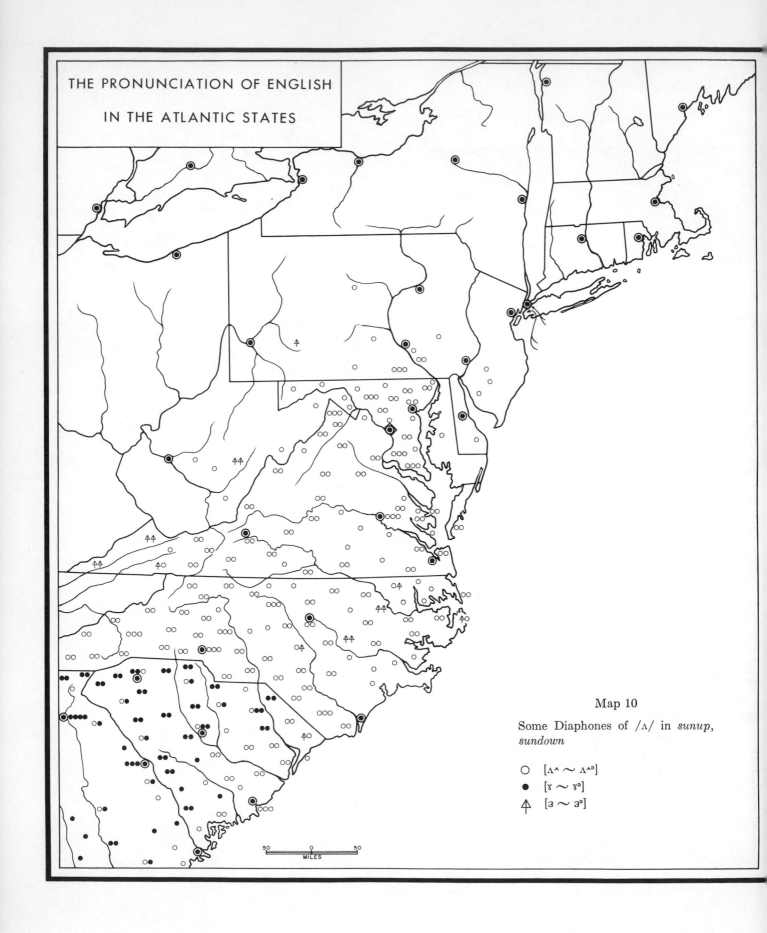

THE PRONUNCIATION OF ENGLISH

IN THE ATLANTIC STATES

Map 10

Some Diaphones of /ʌ/ in *sunup,*
sundown

○   [ʌˆ ∼ ʌˆə]

●   [ɤ ∼ ɤə]

↑   [ɜ ∼ ɜə]

50   0   50

MILES

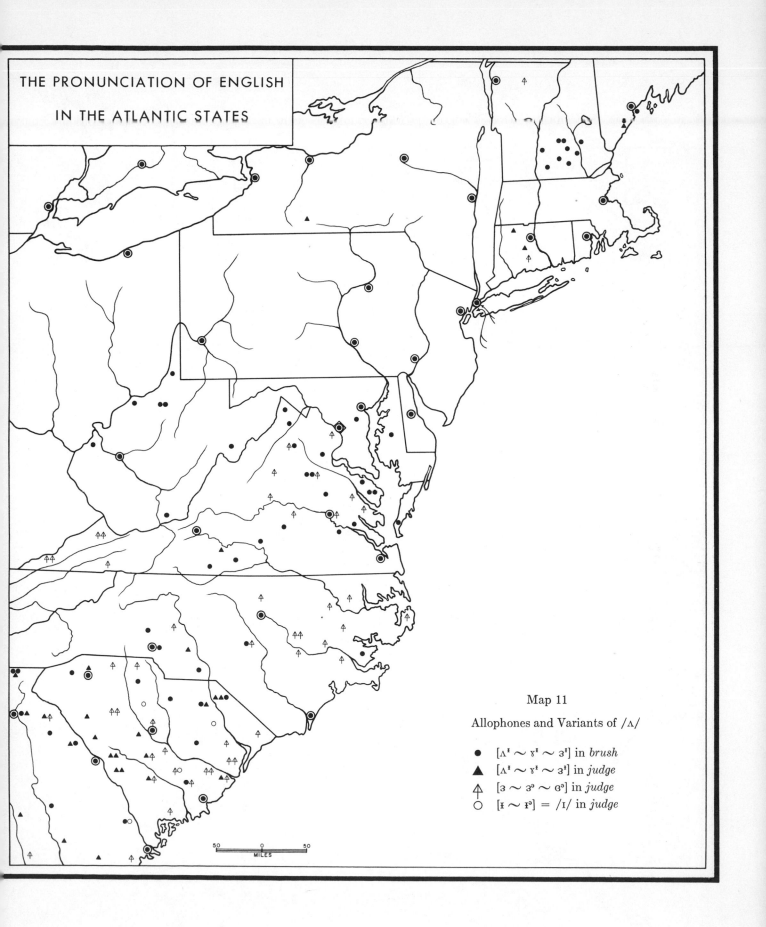

THE PRONUNCIATION OF ENGLISH

IN THE ATLANTIC STATES

Map 11

Allophones and Variants of /ʌ/

- ● [ʌ˕ ∼ ɤ˕ ∼ ɜ˕] in *brush*
- ▲ [ʌ˕ ∼ ɤ˕ ∼ ɜ˕] in *judge*
- ↑ [ɜ ∼ ɜ˒ ∼ ɵ˒] in *judge*
- ○ [ɨ ∼ ɨ˒] = /ɪ/ in *judge*

50 0 50
MILES

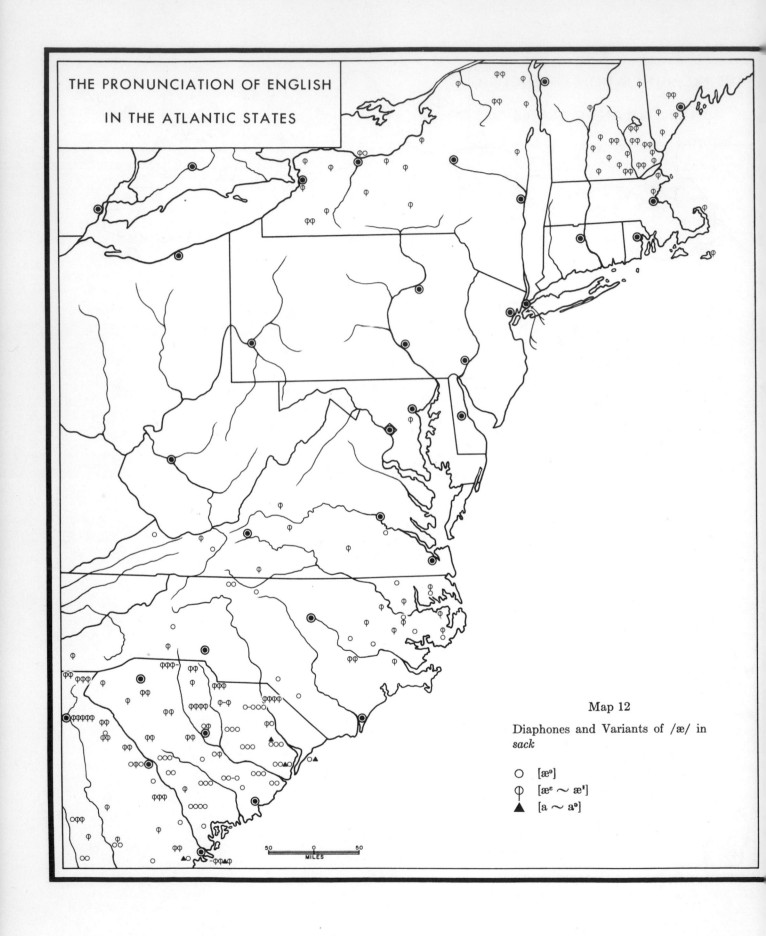

THE PRONUNCIATION OF ENGLISH

IN THE ATLANTIC STATES

Map 12

Diaphones and Variants of /æ/ in
sack

○   [æ^ə]

Φ   [æ^ɛ ~ æ^ɪ]

▲   [a ~ a^ə]

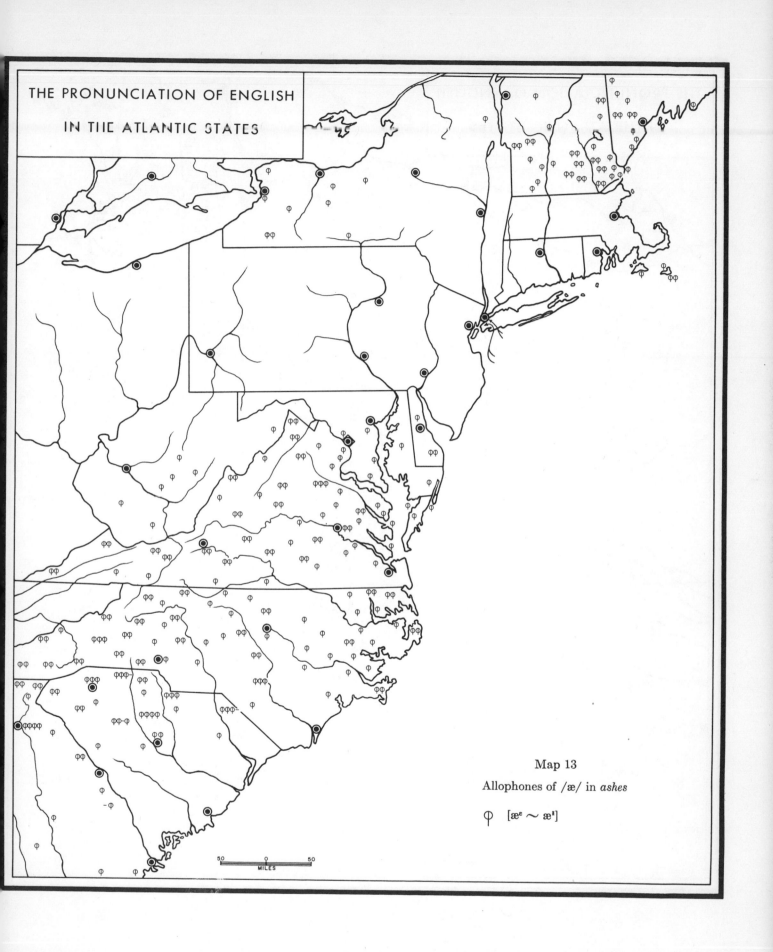

THE PRONUNCIATION OF ENGLISH

IN THE ATLANTIC STATES

Map 13

Allophones of /æ/ in *ashes*

φ [æᵉ ~ æ¹]

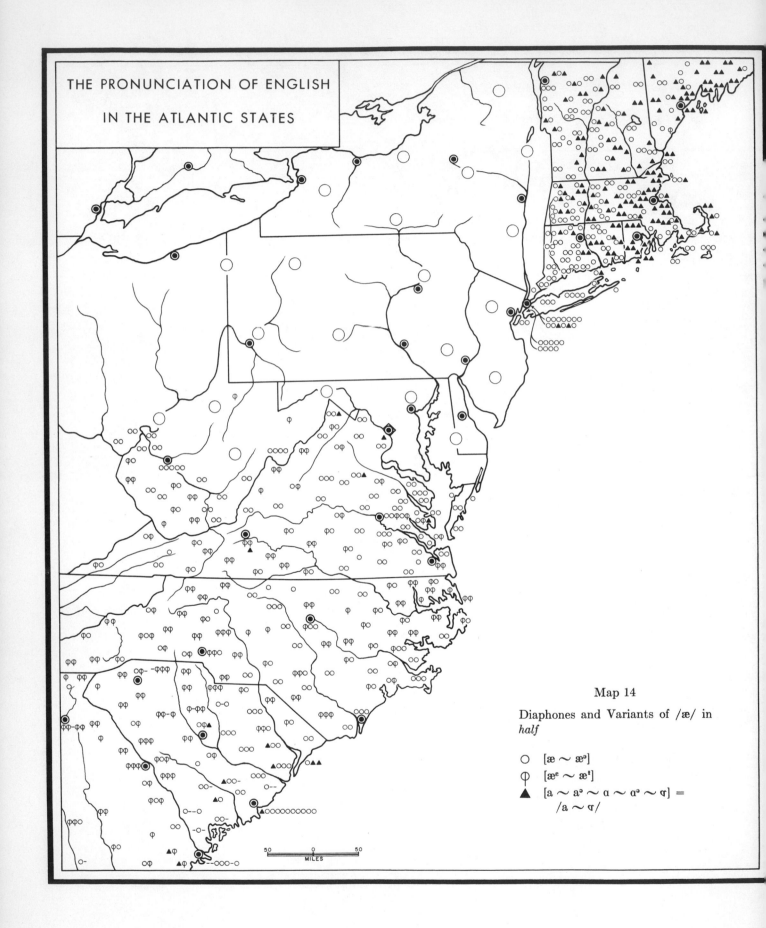

THE PRONUNCIATION OF ENGLISH

IN THE ATLANTIC STATES

Map 14

Diaphones and Variants of /æ/ in
half

○   [æ ∼ æᵊ]

φ   [æᵋ ∼ æᴵ]

▲   [a ∼ aᵊ ∼ ɑ ∼ ɑᵊ ∼ ɒ] =
       /a ∼ ɒ/

50   0   50
MILES

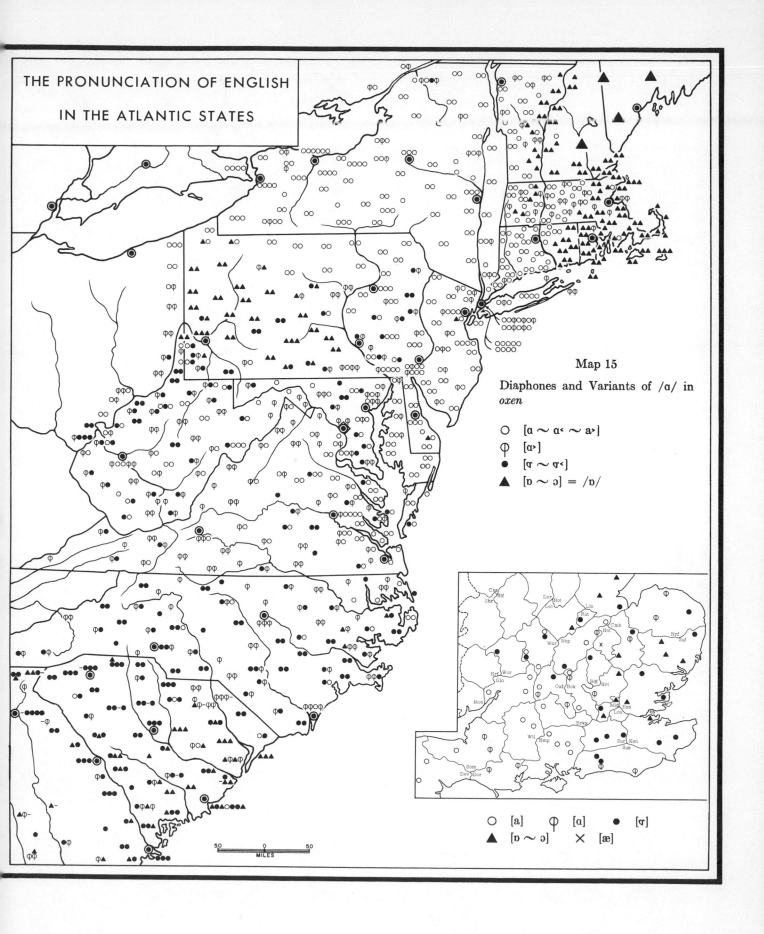

THE PRONUNCIATION OF ENGLISH

IN THE ATLANTIC STATES

Map 15

Diaphones and Variants of /ɑ/ in
oxen

○   [ɑ ∼ ɑ‹ ∼ a›]

φ   [ɑ›]

●   [ɒ ∼ ɒ‹]

▲   [ɒ ∼ ɔ] = /ɒ/

○ [a]   φ [ɑ]   ● [ɒ]

▲ [ɒ ∼ ɔ]   × [æ]

50   0   50
MILES

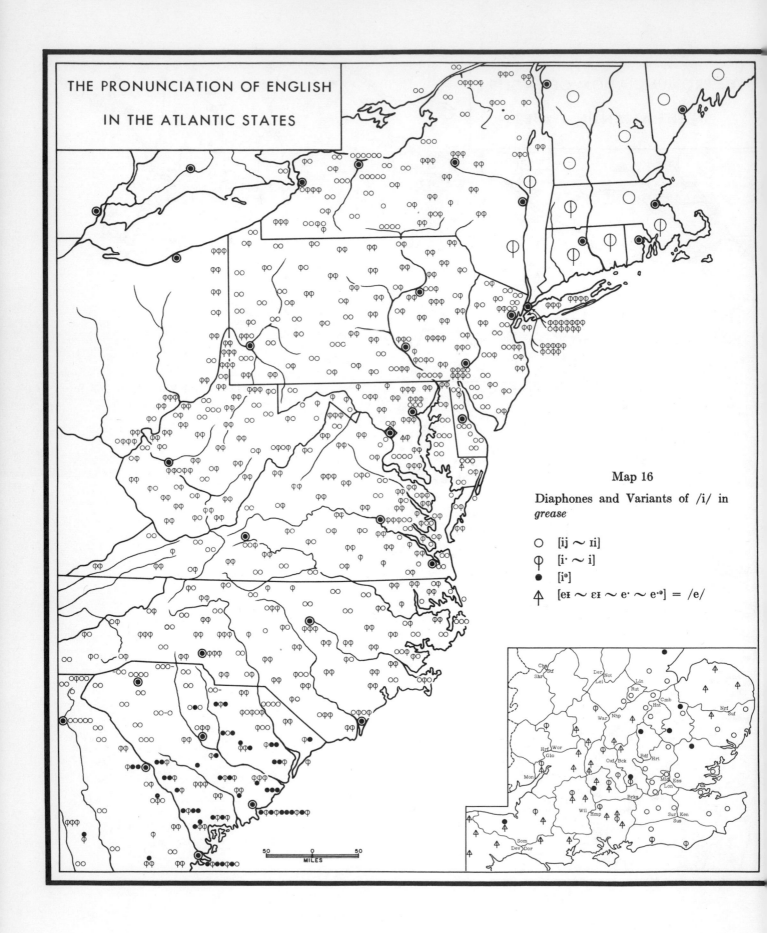

THE PRONUNCIATION OF ENGLISH
IN THE ATLANTIC STATES

Map 16

Diaphones and Variants of /i/ in
grease

○ [ij ~ ɪi]

φ [i· ~ i]

● [iə]

⚲ [eɪ ~ ɛɪ ~ e· ~ e·ə] = /e/

50   0   50
MILES

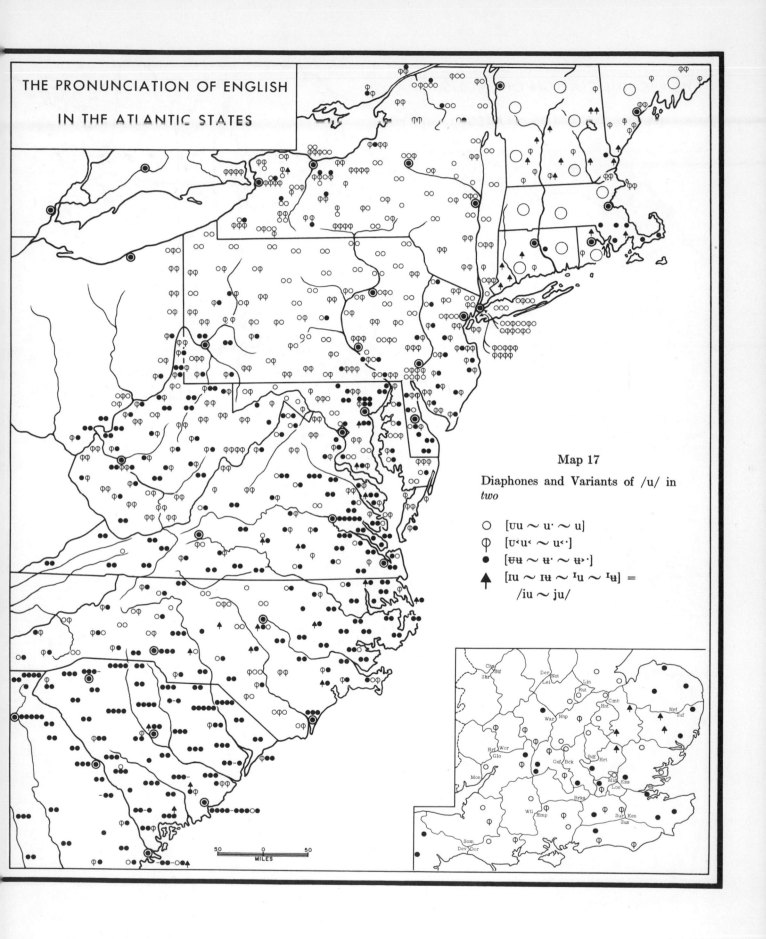

THE PRONUNCIATION OF ENGLISH
IN THE ATLANTIC STATES

Map 17

Diaphones and Variants of /u/ in
two

○ [ʊu ~ u· ~ u]

φ [ʊ‹u‹ ~ u‹·]

● [ʉu ~ ʉ· ~ ʉ·]

▲ [ɪu ~ ɪʉ ~ ɪu ~ ɪʉ] =
/iu ~ ju/

50   0   50
MILES

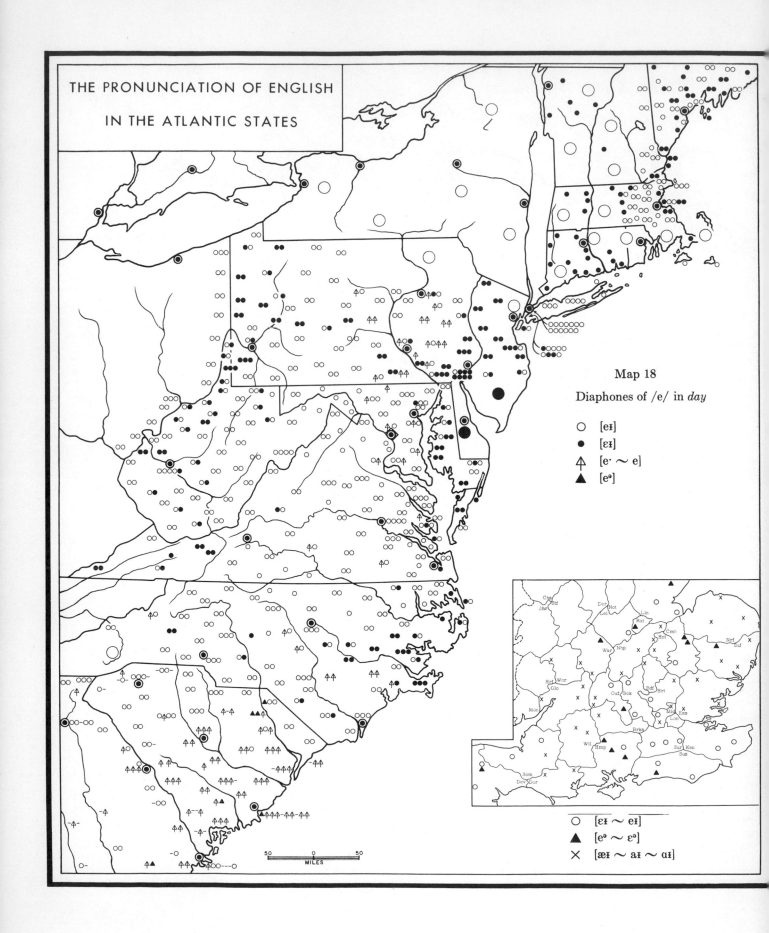

THE PRONUNCIATION OF ENGLISH
IN THE ATLANTIC STATES

Map 18

Diaphones of /e/ in *day*

○ [eɪ]

● [ɛɪ]

⚲ [e· ∼ e]

▲ [eə]

MILES

50 0 50

──── [ɛɪ ∼ eɪ]

▲ [eə ∼ ɛə]

✕ [æɪ ∼ aɪ ∼ ɑɪ]

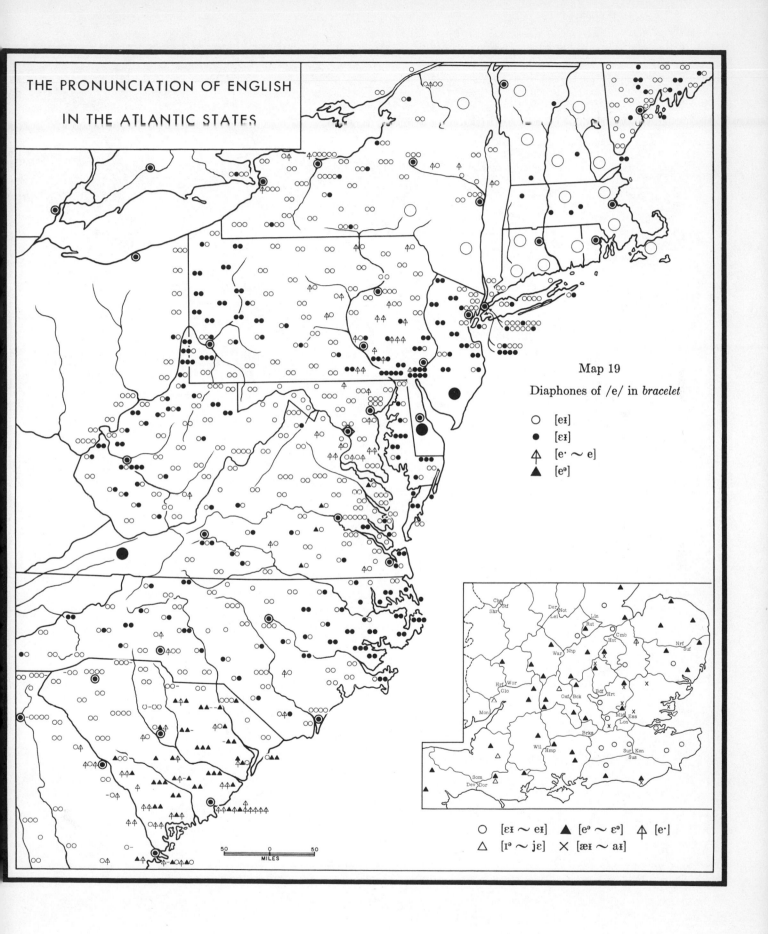

THE PRONUNCIATION OF ENGLISH
IN THE ATLANTIC STATES

Map 19

Diaphones of /e/ in *bracelet*

○ [eɪ]
● [ɛɪ]
⚑ [e· ∼ e]
▲ [eə]

○ [ɛɪ ∼ eɪ]   ▲ [eə ∼ ɛə]   ⚑ [e·]
△ [ɪə ∼ jɛ]   ✕ [æɪ ∼ aɪ]

MILES

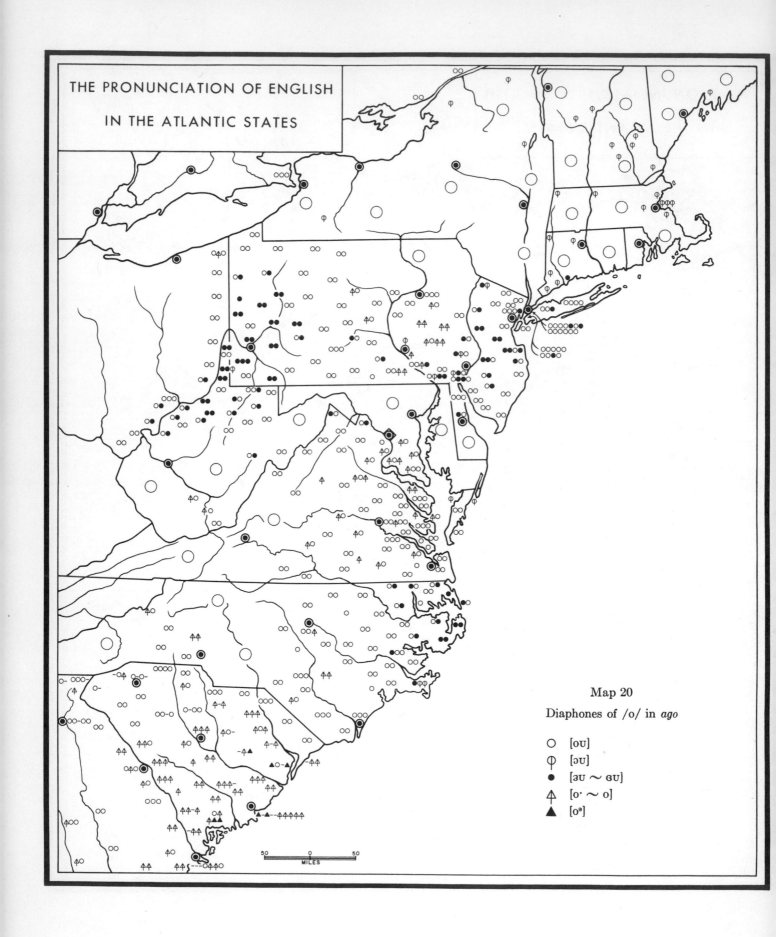

THE PRONUNCIATION OF ENGLISH
IN THE ATLANTIC STATES

Map 20

Diaphones of /o/ in *ago*

O	[oʊ]
φ	[ɔʊ]
●	[ɜʊ ~ ɐʊ]
⋏	[oˑ ~ o]
▲	[oᵊ]

50   0   50

MILES

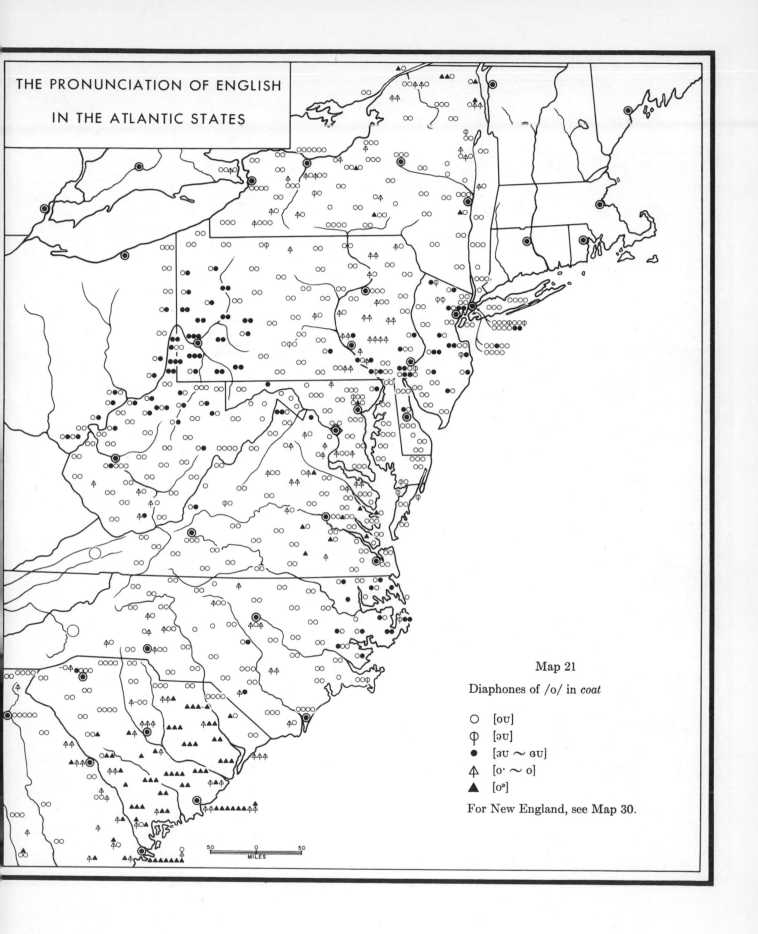

THE PRONUNCIATION OF ENGLISH
IN THE ATLANTIC STATES

Map 21

Diaphones of /o/ in *coat*

O   [oʊ]

φ   [əʊ]

●   [ɜʊ ∼ ɐʊ]

△   [oˑ ∼ o]

▲   [oə]

For New England, see Map 30.

MILES

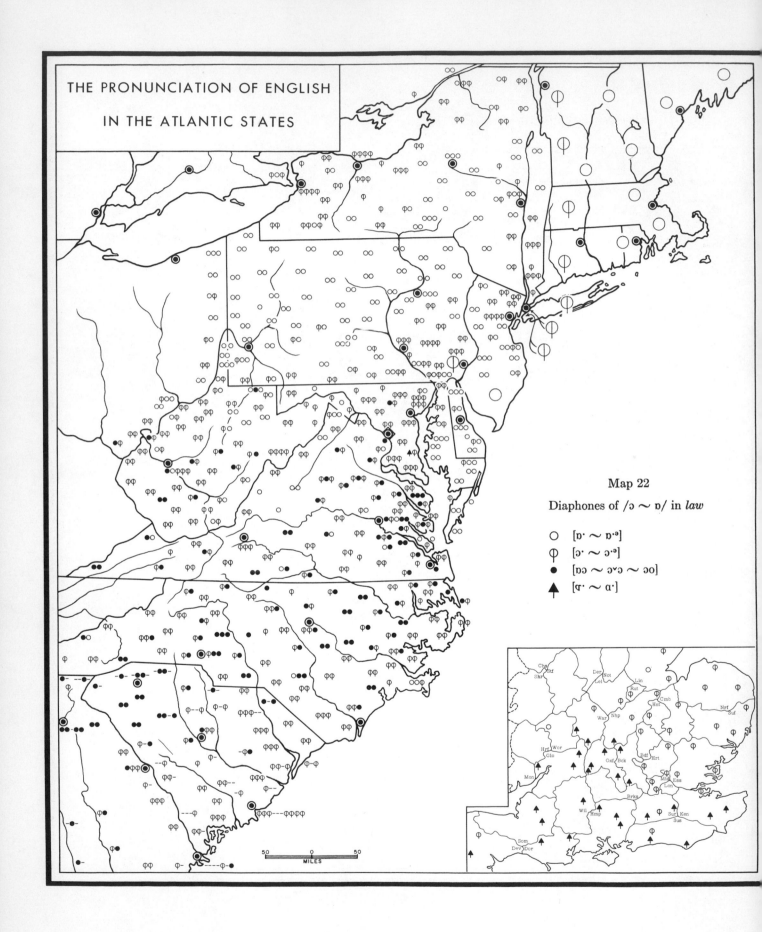

THE PRONUNCIATION OF ENGLISH
IN THE ATLANTIC STATES

Map 22

Diaphones of /ɔ ~ ɒ/ in *law*

○ [ɒ· ~ ɒ·ə]

φ [ɔ· ~ ɔ·ə]

● [ɒɔ ~ ɔ·ɒ ~ ɔɒ]

▲ [ɑ· ~ ɑ·]

MILES

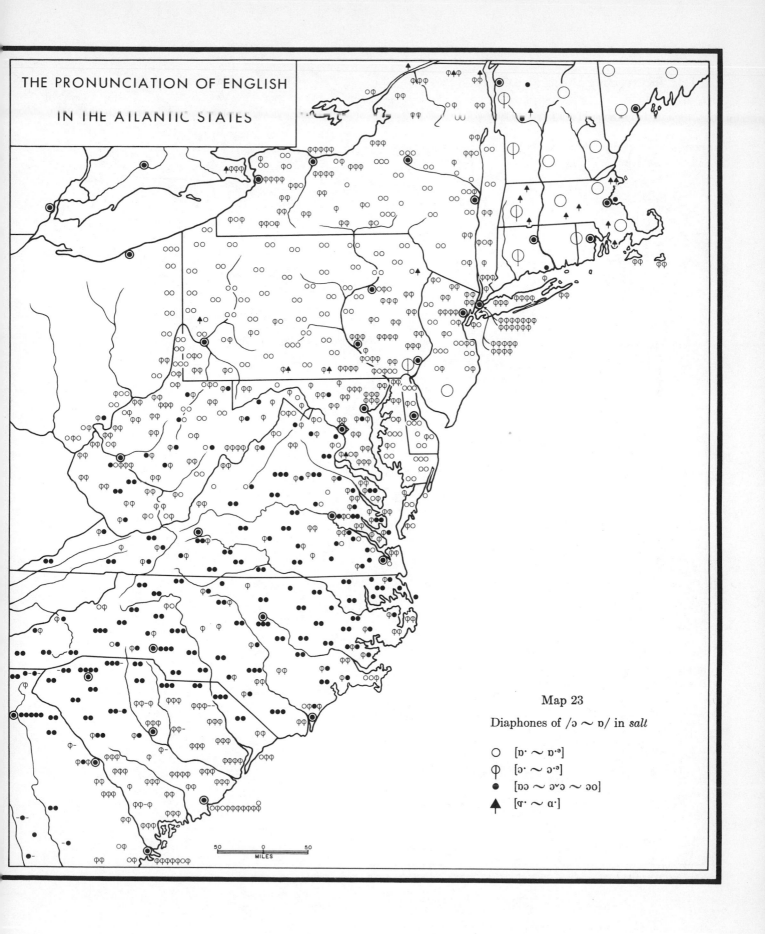

THE PRONUNCIATION OF ENGLISH

IN THE ATLANTIC STATES

Map 23

Diaphones of /ɔ ~ ɒ/ in *salt*

○   [ɒ· ~ ɒ·ə]

ϙ   [ɔ· ~ ɔ·ə]

●   [oɒ ~ ɔʌɔ ~ ɔo]

▲   [ɤ· ~ ɑ·]

50   0   50
MILES

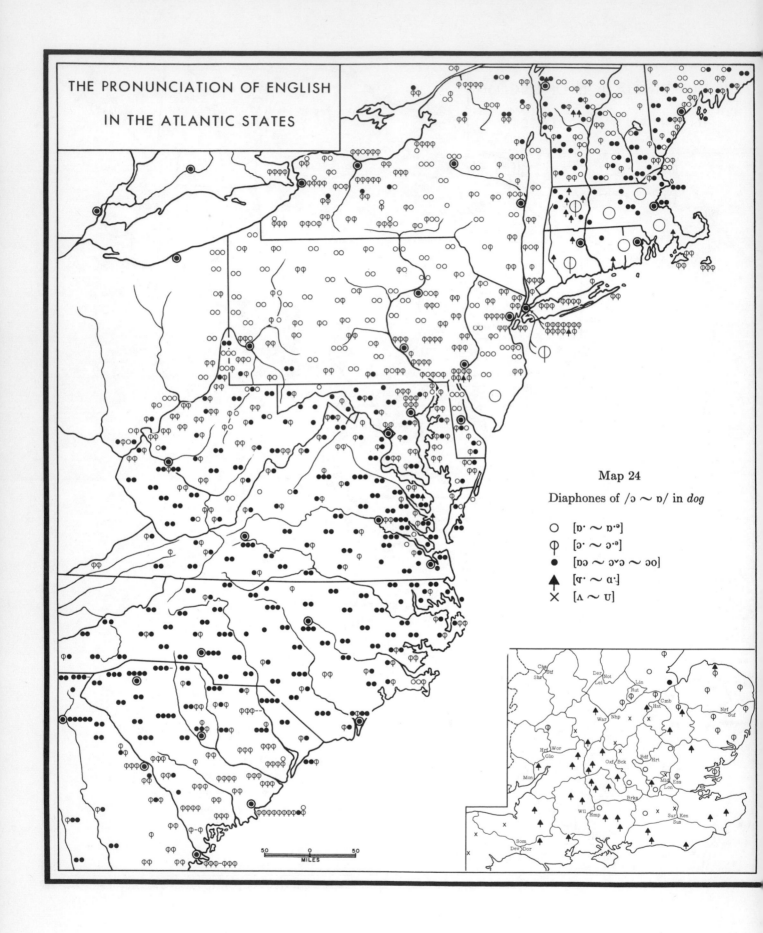

THE PRONUNCIATION OF ENGLISH
IN THE ATLANTIC STATES

Map 24

Diaphones of /ɔ ~ ɒ/ in *dog*

○   [ɒ· ~ ɒ·ə]

Ϙ   [ɔ· ~ ɔ·ə]

●   [ɒɔ ~ ɔ▾ɔ ~ ɔɒ]

▲   [ɑ· ~ ɑ·]

✕   [ʌ ~ ʊ]

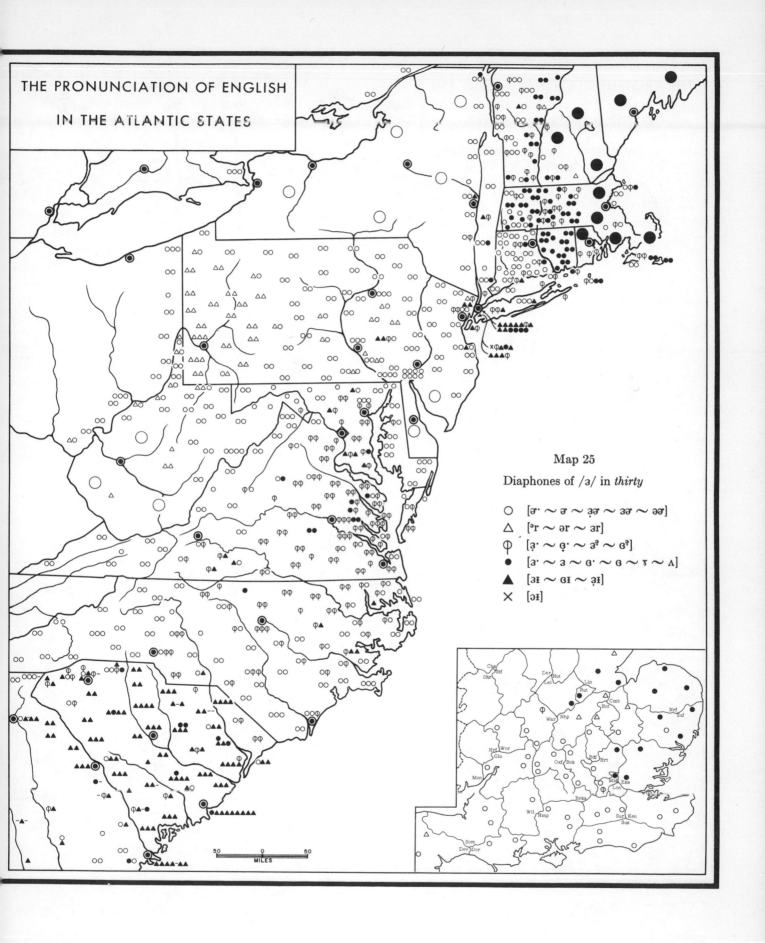

THE PRONUNCIATION OF ENGLISH

IN THE ATLANTIC STATES

Map 25

Diaphones of /ɝ/ in *thirty*

○ [ɝ· ~ ɝ ~ ɜɚ ~ ɜɚ ~ əɚ]

△ [ʰr ~ ər ~ ɜr]

φ [ɜ· ~ ɐ· ~ ɜˀ ~ ɐˀ]

● [ɜ ~ ɜ ~ ɐ· ~ ɐ ~ ɤ ~ ʌ]

▲ [ɜɨ ~ ɐɨ ~ ɜɨ]

✕ [əɨ]

50   50
MILES

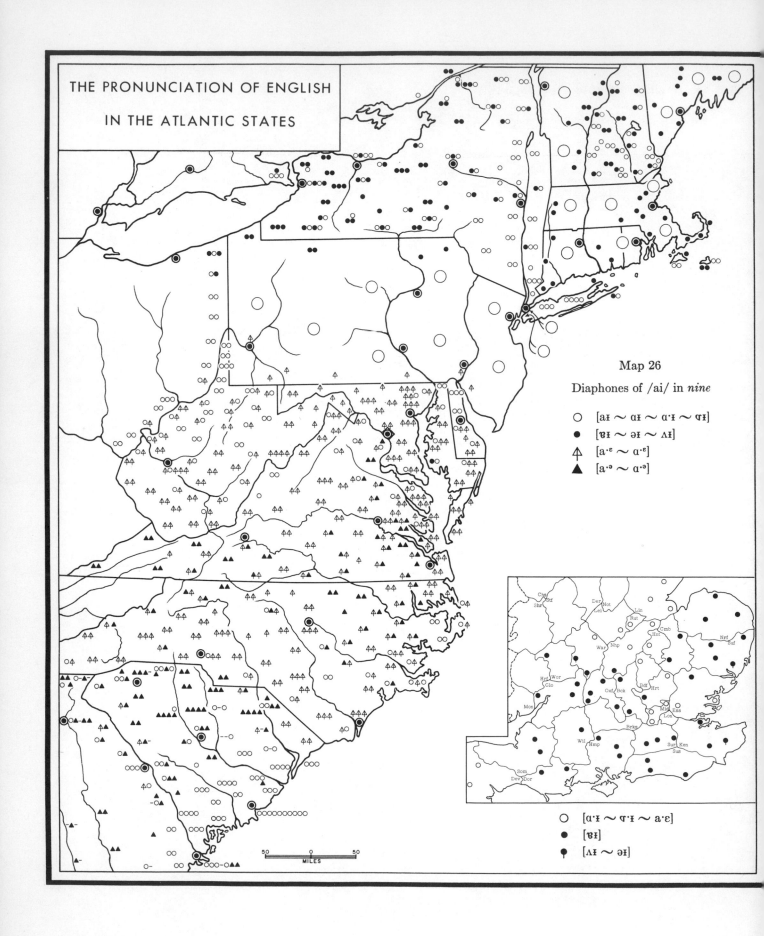

THE PRONUNCIATION OF ENGLISH

IN THE ATLANTIC STATES

Map 26

Diaphones of /ai/ in *nine*

○ [aɪ ~ aɪ ~ ɑ·ɪ ~ ɑɪ]
● [ɐɪ ~ əɪ ~ ʌɪ]
⚑ [a·ᵋ ~ ɑ·ᵋ]
▲ [a·ᵊ ~ ɑ·ᵊ]

○ [ɑ·ɪ ~ ɑ·ɪ ~ a·ɛ]
● [ɐɪ]
♀ [ʌɪ ~ əɪ]

50   0   50
MILES

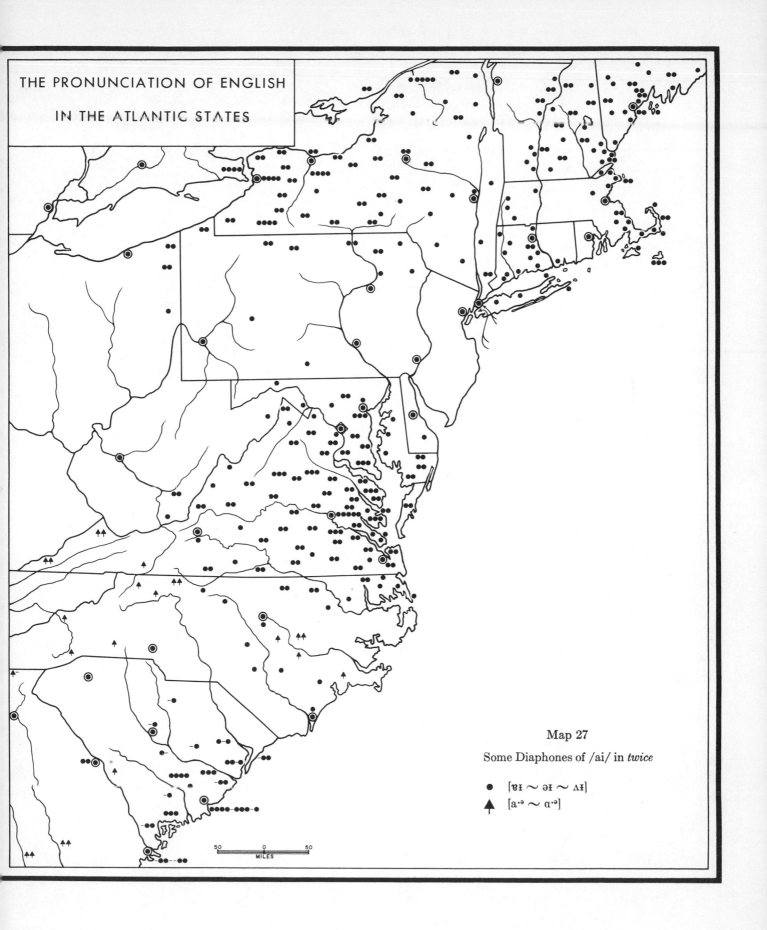

THE PRONUNCIATION OF ENGLISH

IN THE ATLANTIC STATES

Map 27

Some Diaphones of /ai/ in *twice*

● [ɐɪ ~ əɪ ~ ʌɪ]

▲ [a·ə ~ ɑ·ə]

50   0   50
MILES

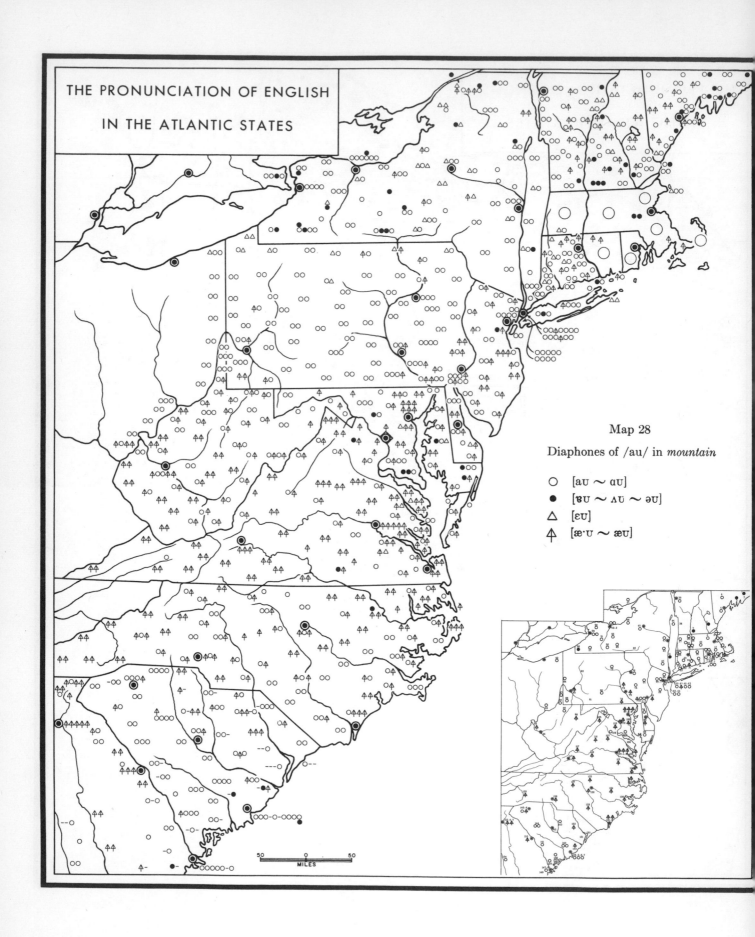

THE PRONUNCIATION OF ENGLISH
IN THE ATLANTIC STATES

Map 28

Diaphones of /au/ in *mountain*

○   [aʊ ~ ɑʊ]

●   [ɐʊ ~ ʌʊ ~ əʊ]

△   [ɛʊ]

⚹   [æ·ʊ ~ æʊ]

50   0   50
MILES

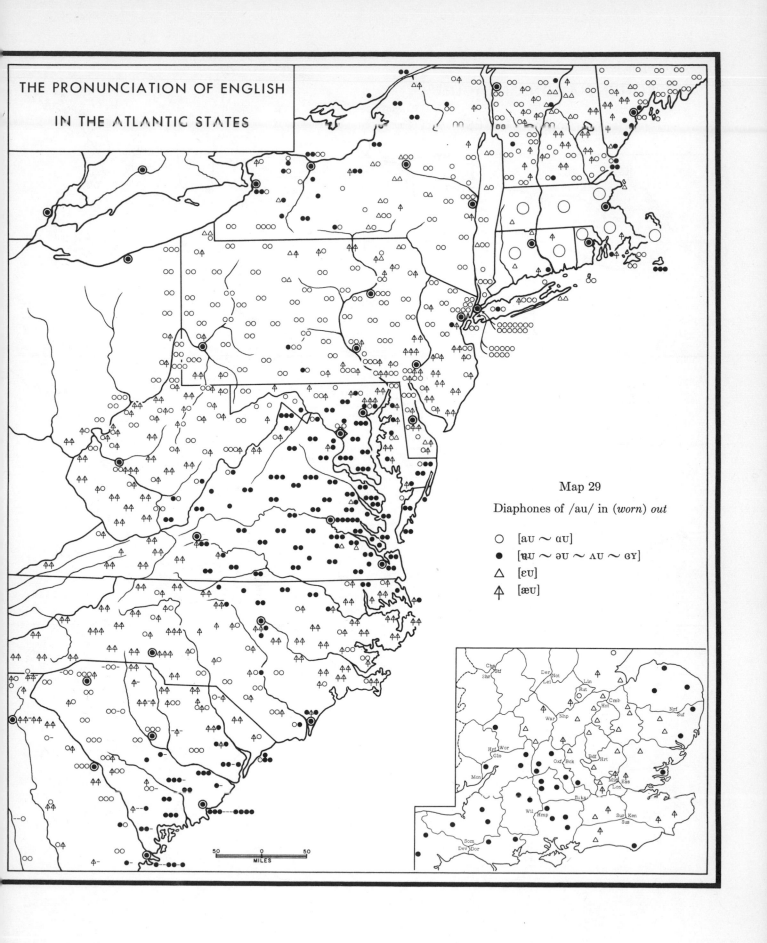

THE PRONUNCIATION OF ENGLISH

IN THE ATLANTIC STATES

Map 29

Diaphones of /au/ in (worn) out

○ [aʊ ~ ɑʊ]

● [ɐʊ ~ əʊ ~ ʌʊ ~ ɵʏ]

△ [ɛʊ]

⋏ [æʊ]

MILES

50 0 50

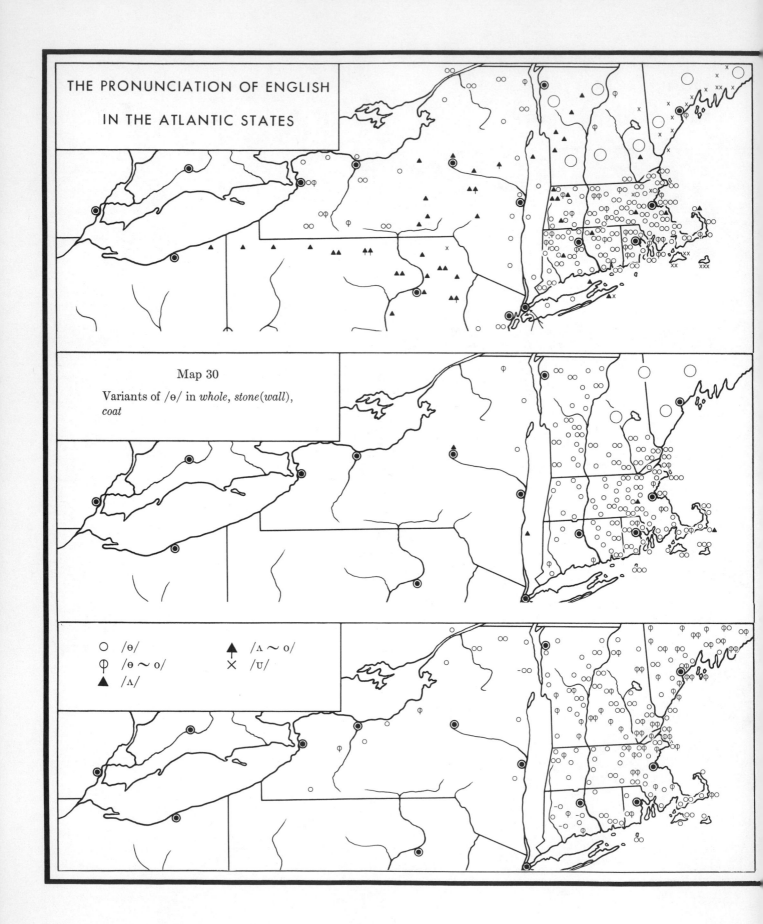

THE PRONUNCIATION OF ENGLISH

IN THE ATLANTIC STATES

Map 30

Variants of /ɵ/ in *whole, stone(wall),*
coat

O	/ɵ/	▲	/ʌ ∼ o/
φ	/ɵ ∼ o/	X	/ʊ/
▲	/ʌ/		

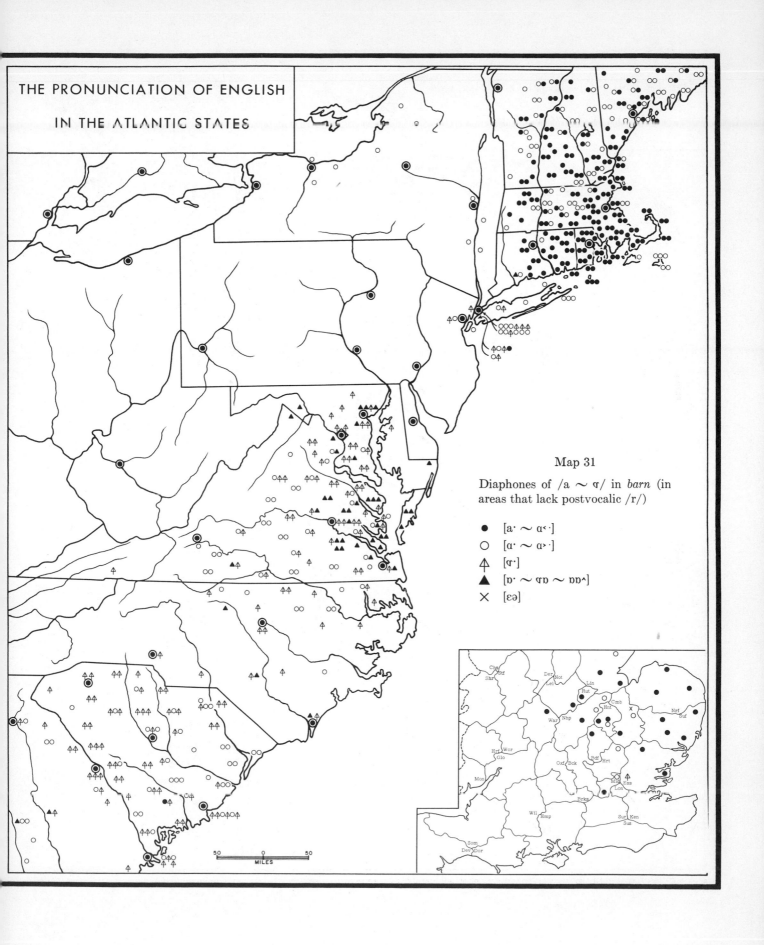

THE PRONUNCIATION OF ENGLISH

IN THE ATLANTIC STATES

Map 31

Diaphones of /a ~ ɑ/ in *barn* (in areas that lack postvocalic /r/)

- ● [aˑ ~ ɑ<ˑ]
- ○ [ɑˑ ~ ɑ>ˑ]
- ⋔ [ɹˑ]
- ▲ [ɒˑ ~ ɑɒ ~ ɒɒ^]
- × [ɛə]

MILES

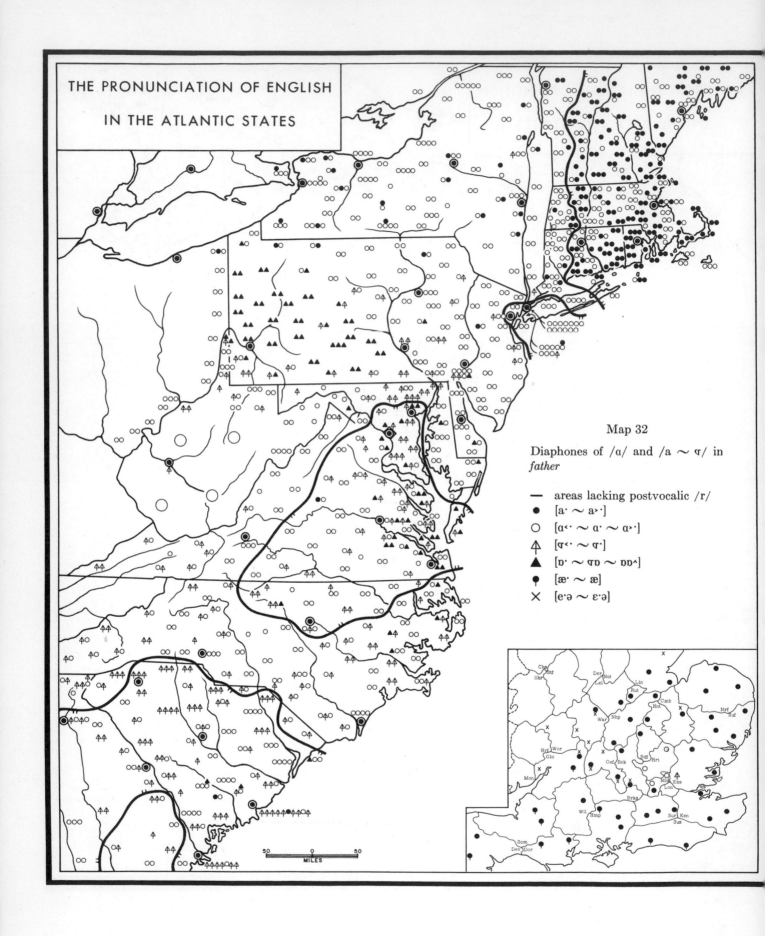

THE PRONUNCIATION OF ENGLISH

IN THE ATLANTIC STATES

Map 32

Diaphones of /ɑ/ and /a ~ ɒ/ in *father*

— areas lacking postvocalic /r/

● [aˑ ~ a>ˑ]

○ [ɑ<ˑ ~ ɑˑ ~ ɑ>ˑ]

⚐ [ɒ<ˑ ~ ɒˑ]

▲ [ɒ ~ ɒɒ ~ ɒɒ^]

♀ [æˑ ~ æ]

✗ [eˑə ~ ɛˑə]

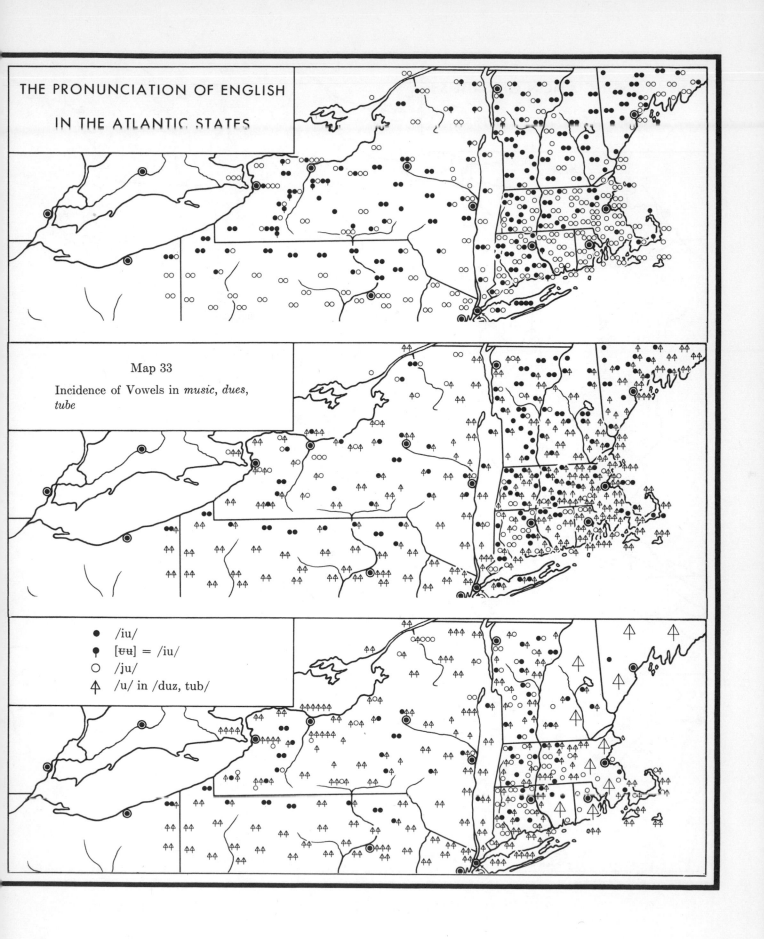

THE PRONUNCIATION OF ENGLISH

IN THE ATLANTIC STATES

Map 33

Incidence of Vowels in *music, dues, tube*

- ● /iu/
- ◐ [ʊu] = /iu/
- ○ /ju/
- ⋏ /u/ in /duz, tub/

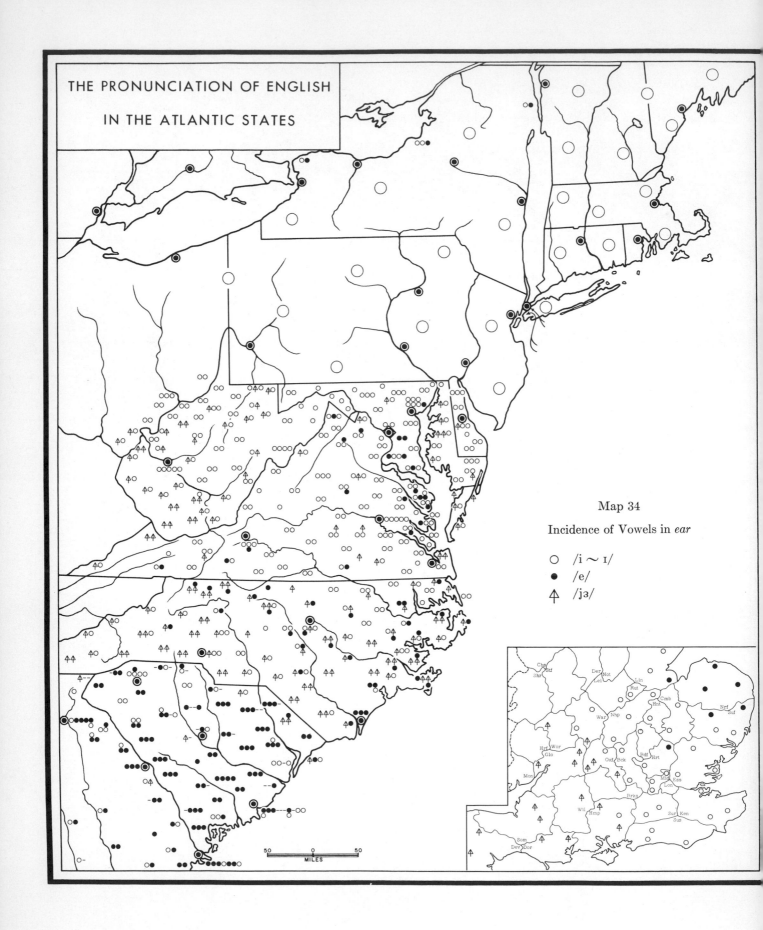

THE PRONUNCIATION OF ENGLISH
IN THE ATLANTIC STATES

Map 34

Incidence of Vowels in *ear*

○ /i ~ ɪ/

● /e/

⋏ /jɜ/

50   0   50
MILES

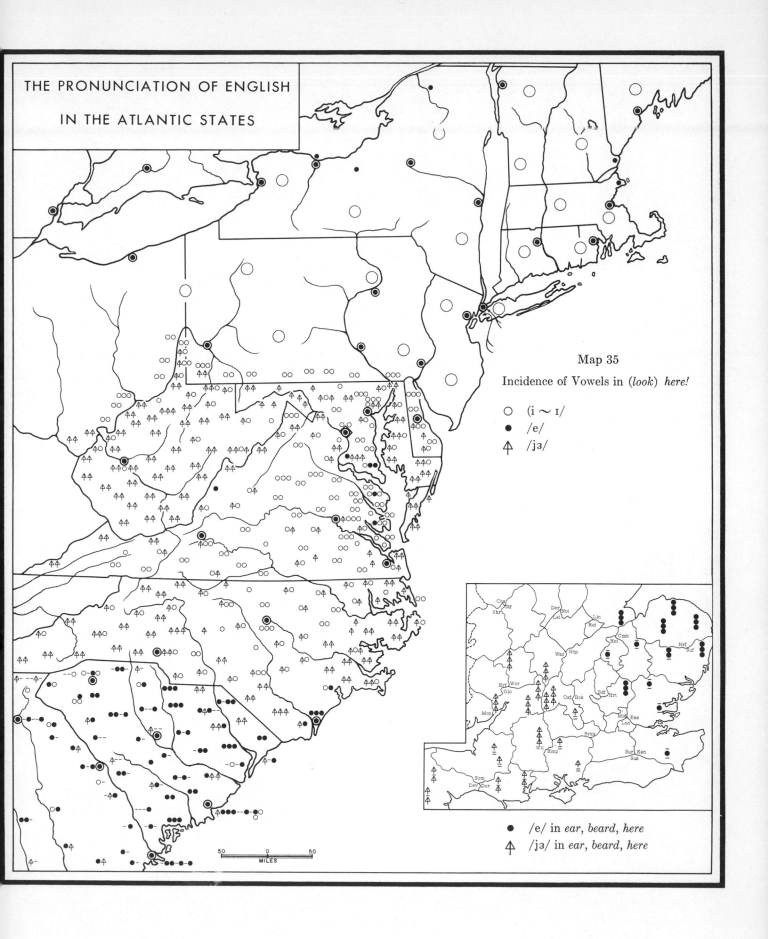

THE PRONUNCIATION OF ENGLISH

IN THE ATLANTIC STATES

Map 35

Incidence of Vowels in (*look*) *here!*

○ (i ∼ ɪ/

● /e/

⚲ /jɜ/

● /e/ in *ear, beard, here*

⚲ /jɜ/ in *ear, beard, here*

MILES

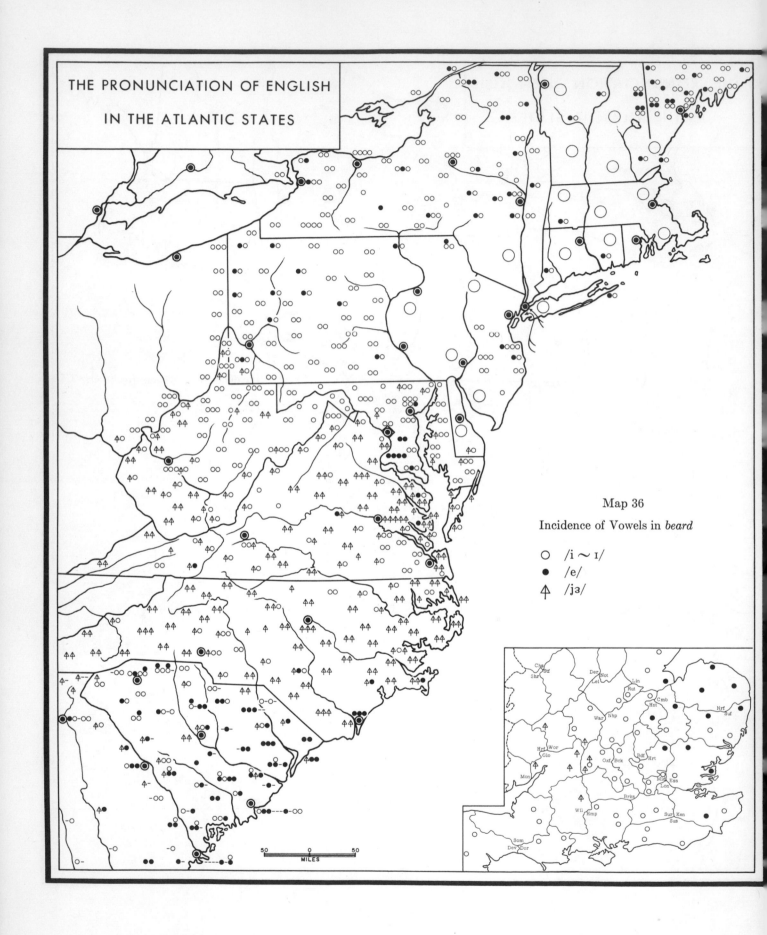

THE PRONUNCIATION OF ENGLISH
IN THE ATLANTIC STATES

Map 36

Incidence of Vowels in *beard*

○ /i ∼ ɪ/

● /e/

⚲ /jɚ/

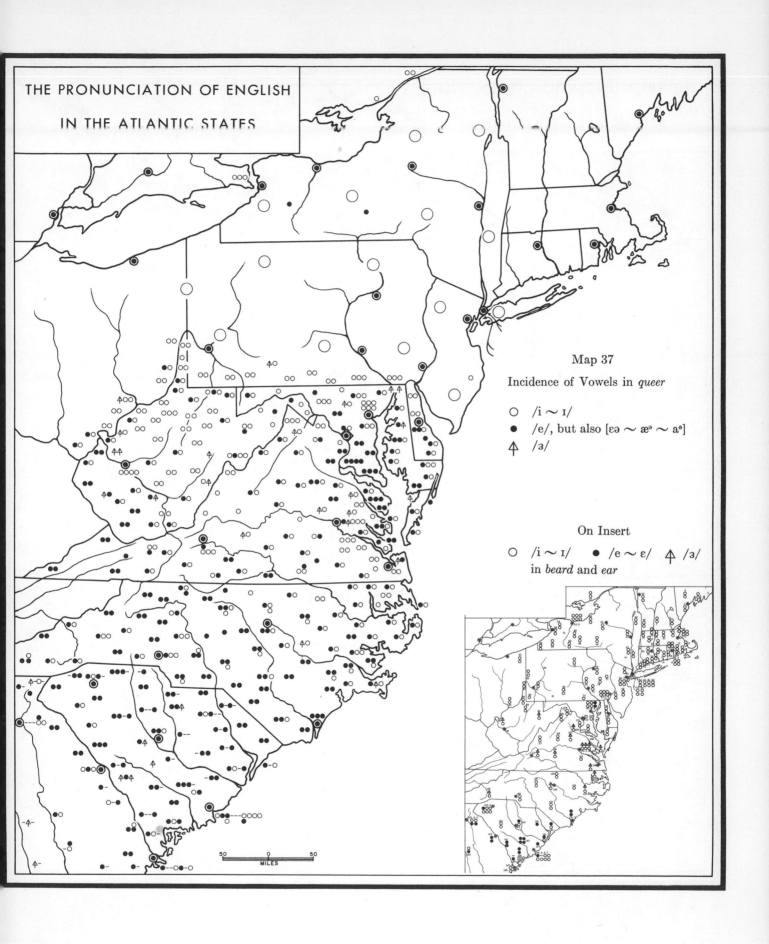

THE PRONUNCIATION OF ENGLISH
IN THE ATLANTIC STATES

Map 37

Incidence of Vowels in *queer*

○ /i ~ ɪ/

● /e/, but also [ɛə ~ æ^ə ~ a^ə]

⚹ /ɜ/

On Insert

○ /i ~ ɪ/   ● /e ~ ɛ/   ⚹ /ɜ/
in *beard* and *ear*

MILES
50   0   50

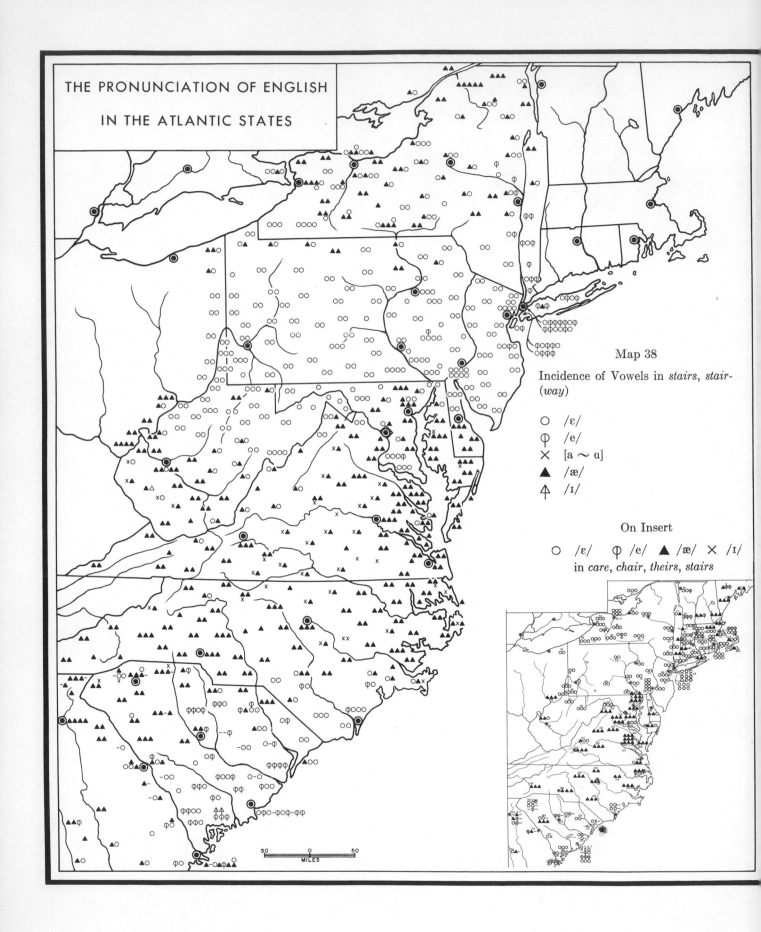

Map 38

Incidence of Vowels in *stairs, stair-(way)*

○ /ɛ/

φ /e/

✕ [a ∼ ɑ]

▲ /æ/

⚐ /ɪ/

On Insert

○ /ɛ/   φ /e/   ▲ /æ/   ✕ /ɪ/

in *care, chair, theirs, stairs*

50   0   50

MILES

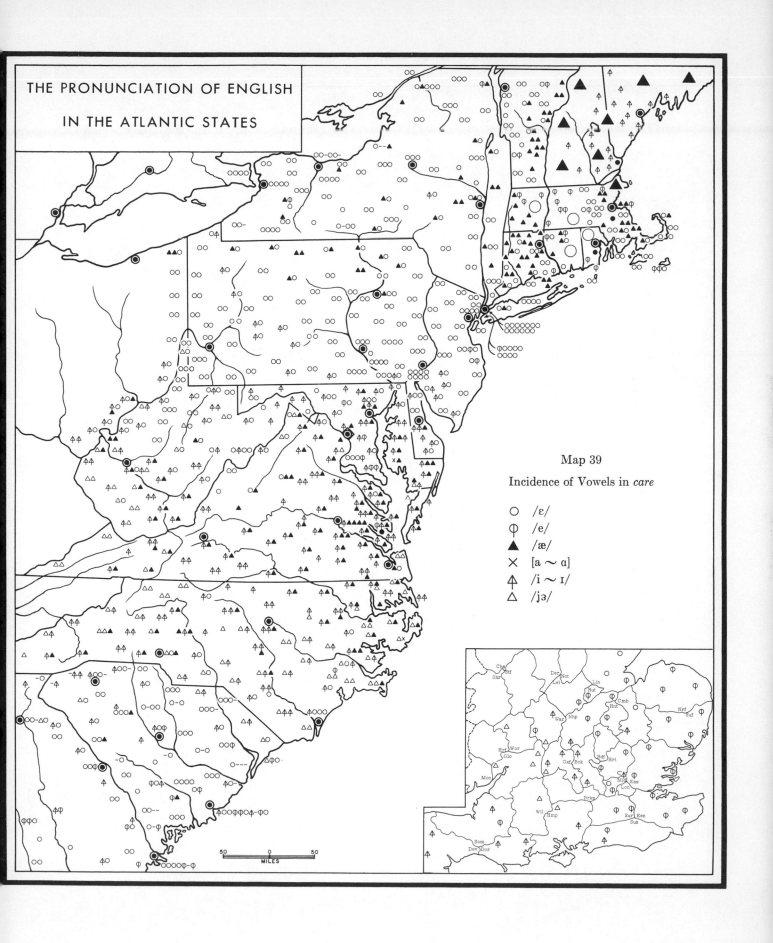

THE PRONUNCIATION OF ENGLISH
IN THE ATLANTIC STATES

Map 39

Incidence of Vowels in *care*

○ /ɛ/
φ /e/
▲ /æ/
× [a ∼ ɑ]
⚹ /i ∼ ɪ/
△ /jɜ/

MILES

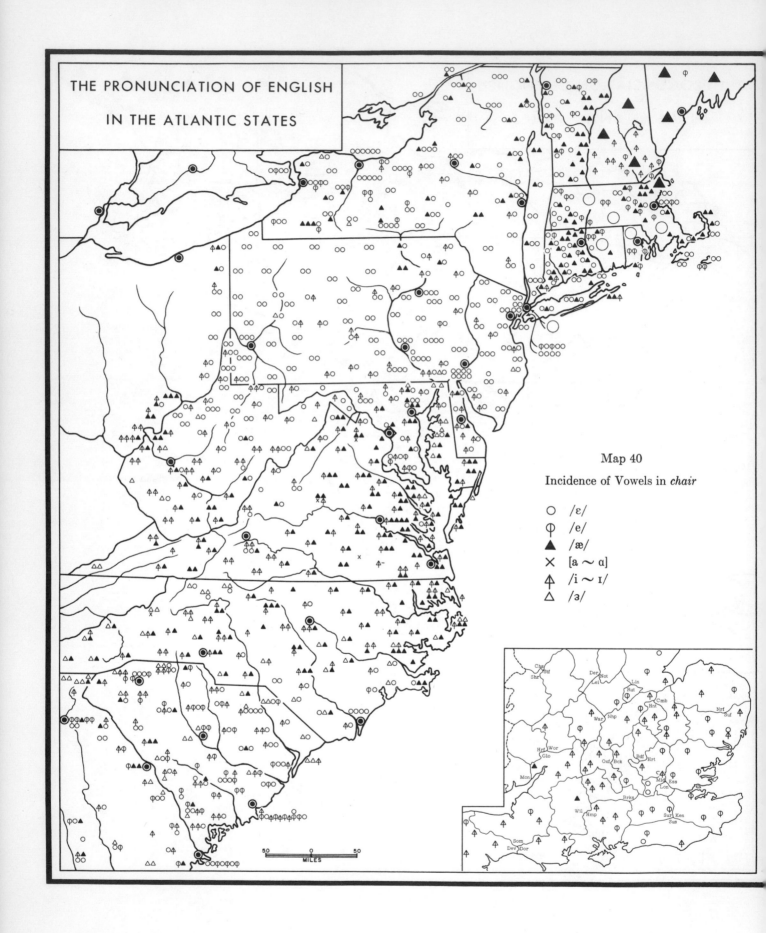

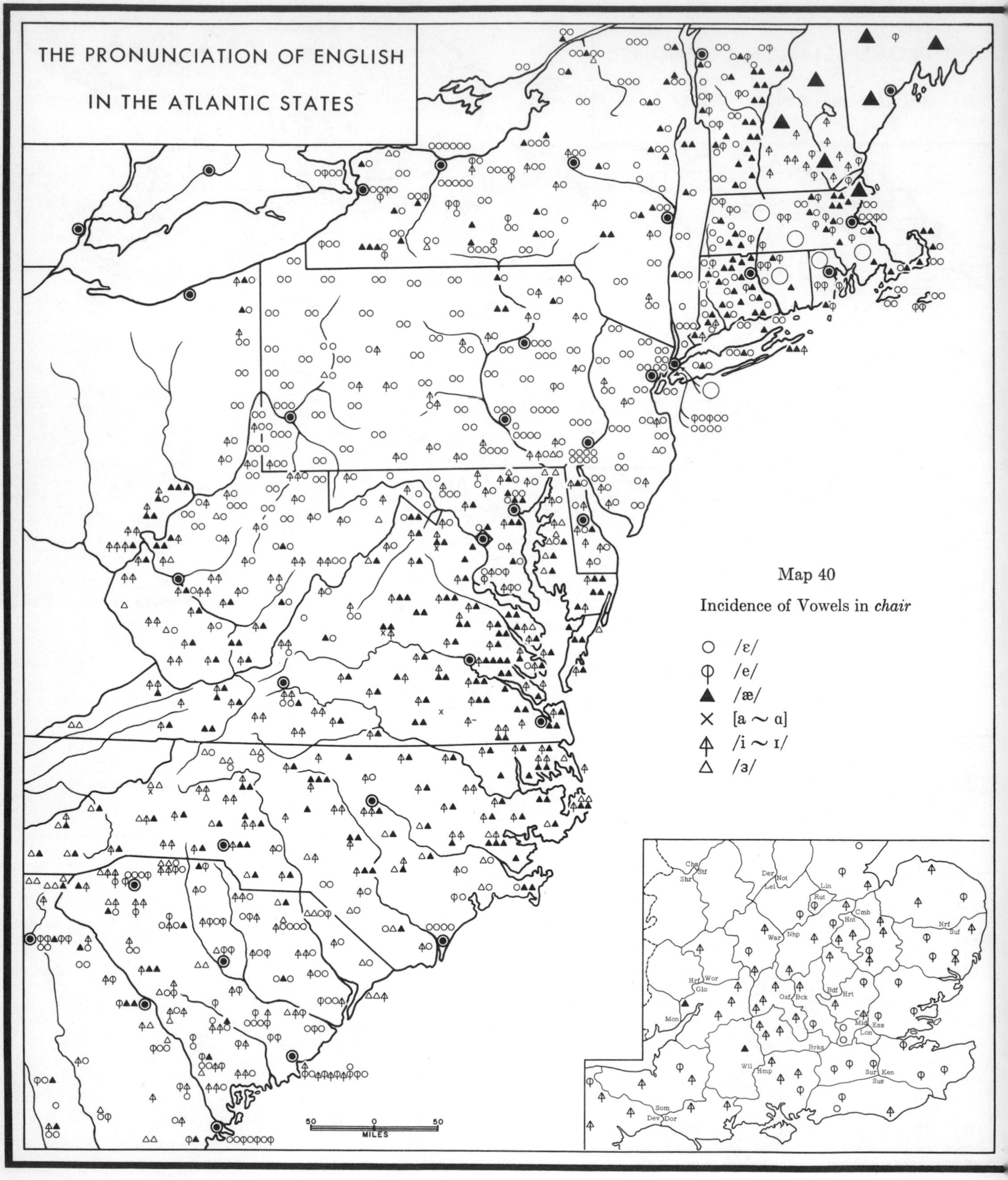
THE PRONUNCIATION OF ENGLISH
IN THE ATLANTIC STATES
Map 40
Incidence of Vowels in *chair*
○ /ɛ/
φ /e/
▲ /æ/
× [a ~ ɑ]
/i ~ ɪ/
△ /ɜ/
50 0 50
MILES
Chs Stf
Shr
Der Not
Lei
Lin
Rut
Cmb
Hnt
Nrf
Suf
War
Nhp
Hrf Wor
Glo
Oxf Bck
Bdf
Hrt
Mon
Mid
Ess
Lon
Brks
Wil
Hmp
Sur Ken
Sus
Som
Dev Dor

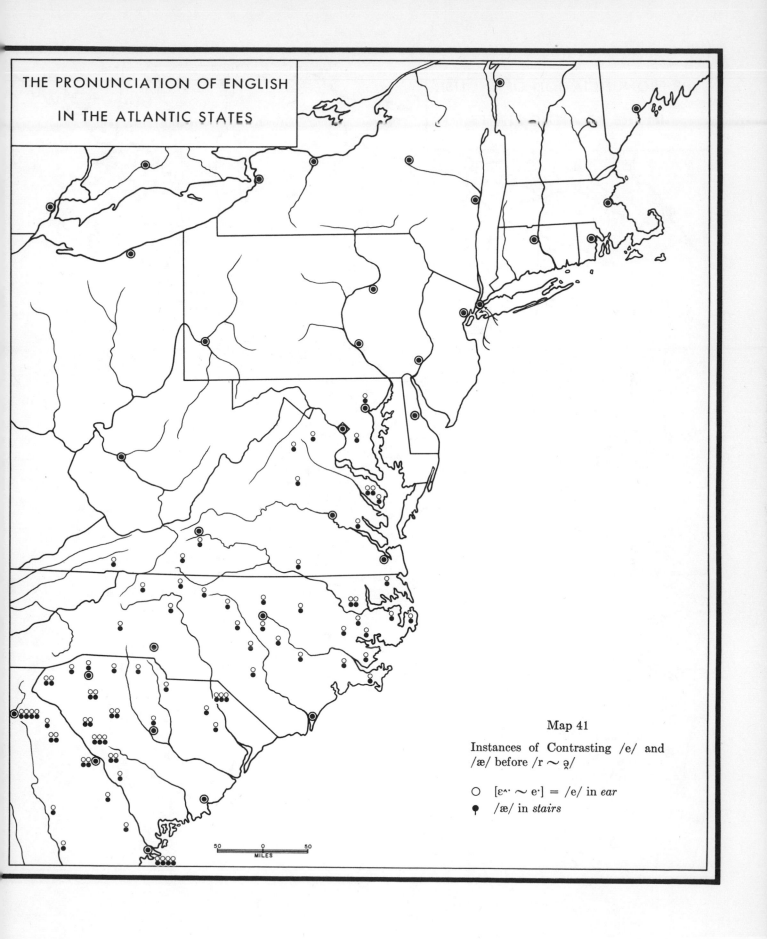

THE PRONUNCIATION OF ENGLISH

IN THE ATLANTIC STATES

Map 41

Instances of Contrasting /e/ and
/æ/ before /r ∼ ə̣/

○   [ɛ^· ∼ e·] = /e/ in *ear*

◕   /æ/ in *stairs*

50   0   50
MILES

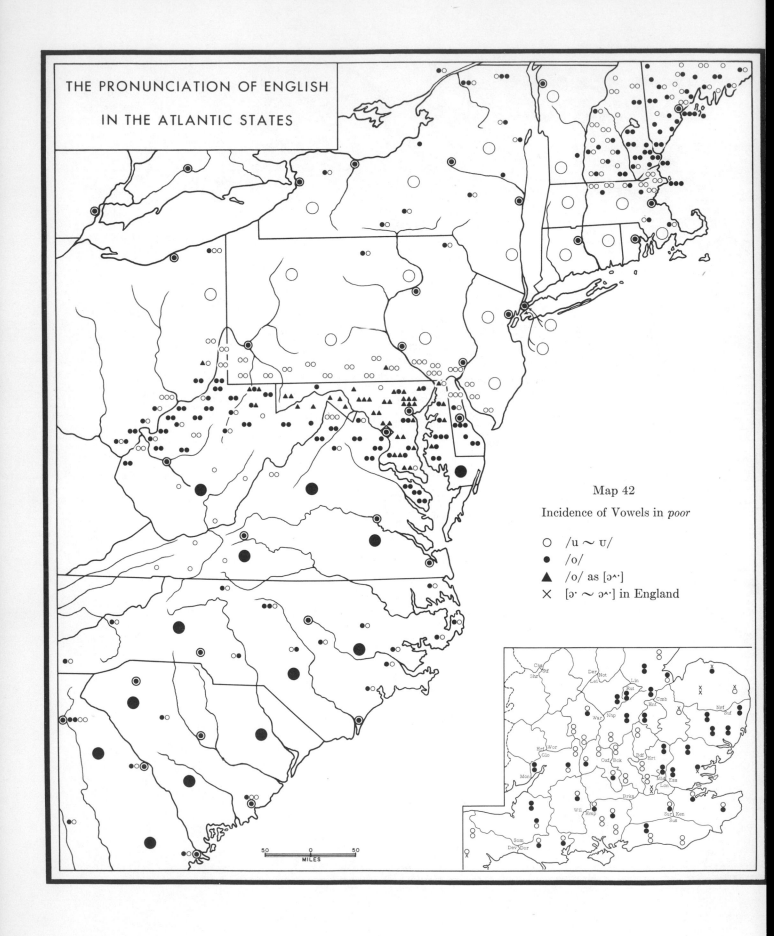

THE PRONUNCIATION OF ENGLISH

IN THE ATLANTIC STATES

Map 42

Incidence of Vowels in *poor*

○   /u ∼ ʊ/

●   /o/

▲   /o/ as [ɔˑ]

✕   [əˑ ∼ ɔˑ] in England

50   0   50
MILES

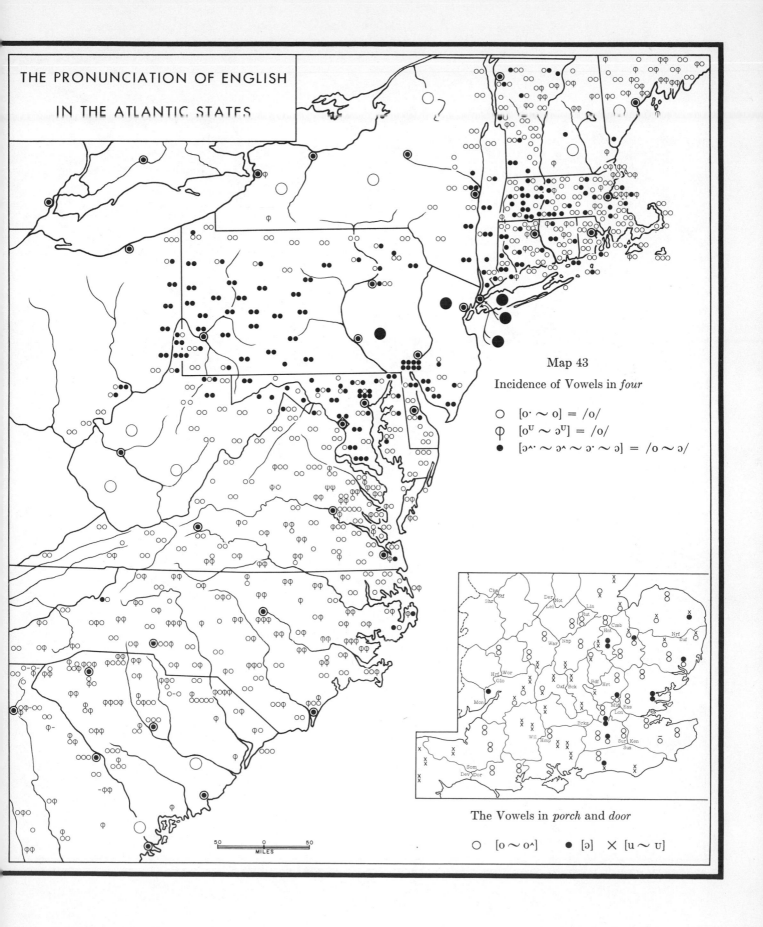

THE PRONUNCIATION OF ENGLISH

IN THE ATLANTIC STATES

Map 43

Incidence of Vowels in *four*

○ [o· ∼ o] = /o/

φ [oᵁ ∼ ɔᵁ] = /o/

● [ɔʌ· ∼ ɔʌ ∼ ɔ· ∼ ɔ] = /o ∼ ɔ/

The Vowels in *porch* and *door*

○ [o ∼ oʌ] ● [ɔ] ✕ [u ∼ ʊ]

MILES
50   0   50

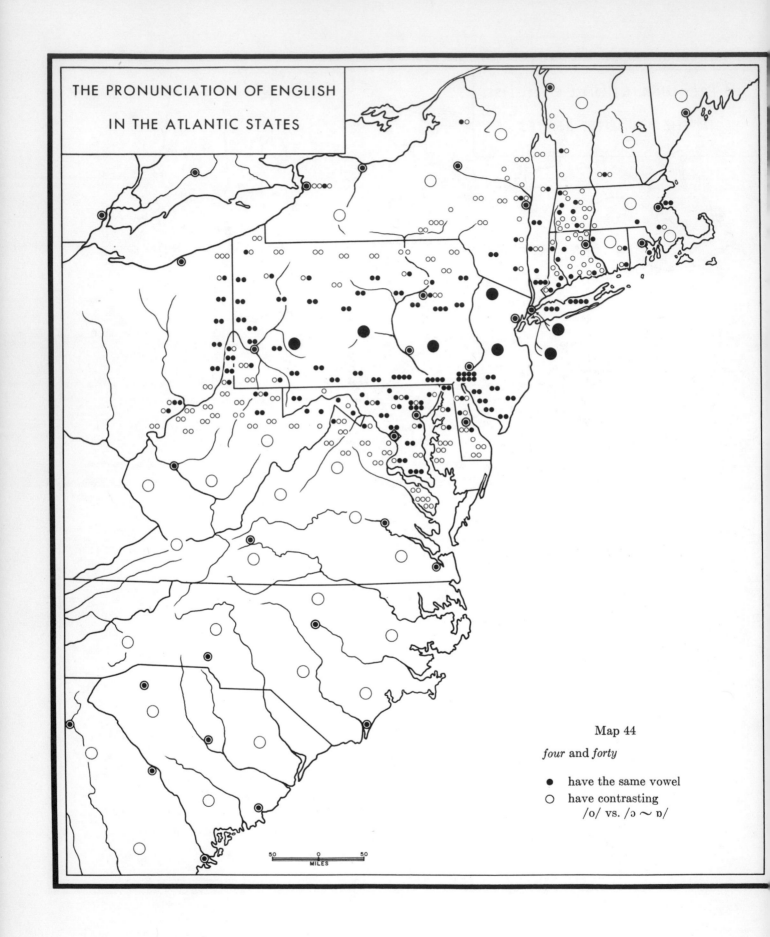

THE PRONUNCIATION OF ENGLISH

IN THE ATLANTIC STATES

Map 44

four and *forty*

● have the same vowel

○ have contrasting
/o/ vs. /ɔ ~ ɒ/

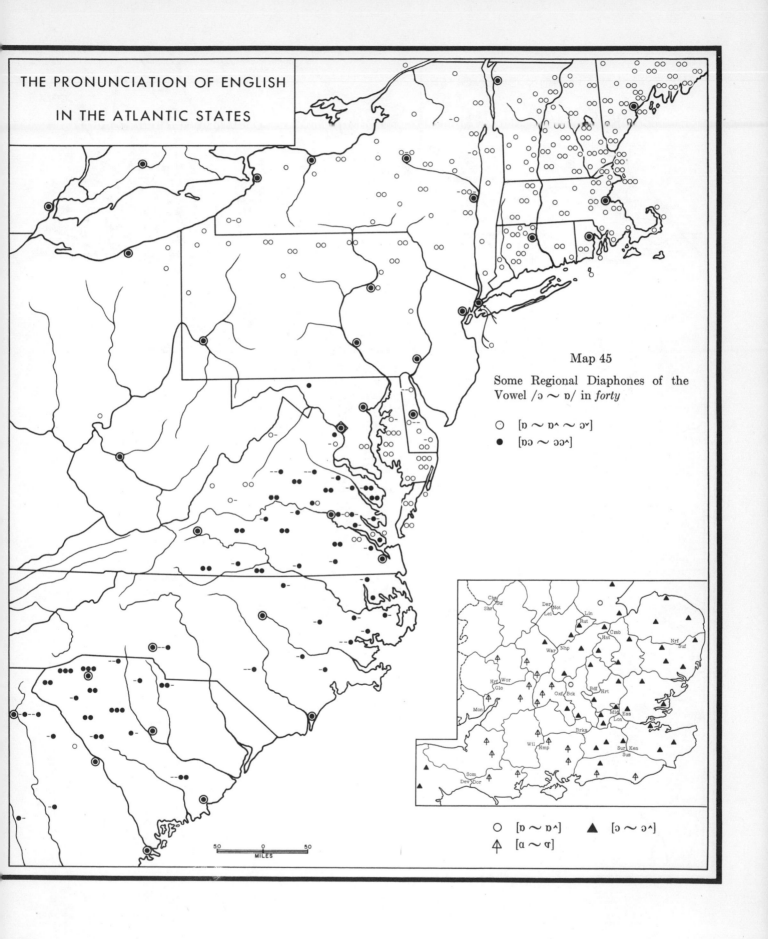

THE PRONUNCIATION OF ENGLISH

IN THE ATLANTIC STATES

Map 45

Some Regional Diaphones of the
Vowel /ɔ ~ ɒ/ in *forty*

○ [ɒ ~ ɒˆ ~ ɔˇ]

● [ɒɔ ~ ɔɔˆ]

○ [ɒ ~ ɒˆ]   ▲ [ɔ ~ ɔˆ]

⚲ [ɑ ~ ɒ]

50   0   50
MILES

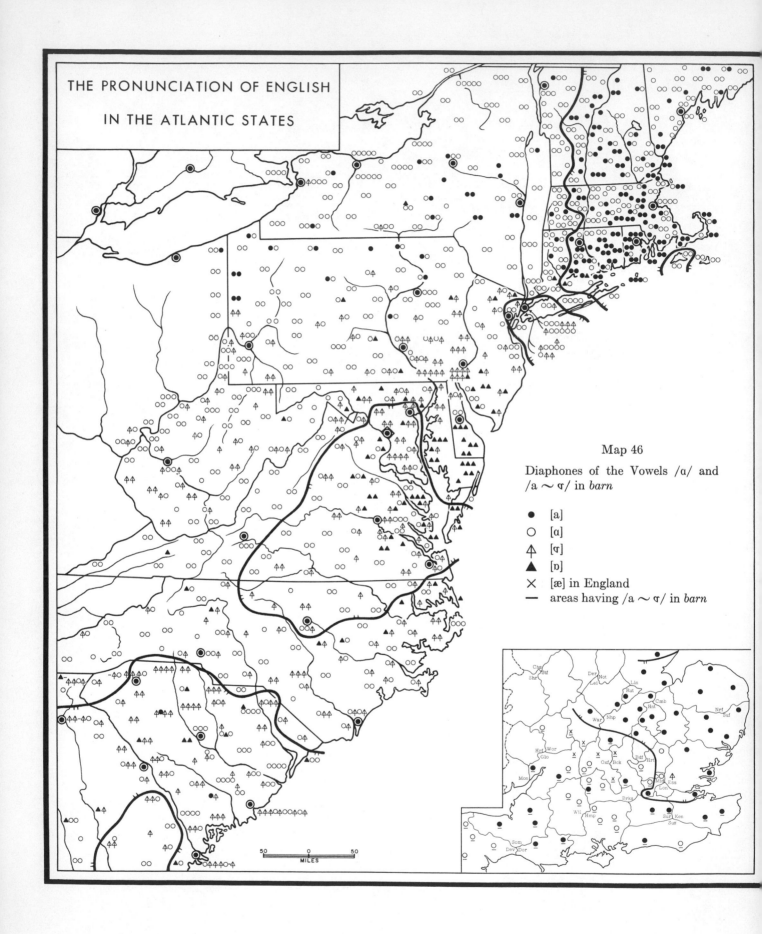

THE PRONUNCIATION OF ENGLISH
IN THE ATLANTIC STATES

Map 46

Diaphones of the Vowels /ɑ/ and
/a ~ ɑ/ in *barn*

●   [a]

○   [ɑ]

⚲   [ɑ]

▲   [ɒ]

✕   [æ] in England

—   areas having /a ~ ɑ/ in *barn*

50   50
MILES

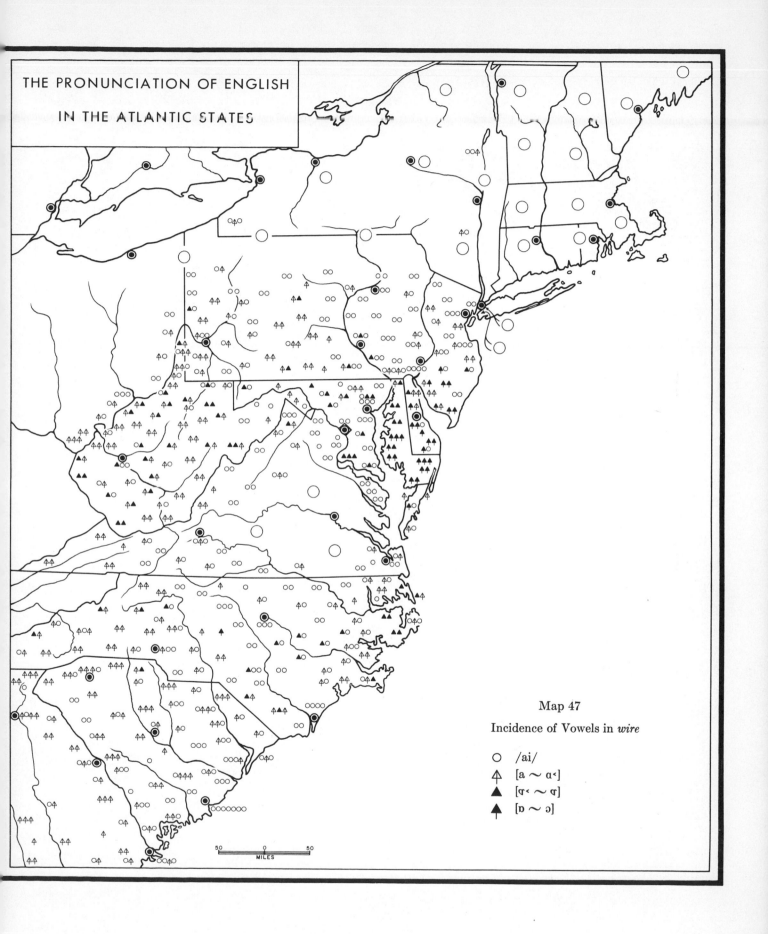

THE PRONUNCIATION OF ENGLISH

IN THE ATLANTIC STATES

Map 47

Incidence of Vowels in *wire*

○   /ai/

↑   [a ∼ ɑ‹]

▲   [ɒ‹ ∼ ɑ]

▲   [ɒ ∼ ɔ]

50   0   50
MILES

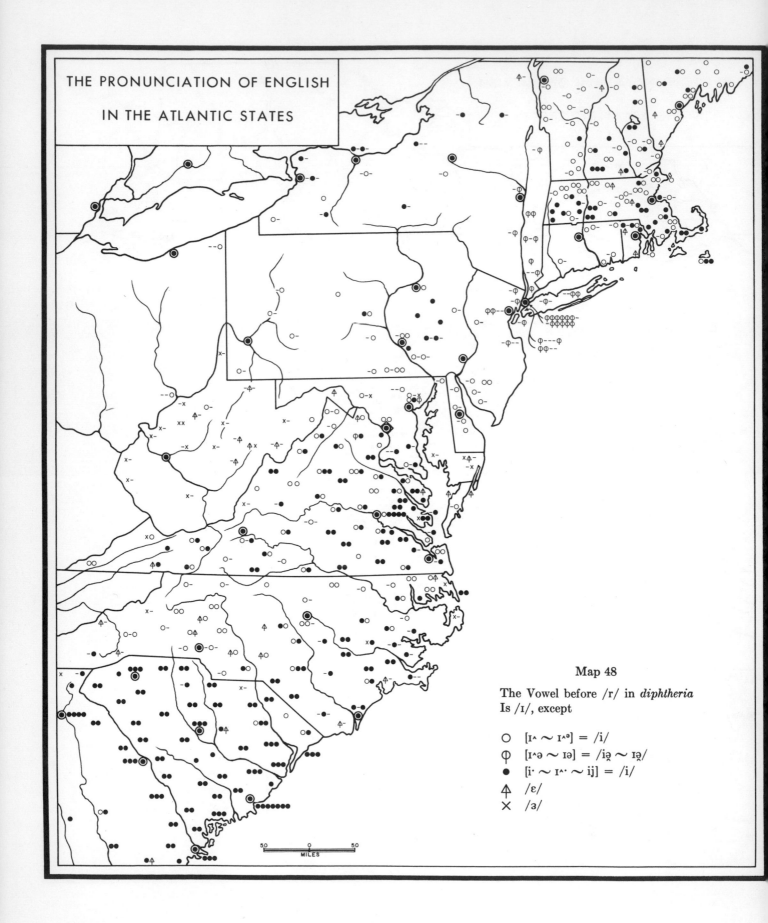

THE PRONUNCIATION OF ENGLISH

IN THE ATLANTIC STATES

Map 48

The Vowel before /r/ in *diphtheria*
Is /ɪ/, except

○   [ɪ^ ∼ ɪ^ə] = /i/

φ   [ɪ^ə ∼ ɪə] = /iɚ ∼ ɪɚ/

●   [i· ∼ ɪ^· ∼ ij] = /i/

⋏   /ɛ/

✕   /ɝ/

50   0   50
MILES

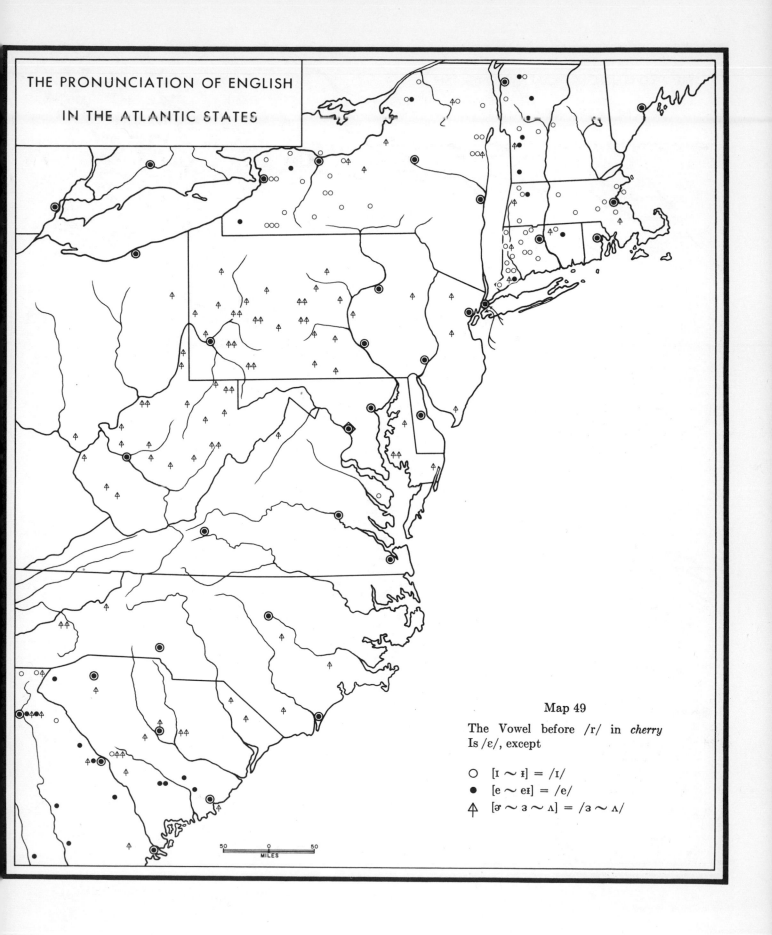

THE PRONUNCIATION OF ENGLISH

IN THE ATLANTIC STATES

Map 49

The Vowel before /r/ in *cherry*
Is /ɛ/, except

O [ɪ ~ ɨ] = /ɪ/

● [e ~ eɨ] = /e/

⚲ [ɝ ~ ɜ ~ ʌ] = /ɜ ~ ʌ/

MILES

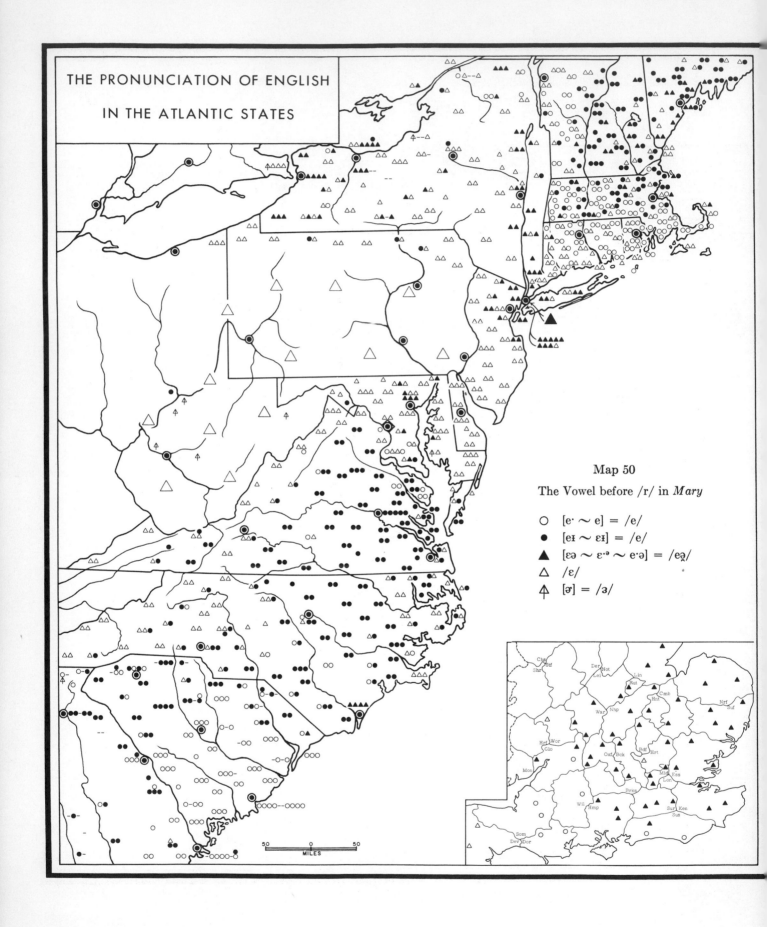

THE PRONUNCIATION OF ENGLISH
IN THE ATLANTIC STATES

Map 50

The Vowel before /r/ in *Mary*

○ [eˑ ~ e] = /e/
● [eɨ ~ ɛɨ] = /e/
▲ [ɛə ~ ɛˑ ~ eˑə] = /eə̯/
△ /ɛ/
⟰ [ɚ] = /ɝ/

MILES

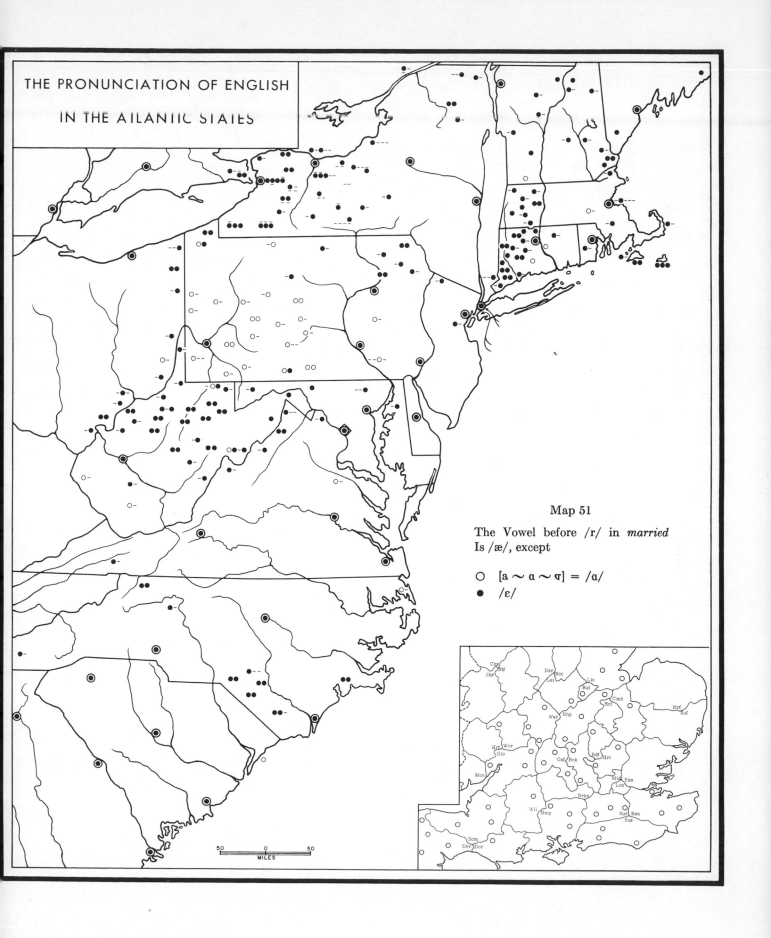

THE PRONUNCIATION OF ENGLISH

IN THE ATLANTIC STATES

Map 51

The Vowel before /r/ in *married*
Is /æ/, except

○ [a ～ ɑ ～ ɒ] = /ɑ/

● /ɛ/

50   0   50
MILES

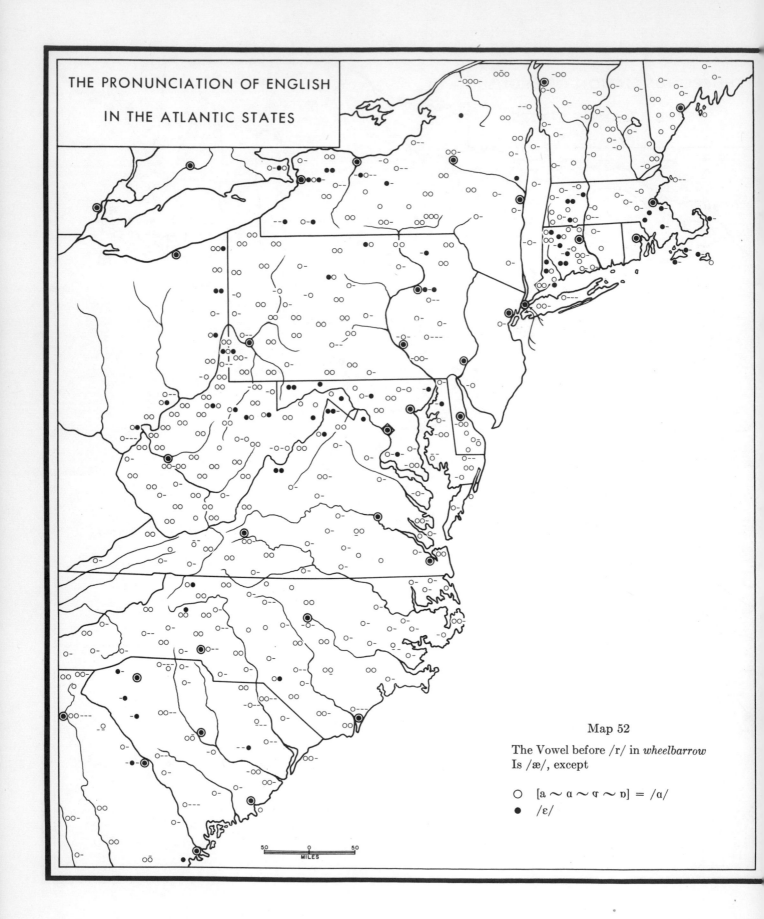

THE PRONUNCIATION OF ENGLISH
IN THE ATLANTIC STATES

Map 52

The Vowel before /r/ in *wheelbarrow*
Is /æ/, except

○   [a ∼ ɑ ∼ ɒ ∼ ɒ] = /ɑ/

●   /ɛ/

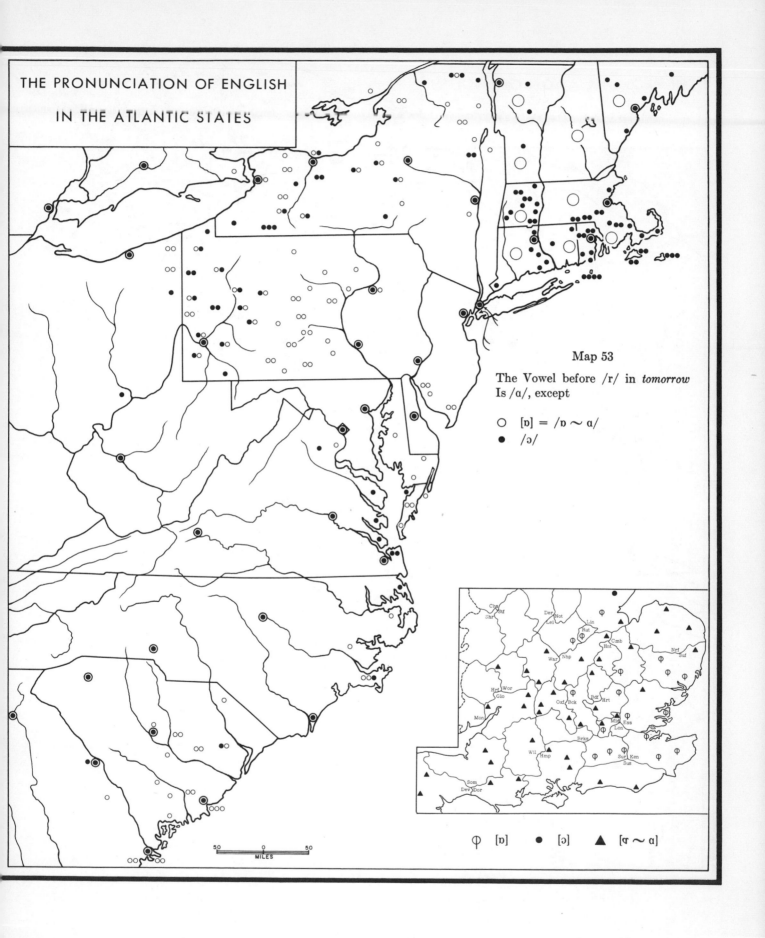

THE PRONUNCIATION OF ENGLISH

IN THE ATLANTIC STATES

Map 53

The Vowel before /r/ in *tomorrow*
Is /ɑ/, except

○   [ɒ] = /ɒ ～ ɑ/

●   /ɔ/

φ   [ɒ]   ●   [ɔ]   ▲   [ɤ ～ ɑ]

MILES
50   0   50

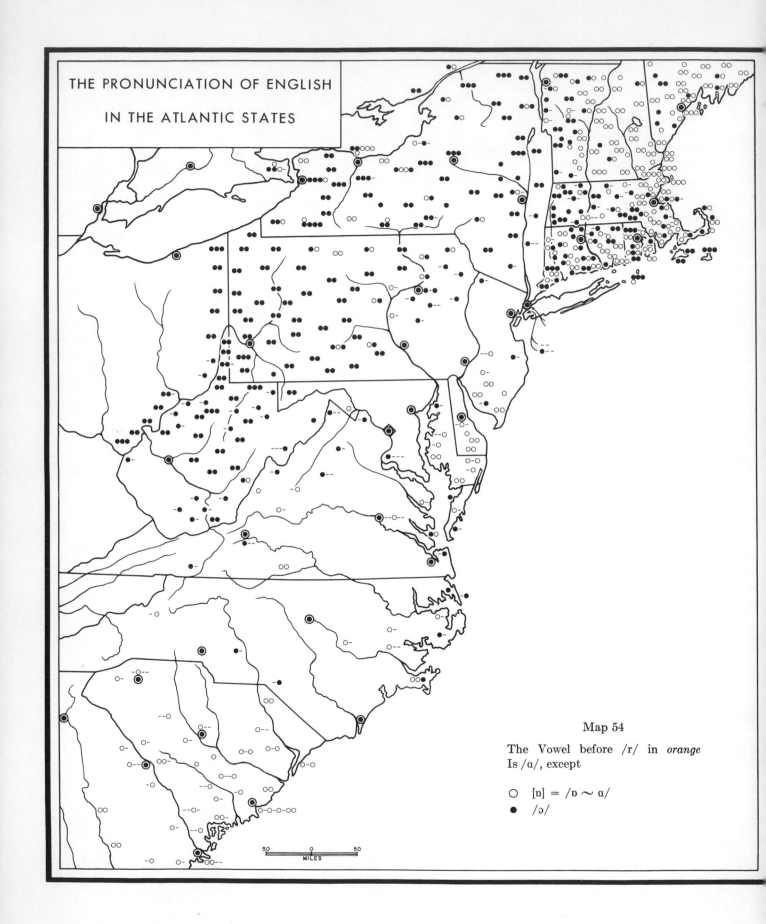

THE PRONUNCIATION OF ENGLISH

IN THE ATLANTIC STATES

Map 54

The Vowel before /r/ in *orange*
Is /ɑ/, except

○ [ɒ] = /ɒ ∼ ɑ/

● /ɔ/

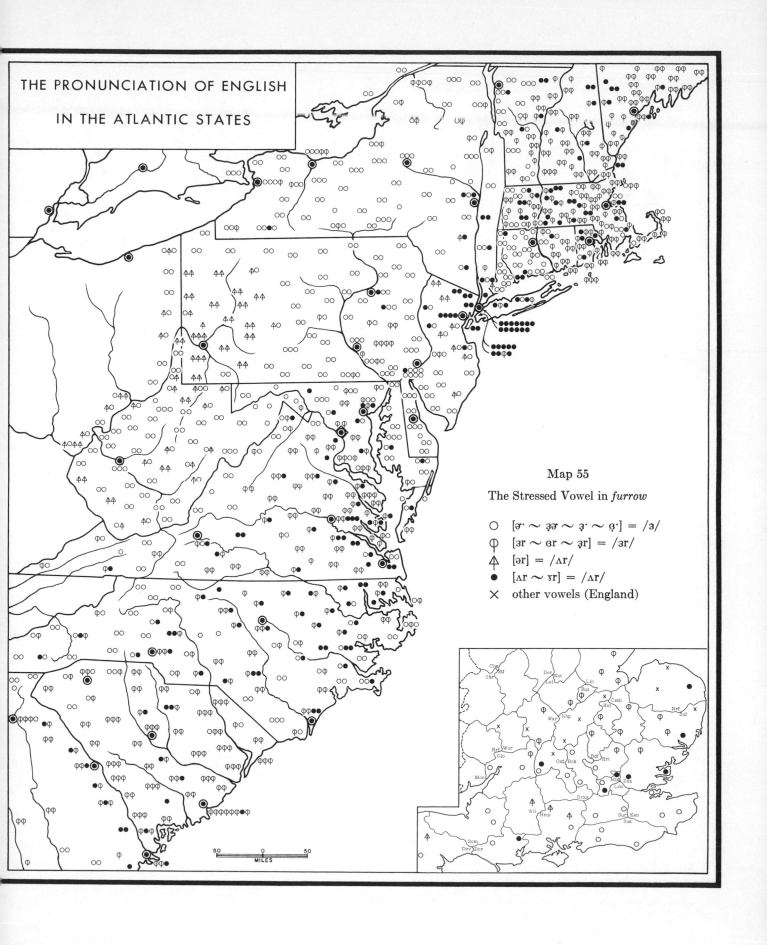

THE PRONUNCIATION OF ENGLISH
IN THE ATLANTIC STATES

Map 55

The Stressed Vowel in *furrow*

○ [ɝˑ ~ ɜɚ ~ ɜˑ ~ ɞˑ] = /ɜ/

Φ [ɜr ~ ɵr ~ ɜr] = /ɜr/

⊥ [ər] = /ʌr/

● [ʌr ~ ɤr] = /ʌr/

✕ other vowels (England)

50   0   50

MILES

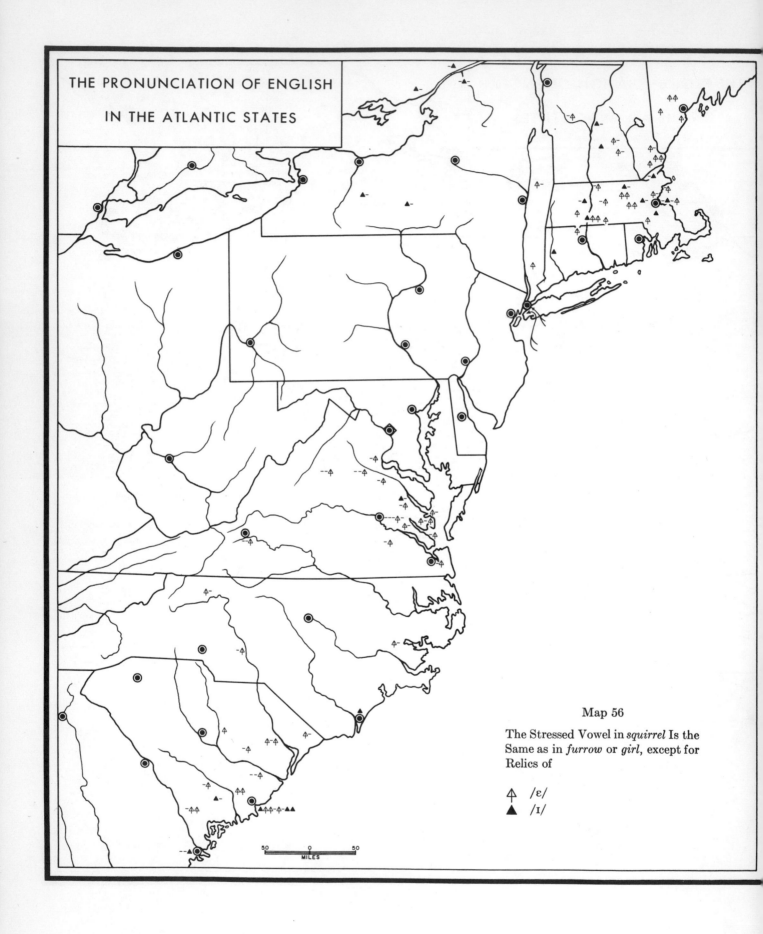

THE PRONUNCIATION OF ENGLISH

IN THE ATLANTIC STATES

Map 56

The Stressed Vowel in *squirrel* Is the
Same as in *furrow* or *girl*, except for
Relics of

⚲ /ɛ/
▲ /ɪ/

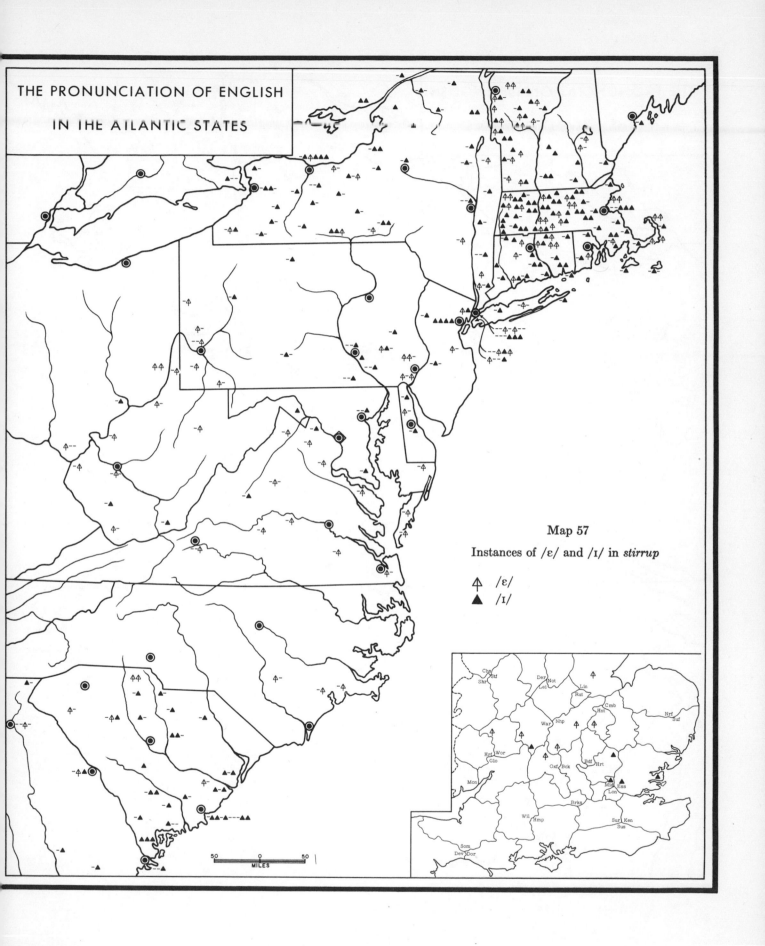

THE PRONUNCIATION OF ENGLISH
IN THE ATLANTIC STATES

Map 57

Instances of /ɛ/ and /ɪ/ in *stirrup*

⚲ /ɛ/
▲ /ɪ/

MILES

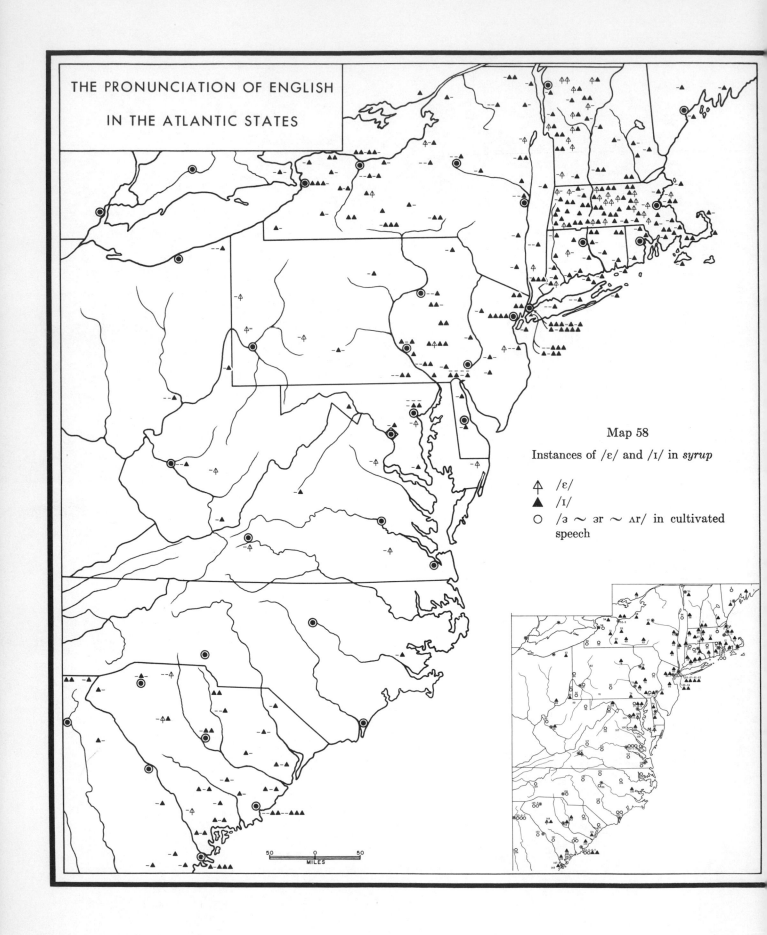

THE PRONUNCIATION OF ENGLISH

IN THE ATLANTIC STATES

Map 58

Instances of /ɛ/ and /ɪ/ in *syrup*

⚘ /ɛ/

▲ /ɪ/

○ /ɜ ~ ɜr ~ ʌr/ in cultivated
speech

MILES

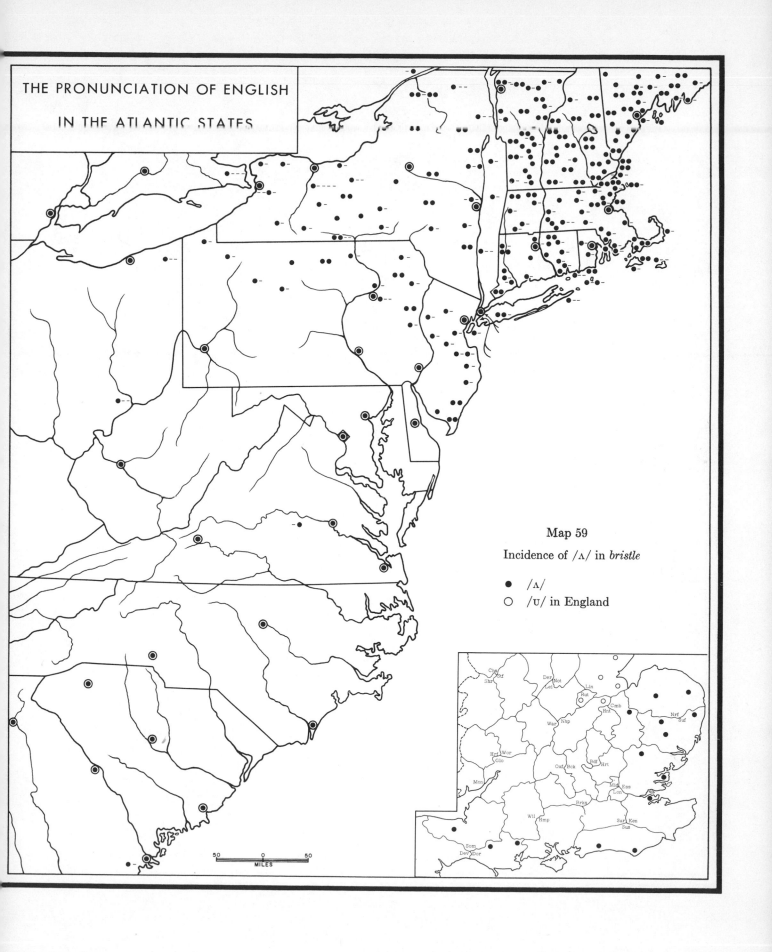

THE PRONUNCIATION OF ENGLISH

IN THE ATLANTIC STATES

Map 59

Incidence of /ʌ/ in *bristle*

● /ʌ/
○ /ʊ/ in England

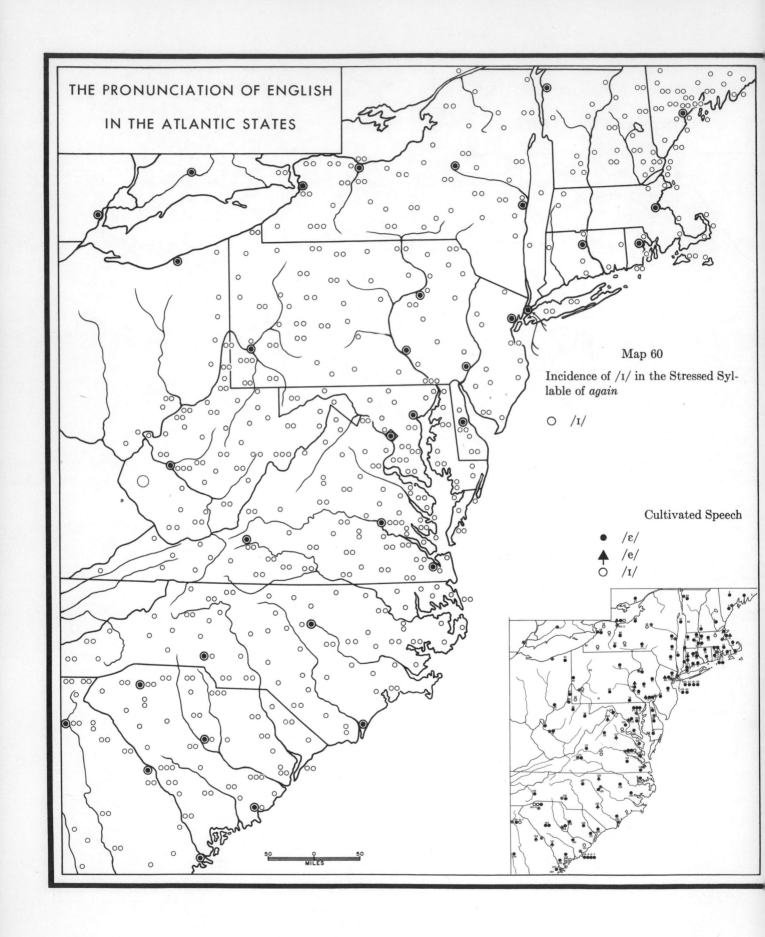

THE PRONUNCIATION OF ENGLISH
IN THE ATLANTIC STATES

Map 60

Incidence of /ɪ/ in the Stressed Syllable of *again*

○   /ɪ/

Cultivated Speech

●   /ɛ/
▲   /e/
○   /ɪ/

50   0   50
MILES

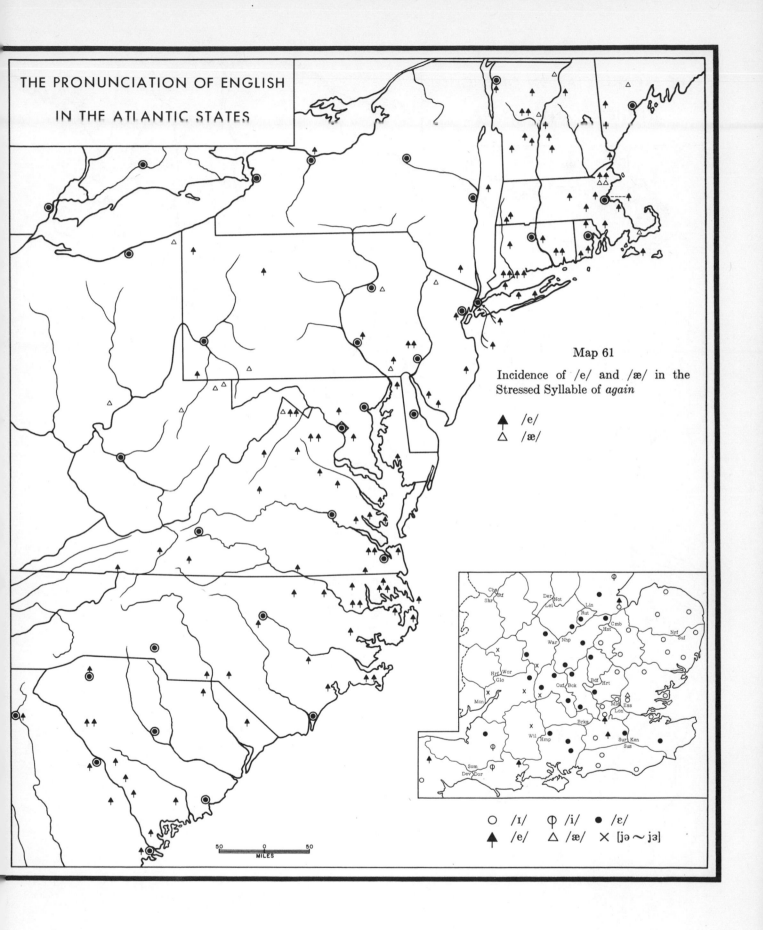

THE PRONUNCIATION OF ENGLISH
IN THE ATLANTIC STATES

Map 61

Incidence of /e/ and /æ/ in the
Stressed Syllable of *again*

▲ /e/

△ /æ/

○ /ɪ/   φ /i/   ● /ɛ/

▲ /e/   △ /æ/   ✕ [jə ～ jɜ]

50   0   50
MILES

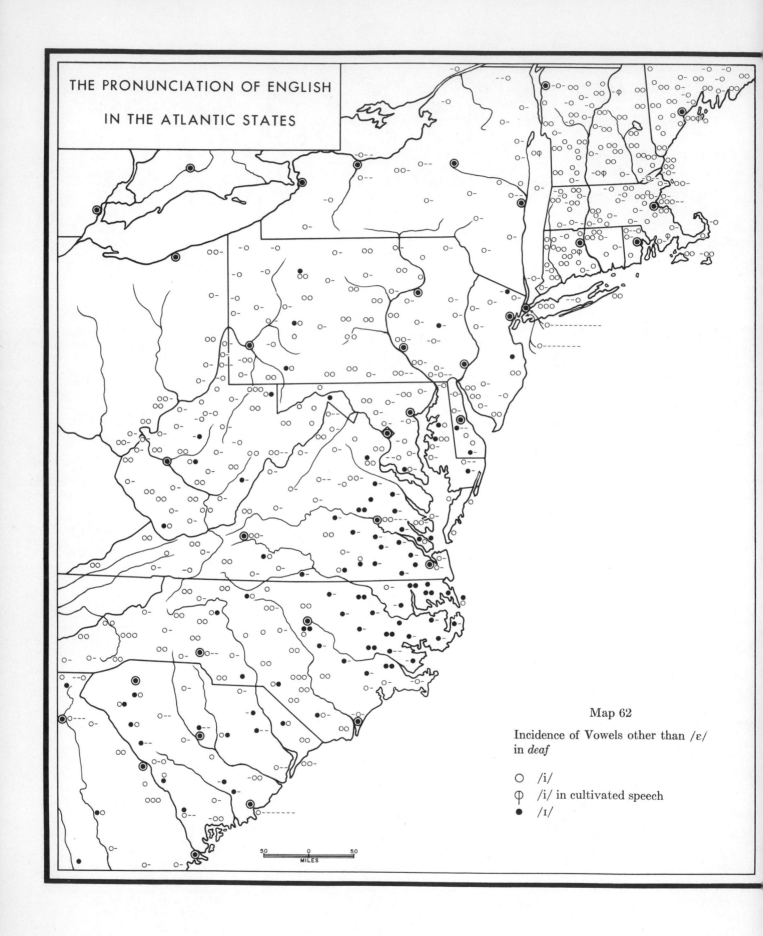

THE PRONUNCIATION OF ENGLISH

IN THE ATLANTIC STATES

Map 62

Incidence of Vowels other than /ɛ/
in *deaf*

○   /i/

φ   /i/ in cultivated speech

●   /ɪ/

50   0   50
MILES

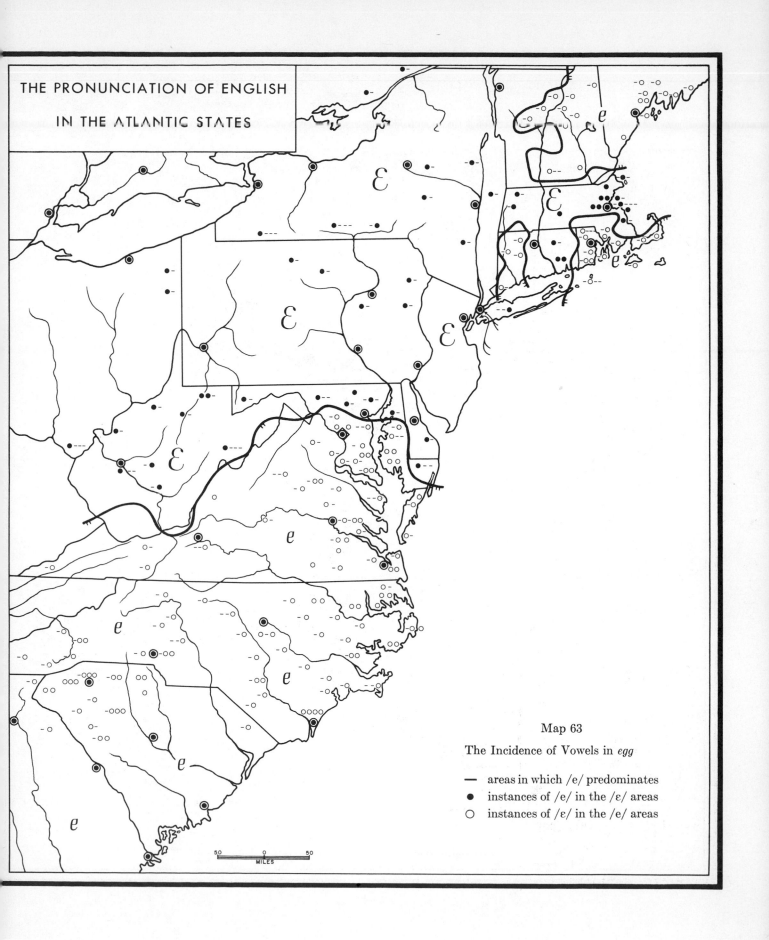

THE PRONUNCIATION OF ENGLISH

IN THE ATLANTIC STATES

Map 63

The Incidence of Vowels in *egg*

— areas in which /e/ predominates

● instances of /e/ in the /ɛ/ areas

○ instances of /ɛ/ in the /e/ areas

50   0   50
MILES

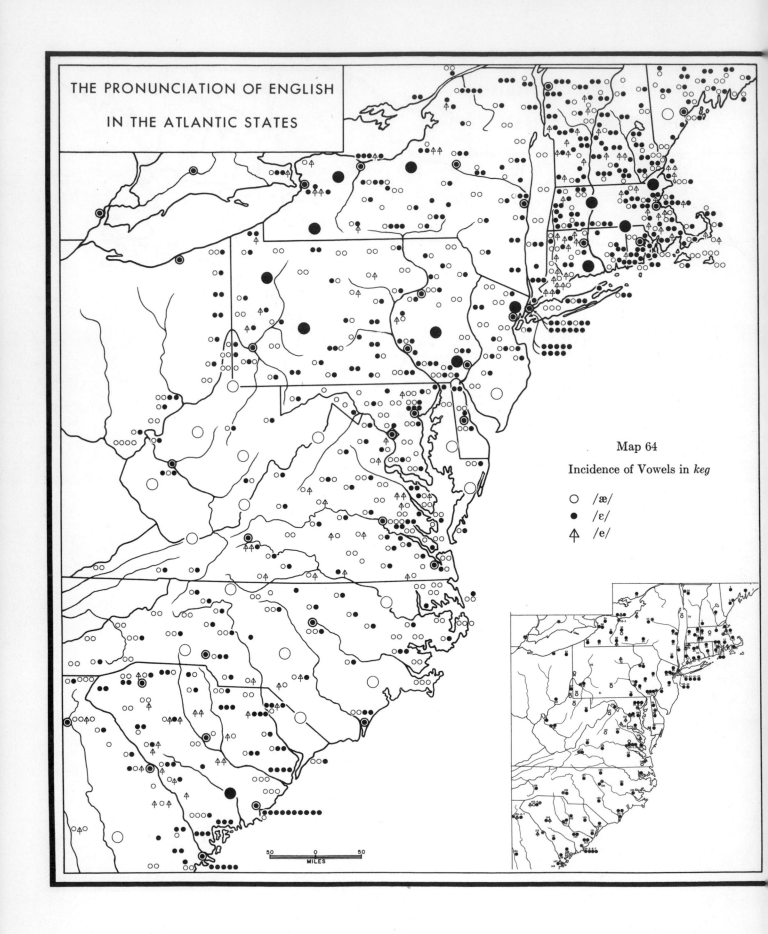

THE PRONUNCIATION OF ENGLISH
IN THE ATLANTIC STATES

Map 64

Incidence of Vowels in *keg*

○ /æ/

● /ɛ/

⋏ /e/

50   0   50
MILES

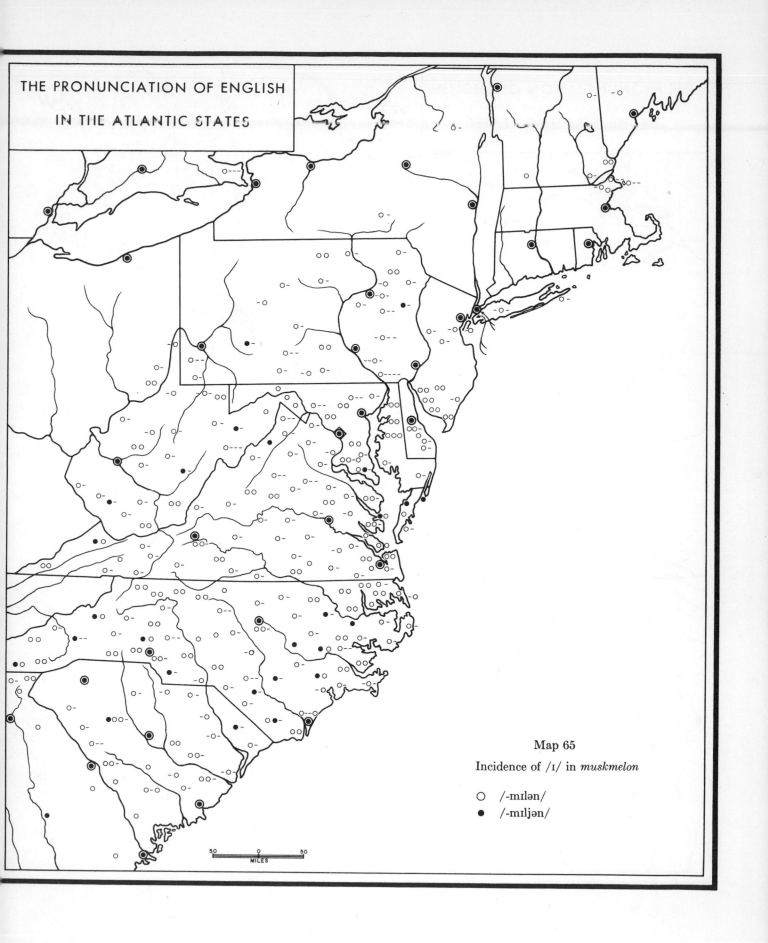

THE PRONUNCIATION OF ENGLISH

IN THE ATLANTIC STATES

Map 65

Incidence of /ɪ/ in *muskmelon*

○ /-mɪlən/

● /-mɪljən/

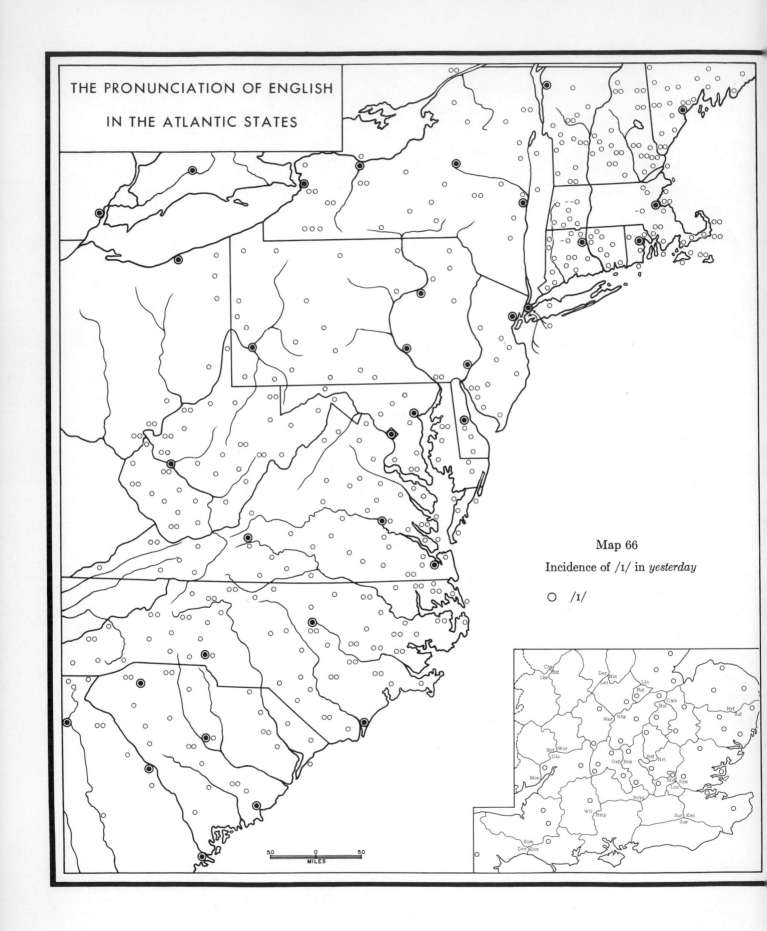

THE PRONUNCIATION OF ENGLISH
IN THE ATLANTIC STATES

Map 66

Incidence of /ɪ/ in *yesterday*

○ /ɪ/

MILES
50   0   50

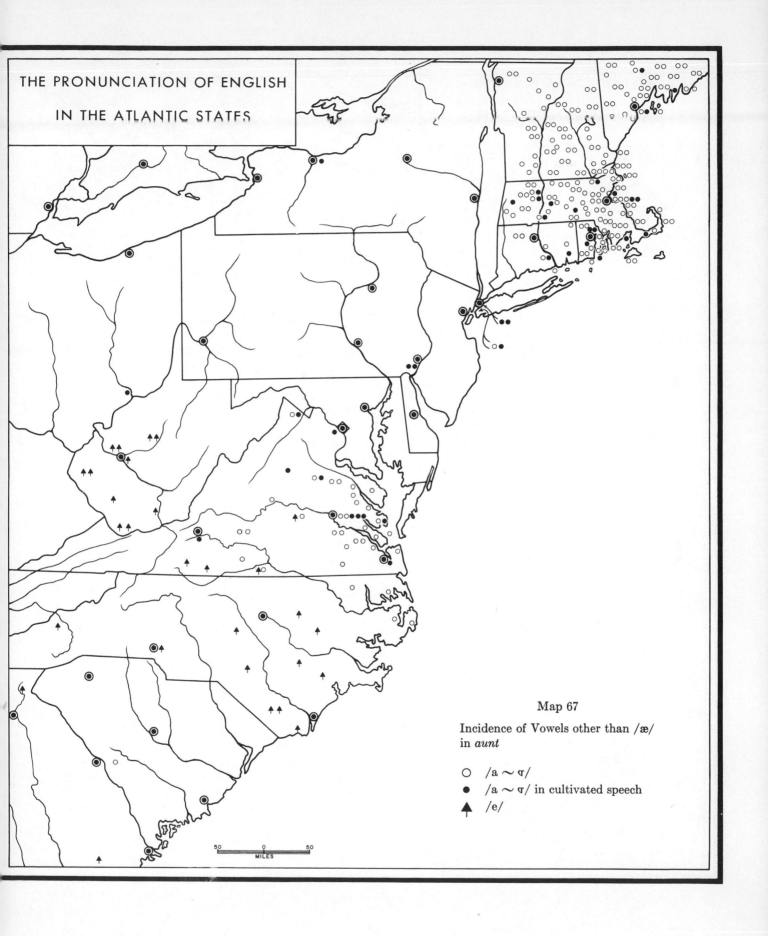

THE PRONUNCIATION OF ENGLISH

IN THE ATLANTIC STATES

Map 67

Incidence of Vowels other than /æ/
in *aunt*

○ /a ~ ɑ/

● /a ~ ɑ/ in cultivated speech

▲ /e/

50   0   50
MILES

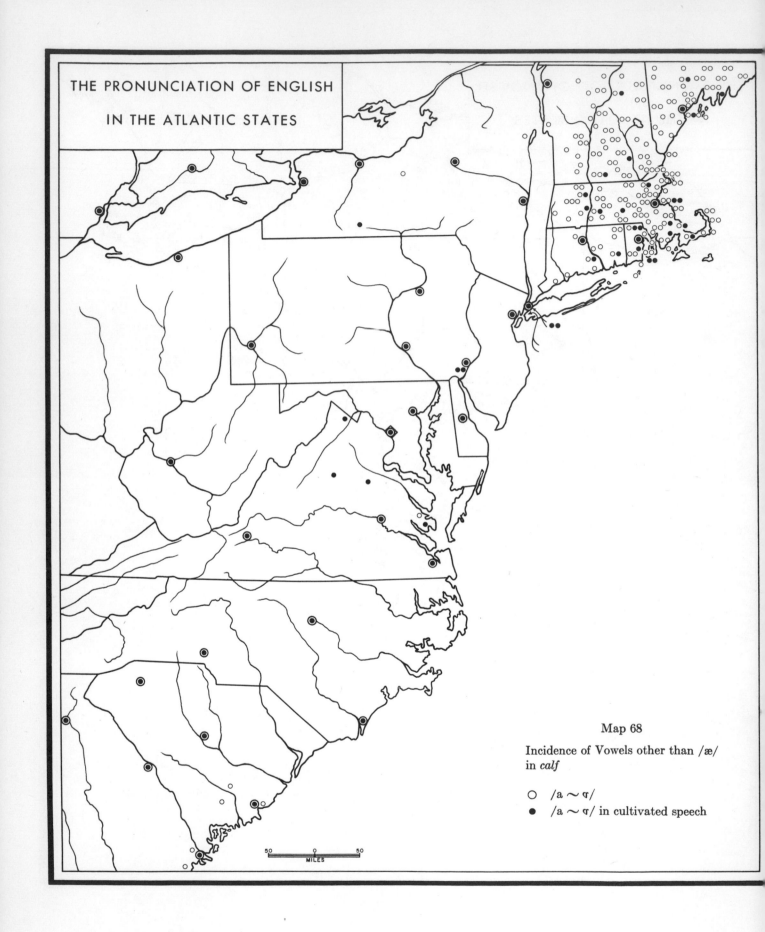

THE PRONUNCIATION OF ENGLISH
IN THE ATLANTIC STATES

Map 68

Incidence of Vowels other than /æ/
in *calf*

○   /a ~ ɑ/

●   /a ~ ɑ/ in cultivated speech

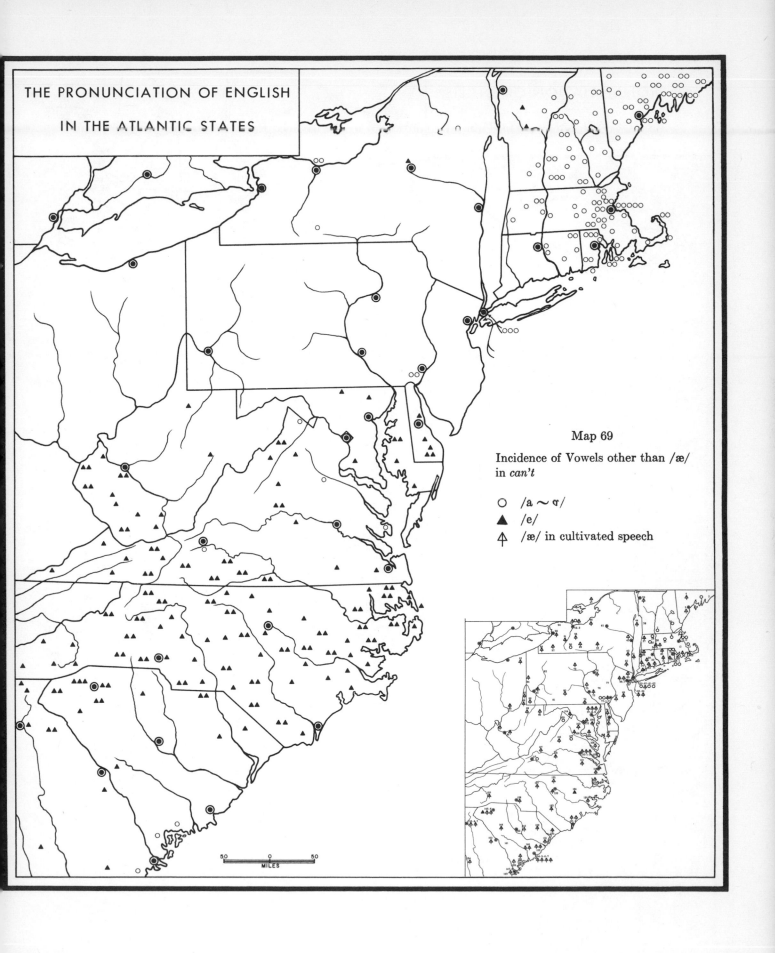

THE PRONUNCIATION OF ENGLISH

IN THE ATLANTIC STATES

Map 69

Incidence of Vowels other than /æ/
in *can't*

○ /a ~ ɑ/

▲ /e/

⚘ /æ/ in cultivated speech

50 0 50
MILES

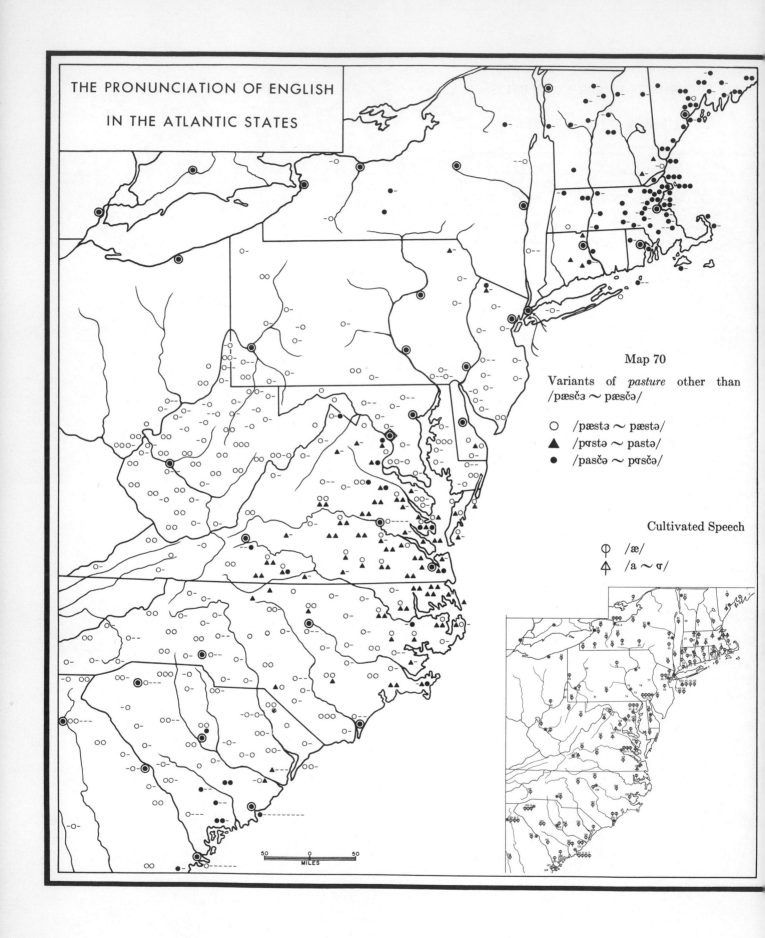

THE PRONUNCIATION OF ENGLISH

IN THE ATLANTIC STATES

Map 70

Variants of *pasture* other than
/pæsčɜ ~ pæsčə/

○ /pæstɜ ~ pæstə/

▲ /pɑstə ~ pastə/

● /pasčə ~ pɑsčə/

Cultivated Speech

φ /æ/

ᵠ /a ~ ɑ/

50   0   50
MILES

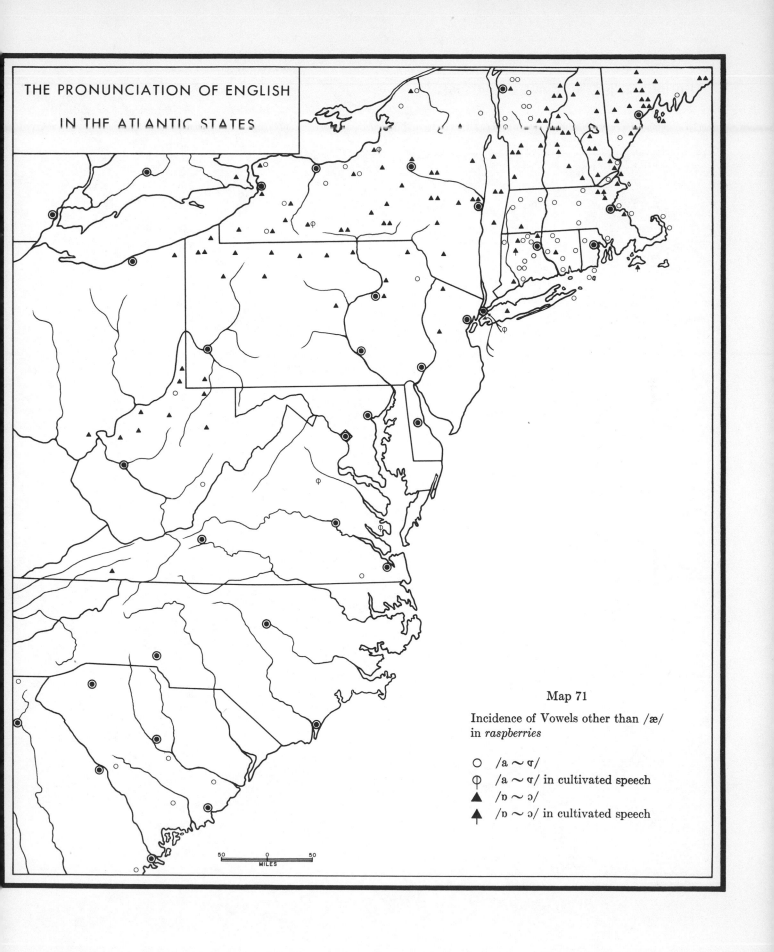

THE PRONUNCIATION OF ENGLISH
IN THE ATLANTIC STATES

Map 71

Incidence of Vowels other than /æ/
in *raspberries*

○ /a ∼ ɑ/
ⵁ /a ∼ ɑ/ in cultivated speech
▲ /ɒ ∼ ɔ/
▲ /ɒ ∼ ɔ/ in cultivated speech

50   0   50
MILES

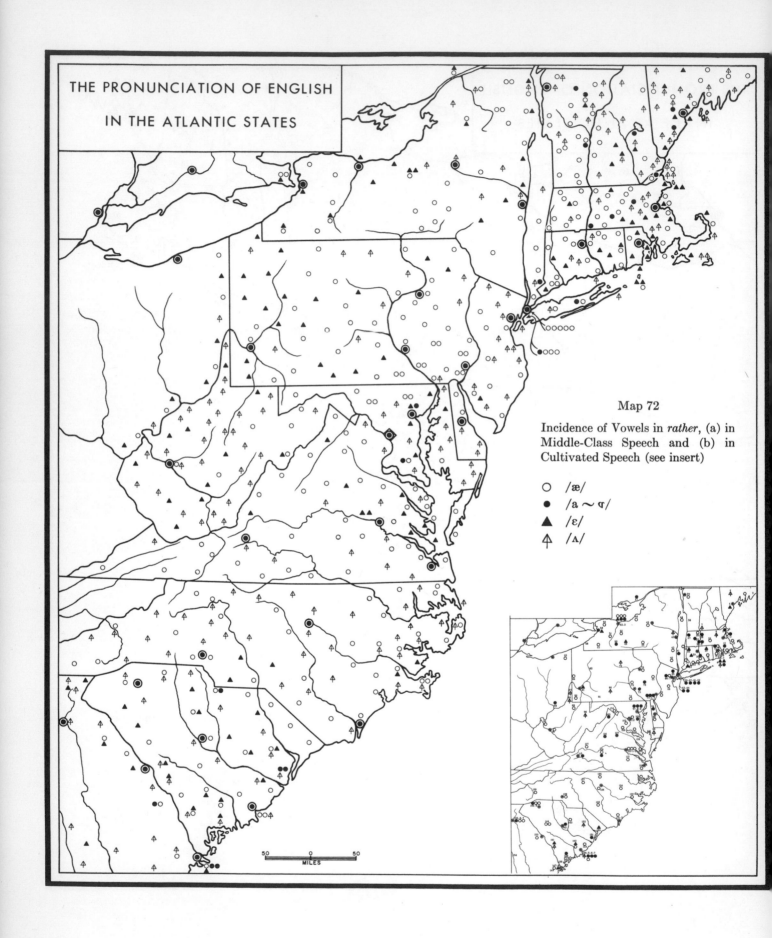

THE PRONUNCIATION OF ENGLISH
IN THE ATLANTIC STATES

Map 72

Incidence of Vowels in *rather*, (a) in
Middle-Class Speech and (b) in
Cultivated Speech (see insert)

○ /æ/
● /a ~ ɑ/
▲ /ɛ/
⅄ /ʌ/

50   0   50
MILES

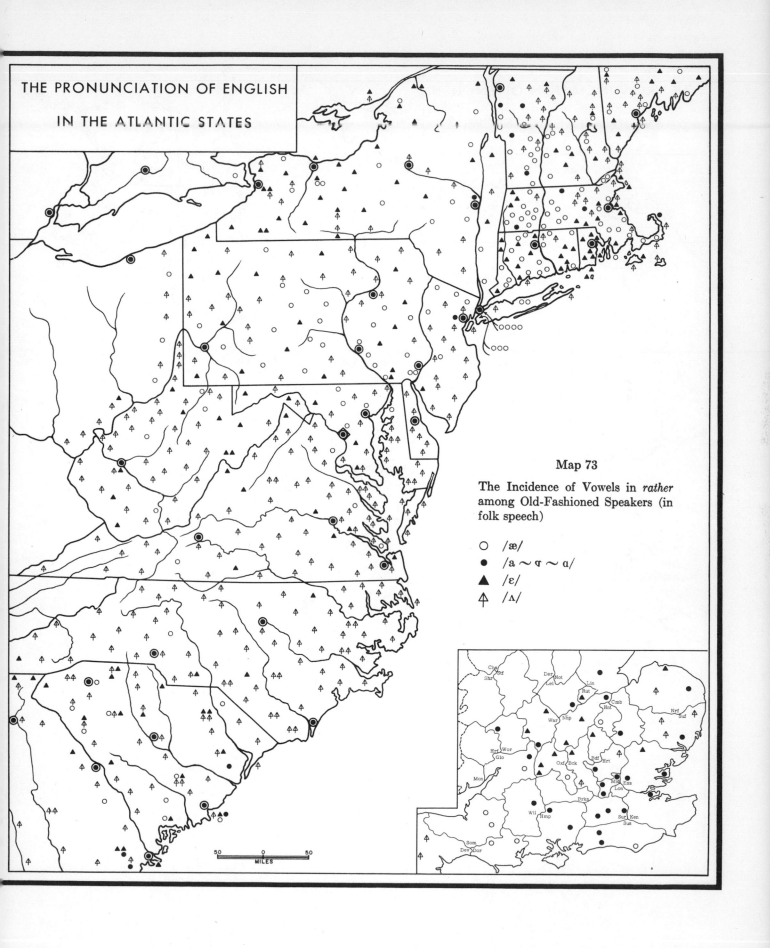

THE PRONUNCIATION OF ENGLISH

IN THE ATLANTIC STATES

Map 73

The Incidence of Vowels in *rather*
among Old-Fashioned Speakers (in
folk speech)

○ /æ/

● /a ~ ɒ ~ ɑ/

▲ /ɛ/

↟ /ʌ/

MILES

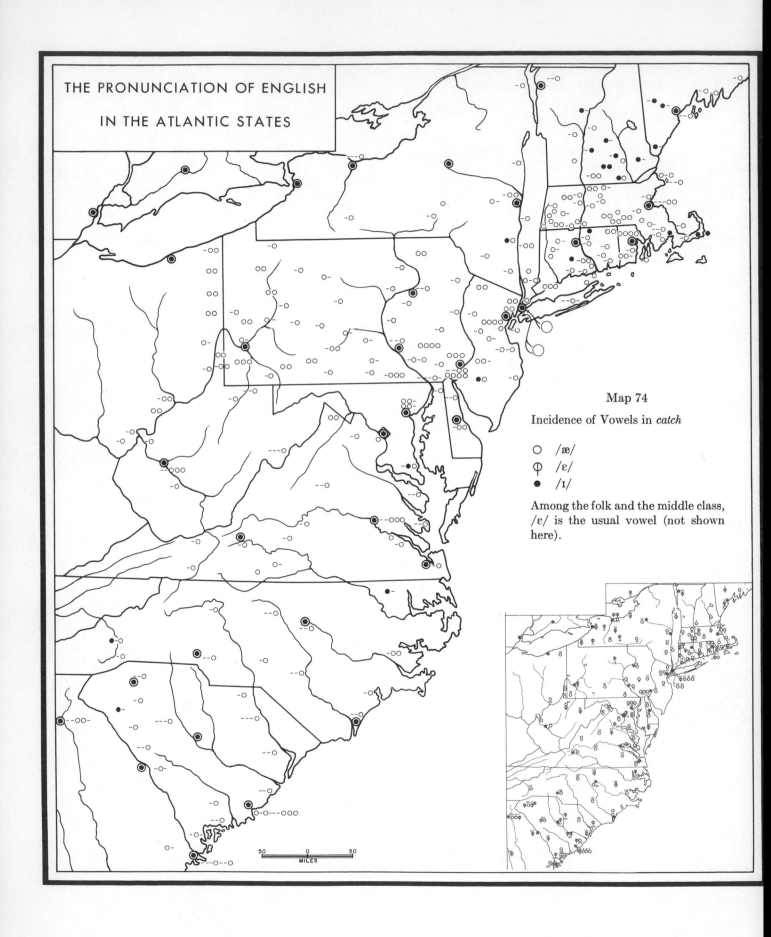

THE PRONUNCIATION OF ENGLISH

IN THE ATLANTIC STATES

Map 74

Incidence of Vowels in *catch*

○ /æ/

φ /ɛ/

● /ɪ/

Among the folk and the middle class, /ɛ/ is the usual vowel (not shown here).

50 0 50
MILES

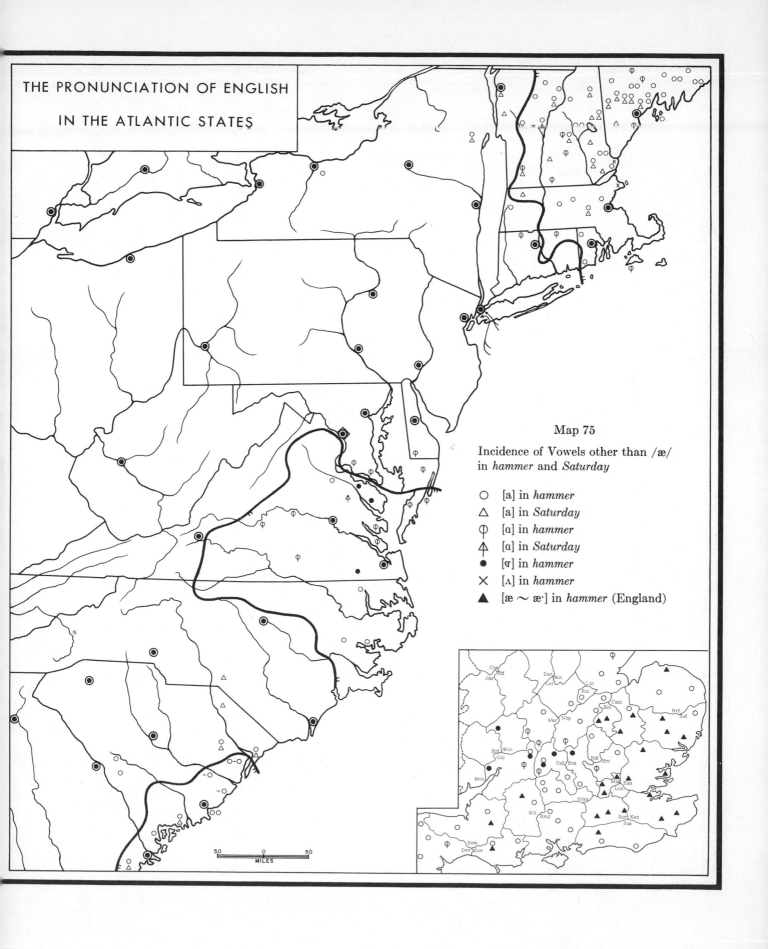

THE PRONUNCIATION OF ENGLISH

IN THE ATLANTIC STATES

Map 75

Incidence of Vowels other than /æ/
in *hammer* and *Saturday*

○ [a] in *hammer*

△ [a] in *Saturday*

Ⴔ [ɑ] in *hammer*

⏃ [ɑ] in *Saturday*

● [ɒ] in *hammer*

✕ [ʌ] in *hammer*

▲ [æ ∼ æ·] in *hammer* (England)

MILES
50   0   50

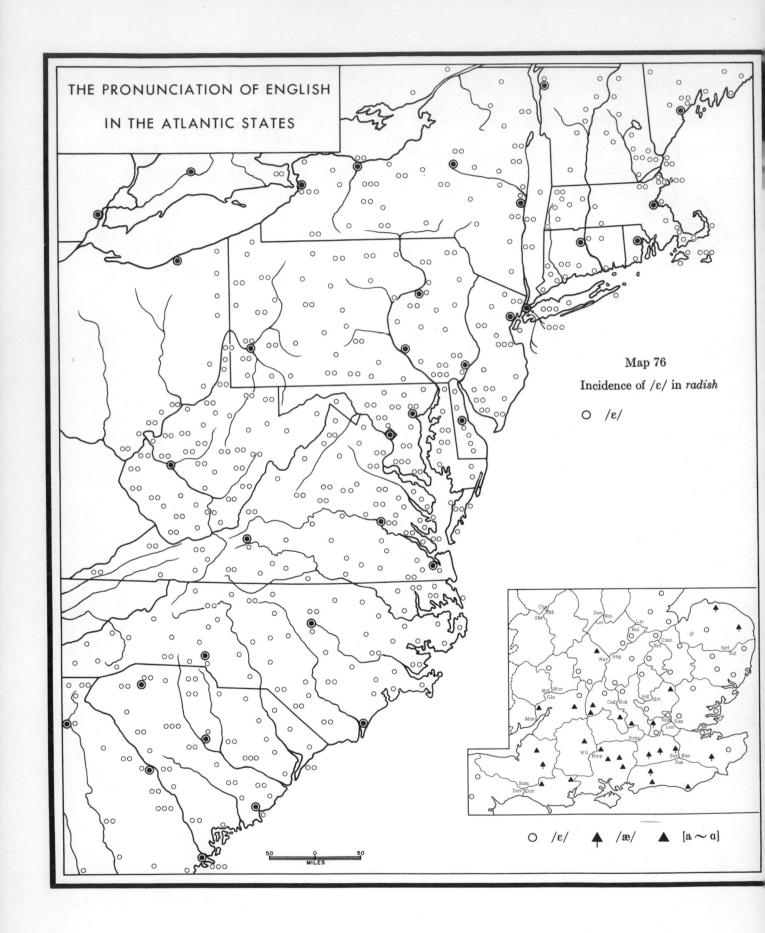

THE PRONUNCIATION OF ENGLISH
IN THE ATLANTIC STATES

Map 76

Incidence of /ɛ/ in *radish*

○ /ɛ/

○ /ɛ/   ▲ /æ/   ▲ [a ~ ɑ]

MILES

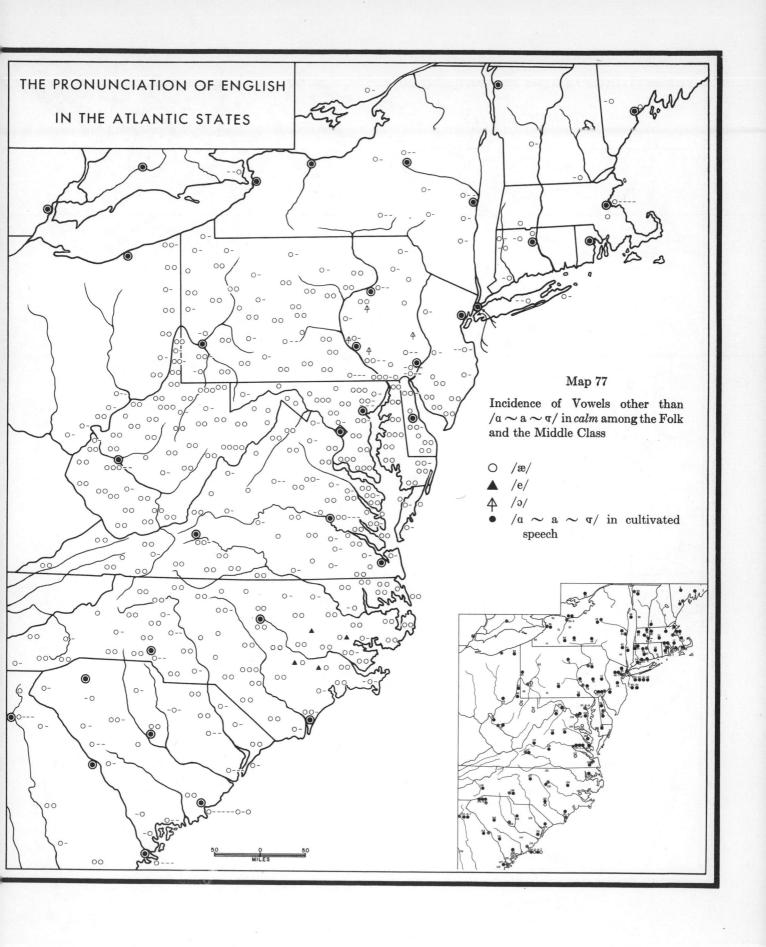

THE PRONUNCIATION OF ENGLISH
IN THE ATLANTIC STATES

Map 77

Incidence of Vowels other than
/ɑ ~ a ~ ɒ/ in *calm* among the Folk
and the Middle Class

○ /æ/

▲ /e/

↑ /ɔ/

● /ɑ ~ a ~ ɒ/ in cultivated
    speech

50   0   50
MILES

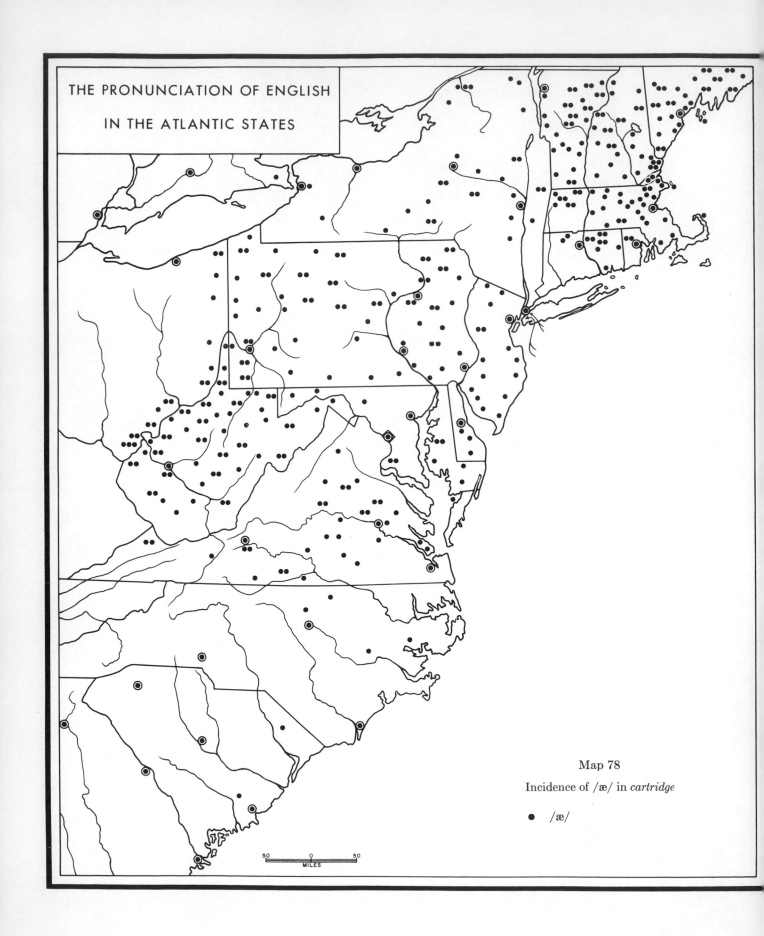

THE PRONUNCIATION OF ENGLISH

IN THE ATLANTIC STATES

Map 78

Incidence of /æ/ in *cartridge*

● /æ/

50 0 50
MILES

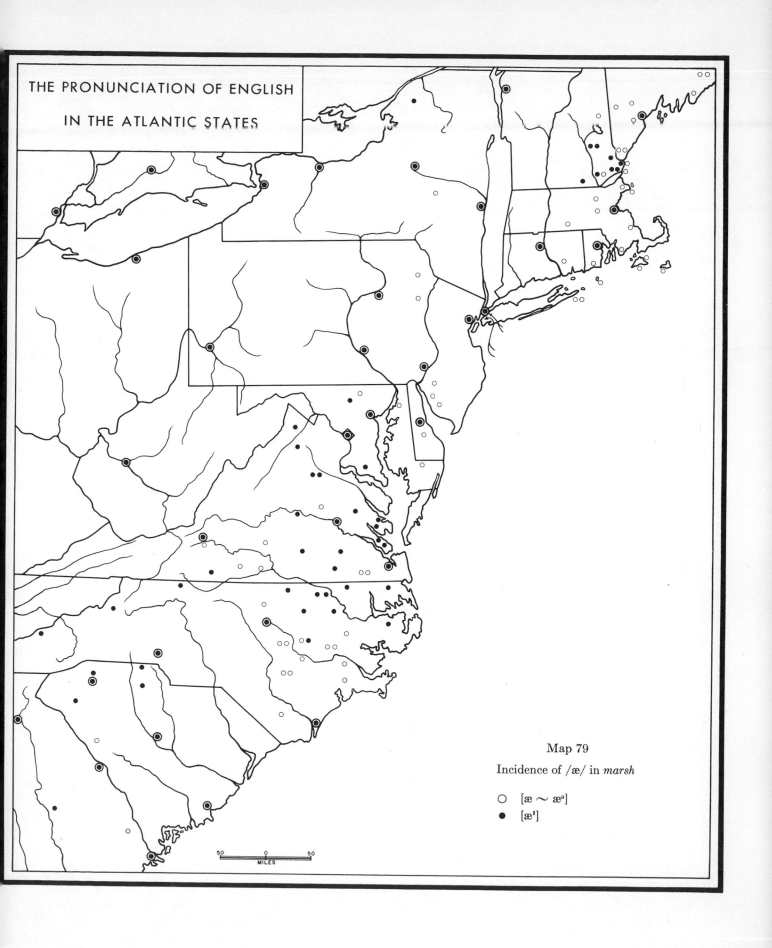

THE PRONUNCIATION OF ENGLISH

IN THE ATLANTIC STATES

Map 79

Incidence of /æ/ in *marsh*

○   [æ ～ æə]

●   [æˡ]

50   0   50

MILES

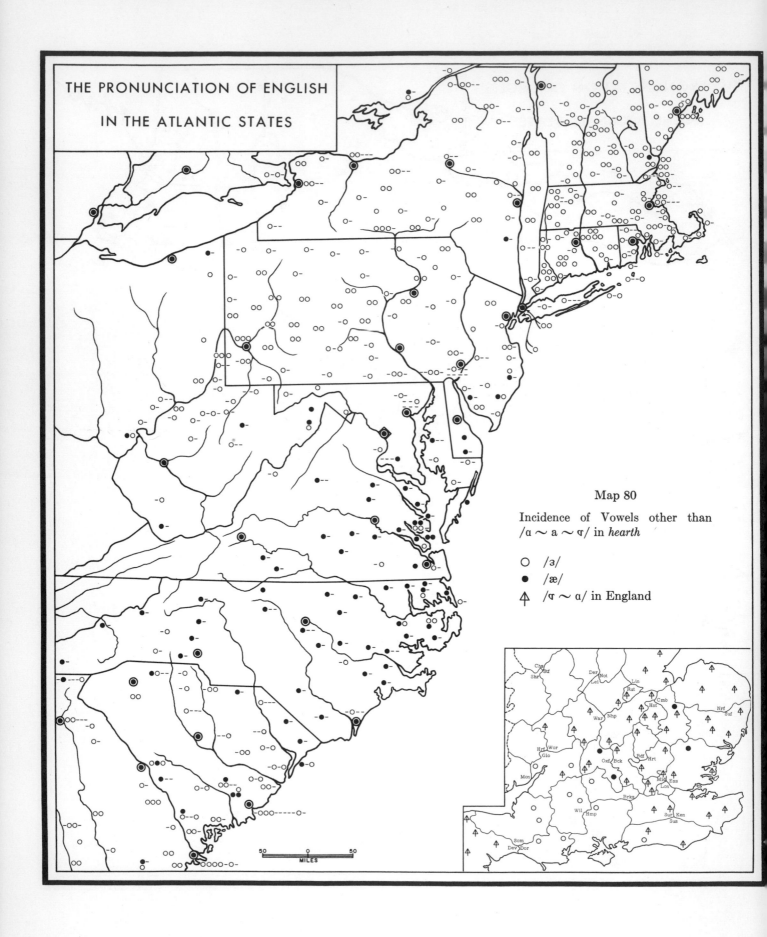

THE PRONUNCIATION OF ENGLISH

IN THE ATLANTIC STATES

Map 80

Incidence of Vowels other than
/ɑ ~ a ~ ɒ/ in *hearth*

○ /ɜ/

● /æ/

⚲ /ɒ ~ ɑ/ in England

50   0   50
MILES

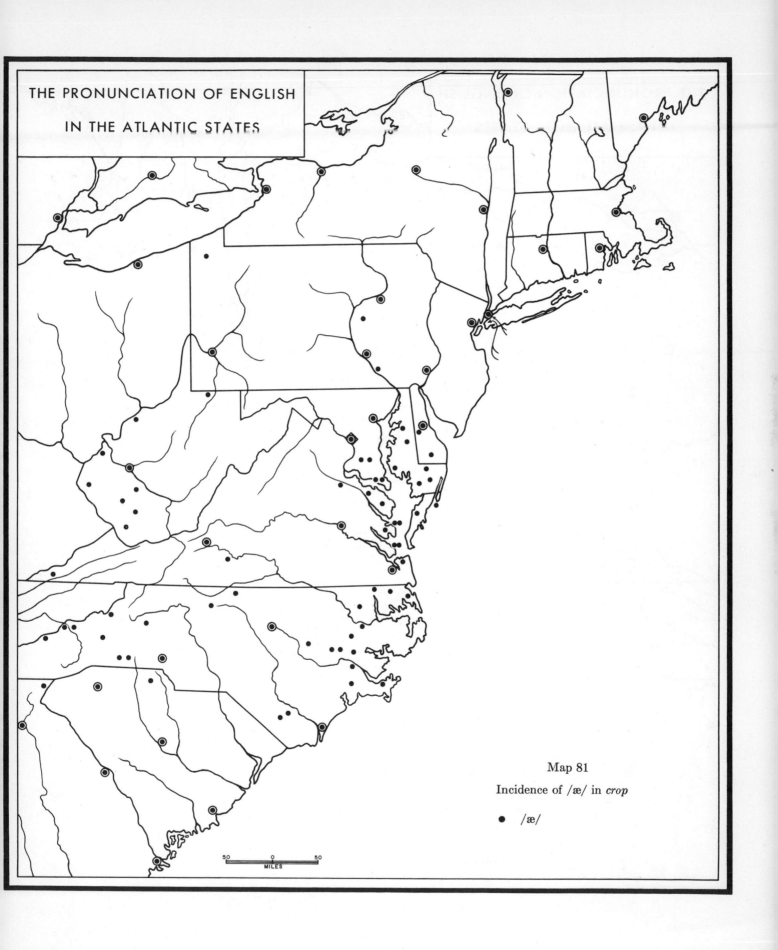

THE PRONUNCIATION OF ENGLISH

IN THE ATLANTIC STATES

Map 81

Incidence of /æ/ in *crop*

● /æ/

50   0   50
MILES

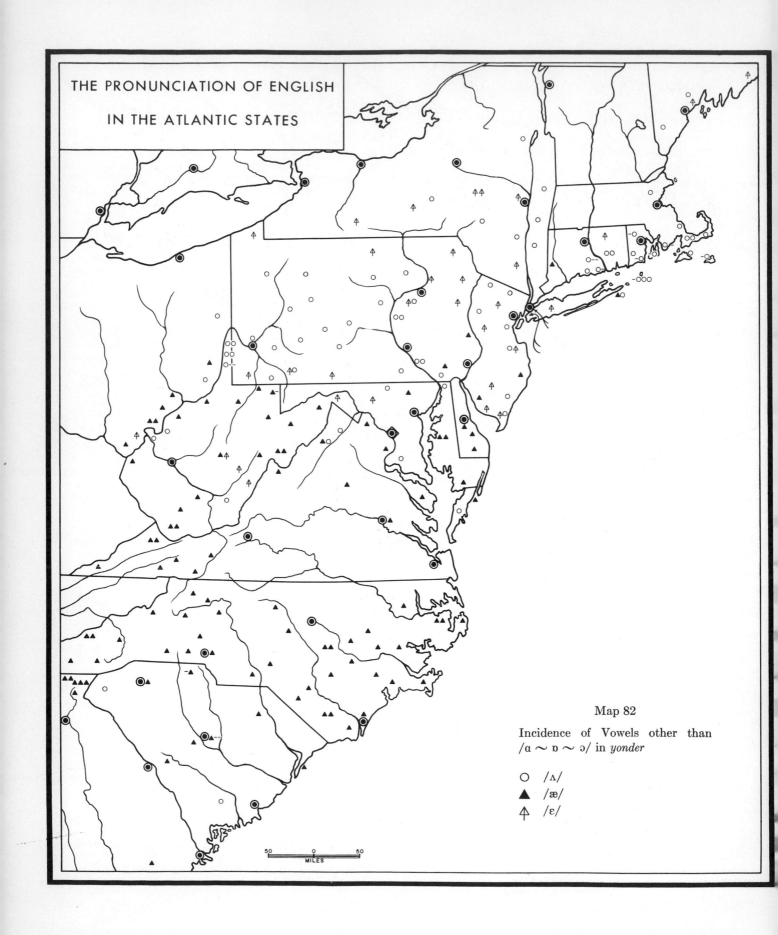

THE PRONUNCIATION OF ENGLISH

IN THE ATLANTIC STATES

Map 82

Incidence of Vowels other than
/ɑ ∼ ɒ ∼ ɔ/ in *yonder*

○ /ʌ/

▲ /æ/

⚓ /ɛ/

50   0   50
MILES

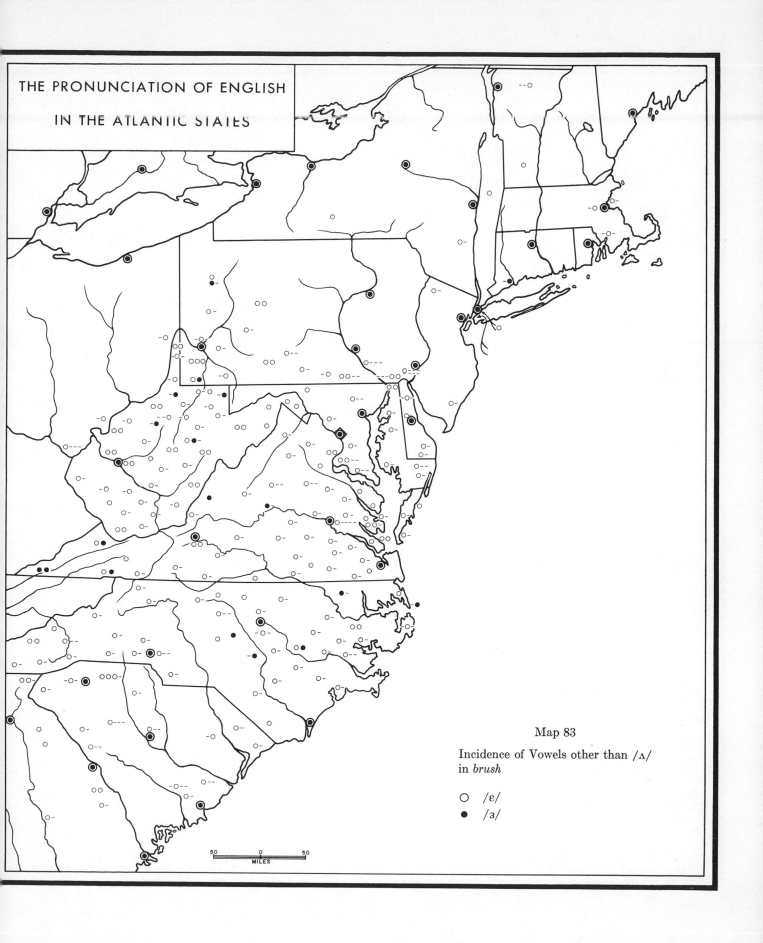

THE PRONUNCIATION OF ENGLISH

IN THE ATLANTIC STATES

Map 83

Incidence of Vowels other than /ʌ/
in *brush*

○   /ɛ/

●   /ɝ/

50   0   50
MILES

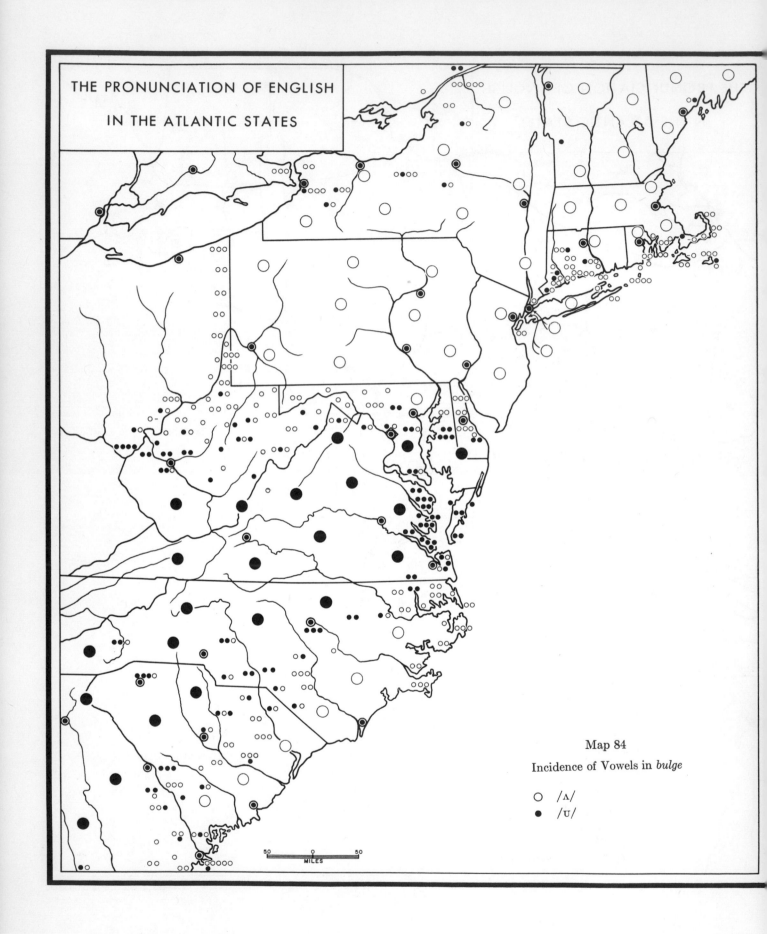

THE PRONUNCIATION OF ENGLISH

IN THE ATLANTIC STATES

Map 84

Incidence of Vowels in *bulge*

○ /ʌ/

● /ʊ/

MILES

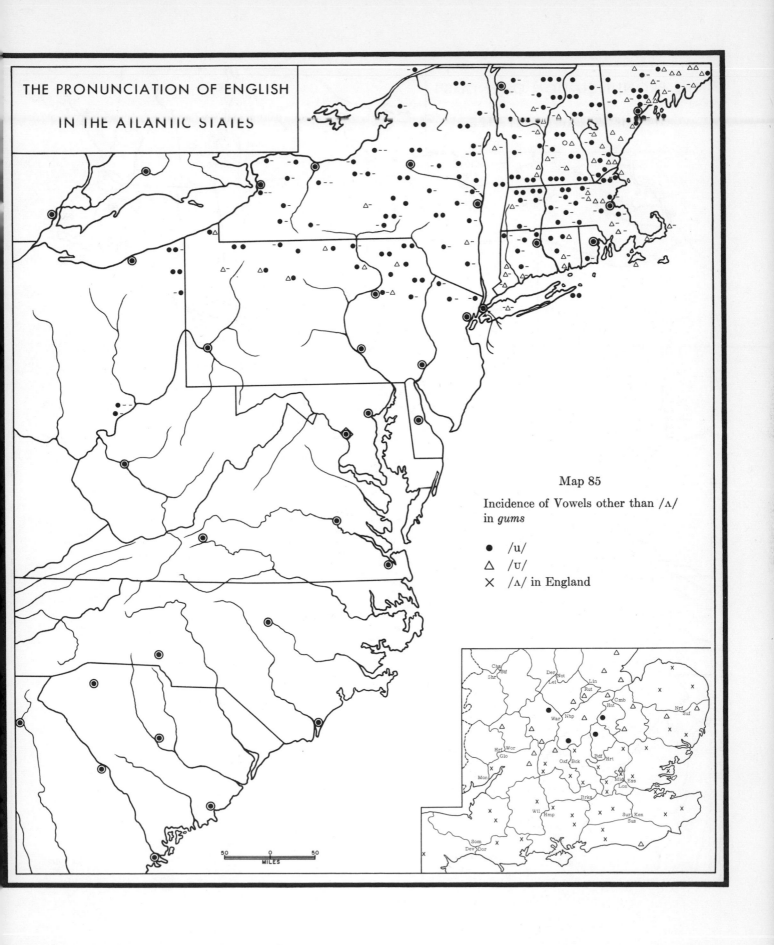

THE PRONUNCIATION OF ENGLISH

IN THE ATLANTIC STATES

Map 85

Incidence of Vowels other than /ʌ/
in *gums*

- ● /u/
- △ /ʊ/
- ✕ /ʌ/ in England

MILES

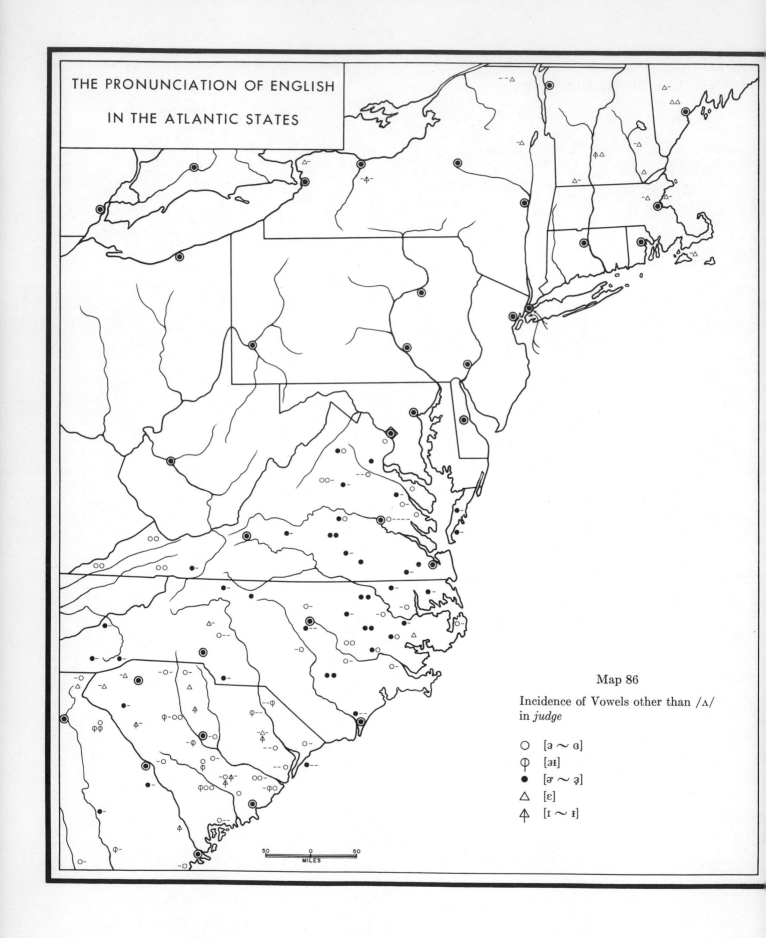

THE PRONUNCIATION OF ENGLISH
IN THE ATLANTIC STATES

Map 86

Incidence of Vowels other than /ʌ/
in *judge*

○ [ɜ ~ ɐ]
 φ [ɜɪ]
● [ɚ ~ ɝ]
△ [ɛ]
⚇ [ɪ ~ ɨ]

MILES
50   0   50

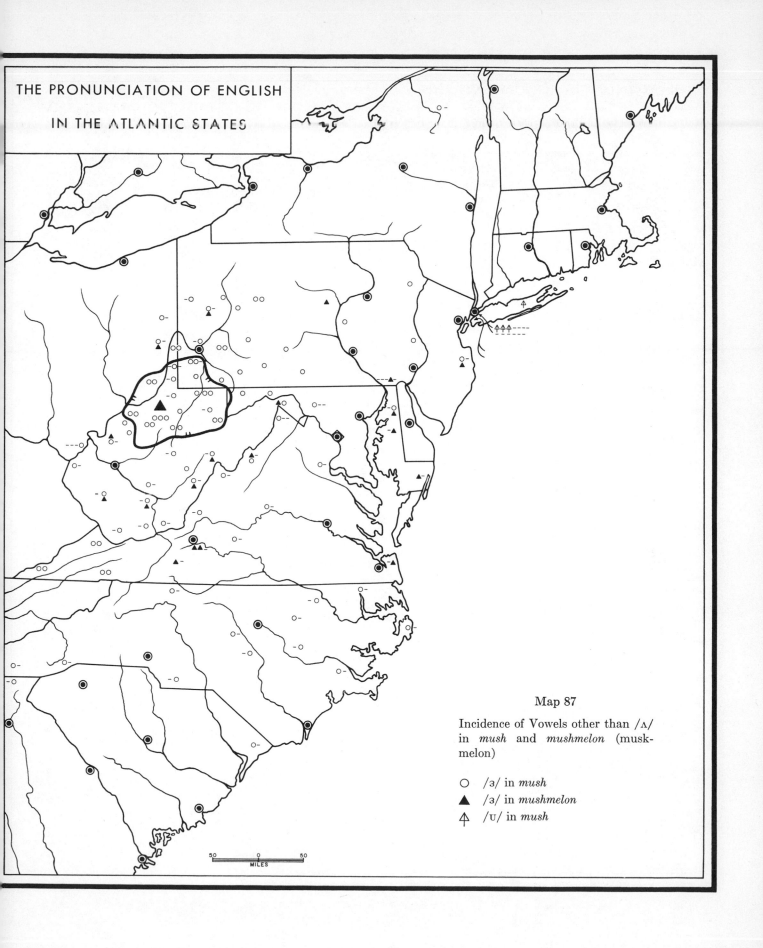

THE PRONUNCIATION OF ENGLISH

IN THE ATLANTIC STATES

Map 87

Incidence of Vowels other than /ʌ/
in *mush* and *mushmelon* (muskmelon)

○   /ɜ/ in *mush*
▲   /ɜ/ in *mushmelon*
⚘   /ʊ/ in *mush*

50   0   50
MILES

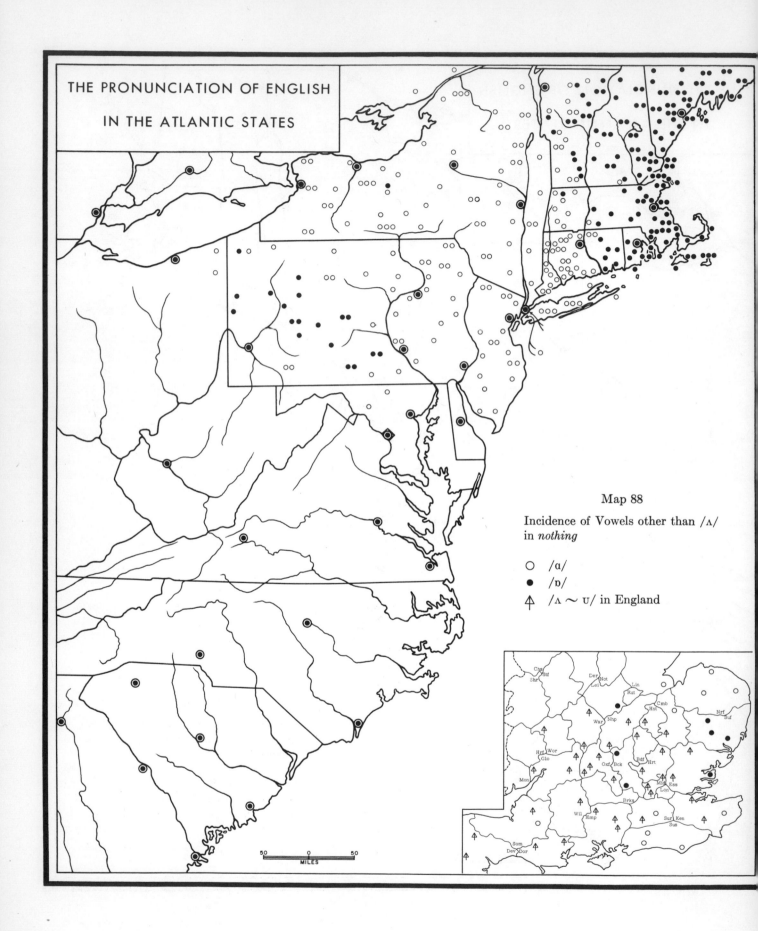

THE PRONUNCIATION OF ENGLISH

IN THE ATLANTIC STATES

Map 88

Incidence of Vowels other than /ʌ/
in *nothing*

○ /ɑ/

● /ɒ/

⌠ /ʌ ~ ʊ/ in England

50   0   50
MILES

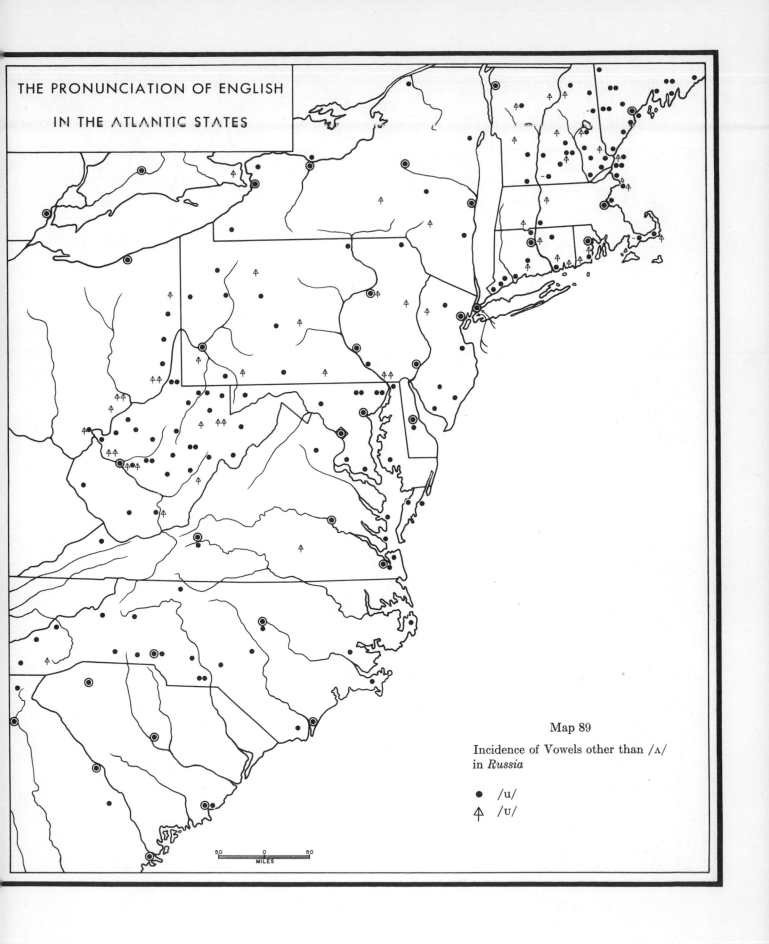

THE PRONUNCIATION OF ENGLISH

IN THE ATLANTIC STATES

Map 89

Incidence of Vowels other than /ʌ/
in *Russia*

● /u/

↑ /ʊ/

50   0   50
MILES

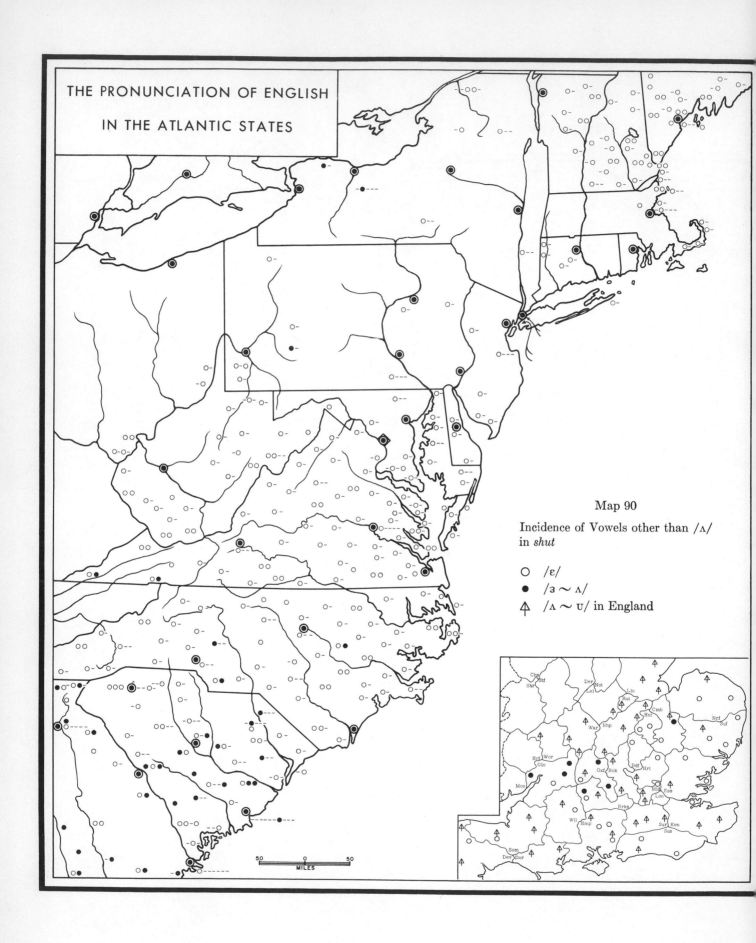

THE PRONUNCIATION OF ENGLISH
IN THE ATLANTIC STATES

Map 90

Incidence of Vowels other than /ʌ/
in *shut*

○ /ɛ/

● /ɜ ~ ʌ/

⚴ /ʌ ~ ʊ/ in England

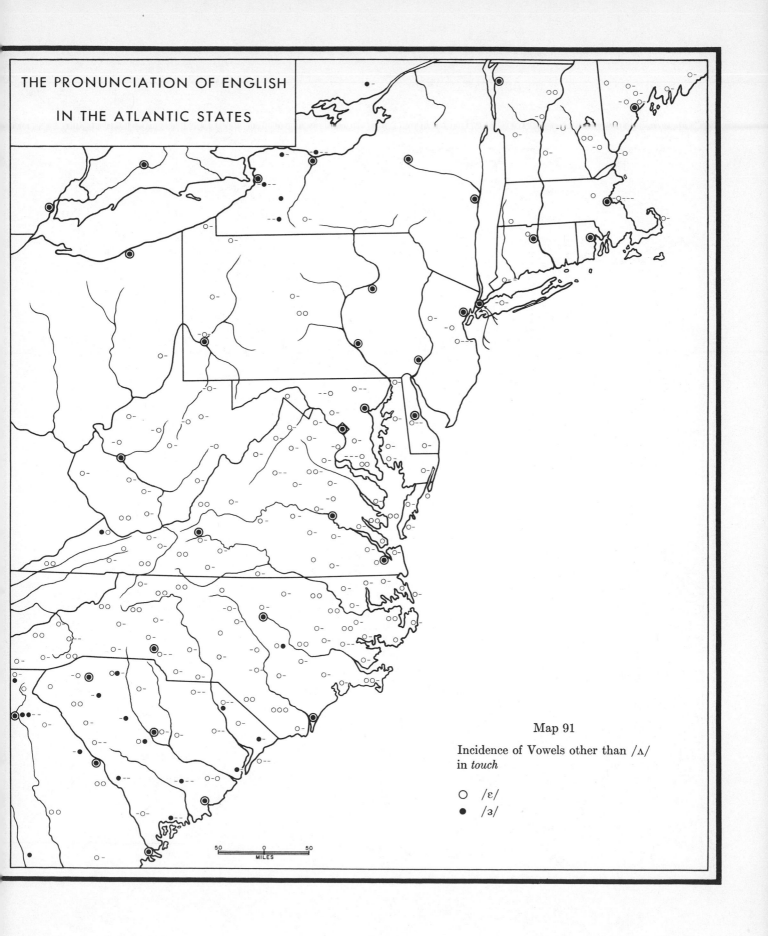

Map 91

Incidence of Vowels other than /ʌ/
in *touch*

○   /ɛ/

●   /ɜ/

50   0   50
MILES

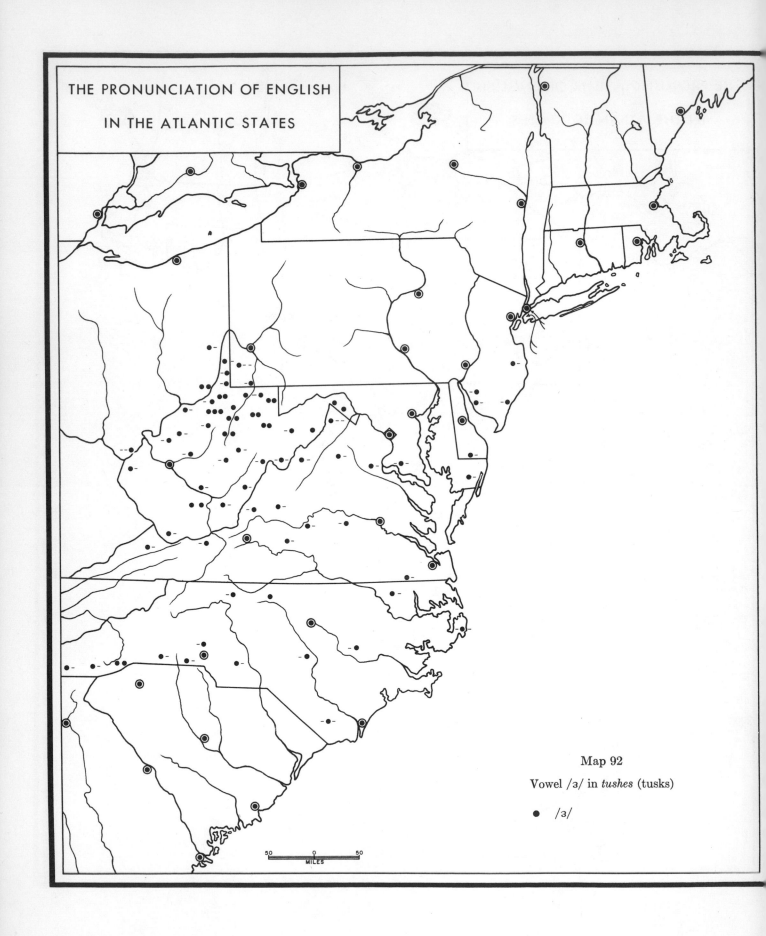

THE PRONUNCIATION OF ENGLISH

IN THE ATLANTIC STATES

Map 92

Vowel /ɜ/ in *tushes* (tusks)

● /ɜ/

50   0   50
MILES

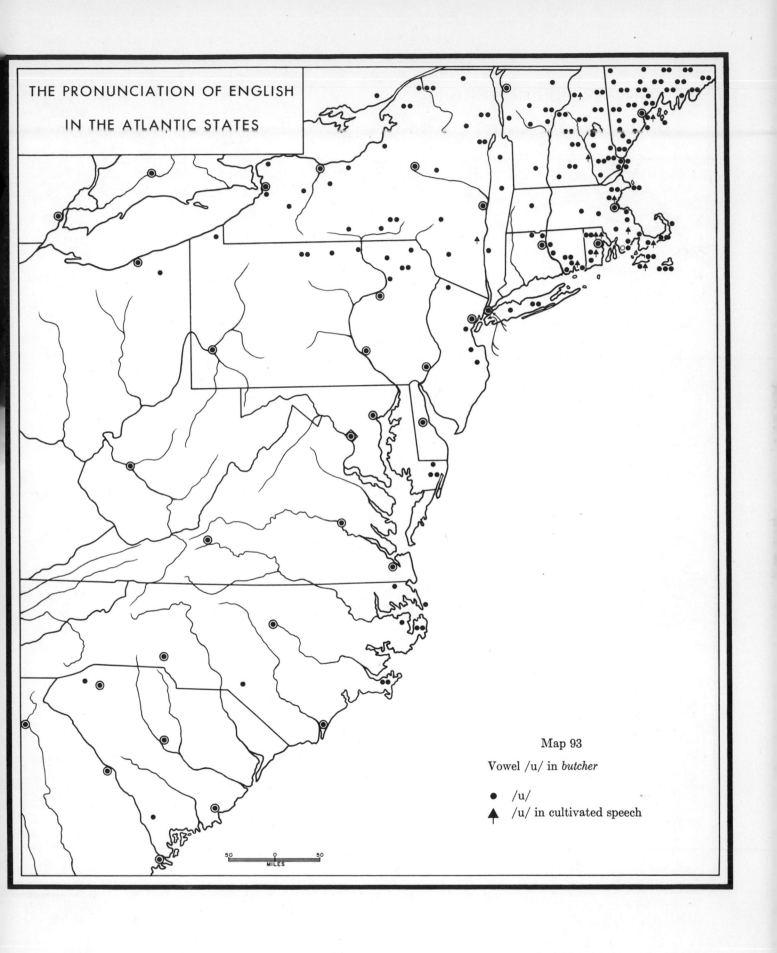

THE PRONUNCIATION OF ENGLISH

IN THE ATLANTIC STATES

Map 93

Vowel /u/ in *butcher*

● /u/

▲ /u/ in cultivated speech

50　0　50
MILES

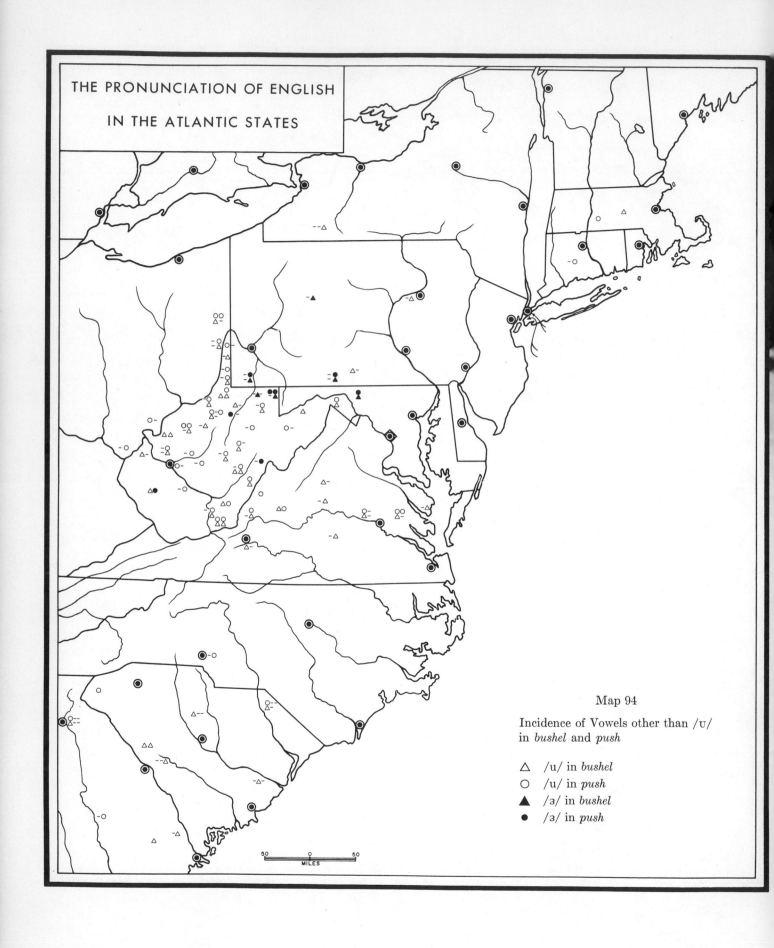

THE PRONUNCIATION OF ENGLISH

IN THE ATLANTIC STATES

Map 94

Incidence of Vowels other than /ʊ/
in *bushel* and *push*

△ /u/ in *bushel*

○ /u/ in *push*

▲ /ɝ/ in *bushel*

● /ɝ/ in *push*

50   0   50
MILES

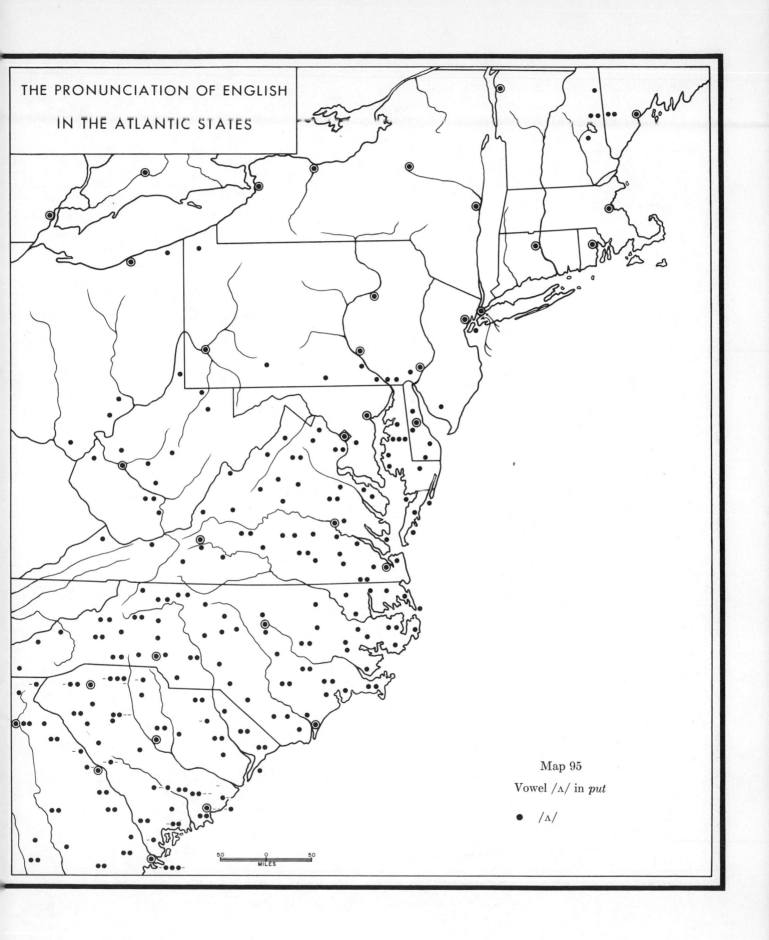

THE PRONUNCIATION OF ENGLISH

IN THE ATLANTIC STATES

Map 95

Vowel /ʌ/ in *put*

● /ʌ/

50   0   50
MILES

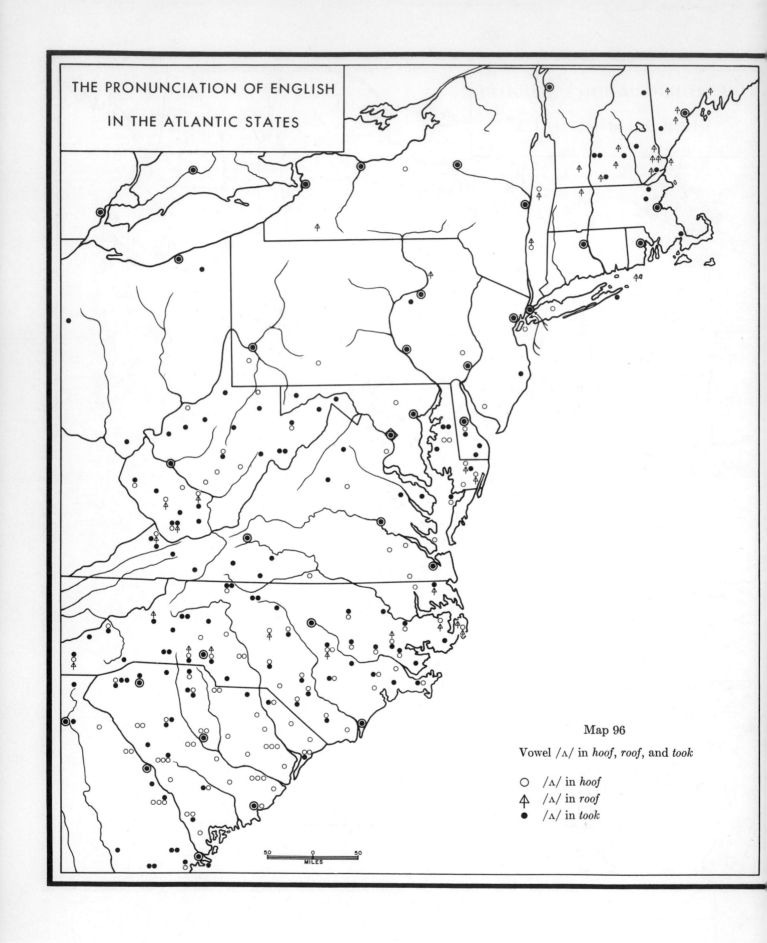

THE PRONUNCIATION OF ENGLISH
IN THE ATLANTIC STATES

Map 96

Vowel /ʌ/ in *hoof*, *roof*, and *took*

○ /ʌ/ in *hoof*
⚔ /ʌ/ in *roof*
● /ʌ/ in *took*

50   0   50
MILES

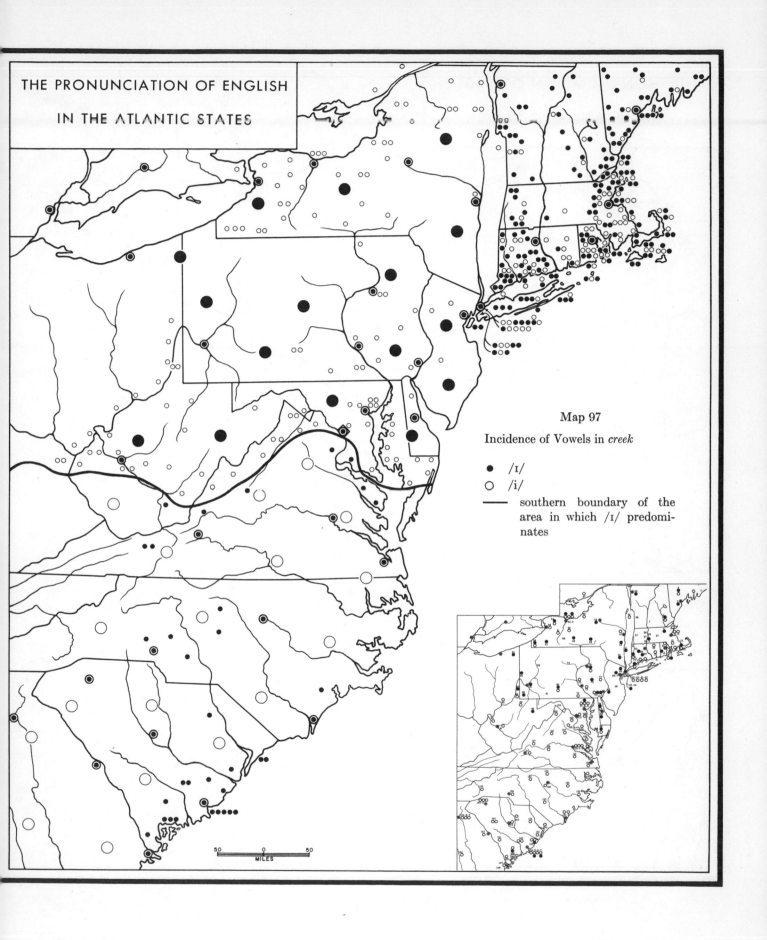

THE PRONUNCIATION OF ENGLISH

IN THE ATLANTIC STATES

Map 97

Incidence of Vowels in *creek*

● /ɪ/

○ /i/

—— southern boundary of the
area in which /ɪ/ predominates

50   0   50
MILES

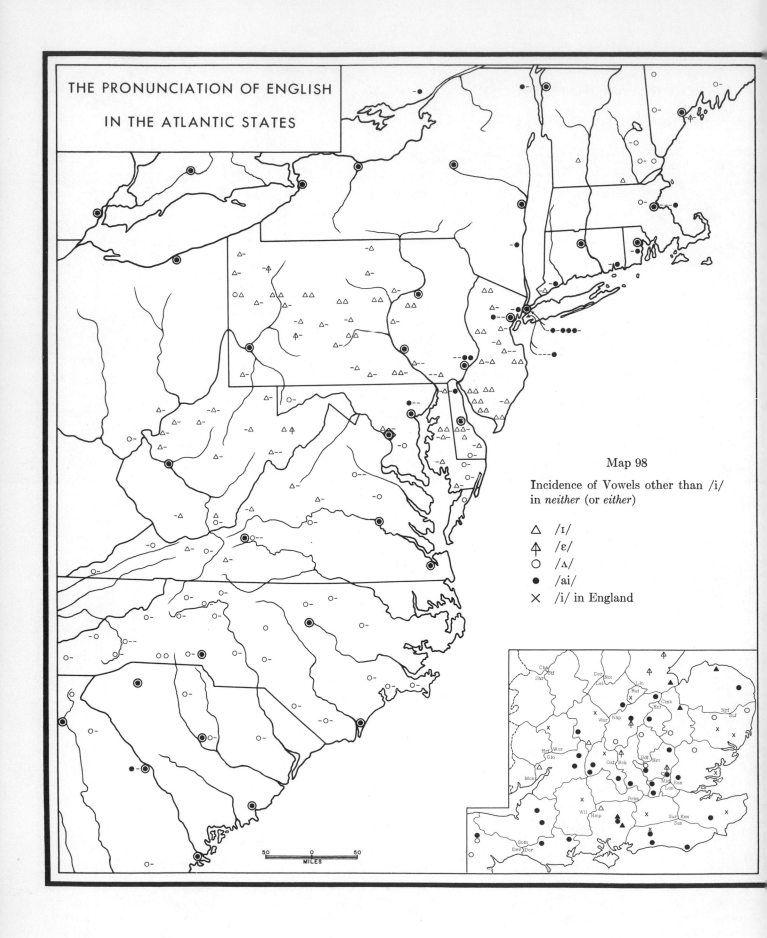

THE PRONUNCIATION OF ENGLISH

IN THE ATLANTIC STATES

Map 98

Incidence of Vowels other than /i/
in *neither* (or *either*)

△   /ɪ/

⚡   /ɛ/

○   /ʌ/

●   /ai/

✕   /i/ in England

50   0   50

MILES

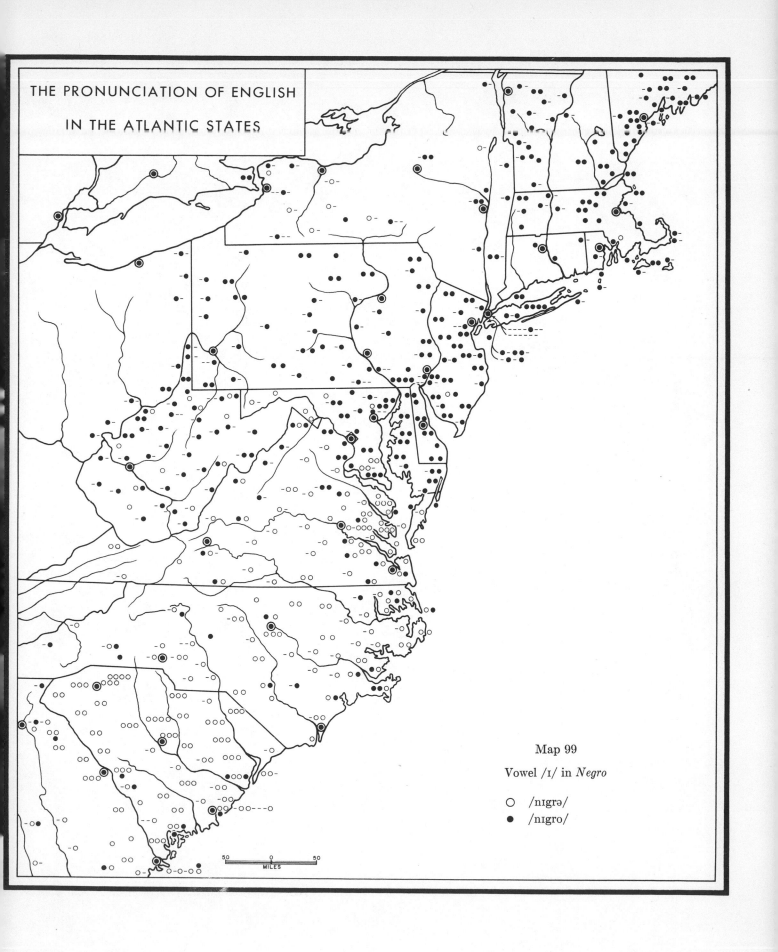

THE PRONUNCIATION OF ENGLISH
IN THE ATLANTIC STATES

Map 99

Vowel /ɪ/ in *Negro*

○   /nɪgrə/

●   /nɪgro/

50   0   50
MILES

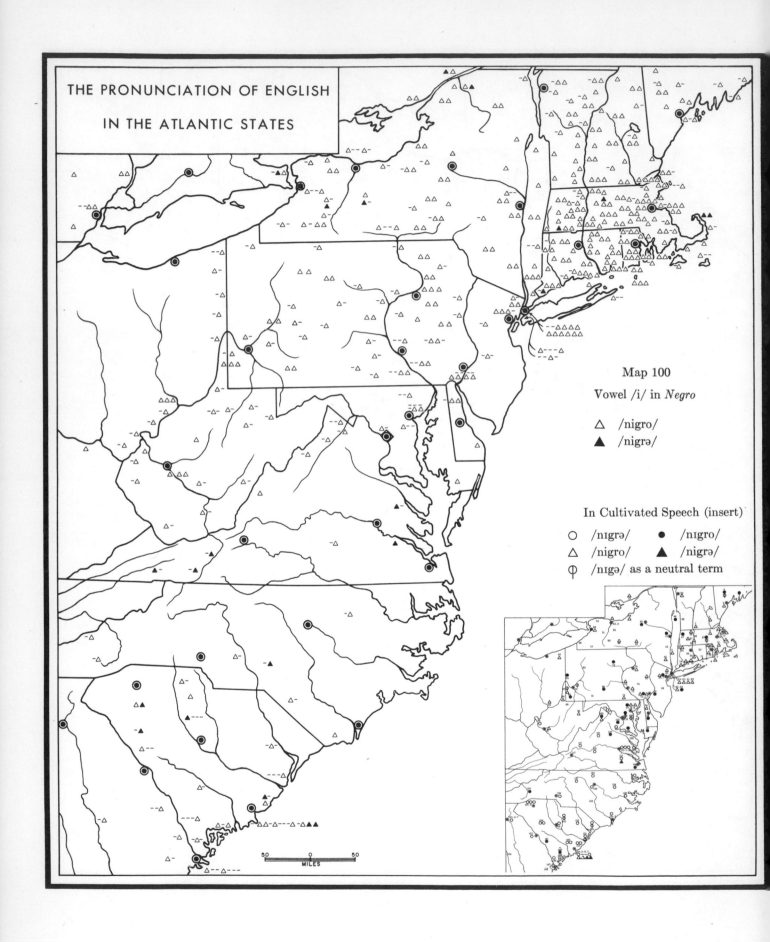

THE PRONUNCIATION OF ENGLISH
IN THE ATLANTIC STATES

Map 100

Vowel /i/ in *Negro*

△ /nigro/

▲ /nigrə/

In Cultivated Speech (insert)

○ /nɪgrə/   ● /nɪgro/

△ /nigro/   ▲ /nigrə/

ϙ /nɪgə/ as a neutral term

MILES

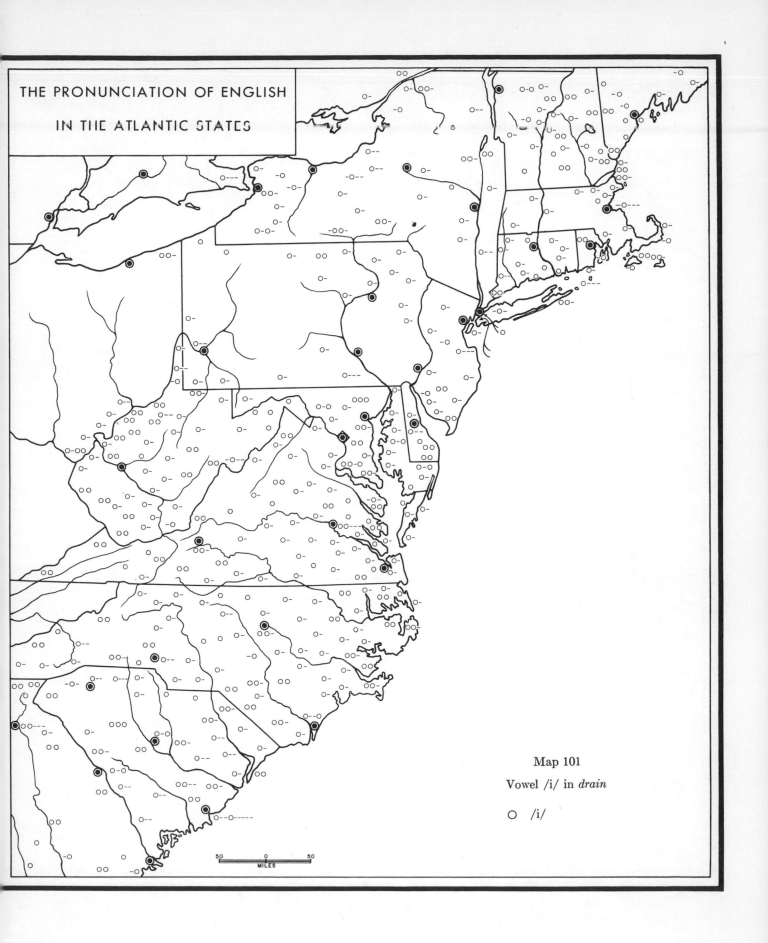

THE PRONUNCIATION OF ENGLISH

IN THE ATLANTIC STATES

Map 101

Vowel /i/ in *drain*

○ /i/

MILES

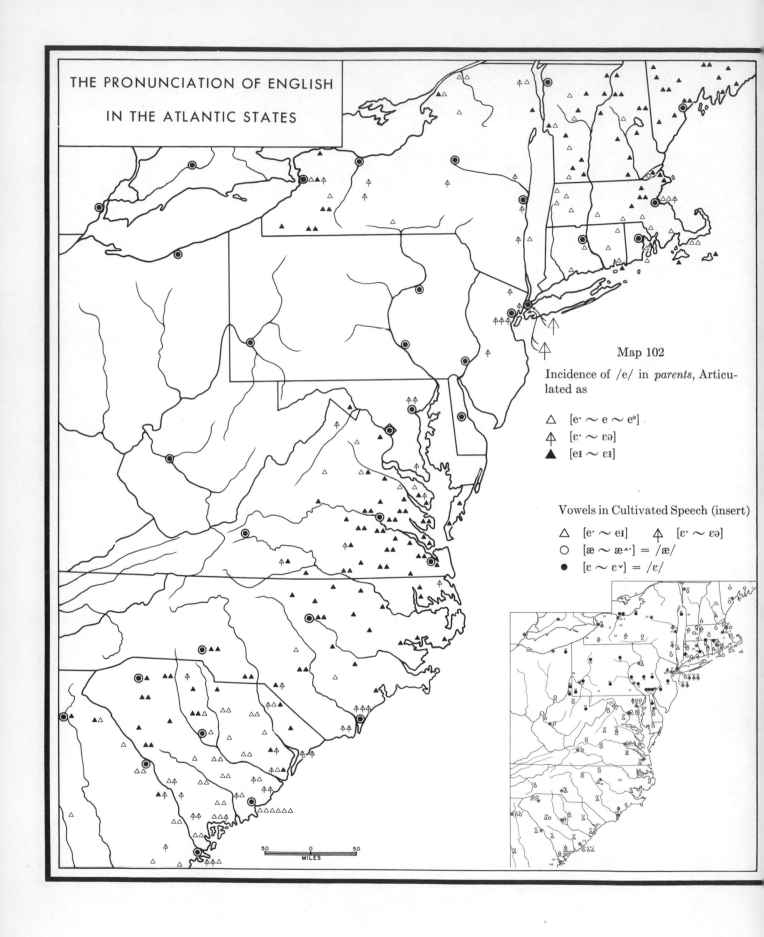

THE PRONUNCIATION OF ENGLISH
IN THE ATLANTIC STATES

Map 102

Incidence of /e/ in *parents*, Articulated as

△ [e· ∼ e ∼ eᵊ]
⋔ [ɛ· ∼ ɛə]
▲ [eɪ ∼ ɛɪ]

Vowels in Cultivated Speech (insert)

△ [e· ∼ eɪ]   ⋔ [ɛ· ∼ ɛə]
○ [æ ∼ æ·ʌ] = /æ/
● [ɛ ∼ ɛˇ] = /ɛ/

50   0   50
MILES

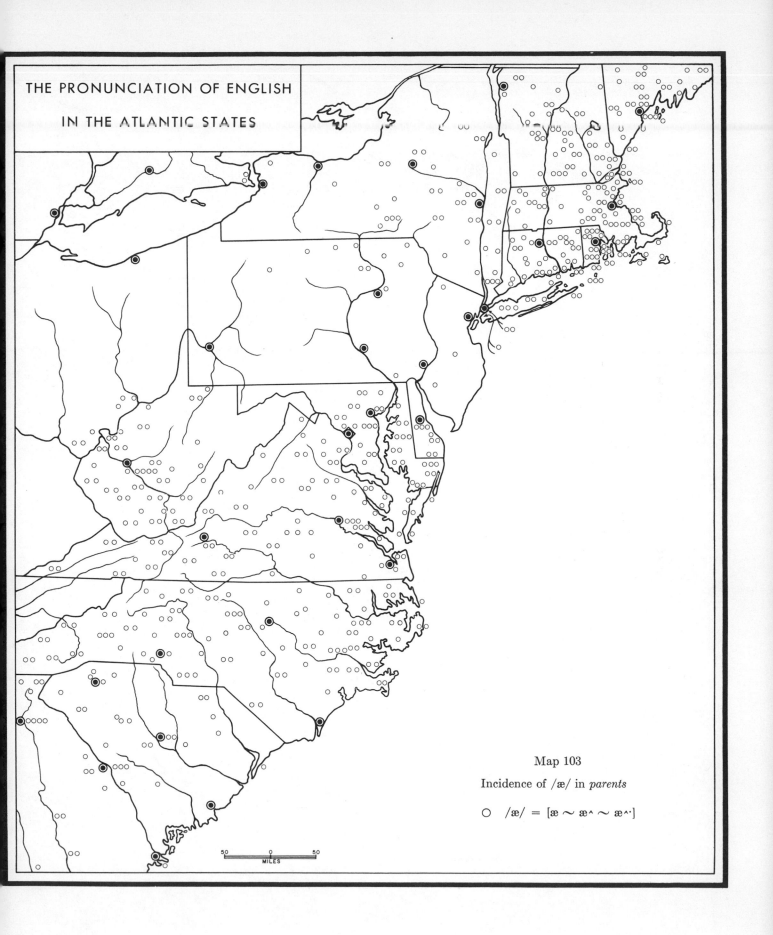

THE PRONUNCIATION OF ENGLISH

IN THE ATLANTIC STATES

Map 103

Incidence of /æ/ in *parents*

O   /æ/ = [æ ∼ æˆ ∼ æˆ·]

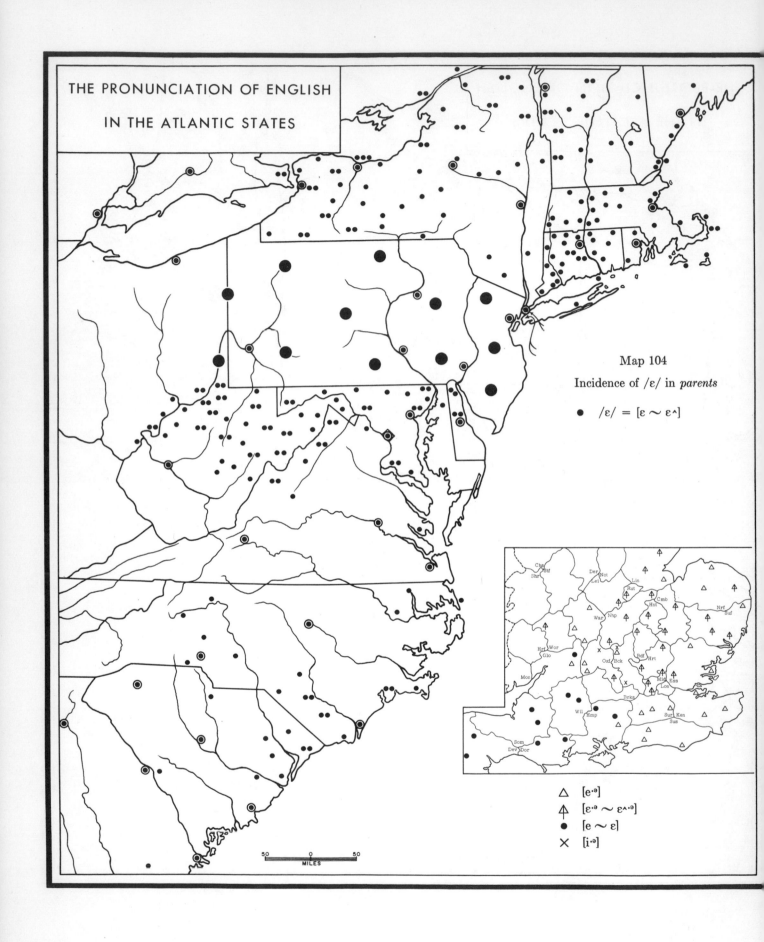

THE PRONUNCIATION OF ENGLISH

IN THE ATLANTIC STATES

Map 104

Incidence of /ɛ/ in *parents*

● /ɛ/ = [ɛ ～ ɛ^]

△ [e·ə]

↑ [ɛ·ə ～ ɛ^·ə]

● [e ～ ɛ]

✕ [i·ə]

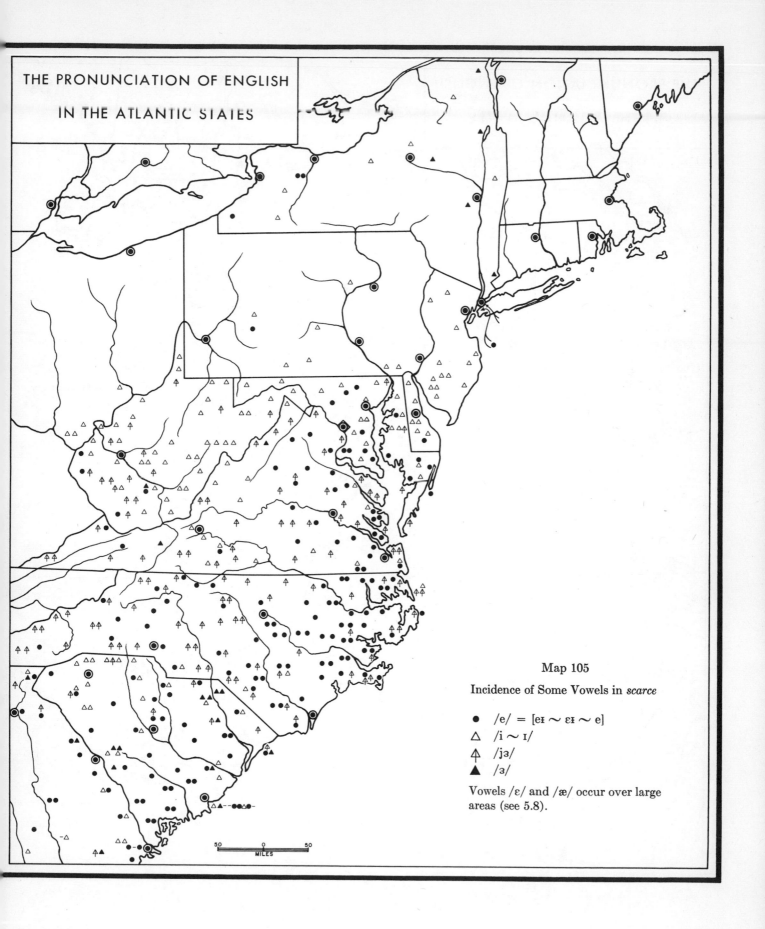

THE PRONUNCIATION OF ENGLISH

IN THE ATLANTIC STATES

Map 105

Incidence of Some Vowels in *scarce*

● /e/ = [eɪ ~ ɛɪ ~ e]

△ /i ~ ɪ/

⏃ /jɜ/

▲ /ɜ/

Vowels /ɛ/ and /æ/ occur over large areas (see 5.8).

MILES
50   0   50

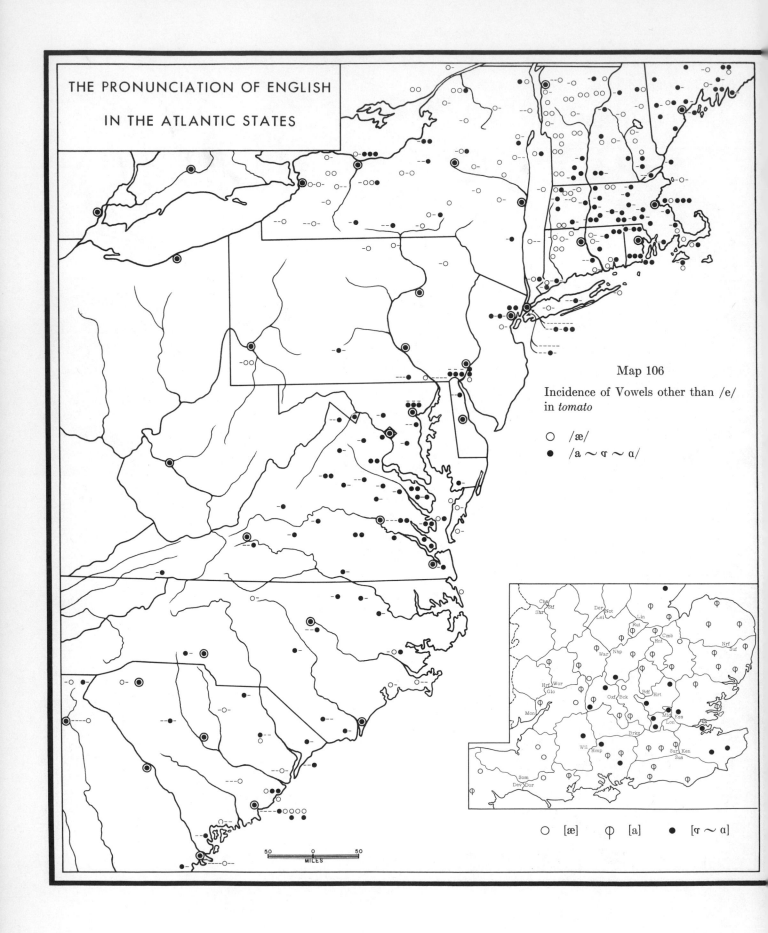

THE PRONUNCIATION OF ENGLISH

IN THE ATLANTIC STATES

Map 106

Incidence of Vowels other than /e/
in *tomato*

○ /æ/

● /a ~ ɒ ~ ɑ/

○ [æ]   φ [a]   ● [ɒ ~ ɑ]

50   0   50
MILES

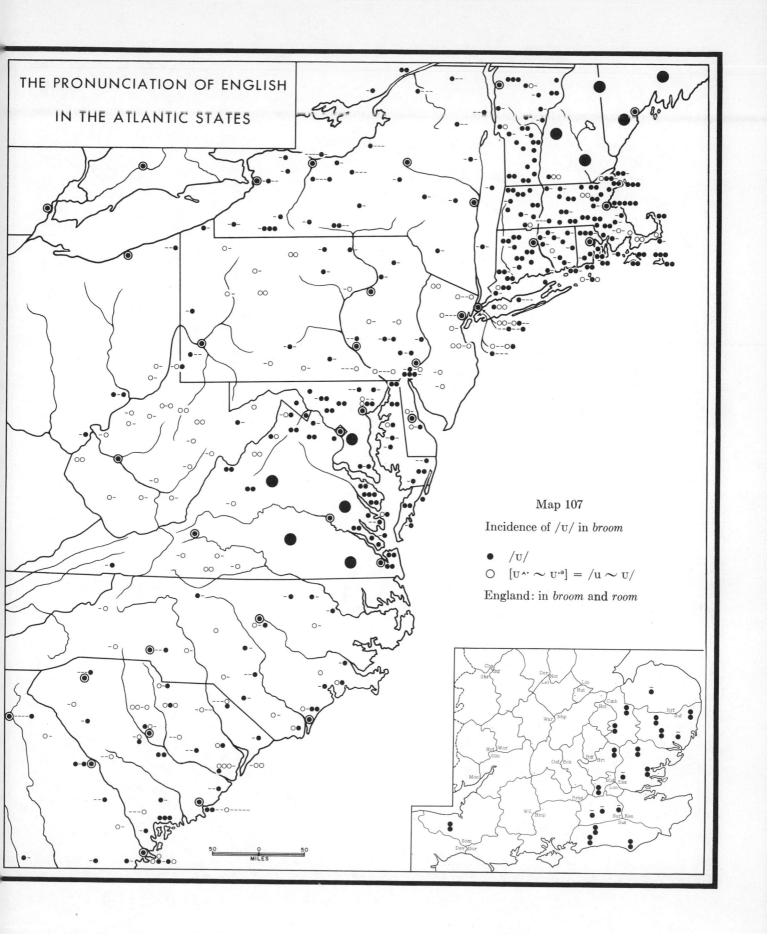

THE PRONUNCIATION OF ENGLISH
IN THE ATLANTIC STATES

Map 107

Incidence of /ʊ/ in *broom*

● /ʊ/

○ [ʊ^· ∼ ʊ·ə] = /u ∼ ʊ/

England: in *broom* and *room*

MILES

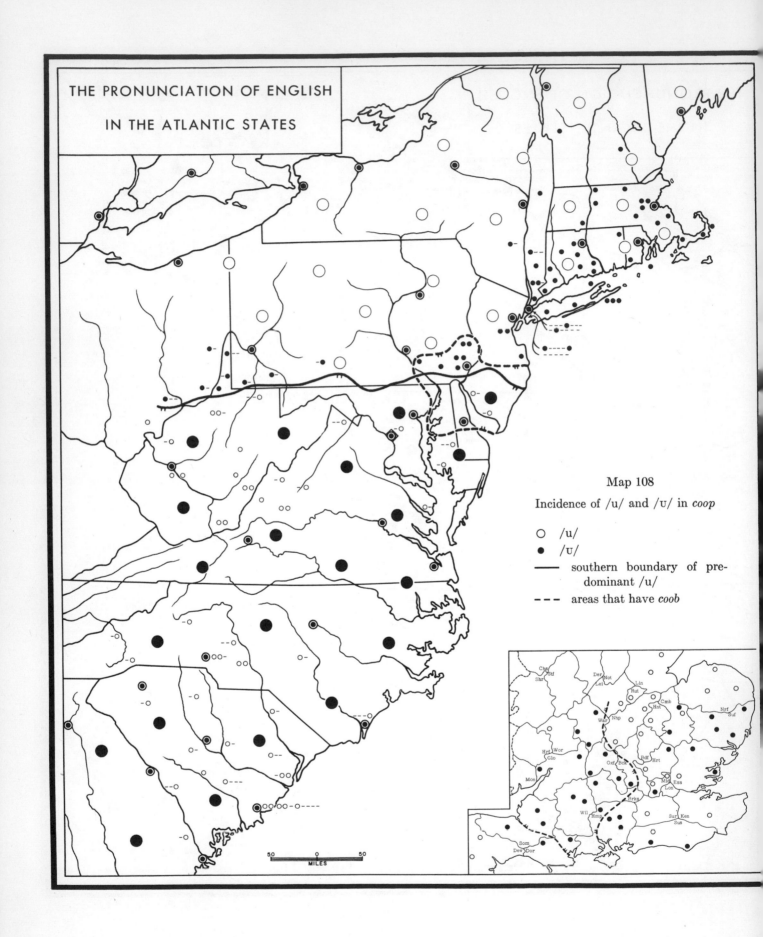

THE PRONUNCIATION OF ENGLISH
IN THE ATLANTIC STATES

Map 108

Incidence of /u/ and /ʊ/ in *coop*

○   /u/

●   /ʊ/

———   southern boundary of pre-
           dominant /u/

– – –   areas that have *coob*

50   0   50

MILES

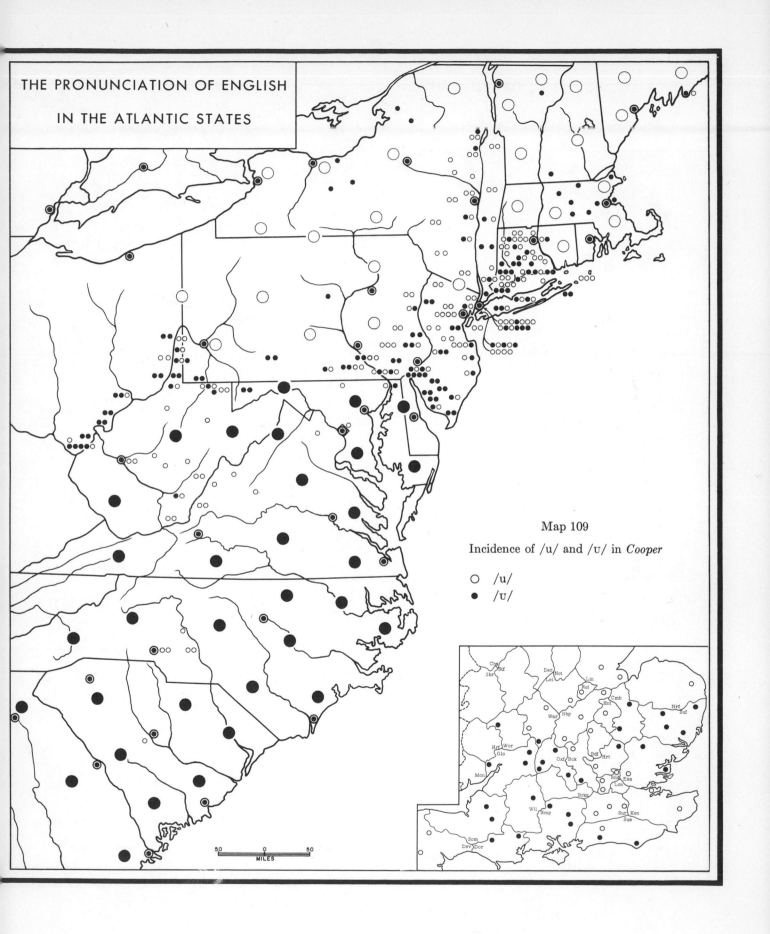

THE PRONUNCIATION OF ENGLISH

IN THE ATLANTIC STATES

Map 109

Incidence of /u/ and /ʊ/ in *Cooper*

○ /u/

● /ʊ/

MILES

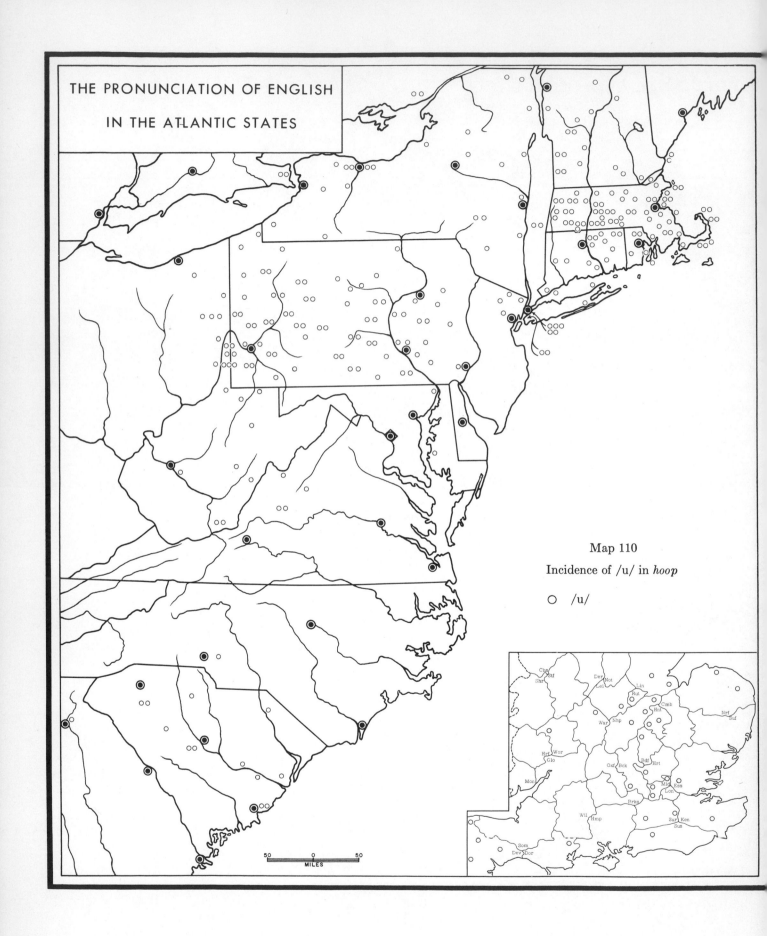

THE PRONUNCIATION OF ENGLISH

IN THE ATLANTIC STATES

Map 110

Incidence of /u/ in *hoop*

○   /u/

MILES

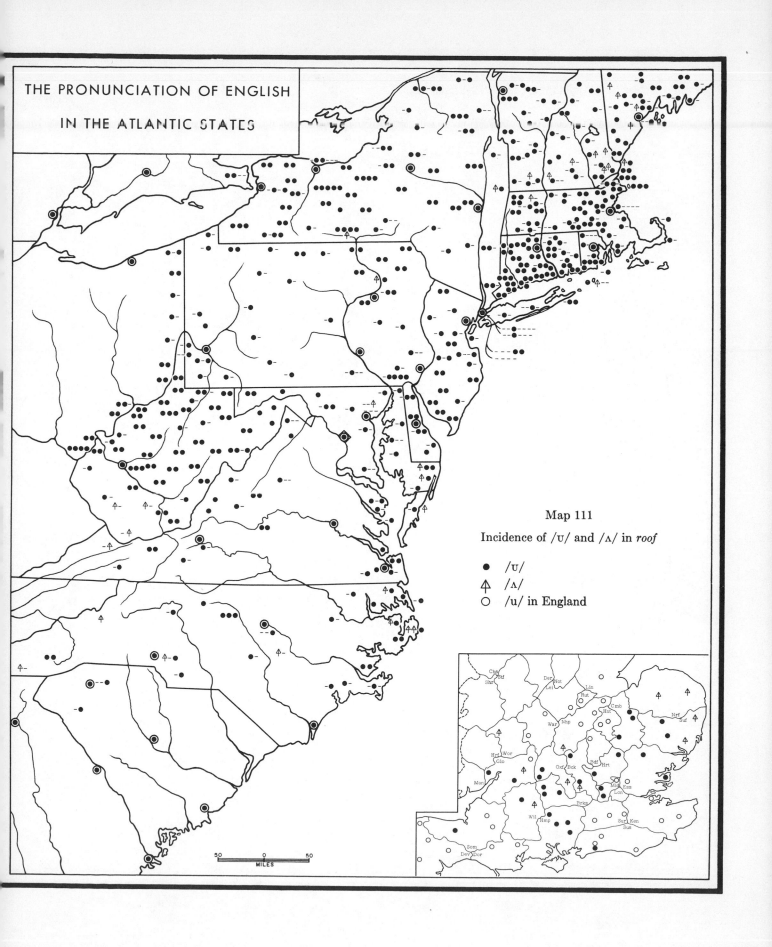

THE PRONUNCIATION OF ENGLISH
IN THE ATLANTIC STATES

Map 111

Incidence of /ʊ/ and /ʌ/ in *roof*

- ● /ʊ/
- ⋔ /ʌ/
- ○ /u/ in England

MILES
50   0   50

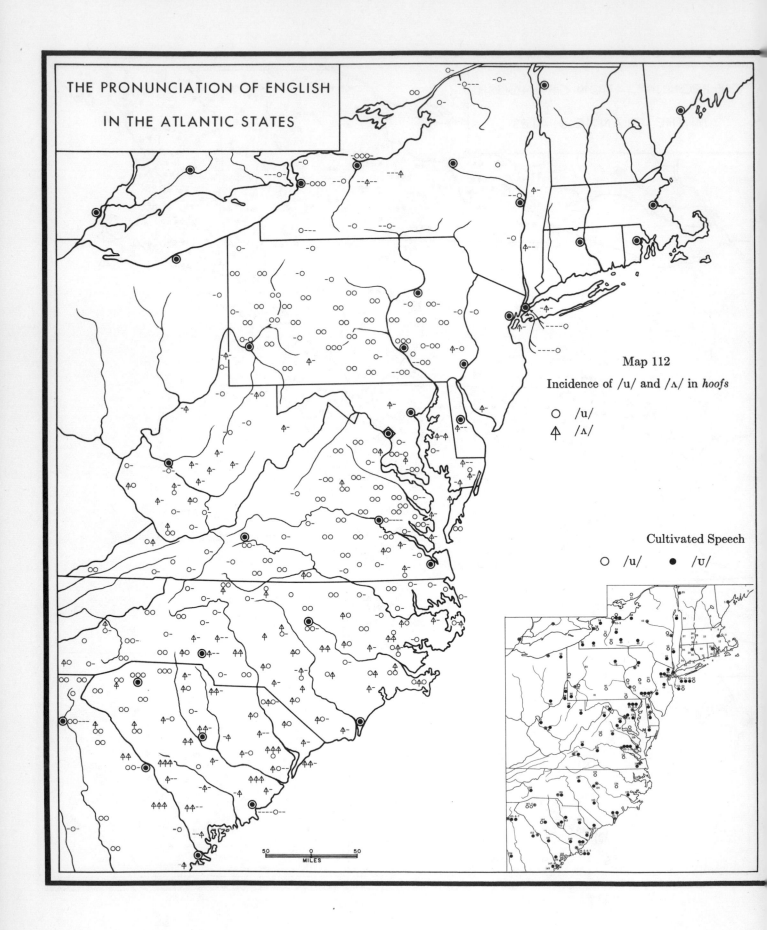

THE PRONUNCIATION OF ENGLISH
IN THE ATLANTIC STATES

Map 112

Incidence of /u/ and /ʌ/ in *hoofs*

○ /u/

⋏ /ʌ/

Cultivated Speech

○ /u/   ● /ʊ/

50   0   50
MILES

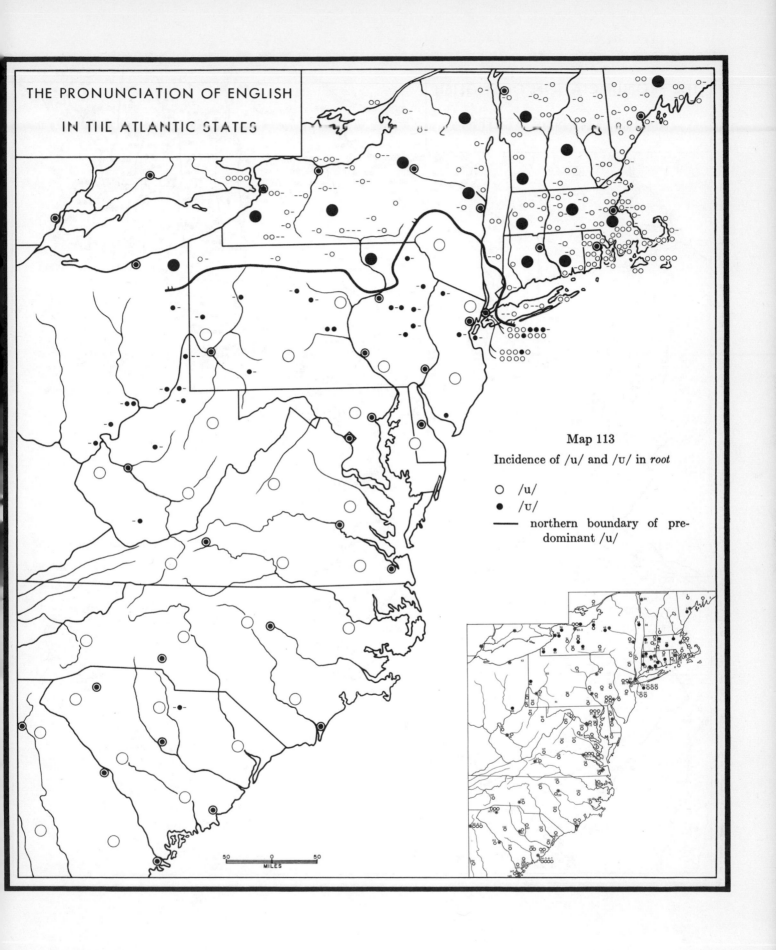

THE PRONUNCIATION OF ENGLISH

IN THE ATLANTIC STATES

Map 113

Incidence of /u/ and /ʊ/ in *root*

○ /u/

● /ʊ/

—— northern boundary of predominant /u/

MILES

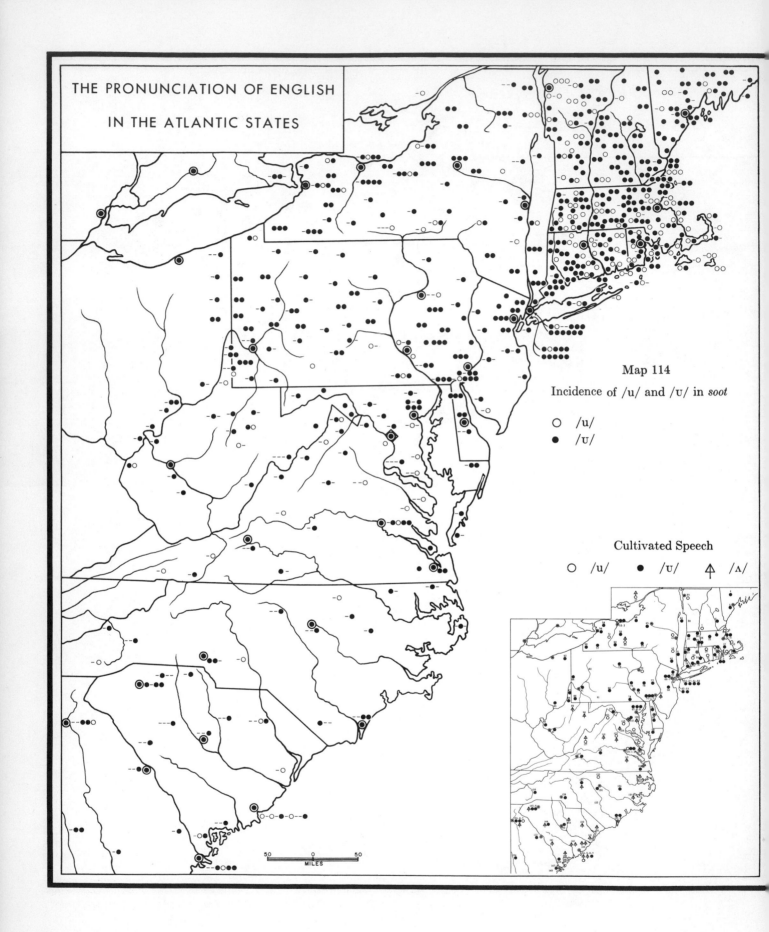

THE PRONUNCIATION OF ENGLISH

IN THE ATLANTIC STATES

Map 114

Incidence of /u/ and /ʊ/ in *soot*

○ /u/

● /ʊ/

Cultivated Speech

○ /u/   ● /ʊ/   ⚶ /ʌ/

50   0   50
MILES

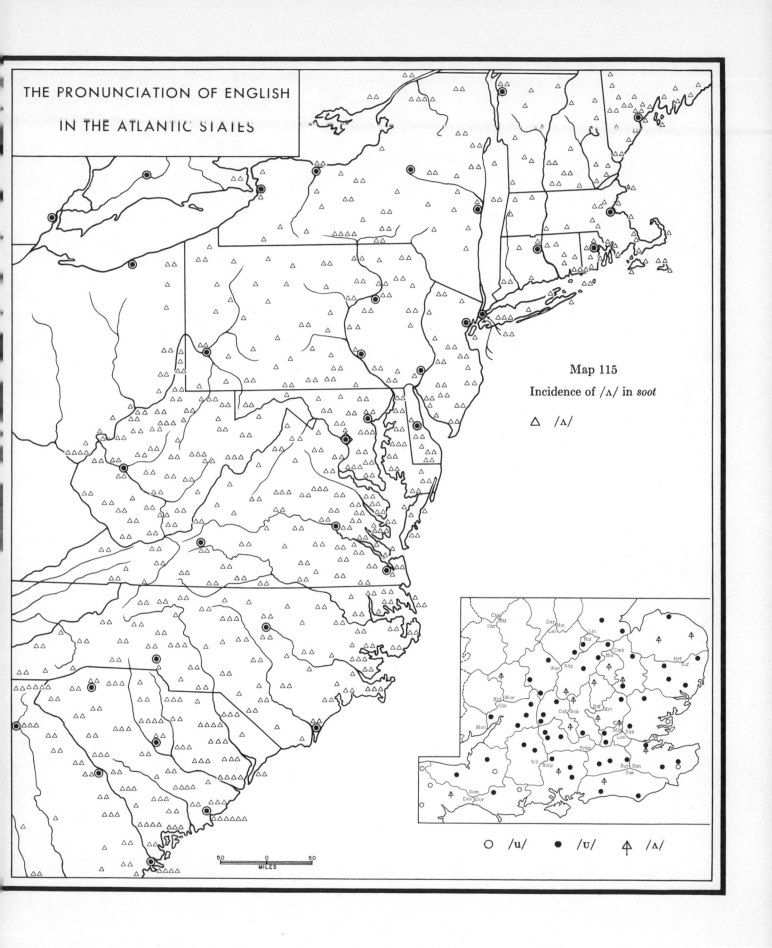

THE PRONUNCIATION OF ENGLISH
IN THE ATLANTIC STATES

Map 115

Incidence of /ʌ/ in *soot*

△ /ʌ/

○ /u/   ● /ʊ/   ⚡ /ʌ/

MILES

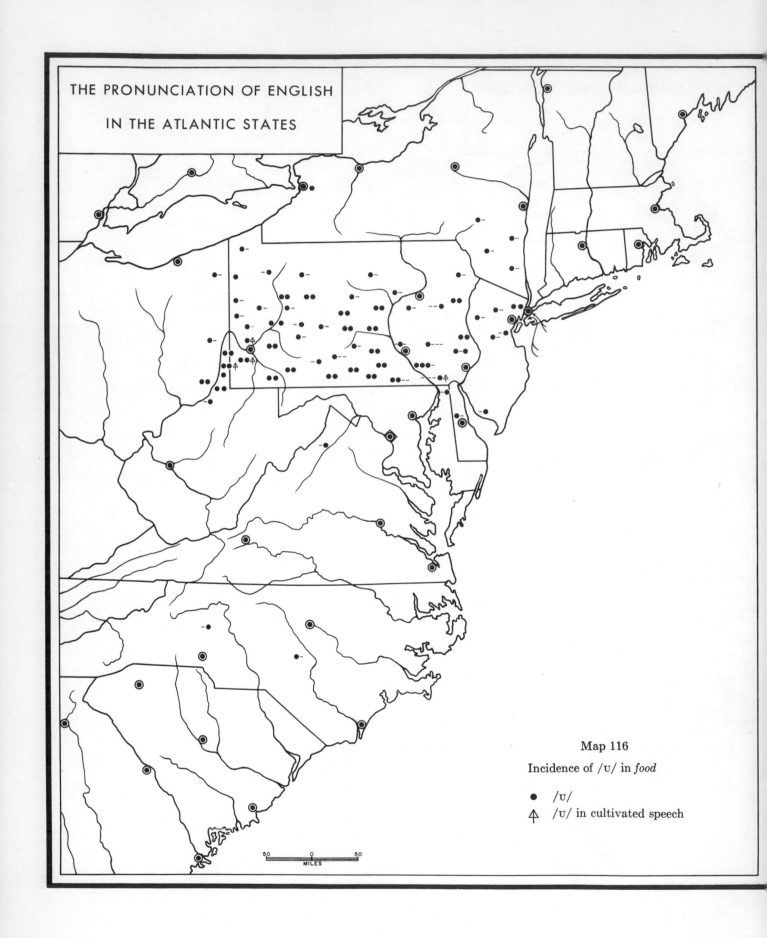

THE PRONUNCIATION OF ENGLISH

IN THE ATLANTIC STATES

Map 116

Incidence of /ʊ/ in *food*

● /ʊ/

⚔ /ʊ/ in cultivated speech

50   0   50

MILES

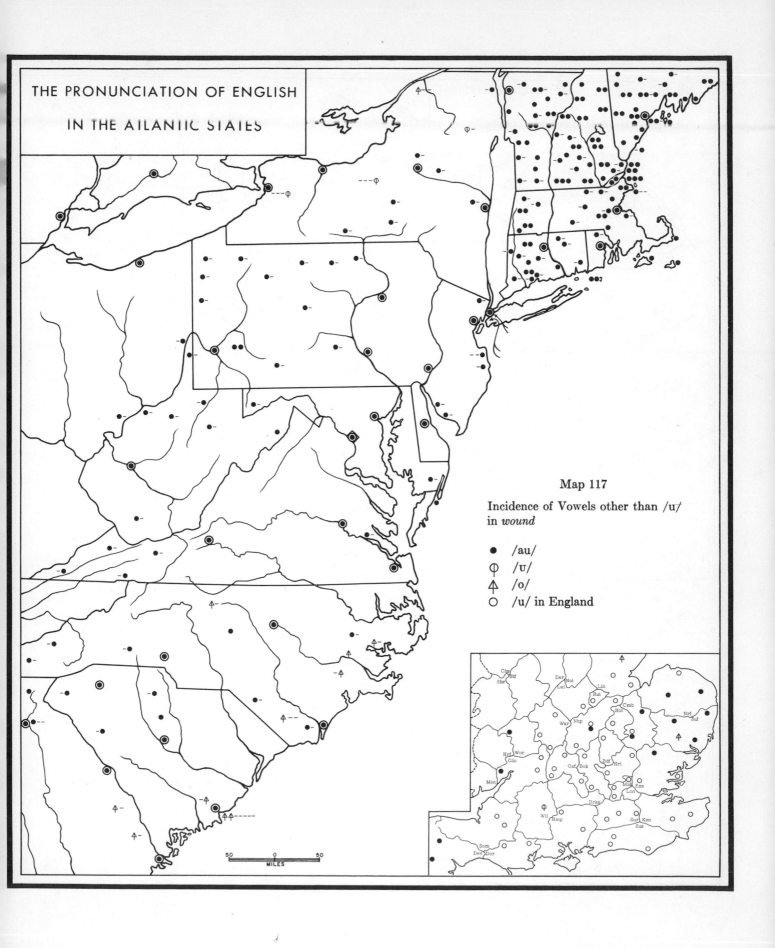

THE PRONUNCIATION OF ENGLISH
IN THE ATLANTIC STATES

Map 117

Incidence of Vowels other than /u/
in *wound*

- ● /au/
- φ /ʊ/
- ⌁ /o/
- ○ /u/ in England

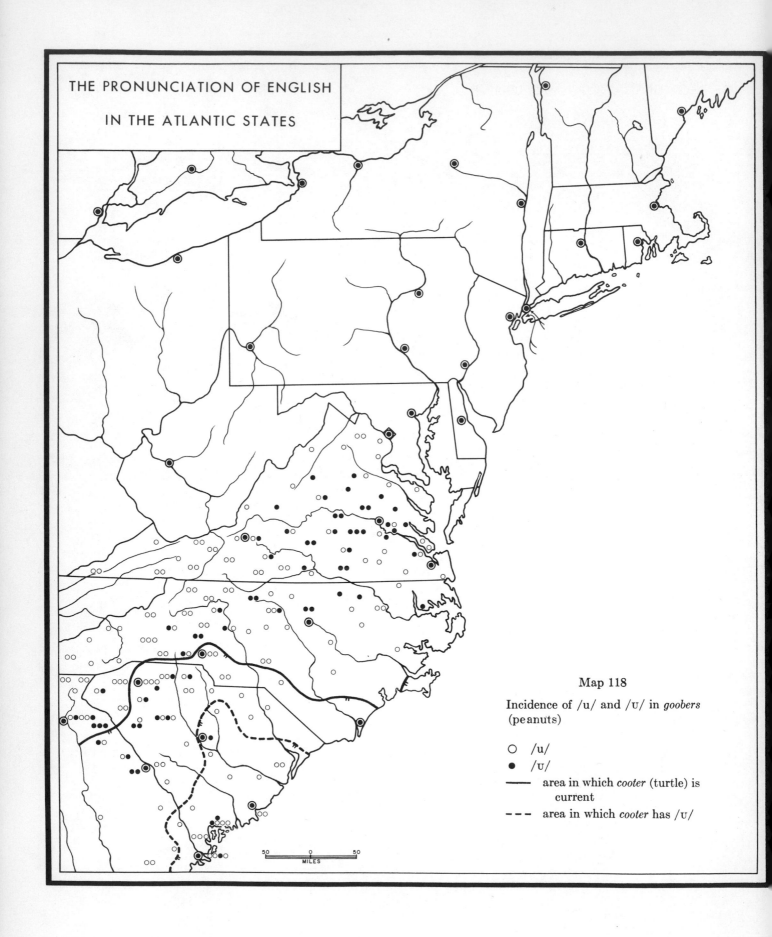

THE PRONUNCIATION OF ENGLISH
IN THE ATLANTIC STATES

Map 118

Incidence of /u/ and /ʊ/ in *goobers*
(peanuts)

○   /u/

●   /ʊ/

———   area in which *cooter* (turtle) is
        current

‐ ‐ ‐   area in which *cooter* has /ʊ/

50   0   50
MILES

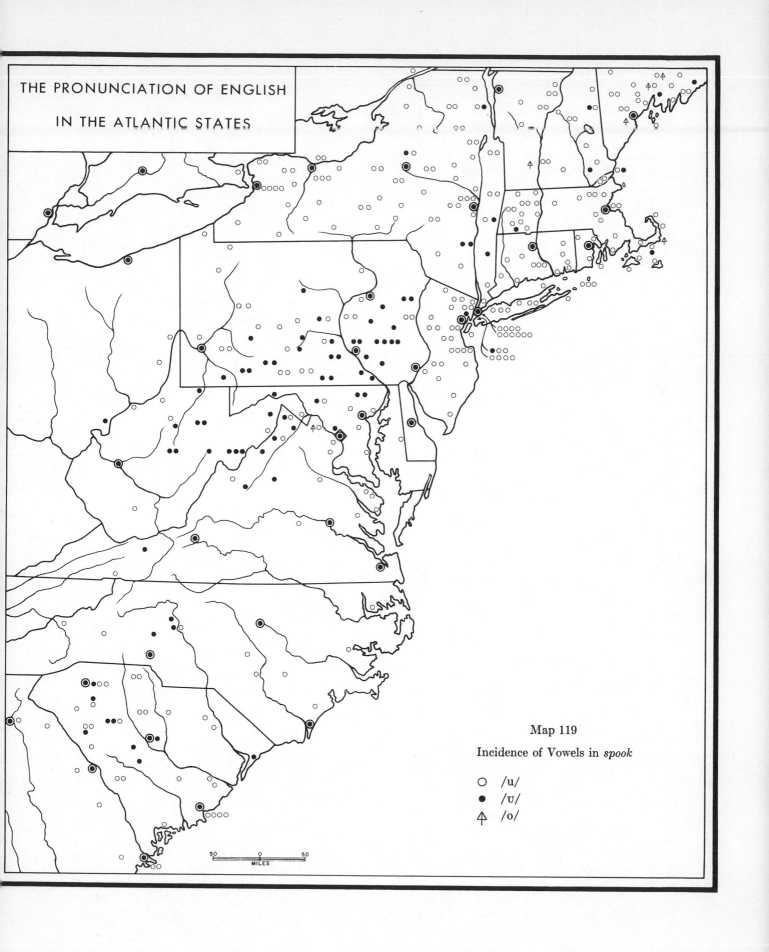

THE PRONUNCIATION OF ENGLISH

IN THE ATLANTIC STATES

Map 119

Incidence of Vowels in *spook*

O   /u/

●   /ʊ/

⚐   /o/

50   0   50
MILES

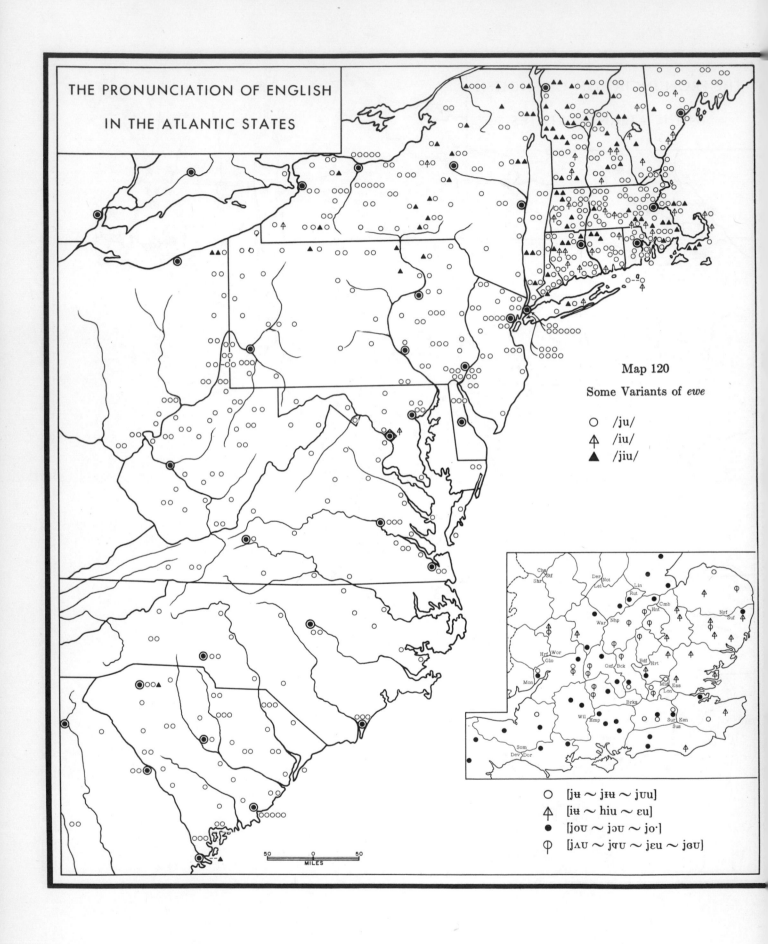

THE PRONUNCIATION OF ENGLISH

IN THE ATLANTIC STATES

Map 120

Some Variants of *ewe*

○ /ju/

⚘ /iu/

▲ /jiu/

○ [jʉ ~ jɪʉ ~ jʊu]

⚘ [iʉ ~ hiu ~ ɛu]

● [joʊ ~ jɔʊ ~ joˑ]

ϙ [jʌʊ ~ jɑʊ ~ jɛu ~ jɐʊ]

50   0   50
MILES

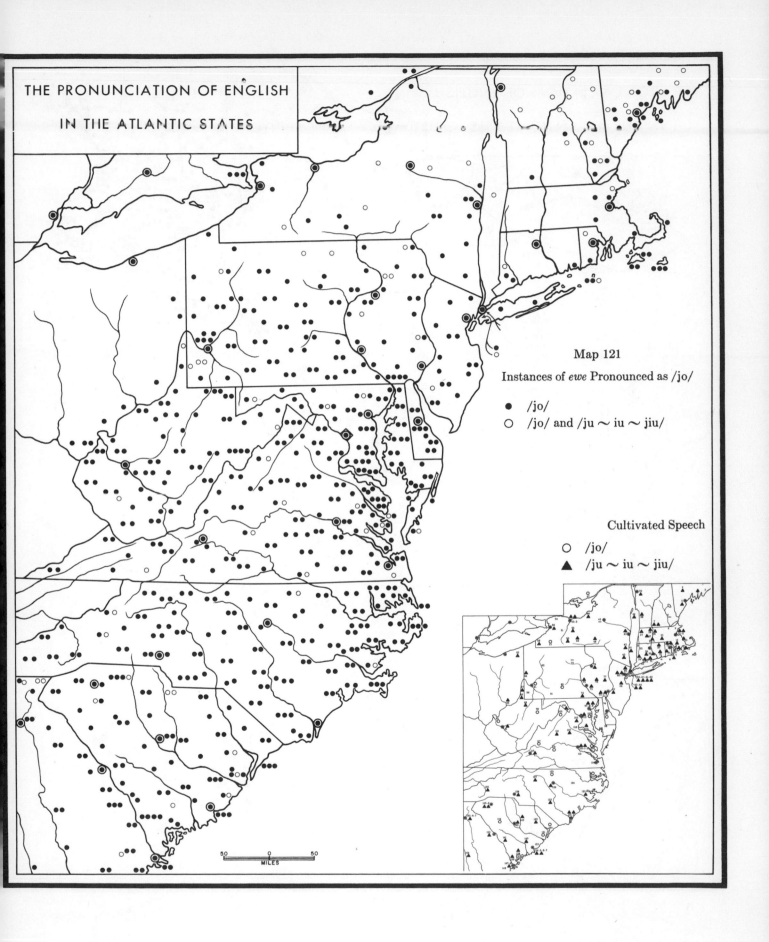

THE PRONUNCIATION OF ENGLISH

IN THE ATLANTIC STATES

Map 121

Instances of *ewe* Pronounced as /jo/

● /jo/

○ /jo/ and /ju ~ iu ~ jiu/

Cultivated Speech

○ /jo/

▲ /ju ~ iu ~ jiu/

50　0　50
MILES

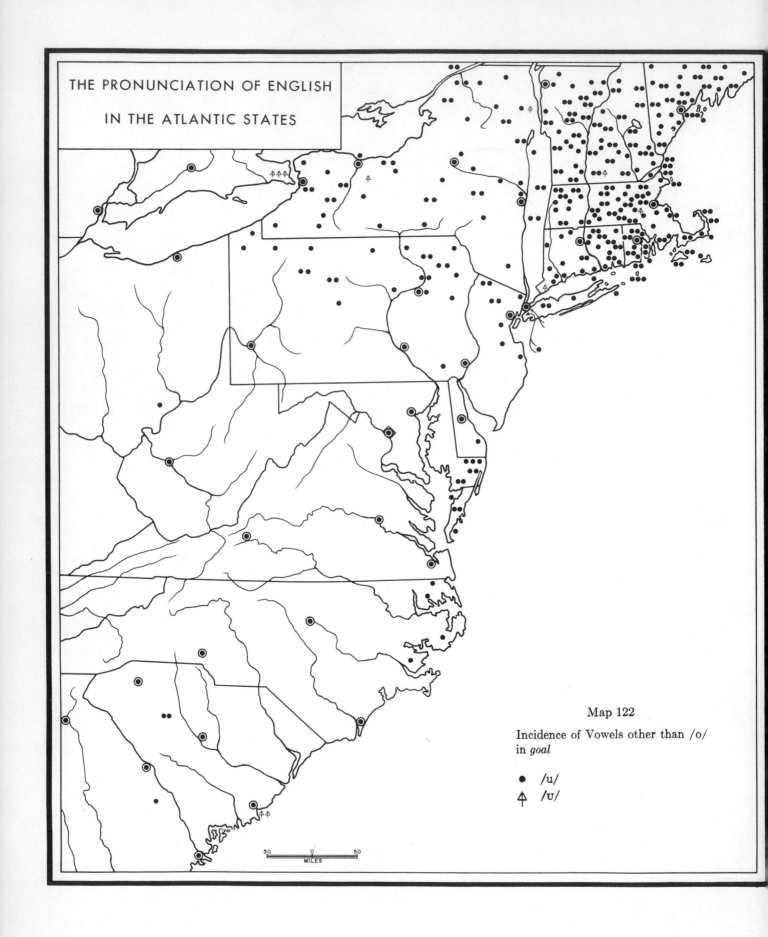

THE PRONUNCIATION OF ENGLISH

IN THE ATLANTIC STATES

Map 122

Incidence of Vowels other than /o/
in *goal*

● /u/

⚑ /ʊ/

50   0   50
MILES

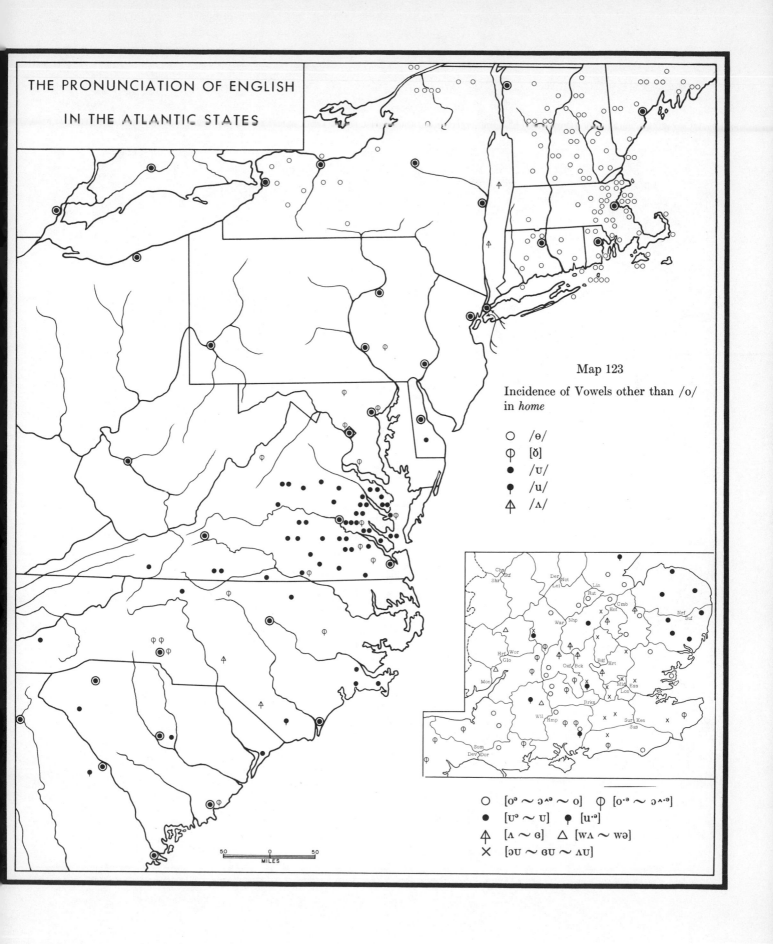

THE PRONUNCIATION OF ENGLISH

IN THE ATLANTIC STATES

Map 123

Incidence of Vowels other than /o/
in *home*

○ /ɵ/

Ⴔ [ð]

● /ʊ/

Ⴁ /u/

Ⴔ /ʌ/

○ [oᵊ ~ ɔ ᴧᵊ ~ o]   Ⴔ [oˑᵊ ~ ɔ ᴧˑᵊ]

● [ʊᵊ ~ ʊ]   Ⴁ [uˑᵊ]

Ⴔ [ʌ ~ ɐ]   △ [wʌ ~ wə]

✗ [ɔʊ ~ ɐʊ ~ ʌʊ]

50   0   50
MILES

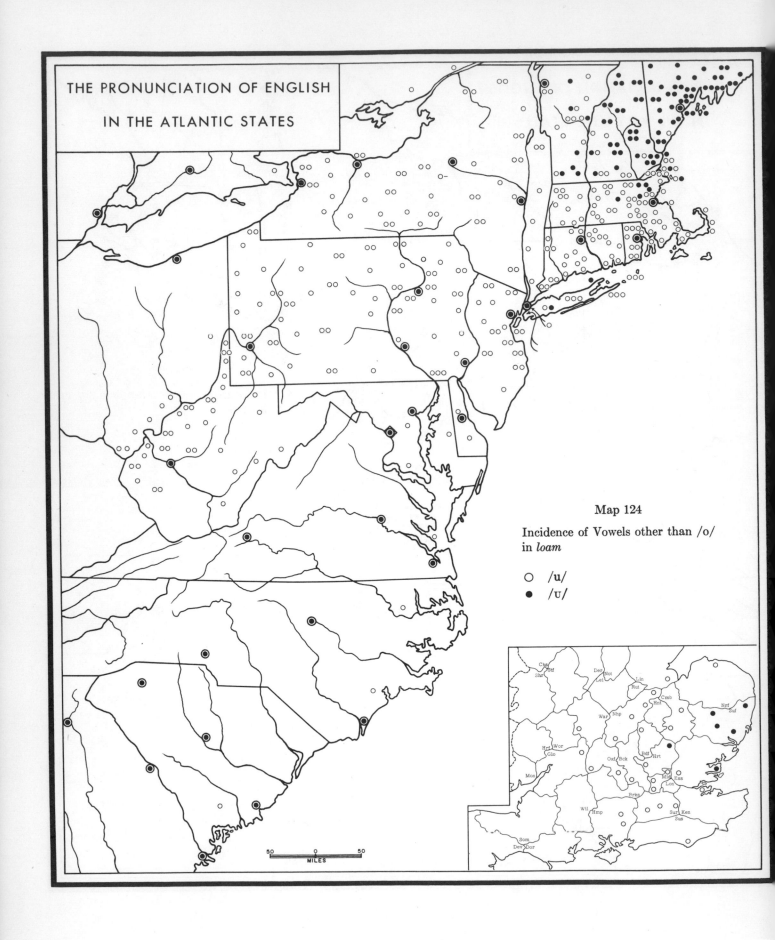

THE PRONUNCIATION OF ENGLISH

IN THE ATLANTIC STATES

Map 124

Incidence of Vowels other than /o/
in *loam*

○ /u/

● /ʊ/

MILES

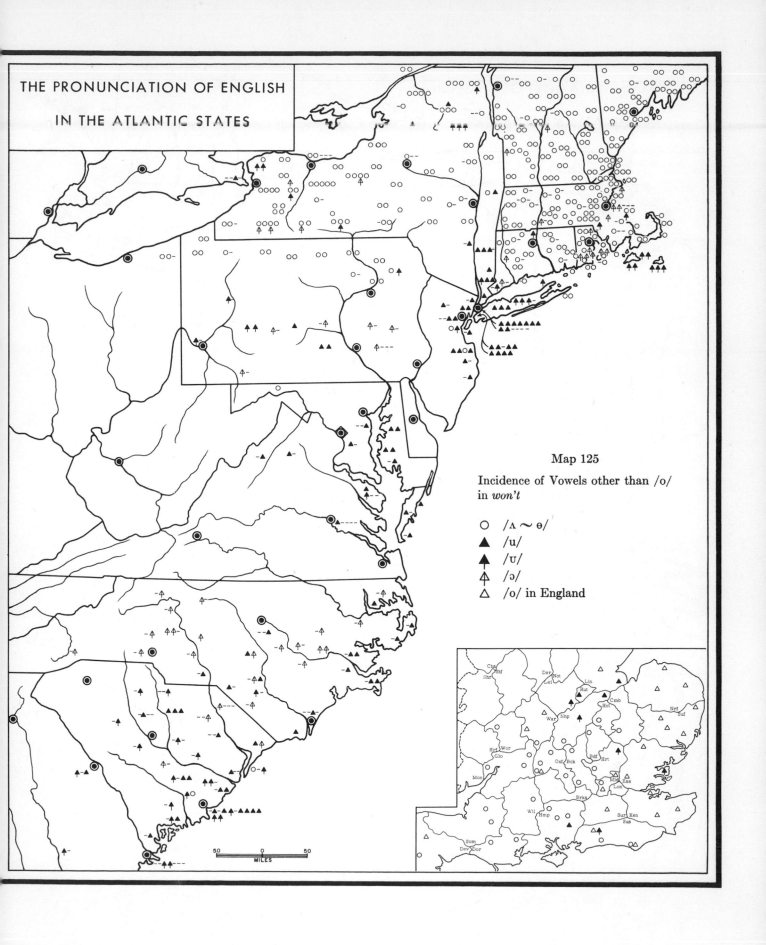

THE PRONUNCIATION OF ENGLISH

IN THE ATLANTIC STATES

Map 125

Incidence of Vowels other than /o/
in *won't*

○   /ʌ ~ ɵ/

▲   /u/

▲   /ʊ/

⚲   /ə/

△   /o/ in England

MILES

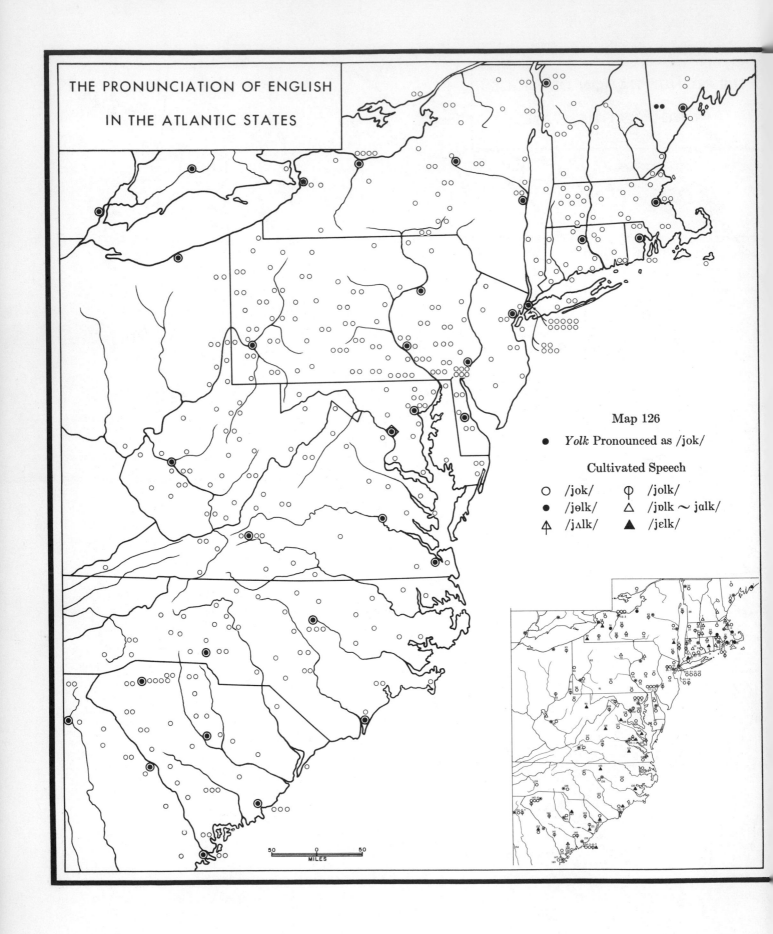

THE PRONUNCIATION OF ENGLISH
IN THE ATLANTIC STATES

Map 126

● *Yolk* Pronounced as /jok/

Cultivated Speech

○ /jok/   ♀ /jolk/

● /jəlk/   △ /jɒlk ~ jɑlk/

⟰ /jʌlk/   ▲ /jɛlk/

50   0   50
MILES

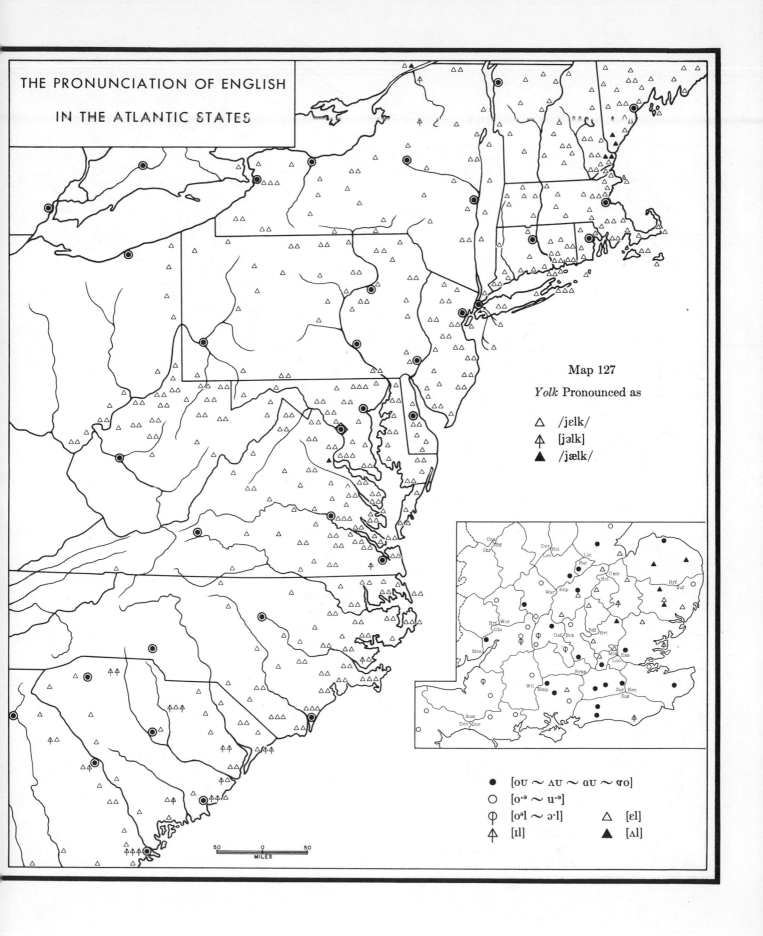

THE PRONUNCIATION OF ENGLISH
IN THE ATLANTIC STATES

Map 127

Yolk Pronounced as

△ /jɛlk/

⟁ [jəlk]

▲ /jælk/

● [oʊ ∼ ʌʊ ∼ ɑʊ ∼ ɤo]

○ [oˑə ∼ uˑə]

φ [oəl ∼ əˑl]   △ [ɛl]

⟁ [ɪl]   ▲ [ʌl]

50   0   50
MILES

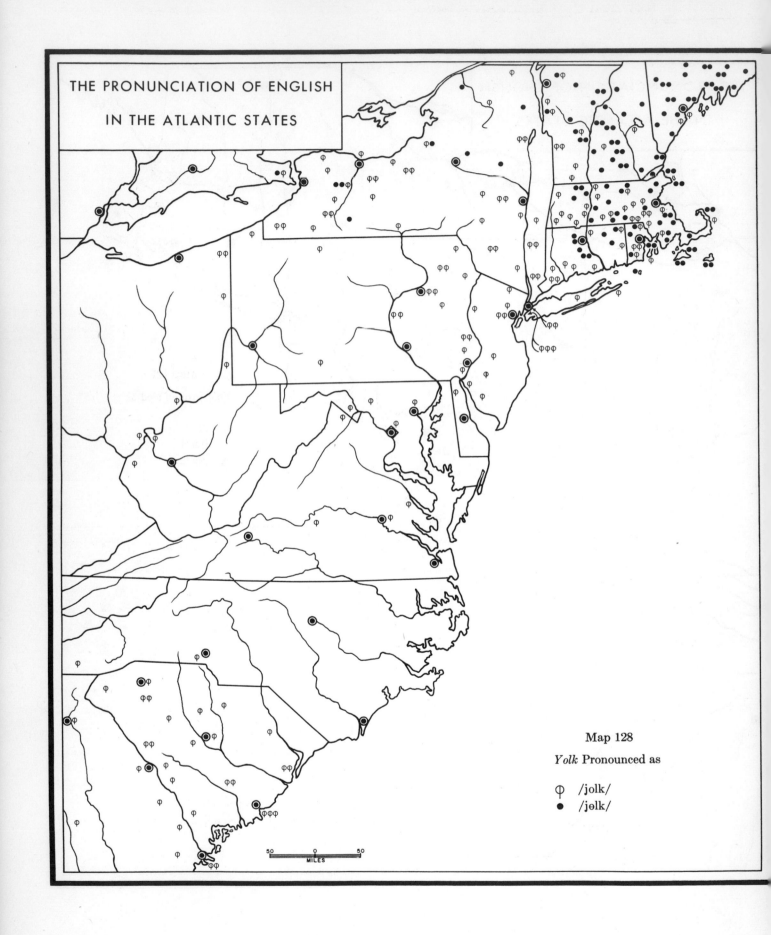

THE PRONUNCIATION OF ENGLISH

IN THE ATLANTIC STATES

Map 128

Yolk Pronounced as

φ /jolk/

● /jəlk/

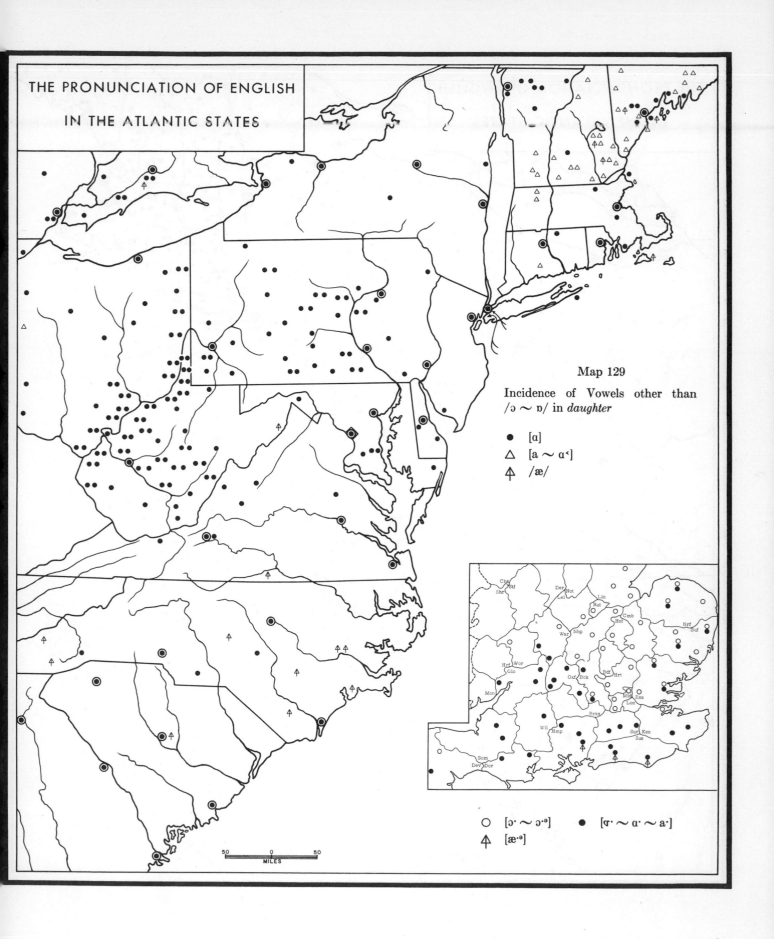

THE PRONUNCIATION OF ENGLISH
IN THE ATLANTIC STATES

Map 129

Incidence of Vowels other than
/ɔ ~ ɒ/ in *daughter*

- ● [ɑ]
- △ [a ~ ɑˎ]
- ⚹ /æ/

○ [ɔˑ ~ ɔˑə] ● [ɒˑ ~ ɑˑ ~ aˑ]
⚹ [æˑə]

50   0   50
MILES

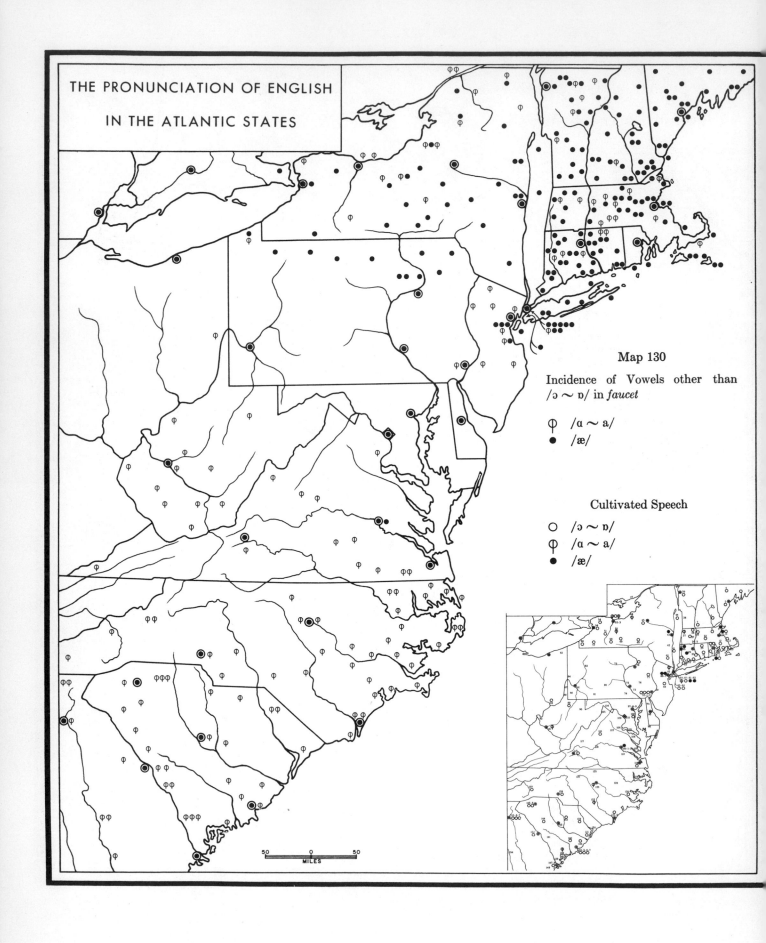

THE PRONUNCIATION OF ENGLISH
IN THE ATLANTIC STATES

Map 130

Incidence of Vowels other than
/ɔ ~ ɒ/ in *faucet*

φ   /ɑ ~ a/

●   /æ/

Cultivated Speech

○   /ɔ ~ ɒ/

φ   /ɑ ~ a/

●   /æ/

50   0   50
MILES

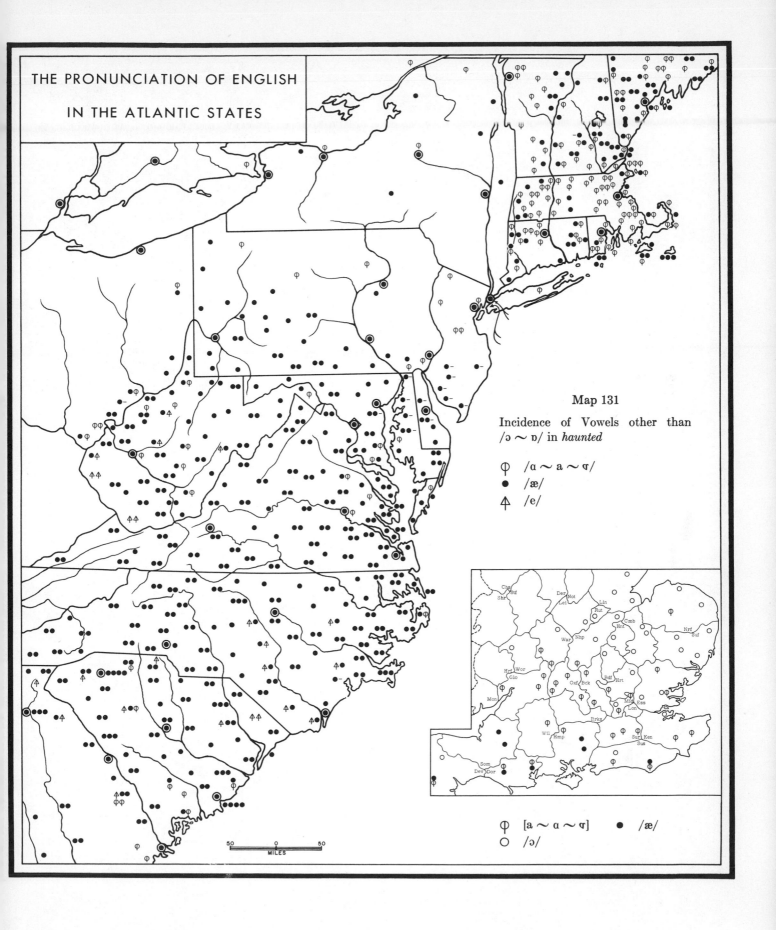

THE PRONUNCIATION OF ENGLISH
IN THE ATLANTIC STATES

Map 131

Incidence of Vowels other than
/ɔ ~ ɒ/ in *haunted*

ɸ   /ɑ ~ a ~ ɒ/
●   /æ/
⅄   /e/

ɸ   [a ~ ɑ ~ ɒ]   ●   /æ/
○   /ɔ/

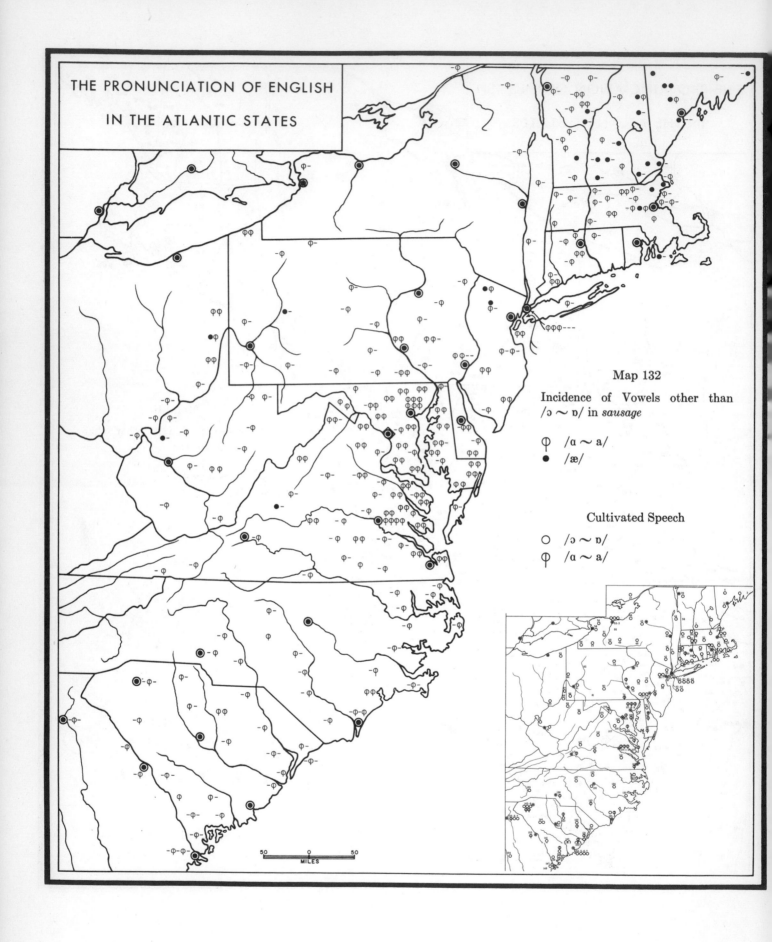

THE PRONUNCIATION OF ENGLISH

IN THE ATLANTIC STATES

Map 132

Incidence of Vowels other than
/ɔ ~ ɒ/ in *sausage*

φ /ɑ ~ a/

● /æ/

Cultivated Speech

○ /ɔ ~ ɒ/

φ /ɑ ~ a/

MILES

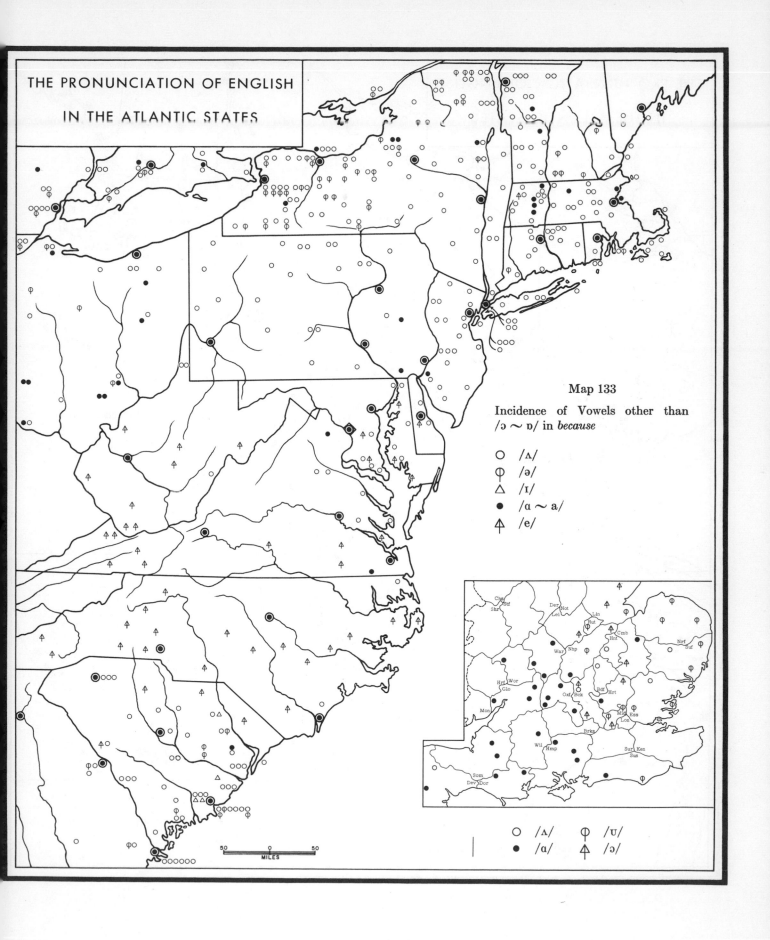

THE PRONUNCIATION OF ENGLISH
IN THE ATLANTIC STATES

Map 133

Incidence of Vowels other than
/ɔ ~ ɒ/ in *because*

○ /ʌ/
φ /ə/
△ /ɪ/
● /ɑ ~ a/
⯕ /e/

○ /ʌ/   φ /ʊ/
● /ɑ/   ⯕ /ɔ/

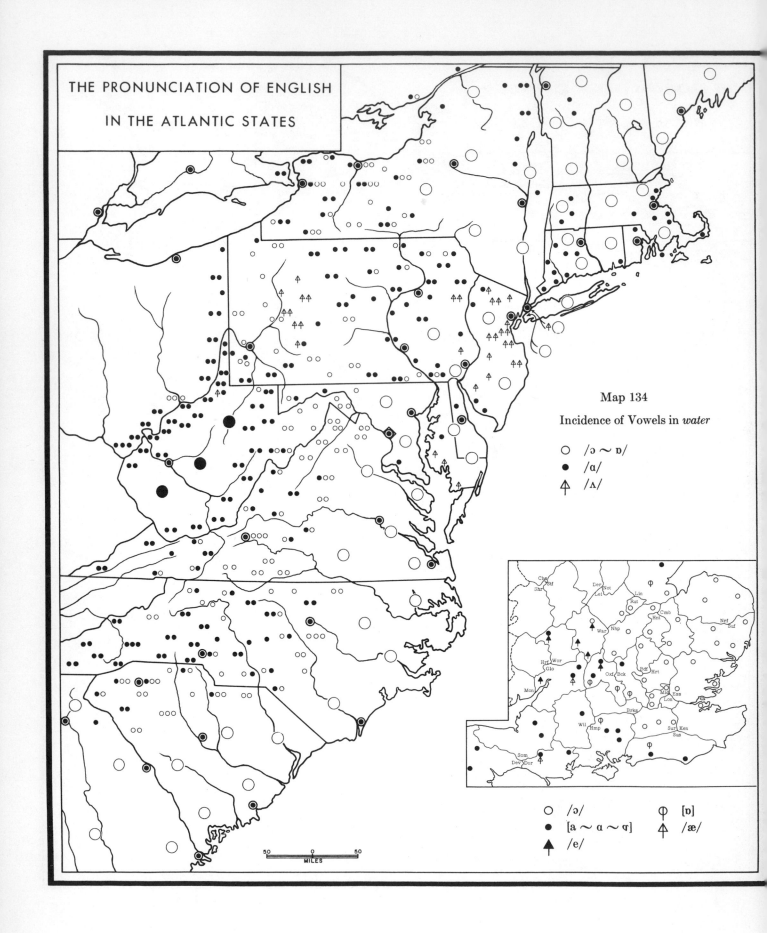

THE PRONUNCIATION OF ENGLISH
IN THE ATLANTIC STATES

Map 134

Incidence of Vowels in *water*

○ /ɔ ~ ɒ/

● /ɑ/

↑ /ʌ/

50   0   50
MILES

○ /ɔ/

● [a ~ ɑ ~ ɐ]

▲ /e/

φ [ɒ]

↑ /æ/

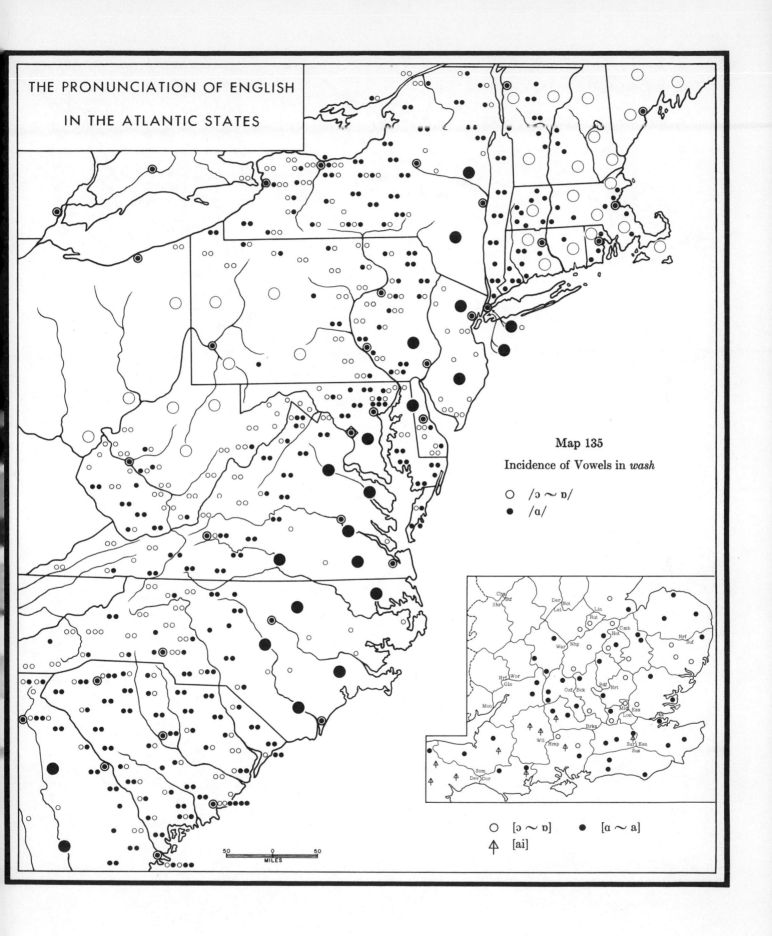

THE PRONUNCIATION OF ENGLISH
IN THE ATLANTIC STATES

Map 135

Incidence of Vowels in *wash*

○ /ɔ ~ ɒ/

● /ɑ/

○ [ɔ ~ ɒ]   ● [ɑ ~ a]

⚲ [ai]

50   0   50
MILES

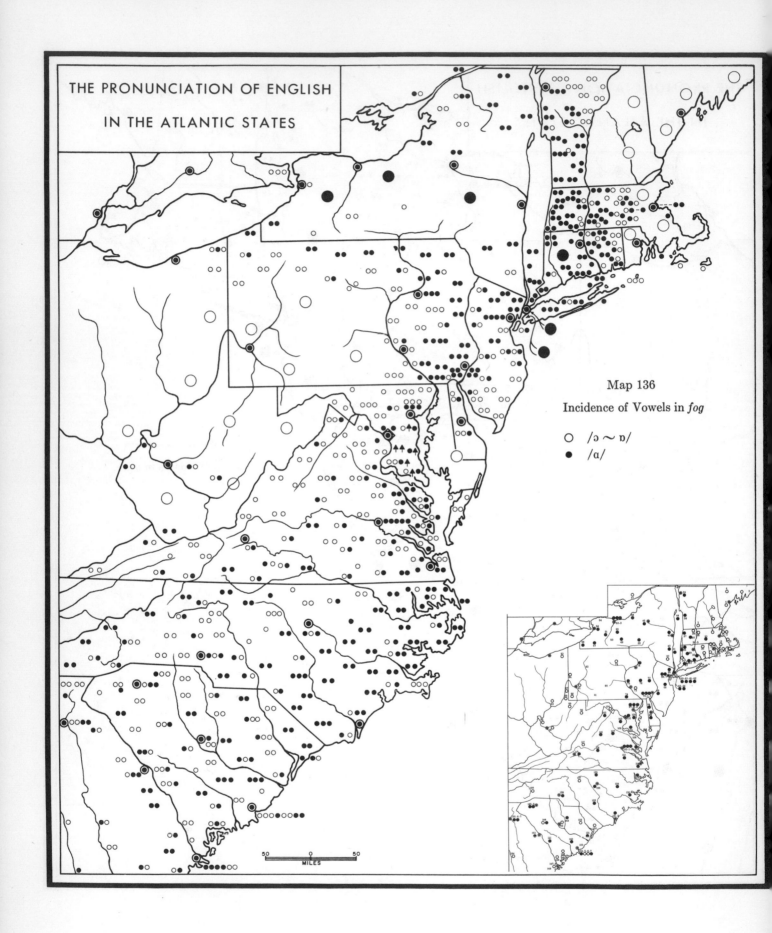

THE PRONUNCIATION OF ENGLISH

IN THE ATLANTIC STATES

Map 136

Incidence of Vowels in *fog*

○ /ɔ ~ ɒ/

● /ɑ/

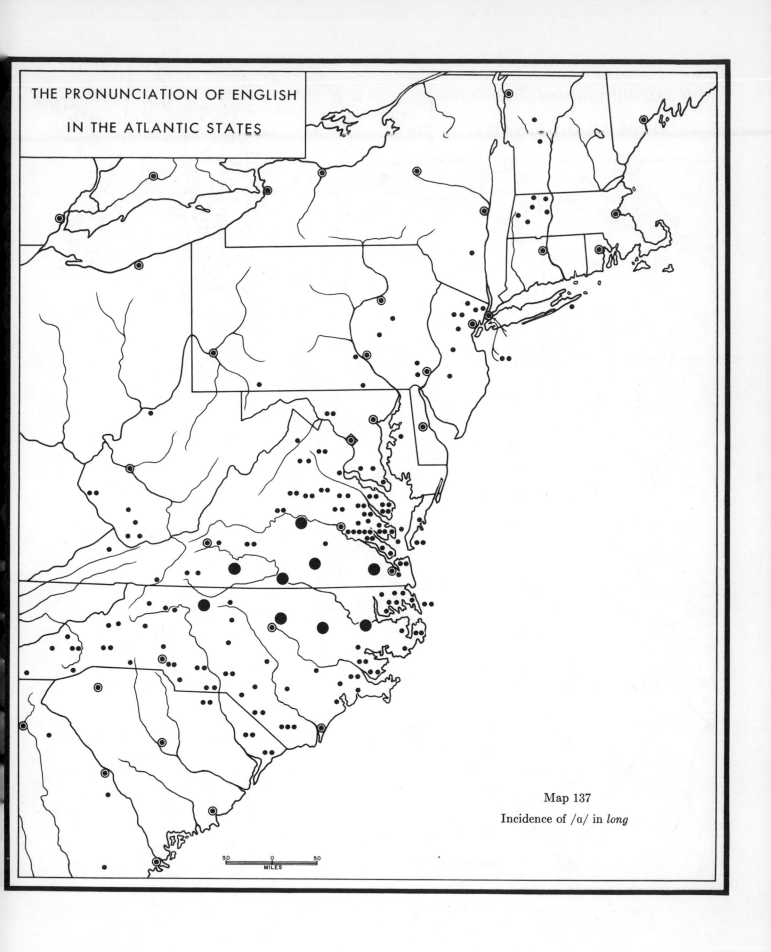

THE PRONUNCIATION OF ENGLISH

IN THE ATLANTIC STATES

Map 137

Incidence of /ɑ/ in *long*

MILES

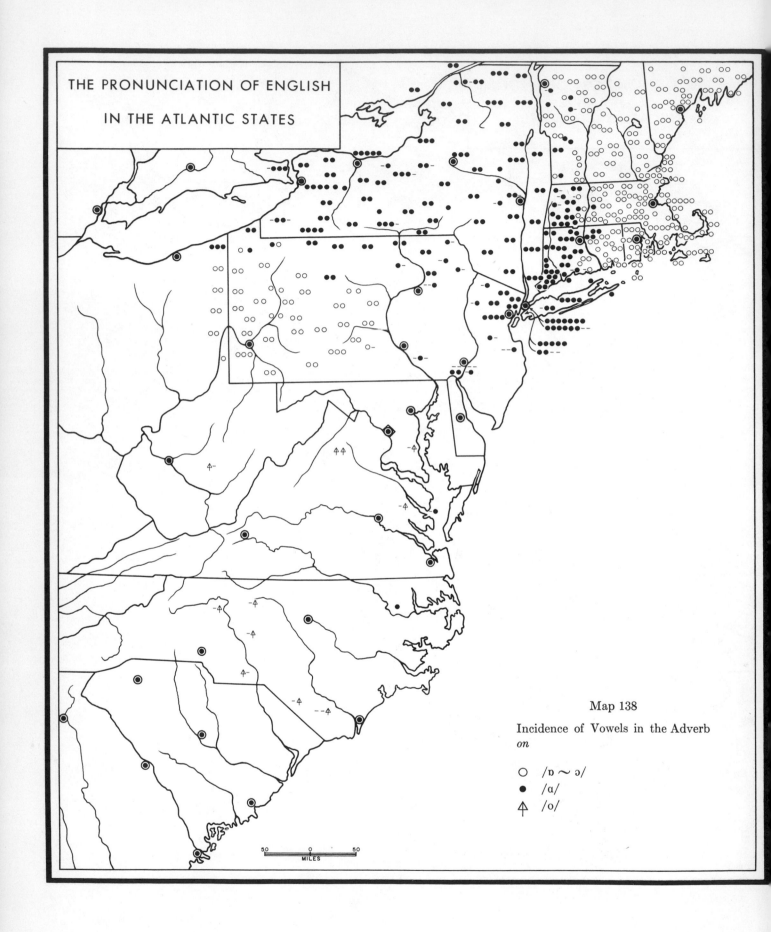

THE PRONUNCIATION OF ENGLISH

IN THE ATLANTIC STATES

Map 138

Incidence of Vowels in the Adverb
on

○ /ɒ ~ ə/

● /ɑ/

⚡ /o/

MILES
50   0   50

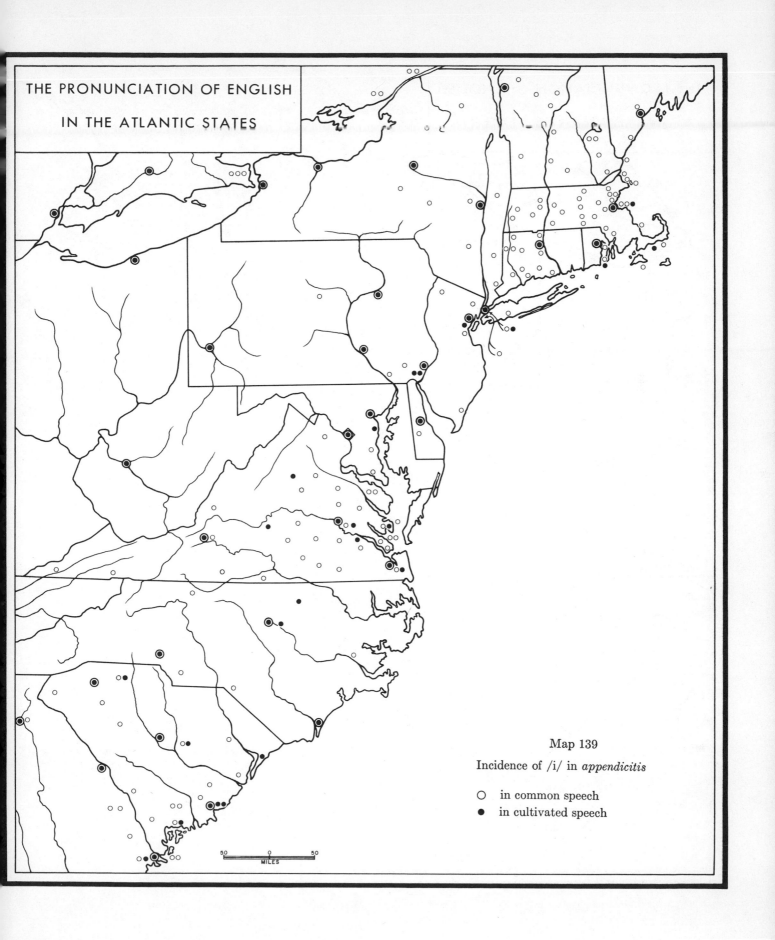

THE PRONUNCIATION OF ENGLISH

IN THE ATLANTIC STATES

Map 139

Incidence of /i/ in *appendicitis*

○   in common speech
●   in cultivated speech

50   0   50
MILES

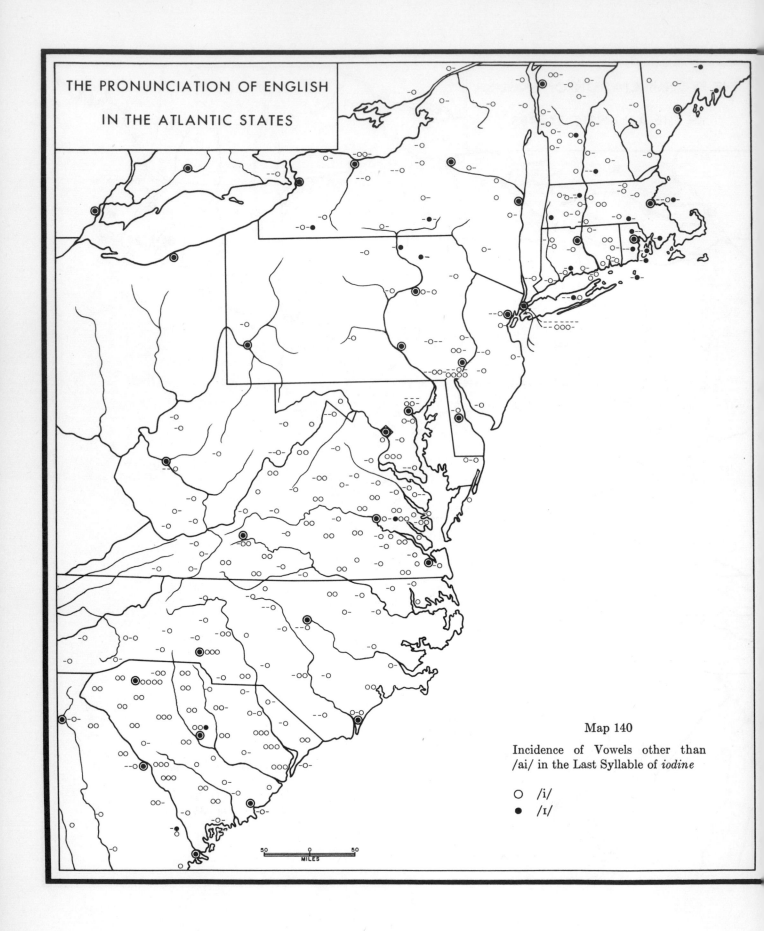

THE PRONUNCIATION OF ENGLISH

IN THE ATLANTIC STATES

Map 140

Incidence of Vowels other than
/ai/ in the Last Syllable of *iodine*

○ /i/

● /ɪ/

MILES

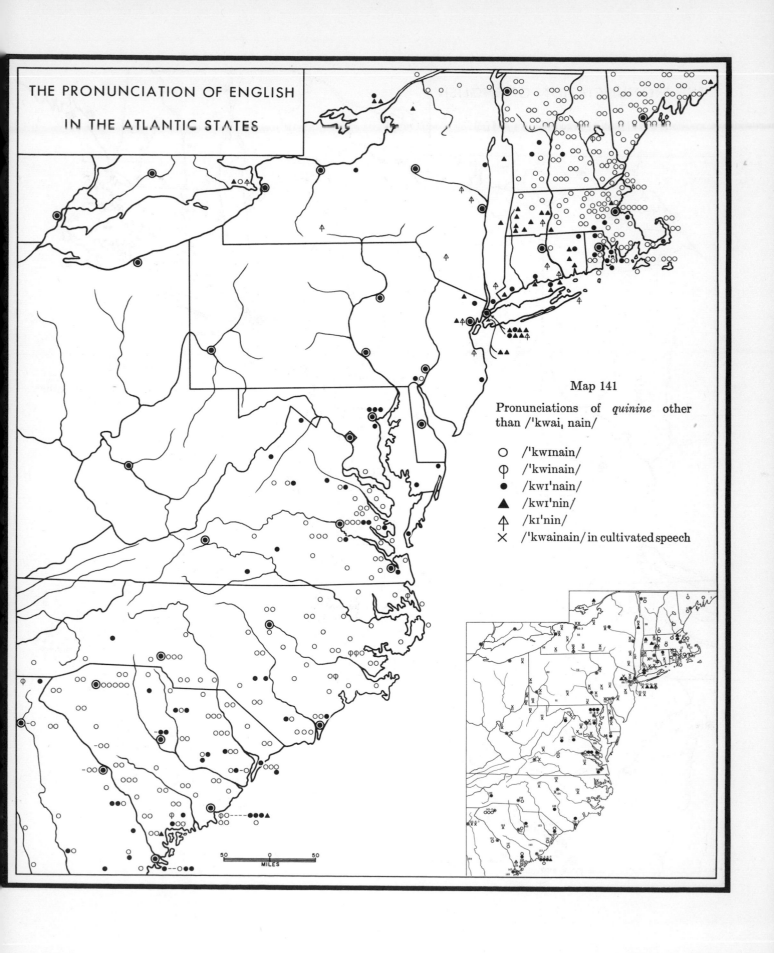

THE PRONUNCIATION OF ENGLISH

IN THE ATLANTIC STATES

Map 141

Pronunciations of *quinine* other than /ˈkwaiˌnain/

○ /ˈkwɪnain/

Ⴔ /ˈkwinain/

● /kwɪˈnain/

▲ /kwɪˈnin/

⚇ /kɪˈnin/

✕ /ˈkwainain/ in cultivated speech

50   0   50
MILES

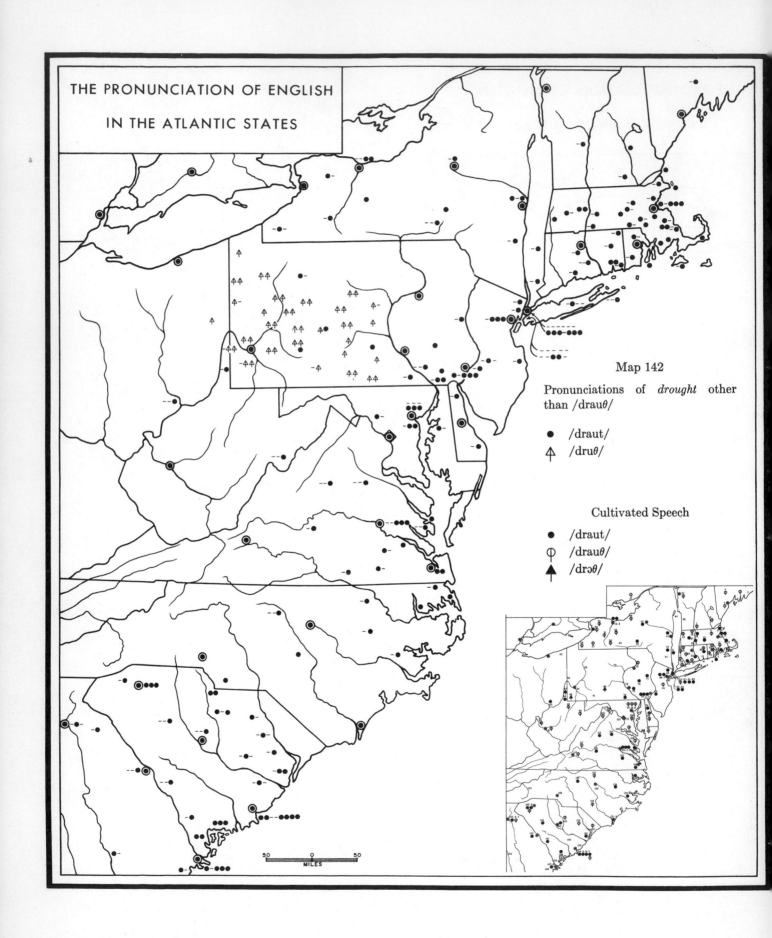

THE PRONUNCIATION OF ENGLISH
IN THE ATLANTIC STATES

Map 142

Pronunciations of *drought* other
than /drauθ/

- /draut/
⚇ /druθ/

Cultivated Speech

- /draut/
φ /drauθ/
▲ /drɔθ/

50   0   50
MILES

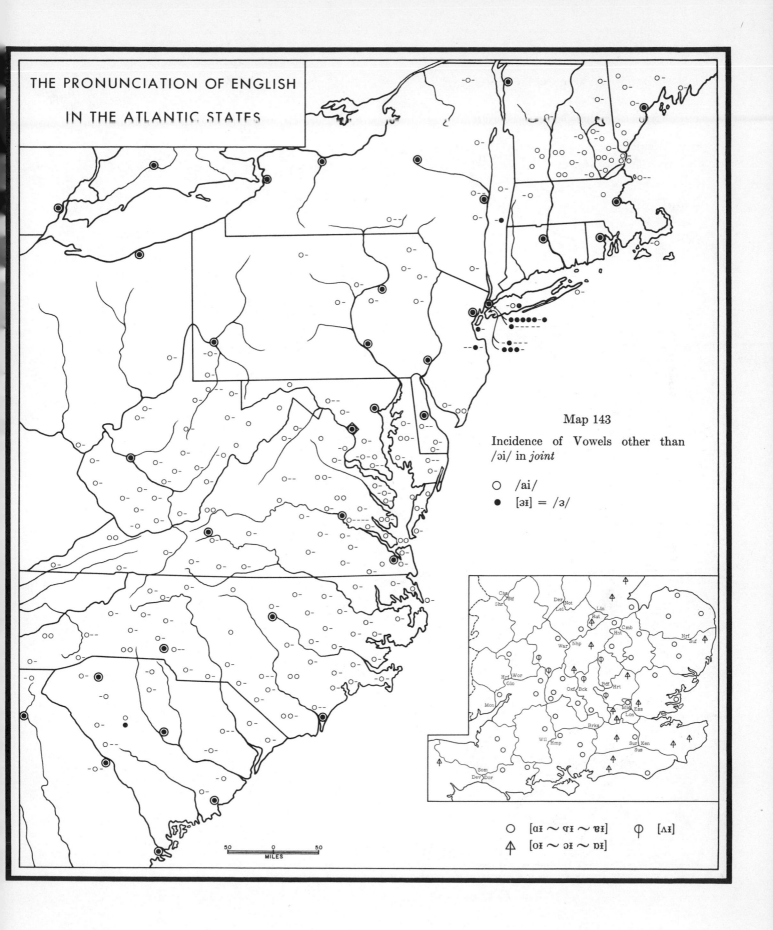

THE PRONUNCIATION OF ENGLISH
IN THE ATLANTIC STATES

Map 143

Incidence of Vowels other than
/ɔi/ in *joint*

○ /ai/

● [ɜɪ] = /ɜ/

○ [ɑɪ ~ ɒɪ ~ ɐɪ ~ ɪɒ]   φ [ʌɪ]

⚡ [ɒɪ ~ ɔɪ ~ ɒɪ]

50   0   50
MILES

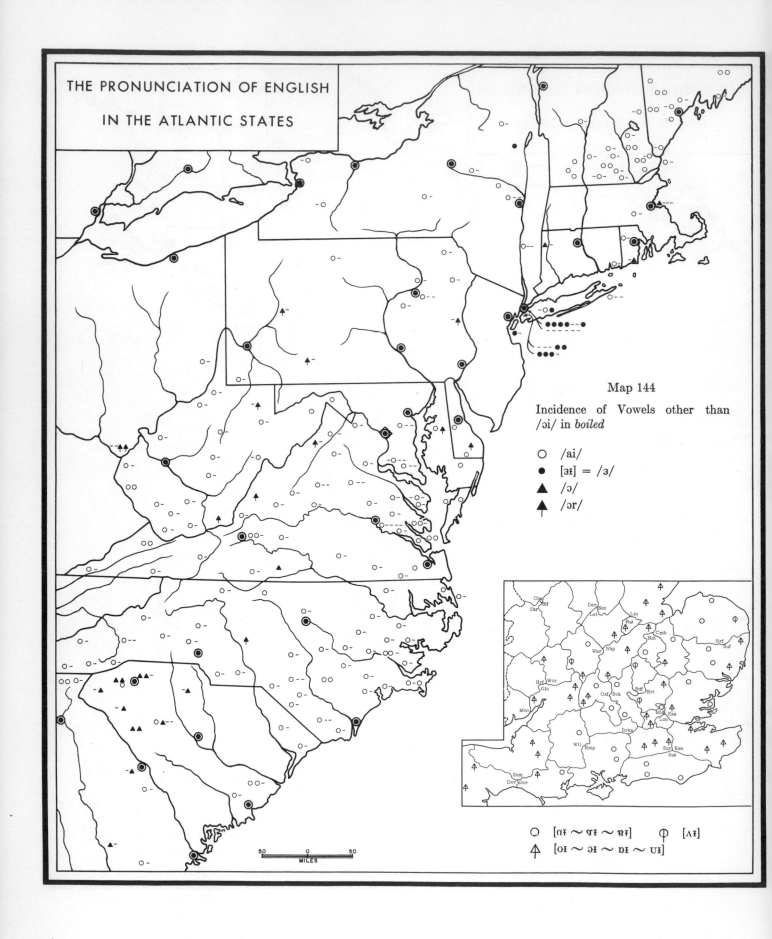

THE PRONUNCIATION OF ENGLISH

IN THE ATLANTIC STATES

Map 144

Incidence of Vowels other than /ɔi/ in *boiled*

○ /ai/
● [ɜɨ] = /ɜ/
▲ /ɔ/
♠ /ɔr/

MILES

○ [ɒɨ ～ ɑɨ ～ ɐɨ]   ⏀ [ʌɨ]
♠ [oɨ ～ ɔɨ ～ ɒɨ ～ ʊɨ]

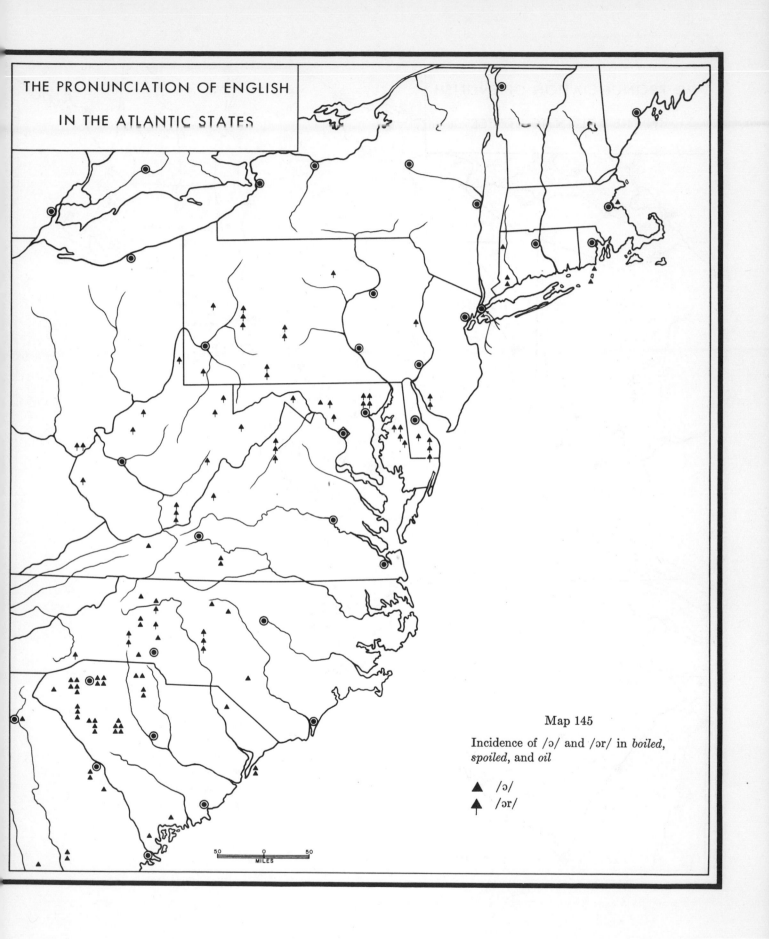

THE PRONUNCIATION OF ENGLISH

IN THE ATLANTIC STATES

Map 145

Incidence of /ɔ/ and /ɔr/ in *boiled*,
spoiled, and *oil*

▲ /ɔ/

⬆ /ɔr/

50   0   50
MILES

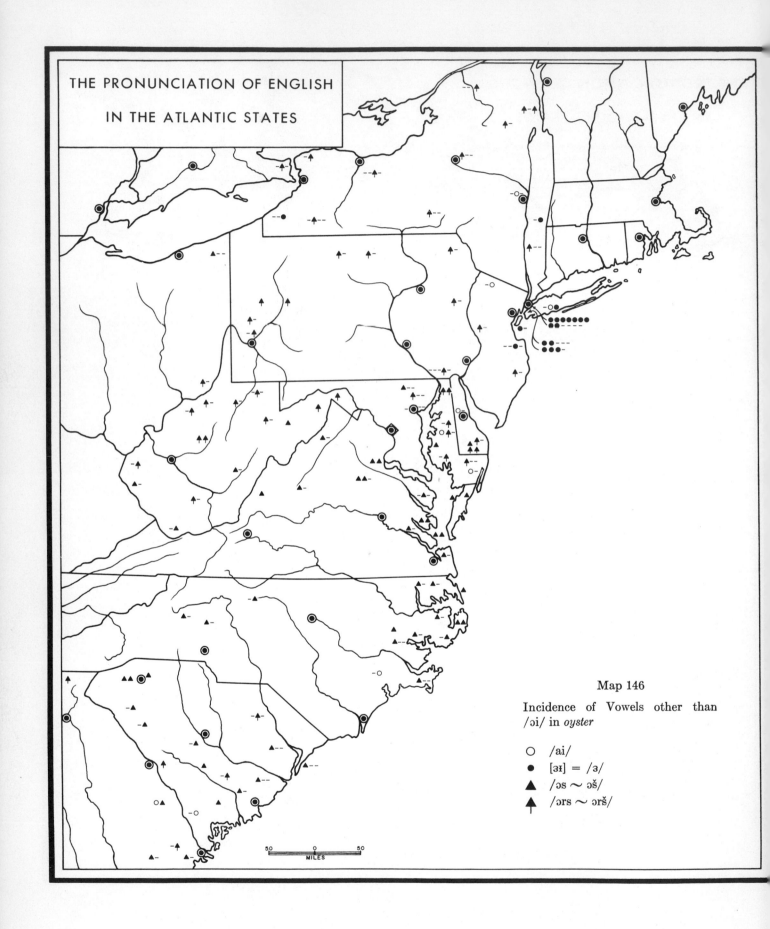

THE PRONUNCIATION OF ENGLISH

IN THE ATLANTIC STATES

Map 146

Incidence of Vowels other than
/ɔi/ in *oyster*

○   /ai/

●   [ɜɪ] = /ɜ/

▲   /ɔs ~ ɔš/

↑   /ɔrs ~ ɔrš/

50   0   50
MILES

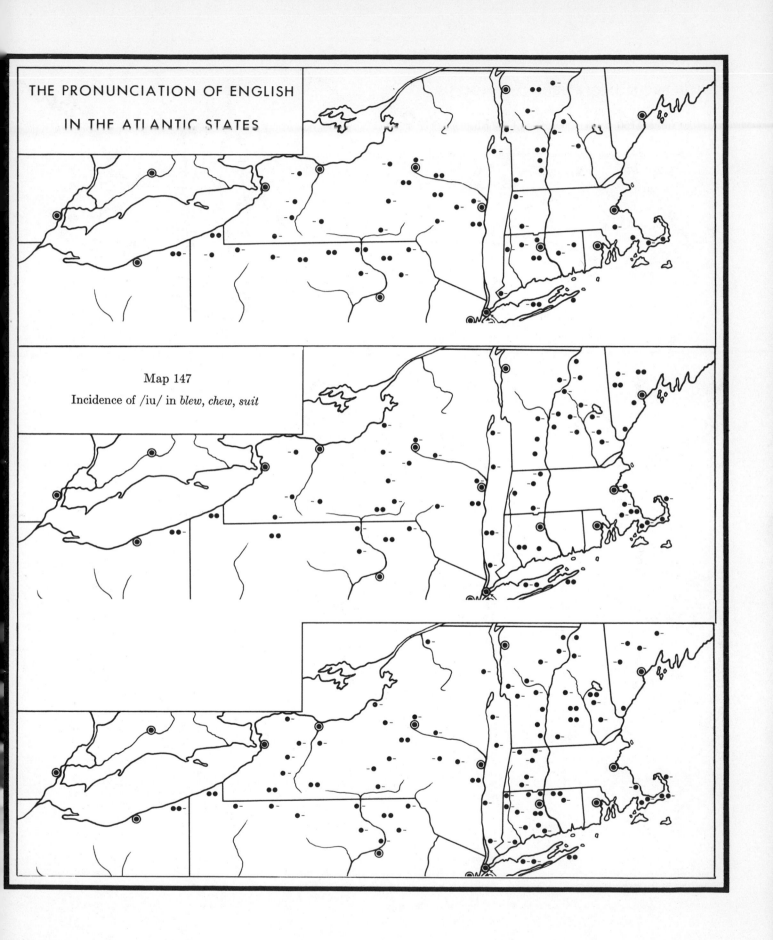

THE PRONUNCIATION OF ENGLISH
IN THE ATLANTIC STATES

Map 147

Incidence of /iu/ in *blew, chew, suit*

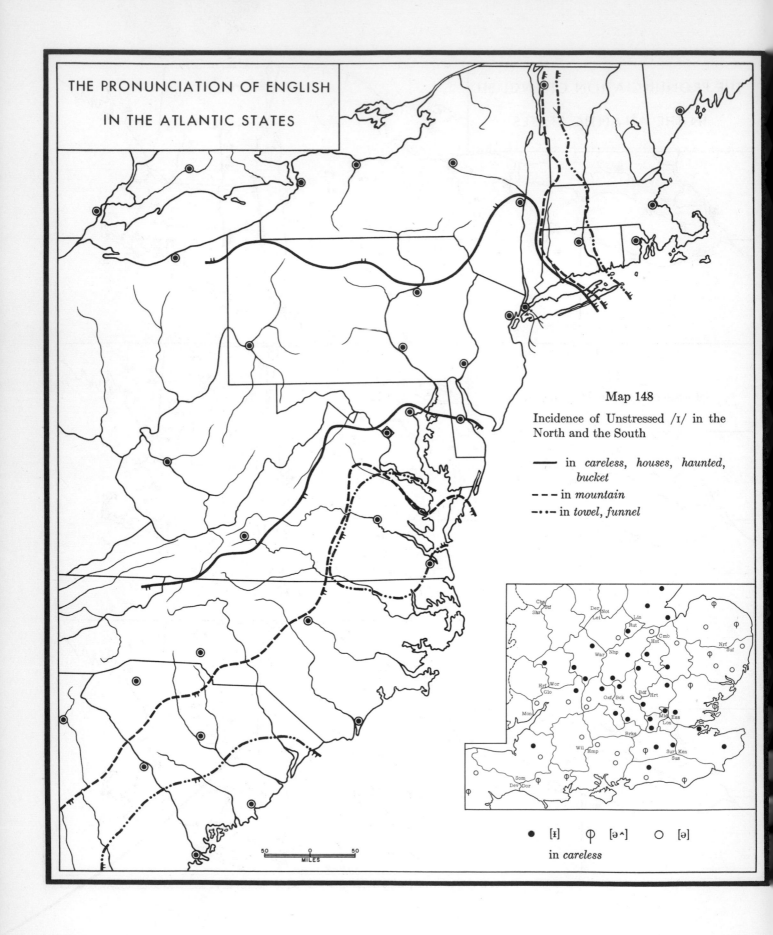

THE PRONUNCIATION OF ENGLISH
IN THE ATLANTIC STATES

Map 148

Incidence of Unstressed /ɪ/ in the
North and the South

——— in *careless, houses, haunted,*
bucket

– – – in *mountain*

–·–·– in *towel, funnel*

● [ɨ]   φ [ə˄]   ○ [ə]

in *careless*

50   0   50
MILES

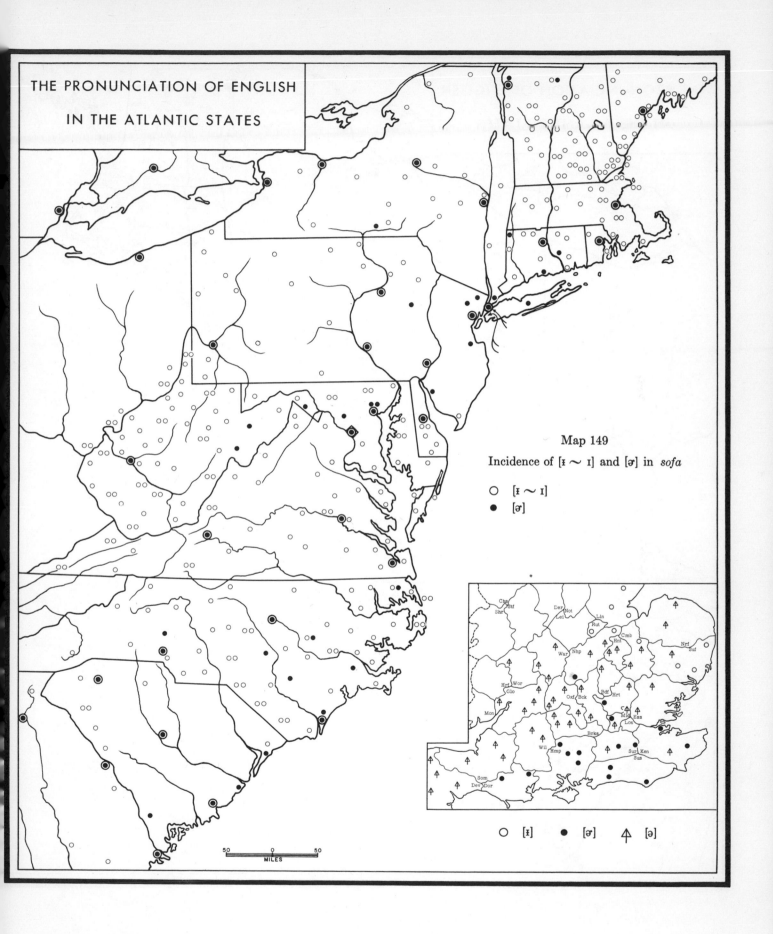

THE PRONUNCIATION OF ENGLISH
IN THE ATLANTIC STATES

Map 149

Incidence of [ɪ ~ ɪ] and [ɚ] in *sofa*

○   [ɪ ~ ɪ]

●   [ɚ]

○   [ɪ]   ●   [ɚ]   ⚲   [ə]

50   0   50
MILES

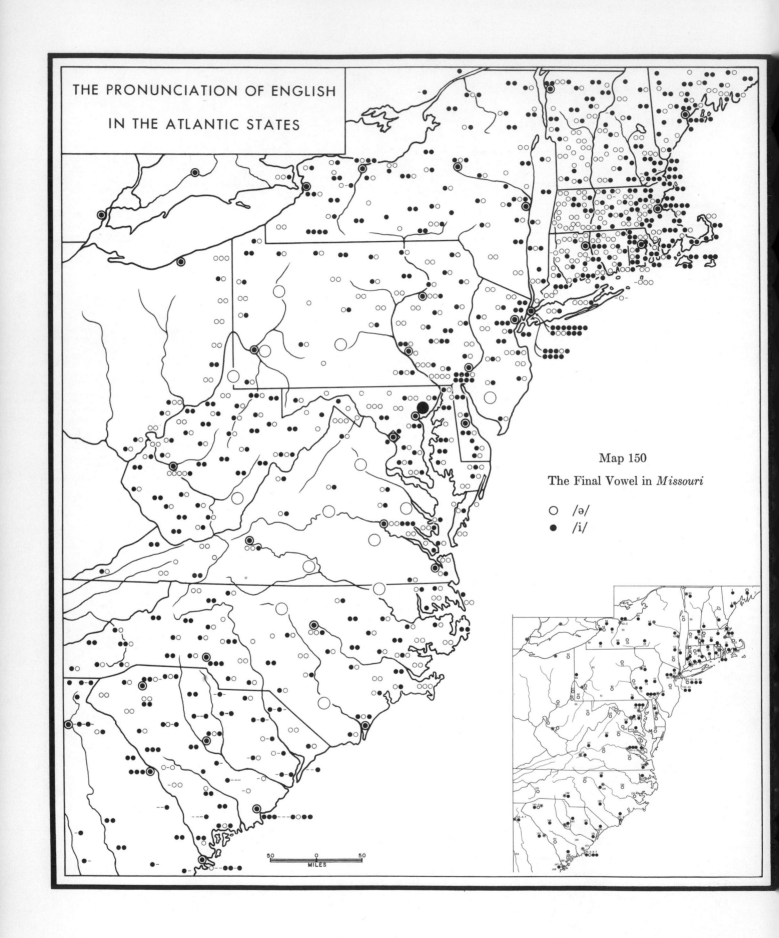

THE PRONUNCIATION OF ENGLISH
IN THE ATLANTIC STATES

Map 150

The Final Vowel in *Missouri*

○ /ə/

● /i/

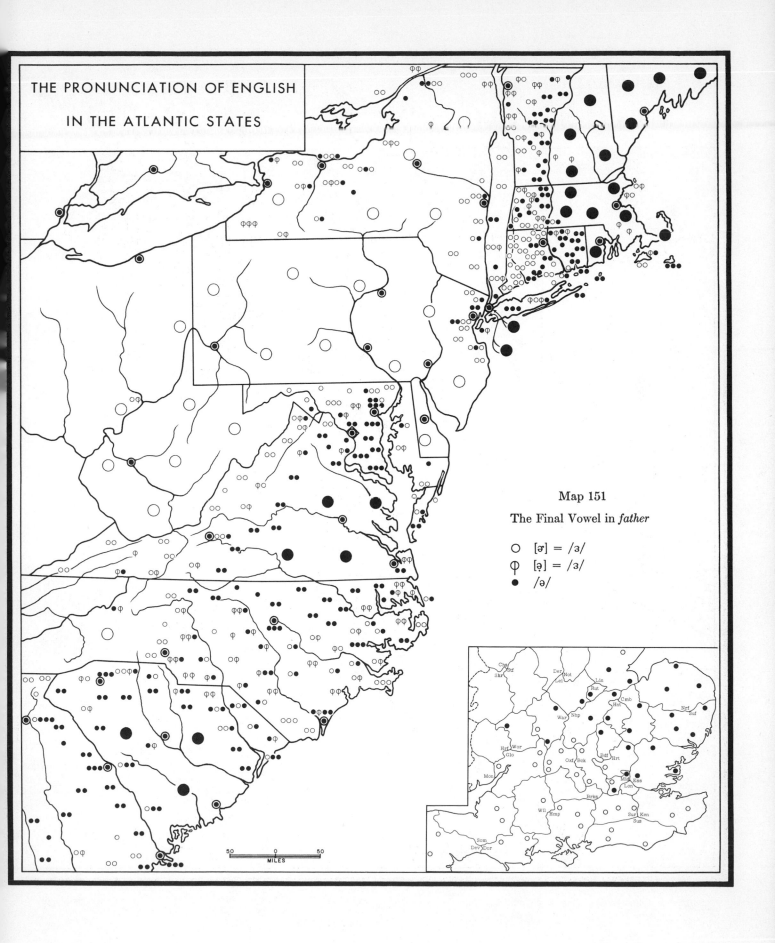

THE PRONUNCIATION OF ENGLISH

IN THE ATLANTIC STATES

Map 151

The Final Vowel in *father*

○ [ɚ] = /ɜ/

φ [ə̣] = /ɜ/

● /ə/

MILES

50   0   50

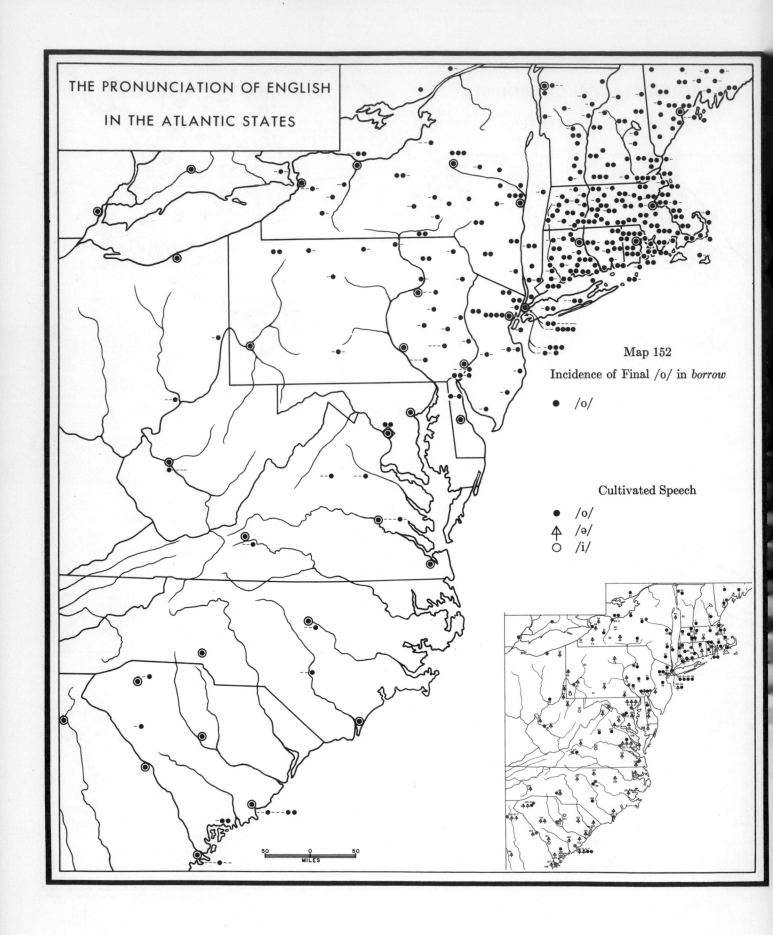

THE PRONUNCIATION OF ENGLISH

IN THE ATLANTIC STATES

Map 152

Incidence of Final /o/ in *borrow*

● /o/

Cultivated Speech

● /o/

⚤ /ə/

○ /i/

50   0   50
MILES

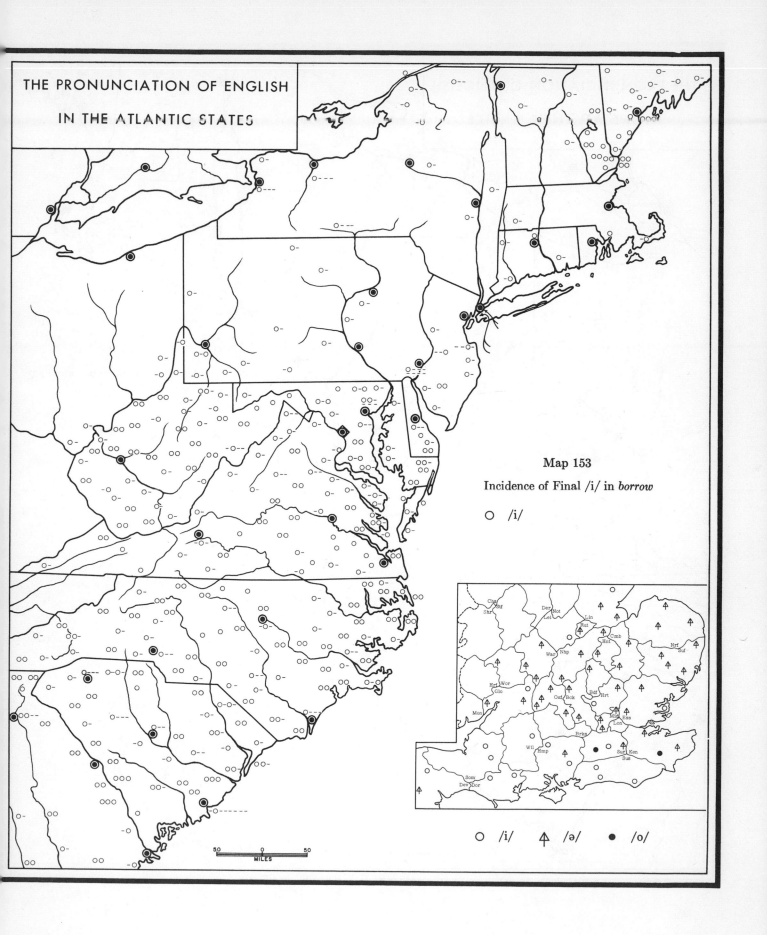

THE PRONUNCIATION OF ENGLISH
IN THE ATLANTIC STATES

Map 153

Incidence of Final /i/ in *borrow*

○ /i/

○ /i/   ⋔ /ə/   ● /o/

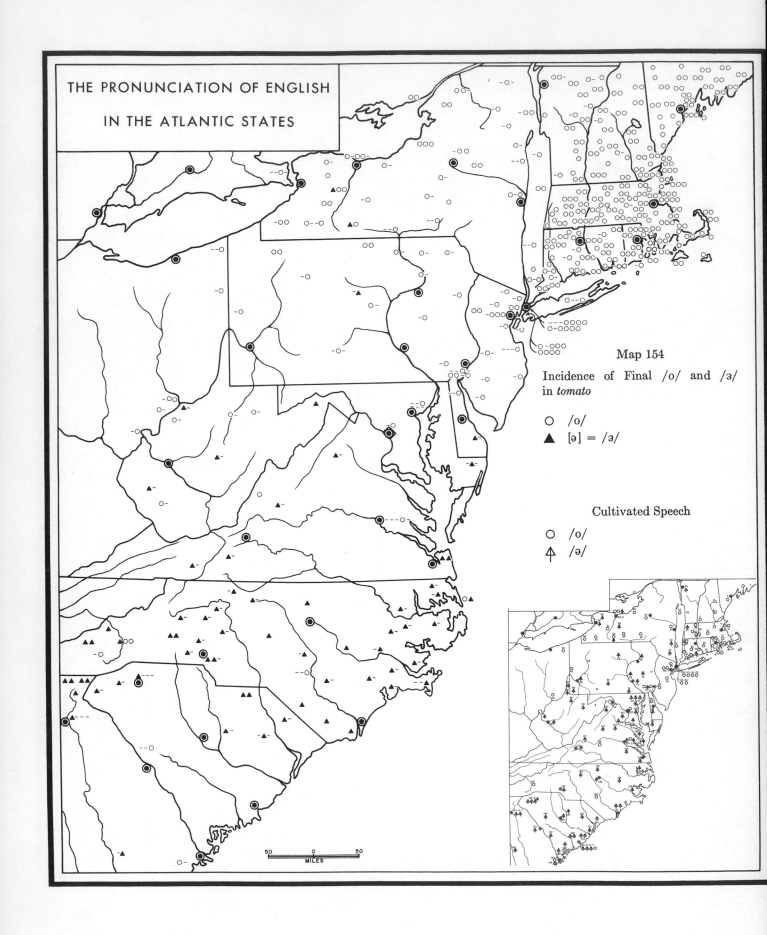

THE PRONUNCIATION OF ENGLISH
IN THE ATLANTIC STATES

Map 154

Incidence of Final /o/ and /ɜ/
in *tomato*

○ /o/
▲ [ə] = /ɜ/

Cultivated Speech

○ /o/
⚐ /ə/

MILES

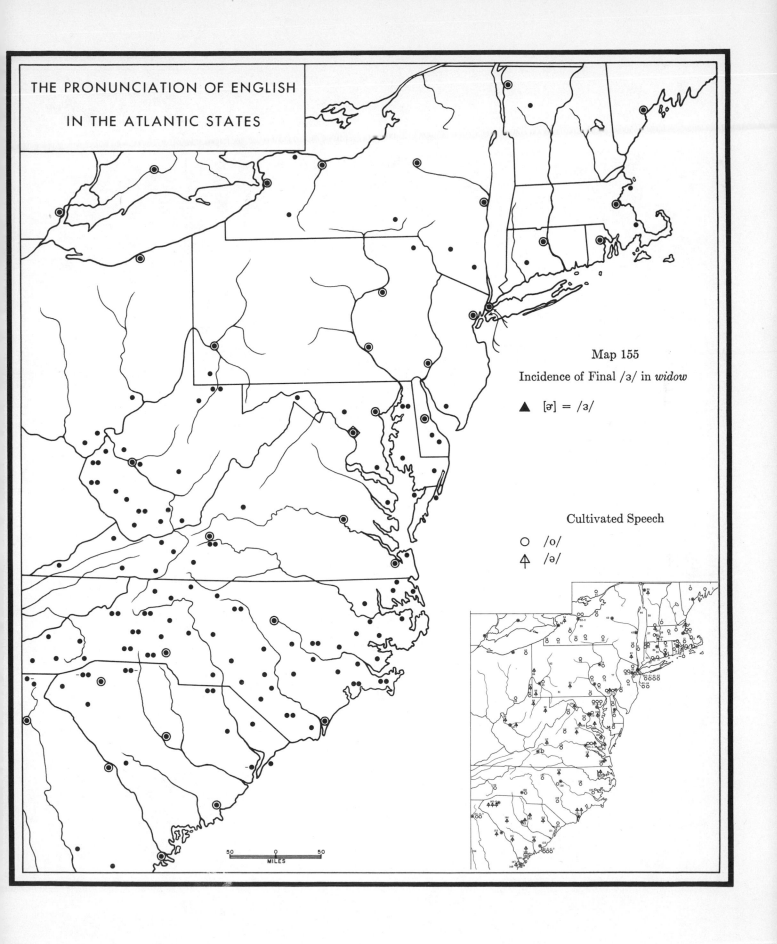

THE PRONUNCIATION OF ENGLISH
IN THE ATLANTIC STATES

Map 155

Incidence of Final /ɝ/ in *widow*

▲ [ɝ] = /ɝ/

Cultivated Speech

○ /o/
⋔ /ə/

MILES

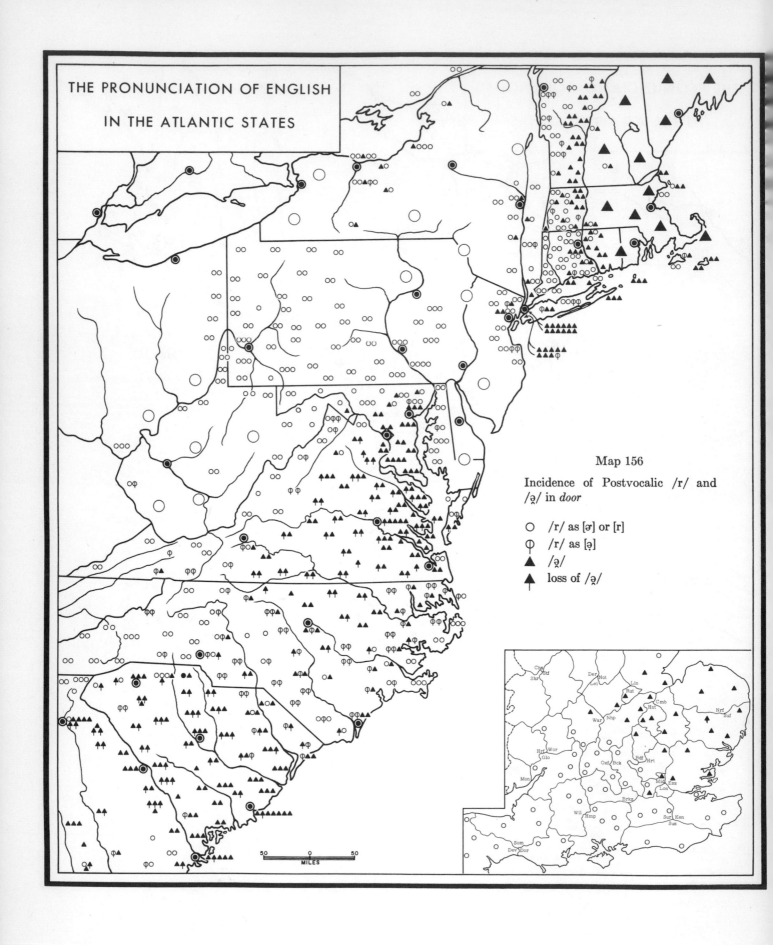

THE PRONUNCIATION OF ENGLISH

IN THE ATLANTIC STATES

Map 156

Incidence of Postvocalic /r/ and /ə/ in *door*

○   /r/ as [ɚ] or [r]

Ⴔ   /r/ as [ə̞]

▲   /ə/

⬆   loss of /ə/

50   50
MILES

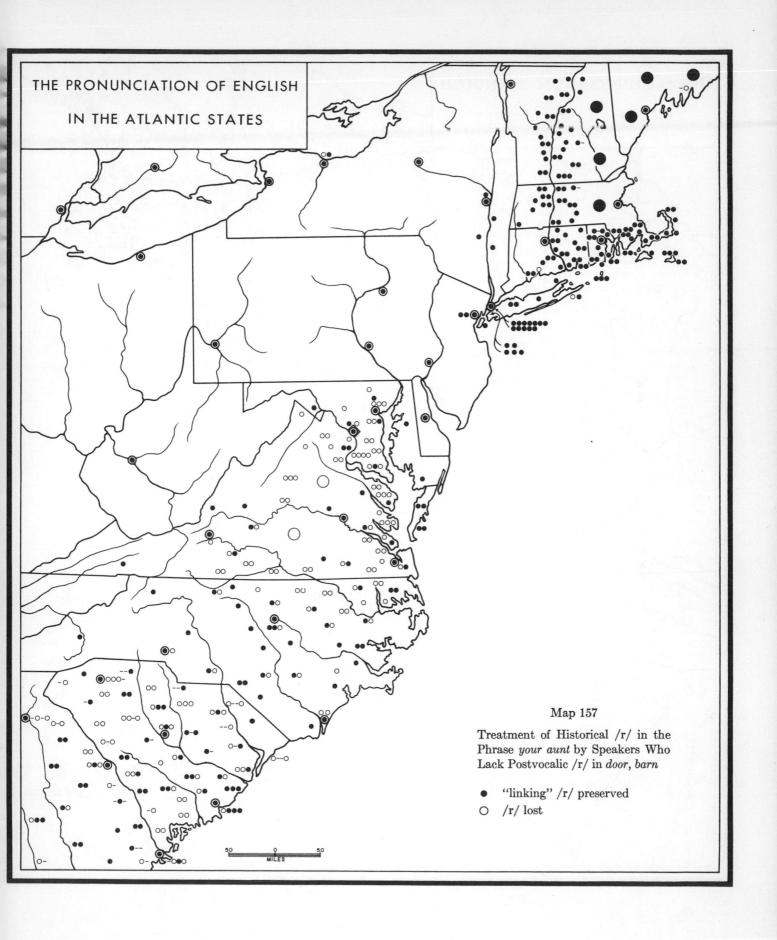

THE PRONUNCIATION OF ENGLISH

IN THE ATLANTIC STATES

Map 157

Treatment of Historical /r/ in the
Phrase *your aunt* by Speakers Who
Lack Postvocalic /r/ in *door, barn*

● "linking" /r/ preserved
○ /r/ lost

50 0   50
   MILES

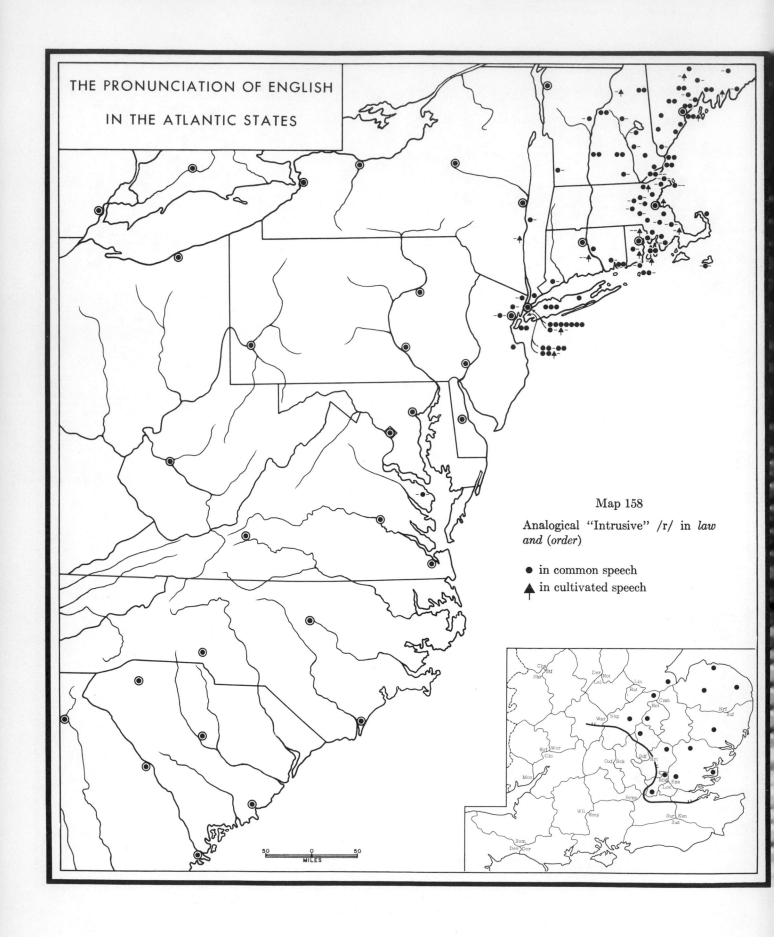

THE PRONUNCIATION OF ENGLISH

IN THE ATLANTIC STATES

Map 158

Analogical "Intrusive" /r/ in *law*
and (*order*)

● in common speech

▲ in cultivated speech

50 0 50
MILES

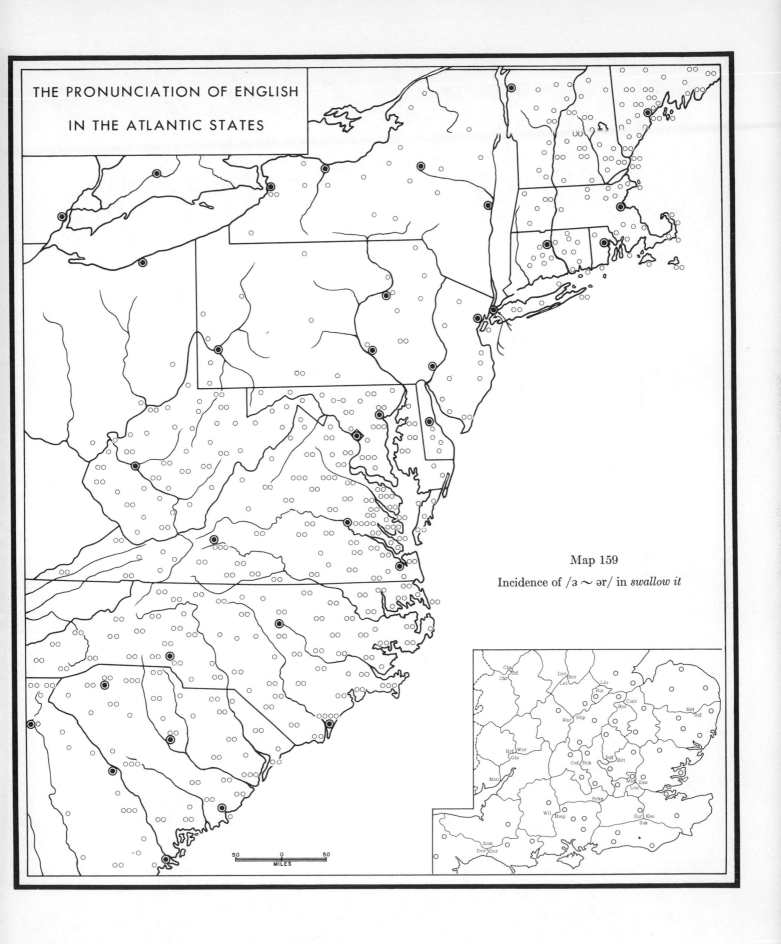

THE PRONUNCIATION OF ENGLISH

IN THE ATLANTIC STATES

Map 159

Incidence of /ɜ ~ ər/ in *swallow it*

50   0   50
MILES

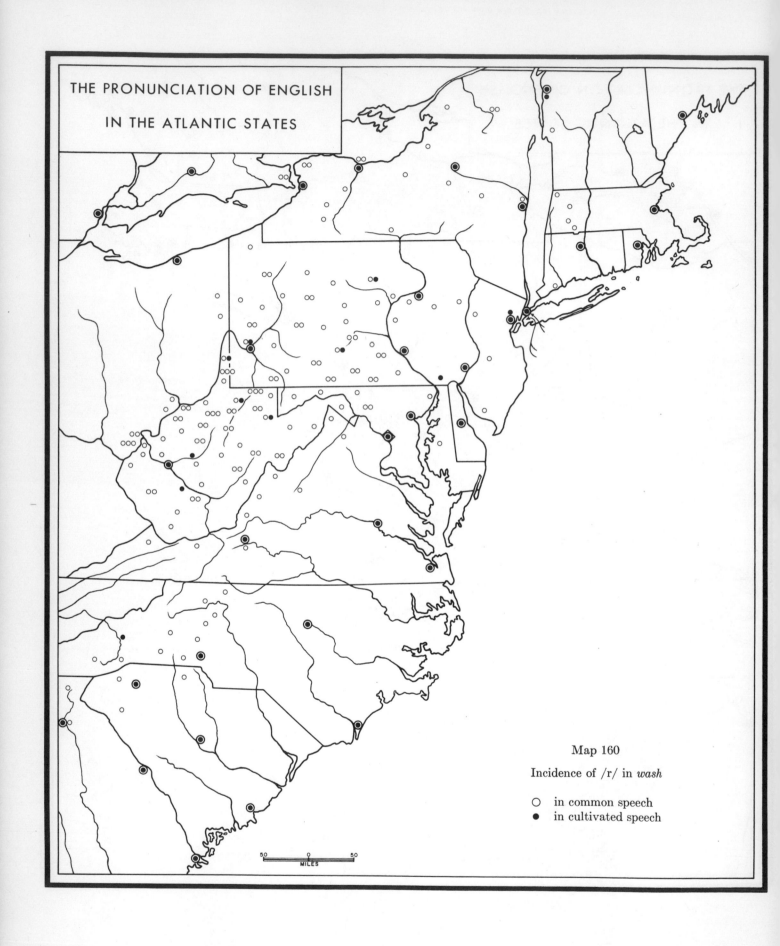

THE PRONUNCIATION OF ENGLISH

IN THE ATLANTIC STATES

Map 160

Incidence of /r/ in *wash*

○   in common speech
●   in cultivated speech

50   0   50
MILES

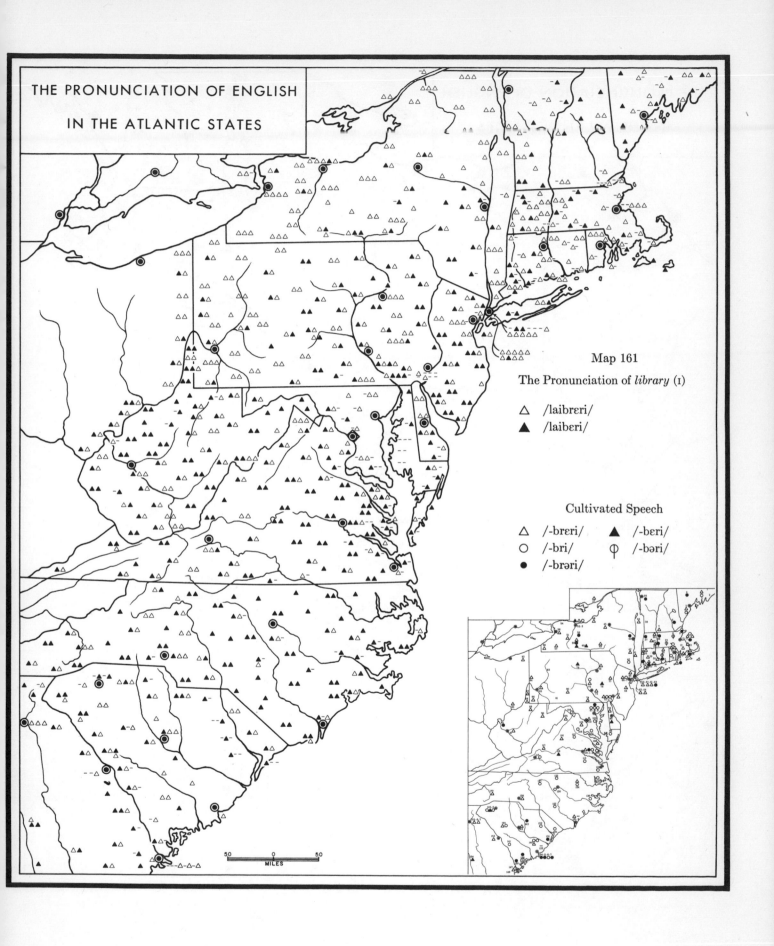

THE PRONUNCIATION OF ENGLISH

IN THE ATLANTIC STATES

Map 161

The Pronunciation of *library* (I)

△ /laibɾeri/

▲ /laibɛri/

Cultivated Speech

△ /-bɾeri/   ▲ /-bɛri/

○ /-bri/   ϙ /-bəri/

● /-bɾəri/

50   0   50
MILES

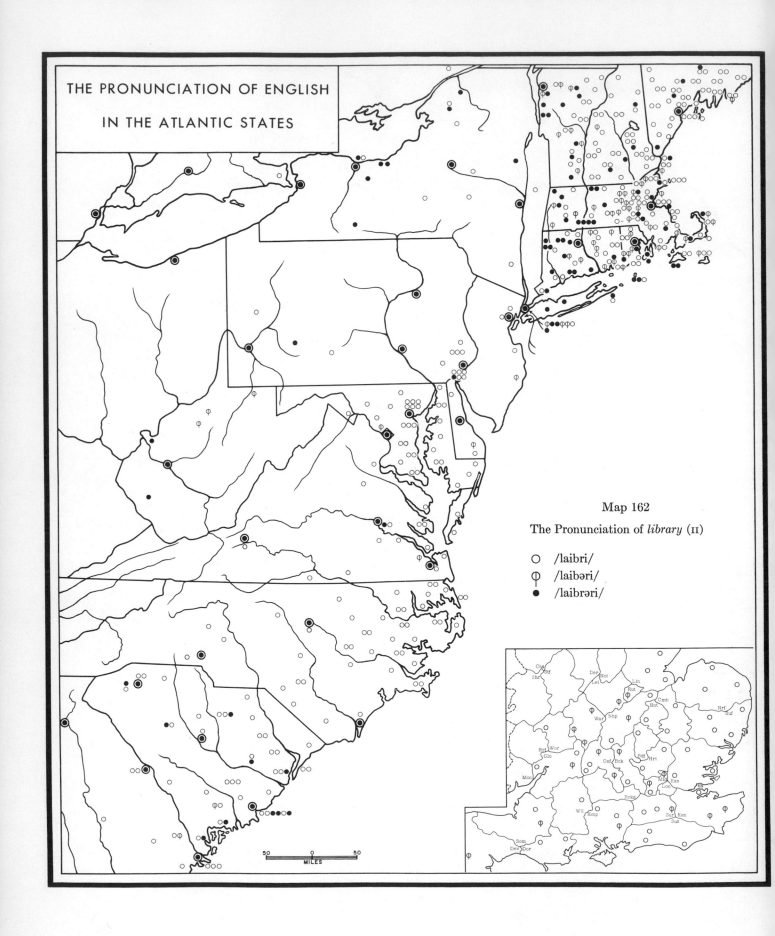

THE PRONUNCIATION OF ENGLISH

IN THE ATLANTIC STATES

Map 162

The Pronunciation of *library* (II)

○ /laibri/

φ /laibəri/

● /laibrəri/

MILES

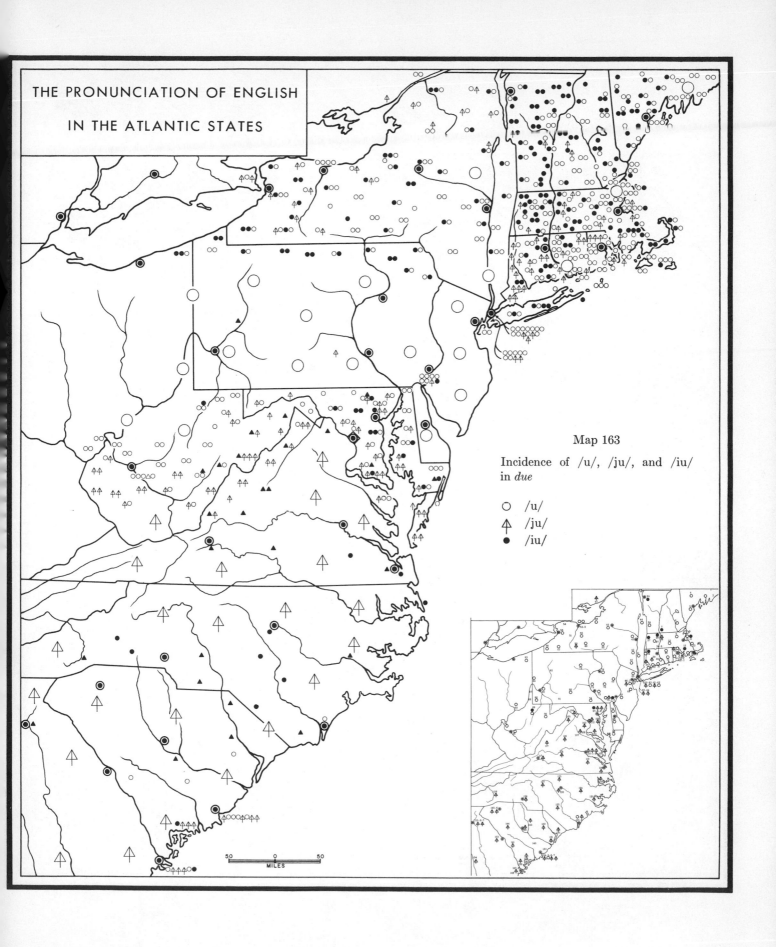

THE PRONUNCIATION OF ENGLISH

IN THE ATLANTIC STATES

Map 163

Incidence of /u/, /ju/, and /iu/
in *due*

○ /u/

⋏ /ju/

● /iu/

50   0   50
MILES

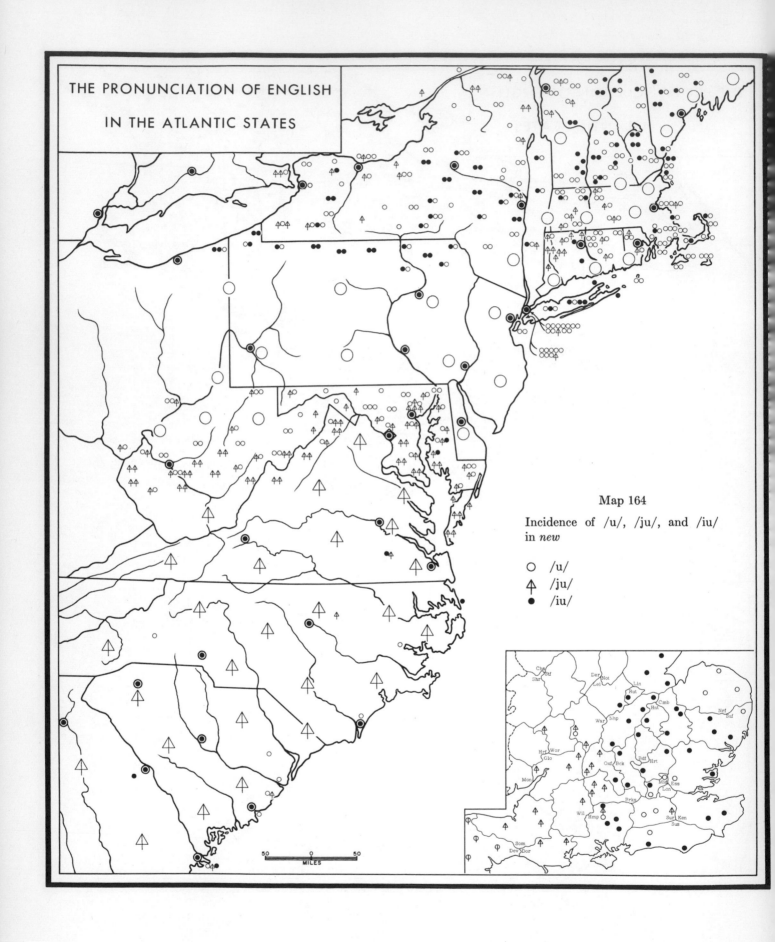

THE PRONUNCIATION OF ENGLISH
IN THE ATLANTIC STATES

Map 164

Incidence of /u/, /ju/, and /iu/
in *new*

○ /u/

⋔ /ju/

● /iu/

50   0   50
MILES

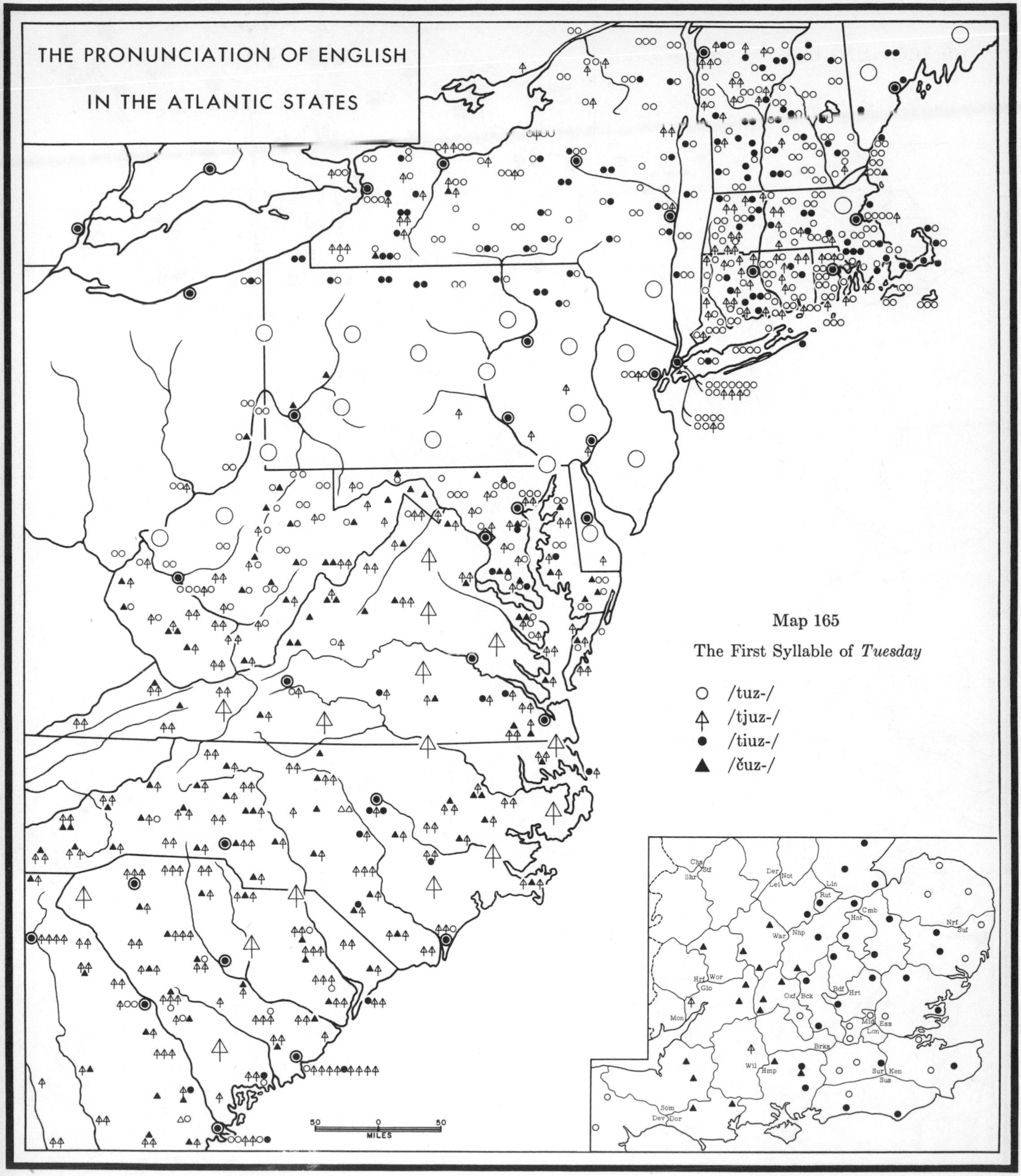
THE PRONUNCIATION OF ENGLISH
IN THE ATLANTIC STATES
Map 165
The First Syllable of *Tuesday*
/tuz-/
/tjuz-/
/tiuz-/
/čuz-/
50
0
50
MILES
Chs
Stf
Shr
Der
Not
Lei
Lin
Rut
Cmb
Hnt
Nrf
Suf
War
Nhp
Hrf
Wor
Glo
Oxf
Bck
Bdf
Hrt
Mon
Mid
Ess
Lon
Brks
Wil
Hmp
Sur
Ken
Sus
Som
Dev
Dor

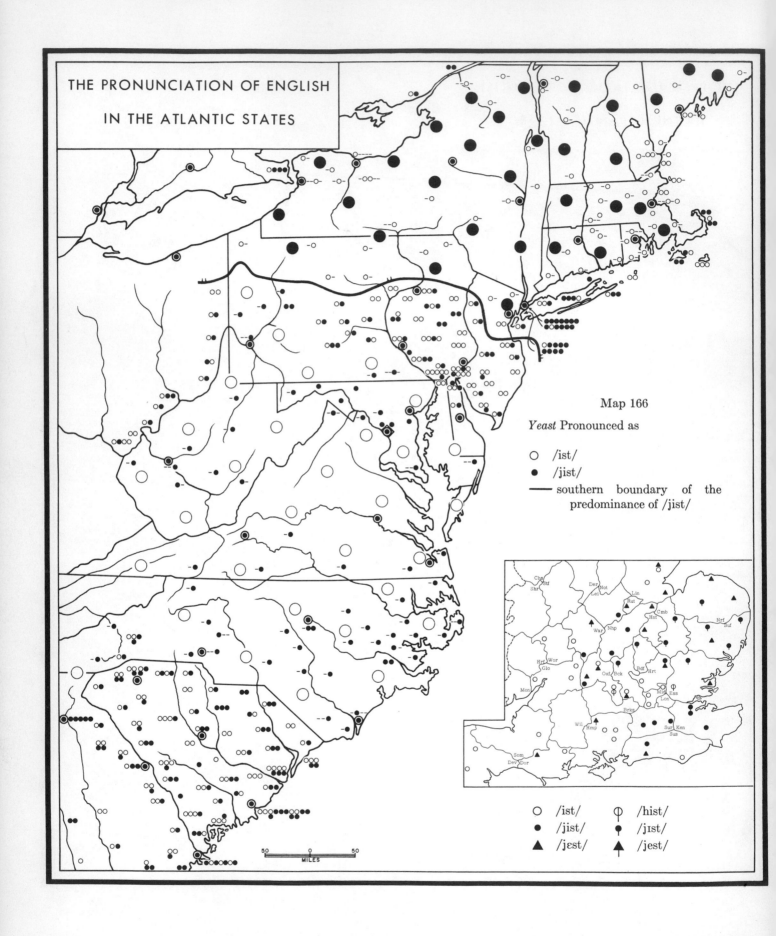

THE PRONUNCIATION OF ENGLISH

IN THE ATLANTIC STATES

Map 166

Yeast Pronounced as

○ /ist/

● /jist/

―――― southern boundary of the predominance of /jist/

50 0 50
MILES

○ /ist/   ⦶ /hist/

● /jist/   ◓ /jɪst/

▲ /jɛst/   ⬆ /jest/

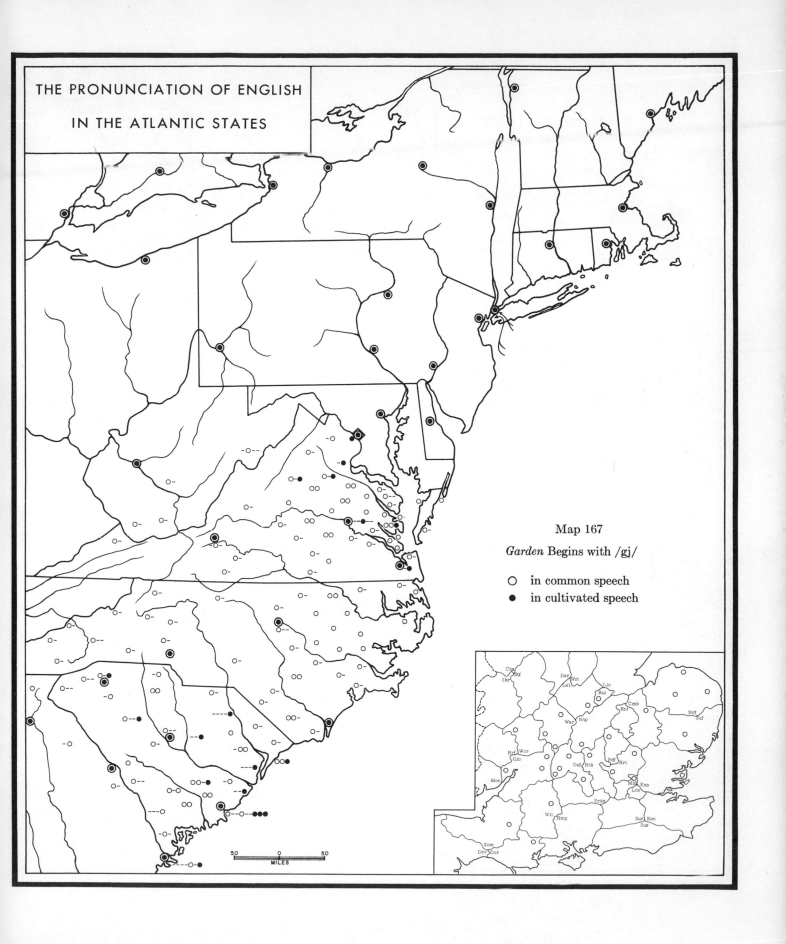

THE PRONUNCIATION OF ENGLISH
IN THE ATLANTIC STATES

Map 167

Garden Begins with /gj/

○   in common speech
●   in cultivated speech

MILES

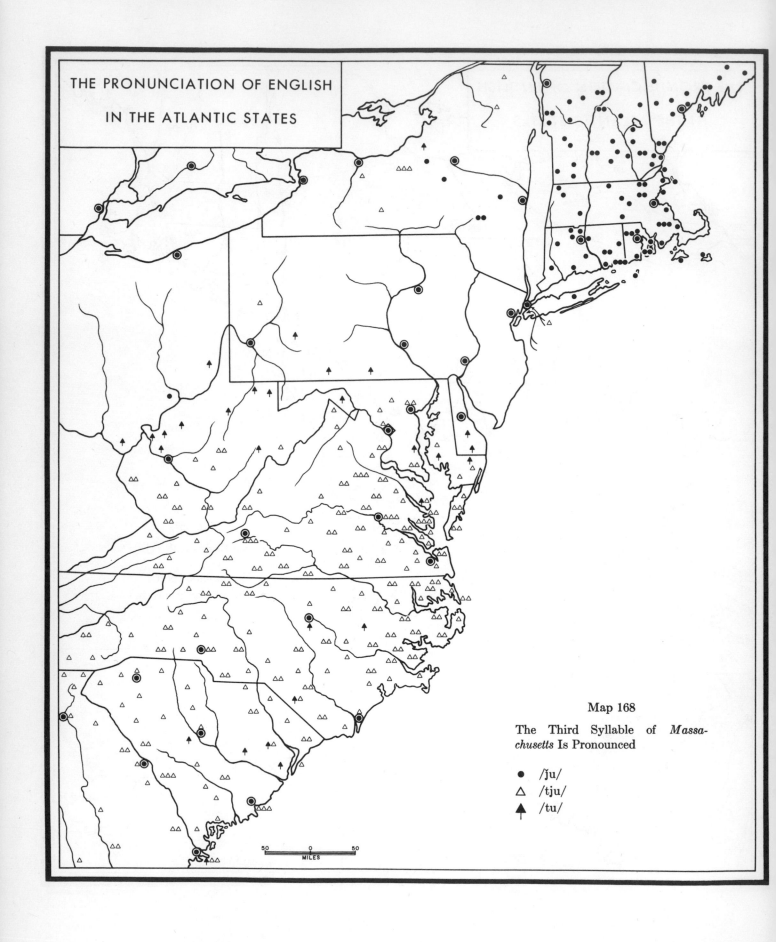

THE PRONUNCIATION OF ENGLISH

IN THE ATLANTIC STATES

Map 168

The Third Syllable of *Massa-chusetts* Is Pronounced

● /ju/

△ /tju/

▲ /tu/

50   0   50
MILES

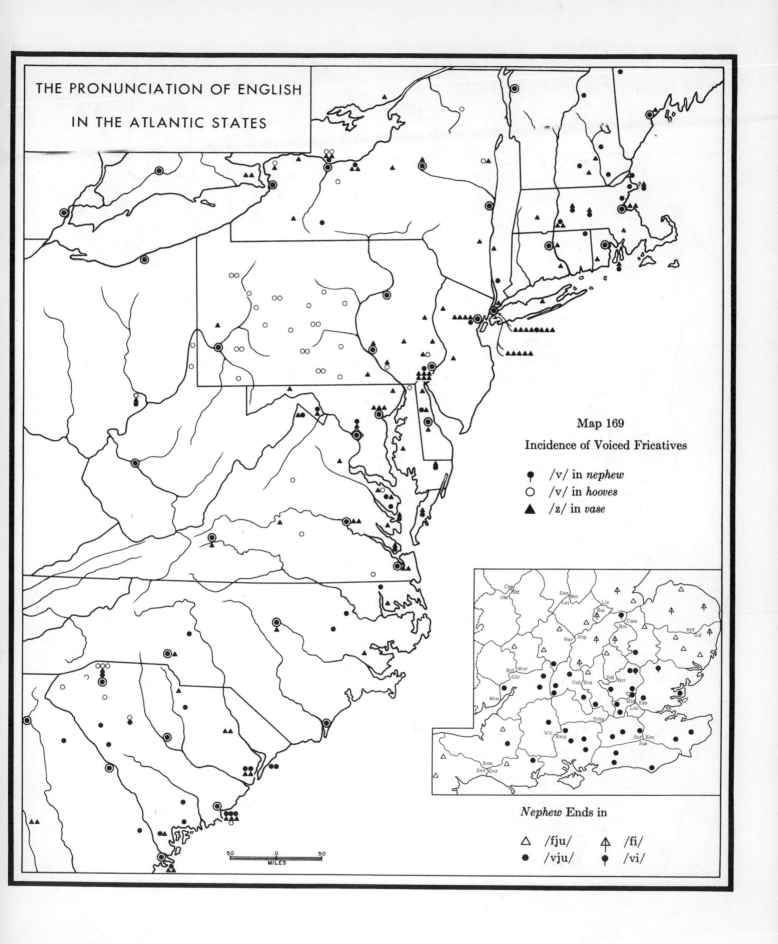

THE PRONUNCIATION OF ENGLISH

IN THE ATLANTIC STATES

Map 169

Incidence of Voiced Fricatives

- /v/ in *nephew*
○ /v/ in *hooves*
▲ /z/ in *vase*

Nephew Ends in

△ /fju/   ⊥ /fi/
● /vju/   ⦶ /vi/

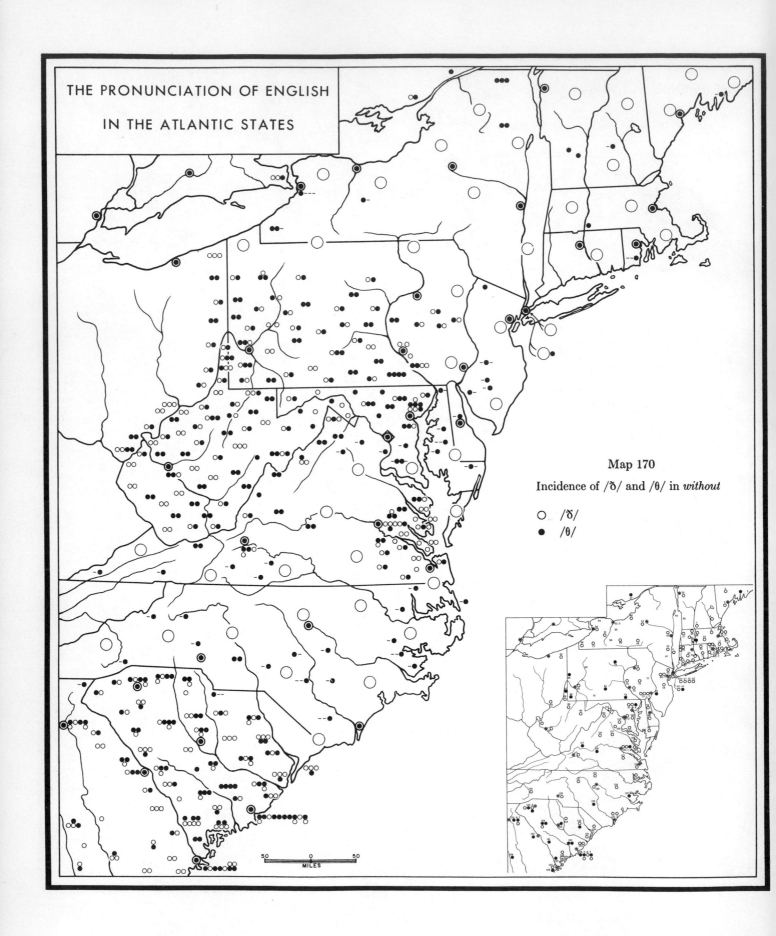

THE PRONUNCIATION OF ENGLISH

IN THE ATLANTIC STATES

Map 170

Incidence of /ð/ and /θ/ in *without*

○ /ð/

● /θ/

50   0   50
MILES

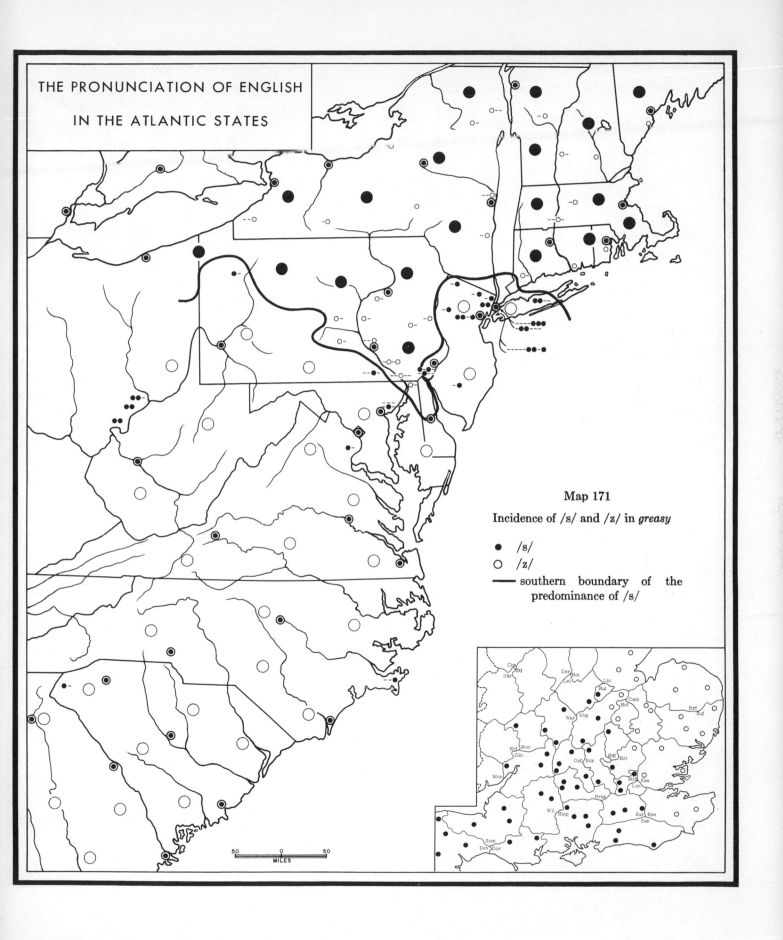

THE PRONUNCIATION OF ENGLISH
IN THE ATLANTIC STATES

Map 171

Incidence of /s/ and /z/ in *greasy*

● /s/

○ /z/

—— southern boundary of the predominance of /s/

MILES
50 0 50

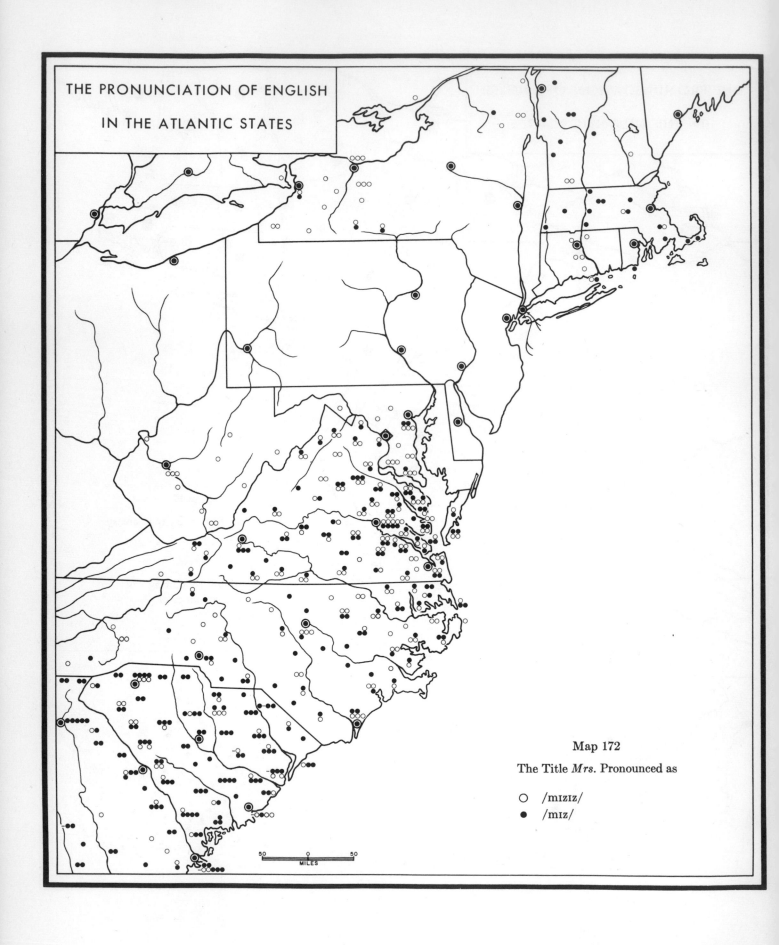

THE PRONUNCIATION OF ENGLISH

IN THE ATLANTIC STATES

Map 172

The Title *Mrs.* Pronounced as

○ /mɪzɪz/

● /mɪz/

50   0   50
MILES

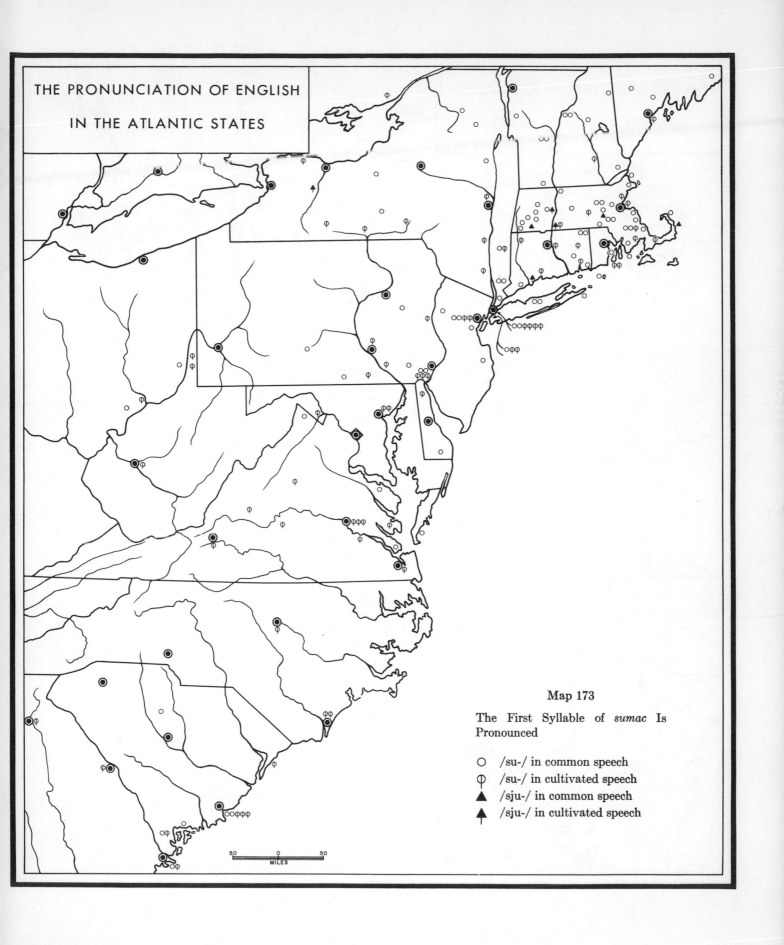

THE PRONUNCIATION OF ENGLISH
IN THE ATLANTIC STATES

Map 173

The First Syllable of *sumac* Is
Pronounced

○   /su-/ in common speech

🝑   /su-/ in cultivated speech

▲   /sju-/ in common speech

☀   /sju-/ in cultivated speech

50   0   50
MILES

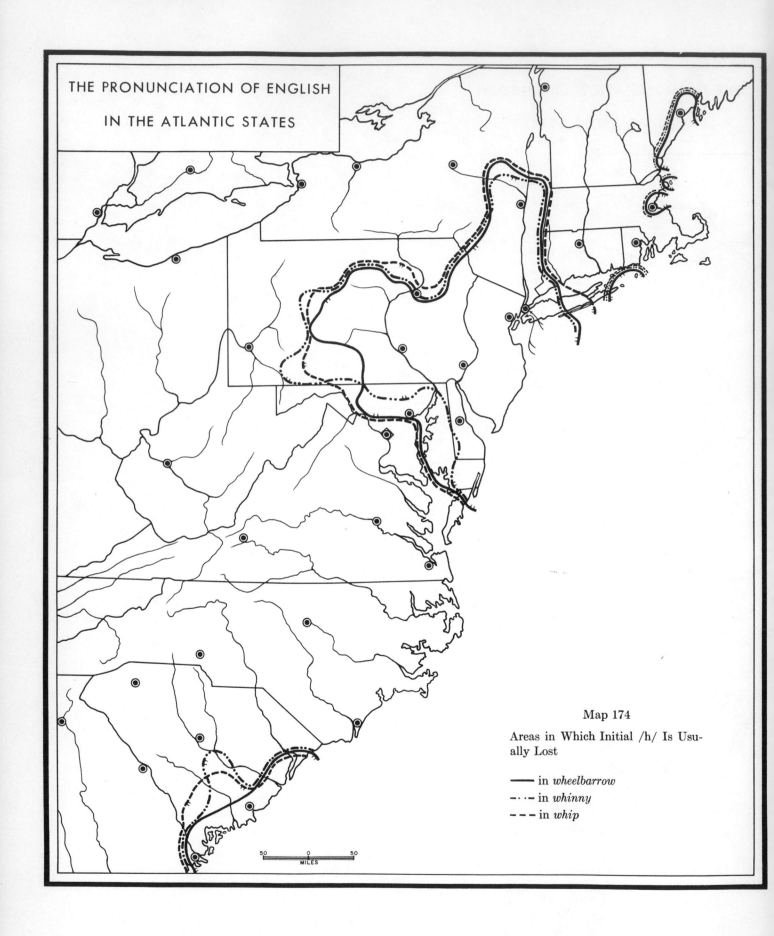

THE PRONUNCIATION OF ENGLISH

IN THE ATLANTIC STATES

Map 174

Areas in Which Initial /h/ Is Usually Lost

——— in *wheelbarrow*

—·—·— in *whinny*

— — — in *whip*

50   0   50

MILES

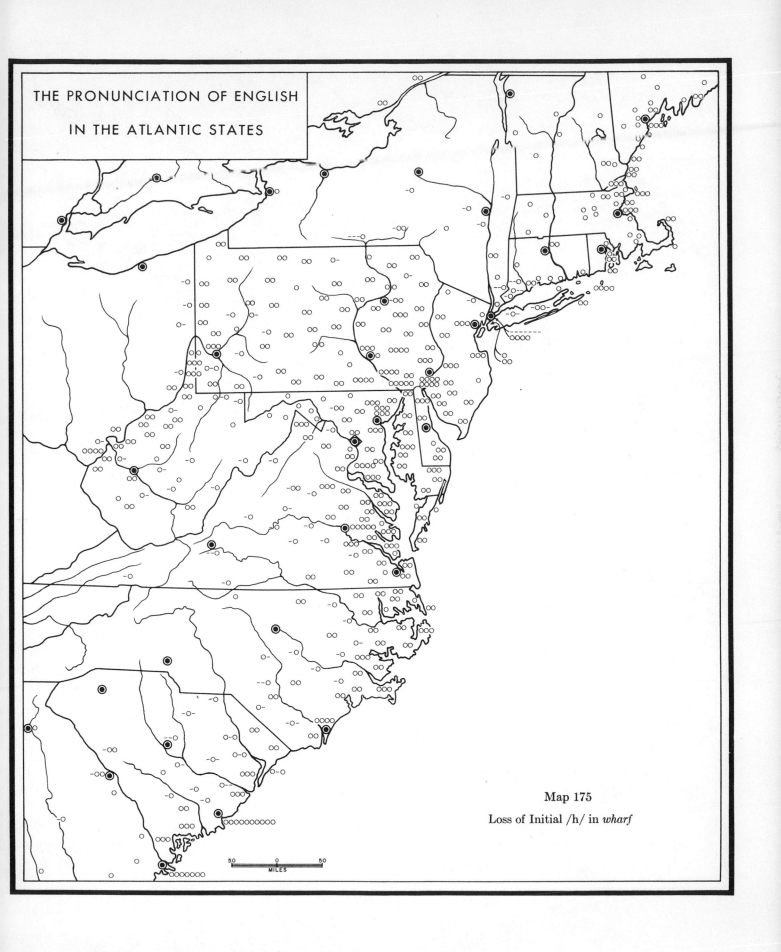

THE PRONUNCIATION OF ENGLISH
IN THE ATLANTIC STATES

Map 175

Loss of Initial /h/ in *wharf*

50   0   50
MILES

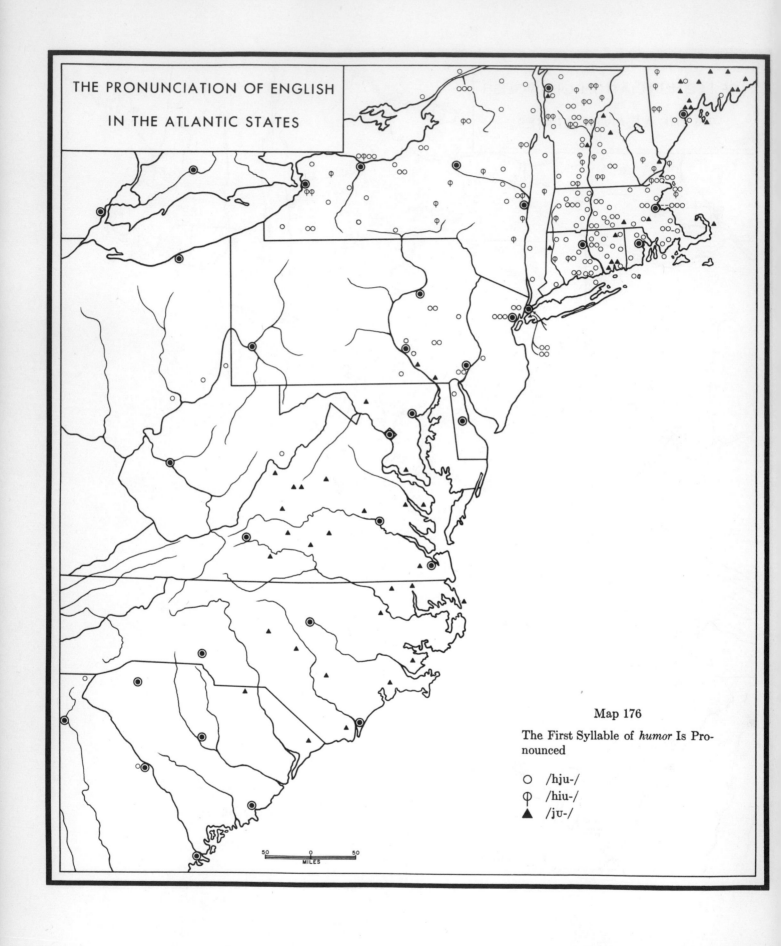

THE PRONUNCIATION OF ENGLISH

IN THE ATLANTIC STATES

Map 176

The First Syllable of *humor* Is Pronounced

○ /hju-/
φ /hiu-/
▲ /ju-/

50   0   50

MILES

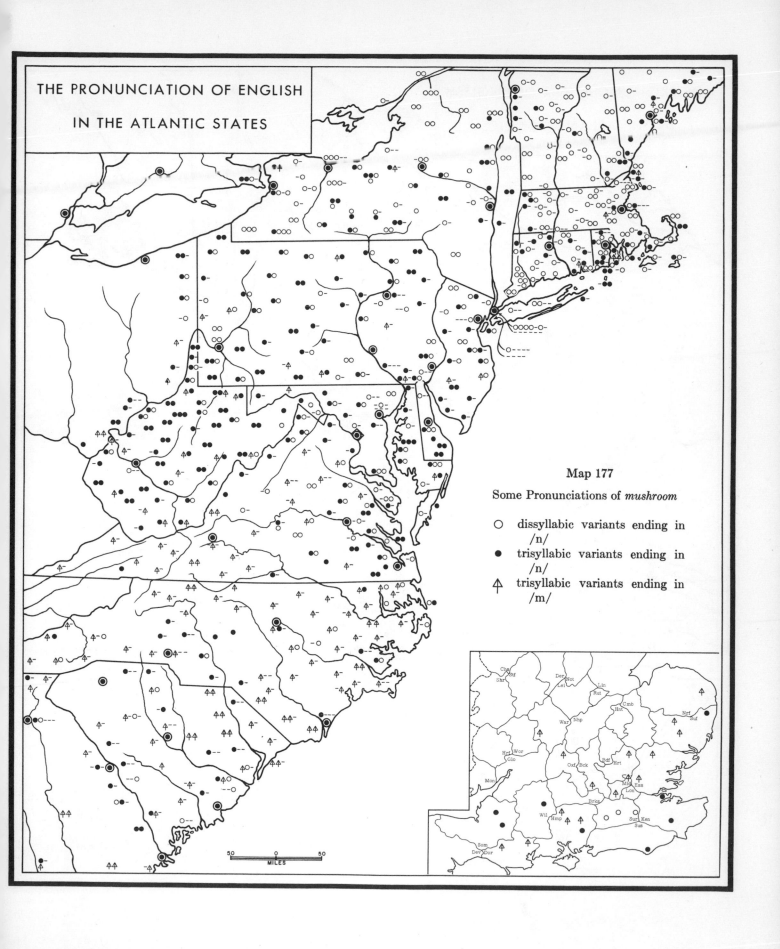

THE PRONUNCIATION OF ENGLISH
IN THE ATLANTIC STATES

Map 177

Some Pronunciations of *mushroom*

○ dissyllabic variants ending in /n/

● trisyllabic variants ending in /n/

⚐ trisyllabic variants ending in /m/

MILES

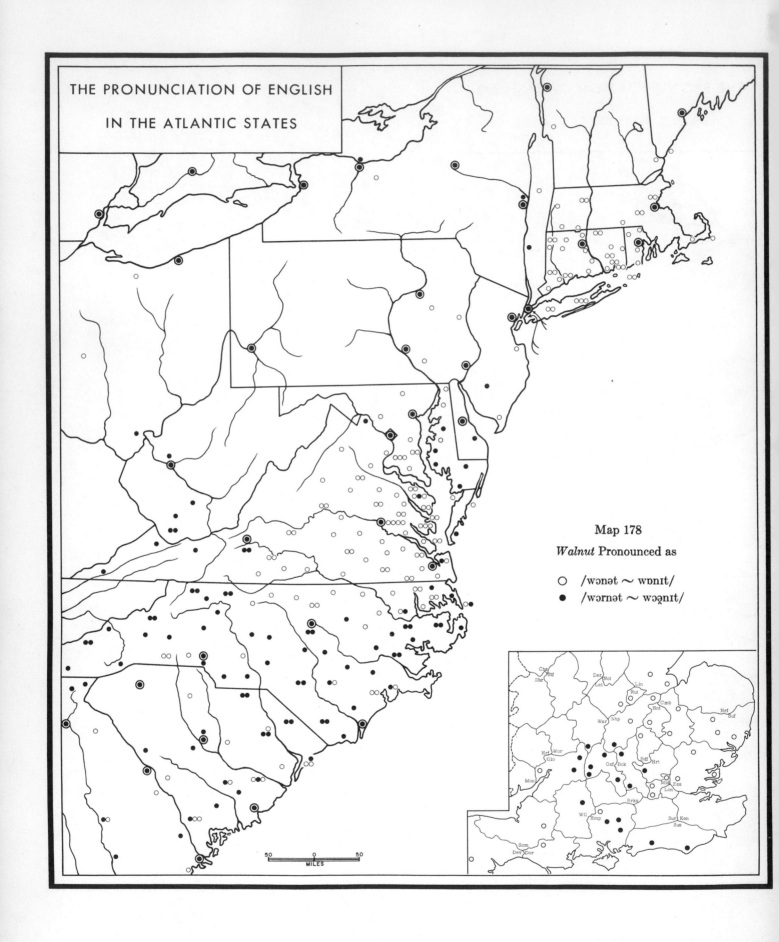

THE PRONUNCIATION OF ENGLISH
IN THE ATLANTIC STATES

Map 178

Walnut Pronounced as

○ /wɔnət ~ wɒnɪt/

● /wɔrnət ~ wɔənɪt/

MILES
50 0 50

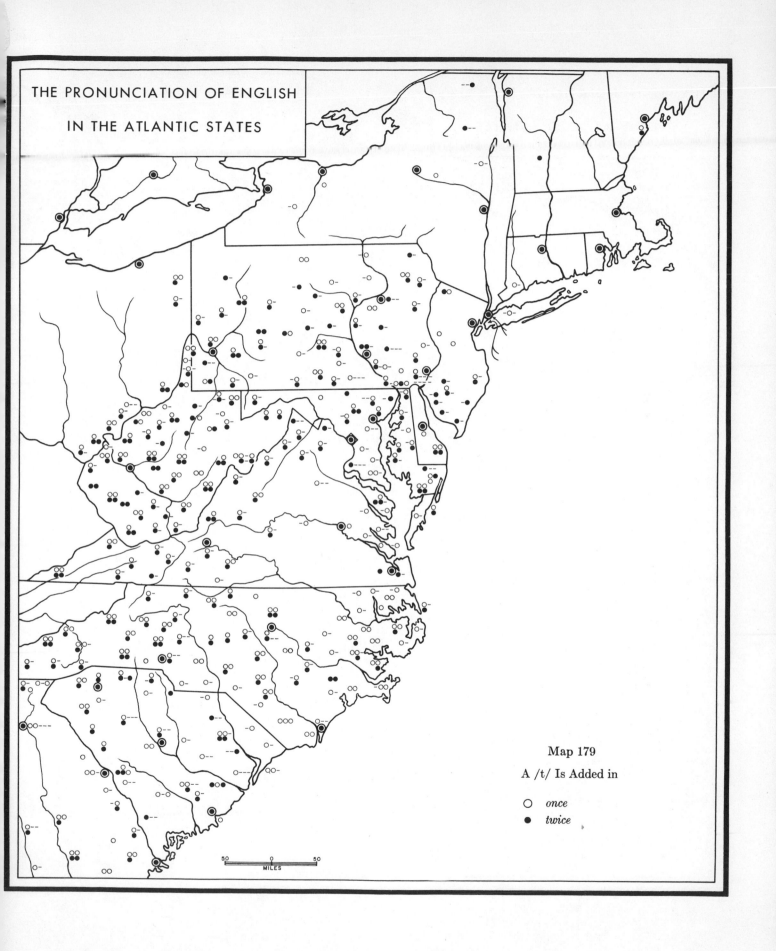

THE PRONUNCIATION OF ENGLISH

IN THE ATLANTIC STATES

Map 179

A /t/ Is Added in

○ *once*

● *twice*

50   0   50

MILES

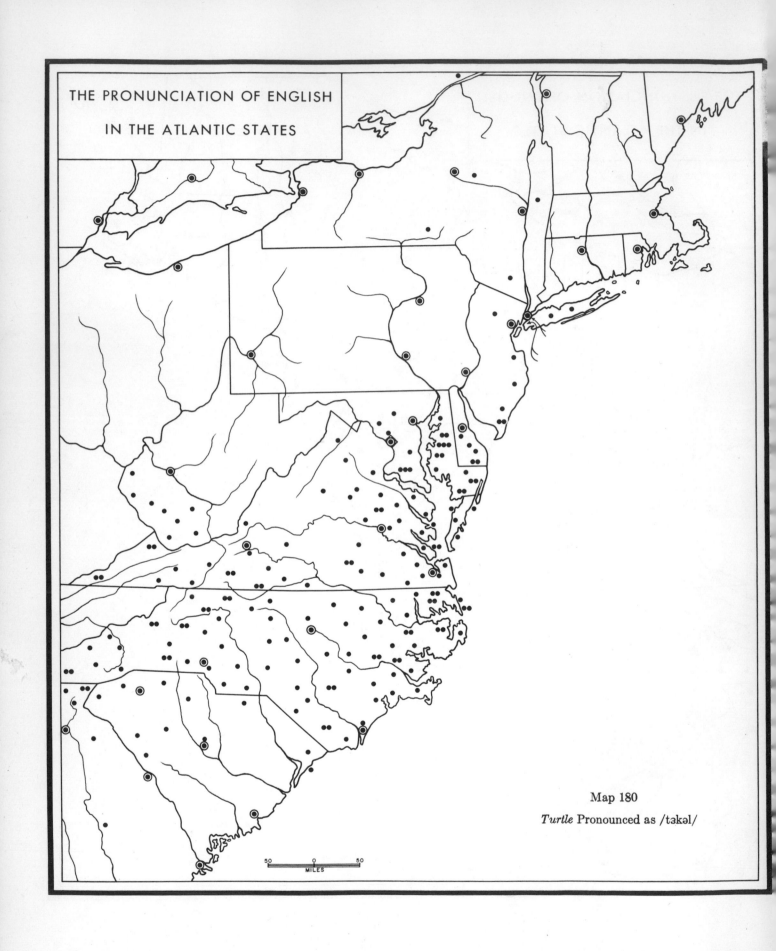

THE PRONUNCIATION OF ENGLISH

IN THE ATLANTIC STATES

Map 180

Turtle Pronounced as /tɜkəl/

50   0   50
MILES